Introduction to
World Philosophies

Introduction to World Philosophies

*Edited, with introductions
and commentaries, by*

Eliot Deutsch

PRENTICE HALL
Upper Saddle River, New Jersey 07458

Library of Congress Cataloging-in-Publication Data

Introduction to world philosophies / [edited with introductions and commentaries by] Eliot
Deutsch.
    p.   cm.
    Includes index.
    ISBN 0-13-227505-8
    1. Philosophy—Introductions.
BD21.I585   1997
100—dc20
                                          96-22934
                                              CIP

Editor-in-chief: Charlyce Jones Owen
Acquisitions editor: Angela Stone
Assistant editor: Jennie Katsaros
Director of production and manufacturing: Barbara Kittle
Managing editor: Jan Stephan/Fran Russello
Editorial production/supervision
   and interior design: Joseph Barron/P. M. Gordon Associates, Inc.
Manufacturing manager: Nick Sklitsis
Cover design: Kiwi Design
Copy editor: Sherry Babbitt
Electronic art creation: Asterisk, Inc.

© 1997 by Prentice-Hall, Inc.
A Pearson Education Company
Upper Saddle River, NJ 07458

Printed in the United States of America

ISBN 0-13-227505-8

Prentice-Hall International (UK) Limited,London
Prentice-Hall of Australia Pty. Limited, Sydney
Prentice-Hall Canada Inc., Toronto
Prentice-Hall Hispanoamericana, S.A., Mexico
Prentice-Hall of India Private Limited, New Delhi
Prentice-Hall of Japan, Inc., Tokyo
Pearson Education Asia Pte. Ltd., Singapore
Editora Prentice-Hall do Brasil, Ltda., Rio de Janeiro

Contents

Preface

TO THE INSTRUCTOR

In some ways, in spirit, this book is properly named. In other ways, in fact, it is misnamed. Let me explain.

This *Introduction to World Philosophies* is dedicated to the idea that philosophy is not the exclusive province of the West, and that indeed other traditions—notably the Asian ones we will be exploring—have a depth, range, and distinctive character that need to be recognized if for no other reason than to enrich considerably our own philosophical background and to enable us to understand better our own tradition. One could, of course, appeal to the fact that since we live in a global society with a highly interdependent economy, and since many nations, including most conspicuously the United States, are rapidly becoming multicultural, to survive well in such a situation we need to know a great deal about different world traditions. The appeal I would make here, however, is a straightforward philosophical one: we can think better and more creatively in philosophy when we understand and appreciate the rich and diverse ways in which basic issues have been dealt with, identified, and defined in different cultures.

This introductory text does not deal with *all* of the philosophical traditions in the world. It should, however, be obvious that no excuse need be given for this lack of comprehensiveness in a single work.

The book is divided into five parts. I have not designated all of them explicitly in terms of the usual branches of philosophy, although the readings quite obviously fall respectively within the areas of philosophical anthropology, ethics and political philosophy, epistemology, metaphysics, and philosophy of religion. I leave it to you, if you choose, to characterize these areas more fully in your own terms to your students, and to explain that the field of philosophy encompasses a great deal more than could possibly be covered in a single course.

I have tried to keep the introductory remarks to the primary selections to a minimum to allow you to proffer your own understanding and interpretation of the texts, except for certain readings relating to non-Western materials, where many of you may not have the same degree of familiarity as you have with the Western sources.

An introductory course could be organized using the book in different ways. You might want to begin with the ethical rather than the anthropological, for example, although biographical information appears only with the first reading by a given author; you might also want to concentrate only on a few of the five parts as the pace of your teaching dictates.

TO THE STUDENT

In this text I do not intend to talk down to you or to assume that you are incapable of joyfully exercising your intellect and feelings to explore difficult ideas and to criticize complex theories. I will assume rather that you are eager to seek a deep understanding of yourself and the world. Although a number of the issues that I will present have topical relevance, this text is designed to introduce you to some of the most exciting ideas put forward by humankind at different times and in diverse cultures and to call for your own creative response to them.

It is often said that "there is nothing new under the sun," that every possibility of thought has already been expressed, that we can, at best, only write footnotes to the great thinkers of the past. I disagree. Philosophy is not history or archaeology or anthropology—important as these disciplines, in their own ways, might be. Philosophy is dedicated to the pursuit of truth and wisdom, which, by its very nature, is an ongoing, highly individualized yet at the same time cooperative enterprise.

Do not be dismayed if during your readings and discussions you find yourself agreeing with one author and then with another, only to discover that the positions argued are incompatible. You can be assured that something very important will follow from that discovery. You will often be confused by what you encounter in philosophy, and you will find unsettling the challenge it presents for you to confront your own deep-seated beliefs in a critical manner. But you can also be assured that this confusion and uncertainty will be a source of intellectual growth and maturity.

Socrates said that the unexamined life is not worth living. Have a worthwhile and productive time in this, your introduction to that examination of life that we call philosophy.

ACKNOWLEDGMENTS

I want to extend my warmest thanks to my research assistant Adrienne C. Cochran for her gracious help throughout the preparation of this book. It would never have reached the final stages of production without her many fine suggestions and hard work.

I would also like to express my appreciation to my reviewers: Mark B. Woodhouse, Georgia State University; John M. Koller, Rensselaer Polytechnic Institute; Richard Sherlock, Utah State University; Marshall Missner, University of Wisconsin, Oshkosh; and John C. Modschiedler, College of du Page.

Introduction: The Nature and Value of Philosophy

The literal meaning of the term "philosophy" is "the love of wisdom" (from the Greek *philein-sophia*). Philosophy, however, has been defined in many ways: as a search for the first principles that underlie and constitute the universe, as the clarification of our fundamental concepts and the justification of our basic beliefs, and as the systematic organization of the results of all the special sciences; it has also been defined as the attempt to resolve the basic mysteries of existence and to provide guidance as to how our lives should be lived. William James, the well known American philosopher and psychologist, understood philosophy to be simply "the unusual obstinate effort to think clearly."

The history of philosophy teaches us that all of these definitions and conceptions of philosophy are "true" in that they have all been held by one or more philosophers at one or more times. Some philosophers—perhaps the majority in the West today—see philosophy as closely aligned to science in its spirit of objectivity if not in its precise methods; others see it as affiliated more with art and religion. James referred to this division in terms of the "tough-minded" versus the "tender-minded" in philosophy. In any event, there is some considerable consensus that philosophy is a *rational* enterprise that seeks an understanding of the most basic principles that inform human experience. It has its grand and ambitious "speculative" side, defined by Alfred North Whitehead as "the endeavor to frame a coherent, logical, necessary system of general ideas in terms of which every element of our experience can be interpreted"; it has its more analytical concerns with our linguistic practices and ways of correct thinking, and much else besides.

There is also some considerable consensus that philosophy has a very special value related to the kinds of interests that it exhibits and the freedom of inquiry that it embodies. Bertrand Russell, a major twentieth-century philosopher, argues in the following selection that the value of philosophy lies in its uncertainty, its aversion to dogmatism, and the freedom from narrow practical concerns that is brought about by "the greatness of the objects it contemplates."

BERTRAND RUSSELL

The Value of Philosophy

It will be well to consider . . . what is the value of philosophy and why it ought to be studied. It is the more necessary to consider this question, in view of the fact that many men, under the influence of science or of practical affairs, are inclined to doubt whether philosophy is anything better than innocent but useless trifling, hair-splitting distinctions, and controversies on matters concerning which knowledge is impossible.

This view of philosophy appears to result, partly from a wrong conception of the ends of life, partly from a wrong conception of the kind of goods which philosophy strives to achieve. Physical science, through the medium of inventions, is useful to innumerable people who are wholly ignorant of it; thus the study of physical science is to be recommended, not only, or primarily, because of the effect on mankind in general. This utility does not belong to philosophy. If the study of philosophy has any value at all for others than students of philosophy, it must be only indirectly, through its effects upon the lives of those who study it. It is in these effects, there-fore, if anywhere, that the value of philosophy must be primarily sought.

But further, if we are not to fail in our endeavour to determine the value of phi-losophy, we must first free our minds from the prejudices of what are wrongly called "practical" men. The "practical" man, as this word is often used, is one who recog-nizes only material needs, who realizes that men must have food for the body, but is oblivious of the necessity of providing food for the mind. If all men were well off, if poverty and disease had been reduced to their lowest possible point, there would still remain much to be done to produce a valuable society; and even in the existing world the goods of the mind are at least as important as the goods of the body. It is exclusively among the goods of the mind that the value of philosophy is to be found; and only those who are not indifferent to these goods can be persuaded that the study of philosophy is not a waste of time.

Philosophy, like all other studies, aims primarily at knowledge. The knowledge it aims at is the kind of knowledge which gives unity and system to the body of the sci-ences, and the kind which results from a critical examination of the grounds of our convictions, prejudices, and beliefs. But it cannot be maintained that philosophy has had any very great measure of success in its attempts to provide definite answers to its questions. If you ask a mathematician, a mineralogist, a historian, or any other man of learning, what definite body of truths has been ascertained by his science, his answer will last as long as you are willing to listen. But if you put the same ques-tion to a philosopher, he will, if he is candid, have to confess that his study has not achieved positive results such as have been achieved by other sciences. It is true that this is partly accounted for by the fact that, as soon as definite knowledge concern-

From *The Problems of Philosophy* by Bertrand Russell (1912). Reprinted by permission of Oxford University Press.

ing any subject becomes possible, this subject ceases to be called philosophy, and becomes a separate science. The whole study of the heavens, which now belongs to astronomy, was once included in philosophy; Newton's great work was called "the mathematical principles of natural philosophy." Similarly, the study of the human mind, which was, until very lately, a part of philosophy, has now been separated from philosophy and has become the science of psychology. Thus, to a great extent, the uncertainty of philosophy is more apparent than real: those questions which are already capable of definite answers are placed in the sciences, while those only to which, at present, no definite answer can be given, remain to form the residue which is called philosophy.

This is, however, only a part of the truth concerning the uncertainty of philosophy. There are many questions—and among them those that are of the profoundest interest to our spiritual life—which, so far as we can see, must remain insoluble to the human intellect unless its powers become of quite a different order from what they are now. Has the universe any unity of plan of purpose, or is it a fortuitous concourse of atoms? Is consciousness a permanent part of the universe, giving hope of indefinite growth in wisdom, or is it a transitory accident on a small planet on which life must ultimately become impossible? Are good and evil of importance to the universe or only to man? Such questions are asked by philosophy, and variously answered by various philosophers. But it would seem that, whether answers be otherwise discoverable or not, the answers suggested by philosophy are none of them demonstrably true. Yet, however slight may be the hope of discovering an answer, it is part of the business of philosophy to continue the consideration of such questions, to make us aware of their importance, to examine all the approaches to them, and to keep alive that speculative interest in the universe which is apt to be killed by confining ourselves to definitely ascertainable knowledge.

Many philosophers, it is true, have held that philosophy could establish the truth of certain answers to such fundamental questions. They have supposed that what is of most importance in religious beliefs could be proved by strict demonstration to be true. In order to judge of such attempts, it is necessary to take a survey of human knowledge, and to form an opinion as to its methods and its limitations. On such a subject it would be unwise to pronounce dogmatically. . . . We cannot, therefore, include as part of the value of philosophy any definite set of answers to such questions. Hence, once more, the value of philosophy must not depend upon any supposed body of definitely ascertainable knowledge to be acquired by those who study it.

The value of philosophy is, in fact, to be sought largely in its very uncertainty. The man who has no tincture of philosophy goes through life imprisoned in the prejudices derived from common sense, from the habitual beliefs of his age or his nation, and from convictions which have grown up in his mind without the cooperation or consent of his deliberate reason. To such a man the world tends to become definite, finite, obvious; common objects rouse no questions, and unfamiliar possibilities are contemptuously rejected. As soon as we begin to philosophise, on the contrary, we find . . . that even the most everyday things lead to problems to which only very incomplete answers can be given. Philosophy, though unable to tell us with certainty what is the true answer to the doubts which it raises, is able to suggest many possibilities which enlarge our thoughts and free them from the tyranny of custom. Thus, while diminishing our feeling of certainty as to what things are, it greatly increases our knowledge as to what they may be; it removes the somewhat arrogant dogmatism of those who have never travelled into the region of liberating doubt, and it keeps alive our sense of wonder by showing familiar things in an unfamiliar aspect.

Apart from its utility in showing unsuspected possibilities, philosophy has a value—perhaps its chief value—through the greatness of the objects which it contemplates, and the freedom from narrow and personal aims resulting from this contemplation. The life of the instinctive man is shut up within the circle of his private interests: family and friends may be included, but the outer world is not regarded except as it may help or hinder what comes within the circle of instinctive wishes. In such a life there is something feverish and confined, in comparison with which the philosophic life is calm and free. The private world of instinctive interests is a small one, set in the midst of a great and powerful world which must, sooner or later, lay our private world in ruins. Unless we can so enlarge our interests as to include the whole outer world, we remain like a garrison in a beleaguered fortress, knowing that the enemy prevents escape and that ultimate surrender is inevitable. In such a life there is no peace, but a constant strife between the insistence of desire and the powerlessness of will. In one way or another, if our life is to be great and free, we must escape this prison and this strife.

One way of escape is by philosophic contemplation. Philosophic contemplation does not, in its widest survey, divide the universe into two hostile camps—friends and foes, helpful and hostile, good and bad—it views the whole impartially. Philosophic contemplation, when it is unalloyed, does not aim at proving that the rest of the universe is akin to man. All acquisition of knowledge is an enlargement of the Self, but this enlargement is best attained when it is not directly sought. It is obtained when the desire for knowledge is alone operative, by a study which does not wish in advance that its objects should have this or that character, but adapts the Self to the characters which it finds in its objects. This enlargement of Self is not obtained when, taking the Self as it is, we try to show that the world is so similar to this Self that knowledge of it is possible without any admission of what seems alien. The desire to prove this is a form of self-assertion, and like all self-assertion, it is an obstacle to the growth of Self which it desires, and of which the Self knows that it is capable. Self-assertion, in philosophic speculation as elsewhere, views the world as a means to its own ends; thus it makes the world of less account than Self, and the Self sets bounds to the greatness of its goods. In contemplation, on the contrary, we start from the not-Self, and through its greatness the boundaries of Self are enlarged; through the infinity of the universe the mind which contemplates it achieves some share in infinity.

For this reason greatness of soul is not fostered by those philosophies which assimilate the universe to Man. Knowledge is a form of union of Self and not-Self; like all union, it is impaired by dominion, and therefore by any attempt to force the universe into conformity with what we find in ourselves. There is a widespread philosophical tendency towards the view which tells us that man is the measure of all things, that truth is man-made, that space and time and the world of universals are properties of the mind, and that, if there be anything not created by the mind, it is unknowable and of no account for us. This view, if our previous discussions were correct, is untrue; but in addition to being untrue, it has the effect of robbing philosophic contemplation of all that gives it value, since it fetters contemplation to Self. What it calls knowledge is not a union with the not-Self, but a set of prejudices, habits, and desires, making an impenetrable veil between us and the world beyond. The man who finds pleasure in such a theory of knowledge is like the man who never leaves the domestic circle for fear his word might not be law.

The true philosophic contemplation, on the contrary, finds its satisfaction in every enlargement of the not-Self, in everything that magnifies the objects contemplated, and thereby the subject contemplating. Everything, in contemplation, that is personal or private, everything that depends upon habit, self-interest, or desire, distorts the object, and hence impairs the union which the intellect seeks. By thus making a barrier between subject and object, such personal and private things become a prison to the intellect. The free intellect will see as God might see, with a *here* and *now,* without hopes and fears, without the trammels of customary beliefs and traditional prejudices, calmly, dispassionately, in the sole and exclusive desire of knowledge—knowledge as impersonal, as purely contemplative, as it is possible for man to attain. Hence also the free intellect will value more the abstract and universal knowledge into which the accidents of private history do not enter, than the knowledge brought by the senses, and dependent, as such knowledge must be, upon an exclusive and personal point of view and a body whose sense-organs distort as much as they reveal.

The mind which has become accustomed to the freedom and impartiality of philosophic contemplation will preserve something of the same freedom and impartiality in the world of action and emotion. It will view its purposes and desires as parts of the whole, with the absence of insistence that results from seeing them as infinitesimal fragments in a world of which all the rest is unaffected by any one man's deeds. The impartiality which, in contemplation, is the unalloyed desire for truth, is the very same quality of mind which, in action, is justice, and in emotion is that universal love which can be given to all, and not only to those who are judged useful or admirable. Thus contemplation enlarges not only the objects of our thoughts, but also the objects of our actions and our affections: it makes us citizens of the universe, not only of one walled city at war with all the rest. In this citizenship of the universe consists man's true freedom, and his liberation from the thraldom of narrow hopes and fears.

Thus, to sum up our discussion of the value of philosophy: Philosophy is to be studied, not for the sake of any definite answers to its questions, since no definite answers can, as a rule, be known to be true, but rather for the sake of the questions themselves, because these questions enlarge our conception of what is possible, enrich our intellectual imagination, and diminish the dogmatic assurance which closes the mind against speculation; but above all because, through the greatness of the universe which philosophy contemplates, the mind also is rendered great, and becomes capable of that union with the universe which constitutes its highest good.

Timeline of Major Historical Philosophers Cited

Lao Tzu (sixth century B.C.E.)

Buddha (563–483 B.C.E.)

Confucius (551–479 B.C.E.)

Plato (428–347 B.C.E.)

Praśastapāda (fourth century B.C.E.)

Chuang Tzu (c. 399–295 B.C.E.)

Aristotle (384–322 B.C.E.)

Mencius (c. 372–289 B.C.E.)

Han Fei Tzu (280–233 B.C.E.)

Saint Augustine (354–430)

Vasubandhu (fourth–fifth centuries)

Śaṃkara (eighth century)

Saint Anselm (c. 1033–1109)

Dōgen (1200–1253)

Saint Thomas Aquinas (1225–1274)

René Descartes (1596–1650)

Blaise Pascal (1623–1662)

Baruch Spinoza (1632–1677)

John Locke (1632–1704)

Gottfried Wilhelm Leibniz (1646–1716)

George Berkeley (1685–1753)

David Hume (1711–1776)

Immanuel Kant (1724–1804)

John Stuart Mill (1806–1873)

William James (1842–1910)

Friedrich Nietzsche (1844–1900)

Sigmund Freud (1856–1939)

Edmund Husserl (1859–1938)

Mahatma Gandhi (1869–1948)

Bertrand Russell (1872–1970)

Martin Buber (1878–1965)

Martin Heidegger (1889–1976)

Jean-Paul Sartre (1905–1980)

Guide to Pronunciation

SANSKRIT

Vowels

a   *a* in *America* or *o* in *come*
ā   *a* in *far* or *father*
i   *i* in *pit* or *pin*
ī   *ee* in *feel* or *i* in *machine*
u   *u* in *put* or *pull*
ū   *u* in *rule*
ri (ṛ)   properly *ur,* but by modern Hindus as *ri* in *river*
e   *ay* in *say* or *a* in *made*
ai   *i* in *rite* or *ai* in *aisle*
o   *o* in *go*
au   *ou* in *loud*

Semivowels

y   *y* in *yonder*
r   *r* in *ram*
l   *l* in *luck*
v   *v* in *clover*

Consonants

Consonants are pronounced approximately as in English, except:
g   *g* in *gun* or *get* (always hard)
ch   *ch* in *church*
ṁ or ṃ   seminasal sound, as *n* in *sing*
sh (ś , ṣ)   *sh* in *sheet* or *shun*

When *h* is combined with another consonant (e.g., *th, bh*), it is aspirated: e.g., *th*—*th* in *boathouse; ph*—*ph* in *uphill.* The palatal *ñ* is like the Spanish *señor* (*jña,* however, is pronounced most often by modern Hindus as *gyah,* with a hard *g*).

Accent

The general rule is to accent the next-to-final syllable, if it is long, or the nearest long syllable preceding it. If none is long, the first syllable is accented. (A long syllable is one that contains a long vowel or a vowel followed by two or more consonants.)

CHINESE

This work employs the Wade-Giles system of romanization, which has traditionally been used in English transliterations of Chinese terms. The *pinyin* system recently introduced in China is now also quite common.

Vowels

a   *a* in *father*
ai   to rhyme with *why*
ao   to rhyme with *now*
e   *e* in *wet*
ê   *u* in *but*
ei   to rhyme with *stay*
yi or *i*   *e* in *me*
ieh   to rhyme with (Oh) *yeh*
o   *o* in *tore*
ou   to rhyme with *know*
u   *u* in *duty*
ü   as in German

Consonants

When aspirated, consonants are pronounced as in English; e.g., *k'*—as *k* in *king* and *ch'*— *ch* in *church*

When unaspirated, they are pronounced as:

ch   *j* in *jam*
eh   *j* in *job*
f   *f* in *faint*
h   *h* in *how*
j   *r* in *ran*
k   *g* in *got*
l   *l* in *lake*
m   *m* in *moon*
n   *n* in *no*
p   *b* in *bad*
r   *r* in *rare*
s   *s* in *snow*

sh   *sh* in *shoulder*
t   *d* in *dub*
ts   *dz* in *adze*
tz   *ds* in *words*
w   *w* in *water*

.

About the Editor

Eliot Deutsch is Professor of Philosophy at the University of Hawaii (Manoa). He is a past editor (1967–1987) of the international journal *Philosophy East and West,* Director of the Sixth East-West Philosophers' Conference, and a past president of the Society for Asian and Comparative Philosophy. Deutsch received his Ph.D. degree from Columbia University and has been a visiting professor at the University of Chicago and Harvard. He has been an invited lecturer at numerous universities and colleges in Asia, Europe, the USSR, and the Americas and is the author of twelve books, including *On Truth: An Ontological Theory; Advaita Vedānta: A Philosophical Reconstruction; Personhood, Creativity and Freedom; Studies in Comparative Aesthetics; Creative Being: The Crafting of Person and World; Religion and Spirituality;* and *Essays on the Nature of Art;* and many articles and reviews in professional journals.

PART

I

WHO AM I?

Who am I? We ask this question when we face moments of crisis (as when we enter a new stage of life with its different demands, opportunities, and expectations), and when we have to make crucial, life-determining decisions (such as whether to get married). We ask it when we make mistakes in our judgments about ourselves, and we ask it especially when we discover that our image of ourselves does not coincide with the image or identification that others have of us. We seem to ask the question "Who am I?" continually but without being able to answer it definitively.

Our experience discloses that there is something in our "I" that is permanent, that endures throughout our experience, and at the same time that our "I" is constantly changing. The photo in the family album of that funny-looking six-year-old is, we believe, "me," and yet everything about "me"—my body, my thoughts, my values—has changed. We are aware that somehow we are persons continuous in time and that we are also made different by out experience—that the "I" of today is the "I" of yesterday, and also that it is not.

We are also aware that at any one time we are at once a single person and many persons, that there is something within us that makes for a unique self-identity, and that we have a rather fantastic potentiality for being different selves according to the different functions that we perform and the responses we make to others' identifications of us. The self that I am as a son or daughter is not the self that I am as a friend; the self that I am with my friends of the same sex is different from the self that I am with my friends of the other sex. In short, we are aware that we are somehow both a continuous "I" and a self in constant change, and both a single "I" and a multiple "I."

And we wonder which among our "I"'s is the most important; which is *truly* "me."

One of the most disconcerting things we face is the experience of not being understood; of being treated, whether by parents, friends, or strangers, as a kind of person we know ourselves not to be. Now this realization that there is a real self, a true "me," seems to take place on many different levels. There is the level of everyday striving for authenticity, and there is the level of deeper spiritual probing. Each of us no doubt has had some powerful and deep experiences in which we feel that we have encountered a truer kind of self than we normally exhibit in our everyday consciousness of ourselves and others. This truer self might be revealed in experiences of loving relation with another person or thing, of intense religious or spiritual insight, of aesthetic contemplation, or of realizations of moral certitude. Apart from the problems of the continuity and unity of the self, then, we also have the question of the relationship between our real or true selves, however they are experienced and conceived, and our phenomenal or everyday selves, no matter how continuous or many the latter may be.

One of the worst forms of punishment is solitary confinement. We are able, it seems, to endure as individuals (to live with ourselves, as it were) only in relation to others. Paradoxically, we seem to be awake as individuals only when we are active as social beings. Does this mean that there is no "I" or real self apart from functional social processes? Does it mean that the individual is dependent upon others for the very being of his or her "I"? And does this social dependency carry over to cultural participation in such a way that it can be said that I have no intrinsic human nature at all apart from my being embedded in a culture and its various traditions?

And yet, we believe ourselves to be free. We believe that, within certain limitations to be sure, we can choose ourselves, we can fashion from the rich possibilities of our being an articulated self that is our own. Whether we are dependent upon others or not for the bare existence of our ego, we are aware that the self is something to be made, to be developed, to be crafted; that it is not simply a given like the color of one's eyes or the shape of one's head. But we are also aware, and here again is the rub, that often we are not as free as we otherwise think ourselves to be; that much of our behavior, our style, our very personality is involuntary; and that despite all effort to the contrary we become, as with intense emotions such as anger and fear, a victim of forces outside of our control and frequently even outside of our awareness. In many ways, it seems, we are in inner conflict with ourselves.

What, then, is the self? Do we have an identity across time? Am I essentially one or many? What is my real or true self? To what extent am I socially constituted and bound in my very nature to my culture? Am I free? These are among the questions that are fundamental to the search for philosophical self-understanding. But before they can be addressed, we must ask whether these questions themselves are culture bound or "universal"? In other words: are questions about the self always raised and addressed from within various cultural assumptions about what it means to be human?

In our Western culture, for example, ever since Genesis, we have accorded ourselves a unique place in the scheme of things, and, despite what many see as the implications of biological evolutionary theory, we continue for the most part to frame questions of personal identity, the relationships of mind and body, and the like on this assumption of human uniqueness. In main-line Indian thought, on the other hand, as we will see, the self-consciousness of human uniqueness is generally missing in favor of an awareness of the continuity of our everyday self and the natural world and the affirmation of the possibility of a radical transcendence of that ego-bound ordinary self. The major problems of the self in Indian philosophy have to do with the nature of our ordinary empirical or everyday self and its relation to other and higher states of consciousness.

And with Chinese philosophical traditions we are apt to find yet a different set of concerns and presuppositions. Problems of the self, for the most part, are governed by ethical considerations. Questions about humanity's "original nature" are indeed asked, but with the intent not of seeking philosophical understanding for its own sake, but of determining the quality of one's moral consciousness. In the main-line Confucian tradition, for example, the self is taken to be thoroughly social in nature. It is not so much that an otherwise autonomous self enters into relations with others as he or she is constituted organically by those very relations. Hence, for the Chinese the problems of understanding the potential quality of human relationships and of providing for the conditions to realize proper self-cultivation become paramount.

We are then compelled, it would seem, to recognize that there are cultural-philosophical presuppositions that influence strongly the formulation of specific philosophical problems of the self and that these problems, in their specificity, are not universal. Put simply, East Asians, South Asians, Westerners, and no doubt others frequently are talking about different things in their various treatments of problems regarding the self. And yet, at a deeper level, we do find and philosophically we are committed, if you will, to believe that there is a common core of human experience, a range of possibilities that cuts across differences between cultures and indeed across differences within the same culture, a range that gets articulated in diverse ways but that nevertheless serves as a kind of deep grammar of human experience.

As human beings we do share a number of important mental and physical factors that, when brought into patterns of relationships with our environment, clearly disclose many similarities between us and enable us to communicate effectively with one another. We oftentimes think we communicate when in fact we do not, but at the same time we could not even come to have that awareness if we always failed to communicate. In short, whenever we ask, "Who am I?," we realize quickly enough that we are persons who are at once mental and physical, living in complex relationships with our environment and each other, destined to perish and yet striving to achieve something meaningful for ourselves and contributory to others. We realize that we are alone and yet always together, quite capable of inflicting great pain upon each other and quite capable as well of acting with extraordinary dignity and grace.

In the selections that follow various questions regarding ourselves in different cultural contexts are addressed. Many contending voices will be heard. These voices are representative, but by no means exhaustive, of our enduring human quest for self-understanding.

Plato

Plato (428–347 B.C.E.) was one of the greatest and most influential philosophers of all time. The eminent twentieth-century mathematician and philosopher Alfred North Whitehead allowed that all philosophy since Plato has been a series of footnotes to his work. Plato wrote primarily dialogues in which his famous teacher Socrates plays a dominant role. The dialogue form enabled Plato to show Socratic thinking as a mutual exploration that sought by way of clear rational thinking to come to some resolution, however tentative, of the deepest questions regarding ourselves and our experience of the world.

What are the fundamental constituents or dimensions of the self, and how are they arranged hierarchically? We are reasoning, feeling, willful, and emotional as well as physical beings. How are these characteristics related to each other? Are they necessarily and always in conflict with one another? Does one of these aspects have a rightful place of prominence over the others? And if so, which, and how, and why?

Plato is deeply concerned with this problem and deals with it in terms of an analysis of the "soul." In reading classical Greek discussions about the soul, it is important to realize at the outset that the word "soul" is a translation of the Greek *psyche* and that *psyche* essentially connotes "life" and "movement." The *psyche* is the animating principle (the Latin translation of *psyche* being *anima*), that which constitutes the dynamic principle of animate being. Plato conceives of the soul as a substantial life-giving principle that underlies and supports the various faculties and as that which, in its highest rational expression, is immortal in human beings. For Plato, "man is a soul who uses a body." The soul has three parts or elements—the rational ("that part . . . whereby it reflects"), the spirited or passionate ("which makes us feel angry and indignant"), and the appetites ("with which it feels hunger and thirst and is distracted by sexual passion and all other desires").

The three divisions set forth in Plato's major work, *The Republic*, correspond to the tripartite pattern put forward in his dialogue *Phaedrus* with its vivid metaphor of the chariot—the charioteer representing reason, which controls the noble horse, the spirited element, and the ignoble horse, the irrational appetites. In the voice of Socrates,

> What manner of thing it [the soul] is would be a long tale to tell, and most assuredly a god alone could tell it; but what it resembles, that a man might tell in briefer compass. Let this therefore be our manner of discourse. Let it be likened

to the union of powers in a team of winged steeds and their winged charioteer. Now all the gods' steeds and their charioteers are good, and of good stock, but with other beings it is not wholly so. With us men, in the first place, it is a pair of steeds that the charioteer controls; moreover one of them is noble and good, and of good stock, while the other has the opposite character, and his stock is opposite. Hence the task of our charioteer is difficult and troublesome. (Plato's *Phaedrus,* trans. with an introduction and commentary by R. Hackforth [New York: The Liberal Arts Press; first published by Cambridge University Press, 1952], p. 69)

The key notion in Plato's conception of the self is the power and duty of reason to rule over both the lower "noble" spirited elements of the self and the "ignoble" desire-based aspects in order to establish a harmony or balance within the self. We are free, according to Plato, when we are self-controlled, when we realize ourselves fully as rational beings. It is then that we are able to act according to what is proper to our nature and to attain that immortality of soul, as set forth so vividly in his dialogue the *Phaedo*, which is our natural birthright.

A medieval rendering of Plato and Socrates. The New York Public Library Picture Collection.

The Three Parts of the Soul

... The soul of a thirsty man, just in so far as he is thirsty, has no other wish than to drink. That is the object of its craving, and towards that it is impelled.

That is clear. ...

Now, is it sometimes true that people are thirsty and yet unwilling to drink?

Yes, often.

What, then, can one say of them, if not that their soul contains something which urges them to drink and something which holds them back, and that this latter is a distinct thing and overpowers the other?

I agree.

And is it not true that the intervention of this inhibiting principle in such cases always has its origin in reflection; whereas the impulses driving and dragging the soul are engendered by external influences and abnormal conditions?

Evidently.

We shall have good reason, then, to assert that they are two distinct principles. We may call that part of the soul whereby it reflects, rational; and the other, with which it feels hunger and thirst and is distracted by sexual passion and all the other desires, we will call irrational appetite, associated with pleasure in the replenishment of certain wants.

Yes, there is good ground for that view.

Let us take it, then, that we have now distinguished two elements in the soul. What of that passionate element which makes us feel angry and indignant? Is that a third, or identical in nature with one of those two?

It might perhaps be identified with appetite.

I am more inclined to put my faith in a story I once heard about Leontius, son of Aglaion. On his way up from the Piraeus outside the north wall, he noticed the bodies of some criminals lying on the ground, with the executioner standing by them. He wanted to go and look at them, but at the same time he was disgusted and tried to turn away. He struggled for some time and covered his eyes, but at last the desire was too much for him. Opening his eyes wide, he ran up to the bodies and cried, "There you are, curse you; feast yourselves on this lovely sight!"

Yes, I have heard that story too.

The point of it surely is that anger is sometimes in conflict with appetite, as if they were two distinct principles. Do we not often find a man whose desires would force him to go against his reason, reviling himself and indignant with this part of his nature which is trying to put constraint on him? It is like a struggle between two factions, in which indignation takes the side of reason. But I believe you have never observed, in yourself or anyone else, indignation make common cause with appetite in behaviour which reason decides to be wrong.

From *The Republic of Plato*, translated by F. M. Cornford (1941). Reprinted by permission of Oxford University Press.

No, I am sure I have not.

Again, take a man who feels he is in the wrong. The more generous his nature, the less can he be indignant at any suffering, such as hunger and cold, inflicted by the man he has injured. He recognizes such treatment as just, and, as I say, his spirit refuses to be roused against it.

That is true.

But now contrast one who thinks it is he that is being wronged. His spirit boils with resentment and sides with the right as he conceives it. Persevering all the more for the hunger and cold and other pains he suffers, it triumphs and will not give in until its gallant struggle has ended in success or death; or until the restraining voice of reason, like a shepherd calling off his dog, makes it relent.

An apt comparison, he said. . . .

Yes, you understand very well what I have in mind. But do you see how we have changed our view? A moment ago we were supposing this spirited element to be something of the nature of appetite; but now it appears that, when the soul is divided into factions, it is far more ready to be up in arms on the side of reason.

Quite true.

Is it, then, distinct from the rational element or only a particular form of it, so that the soul will contain no more than two elements, reason and appetite? . . . Does the spirited element make a third, the natural auxiliary of reason, when not corrupted by bad upbringing?

It must be a third.

Yes, I said, provided it can be shown to be distinct from reason, as we saw it was from appetite.

That is easily proved. You can see that much in children: they are full of passionate feelings from their very birth; but some, I should say, never become rational, and most of them only late in life.

A very sound observation, said I, the truth of which may also be seen in animals. . . .

I entirely agree.

The Immortality of the Soul

"Shall we say there are two kinds of thing, the visible and the invisible?"

"Very well."

"The invisible being always constant, the visible never?"

"We may agree to that too."

"To proceed: we ourselves are partly body, partly soul, are we not?"

From the *Phaedo* by Plato, translated with introduction and commentary by R. Hackforth (1952). Reprinted with the permission of Cambridge University Press.

"Just so."

"Well, which kind of thing shall we say the body tends to resemble and be akin to?"

"The visible kind; anyone can see that."

"And the soul? Is that visible or invisible?"

"Not visible to the human eye, at all events, Socrates."

"Oh well, we were speaking of what is or is not visible to mankind: or are you thinking of some other sort of being?"

"No: of a human being."

"Then what is our decision about the soul, that it can be seen, or cannot?"

"That it cannot."

"In fact it is invisible?"

"Yes."

"Hence soul rather than body is like the invisible, while body rather than soul is like the visible."

"Unquestionably, Socrates."

"Now were we not saying some time ago that when the soul makes use of the body to investigate something through vision or hearing or some other sense—of course investigating by means of the body is the same as investigating by sense—it is dragged by the body towards objects that are never constant, and itself wanders in a sort of dizzy drunken confusion, inasmuch as it is apprehending confused objects?"

"Just so."

"But when it investigates by itself alone, it passes to that other world of pure, everlasting, immortal, constant being, and by reason of its kinship thereto abides ever therewith, whensoever it has come to be by itself and is suffered to do so; and then it has rest from wandering and ever keeps close to that being, unchanged and constant, inasmuch as it is apprehending unchanging objects. And is not the experience which it then has called intelligence?"

"All you have said, Socrates, is true and admirably put."

"Once again, then, on the strength of our previous arguments as well as of this last, which of the two kinds of thing do you find that soul resembles and is more akin to?"

"On the strength of our present line of inquiry, Socrates, I should think that the veriest dullard would agree that the soul has a far and away greater resemblance to everlasting, unchanging being than to its opposite."

"And what does the body resemble?"

"The other kind."

"Now consider a further point. When soul and body are conjoined, Nature prescribes that the latter should be slave and subject, the former master and ruler. Which of the two, in your judgement, does that suggest as being like the divine, and which like the mortal? Don't you think it naturally belongs to the divine to rule and lead, and to the mortal to be ruled and subjected?"

"Yes, I do."

"Then which is soul like?"

"Of course it is obvious, Socrates, that soul is like the divine, and body like the mortal."

"Would you say then . . . that the result of our whole discussion amounts to this: on the one hand we have that which is divine, immortal, indestructible, of a single form, accessible to thought, ever constant and abiding true to itself; and the soul is very like it: on the other hand we have that which is human, mortal, destructible, of many forms, inaccessible to thought, never constant nor abiding true to itself; and the body is very like that. Is there anything to be said against that? . . ."

"Nothing."

"Well then, that being so, isn't it right and proper for the body to be quickly destroyed, but for the soul to be altogether indestructible, or nearly so?"

"Certainly."

Freud

Sigmund Freud (1856–1939), the founder of psychoanalysis, or "depth psychology," was one of the most controversial figures in the twentieth century. His The Interpretation of Dreams *(1900) was a pioneering work that explored the hidden recesses of the subconscious, as did his popular* Psychopathology of Everyday Life *(1901), which argued for the existence of "deeper reasons" for so many of our "unintended" mistakes (e.g., the "slips of the tongue") that we often make in our daily lives. Freud went on to develop therapeutic techniques for the treatment of the various neuroses that he identified and an elaborate psychological theory that emphasized the role of sexuality in human experience.*

Freud was very much concerned about the implications of his psychological theories for a philosophical understanding of humankind and believed that his ideas brought about a major revolution in our conceptions of ourselves. He argued for the existence of an unconscious domain of the self that is essentially irrational and blind, driven as it is by a seething sexual energy, the "libido." This unconscious domain, later termed the "id," exerts, Freud believed, a tremendous influence on everyday waking experience and contributes significantly to many of the damaging conflicts within the ego. The "ego," the individual, waking self, seeks to preserve itself and to adjust to the demands of nature and society, to the "reality principle." It must also confront the "superego," by which Freud means all the internalized rules of conduct and moral attitudes that the child learns from his or her parents and that traditionally was called the "conscience."

Due to the importance of early childhood experiences, one's personality, according to Freud, becomes determined to a high degree at a very early age, in fact, before one has much of an opportunity to do anything about it. Through analytic self-understanding, one may nevertheless achieve a significant liberation from those determining factors and forces that might otherwise paralyze one in one's relations with others and in one's adjustment to the world.

The following selection on "The Dissection of the Personality" is taken from Freud's *New Introductory Lectures on Psychoanalysis,* which were delivered to a general audience and which set forth, in basically nontechnical terms, the main outlines of his theories.

The Dissection of the Personality

We wish to make the ego the matter of our enquiry, our very own ego. But is that possible? After all, the ego is in its very essence a subject; how can it be made into an object? Well, there is no doubt that it can be. The ego can take itself as an object, can treat itself like other objects, can observe itself, criticize itself, and do Heaven knows what with itself. In this, one part of the ego is setting itself over against the rest. So the ego can be split; it splits itself during a number of its functions—temporarily at least. Its parts can come together again afterwards. That is not exactly a novelty, though it may perhaps be putting an unusual emphasis on what is generally known. On the other hand, we are familiar with the notion that pathology, by making things larger and coarser, can draw our attention to normal conditions which would otherwise have escaped us. Where it points to a breach or a rent, there may normally be an articulation present. If we throw a crystal to the floor, it breaks; but not into haphazard pieces. It comes apart along its lines of cleavage into fragments whose boundaries, though they were invisible, were predetermined by the crystal's structure. Mental patients are split and broken structures of this same kind. Even we cannot withhold from them something of the reverential awe which peoples of the past felt for the insane. They have turned away from external reality, but for that very reason they know more about internal, psychical reality and can reveal a number of things to us that would otherwise be inaccessible to us.

We describe one group of these patients as suffering from delusions of being observed. They complain to us that perpetually, and down to their most intimate actions, they are being molested by the observation of unknown powers—presumably persons—and that in hallucinations they hear these persons reporting the outcome of their observation: "now he's going to say this, now he's dressing to go out" and so on. Observation of this sort is not yet the same thing as persecution, but it is not far from it; it presupposes that people distrust them, and expect to catch them carrying out forbidden actions for which they would be punished. How would it be if these insane people were right, if in each of us there is present in his ego an agency like this which observes and threatens to punish, and which in them has merely become sharply divided from their ego and mistakenly displaced into external reality?

I cannot tell whether the same thing will happen to you as to me. Ever since, under the powerful impression of this clinical picture, I formed the idea that the separation of the observing agency from the rest of the ego might be a regular feature of the ego's structure, that idea has never left me, and I was driven to investigate the further characteristics and connections of the agency which was thus separated off. The next step is quickly taken. The content of the delusions of being observed already suggests that the observing is only a preparation for judging and punishing, and we accordingly guess that another function of this agency must be what we call our conscience. There is scarcely anything else in us that we so regularly separate from our ego and so easily set over against it as precisely our conscience. I feel an inclination to do something that I think will give me pleasure, but I abandon it on the ground that my conscience does not allow it. Or I have let myself be persuaded by too great an expectation of pleasure into doing something to which the voice of conscience has objected and after the deed my conscience punishes me with distressing reproaches and causes me to feel remorse for the deed. I might simply say that the special agency which I am beginning to distinguish in the ego is conscience. But it is more prudent to keep the agency as something independent and to suppose that conscience is one of its functions and that self-observation, which is an essential preliminary to the judging activity of conscience, is another of them. And since when we recognize that something has a separate existence we give it a name of its own, from this time forward I will describe this agency in the ego as the "*super-ego.*"

I am now prepared to hear you ask me scornfully whether our ego-psychology comes down to nothing more than taking commonly used abstractions literally and in a crude sense, and transforming them from concepts into things—by which not much would be gained. To this I would reply that in ego-psychology it will be difficult to escape what is universally known; it will rather be a question of new ways of looking at things and new ways of arranging them than of new discoveries. So hold to your contemptuous criticism for the time being and await further explanations. The facts of pathology give our efforts a background that you would look for in vain in popular psychology. So I will proceed.

Hardly have we familiarized ourselves with the idea of a super-ego like this which enjoys a certain degree of autonomy, follows its own intentions and is independent of the ego for its supply of energy, than a clinical picture forces itself on our notice which throws a striking light on the severity of this agency and indeed its cruelty, and on its changing relations to the ego. I am thinking of the condition of melancholia, or, more precisely, of melancholic attacks, which you too will have heard plenty about, even if you are not psychiatrists. The most striking feature of this illness, of whose causation and mechanism we know much too little, is the way in which the super-ego—"conscience," you may call it, quietly—treats the ego. While a melancholic can, like other people, show a greater or lesser degree of severity to himself in his healthy periods, during a melancholic attack his super-ego becomes over-severe, abuses the poor ego, humiliates it and ill-treats it, threatens it with the direst punishments, reproaches it for actions in the remotest past which had been taken lightly at the time—as though it had spent the whole interval in collecting accusations and had only been waiting for its present access of strength in order to bring them up and make a condemnatory judgement on their basis. The super-ego applies the strictest moral standard to the helpless ego which is at its mercy; in general it represents the claims of morality, and we realize all at once that our moral sense of guilt is the expression of the tension between the ego and the super-ego. It is a most remarkable experience to see morality, which is supposed to have been given us by God and thus deeply implanted in us, functioning [in these patients] as a periodic phenomenon. For after a certain number of months the whole moral fuss is over, the criticism of the super-ego is silent, the ego is rehabilitated and again enjoys all the rights of man till the next attack. In some forms of the disease, indeed, something of a contrary sort occurs in the intervals; the ego finds itself in a blissful state of intoxication, it celebrates a triumph, as though the super-ego had lost all its strength or had melted into the ego; and this liberated, manic ego permits itself a truly uninhibited satisfaction of all its appetites. Here are happenings rich in unsolved riddles!

No doubt you will expect me to give you more than a mere illustration when I inform you that we have found out all kinds of things about the formation of the super-ego—that is to say, about the origin of conscience. Following a well-known pronouncement of Kant's which couples the conscience within us with the starry Heavens, a pious man might well be tempted to honour these two things as the masterpieces of creation. The stars are indeed magnificent, but as regards conscience God has done an uneven and careless piece of work, for a large majority of men have brought along with them only a modest amount of it or scarcely enough to be worth mentioning. We are far from overlooking the portion of psychological truth that is contained in the assertion that conscience is of divine origin; but the thesis needs interpretation. Even if conscience is something "within us," yet it is not so from the first. In this it is a real contrast to sexual life, which is in fact there from the beginning of life and not only a later addition. But, as is well known, young children are amoral and possess no internal inhibitions against their impulses striving for pleasure. The part which is later taken on by the super-ego is played to begin with by an external power, by parental authority. Parental influence governs the child by offering proofs of love and by threatening punishments which are signs to the child of loss of love and are bound to be feared on their own account. This realistic anxiety is the precursor of the later moral anxiety. So long as it is dominant there is no need to talk of a super-ego and of a conscience. It is only subsequently that the secondary situation develops (which we are all too ready to regard as the normal one), where the external restraint is internalized and the super-ego takes the place of the parental agency and observes, directs and threatens the ego in exactly the same way as earlier the parents did with the child.

The super-ego, which thus takes over the power, function and even the methods of the parental agency, is however not merely its successor but actually the legitimate heir of its body. It proceeds directly out of it, we shall learn presently by what process. First, however, we must dwell upon a discrepancy between the two. The super-ego seems to have made a one-sided choice and to have picked out only the parents' strictness and severity, their prohibiting and punitive function, whereas their loving care seems not to have been taken over and maintained. If the parents have really enforced their authority with severity we can easily understand the child's in turn developing a severe super-ego. But, contrary to our expectation, experience shows that the super-ego can acquire the same characteristic of relentless severity even if the upbringing had been mild and kindly and had so far as possible avoided threats and punishments. We shall come back later to this contradiction when we deal with the transformations of instinct during the formation of the super-ego. . . .

The basis of the process is what is called an "identification"—that is to say, the assimilation of one ego to another one, as a result of which the first ego behaves like the second in certain respects, imitates it and in a sense takes it up into itself. Identification has been not unsuitably compared with the oral, cannibalistic incorporation of the other person. It is a very important form of attachment to someone else, probably the very first, and not the same thing as the choice of an object. The difference between the two can be expressed in some such way as this. If a boy identifies himself with his father, he wants to *be like* his father; if he makes him the object of his choice, he wants to *have* him, to possess him. In the first case his ego is altered on the model of his father; in the second case that is not necessary. Identification and object-choice are to a large extent independent of each other; it is however possible to identify oneself with someone whom, for instance, one has taken as a sexual object, and to alter one's ego on his model. It is said that the influencing of the ego by the sexual object occurs particularly often with women and is characteristic of femininity. . . . If one has lost an object or has been obliged to give it up, one often compensates oneself by identifying oneself with it and by setting it up once more in one's ego, so that here object-choice regresses, as it were, to identification.

I myself am far from satisfied with these remarks on identification; but it will be enough if you can grant me that the installation of the super-ego can be described as a successful instance of identification with the parental agency. . . .

I hope you have already formed an impression that the hypothesis of the super-ego really describes a structural relation and is not merely a personification of some such abstraction as that of conscience. One more important function remains to be mentioned which we attribute to this super-ego. It is also the vehicle of the ego ideal by which the ego measures itself, which it emulates, and whose demand for ever greater perfection it strives to fulfil. There is no doubt that this ego ideal is the precipitate of the old picture of the parents, the expression of admiration for the perfection which the child then attributed to them. . . .

. . . We have allotted it [the super-ego] the functions of self-observation, of conscience and of [maintaining] the ideal. It follows from what we have said about its origin that it presupposes an immensely important biological fact and a fateful psychological one: namely, the human child's long dependence on its parents and the Oedipus complex, both of which, again, are intimately interconnected. The super-ego is the representative for us of every moral restriction, the advocate of a striving towards perfection—it is, in short, as much as we have been able to grasp psychologically of what is described as the higher side of human life. Since it itself goes back to the influence of parents, educators and so on, we learn still more of its significance if we turn to those who are its sources. As a rule parents and authorities analogous to them follow the precepts of their own super-egos in educating children. Whatever understanding their ego may have come to with their super-ego, they are severe and exacting in educating children. They have forgotten the difficulties of their own childhood and they are glad to be able now to identify themselves fully with their own parents who in the past laid such severe restrictions upon them. Thus a child's super-ego is in fact constructed on the model not of its parents but of its parents' super-ego; the contents which fill it are the same and it becomes the vehicle of tradition and of all the time-resisting judgements of value which have propagated themselves in this manner from generation to generation. You may easily guess what important assistance taking the super-ego into account will give us in our understanding of the social behaviour of mankind—in the problem of delinquency, for instance—and perhaps even what practical hints on education. It seems likely that what are known as materialistic views of history sin in under-estimating this factor. They brush it aside with the remark that human "ideologies" are nothing other than the product and superstructure of their contemporary economic conditions. That is true, but very probably not the whole truth. Mankind never lives entirely in the present. The past, the tradition of the race and of the people, lives on in the ideologies of the super-ego, and yields only slowly to the influences of the present and to new changes; and so long as it operates through the super-ego it plays a powerful part in human life, independently of economic conditions. . . .

. . . Another problem awaits us—at the opposite end of the ego, as we might put it. It is presented to us by an observation during the work of analysis, an observation which is actually a very old one. As not infrequently happens, it has taken a long time to come to the point of appreciating its importance. The whole theory of psycho-analysis is, as you know, in fact built up on the perception of the resistance offered to us by the patient when we attempt to make his unconscious conscious to him. The objective sign of this resistance is that his associations fail or depart widely from the topic that is being dealt with. He may also recognize the resistance *subjectively* by the fact that he has distressing feelings when he approaches the topic. But this last sign may also be absent. We then say to the patient that we infer from his behaviour that he is now in a state of resistance; and he replies that he knows nothing of that, and is only aware that his associations have become more difficult. It turns out that we were right; but in that case his resistance was unconscious too, just as unconscious as the repressed, at the lifting of which we were working. We should long ago have asked the question: from what part of his mind does an unconscious resistance like this arise? The beginner in psycho-analysis will be ready at once with the answer: it is, of course, the resistance of the unconscious. An ambiguous and unserviceable answer! If it means that the resistance rises from the repressed, we must rejoin: certainly not! We must rather attribute to the repressed a strong upward drive, an impulsion to break through into consciousness. The resistance can only be a manifestation of the ego, which originally put the repression into force and now wishes to maintain it. That, moreover, is the view we always took. Since we have come to assume a special agency in the ego, the super-ego, which represents demands of a restrictive and rejecting character, we may say that repression is the work of this super-ego and that it is carried out either by itself or by the ego in obedience to its orders. If then we are met by the case of the resistance in analysis not being conscious to the patient, this means either that in quite important situations the super-ego and the ego can operate unconsciously, or—and this would be still more important—the portions of both of them, the ego and the super-ego themselves, are unconscious. In both cases we have to reckon with the disagreeable discovery that on the one hand (super-) ego and conscious and on the other hand repressed and unconscious are far from coinciding. . . .

. . . In face of the doubt whether the ego and super-ego are themselves unconscious or merely produce unconscious effects, we have, for good reasons, decided in
favour of the former possibility. And it is indeed the case that large portions of the
ego and super-ego can remain unconscious and are normally unconscious. That is
to say, the individual knows nothing of their contents and it requires an expenditure
of effort to make them conscious. It is a fact that ego and conscious, repressed and
unconscious do not coincide. We feel a need to make a fundamental revision of our
attitude to the problem of conscious-unconscious. At first we are inclined greatly to
reduce the value of the criterion of being conscious since it has shown itself so un-
trustworthy. But we should be doing it an injustice. As may be said of our life, it is
not worth much, but it is all we have. Without the illumination thrown by the quality of consciousness, we should be lost in the obscurity of depth-psychology; but we
must attempt to find our bearings afresh.

There is no need to discuss what is to be called conscious: it is removed from all
doubt. The oldest and best meaning of the word "unconscious" is the descriptive
one; we call a psychical process unconscious whose existence we are obliged to assume—for some such reason as that we infer it from its effects—, but of which we
know nothing. In that case we have the same relation to it as we have to a psychical
process in another person, except that it is in fact one of our own. If we want to be
still more correct, we shall modify our assertion by saying that we call a process unconscious if we are obliged to assume that it is being activated *at the moment*, though
at the moment we know nothing about it. This qualification makes us reflect that the
majority of conscious processes are conscious only for a short time; very soon they
become *latent*, but can easily become conscious again. We might also say that they
had become unconscious, if it were at all certain that in the condition of latency
they are still something psychical. So far we should have learnt nothing new; nor
should we have acquired the right to introduce the concept of an unconscious into
psychology. But then comes the new observation that we were already able to make
in parapraxes. In order to explain a slip of the tongue, for instance, we find ourselves obliged to assume that the intention to make a particular remark was present
in the subject. We infer it with certainty from the interference with his remark which
has occurred; but the intention did not put itself through and was thus unconscious.
If, when we subsequently put it before the speaker, he recognizes it as one familiar
to him, then it was only temporarily unconscious to him; but if he repudiates it as
something foreign to him, then it was permanently unconscious. From this experience we retrospectively obtain the right also to pronounce as something unconscious what had been described as latent. A consideration of these dynamic relations permits us now to distinguish two kinds of unconscious—one which is easily,
under frequently occurring circumstances, transformed into something conscious,
and another with which this transformation is difficult and takes place only subject
to a considerable expenditure of effort or possibly never at all. In order to escape
the ambiguity as to whether we mean the one or the other unconscious, whether we
are using the word in the descriptive or in the dynamic sense, we make use of a permissible and simple way out. We call the unconscious which is only latent, and thus
easily becomes conscious, the "preconscious" and retain the term "unconscious" for

the other. We now have three terms, "conscious," "preconscious" and "unconscious," with which we can get along in our description of mental phenomena. Once again: the preconscious is also unconscious in the purely descriptive sense, but we do not give it that name, except in talking loosely or when we have to make a defence of the existence in mental life of unconscious processes in general.

You will admit, I hope, that so far that is not too bad and allows of convenient handling. Yes, but unluckily the work of psycho-analysis has found itself compelled to use the word "unconscious" in yet another, third, sense, and this may, to be sure, have led to confusion. Under the new and powerful impression of there being an extensive and important field of mental life which is normally withdrawn from the ego's knowledge so that the processes occurring in it have to be regarded as unconscious in the truly dynamic sense, we have come to understand the term "unconscious" in a topographical or systematic sense as well; we have come to speak of a "system" of the preconscious and a "system" of the unconscious [*Ucs.*], of a conflict between the ego and the system *Ucs.*, and have used the word more and more to denote a mental province rather than a quality of what is mental. The discovery, actually an inconvenient one, that portions of the ego and super-ego as well are unconscious in the dynamic sense, operates at this point as a relief—it makes possible the removal of a complication. We perceive that we have no right to name the mental region that is foreign to the ego "the system *Ucs.*," since the characteristic of being unconscious is not restricted to it. Very well; we will no longer use the term "unconscious" in the systematic sense and we will give what we have hitherto so described a better name and one no longer open to misunderstanding. . . . We will in future call it the "id." This impersonal pronoun seems particularly well suited for expressing the main characteristic of this province of the mind—the fact of its being alien to the ego. The super-ego, the ego and the id—these, then, are the three realms, regions, provinces, into which we divide an individual's mental apparatus, and with the mutual relations of which we shall be concerned in what follows. . . .

You will not expect me to have much to tell you that is new about the id apart from its new name. It is the dark, inaccessible part of our personality; what little we know of it we have learnt from our study of the dream-work and of the construction of neurotic symptoms, and most of that is of a negative character and can be described only as a contrast to the ego. We approach the id with analogies: we call it a chaos, a cauldron full of seething excitations. We picture it as being open at its end to somatic influences, and as there taking up into itself instinctual needs which find their psychical expression in it, but we cannot say in what substratum. It is filled with energy reaching it from the instincts, but it has no organization, produces no collective will, but only a striving to bring about the satisfaction of the instinctual needs subject to the observance of the pleasure principle. The logical laws of thought do not apply in the id, and this is true above all of the law of contradiction. Contrary impulses exist side by side, without cancelling each other out or diminishing each other: at the most they may converge to form compromises under the dominating economic pressure towards the discharge of energy. There is nothing in the id that could be compared with negation; and we perceive with surprise an exception to the philosophical theorem that space and time are necessary forms of our mental acts. There is nothing in the id that corresponds to the idea of time; there is no recognition of the passage of time, and—a thing that is most remarkable and awaits consideration in philosophical thought—no alteration in its mental processes is produced by the passage of time. Wishful impulses which have never passed beyond the id, but impressions, too, which have been sunk into the id by repression, are virtually immortal; after the passage of decades they behave as though they have just occurred. They can only be recognized as belonging to the past, can only lose their importance and be deprived of their cathexis of energy, when they have been made conscious by the work of analysis, and it is on this that the therapeutic effect of analytic treatment rests to no small extent.

Again and again I have had the impression that we have made too little theoretical use of this fact, established beyond any doubt, of the unalterability by time of the repressed. This seems to offer an approach to the most profound discoveries. Nor, unfortunately, have I myself made any progress here.

The id of course knows no judgements of value: no good and evil, no morality. The economic or, if you prefer, the quantitative factor, which is intimately linked to the pleasure principle, dominates all its processes. Instinctual cathexes seeking discharge—that, in our view, is all there is in the id. It even seems that the energy of these instinctual impulses is in a state different from that in the other regions of the mind, far more mobile and capable of discharge; otherwise the displacements and condensations would not occur which are characteristic of the id and which so completely disregard the *quality* of what is cathected—what in the ego we should call an idea. We would give much to understand more about these things! You can see, incidentally, that we are in a position to attribute to the id characteristics other than that of its being unconscious, and you can recognize the possibility of portions of the ego and super-ego being unconscious without possessing the same primitive and irrational characteristics.

We can best arrive at the characteristics of the actual ego, in so far as it can be distinguished from the id and from the super-ego, by examining its relation to the outermost superficial portion of the mental apparatus, which we describe as the system *Pcpt.-Cs.* [Perceptual-Consciousness]. This system is turned towards the external world, it is the medium for the perceptions arising thence, and during its functioning the phenomenon of consciousness arises in it. It is the sense-organ of the entire apparatus; moreover it is receptive not only to excitations from outside but also to those arising from the interior of the mind. We need scarcely look for a justification of the view that the ego is that portion of the id which was modified by the proximity and influence of the external world, which is adapted for the reception of stimuli and as a protective shield against stimuli, comparable to the cortical layer by which a small piece of living substance is surrounded. The relation to the external world has become the decisive factor for the ego; it has taken on the task of representing the external world to the id—fortunately for the id, which could not escape destruction if, in its blind efforts for the satisfaction of its instincts, it disregarded that supreme external power. In accomplishing this function, the ego must observe the external world, must lay down an accurate picture of it in the memory-traces of its perceptions, and by its exercise of the function of "reality-testing" must put aside whatever in this picture of the external world is an addition derived from internal sources of excitation. The ego controls the approaches to motility under the id's orders; but between a need and an action it has interposed a postponement in the form of the activity of thought, during which it makes use of the mnemic residues of experience. In that way it has dethroned the pleasure principle which dominates the course of events in the id without any restriction and has replaced it by the reality principle, which promises more certainty and greater success. . . .

We are warned by a proverb against serving two masters at the same time. The poor ego has things even worse: it serves three severe masters and does what it can to bring their claims and demands into harmony with one another. These claims are always divergent and often seem incompatible. No wonder that the ego so often fails in its task. Its three tyrannical masters are the external world, the super-ego and the id. When we follow the ego's efforts to satisfy them simultaneously—or rather, to obey them simultaneously—we cannot feel any regret at having personified this ego and having set it up as a separate organism. It feels hemmed in on three sides, threatened by three kinds of danger, to which, if it is hard pressed, it reacts by generating anxiety. Owing to its origin from the experiences of the perceptual system, it is earmarked for representing the demands of the external world, but it strives too to be a loyal servant of the id, to remain on good terms with it, to recommend itself to it as an object and to attract its libido to itself. In its attempts to mediate between the id and reality, it is often obliged to cloak the commands of the id with its own rationalizations, to conceal the id's conflicts with reality, to profess, with diplomatic disingenuousness, to be taking notice of reality even when the id has remained rigid and unyielding. On the other hand it is observed at every step it takes by the strict super-ego, which lays down definite standards for its conduct, without taking any account of its difficulties from the direction of the id and the external world, and which, if those standards are not obeyed, punishes it with tense feelings of inferiority and of guilt. Thus the ego, driven by the id, confined by the super-ego, repulsed by reality, struggles to master its economic task of bringing about harmony among the forces and influences working in and upon it; and we can understand how it is that so often we cannot suppress a cry: "Life is not easy!" If the ego is obliged to admit its weakness, it breaks out in anxiety—realistic anxiety regarding the external world, moral anxiety regarding the super-ego and neurotic anxiety regarding the strength of the passions in the id. . . .

And here is another warning, to conclude these remarks, which have certainly been exacting and not, perhaps, very illuminating. In thinking of this division of the personality into an ego, a super-ego and an id, you will not, of course, have pictured sharp frontiers like the artificial ones drawn in political geography. We cannot do justice to the characteristics of the mind by linear outlines like those in a drawing or in primitive painting, but rather by areas of colour melting into one another as they are presented by modern artists. After making the separation we must allow what we have separated to merge together once more. You must not judge too harshly a first attempt at giving a pictorial representation of something so intangible as psychical processes. It is highly probable that the development of these divisions is subject to great variations in different individuals; it is possible that in the course of actual functioning they may change and go through a temporary phase of involution. Particularly in the case of what is phylogenetically the last and most delicate of these divisions—the differentiation between the ego and the super-ego—something of the sort seems to be true. There is no question but that the same thing results from psychical illness. It is easy to imagine, too, that certain mystical practices may succeed in upsetting the normal relations between the different regions of the mind so that, for instance, perception may be able to grasp happenings in the depths of the ego and in the id which were otherwise inaccessible to it. It may safely be doubted, however, whether this road will lead us to the ultimate truths from which salvation is to be expected. Nevertheless it may be admitted that the therapeutic efforts of psychoanalysis have chosen a similar line of approach. Its intention is, indeed, to strengthen the ego, to make it more independent of the super-ego, to widen its field of perception and enlarge its organization, so that it can appropriate fresh portions of the id. Where id was, there ego shall be. It is a work of culture—not unlike the draining of the Zuider Zee.

Vedānta

In Sanskrit, the classical language of India, philosophy is called *darśana*, which is derived from the root *driś*, which means "to see." This etymology suggests two interrelated ideas about the nature of philosophy in India. First, it suggests that the function of philosophy is to enable its students to see the ultimate depths and truths of life directly; that philosophy, in other words, is a personal vision of life in its widest frame of reference. Second, this seeing idea of philosophy suggests that all systems of thought represent different points of view or perspectives upon the enduring truths of life, and that no one system is the sole possessor of truth. "The truth is One, it is called by many names," is a statement put forward in the earliest Indian literature and remains a constant refrain throughout the tradition. This does not mean, however, that Indian philosophers do not engage one another contentiously in their search for the truth; quite the opposite, they argue endlessly and relentlessly over every conceivable issue. For the most part, though, this argumentation is carried out in a spirit of mutual respect and of keen awareness of the limitations of argument as such to attain and sustain an adequate comprehensive vision.

This intellectual "tolerance" among Indian philosophers traditionally is evident in the way in which a proponent of one *darśana* will carefully summarize an opponent's position in its strongest terms before attempting to substitute a better position in its place. It is also manifested in the close if not at times inseparable relationship between philosophy, as we tend to understand it in the West, and religion. A contemporary Indian philosopher, Sri Aurobindo, for example, has written that "philosophy is the intellectual search for the fundamental truth of things, religion is the attempt to make the truth dynamic in the soul of man. They are essential to each other; a religion that is not the expression of philosophical truth degenerates into superstition and obscurantism, and a philosophy which does not dynamise itself with the religious spirit is a barren light, for it cannot get itself practiced." According to this rather typical Indian idea, philosophical understanding is meaningful only insofar as it can be acted upon. This attitude is expressed in Indian thought perhaps most fully in the philosophy known as Vedānta.

The term "Vedānta" literally means "end of the Veda" and refers to the most influential tradition in Indian philosophy. The Veda consists of collections of various hymns and prose texts, the earliest of which dates back as far as 1400 B.C.E. These collections were handed down from generation to generation through oral transmission. Each collection contains various Upaniṣads, or sacred philosophical texts. The term "Upaniṣad" literally means "to sit down near" and thus connotes sitting near a teacher who is transmitting wisdom. In India traditionally the teacher, or guru, is concerned not so much with imparting information, but with initiating a pupil or disciple into a form of understanding based on the teacher's own direct experience. The Upaniṣads can thus best be read as records of guru-student relationships rather than as "literature" in the usual sense of the term. In other words, the Upaniṣads for the most part are not tightly organized, systematic treatises, although they do indeed offer a wide range of philosophical discussion and show deep insight into the nature and constitution of the self. Further, they became the primary source material for the later schools of Vedāntic philosophy that attempted to bring these discussions and insights into a comprehensive and coherent system of thought and experience.

Over a hundred Upaniṣads have come down to us, but only ten or so are regarded as "Principal Upaniṣads." In one of the oldest, the *Chāndogya Upaniṣad*, it is asserted that the self, in its depth, *is* reality. Through a number of vivid illustrations the teacher brings home to the student the realization that *tat tvam asi*, "You are that"—"You are the Real."

Drawing on other Upaniṣads and related sources, we shall summarize the teachings of Vedānta on the self as they were systematized in the school known as Advaita Vedānta. This is the nondualistic system that was expounded primarily by the great philosopher Śaṃkara (c. 788–820) and that is usually regarded as the most important school in the Indian philosophical tradition. Based on the assertion of the nondifference of the true self (*ātman*) and the supreme and surpassing reality called *Brahman*, Advaita Vedānta elaborates a multileveled theory of consciousness and tries to show how we develop mistaken views regarding the reality and centrality of our ego-based individual selves.

"You Are That"

. . . "Just as the bees prepare honey by collecting the juices of all manner of trees and bring the juice to one unity, and just as the juices no longer distinctly know that the one hails from this tree, the other from that one, likewise, my son, when all these creatures have merged with the Existent they do not know, realizing only that they have merged with the Existent.

"Whatever they are here on earth, tiger, lion, wolf, boar, worm, fly, gnat, or mosquito, they become that.

"It is this very fineness which ensouls all this world, it is the true one, it is the soul. *You are that* [*tat tvam asi*], Śvetaketu."

"Instruct me further, sir."

"So I will, my son," he said.

"The rivers of the east, my son, flow eastward, the rivers of the west flow westward. From ocean they merge into ocean, it becomes the same ocean. Just as they then no

---

longer know that they are this river or that one, just so all these creatures, my son, know no more, realizing only when having come to the Existent that they have come to the Existent. Whatever they are here on earth, tiger, lion, wolf, boar, worm, fly, gnat or mosquito, they become that.

"It is this very fineness which ensouls all this world, it is the true one, it is the soul. *You are that*, Śvetaketu."

"Instruct me further, sir."

"So I will, my son," he said.

"If a man would strike this big tree at the root, my son, it would bleed but stay alive. If he struck it at the middle, it would bleed but stay alive. If he struck it at the top, it would bleed but stay alive. Being entirely permeated by the living soul, it stands there happily drinking its food.

"If this life leaves one branch, it withers. If it leaves another branch, it withers. If it leaves a third branch, it withers. If it leaves the whole tree, the whole tree withers. Know that it is in this same way, my son," he said, "that this very body dies when deserted by this life, but this life itself does not die.

"This is the very fineness which ensouls all this world, it is the true one, it is the soul. *You are that*, Śvetaketu."

"Instruct me further, sir."

"So I will, my son," he said.

"Bring me a banyan fruit."

"Here it is, sir."

"Split it."

"It is split, sir."

"What do you see inside it?"

"A number of rather fine seeds, sir."

"Well, split one of them."

"It is split, sir."

"What do you see inside it?"

"Nothing, sir."

He said to him, "This very fineness that you no longer can make out, it is by virtue of this fineness that this banyan tree stands so big.

"Believe me, my son. It is this very fineness which ensouls all this world, it is the true one, it is the soul. *You are that*, Śvetaketu."

"Instruct me further, sir."

"So I will, my son," he said.

"Throw this salt in the water, and sit with me on the morrow." So he did. He said to him, "Well, bring me the salt that you threw in the water last night." He looked for it, but could not find it as it was dissolved.

"Well, taste the water on this side.—How does it taste?"

"Salty."

"Taste it in the middle.—How does it taste?"

"Salty."

"Taste it at the other end.—How does it taste?"

"Salty."

"Take a mouthful and sit with me." So he did.

"It is always the same."

He said to him, "You cannot make out what exists in it, yet it is there.

"It is this very fineness which ensouls all this world, it is the true one, it is the soul. *You are that*, Śvetaketu."

"Instruct me further, sir."

"So I will, my son," he said.

"Suppose they brought a man from the Gandhāra country, blindfolded, and let him loose in an uninhabited place beyond. The man, brought out and let loose with his blindfold on, would be turned around, to the east, north, west, and south.

"Then someone would take off his blindfold and tell him, 'Gandhāra is that way, go that way.' Being a wise man and clever, he would ask his way from village to village and thus reach Gandhāra. Thus in this world a man who has a teacher knows from him, 'So long will it take until I am free, then I shall reach it.'

"It is this very fineness which ensouls all this world, it is the true one, it is the soul. *You are that*, Śvetaketu."

"Instruct me further, sir."

"So I will, my son," he said.

"When a man is dying, his relatives crowd around him: 'Do you recognize me? Do you recognize me?' As long as his speech has not merged in his mind, his mind in his breath, his breath in Fire, and Fire in the supreme deity, he does recognize.

"But when his speech has merged in the mind, the mind in the breath, the breath in Fire, and Fire in the supreme deity, he no longer recognizes.

"It is this very fineness which ensouls all this world, it is the true one, it is the soul. *You are that*, Śvetaketu."

ELIOT DEUTSCH

The Self in Advaita Vedānta

The central concern of Advaita Vedānta is to establish the oneness of Reality and to lead the human being to a realization of it. Any difference in essence between man and Reality must be erroneous, for one who knows himself knows Reality, and this self-knowledge is a "saving" knowledge; it enables the knower to overcome all pain, misery, ignorance, and bondage. What, though, is the self, the knowledge of which

From *Advaita Vedānta: A Philosophical Reconstruction* by Eliot Deutsch. First published by the East-West Center Press (1969). Reprinted by permission of University of Hawaii Press. Copyright © East-West Center Press.

yields freedom and wisdom? How does it relate to what we ordinarily take to be our self—our physical organization, our mental activities and capacities, our emotional and volitional life? These are the questions Advaita Vedānta is committed to answer; the answers being at the very core of Advaita philosophy.

I

> Bāṣkali asked Bāhva three times about the nature of Brahman: the latter remained silent all the time, but finally replied:—I teach you, but you understand not: silence is the Ātman.

A person's essence is unapproachable through his name; and in the Spirit, in the Absolute where pure silence reigns, all names are rejected.

The application of a label to someone too often implies that in the deepest ontological sense that someone is a "something." Labels are mere conventions and sounds; and to disown all labels in a penetrating inward intuition means not only to recognize the "nothing" that one is but also to become the silence, the "everything" that alone is.

Ātman (or *paramātman*, the highest Self), for Advaita Vedānta, is that pure, undifferentiated self-shining consciousness, timeless, spaceless, and unthinkable, that is not-different from Brahman [the supreme Reality] and that underlies and supports the individual human person.

Ātman is pure, undifferentiated, self-shining consciousness: It is a supreme power of awareness, transcendent to ordinary sense-mental consciousness, aware only of the Oneness of being. Ātman is that state of conscious human being wherein the divisions of subject and object, which characterize ordinary consciousness, are overcome. Nothing can condition this transcendental state of consciousness: among those who have realized it, no doubts about it can arise. Ātman is thus void of differentiation, but for Advaita it is not simply a void: it is the infinite richness of spiritual being.

"This Ātman is self-luminous."

Ātman is timeless: It cannot be said to have arisen in time, to be subject to a "present," or to have an end in time—for all such sayings apply only to what is relative and conditioned. Time, according to Advaita, is a category of the empirical or phenomenal world only. Time, with its before and after, can make no claim on the "eternal Now" which is the state of Ātman realization.

"This intelligent Self is without birth or death."

Likewise it is spaceless: Spatial relations hold between objects of the empirical order; they cannot be extended to constrain that which is the content of spiritual experience.

"It is impossible for the body to be the receptacle of the Self."

And unthinkable: "The eye does not go there, nor speech, nor mind."

"It is great and self-effulgent, and its form is unthinkable."

Thought functions only with forms, in multiplicity; Ātman, being without determinate form and being ultimately simple, cannot be an object knowable by the mind, perceivable by the senses. Thought is a process; Ātman is a state of being. Thought objectifies, Ātman is the pure "subject" that underlies all subject/object distinctions. "The knowledge of the Ātman is self-revealed and is not dependent upon perception and other means of knowledge." . . .

In the depth of my being, then, I am not-different from Reality: the depth of my being, which is not "mine," is Reality. Man, according to Advaita, is not just a conditioned being, so that if you were to strip away his desires, his mental activities, his emotions, and his ego, you would find a mere nothing; he is spirit, he is consciousness, he is free and timeless being.

Ātman cannot be an object of thought, and it cannot be arrived at as the conclusion of a rational argument. In order, however, to orient the mind towards it and to prepare the mind to accept it as a fact of experience, the Advaitin does proffer rational arguments, the most common of which is a sort of *cogito ergo sum* argument. Śaṃkara states that "to refute the Self is impossible, for he who tries to refute it is the Self." No one, Śaṃkara maintains, can doubt the existence of Ātman, for the act of doubting implies the very being of the doubter who must thereby affirm his own existence. Vidyāraṇa [a disciple of Śaṃkara] expresses the argument thus:

> No one can doubt the fact of his own existence. Were one to do so, who could the doubter be?
> Only a deluded man could entertain the idea that he does not exist.

The argument is not without its difficulties. A subtle and unsupported transition is made between the Ātman and the *jīva* (the individual conscious being) so that the argument does not so much prove the Ātman as it does the *jīva*—the *jīva*, which has the kind of self-consciousness described in, and presupposed by, the argument, and not the Ātman, which is pure consciousness. In other words, by establishing the self on the basis of the inability to deny the doubter who would deny the self, the self that is being established, apart from any other difficulty in the argument, is necessarily a qualified one; it is the self in waking consciousness who is aware of an "I" and who, as will be shown, is associated with a qualified reality, the *jīva*, and not with Ātman, the non-dual Reality.

II

> The individual soul is not directly the highest Ātman, because it is seen to be different on account of the upādhis [limiting adjuncts]; nor is it different from the Ātman, because it is the Ātman who has entered as the jīvātman in all the bodies. We may call the jīva as a mere reflection of the Ātman.

The individual human person, the *jīva*, is a combination of reality and appearance. It is "reality" so far as Ātman is its ground; it is "appearance" so far as it is identified as finite, conditioned, relative. The individual self then is empirically real, for it is a datum of objective and subjective experience; but it is transcendentally unreal, for the self, in essence, is identical with the Absolute.

In attempting to understand the status of the *jīva*, Advaita Vedānta proffers two theories or metaphors, both of which as indicated above are suggested by Śaṁkara. A common intent informs these two theories, but the differences between them are instructive. According to the first, which is called *pratibimba-vāda*, the theory of reflection (and which is associated primarily with the Vivaraṇa school of Advaita), the *jīva* is a reflection of Ātman on the mirror of *avidyā*, and as such it is not-different from Ātman in essence. Just as in everyday experience where we know that the face in the mirror is not really different from the face in front of it, that the face in the mirror does not have an independent life of its own, and yet we maintain a distinction between them, so the *jīva* reflected in "ignorance" is not really different from its prototype, the Self, and yet it continues to be a *jīva* until the mirror itself is removed. The *pratibimba*, the reflection, is actually as real as the *bimba*, the prototype, being in essence the same thing; the *pratibimba* is misjudged to be different only because it appears to be located elsewhere than the *bimba*. One attains the truth of nondifference, then, the moment one understands that one is a reflection of Ātman that only appears to be different from it, but is identical with it in reality. And just as the reflection of a person in a body of water varies according to the state of the water, according as the water is calm or turbulent, clean or dirty, so the reflection of the Absolute varies according to the state of *avidyā* upon which it is reflected. The minds of men vary: some are more, some are less, under the influence of passion and desire; some are more, some are less, capable of intellectual discrimination and insight. The Absolute appears differently according to these differences among individuals.

The first description of, or metaphor about, the appearance of the *jīva* has this advantage; it suggests that the clearer the mirror, the more perfect is the relation between the *jīva* and Ātman. As the mirror loses its individual characteristics it reflects better what is presented to it. The *pratibimba-vāda* suggests, then, that rather than being restless, anticipating, and desiring, our minds ought to be like a clear and calm mirror capable of reflecting truth.

The second theory (which is associated with the Bhāmatī school of Advaita) is called *avaccheda-vāda*, the theory of limitation. According to this theory, consciousness that is pure and unqualified, without sensible qualities, cannot be "reflected," and hence the analogy with the mirror breaks down when pressed to the point to which the *pratibimba-vāda* takes it. The individual is not so much a reflection of consciousness as he is a limitation of it; a limitation that is constituted by the *upādhi* of ignorance. The term *upādhi*, translated usually as "limiting adjunct" or "limiting condition," is frequently employed in Advaitic analysis. A *upādhi* generally means the qualification or limitation of one thing by another thing. For Advaita, in the context with which we refer to it, a *upādhi* is the limitation, owing to mental imposition, of infinity by finitude, of unity by multiplicity. It results in the seeing of the Infinite by, and through, limitations or conditions that do not properly belong to the Infinite. As long as ignorance exists, the individual engages in *adhyāsa* (superimposition) and does not see himself as he really is, but as a being separated from other individuals, conditioned and finite. Just as space (*ākāśa*) is really one but is seen through limitations as if it were divided into particular spaces like the space in a pot or a room, so is the Self—it is one but is seen through limitations as if it were multiple. The limitations, grounded in ignorance, are only conceptual: the self is essentially unlimited and real.

Avaccheda-vāda, the theory of limitation, gives a somewhat greater empirical reality to the *jīva* than does *pratibimba-vāda,* the theory of reflection, in this sense that, whereas the *jīva* in the *pratibimba-vāda* is a mere fleeting image, as it were, the *jīva* in the *avaccheda-vāda* is a necessary "practical" reality. Because we are subject to *avidyā,* it is necessary, as a matter of practical convenience, that we perceive individual persons and objects as separate, distinct realities. For both theories, however, the *jīva qua jīva* is an illusory appearance. The existential status of the individual human person, whether as a reflection of Ātman or as a limitation of Ātman, is one of qualified reality; its essential status is that of unqualified reality, of identity with the Absolute. Whereas the world is "false" (*mithyā*), according to Advaita, in that it may completely disappear from consciousness when subrated, the self (*jīva*) is only misperceived: the self is really Brahman. In other words, the self is not so much denied by Brahman as its real nature (as not-different from Brahman) is revealed when Brahman is realized.

III

The analysis of the empirical or phenomenal self in Advaita Vedānta, as we reconstruct it, is primarily a "phenomenology" of consciousness. It is a description of the kinds of awareness that one has of oneself when one is subject to *avidyā.* Advaita does not so much explain the self as it describes the process by which we come to believe that it exists. In short, the Advaitic analysis of the empirical or qualified self is concerned to answer this question: By what process of mis-identification do we form the belief in the reality of what is in fact an illusory appearance?

The first domain of our self-awareness, according to Advaita, is that of our being awake in relation to a world of external objects. We take ourselves as "I" or "me" so far as we are aware of things, events, and processes. Waking consciousness (*jāgarita-sthāna*) or primitive I-consciousness is "intentional": Advaita agrees with existential phenomenology on this point that waking consciousness must have an object in order to be; that being awake means being *awake to.* And this being awake is never static. Waking consciousness ceaselessly shifts its attentive energies to different objects and to different aspects of a single object; it lapses into disinterest and is freshly stimulated by other interests. Waking consciousness is thus time-bound: when in it we do not see things all at once; nor do we think about things in a comprehensive totality; we are constrained to a successive representation, to a considering of things one at a time.

According to the *Māṇḍūkya Upaniṣad,* wherein the analysis of the states of consciousness of the self is given, waking consciousness is directed towards the enjoyment of gross objects. It is involved in desire and consequently is dissatisfied, for no object is capable of sustaining our interest in it; no object is capable of fulfilling the demands that we make upon it. We are aware of ourselves initially, then, as waking, time-bound, and enjoyment-seeking, but subsequently as dissatisfied beings. This self that is so dissatisfied, according to Advaita, is the self that has identified itself with its physical body. In waking consciousness we are aware that we are a part of physical nature, that we are formed from it, that we are sustained by it, and that eventually we return to it. The *Taittirīya Upaniṣad* speaks of this kind of identification as the *annamayakośa*, the "sheath" or "vesture" of food (matter). In waking consciousness we think that "this physical body is me"; and we miss thereby the truth of the Self. The physical body (or what becomes termed the *sthūla-śarīra*, the gross body) cannot be the Self, for it is conditioned, temporal, finite.

The first stage in the development of self-awareness, or the starting point in the phenomenology of consciousness, is that of waking consciousness, the basic standpoint of all philosophy. Advaita is not concerned here to deal with waking consciousness functionally; it is not concerned, that is, to explain the manner of the functioning of waking consciousness in relation to its contents. Advaita is concerned only to identify waking consciousness and to point out the kind of self-identification that follows from it. In waking consciousness the self has forgotten itself. Whereas in reality the self is Ātman, pure "subject," here it takes itself as a mere object. It is some-thing among other things; it is "estranged" from the fullness of its being.

The second level or state of consciousness distinguished by Advaita is that of dream consciousness (*svapna-sthāna*). It is the level of self that is inwardly cognitive of the impressions carried over from the waking state: it is the level of self that draws its sensuous and passional materials from past experience and in turn influences future experience within the waking state. The dream state is the state of fancy and wish-fulfillment and in function, if not in content, it may be equated with the "subconscious" of analytic psychology. Śaṁkara states that "after the cessation in sleep of the activities of the senses, (the individual) creates a subtle body of desires, and shapes his dreams according to the light of his own intellect." The dream state is thus a natural extension of the waking state, but, as further pointed out by Śaṁkara, the waking state lasts until the knowledge of Brahman is attained while the dream state is subrated daily by waking life. In other words, the stuff of dreams, although rooted in the waking life, is not empirically real in the same sense as the content of waking life, for one recognizes it for what it is, namely, fancy and desire (the illusory existent).

Advaita Vedānta attaches a good deal of importance, however, to the phenomenology of dream consciousness in order to show the continuity of consciousness and the persistence of self-awareness throughout all states of consciousness. The independence of the subject of experience from its object is clearly exhibited in the dream state. No matter how deeply involved one is with the objects of dream, one retains an independence from them (as embodied in the judgment "I had a dream") and indeed a greater freedom with respect to them than is possible in waking consciousness. One can violate all the rules of spatial-temporal relationships that hold between empirical objects when one is in the dream state; and one can readily "transpose" one's emotional relations to these objects from one kind of past experience to another. But because one is involved in one's dream as well as being a witness to it, one is committing a fundamental mis-identification of oneself with the contents of one's quasi-liberated consciousness. These contents are called subtle elements (*tanmātras*): not only are they less gross than the objects of waking consciousness, but they also subtlely influence the whole fabric of waking consciousness, constituting as they do the material out of which so much of "personality" is formed. And it is precisely this subtle influence that makes it difficult for the *jīva* to know itself, to become fully aware of the forces that motivate it and that mold its attitudes and values. The contents of the dream state are elusive, and from the standpoint of the experiencer, they are largely involuntary: they present themselves without conscious control or selectivity. Further, so far as the waking state is intimately bound up in the dream state, it too is largely involuntary. A complete freedom to choose the contents of consciousness is thus denied the *jīva*. The Advaitin would agree with Spinoza that we think we are free when we are aware of our desires, but that in fact we are not free as we fail to understand the causes of these desires—which causes, for the Advaitin, are traceable to a root cause of *avidyā*.

According to the Vedānta, the three *kośas* or sheaths that are associated with the dream state of consciousness and that constitute the "subtle body" . . . of the self are the *prāṇamayakośa*, the sheath of "vitality," the *manomayakośa*, the sheath of "mind," and the *vijñānamayakośa*, the sheath of "understanding." The *prāṇamayakośa* is the self identified as a vital being. We identify ourselves initially not only as gross physical beings but also as animate beings. . . . It has been shown in modern psychology (namely, by Freud) that all of us believe that "death is what happens to the other person"; that we cannot imagine what it would mean for our own consciousness to cease; that we believe ourselves to be immortal. This belief is grounded in the *prāṇamayakośa* in our identifying ourselves as persistent vital beings. But there is no genuine, that is to say, spiritual, immortality for the *jīva qua jīva*: it is condemned to "existence," to phenomenal reality, until it realizes Ātman.

The *manomayakośa* and the *vijñānamayakośa* comprise the mental life of the self. They are made up respectively of *manas* and the five organs of perception, and *buddhi* and the five sense organs. A general distinction is made throughout Indian philosophy between two aspects—functions or domains—of mental life: that of *manas* or "sense-mind" and that of *buddhi* or "intellect." The precise meaning and role given to these two domains of mental life differ from system to system as well as in the different stages in the development of a single system, but a core of meaning common enough is present throughout. *Manas*, the sense-mind, is an instrument, sometimes taken as a sense organ itself, which assimilates and synthesizes sense impressions and thus enables the self to make contact with external objects. It is involved with these objects and consequently gives rise to the possessive "my" and "mine." *Manas*, however, is somewhat blind, lacking as it does a discriminating objectivity, and is thus referred to as a mental condition of doubt. *Manas* rushes out through the senses, as it were, toward the form of any object presented to it and assimilates that form to itself. It only furnishes the self with percepts that must be acted upon, transformed, and guided by a higher mental function. This is the work of the *buddhi*, the intellect or reason. The *buddhi* is an instrument of discrimination, a faculty of judgment; it determines our intellectual attitudes, fortifies our beliefs, and makes understanding possible. Whenever one is aware of oneself, then, as a rational being who is capable of intellectual insight and judgment, one is involved in this *vijñānamayakośa*. Both the *manomayakośa* and the *vijñānamayakośa* form the *antaḥkāraṇa* or "internal organ," which is the psychological expression for the totality of mental functions in waking-dream consciousness.

According to Advaita, all the mental activities of the self who identifies himself as a mental being are subject to a pervasive *avidyā*. No true self-knowledge is possible until Ātman is realized, until there is a fundamental change in consciousness. The empirical self, being a subject, cannot be an object to itself. All knowledge that takes place apart from Ātman is within the subject/object situation: the self as knower, within the context of the waking and dream states of consciousness, is a self that necessarily separates itself from the object of knowledge and hence always imposes something of itself upon the object. In short, with *manas* and *buddhi,* with the totality of mental functions, we may be self-possessed but never possessed by the Self.

The next stage of consciousness identified by Vedānta is that of deep sleep (*suṣupti*), which is characterized by a bliss that follows from the holding in abeyance of all distinctions. Its *kośa* counterpart is the *ānandamayakośa* and is referred to as the "causal body" of the self. Deep-sleep consciousness is not "transcendental consciousness," the spiritual consciousness in which oneness is obtained, but it is not to be construed as a void on that account. Defined initially in negative terms as an absence of objects, of desires, and of activities, it is then described in positive terms as a state of joyous consciousness. It is, writes Śaṁkara, "an abundance of joy caused by the absence of the misery involved in the [usual] effort of the mind. . . ." Deep-sleep consciousness is the self as unified and integrated; it is not so much an overcoming of the distinctions that make for activity and desire as it is a harmonization and a being a witness to them. Distinctions, in other words, are not abolished here but are present in a kind of pure potentiality; and for this reason the *jīva* is said here to perceive pure *avidyā*, the cause or source of all distinctions. Further, deep-sleep consciousness . . . is also called "causal"; it is the ground for future actions: the various sheaths that are manifest in the waking and dream states are latent here ready to unfold as prompted by the effects of one's past experience (*karma*).

Lastly, the *Māṇḍūkya Upaniṣad*, through a series of negations and affirmations, describes the pure state of consciousness associated with Ātman.

> They consider the fourth to be that which is not conscious of the internal world, nor conscious of the external world, nor conscious of both the worlds, nor a mass of consciousness, nor simple consciousness, nor unconsciousness; which is unseen, beyond empirical determination, beyond the grasp (of the mind) undemonstrable, unthinkable, indescribable; of the nature of consciousness alone wherein all phenomena cease, unchanging, peaceful and non-dual.

This is transcendental consciousness (*turīya*—lit., "the fourth") the attainment of which leads to self-realization, to freedom (*mokṣa*). . . .

IV

. . . Phenomenally, as *jīvas*, as individual conscious beings, we are multi-personalities. We become the roles and functions that we perform; we become the kinds of persons we conceive ourselves to be; we become the many identifications we form of aspects of our self. Although we recognize the forces and conditions that act upon us, social as well as physical and psychological, we remain their victims: we ascribe ultimacy to them because we know of nothing to take their place. This, according to Advaita Vedānta, is the process through which we come to believe in the independent reality of the individual self and, consequently, to deny the reality of the Self. Its root cause is *avidyā*, ignorance. We are ignorant so far as we make of our physical, our biophysical, and our mental and emotional vestures something substantial, real, and ultimately valuable—without realizing that all being, reality, and value are grounded in, and arise from, our true Self. We are ignorant so far as we take an expression of consciousness (waking, dream, or deep sleep) as constituting the highest development of consciousness—without realizing that our consciousness, being identical with the Absolute, knows no limit.

The Self is One, it is not different from Brahman. This is the central metareligious or metapsychological affirmation of Advaita Vedānta. It means that man is essentially spiritual; that in the most profound dimension of his being he is no longer the "individual" that he ordinarily takes himself to be, but that he is precisely Reality itself. The affirmation is based not on mere speculation, but upon experience supported by a phenomenological analysis of what we erroneously take to be our selves. For Advaita, to affirm oneself as Reality is an act of a free man. The knowledge of non-difference leads to freedom, to the realization of the potentialities of our human being.

Descartes

René Descartes (1596–1650), whose reputation in his own time was based primarily on his work as a mathematician and scientist (he was the founder of analytic geometry and the Cartesian coordinates and made significant contributions to optics and meteorology), is regarded by many today as the father of modern Western philosophy. He set forth a new method that was based entirely on what he took to be the dictates of reason, free from any traditional or received authority. He resolved to doubt everything that could not be sustained by rational certainty. This led him to enunciate his famous cogito ergo sum, *"I think, therefore I am"—his belief that one cannot doubt that the thinking person who is doing the doubting truly exists. For Descartes, a person's essence is "mind," by which he meant not intelligence as such but consciousness, the awareness of one's own mental operations and their objects. Descartes held that human beings are unique in possessing consciousness; all other animals are essentially only machines. Descartes thus sharply divided the mental from the physical and set forth a dualism of mind and body that has haunted so much of modern Western philosophy.*

In his popular *Meditations on First Philosophy* (1641), from which the following selection is taken, Descartes presents his basic ideas with a clarity and directness quite appropriate to his concern with having "clear and distinct ideas." His assertion of the indubitable reality of his self has over the years attracted much attention and has been subject to continual criticism on various grounds, chief among them being that the most Descartes is entitled to assert by his method is that thinking goes on but not that there is a substantial self or "I" that is doing the thinking; and that this one-sided emphasis upon individual self-consciousness cannot make sense of the complex social factors that inform so much of our nature and our experience.

The Nature of the Human Mind

OF THE NATURE OF THE HUMAN MIND; AND THAT IT IS MORE EASILY KNOWN THAN THE BODY

I will . . . proceed by casting aside all that admits of the slightest doubt, not less than if I had discovered it to be absolutely false; and I will continue always in this track until I shall find something that is certain, or at least, if I can do nothing more, until I shall know with certainty that there is nothing certain. Archimedes, that he might transport the entire globe from the place it occupied to another, demanded only a point that was firm and immovable; so also, I shall be entitled to entertain the highest expectations, if I am fortunate enough to discover only one thing that is certain and indubitable.

I suppose, accordingly, that all the things which I see are false (fictitious); I believe that none of those objects which my fallacious memory represents ever existed; I suppose that I possess no senses; I believe that body, figure, extension, motion, and place are merely fictions of my mind. What is there, then, that can be esteemed true? Perhaps this only, that there is absolutely nothing certain.

But how do I know that there is not something different altogether from the objects I have now enumerated, of which it is impossible to entertain the slightest doubt? Is there not a God, or some being, by whatever name I may designate him, who causes these thoughts to arise in my mind? But why suppose such a being, for it may be I myself am capable of producing them? Am I, then, at least not something? But I before denied that I possessed senses or a body; I hesitate, however, for what follows from that? Am I so dependent on the body and the senses that without these I cannot exist? But I had the persuasion that there was absolutely nothing in the world, that there was no sky and no earth, neither minds nor bodies; was I not, therefore, at the same time, persuaded that I did not exist? Far from it; I assuredly existed, since I was persuaded. But there is I know not what being, who is possessed at once of the highest power and the deepest cunning, who is constantly employing all his ingenuity in deceiving me. Doubtless, then, I exist, since I am deceived; and, let him deceive me as he may, he can never bring it about that I am nothing, so long as I shall be conscious that I am something. So that it must, in fine, be maintained, all things being maturely and carefully considered, that this proposition (*pronunciatum*) I am, I exist, is necessarily true each time it is expressed by me, or conceived in my mind.

But I do not yet know with sufficient clearness what I am, though assured that I am; and hence, in the next place, I must take care, lest perchance I inconsiderately substitute some other object in room of what is properly myself, and thus wander from truth, even in that knowledge (cognition) which I hold to be of all others the

From *Meditations on First Philosophy*, II, by René Descartes, translated by John Veitch, in *The Rationalists* (n.d.). Reprinted with acknowledgment to Doubleday & Company, Inc.

René Descartes. The New York
Public Library Picture
Collection.

most certain and evident. For this reason, I will now consider anew what I formerly believed myself to be, before I entered on the present train of thought; and of my previous opinion I will retrench all that can in the least be invalidated by the grounds of doubt I have adduced, in order that there may at length remain nothing but what is certain and indubitable. What then did I formerly think I was? Undoubtedly I judged that I was a man. But what is a man? Shall I say a rational animal? Assuredly not; for it would be necessary forthwith to inquire into what is meant by animal, and what by rational, and thus, from a single question, I should insensibly glide into others, and these more difficult than the first; nor do I now possess enough of leisure to warrant me in wasting my time amid subtleties of this sort. I prefer here to attend to the thoughts that sprung up of themselves in my mind, and were inspired by my own nature alone, when I applied myself to the consideration of what I was. In the first place, then, I thought that I possessed a countenance, hands, arms, and all the fabric of members that appears in a corpse, and which I called by the name of body. It further occurred to me that I was nourished, that I walked, perceived, and thought, and all those actions I referred to the soul; but what the soul itself was I either did not stay to consider, or, if I did, I imagined that it was something extremely rare and subtile, like wind, or flame, or ether, spread through my grosser parts. As regarded the body, I did not even doubt of its nature, but thought I distinctly knew it, and if I had wished to describe it according to the notions I then entertained, I should have explained myself in this manner: By body I understand all that can be terminated by a certain figure; that can be comprised in a certain place, and so fill a certain space as therefrom to exclude every other body; that can be perceived either by touch, sight, hearing, taste, or smell; that can be moved in different ways, not indeed of itself, but by something foreign to it by which it is touched [and from which it receives the impression]; for the power of self-motion, as likewise that of perceiving and thinking, I held as by no means pertaining to the nature of body; on the contrary, I was somewhat astonished to find such faculties existing in some bodies.

But [as to myself, what can I now say that I am], since I suppose there exists an extremely powerful, and, if I may so speak, malignant being, whose whole endeavours are directed towards deceiving me? Can I affirm that I possess any one of all those attributes of which I have lately spoken as belonging to the nature of body? After attentively considering them in my own mind, I find none of them that can properly be said to belong to myself. To recount them were idle and tedious. Let us pass, then, to the attributes of the soul. The first mentioned were the powers of nutrition and walking; but, if it be true that I have no body, it is true likewise that I am capable neither of walking nor of being nourished. Perception is another attribute of the soul; but perception too is impossible without the body: besides, I have frequently, during sleep, believed that I perceived objects which I afterwards observed I did not in reality perceive. Thinking is another attribute of the soul; and here I discover what properly belongs to myself. This alone is inseparable from me. I am—I exist: this is certain; but how often? As often as I think; for perhaps it would even happen, if I should wholly cease to think, that I should at the same time altogether cease to be. I now admit nothing that is not necessarily true: I am therefore, precisely speaking, only a thinking thing, that is, a mind, understanding, or reason,—terms whose signification was before unknown to me. I am, however, a real thing, and really existent; but what thing? The answer was, a thinking thing. The question now arises, am I aught besides? I will stimulate my imagination with a view to discover whether I am not still something more than a thinking being. Now it is plain I am not the assemblage of members called the human body; I am not a thin and penetrating air diffused through all these members, or wind, or flame, or vapour, or breath, or any of all the things I can imagine; for I supposed that all these were not, and, without changing the supposition, I find that I still feel assured of my existence.

But it is true, perhaps, that those very things which I suppose to be non-existent, because they are unknown to me, are not in truth different from myself whom I know. This is a point I cannot determine, and do not now enter into any dispute regarding it. I can only judge of things that are known to me: I am conscious that I exist, and I who know that I exist inquire into what I am. It is, however, perfectly certain that the knowledge of my existence, thus precisely taken, is not dependent on things, the existence of which is as yet unknown to me: and consequently it is not dependent on any of the things I can feign in imagination. Moreover, the phrase itself, I frame an image reminds me of my error; for I should in truth frame one if I were to imagine myself to be anything, since to imagine is nothing more than to contemplate the figure or image of a corporeal thing; but I already know that I exist, and that it is possible at the same time that all those images, and in general all that relates to the nature of body, are merely dreams [or chimeras]. From this I discover that it is not more reasonable to say, I will excite my imagination that I may know more distinctly what I am, than to express myself as follows: I am now awake, and perceive something real; but because my perception is not sufficiently clear, I will of express purpose go to sleep that my dreams may represent to me the object of my perception with more truth and clearness. And, therefore, I know that nothing of all that I can embrace in imagination belongs to the knowledge which I have of myself, and that there is need to recall with the utmost care the mind from this mode of thinking, that it may be able to know its own nature with perfect distinctness.

But what, then, am I? A thinking thing, it has been said. But what is a thinking thing? It is a thing that doubts, understands [conceives], affirms, denies, wills, refuses, that imagines also, and perceives. Assuredly it is not little, if all these properties belong to my nature. But why should they not belong to it? Am I not that very being who now doubts of almost everything; who, for all that, understands and conceives certain things, who affirms one alone as true, and denies the others; who desires to know more of them, and does not wish to be deceived; who imagines many things, sometimes even despite his will; and is likewise percipient of many, as if through the medium of the senses. Is there nothing of all this as true as that I am, even although I should be always dreaming, and although he who gave me being employed all his ingenuity to deceive me? Is there also any one of these attributes that can be properly distinguished from my thought, or that can be said to be separate from myself? For it is of itself so evident that it is I who doubt, I who understand, and I who desire, that it is here unnecessary to add anything by way of rendering it more clear. And I am as certainly the same being who imagines; for, although it may be (as I before supposed) that nothing I imagine is true, still the power of imagination does not cease really to exist in me and to form part of my thoughts. In fine, I am the same being who perceives, that is, who apprehends certain objects as by the organs of sense, since, in truth, I see light, hear a noise, and feel heat. But it will be said that these presentations are false, and that I am dreaming. Let it be so. At all events it is certain that I seem to see light, hear a noise, and feel heat; this cannot be false, and this is what in me is properly called perceiving, which is nothing else than thinking. From this I begin to know what I am with somewhat greater clearness and distinctness than heretofore.

Buddhism

Buddhism originated in India in the fifth century B.C.E. The founder, Siddhartha Gautama (563–486 B.C.E.) was, according to tradition, born as a member of a royal family whose territory lay along the southern edge of Nepal, approximately one hundred miles north of the holy Indian city of Benares. Although the young Siddhartha lived a protected and luxurious life, he left the palace grounds on numerous occasions and was overwhelmed, so the story goes, by the terrible misery, sickness, and ignorance that he observed. One day, in reaction to this, he decided it was his task to come to a deep understanding of life and to find a way to help others escape from their suffering. He then left the palace and sought various teachers, or gurus, for advice and instruction. He was, however, dissatisfied with their teachings and subsequently joined a group of monks who practiced various extreme austerities such as extended fasting—but still he did not attain to the insight that he was seeking. He resolved then to meditate for such a time as was necessary to attain enlightenment ("Buddha" means "the enlightened one"). After considerable effort he did achieve the understanding he was seeking and traveled to Benares, where he delivered his first and most famous sermon which set forth the Four Noble Truths of Buddhism.

The first noble truth states that all life is "suffering" (*duḥkha*)—that everything in life is subject to death and discord; that our desires, being insatiable, are always frustrated; that impermanence is everywhere stamped on existence. The second truth insists that all suffering has a cause—the selfish craving and desire that are founded on our ignorance, and on our belief in a permanent self and our attachment to it. The third truth argues that such suffering caused by selfish craving can be overcome and destroyed. And the fourth truth sets forth an ethical and mental discipline by which *nirvāṇa* (the extinguishing of the flame of desire) may be achieved.

At first Buddhism confined its teachings on ethical and meditational practices to monks who were dedicated to the Buddhist way of life. The early Buddhists rejected the authority of the Hindu scriptures and social practices and refrained from formulating elaborate philosophical doctrines. Over time, however, various systems of thought developed, and one of the main branches of Buddhism, the Theravāda (Way of the Elders) became especially concerned with the rational justification of Buddhist principles. Devotees of this branch believed *nirvāṇa* is attained by individuals who through their own effort follow a rigorous path of disciplined awareness and action. Buddha was regarded as a great teacher; no gods were evoked as objects of worship or as explanatory principles. The other main branch, the Mahāyāna, developed in reaction to the Theravāda's demanding approach. According to its teachings, the fate of each person is connected to the fate of all others. The ideal was the *bodhisattva*, one who, out of compassion, forgoes his own complete enlightenment in order to help others. It was within the Mahāyāna tradition that "popular" Buddhism, with its innumerable divine beings, emerged, and, somewhat ironically, at the same time many of the most sophisticated schools of Buddhist philosophy and logic were developed. By the twelfth century A.C.E., for a variety of both political and philosophical reasons, Buddhism had few followers in India. It continued, however, to grow and gain adherents in other countries across Asia; today the Theravāda tradition is found mainly in Thailand, Laos, Cambodia, and Sri Lanka; the Mahāyāna, in Nepal, China, and Japan.

In striking contrast to both the Vedāntic tradition and Cartesianism, Buddhism, especially in its earliest phases, denied the existence of a substantial self, both empirically and transcendentally. According to its doctrine of *anātman* or "no-self," a person is his or her experience; a person is nothing but the constituents that make up one's empirical being. An individual is thus a pattern of experience, but it is not an "I" who experiences. The impersonal and impermanent elements are of five types (the *pañca-skandhas*): (1) perception (*saṁjñā*); (2) feelings or sensations (*vedanā*); (3) volitional dispositions or impressions (*saṁskāras*)—all the impulses, emotions, and memories that are associated with past experience and dispose one to act in particular ways; (4) consciousness or intelligence (*vijñāna*); and (5) the body (*rūpa*). Upon death nothing persists

Seated Bodhisattva Padmapani, India, ninth–tenth century, gray stone, height twenty-four inches. Honolulu Academy of Arts.

save the psychic continuity produced by *karma*, one's accumulated action, that gives rise to, or forms a continuity with, a new empirical pattern.

Karma, for Buddhism, thus does not involve a transmigration of a self. It does nevertheless constitute the basis of human bondage. We are bound to the results of our actions, and these results bind us in our manner of future activity, by our desires and attachments, by our "clinging" to ourselves. The first "noble truth" of Buddhism, as we have seen, is that all life is suffering (*duḥkha*)—that everything in life is subject to change and decay, and thus that nothing is able to provide any kind of enduring satisfaction. This suffering comes about fundamentally because of the ego-desires that arise out of our ignorance of who we are.

In the *Milindapañha* (a selection from which appears below), the well-known dialogue between the Buddhist monk Nāgasena and the Greco-Bactrian king Milinda, Nāgasena argues that any object, a chariot, for example, is exhaustively accounted for by the elements that make it up as they stand in relation to one another. There is no "chariot" apart from, or underlying, the empirical constituents. As the appended commentaries from other Buddhist sources point out, it is similarly with ourselves. One's very name is a mere name, a convenient and conventional way of pointing to an individual as, and only as, empirically constituted. "There is no Ego there to be found." An individual is only a continuity of elements that arise and perish in causal connectedness.

There Is No Ego or Personal Identity; Rebirth Is Not Transmigration

THERE IS NO EGO

Translated from the *Milindapañha* (25[1])

Then drew near Milinda the king to where the venerable Nāgasena was; and having drawn near, he greeted the venerable Nāgasena; and having passed the compliments of friendship and civility, he sat down respectfully at one side. And the venerable Nāgasena returned the greeting; by which, verily, he won the heart of king Milinda.

And Milinda the king spoke to the venerable Nāgasena as follows:—

"How is your reverence called? Bhante [priest], what is your name?"

"Your majesty, I am called Nāgasena; my fellow-priests, your majesty, address me as Nāgasena: but whether parents give one the name Nāgasena, or Sūrasena, or Vīrasena, or Sīhasena, it is, nevertheless, your majesty, but a way of counting, a term, an appellation, a convenient designation, a mere name, this Nāgasena; for there is no Ego here to be found."

Then said Milinda the king,—

Reprinted with permission of the publishers from *Buddhism in Translation*, translated by Henry Clark Warren (Cambridge, Mass.: Harvard University Press). Copyright © 1896, 1953, by the President and Fellows of Harvard College.

"Listen to me, my lords, ye five hundred Yonakas, and ye eighty thousand priests! Nāgasena here says thus: 'There is no Ego here to be found.' Is it possible, pray, for me to assent to what he says?"

And Milinda the king spoke to the venerable Nāgasena as follows:—

"Bhante Nāgasena, if there is no Ego to be found, who is it then furnishes you priests with the priestly requisites,—robes, food, bedding, and medicine, the reliance of the sick? who is it makes use of the same? who is it keeps the precepts? who is it applies himself to meditation? who is it realizes the Paths, the Fruits, and Nirvana? who is it destroys life? who is it takes what is not given him? who is it commits immorality? who is it tells lies? who is it drinks intoxicating liquor? who is it commits the five crimes that constitute 'proximate karma' [karma that is brought forth in another existence]? In that case, there is no merit; there is no demerit; there is no one who does or causes to be done meritorious or demeritorious deeds; neither good nor evil deeds can have any fruit or result. Bhante Nāgasena, neither is he a murderer who kills a priest, nor can you priests, bhante Nāgasena, have any teacher, preceptor, or ordination. When you say, 'My fellow-priests, your majesty, address me as Nāgasena,' what then is this Nāgasena? Pray, bhante, is the hair of the head Nāgasena?"

"Nay, verily, your majesty."

"Is the hair of the body Nāgasena?"

"Nay, verily, your majesty."

"Are nails . . . teeth . . . skin . . . flesh . . . sinews . . . bones . . . marrow of the bones . . . kidneys . . . heart . . . liver . . . pleura . . . spleen . . . lungs . . . intestines . . . mesentery . . . stomach . . . faeces . . . bile . . . phlegm . . . pus . . . blood . . . sweat . . . fat . . . tears . . . lymph . . . saliva . . . snot . . . synovial fluid . . . urine . . . brain of the head Nāgasena?"

"Nay, verily, your majesty."

"Is now, bhante, form Nāgasena?"

"Nay, verily, your majesty."

"Is sensation Nāgasena?"

"Nay, verily, your majesty."

"Is perception Nāgasena?"

"Nay, verily, your majesty."

"Are the predispositions Nāgasena?"

"Nay, verily, your majesty."

"Is consciousness Nāgasena?"

"Nay, verily, your majesty."

"Are, then, bhante, form, sensation, perception, the predispositions, and consciousness unitedly Nāgasena?"

"Nay, verily, your majesty."

"Is it, then, bhante, something besides form, sensation, perception, the predispositions, and consciousness, which is Nāgasena?"

"Nay, verily, your majesty."

"Bhante, although I question you very closely, I fail to discover any Nāgasena. Verily, now, bhante, Nāgasena is a mere empty sound. What Nāgasena is there here? Bhante, you speak a falsehood, a lie: there is no Nāgasena."

Then the venerable Nāgasena spoke to Milinda the king as follows:—

"Your majesty, you are a delicate prince, an exceedingly delicate prince; and if, your majesty, you walk in the middle of the day on hot sandy ground, and you tread on rough grit, gravel, and sand, your feet become sore, your body tired, the mind is oppressed, and the body-consciousness suffers. Pray, did you come afoot, or riding?"

"Bhante, I do not go afoot: I came in a chariot."

"Your majesty, if you came in a chariot, declare to me the chariot. Pray, your majesty, is the pole the chariot?"

"Nay, verily, bhante."

"Is the axle the chariot?"

"Nay, verily, bhante."

"Are the wheels the chariot?"

"Nay, verily, bhante."

"Is the chariot-body the chariot?"

"Nay, verily, bhante."

"Is the banner-staff the chariot?"

"Nay, verily, bhante."

"Is the yoke the chariot?"

"Nay, verily, bhante."

"Are the reins the chariot?"

"Nay, verily, bhante."

"Is the goading-stick the chariot?"

"Nay, verily, bhante."

"Pray, your majesty, are pole, axle, wheels, chariot-body, banner-staff, yoke, reins, and goad unitedly the chariot?"

"Nay, verily, bhante."

"Is it, then, your majesty, something else besides pole, axle, wheels, chariot-body, banner-staff, yoke, reins, and goad which is the chariot?"

"Nay, verily, bhante."

"Your majesty, although I question you very closely, I fail to discover any chariot. Verily now, your majesty, the word chariot is a mere empty sound. What chariot is there here? Your majesty, you speak a falsehood, a lie: there is no chariot. Your majesty, you are the chief king in all the continent of India; of whom are you afraid that you speak a lie? Listen to me, my lords, ye five hundred Yonakas, and ye eighty thousand priests! Milinda the king here says thus: 'I came in a chariot;' and being requested, 'Your majesty, if you came in a chariot, declare to me the chariot,' he fails to produce any chariot. Is it possible, pray, for me to assent to what he says?"

When he had thus spoken, the five hundred Yonakas applauded the venerable Nāgasena and spoke to Milinda the king as follows:—

"Now, your majesty, answer, if you can."

Then Milinda the king spoke to the venerable Nāgasena as follows:—

"Bhante Nāgasena, I speak no lie: the word 'chariot' is but a way of counting, term, appellation, convenient designation, and name for pole, axle, wheels, chariot-body, and banner-staff."

"Thoroughly well, your majesty, do you understand a chariot. In exactly the same way, your majesty, in respect of me, Nāgasena is but a way of counting, term, appellation, convenient designation, mere name for the hair of my head, hair of my body . . . brain of the head, form, sensation, perception, the predispositions, and consciousness. But in the absolute sense there is no Ego here to be found. And the priestess Vajirā, your majesty, said as follows in the presence of The Blessed One:—

> " 'Even as the word of "chariot" means
> That members join to frame a whole;
> So when the Groups appear to view,
> We use the phrase, "A living being." ' "

"It is wonderful, bhante Nāgasena! It is marvellous, bhante Nāgasena! Brilliant and prompt is the wit of your replies. If The Buddha were alive, he would applaud. Well done, well done, Nāgasena! Brilliant and prompt is the wit of your replies."

Translated from the Visuddhi-Magga (chap. xviii)

Just as the word "chariot" is but a mode of expression for axle, wheels, chariot-body, pole, and other constituent members, placed in a certain relation to each other, but when we come to examine the members one by one, we discover that in the absolute sense there is no chariot; and just as the word "house" is but a mode of expression for wood and other constituents of a house, surrounding space in a certain relation, but in the absolute sense there is no house; and just as the word "fist" is but a mode of expression for the fingers, the thumb, etc., in a certain relation; and the word "lute" for the body of the lute, strings, etc.; "army" for elephants, horses, etc.; "city" for fortifications, houses, gates, etc.; "tree" for trunk, branches, foliage, etc., in a certain relation, but when we come to examine the parts one by one, we discover that in the absolute sense there is no tree; in exactly the same way the words "living entity" and "Ego" are but a mode of expression for the presence of the five attachment groups, but when we come to examine the elements of being one by one, we discover that in the absolute sense there is no living entity there to form a basis for such figments as "I am," or "I"; in other words, that in the absolute sense there is only name and form. The insight of him who perceives this is called knowledge of the truth. . . .

NO CONTINUOUS PERSONAL IDENTITY

Translated from the *Milindapañha* (40[1])

"Bhante Nāgasena," said the king, "is a person when just born that person himself, or is he some one else?"

"He is neither that person," said the elder, "nor is he some one else."

"Give an illustration."

"What do you say to this, your majesty? When you were a young, tender, weakly infant lying on your back, was that your present grown-up self?"

"Nay, verily, bhante. The young, tender, weakly infant lying on its back was one person, and my present grown-up self is another person."

"If that is the case, your majesty, there can be no such thing as a mother, or a father, or a teacher, or an educated man, or a righteous man, or a wise man. . . . Is it one person who is a student, and another person who has finished his education? Is it one person who commits a crime, and another person whose hands and feet are cut off?"

"Nay, verily, bhante. But what, bhante, would you reply to these questions?"

Said the elder, "It was I, your majesty, who was a young, tender, weakly infant lying on my back, and it is I who am now grown up. It is through their connection with the embryonic body that all these different periods are unified."

"Give an illustration."

"It is as if, your majesty, a man were to light a light;—would it shine all night?"

"Assuredly, bhante, it would shine all night."

"Pray, your majesty, is the flame of the first watch the same as the flame of the middle watch?"

"Nay, verily, bhante."

"Is the flame of the middle watch the same as the flame of the last watch?"

"Nay, verily, bhante."

"Pray, then, your majesty, was there one light in the first watch, another light in the middle watch, and a third light in the last watch?"

"Nay, verily, bhante. Through connection with that first light there was light all night."

"In exactly the same way, your majesty, do the elements of being join one another in serial succession: one element perishes, another arises, succeeding each other as it were instantaneously. Therefore neither as the same nor as a different person do you arrive at your latest aggregation of consciousnesses."

"Give another illustration."

"It is as if, your majesty, new milk were to change in process of time into sour cream, and from sour cream into fresh butter, and from fresh butter into clarified butter. And if any one, your majesty, were to say that the sour cream, the fresh butter, and the clarified butter were each of them the very milk itself—now would he say well, if he were to say so?"

"Nay, verily, bhante. They came into being through connection with that milk."

"In exactly the same way, your majesty, do the elements of being join one another in serial succession: one element perishes, another arises, succeeding each other as it were instantaneously. Therefore neither as the same nor as a different person do you arrive at your latest aggregation of consciousnesses."

"You are an able man, bhante Nāgasena."

REBIRTH IS NOT TRANSMIGRATION

Translated from the *Milindapañha* (71[10])

Said the king: "Bhante Nāgasena, does rebirth take place without anything transmigrating [passing over]?"

"Yes, your majesty. Rebirth takes place without anything transmigrating."

"How, bhante Nāgasena, does rebirth take place without anything transmigrating? Give an illustration."

"Suppose, your majesty, a man were to light a light from another light; pray, would the one light have passed over [transmigrated] to the other light?"

"Nay, verily, bhante."

"In exactly the same way, your majesty, does rebirth take place without anything transmigrating."

"Give another illustration."

"Do you remember, your majesty, having learnt, when you were a boy, some verse or other from your professor of poetry?"

"Yes, bhante."

"Pray, your majesty, did the verse pass over [transmigrate] to you from your teacher?"

"Nay, verily, bhante."

"In exactly the same way, your majesty, does rebirth take place without anything transmigrating."

"You are an able man, bhante Nāgasena."

[It is important to realize that the *anātman* teaching has for its aim the attaining of *nirvāna*, or enlightenment. The following selection makes it clear that only a fool would remain attached to the nonexistent, an Ego, and that an understanding of *anātman* yields precisely that nonattachment to self that is essential to the attainment of enlightenment.]

ALL SIGNS OF AN EGO ARE ABSENT

Translated from the *Mahā-Vagga* (i. 6[33])

Then The Blessed One addressed the band of five priests:—

"Form, O priests, is not an Ego. For if now, O priests, this form were an Ego, then would not this form tend towards destruction, and it would be possible to say of form, 'Let my form be this way; let not my form be that way!' But inasmuch, O priests, as form is not an Ego, therefore does form tend towards destruction, and it is not possible to say of form, 'Let my form be this way; let not my form be that way!'

"Sensation ... perception ... the predispositions ... consciousness, is not an Ego. For if now, O priests, this consciousness were an Ego, then would not this consciousness tend towards destruction, and it would be possible to say of consciousness, 'Let my consciousness be this way; let not my consciousness be that way!' But inasmuch, O priests, as consciousness is not an Ego, therefore does consciousness tend towards destruction, and it is not possible to say of consciousness, 'Let my consciousness be this way; let not my consciousness be that way!'

"What think you, O priests? Is form permanent, or transitory?"

"It is transitory, Reverend Sir."

"And that which is transitory—is it evil, or is it good?"

"It is evil, Reverend Sir."

"And that which is transitory, evil, and liable to change—is it possible to say of it: 'This is mine; this am I; this is my Ego'?"

"Nay, verily, Reverend Sir."

"Is sensation ... perception ... the predispositions ... consciousness, permanent, or transitory?"

"It is transitory, Reverend Sir."

"And that which is transitory—is it evil, or is it good?"

"It is evil, Reverend Sir."

"And that which is transitory, evil, and liable to change—is it possible to say of it: 'This is mine; this am I; this is my Ego'?"

"Nay, verily, Reverend Sir."

"Accordingly, O priests, as respects all form whatsoever, past, future, or present, be it subjective or existing outside, gross or subtile, mean or exalted, far or near, the correct view in the light of the highest knowledge is as follows: 'This is not mine; this am I not; this is not my Ego.'

"As respects all sensation whatsoever ... as respects all perception whatsoever ... as respects all predispositions whatsoever ... as respects all consciousness whatsoever, past, future, or present, be it subjective or existing outside, gross or subtile, mean or exalted, far or near, the correct view in the light of the highest knowledge is as follows: 'This is not mine; this am I not; this is not my Ego.'

"Perceiving this, O priests, the learned and noble disciple conceives an aversion for form, conceives an aversion for sensation, conceives an aversion for perception, conceives an aversion for the predispositions, conceives an aversion for consciousness. And in conceiving this aversion he becomes divested of passion, and by the absence of passion he becomes free, and when he is free he becomes aware that he is free; and he knows that rebirth is exhausted, that he has lived the holy life, that he has done what it behooved him to do, and that he is no more for this world."

Hume

*David Hume (1711–1776), a Scottish philosopher and historian, was the most in-
fluential philosopher in the British empiricist tradition and a major thinker in the
so-called Enlightenment movement in eighteenth-century Europe. Hume was
deeply skeptical about religious claims to truth and put forward controversial
ideas in ethics as well. In his* Enquiry Concerning the Principles of Morals, *he tries
to show how reason, while having instrumental force in helping us to decide
how to achieve our aims, is nevertheless a slave of the passions when it comes to
determining our ultimate values and commitments.*

In his most famous work, *A Treatise of Human Nature*, published in 1739, Hume argues,
along lines similar to Buddhism but with a very different non-nirvanic aim, that it is impossible for us to experience and to know ourselves as simple, enduring substantial
selves. Whenever we look into ourselves, Hume maintains, we always come upon some
particular idea or feeling; we never grasp the "real self" that we ordinarily (but erroneously) believe ourselves to be. An individual, in the final analysis, is just a bundle of
perceptions that are in constant flux.

According to Hume, every idea that we have in the mind must, if it is to be anything
other than an empty abstraction, have a corresponding sense-impression. By "impression" Hume means any lively perception, any sensation, emotion, or feeling. Ideas come
from this domain of experience; they *copy* impressions.

In his analysis of the self Hume attacks the notion that one can know, or have a true
idea about, the identity and simplicity of the self. He asks from what impression we can
derive this idea of a self. Finding none, he concludes that we cannot rightly assert the
existence of such a self.

Of Personal Identity

There are some philosophers, who imagine we are every moment intimately conscious of what we call our SELF; that we feel its existence and its continuance in existence; and are certain, beyond the evidence of a demonstration, both of its perfect identity and simplicity. The strongest sensation, the most violent passion, say they, instead of distracting us from this view, only fix it the more intensely, and make us consider their influence on *self* either by their pain or pleasure. To attempt a farther proof of this were to weaken its evidence; since no proof can be deriv'd from any fact, of which we are so intimately conscious; nor is there any thing, of which we can be certain, if we doubt of this.

Unluckily all these positive assertions are contrary to that very experience, which is pleaded for them, nor have we any idea of *self*, after the manner it is here explain'd. For from what impression cou'd this idea be deriv'd? This question 'tis impossible to answer without a manifest contradiction and absurdity; and yet 'tis a question, which must necessarily be answer'd, if we wou'd have the idea of self pass for clear and intelligible. It must be some one impression, that gives rise to every real idea. But self or person is not any one impression, but that to which our several impressions and ideas are suppos'd to have a reference. If any impression gives rise to the idea of self, that impression must continue invariably the same, thro' the whole course of our lives; since self is suppos'd to exist after that manner. But there is no impression constant and invariable. Pain and pleasure, grief and joy, passions and sensations succeed each other, and never all exist at the same time. It cannot, therefore, be from any of these impressions, or from any other, that the idea of self is deriv'd; and consequently there is no such idea.

But farther, what must become of all our particular perceptions upon this hypothesis? All these are different, and distinguishable, and separable from each other, and may be separately consider'd, and may exist separately, and have no need of any thing to support their existence. After what manner, therefore, do they belong to self; and how are they connected with it? For my part, when I enter most intimately into what I call *myself*, I always stumble on some particular perception or other, of heat or cold, light or shade, love or hatred, pain or pleasure. I never can catch *myself* at any time without a perception, and never can observe any thing but the perception. When my perceptions are remov'd for any time, as by sound sleep; so long am I insensible of *myself*, and may truly be said not to exist. And were all my perceptions remov'd by death, and cou'd I neither think, nor feel, nor see, nor love, nor hate after the dissolution of my body, I shou'd be entirely annihilated, nor do I conceive what is farther requisite to make me a perfect non-entity. If any one upon serious and unprejudic'd reflexion, thinks he has a different notion of *himself*, I must confess I can reason no longer with him. All I can allow him is, that he may be

---

in the right as well as I, and that we are essentially different in this particular. He may, perhaps, perceive something simple and continu'd, which he calls *himself*; tho' I am certain there is no such principle in me.

But setting aside some metaphysicians of this kind, I may venture to affirm of the rest of mankind, that they are nothing but a bundle or collection of different perceptions, which succeed each other with an inconceivable rapidity, and are in a perpetual flux and movement. Our eyes cannot turn in their sockets without varying our perceptions. Out thought is still more variable than our sight; and all our other senses and faculties contribute to this change; nor is there any single power of the soul, which remains unalterably the same, perhaps for one moment. The mind is a kind of theatre, where several perceptions successively make their appearance; pass, re-pass, glide away, and mingle in an infinite variety of postures and situations. There is properly no *simplicity* in it at one time, nor *identity* in different; whatever natural propension we may have to imagine that simplicity and identity. The comparison of the theatre must not mislead us. They are the successive perceptions only, that constitute the mind; nor have we the most distant notion of the place, where these scenes are represented, or of the materials, of which it is compos'd.

What then gives us so great a propension to ascribe an identity to these successive perceptions, and to suppose ourselves possest of an invariable and uninterrupted existence thro' the whole course of our lives? In order to answer this question, we must distinguish betwixt personal identity, as it regards our thought or imagination, and as it regards our passions or the concern we take in ourselves. The first is our present subject; and to explain it perfectly we must take the matter pretty deep, and account for that identity, which we attribute to plants and animals; there being a great analogy betwixt it, and the identity of a self or person.

We have a distinct idea of an object, that remains invariable and uninterrupted thro' a suppos'd variation of time; and this idea we call that of *identity* or *sameness*. We have also a distinct idea of several different objects existing in succession, and connected together by a close relation; and this to an accurate view affords as perfect a notion of *diversity*, as if there was no manner of relation among the objects. But tho' these two ideas of identity, and a succession of related objects be in themselves perfectly distinct, and even contrary, yet 'tis certain, that in our common way of thinking they are generally confounded with each other. That action of the imagination, by which we consider the uninterrupted and invariable object, and that by which we reflect on the succession of related objects, are almost the same to the feeling, nor is there much more effort of thought requir'd in the latter case than in the former. The relation facilitates the transition of the mind from one object to another, and renders its passage as smooth as if it contemplated one continu'd object. This resemblance is the cause of the confusion and mistake, and makes us substitute the notion of identity, instead of that of related objects. However at one instant we may consider the related succession as variable or interrupted, we are sure the next to ascribe to it a perfect identity, and regard it as invariable and uninterrupted. Our propensity to this mistake is so great from the resemblance above-mention'd, that we fall into it before we are aware; and tho' we incessantly correct ourselves by reflexion, and return to a more accurate method of thinking, yet we cannot long sustain our philosophy, or take off this biass from the imagination. Our last resource is to yield to it, and boldly assert that these different related objects are in effect the same, however interrupted and variable. In order to justify to ourselves this absurdity, we often feign some new and unintelligible principle, that connects the objects together, and prevents their interruption or variation. Thus we feign the continu'd existence of the perceptions of our senses, to remove the interruption; and run into the notion of a *soul*, and *self*, and *substance*, to disguise the variation. But we may farther observe, that where we do not give rise to such a fiction, our propension to confound identity with relation is so great, that we are apt to imagine something unknown and mysterious, connecting the parts, beside their relation; and this I take to be the case with regard to the identity as ascribe to plants and vegetables. And even when this does not take place, we still feel a propensity to confound these ideas, tho' we are not able fully to satisfy ourselves in that particular, nor find any thing invariable and uninterrupted to justify our notion of identity.

Thus the controversy concerning identity is not merely a dispute of words. For when we attribute identity, in an improper sense, to variable or interrupted objects, our mistake is not confin'd to the expression, but is commonly attended with a fiction, either of something invariable and uninterrupted, or of something mysterious and inexplicable, or at least with a propensity to such fictions. What will suffice to prove this hypothesis to the satisfaction of every fair enquirer, is to shew from daily experience and observation, that the objects, which are variable or interrupted, and yet are suppos'd to continue the same, are such only as consist of a succession of parts, connected together by resemblance, contiguity, or causation. For as such a succession answers evidently to our notion of diversity, it can only be by mistake we ascribe to it an identity; and as the relation of parts, which leads us into this mistake, is really nothing but a quality, which produces an association of ideas, and an easy transition of the imagination from one to another, it can only be from the resemblance, which this act of the mind bears to that, by which we contemplate one continu'd object, that the error arises. Our chief business, then, must be to prove, that all objects, to which we ascribe identity, without observing their invariableness and uninterruptedness, are such as consist of a succession of related objects.

In order to this, suppose any mass of matter, of which the parts are contiguous and connected, to be plac'd before us; 'tis plain we must attribute a perfect identity to this mass, provided all the parts continue uninterruptedly and invariably the same, whatever motion or change of place we may observe either in the whole or in any of the parts. But supposing some very *small* or *inconsiderable* part to be added to the mass, or substracted from it; tho' this absolutely destroys the identity of the whole, strictly speaking; yet as we seldom think so accurately, we scruple not to pronounce a mass of matter the same, where we find so trivial an alteration. The passage of the thought from the object before the change to the object after it, is so smooth and easy, that we scarce perceive the transition, and are apt to imagine, that 'tis nothing but a continu'd survey of the same object. . . .

We may also consider the two following phænomena, which are remarkable in their kind. The first is, that tho' we commonly be able to distinguish pretty exactly betwixt numerical and specific identity, yet it sometimes happens, that we confound them, and in our thinking and reasoning employ the one for the other. Thus a man, who hears a noise, that is frequently interrupted and renew'd, says, it is still the same noise; tho' 'tis evident the sounds have only a specific identity or resemblance, and there is nothing numerically the same, but the cause, which produc'd them. In like manner it may be said without breach of the propriety of language, that such a church, which was formerly of brick, fell to ruin, and that the parish rebuilt the same church of free-stone, and according to modern architecture. Here neither the form nor materials are the same, nor is there any thing common to the two objects, but their relation to the inhabitants of the parish; and yet this alone is sufficient to make us denominate them the same. But we must observe, that in these cases the first object is in a manner annihilated before the second comes into existence; by which means, we are never presented in any one point of time with the idea of difference and multiplicity; and for that reason are less scrupulous in calling them the same.

Secondly, We may remark, that tho' in a succession of related objects, it be in a manner requisite, that the change of parts be not sudden nor entire, in order to preserve the identity, yet where the objects are in their nature changeable and inconstant, we admit of a more sudden transition, than wou'd otherwise be consistent with that relation. Thus as the nature of a river consists in the motion and change of parts; tho' in less than four and twenty hours these be totally alter'd; this hinders not the river from continuing the same during several ages. What is natural and essential to any thing is, in a manner, expected; and what is expected makes less impression, and appears of less moment, than what is unusual and extraordinary. A considerable change of the former kind seems really less to the imagination, than the most trivial alteration of the latter; and by breaking less the continuity of the thought, has less influence in destroying the identity.

We now proceed to explain the nature of *personal identity*, which has become so great a question in philosophy. . . .

. . . 'Tis evident, that the identity, which we attribute to the human mind, however perfect we may imagine it to be, is not able to run the several different perceptions into one, and make them lose their characters of distinction and difference, which are essential to them. 'Tis still true, that every distinct perception, which enters into the composition of the mind, is a distinct existence, and is different, and distinguishable, and separable from every other perception, either contemporary or successive. But, as, notwithstanding this distinction and separability, we suppose the whole train of perceptions to be united by identity, a question naturally arises concerning this relation of identity; whether it be something that really binds our several perceptions together, or only associates their ideas in the imagination. That is, in other words, whether in pronouncing concerning the identity of a person, we observe some real bond among his perceptions, or only feel one among the ideas we form of them. This question we might easily decide, if we wou'd recollect what has been already prov'd at large, that the understanding never observes any real connexion among objects, and that even the union of cause and effect, when strictly examin'd, resolves itself into a customary association of ideas. For from thence it evidently follows, that identity is nothing really belonging to these different perceptions, and uniting them together; but is merely a quality, which we attribute to them, because of the union of their ideas in the imagination, when we reflect upon them. Now the only qualities, which can give ideas an union in the imagination, are these three relations above-mention'd. These are the uniting principles in the ideal world, and without them every distinct object is separable by the mind, and may be separately consider'd, and appears not to have any more connexion with any other object, than if disjoin'd by the greatest difference and remoteness. 'Tis, therefore, on some of these three relations of resemblance, contiguity and causation, that identity depends; and as the very essence of these relations consists in their producing an easy transition of ideas; it follows, that our notions of personal identity, proceed entirely from the smooth and uninterrupted progress of the thought along a train of connected ideas, according to the principles above-explain'd.

The only question, therefore, which remains, is, by what relations this uninterrupted progress of our thought is produc'd, when we consider the successive existence of a mind or thinking person. And here 'tis evident we must confine ourselves to resemblance and causation, and must drop contiguity, which has little or no influence in the present case.

To begin with *resemblance*; suppose we cou'd see clearly into the breast of another, and observe that succession of perceptions, which constitutes his mind or thinking principle, and suppose that he always preserves the memory of a considerable part of past perceptions; 'tis evident that nothing cou'd more contribute to the bestowing a relation on this succession amidst all its variations. For what is the memory but a faculty, by which we raise up the images of past perceptions? And as an image necessarily resembles its object, must not the frequent placing of these resembling perceptions in the chain of thought, convey the imagination more easily from one link to another, and make the whole seem like the continuance of one object? In this particular, then, the memory not only discovers the identity, but also contributes to its production, by producing the relation of resemblance among the perceptions. The case is the same whether we consider ourselves or others.

As to *causation*; we may observe, that the true idea of the human mind, is to consider it as a system of different perceptions or different existences, which are link'd together by the relation of cause and effect, and mutually produce, destroy, influence, and modify each other. Our impressions give rise to their correspondent ideas; and these ideas in their turn produce other impressions. One thought chaces [*sic*] another, and draws after it a third, by which it is expell'd in its turn. In this respect, I cannot compare the soul more properly to any thing than to a republic or commonwealth, in which the several members are united by the reciprocal ties of government and subordination, and give rise to other persons, who propagate the same republic in the incessant changes of its parts. And as the same individual republic may not only change its members, but also its laws and constitutions; in like manner the same person may vary his character and disposition, as well as his impressions and ideas, without losing his identity. Whatever changes he endures, his several parts are still connected by the relation of causation. And in this view our identity with regard to the passions serves to corroborate that with regard to the imagination, by the making our distant perceptions influence each other, and by giving us a present concern for our past or future pains or pleasures.

As memory alone acquaints us with the continuance and extent of this succession of perceptions, 'tis to be consider'd, upon that account chiefly, as the source of personal identity. Had we no memory, we never shou'd have any notion of causation, nor consequently of that chain of causes and effects, which constitute our self or person. But having once acquir'd this notion of causation from the memory, we can extend the same chain of causes, and consequently the identity of our persons beyond our memory, and can comprehend times, and circumstances, and actions, which we have entirely forgot, but suppose in general to have existed. For how few of our past actions are there, of which we have any memory? Who can tell me, for instance, what were his thoughts and actions on the first of *January* 1715, the 11th of *March* 1719, and the 3d of *August* 1733? Or will he affirm, because he has entirely forgot the incidents of these days, that the present self is not the same person with the self of that time; and by that means overturn all the most establish'd notions of personal identity? In this view, therefore, memory does not so much *produce* as *discover* personal identity, by shewing us the relation of cause and effect among our different perceptions. 'Twill be incumbent on those, who affirm that memory produces entirely our personal identity, to give a reason why we can thus extend our identity beyond our memory.

The whole of this doctrine leads us to a conclusion, which is of great importance in the present affair, *viz.* that all the nice and subtile questions concerning personal identity can never possibly be decided, and are to be regarded rather as grammatical than as philosophical difficulties. Identity depends on the relations of ideas; and these relations produce identity, by means of that easy transition they occasion. But as the relations, and the easiness of the transition may diminish by insensible degrees, we have no just standard, by which we can decide any dispute concerning the time, when they acquire or lose a title to the name of identity. All the disputes concerning the identity of connected objects are merely verbal, except so far as the relation of parts gives rise to some fiction or imaginary principle of union, as we have already observ'd.

Grimshaw

Jean Grimshaw is a Senior Lecturer at Bristol Polytechnic in England. She has written extensively on feminist issues in philosophy and is the author of Philosophy and Feminist Thinking, *from which the following section is taken.*

One of the most interesting and difficult issues regarding the question "Who am I?" has arisen with considerable force in recent times by way of feminist concerns with the status of women in our society. Do women have a distinctive nature of their own that leads to and justifies certain social and political practices? If so, is this distinctive nature biologically grounded or primarily a result of socialization? If not, are there various central universal dimensions of humankind, namely focusing on capacities of reason, that remain paramount for both sexes? There is considerable disagreement on this issue among feminist philosophers, many today strongly favoring an approach that sees whatever important gender differences that do obtain arising in, and some would say caused by, specific cultural contexts having to do with necessities of work, mating, nurturing, and so on. Those who situate themselves more in a liberal political tradition see the possibilities of women attaining full social and political equality by accepting a more universalist orientation that extols common capacities and abilities between men and women; others, of a more "radical" perspective, argue for the existence of a distinctive (and some even say "superior") women's nature based on special features of women's experience.

In the following Grimshaw takes a somewhat middle-ground approach and surveys critically some of the leading contending positions on this controversial subject.

Human Nature and Women's Nature

Theories of human nature have had a central importance in philosophy. Their importance arises out of the frequent concern, in moral and political philosophy, to try and spell out a conception of a form of life for human beings, a mode of political and social arrangements, an ideal of human development, which is both possible and desirable.

The question of *possibility* is raised by asking whether there are limits or constraints set by "human nature" on the sorts of social arrangements which can be seen as feasible. It is this sort of question which commonly underpins commonsense or colloquial remarks about human nature; thus phrases such as "It's natural . . ." or "It's only human nature" are often used to express a conviction that some feature of human life is inevitable or at least very deep-rooted ("It's only human nature to look after yourself first"; "It's natural for a woman to do the housework"; and so forth).

The *sort* of appeal to "nature" involved in such remarks is, however, quite complex. In particular, it does not always imply that human *behaviour* is unchangeable or that motives seen as fundamental to human nature always lead to the same sorts of behaviour. Consider, for example, the commonsense view that "It's only human nature to look after yourself first." Those who express such a view are not necessarily discomfited by being shown examples of behaviour which is apparently self-sacrificing or altruistic. What they are likely to claim, rather, is that behaviour which appears on the face of it to be altruistic is in fact motivated by self-interest or can be explained by reference to this. . . .

No theory of human nature claims, so far as I am aware, that any aspect of human behaviour is totally unalterable. It is important to grasp this, since the debate about "human nature" is not usually one in which a belief in the complete fixity of human behaviour is starkly opposed to a belief in its plasticity or flexibility. It is usually, rather, a debate about what *underlies* human behaviour, about how it is to be explained, and about the social consequences that are seen as following from such explanations. Sociobiological theory, for example, which claims that females are "naturally" more inclined than males to invest more energy in the care of their offspring, does not claim that all women actually want to invest their energy in this way, nor does it deny that social experiments in shared child-care can be undertaken. What is commonly argued is that such experiments in changing human behaviour are "against nature," that they "deny nature," and that they are "unnatural" (and hence will be ineffective in the long run). And the idea of "nature" here involves a claim that it is possible in some way to identify some sort of basic or fundamental human motives, drives, desires, which are universal in the sense that they can be thought of as the same in all historical circumstances. Human culture has to negotiate them, and their behavioural expression may vary; but they nevertheless underlie all cultures.

The concept of "un-natural" behaviour is clearly not compatible with a belief in the absolute fixity of human behaviour; "nature" is not something which dictates or determines everything that humans do. What does it mean, then, to claim that behaviour is "unnatural"? Commonly, the idea of "unnatural" behaviour suggests several things. First, it suggests that there is some sort of *hierarchy* of human drives or motives. For example, it might be argued that while some women may want and seek equality with men in the short term, in the long run the need of women to care for their offspring under male protection is a more "fundamental" aspect of female nature and will defeat efforts to seek equality. Second, it allows that there may indeed be *conflicts* between different human desires or motives, or conflicts between different groups. But third, it suggests that these conflicts should be resolved in a way that is *compatible* with "human nature"; attempts to organise a society along lines that are incompatible with human nature will not only in the long run be self-defeating, they may also lead to problems of social order and social control. . . .

In the history of philosophy, the notion of "human nature" has often been a normative one; being fully or truly "human" is seen as a goal to be achieved. Notions of "human-ness" have often been linked to a conception of characteristics that are seen as distinctively or typically human, which differentiate human beings from other species. The enterprise of trying to identify what is truly or distinctively human, and of using this as a way of conceptualising unrealised human potential and evaluating social arrangements is one that has constantly recurred in philosophical and social thought. Commonly, this enterprise has been associated with either or both of two beliefs: first, the belief that distinctively "human" nature can be seen to reside only in those human activities and characteristics for which there is no analogy in other species, and second, that it is possible to identify human needs or motives or characteristics which are universal and can be understood as the same across all cultures. . . .

SOME PROBLEMS IN ARGUING ABOUT HUMAN NATURE

I want now to consider some general problems that arise when discussing the concept of "human nature," before moving on to look at questions about gender and human nature, and at the ways in which conceptions of human nature and of male and female nature have figured in some important feminist arguments.

In some sense, it would be absurd to deny that there is such a thing as "human nature." By this I mean that it cannot sensibly be denied that human life is constrained in some ways by such things as the biological characteristics of the human species, by such things as birth, death, sickness and ageing, and by the need for human beings to work in order to produce their own means of subsistence. There is room for a great deal of disagreement about what these constraints actually are, and the constraints may change historically. Thus, for example, the advent of more reliable contraception and the possibility of different technological means of reproduction changes the nature of the constraints pregnancy and birth lay on human life. Nevertheless, questions about the limits laid on possible forms of social organisation by the nature of the human species should not be seen as questions about whether there are any limits or constraints at all, but rather as questions about the nature and form of these constraints. What has usually been seen as most contentious is the claim that human nature dictates the inevitability or necessity of certain very specific sorts of social roles (male and female ones, for example); that it determines certain very specific psychological characteristics of human beings, or of males and females; and that it dictates the necessity for certain sorts of social controls.

Arguments that human nature dictates these things have taken very different forms. Some arguments, such as that of the philosopher Hobbes, have proceeded by what is basically an exercise in abstraction; that is to say, trying to "think away" social controls and asking what would be likely to happen if they were not present. Hobbes argued that in a "state of nature"—that is to say, a condition of human life without the coercion and authority of the state—life would be "nasty, brutish and short." He assumed an egoism of motivation—that human beings could only be motivated to act in their own individual interests. This assumption was based partly on a sort of conceptual legislation—that, for example, the concept of "one's own interests" can only be *understood* in an egoistic or individualistic sense—and partly on arguments which appealed to commonsense considerations such as the fact that people take care to lock their houses and do not trust other people.

William Golding's novel, *Lord of the Flies,* is, rather similarly, an attempt to "think away" normal social controls by the fictional device of supposing a group of schoolboys stranded without adults on a desert island. The picture Golding draws is of a reversion to savagery, in which deep human propensities for violence, domination, tribalism and various forms of superstition and primitivism erupt, with the declining influence of the taboos instilled by social controls.

Many accounts of human nature (including those which have often most exercised feminist thinking) have appealed directly to biology. The appeal to biology has recently most commonly been made in the context of an appeal to evolutionary theory, and to the idea that certain motivational and behavioural patterns or propensities have been genetically "coded" into human beings as they have proved in the past to be evolutionarily advantageous.

Now one common response to theories which argue, either via an exercise in abstraction or via an appeal to biology and evolution, that certain behavioural propensities or patterns are "natural," is that far from being "natural" in the sense of endemic or universal in human beings, such patterns are the result of specific forms of human socialisation and social relationships. Thus it might be argued that even if William Golding's novel were to be "tested," in the sense that something like the events described did actually take place, that would not show us anything about a universal human nature. It would show us, rather, something about the character structure and particular forms of socialisation of public schoolboys. This creates a necessary complexity in many arguments about human nature, since they appeal not simply to what people actually do or are like, but to what they *would or might* do in other circumstances, or to ways in which they might be different if human societies were different. And it is not always easy to see what sorts of evidence would be relevant to such claims.

Now the idea that the "nature" of human beings (the sorts of psychological characteristics and motives they have and the sorts of behaviour they display) is a product of particular forms of socialisation and social conditions is one that *seems* to be incompatible with talk of a universal human nature. It is therefore one that has a particular appeal to anyone who wants to deny the idea of a universal human nature, and thereby deny that certain patterns of behaviour or human motivations are endemic or inevitable. But it is also one that raises its own problems. The first problem is that under some interpretations it seems to suggest that the nature of human beings is fundamentally malleable; that is to say, it can be shaped in very different ways according to the nature and norms of any particular society (subject perhaps to the general constraints governing human existence such as the need to produce, and so forth). But if this is so, then it may appear to be difficult to conceptualise the idea that a society does not meet human needs. If human needs and human nature are shaped by society, how can we give expression to the idea that there are needs that society does *not* meet, or that there are human potentialities which are unrecognised in a way that amounts to a *distortion* or a *stunting* of human personality?

It is considerations like this which have led many people towards normative theories of human nature or basic human needs which are derived from "the human condition" as such, rather than from any particular set of social circumstances. Many theories of self similarly suppose that it is only possible to criticise social norms or institutions for stunting the growth of self if an "inner self" or a "real self" can be postulated, which is something conceptually distinct from the "social self," which may be seen merely as the product of processes of "conditioning" and the like.

Some of the fundamental problems, then, with which discussions about human nature have to engage, are these. Is it possible to identify characteristics of "human nature," human motives, desires, drives, behaviour patterns which are universal, common to all known cultures, and bound to be endemic in all possible ones? If such a view is rejected, how can one do justice to the constraints laid on human life by things such as biology and the need to support material life? And if it is argued that such desires, behaviour patterns, and so forth, are in some way the product of particular cultural patterns or ways of socialisation, how can human *resistance* to these patterns be conceptualised, and how can we give expression to the idea of the blocking or stunting of fundamental human potentialities? Is it necessary to postulate a conception of basic and universal human needs or of a "real" self distinct from the socialised self in order to do so?

FEMINISM AND HUMAN NATURE

One of the central concerns of feminism has been to argue, in different ways, that women's potentialities have been thwarted or blocked by oppressive social relationships, and that theories of human nature in general, but more especially of the nature of women, which see this as intrinsically tied to specific social roles or gender characteristics, have been instrumental in this thwarting. A centrally important philosophical task for feminism, therefore, is to consider such conceptions of human nature, and of male and female nature. It is important because such conceptions may provide a rationale or impetus for particular social or political strategies or goals. This is as true with feminism as it is for anti-feminist views. Arguments about women's nature have been used to support or legitimate various forms of exclusion and oppression of women (just as arguments about human nature have been used to legitimate racist social policies). But there is substantial disagreement within feminist thinking on questions about male and female nature. What feminists share, I think, is a *concern* about the thwarting of women's potentialities and about theories of women's nature which consign women to subordinate roles. But feminists differ greatly in their political strategies and proposals, and some of these strategies and proposals have a close relationship to views about male and female nature. I want now, therefore, to map out what I think are some of the central themes and conflicts in feminist accounts of this nature, and to discuss the ways in which feminist argument has tried to negotiate the problems I referred to in the previous paragraph.

Conceptions of human nature have been gendered, or had implications for gender, in what I think are two main ways. First, . . . ideals of human potentiality have often been masculine in the sense that they have excluded those qualities or characteristics seen as characteristically female or have believed women to be incapable of fully or truly "human" excellence or self-realisation. But second, some theories of human nature have suggested that the *constraints* operating on men and women are different, and that these constraints account both for differences in the social roles and psychological characteristics of men and women, and for quite general features of human social relationships.

The single most important thing that has been seen as determining these differences is the fact that women, and not men bear children. The ways in which this fact is seen as constraining women's lives have varied. Thus in Freud's theories it is supposed that the desire for a (male) baby becomes the fundamental one around which a woman's life is orientated; it is a substitute for the penis she does not possess, and if a women devotes her life to other things, these will be interpreted as a psychic *substitute,* a sublimation of the wish for a baby, which can never adequately replace actually having one. A great deal of psychoanalytic theorising has assumed, with Freud, that a woman's fulfilment can only come through children. Other theories, however, do not stress a woman's *desire* for a child so much as the different "investment" by males and females in the care of children, which is seen as the evolutionary consequence of their different relationship to conception. In one way or another, however, the biological differences between men and women, especially those related to reproduction, are seen as determining, not necessarily how all women will actually behave, but what their deepest feelings and motivations will be and what forms of relationships between men and women will ultimately be viable. "Biology" is often seen as the rock on which feminism will inevitably founder.

The relationship of feminist thinking to questions about biology and reproduction has been a complex one. I want first to outline some central features of two sorts of arguments which, in different, though related ways, argue that "biology" does not determine anything about human life or about women's fundamental nature or social role.

Sex and Gender

One of the most common distinctions made in feminist writing is that between sex and gender. And one of the clearest statements of it was made by Ann Oakley in her book, *Sex, Gender and Society.* Thus, she says:

> On the whole, Western society is organised around the assumption that the differences between the sexes are more important than any qualities they have in common. When people try to justify this assumption in terms of "natural"

differences, two separate processes become confused; the tendency to differentiate by sex, and the tendency to differentiate in a particular way by sex. The first is genuinely a constant feature of human society, but the second is not, and its inconstancy marks the division between "sex" and "gender": sex differences may be "natural" but gender differences have their source in culture, not nature.

Oakley produces a great deal of evidence from anthropology, studies of different socialisation patterns and the like, to show the immense variability of gender distinctions. She argues that the supposition that any particular version of these gender differences is "natural" (i.e. dictated by biological sex) is often used to oppress women, to put them in positions of dependence and inequality.

The distinction between sex and gender has often been used to support some ideal of "androgyny." The ideal of androgyny often supposes a world where biology will be, as it were "mere"; a "mere" matter of physiological differences, of "naturally given" biological features, whose social consequences will be minimal. They can never be non-existent; thus if women and not men give birth, special arrangements will need to be made for this. But beyond this we might suppose a society where sexual difference is a matter of little importance, and where social roles and psychological characteristics are distributed among human beings regardless of sex.

A feature of Oakley's argument that I shall note here, and return to later, is the fact that it is premised on sharp distinctions between "nature" and "culture," between what is "biological" and what is "cultural." "Sex" is seen as "biological," "gender" as "cultural." I shall discuss this distinction further later on in this chapter.

Women and "Human" Potentialities

As I have already said, philosophical discussions of human nature have often been orientated around an attempt to identify those traits or capacities or activities which are distinctively "human," and one sort of approach to this question has been to identify as distinctively human those capacities or activities for which there is no analogy or comparable capacity or activity in other species. There is an important strand in feminist thinking which argues that in their relegation to certain activities and spheres of life and exclusion from others, women have, in effect, been debarred from developing the most fully human capacities. . . .

Alison Jaggar argues that underlying the philosophy of political liberalism is a kind of dualism. Sometimes this has been connected to a metaphysical dualism; that is to say, to a belief that the human mind and the human body represent two different kinds of being which are only contingently connected to each other. But even where there is no commitment to metaphysical dualism, political liberalism has rested on what Jaggar calls "normative dualism":

> Normative dualism is the belief that what is especially valuable about human beings is a particular "mental" capacity, the capacity for rationality. . . . Contemporary liberal theorists ascribe political rights on the basis of what they

take to be the specifically human capacity for rationality, and disregard what they conceive as "merely physical" capacities and incapacities.

Women, it is thought, have been prevented from developing or exercising their human potentialities for reason by the various forms of oppression and discrimination that they have suffered. Mary Wollstonecraft emphasised time and time again the ways in which she thought that women's minds had been trivialised and prevented from being able to reason properly by the sorts of constraints from which they had suffered. John Stuart Mill argued that the supposition that women were not rational ignored the ways in which they had not been allowed the opportunities to *develop* their reason. And while he and other liberals have expressed an official agnosticism about what women might achieve if given equal opportunities with men, they have thought that gendered characteristics might well disappear with the full flowering of "human" potential and the capacity to reason. Sex would be a biological "accident" which, while it would continue to have certain inevitable social consequences, would be irrelevant to the full development of human nature.

The sorts of normative conceptions of human nature that I have sketched here therefore rest on a distinction between sex and gender and between the "biological" or "physical" aspects of human life which are not seen as constituting specifically human nature. And this human nature itself is not seen as gendered; it is something which is the same in men and women. . . .

MALE NATURE

Sometimes it is argued that males have a nature that is simply to be ascribed to their biology. A clear example of this is the work of Susan Brownmiller on rape. Brownmiller documents the ways in which rape and violence against women have indeed been endemic in human history. But she sees the fundamental explanation as lying in male biology: "What it all boils down to is that the human male can rape. When men discovered that they could rape, they proceeded to do it." The biological ability to rape leads, she suggests, directly and inevitably to the desire to rape. And rape is a conscious process of intimidation by which *all* men keep *all* women in a state of fear. All men benefit from rape, even if they do not themselves rape. Brownmiller is, I think, really suggesting that in some sense all men are really rapists "deep down," and presumably are only kept from rape by fear of the consequences to themselves or by a precarious "veneer" of socialisation which suggests that rape is wrong. The result is that she sees relations between the sexes as necessarily taking the form of a power struggle. Men will always rape if they can get away with it, and the only answer is for women to take power themselves. Hence her political solution to the question of rape proposes what is in effect an army of armed female vigilantes.

Not all accounts of an essential male nature are as explicitly biological as that of Brownmiller, and they may have an appearance of history. Sometimes this is achieved by using the concept of "patriarchy." "Patriarchy" sometimes functions as what can be called a "pseudo-historical" notion. It appears to refer to a specific form of social organisation. Often, however, it is used in an undifferentiated way to cover the whole of human history. In *Gyn/Ecology* for example, Mary Daly writes:

> *Patriarchy is itself the prevailing religion of the entire planet* and its essential message is necrophilia. All of the so-called religions legitimating patriarchy are mere sects subsumed under its vast umbrella/canopy. They are essentially similar, despite the variations. All—from buddhism and hinduism to islam, judaism, christianity—to secular derivatives such as freudianism, jungianism, marxism and maoism—are infrastructures of the edifice of patriarchy. All are erected as part of the male's shelter against anomie. And the symbolic message of all the sects of the religion which is patriarchy is this; Women are the dreaded anomie. Consequently, women are the objects of male terror, the projected personifications of "the Enemy," the real objects under attack in all the wars of patriarchy.

Daly is here postulating a universal and fundamental male need (shelter against anomie) and male fear (of women). What the origins of these are is not explained. They are just postulated as "universals" which enter into all human societies and into all male actions and beliefs. They lead to a universal and basic male motivation, fundamental to all male enterprises, to attack women and see them as "the Enemy."

Rather similarly, in her book on pornography, Andrea Dworkin sees pornography as the quintessential expression of the "unchanging faith" of men in their right to power and to the sexual objectification and domination of women. Terror, based on power, is the theme of male history and culture: "Terror issues forth from the male, illuminates his essential nature and basic purpose." Despite his power, the male is really a parasite on women; he drains their resources and their Being for his own purposes. As a child, Dworkin argues, the first female self he drains is that of his mother; then he transfers his parasitism of the mother to other females.

At times Dworkin denies that this male violence and desire to degrade women is inevitable or that it has biological roots. But it is all the same difficult to avoid concluding that she still sees it as endemic and fundamental in male nature:

> In every realm of male experience and action, violence is experienced and articulated as love and freedom. Pacifist men are only apparent exceptions; repelled by some forms of violence as nearly all men are, they remain impervious to sexual violence as nearly all men do.

Daly, similarly, is unwilling to allow that there could be "exceptions"—males whose aim was *not* to terrorise or degrade women. Seeing some men as exceptions is, she suggests, female self-deception, cowardice or bad faith: "Some feel a fake need to draw distinctions; for example, 'I am anti-patriarchal, but not anti-male.' The courage to be logical—the courage to name—would require that we admit to ourselves that males and males only are the originators, planners, controllers and legitimators of patriarchy."

What Dworkin and Daly both seem to propose is that there are universal male needs or desires which are an essential aspect of male nature and are the same throughout human history.

A rather similar sort of account of universal male needs, desires or unconscious fears is in fact found in a considerable amount of feminist writing. Adrienne Rich, for example, writes, "There is much to suggest that the male mind has always been haunted by the force of the idea of *dependence on a woman for life itself,* the son's constant effort to assimilate, compensate for, or deny that he is 'of woman born.' " It is the *idea* of dependence on a woman for life that is seen as the crucial thing here, not simply the "mere" biological fact, but the nature and power of such an idea is seen as endemic in human life, as part of "the human condition" (and, in this case, the male condition in particular).

The notion of universal (though maybe unconscious) needs and desires and fears is one that owes a lot to psychoanalysis. Freud, while believing that human biology could not be abstracted from human consciousness, also believed that psychic life followed certain universal patterns, which were part of human entry into culture. And while feminist writers have dissociated themselves from many of Freud's particular theories (e.g. the theory of female penis envy), they have nevertheless often explicitly or implicitly subscribed to a view that certain features of human life lead inevitably to the predominance of certain psychic needs, fears and desires which are gender differentiated. . . .

The most common form of belief then in a universal male nature is, I think, one which holds there to be male beliefs, needs, fears and so forth, which are seen as a result of certain features of "the human condition" (such as women giving birth), that results in a genderically differectiated male and female consciousness.

FEMALE NATURE

It is useful to see a number of feminist accounts of female nature as orientated around two central and related themes: first that of woman as victim and second, that of a "true" or "essential" nature of woman.

Women are seen as victimised in two ways: by the physical brutality and coercion of a great deal of male treatment of women, and also by the force of male ideology, by which they are conditioned or indoctrinated. The result of this brutality and indoctrination is that the *humanity* of women has been destroyed. Andrea Dworkin sees pornography as the quintessential symptom of, and as part of the process of, this destruction of women's humanity:

> Woman is not born, she is made. In the making her humanity is destroyed. She becomes symbol of this, symbol of that, mother of the earth, slut of the universe; but she never becomes herself because it is forbidden for her to do so. No act of hers can overturn the way in which she is consistently perceived as some sort of thing. No sense of her own purpose can supercede, finally, the

male's sense of her purpose; to be that thing that enables them to experience raw phallic power.

In *Gyn/Ecology* Mary Daly presents a vivid picture of what she sees as the state of women under patriarchy. A great deal of the book is devoted to an indictment of the brutalities such as suttee, clitoridectomy and footbinding which have been inflicted on women; but Daly does not see this brutality as merely physical. Patriarchy, she argues, has led as well to spiritual death, to the rape and brutalising of the minds of women, not just of their bodies. Women have been spiritually possessed and invaded. They have become domesticated, controlled, docile, submissive, dull, insipid, serving the purposes of others. They have become what Daly calls "fembots": robotised, moronised, lobotomised. They are, she writes, like *mutants*: the "puppets of Papa." The power of the Fathers prevents women even realising the depths of the degradation to which they have sunk. And Daly's view of male nature is revealed in the way in which she uses semen itself as a symbol or metaphor for pollution. When talking of "male" language, she writes: "Exorcism requires naming this environment of spirit/mind rape, refusing to be receptacles for semantic semen." Women she says, are led into "unwholesome alliance with alienating intercourse. . . . Having lost touch with their selves, they are impregnated by the holy spirit of alienation, the discouraging, dispiriting sperm that expels the self." Daly is here aligning herself with the line of feminist thinking which sees men as "the Enemy" and all forms of collaboration with them, sexual, or otherwise, as leading to the danger of selling one's soul. . . .

Daly's language of "mutants" seems to imply that behind the mutant form there is some real or true shape which has become perverted or distorted. And, indeed, Daly does suppose that behind the robotised facade there is a true female nature. Daly's descriptions of this are couched in religious metaphors of salvation and rebirth. The genuine self (which corresponds to true female nature) has to be reborn by a process that is variously described, for example, as cleansing, exorcising, depolluting, unveiling or unwinding, dispossessing the internalised possessor.

The true or authentic female nature that will be unveiled by the removal of the "shrouds" of patriarchy bears little relation to the historical lives and activities of women. Daly's history of patriarchy is one which so emphasises degradation and brutalisation (as does Dworkin's account of pornography) that it is difficult to see how the "fembots" of her analysis could provide any source or resource for women to turn to. . . .

But there are other accounts of female nature which have wanted to reverse this emphasis, and which, while not at all denying or minimising male power and brutality, have suggested that there is a "womanculture" which is a source for an understanding of authentic and autonomous female values. Or they have suggested that there are forms of female experience which, if stripped of their patriarchal meanings, can reveal something about the nature of woman.

Adrienne Rich distinguished between motherhood as experience and motherhood as institution. There is no question that motherhood has been institutionalised in ways that have been oppressive and damaging to women. But in her account of "experience," Rich seems to posit an essential female nature, related to female biology, which has been suppressed by patriarchy:

> I have come to believe, as will be clear throughout this book, that female biology—the diffuse, intense sensuality radiating out from clitoris, breasts, uterus, vagina; the lunar cycles of menstruation; the gestation and fruition of the life which can take place in the female body—has far more radical implications than we have yet come to appreciate. Patriarchal thought has limited female biology to its own narrow specifications. . . . In order to live a fully human life we require not only *control* of our bodies (though control is a prerequisite); we must touch the unity and resonance of our physicality, our bond with the natural order, the corporeal ground of our intelligence.

Rich is here suggesting, I think, that the biology of women of itself, if divested of the trappings of patriarchy, gives rise to a distinctively female nature and to a distinctively female bond *with* nature. . . .

RETHINKING BIOLOGY

Biology, then is often conceived of in various ways as a sort of *substratum* of human life; a *base* which is that which is most fundamental about human nature; a realm of "nature" which *confronts* human culture and socialisation. And this sort of view of biology (or of the desires and needs which are seen as flowing directly from biology), underpins views of male and female nature which are, on the face of it, very different. It underpins conceptions of social arrangements which see these as limited or determined, at least in the long run, by the inevitability of male dominance and of the female childrearing role. It underpins views of male and female nature which see a radical asymmetry between male and female psychology as resulting directly from biological difference, or which posit a realm of "natural" power, feeling or sensation, a "natural life" of women, which flows from the female organism if "untainted" by patriarchal culture or conditioning. But it also lies at the root of sharp distinctions between "sex" and "gender," in which "sex" is seen as "biological" and "gender" as "cultural."

It is arguable that the view of biology as substratum has become part of "commonsense" about human nature. It is given its power partly by the difficulties inherent in some views which can seem to be denying the importance of biology, or suggesting that such things as the bodily constitution of human beings, the differences in reproductive biology, are of minimal importance in either determining or explaining the patterns taken by human culture and social arrangements. Surely, it is felt, the fact that women and not men bear children is of *fundamental* importance in human life, and not something that can be dismissed as "mere" biology, as a sort of "accident" with few necessary social consequences. Or it is felt that there is a *givenness*, an ineluctable quality, about the biological aspects of human life, and that these have to be negotiated by human social relations and cannot be reduced to them.

Within Marxism, there has been a debate about biology and human nature which is of central relevance to feminism. In the *Theses on Feuerbach* Marx argued that there was no "human essence," no fixed human nature, but that the self was the ensemble of social relations. What it means to say this, however, needs making clear. And some interpretations of Marxism, in the attempt to suggest directions for a Marxist psychology which did not assume any theory of fixed biological instincts or drives, have appeared to *reduce* the biological aspects of human existence to social relations. Lucien Seve for example, argued that all needs are always "social"—including needs such as eating. The problem with a view like that of Seve was, again, that it seemed to ignore the way in which human biology can appear to *impose* constraints and requirements on social arrangements, and can enter into individual lives in the form of brute and inevitable contingency. . . .

It sometimes seems, therefore, that we are faced with a choice. We can submerge biology in social relations; but we may then seem to be denying what may appear as the intractability and inevitability of biological processes such as birth, reproduction and death. Or we see biology as a sort of substratum; in which case the constraints it lays on human life may appear as things which are passively experienced and allow no scope for change.

In fact, I think this choice should be rejected; it does not exhaust the options. And the first step in such a rejection is to think again about the concept of the "biological." The "biological" is thought of in a number of ways. It is thought of as the realm of that which is genetically inherited (and is therefore often assumed to be unchangeable). It is thought of more generally as the realm of the "bodily"—and biology is conceived of as the science which tells us about human bodies. And it is thought of, as I have said, as that which lays specific constraints on human existence and sets absolute limits to the possibilities of human social arrangements. In all of these ways, the notion of biology as a substratum is often a powerful one—and it is *that* which has, I think to be questioned. The central argument against the idea of biology as a substratum is that it is not possible to identify an absolutely clear, non-social sense of "biology"; the biological is not a realm or sphere which can be isolated as a cause of any feature of human life. But neither is it possible to identify a clear non-biological sense of "the social." The biological and social are not entirely distinct and separable things which can simply be seen as "interacting," nor can one be seen as in any way more fundamental than the other. . . .

Human biological differences, and the human biological constitution, are themselves partly the product of human social evolution, including not merely such things as general physical structure but also things such as hormonal differences. The human body should not be thought of as an entity which can be understood by a "biology" which is abstracted from the consideration of social phenomena. It is itself a site of the interplay between biology and culture—not only in terms of the more general evolution of the human species but also in terms of the way in which the psychic and emotional history of individuals (related to the social circumstances in which they live) may influence their bodily being. Central to Freud's early work, for example, was his view of the physical symptoms of "hysteria" in women as inexplicable by purely physiological causes. Wilhelm Reich argued that the affective histories of individuals could be traced in the muscular structures and dispositions of their bodies.

If this view of the dialectical and historical relationship between human biology and human culture is accepted, it has a number of consequences for feminist argument. It leads to the rejection of biological determinism; that is to say, of any view that sees particular aspects of human behaviour or particular social roles as the inevitable outcome of a biology considered as a substratum. It leads also to the view that no sort of human behaviour is more "natural" than any other; there is not, in human life, a viable distinction between those activities or behaviours which are "natural" as opposed to those which are social. But this implies that the distinction made in some forms of feminist argument between those activities which are fully or distinctively human and those which are more natural or animal or biological is also not a viable one. "Humanness" is not a property reserved for those activities which can be seen in some way as more remote from the biological contingencies of human life. It has been quite common in philosophy for human reproduction, for example, to be seen as "natural" or "biological"; in fact, as Mary O'Brien points out, the biological aspects of human conception and birth cannot be isolated or abstracted from human consciousness of these.

But if there is a dialectical relationship between human biology and human culture, it follows also that the biological dimension of human life cannot be dismissed as of relatively little importance, as has tended to happen with some versions of the distinction between sex and gender. Human life is always embodied. Marx argued that humans produced their own humanity and their relationships with each other in the course of producing their own material means of subsistence. Without the need to produce there would be no recognisably human life. Marx did not pay a great deal of attention to the process of human reproduction, but human life is conditioned as much by the biological dimensions of birth and sex as by the need to produce the means of subsistence. Unlike production, reproduction is a sexually differentiated process. This I think has consequences for the idea of an "androgynous" human personality, which is "merely" differentiated by sex but not by gender.

Sexual difference itself is not something which is simply given; it is something which can change historically and is conditioned by culture. But neither is sexual difference or reproductive difference simply reducible to culture; and insofar as it is not, there seem to me to be good reasons for supposing it likely that it will always lead, for example, to some sorts of psychological differences between males and females—a difference, perhaps, in such things as feelings about children or about sex. The "meaning" of sexual differentiation may perhaps never be identical for the different sexes. . . .

SECOND NATURE AND THE HUMAN SELF

Marx argued, as I have said, that the human self was the ensemble of social relations, but what it means to say this is not immediately clear. What is clearest is what Marx meant to deny; namely, that there is an "essential" human nature, thought of as a set of attributes or characteristics which are constitutive of human nature for all time. Marx indeed wrote frequently of the "inhumanity" of capitalism, and of the way in which what he called the "species being" of human beings was unrealised under conditions of alienated and exploitative labour. But this "species-being" is not to be thought of as a set of specific characteristics or attributes; the "species-being" of human beings was denied when the products of their own *human* labour came to appear to be set against them as alien "inhuman" forces. In a rather similar way, the human character of reproduction is denied when it is conceived of as a merely biological event which simply "happens" to human beings.

There are, however, some possible interpretations of a view that the self is constituted by social relationships which are problematic. First, as I have already argued, there are problems with any view which tries to *reduce* the biological dimension of human existence to social relations. But second, there are problems with any type of theory which sees the human self as in some way simply *reflecting* any particular set of social arrangements—or which sees human needs as determined, without remainder, by prevailing cultural forms or patterns. Just as the appeal to biology as a substratum has sometimes appeared as the only alternative to a view of human nature which appears to deny the importance of biology, so a view of "basic" or "universal" human needs or of an "essential" human nature has sometimes appeared as the only alternative to an "oversocialised" view of human beings which seems to make it impossible to understand how people can experience certain social forms as failing to meet their needs. Within feminist thinking, this opposition has sometimes appeared in the form of a contrast between a conception of women as totally victimised, conditioned or indoctrinated, and the free, pure or authentic woman who can emerge if patriarchal indoctrination is smashed or rejected, or who can reestablish contact with an essential femaleness that is buried under the layers of conditioning.

If one rejects such an opposition, it has consequences for one's understanding of the lives and needs of women. It is, I think, indeed often true that women may internalise damaging and oppressive conceptions of themselves. They may, for example, construct a sense of their own identity around a precarious conception of "attractiveness" to men, or around a sense of a life devoted to serving others in which any desire for things for oneself is seen as "selfish." (And, of course, men may construct *their* identity around conceptions of masculinity which see this as centered on such things as an aggressive sexual style, or domination of women.)

But a critique of such internalised conceptions should not be carried out in the name of a "real self" or a "real nature" which is seen as "underlying" the socially produced self (in rather the same sort of way as biology is often seen as underlying socialisation). Marilyn Frye argued that "left to themselves" women would not want to serve men, and would pursue their own interests. But to put it like this supposes a "real" or "natural" self which, if simply "left alone," would spontaneously or autonomously produce its "real" needs or desires. It ignores the way in which *all* needs and desires are socially mediated.

Furthermore, to say that women, for instance, are not "naturally" subservient, or men "naturally" aggressive or dominant, that it is not "human nature" that these things should be so, should not at all be taken to imply that such characteristics are necessarily superficial ones. It is sometimes assumed that to say that human beings are not "naturally" aggressive or competitive or subservient, and so forth, is necessarily to propound a facile optimism or utopianism—against which is to be set the "hardheadedness" and common sense of those who pay due attention to the apparently endemic nastier features of human behaviour. And there are theories of human nature and the self which *do* engage in such a facile optimism. A great deal of the theory of humanistic psychology, for example, and the therapeutic techniques with which it has been associated, uses the language of "roles," "masks," "facades," and so forth, as if these were relatively superficial things which could simply be peeled away, given the help, perhaps, of the odd encounter group, to reveal the "real person" within (who is assumed to be basically "good" and desirous of "growth"). But the denial of an essential human nature should not be taken to imply such a view. It may not be "human nature" for men, say, to be aggressive or dominant, but in particular people in particular social circumstances, these characteristics may be so deeply rooted, and so constitutive of a person's sense of their own identity, that they can be said to constitute the "nature" of that person. The concept of "second nature" is a useful one here; "second nature" is that which is so deeply rooted in a person's psyche or sense of themselves that it may in some circumstances be impossible, or exceedingly difficult, to change.

This "second nature" has to be understood historically; it is, so to speak, sedimented history, both the broader history of the network of social relationships in which people are located and the more particular history of their own personal and affective biographies. Gramsci argued that the process of understanding oneself was intrinsically a historical one: "The starting point of critical elaboration is the consciousness of what one really is, and is 'knowing thyself' as a product of the historical process to date which has deposited in you an infinity of traces, without leaving an inventory." But this history is one of contradictions and conflicts, both in material and in ideological terms. And the nature of these conflicts changes over time.

Women's lives have been lived under many of these contradictions and conflicts. Women have, for example, often been faced with trying to make sense of contradictory conceptions of themselves. They are human beings and participate with men in human tasks—yet they have been seen by philosophical theories as not capable of full humanity. They have often been powerless—yet they have also been seen as too powerful, by virtue of the sexual power they hold over men. They have been dependent—yet seen as having an enviable "freedom" to amuse themselves or do as they like within the confines of their own home. They have been seen as asexual—yet the illnesses and disorders from which they have suffered have been seen as having sexual causes. Notoriously, they have been seen both as madonna and whore, as virgin and slut, and they have had to try to reconcile contradictory imperatives, such as those of being *both* chaste and modest, yet *also* sexually available.

Women have also experienced often barely articulated contradictions between thought and action. They have, perhaps, been fully aware of their own competence, yet publicly declared themselves to be weak and helpless, so as not to deflate the ego of a man. Or they have *believed* in their own lack of competence (or not defined the skills they *did* possess as constituting "competence"). Such contrasts between thought and action, if they are widespread, are, Gramsci argued, indications of profounder socio-historical contrasts—they are more than just an indication of discrepancy in the life of an individual. They signify, he argued, that the social group in question:

> has, for reasons of submission and intellectual subordination, adopted a conception which is not its own but is borrowed from another group; and it affirms this conception verbally and believes itself to be following it, because this is the conception which it follows in "normal times"—that is when its conduct is not independent and autonomous, but submissive and subordinate.

But to develop one's "own" conception, to become autonomous, is not a matter of discovering a spontaneously authentic or "real" self, and that which is seen as autonomous or independent should not be thought of in any way as "less social." Gramsci contrasted what he called a disjointed and episodic conception of the world with a critical and coherent one. A disjointed and episodic conception is one in which the contradictions and conflicts in dominant and commonsense conceptions of the world are simply lived with, negotiated in everyday life perhaps, but not questioned. A critical conception of the world is one which questions them. But this questioning necessitates not merely intellectual questioning, but new forms of social practice.

Gramsci did not much consider the situation of women. But I think that many of his ideas can illuminatingly be applied to their lives. Consider, for example, the question of power. Women have often been in the power of men; at the same time, they have sometimes also had power over men. But the associations of "power" in each case have tended to be different. The power of men over women has often been a matter of authority, of force and of violence. The power of women over men has often depended on wiles and cunning and on devious strategies to conceal that power. But women have wanted to "empower" themselves to act in new ways and reject old definitions of themselves; yet the old associations of "power" may seem inadequate for this. The meeting of women in feminism has sometimes suggested new ways to think about "power"; about the "empowering" of women in ways that do not recapitulate the dominant institutionalised forms of hierarchy, violence or cunning. Conceptions of unrealised potentialities, of new social forms and patterns, and of the development of self, go hand in hand. And these new conceptions arise in the space left, as it were, by old contrasts or contradictions, and by the way in which the latter are inadequate to conceptualise new social forms or more coherently articulated personal goals.

Thus insofar as the notion of the "real self" or "authentic nature" of a person is a useful one, it should be used, I think, to express the idea of a more coherent, less fragmented conception of oneself, more critically aware of those things which have deposited in oneself the "traces" of which Gramsci wrote, of the contradictions one may have been living in one's life, and of potential ways in which these might be resolved. In this sense, it is best represented as an achievement rather than a discovery of something that was "already there." It can be represented as the possibility of transcending, in certain circumstances, what had been "second nature."

Sartre

Jean-Paul Sartre (1905–1980), philosopher, playwright, novelist, was France's fore-most existentialist. He published his first novel, Nausea, *in 1938 and his major philosophical work,* Being and Nothingness, *in 1943, at the time of the German occupation of Paris. Sartre was deeply involved in politics as well as philosophy and literature and claimed, at one time, allegiance to Marxism. Upon his death in 1980, thousands of Parisians mourned their leading and rather fearless intellectual.*

It is difficult to speak of *the* existentialist view of the self, as there are many areas of wide disagreement among those thinkers usually labeled as "existentialists." The view of the self put forward by Sartre, however, is generally considered a kind of paradigm or model of the existentialist position. In both his highly technical and more popular works Sartre argues that we are our deeds; that we determine our own nature from out of our basic freedom. This freedom to which, according to Sartre, we are "condemned," obtains not because of some deep accord we have with an essential principle of natural-ness but because nothing determines us in our "human nature." We choose ourselves and thus we bear a heavy responsibility, for in choosing ourselves we choose by impli-cation an ideal for all others. Sartre is an outspoken atheist and acknowledges that much of his thinking about persons is a drawing out of an implications of a radical re-jection of the Judeo-Christian theistic outlook. There is no God or absolute principle of any kind that determines our conduct or makes us who we become. One is able, there-fore, to live authentically as a person only insofar as one accepts one's freedom and commits oneself to the choices one makes. At the same time, however, one is never re-ducible either to the mere givens of one's nature—one's mental capacities, physical conditions, social background, and so on (one's "facticity") or to one's present chosen situation. One is always more that what one presently is; one would be in what Sartre calls "bad faith" if one believed and acted otherwise.

Unhappily, though, "others" always press their identifications upon us and thereby restrict our conscious being, even when these identifications do seem to accord with our behavior. In his *Being and Nothingness,* Sartre gives many vivid examples of this im-position of self-identity; for example, that of the voyeur or "Peeping Tom," who to him-self, while looking through a keyhole in a hotel room, is only an observer of a certain scene, but who, when noticed by someone coming down the hallway, becomes a "voyeur." He is that—but that is not all that he is or may become. In this play *No Exit* Sartre develops this imposing role of the other and concludes that "Hell is other peo-ple."

In the following selections from his popular essay *Existentialism (Is a Humanism)* (1946), Sartre sets forth in clear terms some of the essentials of his thinking.

An Existentialist View of the Self

Atheistic existentialism, of which I am a representative, declares with greater consistency that if God does not exist there is at least one being whose existence comes before its essence, a being which exists before it can be defined by any conception of it. That being is man. . . . What do we mean by saying that existence precedes essence? We mean that man first of all exists, encounters himself, surges up in the world—and defines himself afterwards. If man as the existentialist sees him is not definable, it is because to begin with he is nothing. He will not be anything until later, and then he will be what he makes of himself. Thus, there is no human nature, because there is no God to have a conception of it. Man simply is. Not that he is simply what he conceives himself to be, but he is what he wills, and as he conceives himself after already existing—as he wills to be after that leap towards existence. Man is nothing else but that which he makes of himself. That is the first principle of existentialism. And this is what people call its "subjectivity," using the word as a reproach against us. But what do we mean to say by this, but that man is of a greater dignity than a stone or a table? For we mean to say that man primarily exists—that man is, before all else, something which propels itself towards a future and is aware that it is doing so. Man is, indeed, a project which possesses a subjective life, instead of being a kind of moss, or a fungus or a cauliflower. Before that projection of the self nothing exists; not even in the heaven of intelligence: man will only attain existence when he is what he purposes to be. Not, however, what he may wish to be. For what we usually understand by wishing or willing is a conscious decision taken—much more often than not—after we have made ourselves what we are. I may wish to join a party, to write a book or to marry—but in such a case what is usually called my will is probably a manifestation of a prior and more spontaneous decision. If, however, it is true that existence is prior to essence, man is responsible for what he is. Thus, the first effect of existentialism is that it puts every man in possession of himself as he is, and places the entire responsibility for his existence squarely upon his own shoulders. And, when we say that man is responsible for himself, we do not mean that he is responsible only for his own individuality, but that he is responsible for all men. The word "subjectivism" is to be understood in two senses, and our adversaries play upon only one of them. Subjectivism means, on the one hand, the freedom of the individual subject and, on the other, that man cannot pass beyond human subjectivity. It is the latter which is the deeper meaning of existentialism. When we say

From *Existentialism* by Jean-Paul Sartre, translated by Philip Mairet (c. 1946). Reprinted by permission of Methuen & Co.

that man chooses himself, we do mean that everyone of us must choose himself; but by that we also mean that in choosing for himself he chooses for all men. For in effect, of all the actions a man may take in order to create himself as he wills to be, there is not one which is not creative, at the same time, of an image of man such as he believes he ought to be. To choose between this or that is at the same time to affirm the value of that which is chosen; for we are unable ever to choose the worse. What we choose is always the better; and nothing can be better for us unless it is better for all. If, moreover, existence precedes essence and we will to exist at the same time as we fashion our image, that image is valid for all and for the entire epoch in which we find ourselves. Our responsibility is thus much greater than we had supposed, for it concerns mankind as a whole. If I am a worker, for instance, I may choose to join a Christian rather than a Communist trade union. And if, by that membership, I choose to signify that resignation is, after all, the attitude that best becomes a man, that man's kingdom is not upon this earth, I do not commit myself alone to that view. Resignation is my will for everyone, and my action is, in consequence, a commitment on behalf of all mankind. Or if, to take a more personal case, I decide to marry and to have children, even though this decision proceeds simply from my situation, from my passion or my desire, I am thereby committing not only myself, but humanity as a whole, to the practice of monogamy. I am thus responsible for myself and for all men, and I am creating a certain image of man as I would have him to be. In fashioning myself I fashion man. . . .

. . . For if indeed existence precedes essence, one will never be able to explain one's action by reference to a given and specific human nature; in other words, there is no determinism—man is free, man *is* freedom. Nor, on the other hand, if God does not exist, are we provided with any values or commands that could legitimize our behavior. Thus we have neither behind us, nor before us in a luminous realm of values, any means of justification or excuse. We are left alone, without excuse. That is what I mean when I say that man is condemned to be free. Condemned, because he did not create himself, yet is nevertheless at liberty, and from the moment that he is thrown into this world he is responsible for everything he does. The existentialist does not believe in the power of passion. He will never regard a grand passion as a destructive torrent upon which a man is swept into certain actions as by fate, and which, therefore, is an excuse for them. He thinks that man is responsible for his passion. Neither will an existentialist think that a man can find help through some sign being vouchsafed upon earth for his orientation: for he thinks that the man himself interprets the sign as he chooses. He thinks that every man, without any support or help whatever, is condemned at every instant to invent man. As Ponge has written in a very fine article, "Man is the future of man." That is exactly true. Only, if one took this to mean that the future is laid up in Heaven, that God knows what it is, it would be false, for then it would no longer even be a future. If, however, it means that, whatever man may now appear to be, there is a future to be fashioned, a virgin future that awaits him—then it is a true saying. But in the present one is forsaken. . . .

. . . In reality and for the existentialist, there is no love apart from the deeds of love; no potentiality of love other than that which is manifested in loving; there is no genius other than that which is expressed in works of art. The genius of Proust is the totality of the works of Proust; the genius of Racine is the series of his tragedies, outside of which there is nothing. Why should we attribute to Racine the capacity to write yet another tragedy when that is precisely what he did not write? In life, a man commits himself, draws his own portrait and there is nothing but that portrait. No doubt this thought may seem comfortless to one who has not made a success of his life. On the other hand, it puts everyone in a position to understand that reality alone is reliable; that dreams, expectations and hopes serve to define a man only as deceptive dreams, abortive hopes, expectations unfulfilled; that is to say, they define him negatively, not positively. Nevertheless, when one says, "You are nothing else but what you live," it does not imply that an artist is to be judged solely by his works of art; for a thousand other things contribute no less to his definition as a man. What we mean to say is that a man is no other than a series of undertakings, that he is the sum, the organization, the set of relations that constitute these undertakings.

In the light of all this, what people reproach us with is not, after all, our pessimism, but the sternness of our optimism. If people condemn our works of fiction, in which we describe characters that are base, weak, cowardly and sometimes even frankly evil, it is not only because those characters are base, weak, cowardly or evil. For suppose that, like Zola, we showed that the behavior of these characters was caused by their heredity, or by the action of their environment upon them, or by determining factors, psychic or organic. People would be reassured, they would say, "You see, that is what we are like, no one can do anything about it." But the existentialist, when he portrays a coward, shows him as responsible for his cowardice. He is not like that on account of a cowardly heart or lungs or cerebrum, he has not become like that through his physiological organism; he is like that because he has made himself into a coward by his actions. There is no such thing as a cowardly temperament. There are nervous temperaments; there is what is called impoverished blood, and there are also rich temperaments. But the man whose blood is poor is not a coward for all that, for what produces cowardice is the act of giving up or giving way; and a temperament is not an action. A coward is defined by the deed that he has done. What people feel obscurely, and with horror, is that the coward as we present him is guilty of being a coward. What people would prefer would be to be born either a coward or a hero.

MacIntyre

Alasdair MacIntyre, currently a professor at the University of Notre Dame, has previously held positions of distinction of Boston University and Vanderbilt University. He has also taught philosophy at Oxford University. MacIntyre's book After Virtue *was hailed as one of the most important contemporary works in moral philosophy. Among his other notable books are* A Short History of Ethics *(1966) and* Whose Justice? Which Rationality? *(1988).*

In *After Virtue,* MacIntyre agrees with Sartre on the importance of our actions in shaping the person that we become, but he moves away from Sartre's rather radical subjectivity and self-consciousness toward the social contexts and traditions in which a person is embedded and through which the person develops his or her own narrative or life-story. This shift to the social, the historical, and the cultural leads us, according to MacIntyre, to a different kind and degree of responsibility that involves holding oneself, and others, accountable for the stories of our lives that become constitutive of our very being.

A Narrative Conception of Selfhood

We live out our lives, both individually and in our relationships with each other, in the light of certain conceptions of a possible shared future, a future in which certain possibilities beckon us forward and others repel us, some seem already foreclosed and others perhaps inevitable. There is no present which is not informed by some image of some future and an image of the future which always presents itself in the form of a *telos*—or of a variety of ends or goals—towards which we are either moving or failing to move in the present. Unpredictability and teleology therefore coexist as part of our lives; like characters in a fictional narrative we do not know what will happen next, but none the less our lives have a certain form which projects itself towards our future. Thus the narratives which we live out have both an unpredictable and a partially teleological character. If the narrative of our individual and social lives is to continue intelligibly—and either type of narrative may lapse into unintelligibility—it is always both the case that there are constraints on how the story can continue *and* that within those constraints there are indefinitely many ways that it can continue.

A central thesis then begins to emerge: man is in his actions and practice, as well as in his fictions, essentially a story-telling animal. He is not essentially, but becomes through his history, a teller of stories that aspire to truth. But the key question for men is not about their authorship; I can only answer the question "What am I to do?" if I can answer the prior question "Of what story or stories do I find myself a part?" We enter human society, that is, with one or more imputed characters—roles into which we have been drafted—and we have to learn what they are in order to be able to understand how others respond to us and how our responses to them are apt to be construed. It is through hearing stories about wicked stepmothers, lost children, good but misguided kings, wolves that suckle twin boys, youngest sons who receive no inheritance but must make their own way in the world and eldest sons who waste their inheritance on riotous living and go into exile to live with the swine, that children learn or mislearn both what a child and what a parent is, what the cast of characters may be in the drama into which they have been born and what the ways of the world are. Deprive children of stories and you leave them unscripted, anxious stutterers in their actions as in their words. Hence there is no way to give us an understanding of any society, including our own, except through the stock of stories which constitute its initial dramatic resources. Mythology, in its original sense, is at the heart of things. . . .

I [have] . . . suggested that "an" action is always an episode in a possible history: I would now like to make a related suggestion about another concept, that of personal identity. . . . (Am I the same man at fifty as I was at forty in respect of memory, intellectual powers, critical responses? More or less.) But what is crucial to human beings as characters in enacted narratives is that, possessing only the resources of psychological continuity, we have to be able to respond to the imputation of strict identity. I am forever whatever I have been at any time for others—and I may at any time be called upon to answer for it—no matter how changed I may be now. There is no way of *founding* my identity—or lack of it—on the psychological continuity or discontinuity of the self. The self inhabits a character whose unity is given as the unity of a character. Once again there is a crucial disagreement with empiricist or analytical philosophers on the one hand and with existentialists on the other.

Empiricists, such as Locke or Hume, tried to give an account of personal identity solely in terms of psychological states or events. Analytical philosophers, in so many ways their heirs as well as their critics, have wrestled with the connection between those states and events and strict identity. . . . Both have failed to see that a background has been omitted, the lack of which makes the problems insoluble. That background is provided by the concept of a story and of that kind of unity of character which a story requires. Just as a history is not a sequence of actions, but the concept of an action is that of a moment in an actual or possible history abstracted for some purpose from that history, so the characters in a history are not a collection of persons, but the concept of a person is that of a character abstracted from a history.

What the narrative concept of selfhood requires is thus twofold. On the one hand, I am what I may justifiably be taken by others to be in the course of living out a story that runs from my birth to my death; I am the *subject* of a history that is my own and no one else's, that has its own peculiar meaning. When someone complains—as do some of those who attempt or commit suicide—that his or her life is meaningless, he or she is often and perhaps characteristically complaining that the narrative of their life has become unintelligible to them, that it lacks any point, any movement towards a climax or a *telos*. Hence the point of doing any one thing rather than another at crucial junctures in their lives seems to such a person to have been lost.

To be the subject of a narrative that runs from one's birth to one's death is, I remarked earlier, to be accountable for the actions and experiences which compose a narratable life. It is, that is, to be open to being asked to give a certain kind of account of what one did or what happened to one or what one witnessed at any earlier point in one's life the time at which the question is posed. Of course someone may have forgotten or suffered brain damage or simply not attended sufficiently at the relevant times to be able to give the relevant account. But to say of someone under some one description ("The prisoner of the Chateau d'If") that he is the same person as someone characterised quite differently ("The Count of Monte Cristo") is precisely to say that it makes sense to ask him to give an intelligible narrative account enabling us to understand how he could at different times and different places be one and the same person and yet be so differently characterised. Thus personal identity is just that identity presupposed by the unity of the character which the unity of a narrative requires. Without such unity there would not be subjects of whom stories could be told.

The other aspect of narrative selfhood is correlative: I am not only accountable, I am one who can always ask others for an account, who can put others to the question. I am part of their story, as they are part of mine. The narrative of any one life is part of an interlocking set of narratives. Moreover this asking for and giving of accounts itself plays an important part in constituting narratives. Asking you what you did and why, saying what I did and why, pondering the differences between your account of what I did and my account of what I did, and *vice versa*, these are essential constituents of all but the very simplest and barest of narratives. Thus without the accountability of the self those trains of events that constitute all but the simplest and barest of narratives could not occur; and without that same accountability narratives would lack that continuity required to make both them and the actions that constitute them intelligible.

It is important to notice that I am not arguing that the concepts of narrative or of intelligibility or of accountability are *more* fundamental than that of personal identity. The concepts of narrative, intelligibility and accountability presuppose the applicability of the concept of personal identity, just as it presupposes their applicability and just as indeed each of these three presupposes the applicability of the two others. The relationship is one of mutual presupposition. It does follow of course that all attempts to elucidate the notion of personal identity independently of and in isolation from the notions of narrative, intelligibility and accountability are bound to fail. As all such attempts have.

It is now possible to return to the question from which this inquiry into the nature of human action and identity started: In what does the unity of an individual life consist? The answer is that its unity is the unity of a narrative embodied in a single life. To ask "What is the good for me?" is to ask how best I might live out that unity and bring it to completion. To ask "What is the good for man?" is to ask what all answers to the former question must have in common. But now it is important to emphasise that it is the systematic asking of these two questions and the attempt to answer them in deed as well as in word which provide the moral life with its unity. The unity of a human life is the unity of a narrative quest. Quests sometimes fail, are frustrated, abandoned or dissipated into distractions; and human lives may in all these ways also fail. But the only criteria for success or failure in a human life as a whole are the criteria of success or failure in a narrated or to-be-narrated quest. A quest for what?

Two key features of the medieval conception of a quest need to be recalled. The first is that without some at least partly determinate conception of the final *telos* there could not be any beginning to a quest. Some conception of the good for man is required. Whence is such a conception to be drawn? Precisely from those questions which led us to attempt to transcend that limited conception of the virtues which is available in and through practices. It is in looking for a conception of *the* good which will enable us to order other goods, for a conception of *the* good which will enable us to extend our understanding of the purpose and content of the virtues, for a conception of *the* good which will enable us to understand the place of integrity and constancy in life, that we initially define the kind of life which is a quest for the good. But secondly it is clear the medieval conception of a quest is not at all that of a search for something already adequately characterised, as miners search for gold or geologists for oil. It is in the course of the quest and only through encountering and coping with the various particular harms, dangers, temptations and distractions which provide any quest with its episodes and incidents that the goal of the quest is finally to be understood. A quest is always an education both as to the character of that which is sought and in self-knowledge.

The virtues therefore are to be understood as those dispositions which will not only sustain practices and enable us to achieve the goods internal to practices, but which will also sustain us in the relevant kind of quest for the good, by enabling us to overcome the harms, dangers, temptations and distractions which we encounter, and which will furnish us with increasing self-knowledge and increasing knowledge of the good. The catalogue of the virtues will therefore include the virtues required to sustain the kind of households and the kind of political communities in which men and women can seek for the good together and the virtues necessary for philosophical enquiry about the character of the good. We have then arrived at a provisional conclusion about the good life for man: the good life for man is the life spent in seeking for the good life for man, and the virtues necessary for the seeking are those which will enable us to understand what more and what else the good life for man is. We have also completed the second stage in our account of the virtues, by situating them in relation to the good life for man and not only in relation to practices. But our enquiry requires a third stage.

For I am never able to seek for the good or exercise the virtues only *qua* individual. This is partly because what it is to live the good life concretely varies from circumstance to circumstance even when it is one and the same conception of the good life and one and the same set of virtues which are being embodied in a human life. What the good life is for a fifth-century Athenian general will not be the same as what it was for a medieval nun or a seventeenth-century farmer. But it is not just that different individuals live in different social circumstances; it is also that we all approach our own circumstances as bearers of a particular social identity. I am someone's son or daughter, someone else's cousin or uncle; I am a citizen of this or that city, a member of this or that guild or profession; I belong to this clan, that tribe, this nation. Hence what is good for me has to be the good for one who inhabits these roles. As such, I inherit from the past of my family, my city, my tribe, my nation, a variety of debts, inheritances, rightful expectations and obligations. These constitute the given of my life, my moral starting point. This is in part what gives my life its own moral particularity.

This thought is likely to appear alien and even surprising from the standpoint of modern individualism. From the standpoint of individualism I am what I myself choose to be. I can always, if I wish to, put in question what are taken to be the merely contingent social features of my existence. I may biologically be my father's son; but I cannot be held responsible for what he did unless I choose implicitly or explicitly to assume such responsibility. I may legally be a citizen of a certain country; but I cannot be held responsible for what my country does or has done unless I choose implicitly or explicitly to assume such responsibility. Such individualism is expressed by those modern Americans who deny any responsibility for the effects of slavery upon black Americans, saying "I never owned any slaves." It is more subtly the standpoint of those other modern Americans who accept a nicely calculated responsibility for such effects measured precisely by the benefits they themselves as individuals have indirectly received from slavery. In both cases "being an American" is not in itself taken to be part of the moral identity of the individual. And of course there is nothing peculiar to modern Americans in this attitude: the Englishman who says, "*I* never did any wrong to Ireland; why bring up that old history as though it had something to do with *me?*" or the young German who believes that being born after 1945 means that what Nazis did to Jews has no moral relevance to his relationship to his Jewish contemporaries, exhibit the same attitude, that according to which the self is detachable from its social and historical roles and statuses. And the self so detached is of course a self very much at home in either Sartre's or Goffman's perspective, a self that can have no history. The contrast with the narrative view of the self is clear. For the story of my life is always embedded in the story of those communities from which I derive my identity. I am born with a past; and to try to cut myself off from that past, in the individualist mode, is to deform my present relationships. The possession of an historical identity and the possession of a social identity coincide. Notice that rebellion against my identity is always one possible mode of expressing it.

Notice also that the fact that the self has to find its moral identity in and through its membership in communities such as those of the family, the neighbourhood, the city and the tribe does not entail that the self has to accept the moral *limitations* of the particularity of those forms of community. Without those moral particularities to begin from there would never be anywhere to begin; but it is in moving forward from such particularity that the search for the good, for the universal, consists. Yet particularity can never be simply left behind or obliterated. . . .

What I am, therefore, is in key part what I inherit, a specific past that is present to some degree in my present. I find myself part of a history and that is generally to say, whether I like it or not, whether I recognise it or not, one of the bearers of a tradition. It was important when I characterised the concept of a practice to notice that practices always have histories and that at any given moment what a practice is depends on a mode of understanding it which has been transmitted often through many generations. And thus, insofar as the virtues sustain the relationships required for practices, they have to sustain relationships to the past—and to the future—as well as in the present. But the traditions through which particular practices are transmitted and reshaped never exist in isolation for larger social traditions. What constitutes such traditions? . . .

. . . A living tradition is an historically extended, socially embodied argument, and an argument precisely in part about the goods which constitute that tradition. Within a tradition the pursuit of goods extends through generations, sometimes through many generations. Hence the individual's search for his or her good is generally and characteristically conducted within a context defined by those traditions of which the individual's life is a part, and this is true both of those goods which are internal to practices and of the goods of a single life. Once again the narrative phenomenon of embedding is crucial: the history of a practice in our time is generally and characteristically embedded in and made intelligible in terms of the larger and longer history of the tradition through which the practice in its present form was conveyed to us; the history of each of our own lives is generally and characteristically embedded in and made intelligible in terms of the larger and longer histories of a number of traditions.

Confucianism

K'ung fu-tzu (551–479 B.C.E.), whose name was Latinized as "Confucius," was the founder of the Confucian school of philosophy. He was considered to be the most influential thinker in China, especially with regard to his articulation of the principles of good government and his pronouncements regarding the manner in which exemplary or authoritative (not to be confused with authoritarian) persons were to be cultivated. Confucius believed that through disciplined ritual practice and liberal education one could achieve a genuine concern for, and sensitivity to, the welfare of others. This achievement qualifies an exemplary person (*chün-tzu*) to become a proper administrator and ruler.

Various myths have gathered around the historical Confucius, but it is generally accepted that, although of modest family background, he became a rather unsuccessful official of the state of Lu and brought together a group of young followers with whom he shared his ideas. Frustrated that his ideas for human relations and governance were not being heeded by the Lu government, Confucius, with a group of his most avid students, traveled to other states for a period of thirteen years seeking to influence the rulers. Unsuccessful once again in effecting the desired changes in governmental structures and attitudes, Confucius returned to Lu, continued his teaching, and began working on his major project, the *Lun-yu*, or the *Analects*. Eventually the school of Confucianism gained the support of the government and became the dominant tradition in Chinese culture for many centuries.

Am I basically good or basically evil? What is my original nature? And how may I cultivate or redirect it? To what extent am I intrinsically a social being?

These are among the basic questions that inform Chinese thinking about the nature of humankind. These questions are also at the heart of political-social theory and have tremendous implications for the philosophy and practice of education. If I am basically good, naturally inclined toward identifying with and helping others, then the best government would be one that was made up of persons of culture and learning who could serve as models for me and others and who would provide the conditions for the mature expression or unfolding of my nature; my education would allow me the maximum expression of my native reason and insight. If, on the other hand, I am basically evil, predisposed to secure my own ends at any cost, then the best government would be one that restrained my natural inclinations (through laws and penalties, or direct force); my education would be one of molding me to conform to a social ideal.

Confucian answers to the fundamental questions are diverse. Confucius seemed to hold that human beings are basically good or at any rate that they can attain a "sageliness within" that they can exhibit through all aspects of social living. It was Mencius

(c. 372–289 B.C.E.), of whom very little is known, who set forth what became the classical Confucian position regarding basic human nature. Mencius argued that all persons are basically good, for their original nature is endowed with feelings of commiseration, shame and dislike, respect and reverence, and right and wrong. These give rise to and are correlated with the four moral virtues of basic humanness (*jen*), righteousness (*i*), propriety (*li*), and wisdom (*chih*). Each person is complete in himself or herself, according to Mencius, and all persons are basically equal in their original nature. The evil person is the undeveloped person. The wise person is one who, through controlling his or her passional self and developing his or her mind, realizes to the full his or her basic feelings and dispositions.

In the following selection, Wing-tsit Chan (1901–1994), the twentieth-century dean of Chinese philosophical studies, discusses the importance of Confucius's teaching for Chinese civilization and calls attention to the importance of the concepts of *jen* and the *chün-tzu*, the ideal person. Selections from some central teachings of Mencius are also presented.

This is followed by an exposition of the meaning of the self in Confucianism by Roger T. Ames, Professor of Philosophy and Director of the Center for Chinese Studies at the University of Hawaii. Ames argues that for Confucianism a person is "irreducibly social"—that one is always in relationship to others. For Sartre Hell might be other people, but for Confucianism, I am who I am by virtue of my social being. Confucianism thus presses MacIntyre's claim that a person has an identity only as embedded in traditions to its furthest limit.

WING-TSIT CHAN

The Humanism of Confucius

Confucius (551–479 B.C.E) can truly be said to have molded Chinese civilization in general. It may seem far-fetched, however, to say that he molded Chinese philosophy in particular—that he determined the direction or established the pattern of later Chinese philosophical developments—yet there is more truth in the statement than is usually realized.

Judging on the basis of the *Analects* alone, we find that Confucius exerted great influence on Chinese philosophical development in that, first of all, he determined its outstanding characteristic, namely, humanism.

. . . The humanistic tendency had been in evidence long before his time. But it was Confucius who turned it into the strongest driving force in Chinese philosophy. He did not care to talk about spiritual beings or even about life after death. Instead, believing that man "can make the Way (Tao) great," and not that "the Way can make man great," he concentrated on man. His primary concern was a good society based

From Chan, Wing-tsit, comp. and trans., *A Source Book in Chinese Philosophy.* Copyright © 1963 renewed © Princeton University Press. Reprinted by permission of Princeton University Press.

on good government and harmonious human relations. To this end he advocated a good government that rules by virtue and moral example rather than by punishment or force. His criterion for goodness was righteousness as opposed to profit. For the family, he particularly stressed filial piety and for society in general, proper conduct or *li* (propriety, rites).

More specifically, he believed in the perfectibility of all men, and in this connection he radically modified a traditional concept, that of the *chün-tzu,* or superior man. Literally "son of the ruler," it came to acquire the meaning of "superior man," on the theory that nobility was a quality determined by status, more particularly a hereditary position. The term appears 107 times in the *Analects.* In some cases it refers to the ruler. In most cases, however, Confucius used it to denote a morally superior man. In other words, to him nobility was no longer a matter of blood, but of character—a concept that amounted to social revolution. Perhaps it is more correct to say that it was an evolution, but certainly it was Confucius who firmly established the new concept. His repeated mention of sage-emperors Yao and Shun and Duke Chou as models seems to suggest that he was looking back to the past. Be that as it may, he was looking to ideal men rather than to a supernatural being for inspiration. . . .

. . . In the first place, Confucius made *jen* [humanity] the main theme of his conversations. In the *Analects* fifty-eight of 499 chapters are devoted to the discussion of *jen,* and the word appears 105 times. No other subject, not even filial piety, engaged so much attention of the Master and his disciples. Furthermore, instead of perpetuating the ancient understanding of *jen* as a particular virtue, he transformed it into general virtue. It is true that in a few cases *jen* is still used by Confucius as a particular virtue, in the sense of benevolence. But in most cases, to Confucius the man of *jen* is the perfect man. He is the true *chün-tzu.* He is a man of the golden rule, for, "wishing to establish his own character, he also establishes the character of others, and wishing to be prominent himself, he also helps others to be prominent." In these balanced and harmonized aspects of the self and society, *jen* is expressed in terms of *chung* and *shu,* or conscientiousness and altruism, which is the "one thread" running through Confucius's teachings, and which is in essence the golden mean as well as the golden rule. It was the extension of this idea of *jen* that became the Neo-Confucian doctrine of man's forming one body with Heaven, or the unity of man and Nature, and it was because of the character of *jen* in man that later Confucianists have adhered to the theory of the original good nature of man.

MENCIUS

Human Nature Is Naturally Good

Kao Tzu said, "Human nature is like the willow tree, and righteousness is like a cup or a bowl. To turn human nature into humanity and righteousness is like turning the willow into cups and bowls." Mencius said, "Sir, can you follow the nature of the willow tree and make the cups and bowls, or must you violate the nature of the willow tree before you can make the cups and bowls? If you are going to violate the nature of the willow tree in order to make cups and bowls, then must you also violate human nature in order to make it into humanity and righteousness? Your words, alas! would lend all people in the world to consider humanity and righteousness as calamity [because they required the violation of human nature]!"

Kao Tzu said, "Man's nature is like whirling water. If a breach in the pool is made to the east it will flow to the east. If a breach is made to the west it will flow to the west. Man's nature is indifferent to good and evil, just as water is indifferent to east and west." Mencius said, "Water, indeed, is indifferent to the east and west, but is it indifferent to high and low? Man's nature is naturally good just as water naturally flows downward. There is no man without this good nature; neither is there water that does not flow downward. Now you can strike water and cause it to splash upward over your forehead, and by damming and leading it, you can force it uphill. Is this the nature of water? It is the forced circumstance that makes it do so. Man can be made to do evil, for his nature can be treated in the same way.". . .

Mencius said, "If you let people follow their feelings (original nature), they will be able to do good. This is what is meant by saying that human nature is good. If man does evil, it is not the fault of his natural endowment. The feeling of commiseration is found in all men; the feeling of shame and dislike is found in all men; the feeling of respect and reverence is found in all men; and the feeling of right and wrong is found in all men. The feeling of commiseration is what we call humanity [*jen*], the feeling of shame and dislike is what we called righteousness [*i*]; the feeling of respect and reverence is what we called propriety [*li*]; and the feeling of right and wrong is what we called wisdom [*chih*]. Humanity, righteousness, propriety, and wisdom are not drilled into us from outside. We originally have them with us. Only we do not think [to find them]. Therefore it is said, 'Seek and you will find it, neglect and you will lose it.' ". . .

Mencius said, "In good years most of the young people behave well. In bad years most of them abandon themselves to evil. This is not due to any difference in the natural capacity endowed by Heaven. The abandonment is due to the fact that the mind is allowed to fall into evil. Take for instance the growing of wheat. You sow

---

the seeds and cover them with soil. The land is the same and the time of sowing is also the same. In time they all grow up luxuriantly. When the time of harvest comes, they are all ripe. Although there may be a difference between the different stalks of wheat, it is due to differences in the soil, as rich or poor, to the unequal nourishment obtained from the rain and the dew, and to differences in human effort. Therefore all things of the same kind are similar to one another. Why should there be any doubt about men? The sage and I are the same in kind. . . ."

Kung-tu Tzu asked, "We are all human beings. Why is it that some men become great and others become small?" Mencius said, "Those who follow the greater qualities in their nature become great men and those who follow the smaller qualities in their nature become small men." "But we are all human beings. Why is it that some follow their greater qualities and others follow their smaller qualities?" Mencius replied, "When our senses of sight and hearing are used without thought and are thereby obscured by material things, the material things act on the material senses and lead them astray. That is all. The function of the mind is to think. If we think, we will get them (the principles of things). If we do not think, we will not get them. This is what Heaven has given to us. If we first build up the nobler part of our nature, then the inferior part cannot overcome it. It is simply this that makes a man great." . . .

Mencius said, "All men have the mind which cannot bear [to see the suffering of] others. . . . When a government that cannot bear to see the suffering of the people is conducted from a mind that cannot bear to see the suffering of others, the government of the empire will be as easy as making something go round in the palm."

"When I say that all men have the mind which cannot bear to see the suffering of others, my meaning may be illustrated thus: Now, when men suddenly see a child about to fall into a well, they all have a feeling of alarm and distress, not to gain friendship with the child's parents, nor to seek the praise of their neighbors and friends, nor because they dislike the reputation [of lack of humanity if they did not rescue the child]. From such a case, we see that a man without the feeling of commiseration is not a man; a man without the feeling of shame and dislike is not a man; a man without the feeling of deference and compliance is not a man; and a man without the feeling of right and wrong is not a man. The feeling of commiseration is the beginning of humanity; the feeling of shame and dislike is the beginning of righteousness; the feeling of deference and compliance is the beginning of propriety; and the feeling of right and wrong is the beginning of wisdom. Men have these Four Beginnings just as they have their four limbs. Having these Four Beginnings, but saying that they cannot develop them is to destroy themselves. . . ."

Mencius said, "All things are already complete in oneself. There is no greater joy than to examine oneself and be sincere. When in one's conduct one vigorously exercises altruism, humanity is not far to seek, but right by him."

ROGER T. AMES

The Focus-Field Self in Classical Confucianism

Arthur Danto, a distinguished philosopher (and friend), in the context of discussing the difficulty in interpreting a philosophical text, remarks:

> one of my favorite passages in the *Analects* is where Confucius says that if he gives someone *three* corners who cannot find the *fourth* corner for himself, he cannot teach that person. (Emphasis mine)

Of course, the passage that Danto is referring to in fact reads:

> If I have shown someone *one* corner of a square and he is not able to infer from it the other *three*, I will not show him a second time. (Emphasis mine)

Apart from the rather obvious and amusing irony of getting the passage wrong when you are trying to tell people how to read a text, Danto is certainly understating the effort required to put the square together.

In this essay, I want to begin by looking critically at several interpretations of the Confucian conception of self, claiming that none of them is successful in giving Confucius his square. I then want to develop my own model of the Confucian self, and to argue that, in fact, what Confucius was really looking for was a circle, anyway.

THE HOLLOW MEN

In the early nineteenth century, Hegel, witnessing the European assault on a seemingly passive China, read the situation from a distance. I cite him at some length here because, although the tenor of his commentary might be blunt and offensive, in substance, it resonates rather closely with much of what is being said today. Describing the traditional Chinese conception of self, Hegel reports:

> moral distinctions and requirements are expressed as Laws, but so that the subjective will is governed by these Laws as by an external force. Nothing subjective in the shape of disposition, Conscience, formal Freedom, is recognized. Justice is administered only on the basis of external morality, and Government exists only as the prerogative of compulsion. . . . Morality is in the East likewise a subject of positive legislation, and although moral prescriptions

Excerpted from "The Focus-Field Self in Classical Confucianism" by Roger T. Ames, in *Self as Person in Asian Theory and Practice*, edited by Roger T. Ames with Wimal Dissanayake and Thomas P. Kasulis (1994). Reprinted by permission of the State University of New York Press, © 1994.

(the *substance* of their Ethics) may be perfect, what should be internal subjective sentiment is made a matter of external arrangement. . . . While *we* obey, because what we are required to do is confirmed by an *internal* sanction, there the Law is regarded as inherently and absolutely valid without a sense of the want of this subjective confirmation.

Hegel's perception of the Chinese as animated by a top-down "totalitarianism" and hence as being shaped and justified entirely from without, is hardly obsolete. In fact, its most recent application is in the contemporary discussions on the Chinese response to human-rights talk.

Much if not most of the contemporary commentary available on Chinese attitudes toward human rights has interpreted the fundamental presupposition that the Chinese "self" is qualified by a kind of self-abnegation or "selflessness" in a manner that, in a more modern and subtle way, echoes the Hegelian "hollow men" characterization of the Chinese person cited above. Donald J. Munro, for example, argues that

> selflessness . . . is one of the oldest values in China, present in various forms in Taoism and Buddhism, but especially in Confucianism. The selfless person is always willing to subordinate his own interests, or that of some small group (like a village) to which he belongs, to the interest of a larger social group.

. . . Munro . . . and the legion of scholars who seem to share this interpretation are certainly right in assuming that the Chinese tradition has been largely persuaded by a Confucian-based relational—and hence social—definition of person, rather than by any notion of discrete individuality. And they are again unassailable in their assumption that this fact has profound implications for the way in which China has responded to any doctrine of human rights. But where we must take issue is with the assumption that, in the Chinese context, community interest and self-interest are mutually exclusive.

We can allow that there does not seem to be an adequate philosophical basis to justify self as a locus of interests independent of and prior to society. Under the sway of this relational understanding of human being, the mutuality and interdependence of personal, societal, and political realization in the classical Chinese model can and has been generally conceded. But it certainly does not follow that the consequence of this interdependence is selflessness. Under scrutiny, the consequence of attributing "selflessness" as an ideal to the Chinese tradition is to sneak in both the public/private and the individual/society distinctions by the back door. To be "selfless" in the sense presupposed by these commentators requires that an individual self first exist and then . . . that it be sacrificed for some higher public interest. And the suggestion that there are "higher interests" on the part of either person or society covertly establishes a boundary between them that justifies an adversarial relationship. The "selfless" interpretation of these commentators does not support the claim that "person" in the Chinese tradition is irreducibly social; ironically, it vitiates it.

These several commentators, in imposing a "selfless" ideal on the Chinese tradition, are appealing to a contest between state and individual—the struggle between advocates of group interests over the priority of individual interests—that has in large measure separated collectivist thinkers from the liberal democratic in the Western experience, but has perhaps only limited applicability to the Chinese model. While it is true that for the traditional Chinese model, self-realization does not require a high degree of individual autonomy, it does not follow that the alternative to autonomy is capitulation to the general will. Rather, Confucian "personalism," to use William Theodore de Bary's felicitous term, involves benefiting and being benefited by membership in a world of reciprocal loyalties and obligations that surround and stimulate a person and define a person's own worth.

This attribution of "selflessness" to the Chinese tradition, both ancient and modern, seems to arise out of an unfortunate equivocation between "selfish" and "selfless." To eschew selfish concerns does not necessarily lead to self-abnegation. The classical Confucian position, as I understand it, contends that, because self-realization is fundamentally a social undertaking, "selfish" concerns are to be rejected as an impediment to one's own growth and self-realization.

In Chinese philosophy, a perennial issue that has spanned the centuries has been the likelihood of conflict between the pursuit of selfish advantage (*li*), and negotiation of that which is appropriate and meaningful to all concerned (*yi*), including oneself. Concern for selfish personal advantage is associated with retarded personal development (*hsiao-jen*) while the pursuit of what is broadly "appropriate"—including, of course, one's own interests—is the mainstay of the self-realized and exemplary person (*chün-tzu*).

It can be argued that "self" does necessarily entail a notion of individuality. But, exposed in the differences we have discovered between being "nonselfish" and being "selfless," there is an unnoticed conceptual equivocation on the term *individual* that plagues this whole discussion. "Individual" can mean either one of a *kind*, like one human being as a member of a class of human beings, or *one* of a kind, like Turner's unique *Seastorm*. That is, "individual" can refer to a single, separate and indivisible thing that, by virtue of some essential property or properties, qualifies as a member of a class. By virtue of its membership in a "kind," it is substitutable—"equal before the law," "entitled to equal opportunity," "a locus of unalienable rights," "one of God's children," and so on. It is this definition of individual that generates notions like autonomy, equality, liberty, freedom, and individuated will. By virtue of both its separability and its indivisibility, it relates to its world only extrinsically and hence, where animate, has dominion over its own interiority.

Individual can alternatively also mean uniqueness: the character of a single and unsubstitutable particular, such as a work of art, where it might be quantitatively comparable to other particulars but where it has literally nothing qualitatively in common with them. Under this definition of individual, equality can only mean parity—a comparable excellence.

In the model of the unique individual, determinacy, far from being individuation, lies in the achieved quality of a person's relationships. A person becomes "recognized," "distinguished" or "renowned" by virtue of one's relations and their quality. Much of the effort in coming to an understanding of the traditional Confucian conception of self has to do with clarifying this distinction and reinstating the unique individual in the Confucian picture. While the definition of self as "irreducibly social" certainly precludes autonomous individuality, it does not rule out the second, less familiar notion of unique individuality. . . .

SELF AS FOCUS AND FIELD IN A FOCUS-FIELD MODEL

As I have noted above, the Chinese assumption is that personal, societal, and political order are coterminous and mutually entailing. One method of outlining the focus-field model of self, then, is to follow Plato in using the analogy of political order to describe the articulation of the particular person.

The first volume of the *Cambridge History of China* describes the career of the Han empire from its emergence under Liu Pang to its gradual disintegration three and a half centuries later. In this volume, Yü Ying-shih uses the "five zones" (*wu-fu*) of submission as a device for describing the dynamics of the Han world order:

> According to this theory, China since the Hsia dynasty had been divided into five concentric and hierarchical zones or areas. The central zone (*tien-fu*) was the royal domain, under the direct rule of the king. The royal domain was immediately surrounded by the Chinese states established by the king, known collectively as the lords' zone (*hou-fu*). Beyond the *hou-fu* were Chinese states conquered by the reigning dynasty, which constituted the so-called pacified zone (*sui-fu* or *pin-fu*, guest zone). The last two zones were reserved for the barbarians. The Man and I barbarians lived outside the *sui-fu* or *pin-fu* in the controlled zone (*yao-fu*) which was so called because the Man and I were supposedly subject to Chinese control, albeit of a rather loose kind. Finally, beyond the controlled zone lay the Jung and Ti barbarians, who were basically their own master in the wild zone (*huang-fu*) where the sinocentric world order reached its natural end.

This hierarchical scheme also describes the descending degree of tribute—local products and services—provided to the court at the center. Although this five zone theory seems more complex, it is really a distinction that defines the relative focus of an "inner-outer (*nei-wai*)" circle:

> China was the inner region relative to the outer region of the barbarians, just as the royal domain was, relative to the outer lords' zone, an inner zone, and the controlled zone became the inner area relative to the wild zone on the periphery of Chinese civilization.

This solar system of a centripetal harmony with patterns of deference articulating a central focus seems pervasive in Chinese society. These concrete, functioning patterns of deference "contribute" in varying degrees and are constitutive of the authority at the center, shaping and bringing into focus the character of the social and political entity—its standards and values. This determinate, detailed, "center-seeking" focus fades off into an increasingly indeterminate and untextured field. The attraction of the center is such that, with varying degrees of success, it draws into its field and suspends the disparate and diverse centers that constitute its world. The dynamic tension that obtains among these various centers articulate and inscribes the Han character. Importantly, the quality of these suspended centers are constitutive of the harmony of the field.

This sense of order in which all of the diversity and difference characteristic of the multiple, competing centers of the Warring States period are lifted into the harmony of the Han dynasty translates readily into intellectual world. The intellectual geography of the Hundred Schools in the pre-Ch'in period gives way to a syncretic Confucianism-centered doctrine that absorbs into itself and to some degree conceals the richness of what were competing elements to articulate the philosophical character of the period. This shift is better expressed in the language of incorporation and accommodation than of suppression.

As the centripetal center weakens in the second century A.D. and as the political order gradually dissolves into a period of disunity, the disparate centers precipitate out of the harmony to reassert themselves, and what was their contribution to the now-weakened center becomes the energy of contest. What was a tightening spire in the early Han becomes a gyre, disgorging itself of its disassociated contents. In the same period, there is a resurgence and interplay of competing philosophical schools and religious movements that reflect a disintegration of the centrally driven intellectual harmony.

Reflection, I believe, would persuade us that this focus-field notion of order is precisely that captured in the fundamental Confucian concept of ritually ordered community, where ritual (*li*), defined at the center by the authority of the tradition, not only demands personalization and participation but, further, is always reflective of the quality of its participants. Similarly, the extent to which a "zone" is active or passive with respect to configuring order is a function of its own distinctive achievement and the quality of its contribution. In fact, in the language of this tradition, the meaning of ritually ordered community itself is made literal from the image of *she-hui:* "a deferential assembly gathering around the sacred pole erected in the center of the community." Nishijima Sadao tells us:

> Such community life, based on the hamlet, had its religious center in the altar (*she*) where the local deity was enshrined. In the same way there was an altar for the state community (*kuo-she*), and each county and district also had its own altar. The religious festivals which took place at the hamlet altar (*li-she*), at which meat was distributed to the participants, helped to strengthen the community spirit.

Above we have employed the Han court analogy as a means of articulating the Confucian self as a "field of selves," but then the court analogy is itself derived from the all-pervasive family model. The "family" as the Chinese model of order is a variation on this notion of a graduated, centripetal harmony. Ambrose King argues persuasively that in the Chinese world, all relationships are familial:

> Among the five cardinal relations, three belong to the kinship realm. The remaining two, though not family relationships, are conceived in terms of the family. The relationship between the ruler and the ruled is conceived of in terms of father (*chün-fu*) and son (*tzu-min*), and the relationship between friend and friend is stated in terms of elder brother (*wu-hsiung*) and younger brother (*wu-ti*).

The family as the "in-group," is determinate and focused at the center, but becomes increasingly vague as it stretches out both diachronically in the direction of one's lineage and synchronically as a society full of "uncles" and "aunties." It is articulated in terms of *lun,* a ritual "wheel" (*lun*) of social relations that "ripple out" (*lun*) in a field of discourse (*lun*) to define the person as a network of roles. King's critique on this model is insightful:

> What must be emphasized here is that while Confucian ethics teach how the individual should be related to other particular roles through the proper *lun,* the issue of how the individual should be related to the "group" is not closely examined. In other words, the individual's behavior is supposed to be *lun*-oriented; the *lun*-oriented role relations, however, are seen as personal, concrete, and particularistic in nature.

While King's insistence that the Confucian model of self is constructed in concrete, particular, and differentiated relationships between self and "other" is certainly on the mark, this allowedly parochial self is not entirely devoid of a sense of group. We must give King the observation that the concreteness and immediacy of one's own definition is, like graduated love, necessitated by the unwillingness in this tradition to disengage the theoretical from experience. A role is not something you "are" but something you "do." But King goes too far in suggesting that the self's sense of group is so vague as to preclude the possibility of a broader civil ethic. He states:

> It seems to me that Confucian social ethics has failed to provide a "viable linkage" between the individual and *ch'ün;* the nonfamilistic group. The root of the Confucian *Problematik* lies in the fact that the boundary between the self and the group has not been conceptually articulated.

King, in missing the link, echoes Bertrand Russell's reservations about the weight given to family relations in the Chinese world:

> Filial piety, and the strength of the family generally, are perhaps the weakest point in Confucian ethics, the only point where the system departs seriously

from common sense. Family feeling has militated against public spirit, and the authority of the old has increased the tyranny of ancient customs. . . . In this respect, as in certain others, what is peculiar to China is the preservation of the old custom after a very high level of civilization had been attained.

The link that both King and Russell overlook here is that although the family, the society, the state, and even the tradition itself, as the extended "group" or "field," is indeed ambiguous *as a group or field,* the vagueness of the abstract nexus is focused and made immediate in the embodiment of the group or field by the particular father, the social exemplar, the ruler, and the historical model. The meaning of the group is made present in my father, my teacher, Mao Tse-tung, and Confucius. Each *lun* as the focus and articulation of a particular field of roles is holographic in that it construes its own field. Although the concreteness and immediacy of the centripetal center precludes any but the vaguest and indeterminate definitions of "Chineseness," this notion comes alive *to me* in the image of a Tseng Kuo-fan or a Yang Yu-wei. The totality is nothing more than the full range of particular foci, each focus defining itself and its own particular field.

A final foray. . . . We really must question the appropriateness of using "concept" language to discuss the Confucian self. Concept belongs to the one-many model, where "self" can be understood as having some univocal and hence formal definition—it reifies or entifies self as an ego or an ideal. Concept is dependent upon formal abstraction. Given the dependency of the Confucian model on the particular image, then, we might have to allow that the Confucian self is precisely that particular and detailed portrait of Confucius found in the middle books of the *Analects,* where each passage is a remembered detail contributed by one of the disciples who belonged to the conversation. And this portrait, as it attracts more disciples and plays a role in shaping unique self-images in the tradition, does the work of concept.

In our *Thinking Through Confucius,* David L. Hall and I argue for the dominance of what we call an "aesthetic" order as the signature of the Confucian sensibility. It is this aesthetic sensibility that demands the particular detail and precludes the definition of self in abstract terms. It is not unexpected, then, that Rudolf Arnheim, in his reflections on the visual arts, provides us with a useful vocabulary for exploring the Confucian model of order. Arnheim is persuaded that the nature of composition in the visual arts reflects an underlying cosmological tendency: "Cosmically, we find that matter organizes around centers, which are often marked by a dominant mass. Such systems come about whenever their neighbors allow them sufficient freedom." This phenomenon, observes Arnheim, is true of both the vast astronomical space and the microscopic realm. The center that is so constituted is "the center of a field of forces, a focus from which forces issue and towards which forces converge." These centers, then, relate to each other as a calculus of centers, which, from their interplay, produce a balancing centripetal center, which tends to distribute the forces of its field symmetrically around its own center:

> Overcoming the egocentric view amounts to realizing that a center is not always in the middle. . . . More often, the environment is dominated by other

centers, which force the self into a subordinate position. . . . Speaking generally, one can assert that every visual field comprises a number of centers, each of which attempts to draw the others into subservience. The self as viewer is just one of these centers. . . . The overall balance of all these competing aspirations determines the structure of the whole, and that total structure is organized around what I will call the balancing center.

The notion of composition that Arnheim is elaborating here describes abstractly the composition of the Confucian self and the various foci that define that world. But the clearest expression of this Confucian self is not abstract or theoretical. It is available only at the interface between the inspirational biographies and models that define a particular cultural tradition and the unique individuals that populate any particular historical moment.

WHAT IS THE AIM OF LIFE? HOW TO BE ETHICALLY, HOW TO BE POLITICALLY

One of the most enduring human questions we ask at various times throughout our life is: "What is the meaning or aim of life?" We ask this question with a kind of wonderment, for we are aware that no answer is immediately evident or easily forthcoming and that, although many answers have been given by knowledgeable and wise persons in different cultures, none has been accorded anything like universal acceptance. Some among us believe that we are fundamentally biologically driven, pleasure-seeking creatures, the aim of our life thereby becoming the maximizing of various material and other satisfactions. Because none of us lives, however, in radical isolation and independence from others, the question naturally arises how can some kind of harmony or adjudication be achieved between our own private satisfactions and those of others?

There are also many among us who reject the whole pleasure-based idea of life in favor of a commitment to more strictly rational demands concerning our duty to ourselves and to others or to religious conceptions that cast our human destiny in larger cosmic contexts.

It should be evident that the fundamental values we espouse regarding the meaning or aim of life are intimately connected with our views of human nature and our situation as social beings. Philosophical thinking strives to address these interconnections in a highly self-conscious way and to look deeply into the basic assumptions we make when we acknowledge—and hopefully live by—the answers we give to the questions: What values do I stand by? What goals are worth pursuing? How can I fulfill my potentialities as a social being who is grounded in a particular cultural place and historical time?

It also becomes rather evident on reflection that our values and our life experience are closely related. We do not just sit down one day and decide how we should live our lives as individuals in our social matrix, for our values are part and parcel of the whole process of how we become a person; they are formed within our ongoing experience and in turn center us, as it were, in all that we do and inform deeply the story of our individual lives as human beings.

Does this mean, though, that basic values and prescriptions for social behavior can never be rationally sustained as such? Does this also mean that all values and ethical principles are necessarily relative? A wide range of arguments have developed in philosophy around these controversial issues. There has been a strong tendency to attempt to determine the rational grounds for our primary values and principles in ways that show their necessity and universality. There has also been a strong aversion to this rationalist quest from many quarters. Today many feminists see this universalizing demand as part of a male-centered way of thinking that is blind to the many differences that obtain between male and female experience, which differences require us to give greater attention to the particularities of individual experience. Also, many anthropologically oriented thinkers who are keenly aware of multicultural and cross-cultural experience take exception to the idea that there is, or indeed ought to be, a single, universal value-scheme or morality, arguing that any such scheme cannot but be imperialistic in nature, something that is imposed upon others who would otherwise be quite content with cultural patterns of their own.

The debates that today rage sometimes wildly, sometimes thoughtfully, over the difficult issues of abortion, capital punishment, euthanasia, and so on are indicative of the fundamental differences among us concerning basic values and human obligations. Is human life sacred in some absolute sense? Indeed, do animals—being sentient creatures like ourselves—have rights of their own? What circumstances might allow us to intervene in the dying of a consent-giving person suffering horrible pain in what appears to be a hopeless situation? The issues in practical ethics today are many and far-reaching and oftentimes arise out of our confusions regarding the proper private and public domains of our existence.

This brings us to the "political," the arena where this confusion plays itself out most conspicuously. Going back at least to the ancient Greeks, part of the very definition of what it means to be human is that of being a participant in some order or other of public relations with others. Traditionally the "political" has focused on the justification of different types of government and the rights, if any, and obligations, often many, of individuals who are part of a tribal, national, or other recognized social group. Today, however, the meaning of the political tends to be extended to include the power relations that exist in our workplace, our families, and the small communities, such as neighborhoods or professional organizations, in which we might participate. The fundamental style of our acting politically not just as a citizen of a state but throughout the domain of our actions with others thus becomes a central concern.

Political philosophers have often investigated the origins of the coming together of human beings as members of a society in terms of the benefits they hope to acquire. Some have seen this as a kind of contract among persons who are willing to give up the unrestrained freedom of action to do whatever they want whenever they can prevail over others for the sake of the fruits of security and other benefits afforded by civilization. Others have seen this coming together as simply a natural expression of a regard for and feeling of community with others. In any event, certain questions inescapably arise: What rights do we have as individuals with respect to the collective will? How can we frame a conception of our obligations to the political order? What, in short, is the proper meaning of "justice" in human affairs?

The concept of justice has proven to be a central one in political thought and, once again, is closely related to our most fundamental notions of what it means to be a value-seeking and valued human being engaged in the world with others and in various sustaining natural environments. It has often been suggested that we all know something about what justice means—and more powerfully, that we all know more about what *injustice* means—from a kind of primitive sense of our dignity and right to be treated fairly. How, though, can this sense be rationally justified and brought into a central place in our political action?

As with practical ethics, in the political domain a host of issues of pressing concern have arisen and, under rapidly changing social situations and technological advances, continue to arise in unexpected ways. As a citizen, for example, of a liberal democracy, why must I be subject to military service for a cause to which I might take great exception? Why should I pay taxes for anything other than the direct benefits that governmental services offer to me? Or am I obligated in some other way for ensuring the material well-being of those less fortunate or otherwise unable to provide for themselves? These are the kinds of issues that get played out in public debate and that rest quite clearly on a number of philosophical concepts regarding the nature of our values and our ethical principles.

In the following selections, we will once again encounter a rich diversity of viewpoints from within different cultural traditions. Some will argue for an identifiable rational purpose to life and set forth principles for acquiring those virtues that allow us to fulfill our highest potentialities; others will set forth a religiously based account of our moral duties and responsibilities; while still others will reject both a rationalistic and theistic stance in favor of a radical humanism that calls upon each of us to choose for ourselves in full freedom and responsibility. Within ethical theory as such one of the great divides between an ethic of duty based on overarching rational principles and one based on attendance to the consequences of one's actions will be explored. And within the political, arguments for the rightness of liberal democratic principles will be set forth against the claims for the need for authoritarian practices. Arguments will be articulated as well for the abolishing of all forms of governmental coercion.

The famous Greek philosopher Aristotle, as we will see, insisted that the degree of clarity and precision in our thought that we can hope to attain is always relative to the subject that we are investigating. Although the precision and rigor of, say, a mathematical demonstration or logical proof will be lacking in philosophical thinking about values and about ethical and political issues, possibilities of enriched understanding and better living will, hopefully, clearly be present.

Aristotle

Aristotle (384–322 B.C.E.) was an outstanding ancient Greek thinker who was known in medieval times simply as "The Philosopher." Besides his respected and major works in ethics, metaphysics, and aesthetics, Aristotle virtually defined the fields of logic, biology, and the study of language. A student of Plato, he was a member of Plato's Academy for about twenty years. Aristotle, however, disagreed with his famous teacher on many important issues and, although highly dependent upon Plato, set his own philosophical course. Around the year 342 B.C.E, Aristotle traveled to Macedonia and became the tutor of King Philip's son, Alexander, who later became known as Alexander the Great. After a few years Aristotle returned to Athens and established his own school called the Lyceum.

The aim of human life, for Aristotle, its final end or purpose, is happiness (*eudaimonia*). It is, he says, that which is desired only for its own sake, with everything else desired for its sake. Our happiness must be found, according to Aristotle, in that which is most natural and unique to humankind, and he finds this to consist in our living in accordance with a rational ideal or principle of virtue.

Aristotle divides the concept of virtue into two kinds, the intellectual and the moral. The intellectual virtues are those acquired through education and are grounded in wisdom and understanding, the highest among them—which is the ultimate aim of human life—being that of philosophic contemplation. The moral virtues, on the other hand, such as liberality and temperance, to which Aristotle pays the greater attention in his work, arise through habit. One becomes one's habits so that good actions are those performed by good persons. They are to be guided by a rational awareness of what is right and appropriate for every situation, or what Aristotle refers to as a "mean" between various extremes.

Virtue and the Good Life

Every art and every inquiry, and similarly every action and pursuit, is thought to aim at some good; and for this reason the good has rightly been declared to be that at which all things aim. . . . Now, as there are many actions, arts, and sciences, their ends also are many; the end of the medical art is health, that of shipbuilding a vessel, that of strategy victory, that of economics wealth. . . .

If, then, there is some end of the things we do, which we desire for its own sake (everything else being desired for the sake of this), . . . clearly this must be the good and the chief good. Will not the knowledge of it, then, have a great influence on life? Shall we not, like archers who have a mark to aim at, be more likely to hit upon what is right?. . .

Our discussion will be adequate if it has as much clearness as the subject-matter admits of, for precision is not to be sought for alike in all discussions, any more than in all the products of the crafts. . . . It is the mark of an educated man to look for precision in each class of things just so far as the nature of the subject admits; it is evidently equally foolish to accept probable reasoning from a mathematician and to demand from a rhetorician scientific proofs. . . .

Let us resume our inquiry and state, in view of the fact that all knowledge and every pursuit aims at some good, what it is that . . . is the highest of all goods achievable by action. Verbally there is very general agreement; for both the general run of men and people of superior refinement say that it is happiness, and identify living well and doing well with being happy; but with regard to what happiness is they differ, and the many do not give the same account as the wise. For the former think it is some plain and obvious thing, like pleasure, wealth, or honour; they differ, however, from one another—and often even the same man identifies it with different things, with health when he is ill, with wealth when he is poor; but, conscious of their ignorance, they admire those who proclaim some great ideal that is above their comprehension. Now some thought that apart from these many goods there is another which is self-subsistent and causes the goodness of all these as well. To examine all the opinions that have been held were perhaps somewhat fruitless; enough to examine those that are most prevalent or that seem to be arguable. . . .

. . . To judge from the lives that men lead, most men, and men of the most vulgar type, seem (not without some ground) to identify the good, or happiness, with pleasure; which is the reason why they love the life of enjoyment. . . . Now the mass of mankind are evidently quite slavish in their tastes, preferring a life suitable to beasts. . . . A consideration of the prominent types of life shows that people of superior refinement and of active disposition identify happiness with honour; for this is,

From *Nicomachean Ethics* by Aristotle, translated by W. D. Ross, in *The Oxford Translation of Aristotle*, vol. 9 (1925). Reprinted by permission of Oxford University Press.

roughly speaking, the end of the political life. But it seems too superficial to be what we are looking for, since it is thought to depend on those who bestow honour rather than on him who receives it, but the good we divine to be something proper to a man and not easily taken from him. . . .

The life of money-making is one undertaken under compulsion, and wealth is evidently not the good we are seeking; for it is merely useful and for the sake of something else. And so one might rather take the aforenamed objects to be ends; for they are loved for themselves. But it is evident that not even these are ends; yet many arguments have been thrown away in support of them. Let us leave this subject, then. . . .

Let us again return to the good we are seeking, and ask what it can be. It seems different in different actions and arts; it is different in medicine, in strategy, and in the other arts likewise. What then is the good of each? Surely that for whose sake everything else is done. In medicine this is health, in strategy victory, in architecture a house, in any other sphere something else, and in every action and pursuit the end; for it is for the sake of this that all men do whatever else they do. Therefore, if there is an end for all that we do, this will be the good achievable by action, and if there are more than one, these will be the goods achievable by action.

So the argument has by a different course reached the same point; but we must try to state this even more clearly. Since there are evidently more than one end, and we choose some of these (e.g. wealth, flutes, and in general instruments) for the sake of something else, clearly not all ends are final ends; but the chief good is evidently something final. Therefore, if there is only one final end, this will be what we are seeking, and if there are more than one, the most final of these will be what we are seeking. Now we call that which is in itself worthy of pursuit more final than that which is worthy of pursuit for the sake of something else, and that which is never desirable for the sake of something else more final than the things that are desirable both in themselves and for the sake of that other thing, and therefore we call final without qualification that which is always desirable in itself and never for the sake of something else.

Now such a thing happiness, above all else, is held to be; for this we choose always for itself and never for the sake of something else, but honour, pleasure, reason, and every virtue we choose indeed for themselves (for if nothing resulted from them we should still choose each of them), but we choose them also for the sake of happiness, judging that by means of them we shall be happy. Happiness, on the other hand, no one chooses for the sake of these, nor, in general, for anything other than itself.

From the point of view of self-sufficiency the same result seems to follow; for the final good is thought to be self-sufficient. Now by self-sufficient we do not mean that which is sufficient for a man by himself, for one who lives a solitary life, but also for parents, children, wife, and in general for his friends and fellow citizens, since man is born for citizenship. . . . The self-sufficient we now define as that which when isolated makes life desirable and lacking in nothing; and such we think happiness to be; and further we think it most desirable of all things, without being counted as one good thing among others—if it were so counted it would clearly be made more desirable by the addition of even the least of goods; for that which is added becomes an excess of goods, and of goods the greater is always more desirable. Happiness, then, is something final and self-sufficient, and is the end of action.

Presumably, however, to say that happiness is the chief good seems a platitude, and a clearer account of what it is is still desired. This might perhaps be given, if we could first ascertain the function of man. For just as for a flute-player, a sculptor, or any artist, and, in general, for all things that have a function or activity, the good and the "well" is thought to reside in the function, so would it seem to be for man, if he has a function. Have the carpenter, then, and the tanner certain functions or activities, and has man none? Is he born without a function? Or as eye, hand, foot, and in general each of the parts evidently has a function, may one lay it down that man similarly has a function apart from all these? What then can this be? Life seems to be common even to plants, but we are seeking what is peculiar to man. Let us exclude, therefore, the life of nutrition and growth. Next there would be a life of perception, but *it* also seems to be common even to the horse, the ox, and every animal. There remains, then, an active life of the element that has a rational principle; of this, one part has such a principle in the sense of being obedient to one, the other in the sense of possessing one and exercising thought. And, as "life of the rational element" also has two meanings, we must state that life in the sense of activity is what we mean; for this seems to be the more proper sense of the term. Now if the function of man is an activity of soul which follows or implies a rational principle, and if we say "a so-and-so" and "a good so-and-so" have a function which is the same in kind, e.g. a lyre-player and a good lyre-player, and so without qualification in all cases, eminence in respect of goodness being added to the name of the function (for the function of a lyre-player is to play the lyre, and that of a good lyre-player is to do so well): if this is the case, [and we state the function of man to be a certain kind of life, and this to be an activity or actions of the soul implying a rational principle, and the function of a good man to be the good and noble performance of these, and if any action is well performed when it is performed in accordance with the appropriate excellence: if this is the case,] human good turns out to be activity of soul in accordance with virtue, and if there are more than one virtue, in accordance with the best and most complete. . . .

Virtue, then, being of two kinds, intellectual and moral, intellectual virtue in the main owes both its birth and its growth to teaching (for which reason it requires experience and time), while moral virtue comes about as a result of habit. . . . From this it is also plain that none of the moral virtues arises in us by nature; for nothing that exists by nature can form a habit contrary to its nature. For instance the stone which by nature moves downwards cannot be habituated to move upwards, not even if one tries to train it by throwing it up ten thousand times; nor can fire be habituated to move downwards, nor can anything else that by nature behaves in one way be trained to behave in another. Neither by nature, then, nor contrary to nature do the virtues arise in us; rather we are adapted by nature to receive them, and are made perfect by habit.

Again, of all the things that come to us by nature we first acquire the potentiality and later exhibit the activity (this is plain in the case of the senses for it was not by often seeing or often hearing that we got these senses, but on the contrary we had them before we used them, and did not come to have them by using them); but the virtues we get by first exercising them, as also happens in the case of the arts as well. For the things we have to learn before we can do them, we learn by doing them, e.g. men become builders by building and lyre-players by playing the lyre; so too we become just by doing just acts, temperate by doing temperate acts, brave by doing brave acts. . . .

The question might be asked, what we mean by saying that we must become just by doing just acts, and temperate by doing temperate acts; for if men do just and temperate acts, they are already just and temperate, exactly as, if they do what is in accordance with the laws of grammar and of music, they are grammarians and musicians. . . .

Actions, then, are called just and temperate when they are such as the just or the temperate man would do; but it is not the man who does these that is just and temperate, but the man who also does them *as* just and temperate men do them. It is well said, then, that it is by doing just acts that the just man is produced, and by doing temperate acts the temperate man; without doing these no one would have even a prospect of becoming good. . . .

Next we must consider what virtue is. Since things that are found in the soul are of three kinds—passions, faculties, states of character, virtue must be one of these. By passions I mean appetite, anger, fear, confidence, envy, joy, friendly feeling, hatred, longing, emulation, pity, and in general the feelings that are accompanied by pleasure or pain; by faculties the things in virtue of which we are said to be capable of feeling these, e.g. of becoming angry or being pained or feeling pity; by states of character the things in virtue of which we stand well or badly with reference to the passions, e.g. with reference to anger we stand badly if we feel it violently or too weakly, and well if we feel it moderately; and similarly with reference to the other passions.

Now neither the virtues nor the vices are *passions,* because we are not called good or bad on the ground of our passions, but are so called on the ground of our virtues and our vices, and because we are neither praised nor blamed for our passions (for the man who feels fear or anger is not praised, nor is the man who simply feels anger blamed, but the man who feels it in a certain way), but for our virtues and our vices we *are* praised or blamed.

Again, we feel anger and fear without choice, but the virtues are modes of choice or involve choice. Further, in respect of the passions we are said to be moved, but in respect of the virtues and the vices we are said not to be moved but to be disposed in a particular way.

For these reasons also they are not *faculties;* for we are neither called good nor bad, nor praised nor blamed, for the simple capacity of feeling the passions; again, we have the faculties by nature, but we are not made good or bad by nature; we have spoken of this before.

If, then, the virtues are neither passions nor faculties, all that remains is that they should be *states of character.*

Thus we have stated what virtue is in respect of its genus.

·   ·   ·

We must, however, not only describe virtue as a state of character, but also say what sort of state it is. We may remark, then, that every virtue or excellence both brings into good condition the thing of which it is the excellence and makes the work of that thing be done well; e.g. the excellence of the eye makes both the eye and its work good; for it is by the excellence of the eye that we see well. Similarly the excellence of the horse makes a horse both good in itself and good at running and at carrying its rider and at awaiting the attack of the enemy. Therefore, if this is true in every case, the virtue of man also will be the state of character which makes a man good and which makes him do his own work well.

How this is to happen we have stated already, but it will be made plain also by the following consideration of the specific nature of virtue. In everything that is continuous and divisible it is possible to take more, less, or an equal amount, and that either in terms of the thing itself or relatively to us; and the equal is an intermediate between excess and defect. By the intermediate in the object I mean that which is equidistant from each of the extremes, which is one and the same for all men; by the intermediate relatively to us that which is neither too much nor too little—and this is not one, not the same for all. For instance, if ten is many and two is few, six is the intermediate, taken in terms of the object; for it exceeds and is exceeded by an equal amount; this is intermediate according to arithmetical proportion. But the intermediate relatively to us is not to be taken so; if ten pounds are too much for a particular person to eat and two too little, it does not follow that the trainer will order six pounds; for this also is perhaps too much for the person who is to take it, or too little. . . . The same is true of running and wrestling. Thus a master of any art avoids excess and defect, but seeks the intermediate and chooses this—the intermediate not in the object but relatively to us.

If it is thus, then, that every art does its work well—by looking to the intermediate and judging its works by this standard (so that we often say of good works of art that it is not possible either to take away or to add anything, implying that excess and defect destroy the goodness of works of art, while the mean preserves it; and good artists, as we say, look to this in their work), and if, further, virtue is more exact and better than any art, as nature also is, then virtue must have the quality of aiming at the intermediate. I mean moral virtue; for it is this that is concerned with passions and actions, and in these there is excess, defect, and the intermediate. For instance, both fear and confidence and appetite and anger and pity and in general pleasure and pain may be felt both too much and too little, and in both cases not well; but to feel them at the right times, with reference to the right objects, towards the right people, with the right motive, and in the right way, is what is both intermediate and best, and this is characteristic of virtue. Similarly with regard to actions also there is excess, defect, and the intermediate. Now virtue is concerned with passions and actions, in which excess is a form of failure, and so is defect, while the intermediate is praised and is a form of success; and being praised and being successful are both characteristics of virtue. Therefore virtue is a kind of mean, since, as we have seen, it aims at what is intermediate.

Again, it is possible to fail in many ways (for evil belongs to the class of the unlimited, as the Pythagoreans conjectured, and good to that of the limited), while to succeed is possible only in one way (for which reason also one is easy and the other difficult—to miss the mark easy, to hit it difficult); for these reasons also, then, excess and defect are characteristic of vice, and the mean of virtue;

> For men are good in but one way, but bad in many.

Virtue, then, is a state of character concerned with choice, lying in a mean, i.e. the mean relative to us, this being determined by a rational principle, and by that principle by which the man of practical wisdom would determine it. Now it is a mean between two vices, that which depends on excess and that which depends on defect; and again it is a mean because the vices respectively fall short of or exceed what is right in both passions and actions, while virtue both finds and chooses that which is intermediate. Hence in respect of its substance and the definition which states its essence virtue is a mean, with regard to what is best and right an extreme.

But not every action nor every passion admits of a mean; for some have names that already imply badness, e.g. spite, shamelessness, envy, and in the case of actions adultery, theft, murder; for all of these and suchlike things imply by their names that they are themselves bad, and not the excesses or deficiencies of them. It is not possible, then, ever to be right with regard to them; one must always be wrong. Nor does goodness or badness with regard to such things depend on committing adultery with the right woman, at the right time, and in the right way, but simply to do any of them is to go wrong. It would be equally absurd, then, to expect that in unjust, cowardly, and voluptuous action there should be a mean, an excess, and a deficiency; for at that rate there would be a mean of excess and of deficiency, an excess of excess, and a deficiency of deficiency. But as there is no excess and deficiency of temperance and courage because what is intermediate is in a sense an extreme, so too of the actions we have mentioned there is no mean nor any excess and deficiency, but however they are done they are wrong; for in general there is neither a mean of excess and deficiency, nor excess and deficiency of a mean.

We must, however, not only make this general statement, but also apply it to the individual facts. For among statements about conduct those which are general apply more widely, but those which are particular are more genuine, since conduct has to do with individual cases, and our statements must harmonize with the facts in these cases. We may take these cases from our table. With regard to feelings of fear and confidence courage is the mean; of the people who exceed, he who exceeds in fearlessness has no name (many of the states have no name), while the man who exceeds in confidence is rash, and he who exceeds in fear and falls short in confidence is a coward. With regard to pleasures and pains—not all of them, and not so much with regard to the pains—the mean is temperance, the excess self-indulgence. Persons deficient with regard to the pleasures are not often found; hence such persons also have received no name. But let us call them "insensible."

With regard to giving and taking of money the mean is liberality, the excess and the defect prodigality and meanness. In these actions people exceed and fall short in contrary ways; the prodigal exceeds in spending and falls short in taking, while the mean man exceeds in taking and falls short in spending. . . . With regard to money there are also other dispositions—a mean, magnificence (for the magnificent man differs from the liberal man; the former deals with large sums, the latter with small ones), an excess, tastelessness and vulgarity, and a deficiency, niggardliness; these differ from the states opposed to liberality, and the mode of their difference will be stated later.

With regard to honour and dishonour the mean is proper pride, the excess is known as a sort of "empty vanity," and the deficiency is undue humility. . . .

With regard to anger also there is an excess, a deficiency, and a mean. Although they can scarcely be said to have names, yet since we call the intermediate person good-tempered let us call the mean good temper; of the persons at the extremes let the one who exceeds be called irascible, and his vice irascibility, and the man who falls short an inirascible sort of person, and the deficiency inirascibility.

That moral virtue is a mean, then, and in what sense it is so, and that it is a mean between two vices, the one involving excess, the other deficiency, and that it is such because its character is to aim at what is intermediate in passions and in actions, has been sufficiently stated. Hence also it is no easy task to be good. For in everything it is no easy task to find the middle, e.g. to find the middle of a circle is not for every one but for him who knows; so, too, any one can get angry—that is easy—or give or spend money; but to do this to the right person, to the right extent, at the right time, with the right motive, and in the right way, *that* is not for every one, nor is it easy; wherefore goodness is both rare and laudable and noble. . . .

If happiness is activity in accordance with virtue, it is reasonable that it should be in accordance with the highest virtue; and this will be that of the best thing in us. Whether it be reason or something else that is this element which is thought to be our natural rule and guide and to take thought of things noble and divine, whether it be itself also divine or only the most divine element in us, the activity of this in accordance with its proper virtue will be perfect happiness. That this activity is contemplative we have already said.

Now this would seem to be in agreement both with what we said before and with the truth. For, firstly, this activity is the best (since not only is reason the best thing in us, but the objects of reason are the best of knowable objects); and, secondly, it is the most continuous, since we can contemplate truth more continuously than we can *do* anything. And we think happiness has pleasure mingled with it, but the activity of philosophic wisdom is admittedly the pleasantest of virtuous activities; at all events the pursuit of it is thought to offer pleasures marvellous for their purity and their enduringness, and it is to be expected that those who know will pass their time more pleasantly than those who inquire. And the self-sufficiency that is spoken of must belong most to the contemplative activity. For while a philosopher, as well as a just man or one possessing any other virtue, needs the necessaries of life, when they are sufficiently equipped with things of that sort the just man needs people towards whom and with whom he shall act justly, and the temperate man, the brave man, and each of the others is in the same case, but the philosopher, even when by himself, can contemplate truth, and the better the wiser he is; he can perhaps do so better if he has fellow-workers, but still he is the most self-sufficient. And this activity alone would seem to be loved for its own sake; for nothing arises from it apart from the contemplating, while from practical activities we gain more or less apart from the action. And happiness is thought to depend on leisure; for we are busy that we may have leisure, and make war that we may live in peace. Now the activity of the practical virtues is exhibited in political or military affairs, but the actions concerned with these seem to be unleisurely. Warlike actions are completely so (for no one chooses to be at war, or provokes war, for the sake of being at war; any one would seem absolutely murderous if he were to make enemies of his friends in order to bring about battle and slaughter); but the action of the statesman is also unleisurely, and—apart from the political action itself—aims at despotic power and honours, or at all events happiness, for him and his fellow citizens—a happiness different from political action, and evidently sought as being different. So if among virtuous actions political and military actions are distinguished by nobility and greatness, and these are unleisurely and aim at an end and are not desirable for their own sake, but the activity of reason, which is contemplative, seems both to be superior in serious worth and to aim at no end beyond itself, and to have its pleasure proper to itself (and this augments the activity), and the self-sufficiency, leisureliness, unweariedness (so far as this is possible for man), and all the other attributes ascribed to the supremely happy man are evidently those connected with this activity, it follows that this will be the complete happiness of man, if it be allowed a complete term of life (for none of the attributes of happiness is *in*complete).

But such a life would be too high for man; for it is not in so far as he is man that he will live so, but in so far as something divine is present in him; and by so much as this is superior to our composite nature is its activity superior to that which is the exercise of the other kind of virtue. If reason is divine, then, in comparison with man, the life according to it is divine in comparison with human life. But we must not follow those who advise us, being men, to think of human things, and, being mortal, of mortal things, but must, so far as we can, make ourselves immortal, and strain every nerve to live in accordance with the best thing in us; for even if it be small in bulk, much more does it in power and worth surpass everything. This would seem, too, to be each man himself, since it is the authoritative and better part of him. It would be strange, then, if he were to choose not the life of his self but that of something else. And what we said before will apply now; that which is proper to each thing is by nature best and most pleasant for each thing; for man, therefore, the life according to reason is best and pleasantest, since reason more than anything else *is* man. This life therefore is also the happiest.

The *Bhagavad Gītā*

The *Bhagavad Gītā*, or "Song of the Lord," was composed sometime between the fifth and second centuries B.C.E. and forms part of the great Indian epic the *Mahābhārata*, whose authorship has not been accurately determined. The *Gītā*, as it is usually simply referred to, is a religious-philosophical poem with pronounced ethical and social dimensions. It is by far the single most popular text in Hindu culture.

The *Gītā* sets forth various paths, or *yogas*, that persons of various spiritual capacities can follow to achieve a freedom appropriate to their nature. Human beings are in bondage to the degree to which they are victims of their own desires, passions, and ignorance, which encompass the entire range of their ego-based action and thought. According to Indian thought in general, one's own past and present actions always influence strongly one's future actions, and accordingly karmic bonds grow stronger with experience. How, then, can we attain freedom in action in such a way as to fulfill our deepest ethical and spiritual potentialities? The text will show how, through knowledge of ourselves and of the necessities in the divine nature, we can achieve a style of acting and thinking that overcomes all ego-based experience and allows for the realization of genuine freedom.

The work opens within a dramatic context in which the warrior Arjuna, who is compelled to fight in a just war, realizes suddenly the horror of war—some of his own family and friends are in the opposing army—lays down his weapons, and refuses to fight. His charioteer, Kṛṣṇa, who is represented as a manifestation of the great Hindu god Viṣṇu, instructs Arjuna on how and in what manner he must fulfill his duty as a warrior in order to attain freedom. The fundamental questions, then, that are addressed in this extraordinary text are: Ought one to carry out actions that may be injurious or even fatal to others when called upon to do so because of one's social duty? And, if so, in what manner should these actions be carried out? In answering these questions Kṛṣṇa presents to Arjuna, and enables him to experience directly, a theistically grounded view of the nature of the universe as well as an understanding of the self and its ethical obligations that must inform all experience.

This approach is set forth in terms of a number of key concepts that are outlined below. It is followed by selections from the *Gītā* itself, together with brief interposed commentaries, in a translation by Eliot Deutsch.

ELIOT DEUTSCH

Some Key Terms and Concepts in the Bhagavad Gītā

DHARMA

The concept of *dharma*—"duty," "law," "righteousness," "moral merit"—is exceedingly rich in Indian thought in general and in the *Bhagavad Gītā* in particular. The term connotes religious and social duties; that which one ought to perform by virtue of the place which one occupies in the social order, and it further suggests a law of one's own nature, which is understood to be a reflection of one's particular mental-spiritual development. The concept of *dharma* is thus articulated in terms of one's station in life, since this ideally expresses the level of one's development as a spiritual being.

Hindu society is organized traditionally in terms of three interrelated schema: the four "stages of life," the four "aims of life," and the four "social classes" or "castes." According to the first schema, a person's life naturally falls into the various, rather distinct, divisions of youth, maturity, and old age, and one's life ought to be so organized that a fulfillment proper to each stage may be obtained. The term *āśrama* ["stages"] comes from *śram,* "to toil," "to exert oneself," and suggests that there is a special kind of work in the world which corresponds to each of the natural divisions of one's life in the world. The four *āśramas* are (1) the student stage, (2) the householder, (3) retirement, and (4) renunciation of the social order. During the student stage, one's *dharma* is to become educated; it is to learn to be a man (the text employs gender language reflective of its time), and this means studying the Vedic scriptures as well as training one's capacities and talents so that one can function in society with maximum effectiveness. The householder enters into society; he marries, has children, and engages in an occupation which supports his family. When the time comes, however, when he no longer finds satisfaction in this, and when his services are no longer essential to the maintenance of the family, he enters into retirement. He still has the responsibility of offering his guidance in family and community affairs, but he is encouraged to spend his time in study and meditation. Lastly, he is to become a *sannyāsin*—one who renounces the entire social order for the sake of striving for spiritual freedom. The duties enjoined upon him by his previous stages no longer are binding upon him. His only obligation is to seek a self-knowledge and knowledge of reality.

The four aims of life, *puruṣārthas* (literally, "what is sought by men"), are based upon the recognition that there are different basic drives that condition human experience and which need to be satisfied, redirected, and transcended at appropriate times in one's life. The four aims are (1) *artha* or "wealth," (2) *kāma* or

Kṛṣṇa fluting. Kṛṣṇa, the Lord whose song relates the way to human freedom, is a popular deity in Hinduism and performs many functions in the tradition. In addition to being the great teacher, he is often depicted as the supreme lover who beckons his companions to him through the intoxicating and seductive sounds of his flute. From the collection of Eliot Deutsch.

"pleasure," (3) *dharma* or "social duty" (which is related to, but not to be identified with, the general concept of *dharma*), and (4) *mokṣa* or "release," "liberation," "freedom." . . .

Artha is the aim of accumulating and enjoying material things. It is the goal of attaining material necessities and luxuries and of gaining economic and political power. *Kāma* is the aim of having pleasurable experiences such as physical love and aesthetic delight. The term literally means "desire" and, in this context of the *puruṣārthas*, suggests primarily the aim of satisfying sensual desire. *Artha* and *kāma* are essentially egocentric aims. They pertain to the individual who takes his own needs and desires as the central fact of existence. And hence the necessity for *dharma*, the third aim, which involves an awareness of one's dependence upon others and the consequent recognition that one must adjust one's own needs and desires to those of others; that one must work for the good of all as well as for oneself. *Dharma*, which is to inform the other two aims, represents the aim of one who knows that the individual does not stand alone but is rather a member of a social order which demands that he assume various responsibilities in it. The aim of *moksha* is different in kind from the other three. It corresponds precisely to the last stage of life and involves the quest for the realization of a supreme spiritual value to which all other values are subordinated.

The four aims represent a progressive maturing of the self. They are descriptive of the natural growth of a man and, especially with *dharma* and *moksha*, they are prescriptive of the proper development of moral consciousness. As a man passes from studentship to old age, he must transform and transcend just those drives which bind him to his lower nature.

The last of the schema is that of the four *varnas* or "castes." . . .

As in Plato's *Republic*, the dividing of men into four classes was originally intended to suggest that human nature may quite naturally be divided into intellectuals and priests (*brahmins*); rulers, warriors, statesmen (*kshatriyas*); businessmen and managers (*vaiśyas*); and workers and servants (*śūdras*)—and that a society as a whole functions best when each person in it knows his "place" and works within it for his own self-fulfillment and for the good of all. Each "caste" has its appropriate responsibilities to society and its appropriate rights and privileges. Until such time as one abandons society and becomes a *sannyāsin*, one is obligated to work within the social structure. A man's position in society is determined by his nature, capacities, talents, and interests.

In sum, then, *dharma* refers to the norms which make a social order; to the duties of an individual in society with respect to his particular stage in life, his aims in life, and his class position—as this is determined ideally by his own natural capacities and mental-moral-spiritual development. . . .

YOGA

The term *yoga* is used extensively in the *Gītā* and in a number of different senses. The term is probably derived from the root *yuj*, which means to "yoke" or "harness," and carries the general connotation of "joining" or "uniting oneself with." Following the usage in the *Katha Upaniṣad* (I, 2, 12), where the expression *adhyātma-yoga* ("yoking with one's real self" or "disciplined meditation on the self") appears, the *Gītā* generally uses *yoga* to mean the controlling of one's lower sensuous nature and the realization of one's higher spiritual nature. It means a *disciplined* detachment from the lower self of desires, of passions, of obsessions, and a realized attachment to that higher self which transcends the will, the emotions, and even the intellect, and which cannot be identified with them.

Yoga is also used as the name for various specific philosophical-religious "disciplines" or "ways" to self-realization. Among the various types of *yogas* distinguished are *karma yoga*, or the "way of action," *bhakti yoga*, or the "path of devotion," and *jñāna yoga*, or the "discipline of knowledge."

The *Gītā* also uses the term *yoga* to denote the system of Indian philosophy which was allegedly founded by Patañjali, a system also known as *rāja yoga*. In it *yoga* is defined as the "cessation of mental modifications": it is primarily a psychological discipline which also involves various physical postures and breath control and which seeks a state of complete self-integration and freedom. (Most modern writers use the term *yoga* to refer to just this system.)

Lastly, *yoga* is sometimes employed in the *Gītā* as a synonym for "divine power." When Krishna, as the Lord, speaks of his *yoga* (as in Chapters X and XI) he does not mean his "way" or "path" but his "creative power."

(Each chapter of the *Gītā* is entitled "The *yoga* of . . . ," but the term is employed here for the most part only in an honorific sense.)

SĀṀKHYA, PURUṢA, PRAKṚTI

The term *sāṁkhya* is used in the *Gītā* primarily to mean "mental discrimination" or "intellectual understanding." It is thus at times made synonymous with the word *jñāna* ("knowledge," "spiritual understanding").

Sāṁkhya, however, is also a name for another of the classical systems of Indian philosophy. The Sāṁkhya system developed a theory of cosmic evolution or emanation wherein everything in the universe was explained in terms of two basic original principles called *prakṛti* ("matter," "unconscious force") and *puruṣa* ("soul, "spirit," "consciousness"). Through an interaction of these principles, *prakṛti* brings forth and constitutes all the things and powers of the world in an ordered succession, and *puruṣa* is differentiated into a plurality of individual conscious selves.

Now one of the confusing things here is that the *Gītā* will draw heavily upon this system when formulating various conceptual descriptions and schemata. It will make a distinction between *prakṛti* and *puruṣa* and, although it will try to overcome the rigid dualism of Sānkhya, it will follow this system closely in describing the constituents of Nature and the basic categories of existence.

The term *sāṁkhya*, though, when it appears in the *Gītā*, is not intended to denote the Sāṁkhya system; rather, it denotes "intellectual understanding," "analytic discrimination," or "knowledge."

BRAHMAN

The word *Brahman* first appears in the Rig Veda (*c.* 1200 B.C.E.) in the context of various utterances that were believed to have a special magical power. Originally, then, *Brahman* may have signified only "spell" or "prayer"—an invocation for the attainment of worldly wishes (rain, prosperity, fertility) and other worldly bliss. In some places *Brahman* was objectified and was regarded as arising from *ṛta* ("order," "truth") and as thus having a universal significance. Later, and as a development of this, *Brahman* came to signify that principle which stands behind the gods as their ground, and in the *Upaniṣads* generally it becomes the unitary, undifferentiated principle of all being, the knowledge of which liberates one from finitude.

In the *Gītā*, *Brahman* is used in several senses. In some passages it is used as a substitute for the term *prakṛti* ("unconscious nature") and in others as a synonym for the term *Veda*. The general Upaniṣadic metaphysical meaning of *Brahman*, though, is retained and unless otherwise noted, it has this signification.

KARMA

The term *karma* means "deed," "work," "action" and is used in the Hindu tradition to mean both any action which produces tendencies or impressions (*samskāras*) in the actor, which then function as determinants to his future action, and specific ritual actions which are performed in the context of Vedic ceremonial religion. Further, according to most of the Indian philosophical systems, *karma* suggests a "law" of moral nature which holds that actions necessarily produce effects and that this is enacted over a period of innumerable births, deaths, and rebirths. Every action must produce its results—if not immediately, then at some future time—and every disposition to act is the result of one's past action. One is completely responsible for oneself. A man's present condition is the result of his past action over many lives, and his future condition will result from his past and present action.

GUṆA

The concept of *guṇa*—"strand," "quality," "constituent"—was developed most fully in ancient Indian philosophy by the Sāṃkhya system, and it is the Sāṃkhyan meaning of the term which the *Gītā* generally follows. Nature (*prakṛti*), according to Sāṃkhya, is composed of several basic strands or "energy fields" which are called *sattva* or "dynamic equilibrium," *rajas* or "turbulence," and *tamas* or "dullness." Everything in Nature represents some special combination of these three factors. The *guṇas*, however, are taken, and especially in the *Gītā*, not only as fields or dimensions of physical Nature, but also as qualities of psychic being and moral consciousness. *Sattva* stands here for a preponderance of intelligence and objectivity and is considered to be "good"; *rajas* stands for a preponderance of emotion and subjectivity and is considered to be that which is capable of becoming either "good" or "bad," depending upon how and where it is directed (but in any case remains less good than *sattva*); and *tamas* stands for a preponderance of ignorance, insensibility, and lethargy and is judged to be "bad." The criterion of "good" and "bad" implicit in this context is: that which is most conducive to spiritual realization is "good"; that which most stands in its way is "bad."

According to the *Gītā*, men tend naturally toward various "types" which are founded on the relative distribution of the *guṇas* within them. Men of a predominantly *sattvic* disposition are by their nature contemplative, philosophical, moral; men of a predominantly *rajasic* disposition tend to be active, ambitious, strong-willed; and those of a *tamasic* disposition tend to be slothful, dimwitted, and prone to simple sensuality. When the term *guṇa* is used in the *Gītā* it is necessary to look closely at the context in which it is employed in order to see whether the physical, psychological, or moral aspect is emphasized. When it refers primarily to physical Nature it suggests various energy states which constitute Nature and which are the locus of its order and "determinism"; when it refers primarily to psychological dispositions and morality it suggests "character types" and basic volitional attitudes.

JÑĀNA

Jñāna means "knowledge," "intuition," "spiritual understanding," and is often used in conjunction with *yoga* to denote the spiritual path by means of which men of strong intellectual or philosophical (*sattvic*) disposition seek self-realization. *Jñāna yoga* is the discipline associated most closely with Advaita Vedānta, the non-dualistic system expounded primarily by Śaṁkara. It demands a rigorous intellectual discrimination between the phenomenal world and the real world of Brahman, and culminates in an intuitive identification which shatters the independent existence of everything but the non-dual One. The *Gītā* speaks highly of this path but suggests that in its pure form it is meaningful for only a very few persons, and that by itself it cannot lead to the special sort of world-affirmation with which the *Gītā* is concerned.

BHAKTI

Bhakti means "love" or "devotion" and refers to that special intensity by which man reaches out to the Divine. *Bhakti* is the loving adoration for a personal divinity. Psychologically it may be said to represent a sublimation of passions, desires, emotions—their redirection from natural ends to a divine being—and an intensification of that natural religious emotion which seeks fulfillment through spiritual unity. *Bhakti* does not mean interpersonal human love or a love for man which follows from a love of God; it means, rather, an intense devotion which seeks to obtain unity with the Divine Being to whom the devotion is directed. *Bhakti*, when conjoined with *yoga*, thus means "the path of devotion." According to the *Gītā*, *bhakti yoga* is the means by which most persons are able to plumb the depths of religious experience.

Selections from the Bhagavad Gītā

[Arjuna, on the battlefield, is prepared to renounce his duty as a member of the warrior class upon his feeling aversion to killing others.]

Arjuna saw standing there fathers and grandfathers, teachers, uncles, brothers, sons and grandsons, and also companions;

And fathers-in-law and friends in both the armies. Seeing all these kinsmen thus arrayed, Arjuna,

Filled with the utmost compassion, sorrowfully spoke: Seeing my own kinsmen, O Kṛṣṇa, arrayed and wishing to fight,

My limbs collapse, my mouth dries up, there is trembling in my body and my hair stands on end;

The bow . . . slips from my hand and my skin also is burning; I am not able to stand still, my mind is whirling.

And I see evil portents, O Kṛṣṇa, and I foresee no good in slaying my own kinsmen in the fight.

I do not desire victory, O Kṛṣṇa, nor kingdom, nor pleasure. Of what use is kingdom to us, O Kṛṣṇa, of what use pleasure or life?

Those for whose sake we desire kingdom, pleasures and happiness, they are arrayed here in battle, having renounced their lives and riches.

Teachers, fathers, sons, and also grandfathers; uncles, fathers-in-law, grandsons, brothers-in-law and other kinsmen;

These I do not wish to kill, though they kill me, O Kṛṣṇa; even for the kingdom of the three worlds; how much less then for the sake of the earth! (I, 26–35) . . .

[Kṛṣṇa, his divine mentor, explains to Arjuna that the human soul is immortal and timeless and thus cannot, in fact, be destroyed. He sets the stage for directing Arjuna's awareness to the larger cosmic context within which all human action occurs.]

The Blessed Lord said:

Thou grievest for those thou shouldst not grieve for, and yet thou speakest words that sound like wisdom. Wise men do not mourn for the dead or for the living.

Never was there a time when I did not exist, nor thou, nor these rulers of men; nor will there ever be a time hereafter when we shall all cease to be.

As the soul in the body passes through childhood, youth and old age, so (after departure from this body) it passes on to another body. The sage is not bewildered by this.

Contacts with the objects of the senses, O Arjuna, give rise to cold and heat, pleasure and pain. They come and go, they are impermanent; endure them, O Arjuna.

From *The Bhagavad Gītā*, translated with an introduction and critical essays by Eliot Deutsch (1968). Reprinted by permission of Holt, Rinehart & Winston. Copyright © 1968 by Eliot Deutsch

The man who is not troubled by these contacts, O Arjuna, who treats alike pleasure and pain, who is wise; he is fit for immortality.

Of non-being there is no coming to be; of being there is no ceasing to be. The truth about both is seen by the seers of truth.

Know that by which all this is pervaded is indestructible, and that no one can cause the destruction of this immutable being.

It is said that (only) these bodies of the eternal embodied soul, which is indestructible and incomprehensible, are perishable. Therefore fight, O Arjuna!

He who thinks that this soul is a slayer, and he who thinks that this soul is slain; both of them are ignorant. This soul neither slays nor is slain.

It is never born, nor does it die, nor having once been, will it again cease to be. It is unborn, eternal, and everlasting. This primeval one is not slain when the body is slain.

He who knows that it is indestructible and eternal, unborn and unchanging, how can that man slay, O Arjuna, or cause another to slay?

Just as a man casts off worn-out clothes and takes on others that are new, so the embodied soul casts off worn-out bodies and takes on others that are new.

Weapons do not cut it, nor does fire burn it; waters do not make it wet, nor does wind make it dry.

It is uncleavable; it cannot be burnt, it can neither be wetted nor dried. It is eternal, omnipresent, unchanging and immovable. It is everlasting.

It is called unmanifest, unthinkable and immutable; therefore, knowing it as such, thou shouldst not grieve. (II, 11–25)

[Krṣṇa then instructs Arjuna in the rudiments of *karma-yoga,* the discipline of acting without ego-centeredness and attachment to the fruits of one's action. This *yoga* is based on the notion that it is only when one is in ignorance that one believes that one is a real source of action, for in fact one is only, at this level of experience, a passive victim of the forces of nature operating within one and determining one's action. This instruction goes beyond the moral injunctions for correct behavior given in the ancient scriptures (the Vedas) but nevertheless enables one to perform one's "allotted work" in the world.]

As much use as there is for a pond when there is everywhere a flood, so much is there in all the Vedas for a Brahmin who understands.

In action only hast thou a right and never in its fruits. Let not thy motive be the fruits of action; nor let thy attachment be to inaction.

Fixed in *yoga,* O Arjuna, perform actions, abandoning attachment and remaining evenminded in success and failure; for serenity of mind is called *yoga.*

Mere action is far inferior to the discipline of intelligence, O Arjuna. Seek refuge in intelligence; pitiful are those whose motive is the fruit of action.

One who has disciplined his intelligence leaves behind in this world both good and evil deeds. Therefore strive for *yoga,* for *yoga* is skill in action.

Having disciplined their intelligence and having abandoned the fruit born of their action, the wise are freed from the bondage of birth and attain the state that is free from sorrow.

When thy intelligence shall cross the tangle of delusion, then thou shalt become indifferent to what shall be heard and to what has been heard (in the Veda).

When their intelligence, which is now perplexed by the Vedic texts, shall stand immovable and be fixed in concentration, then shalt thou attain *yoga.* (II, 46–53)

In this world, O Arjuna, a twofold path has been taught before by Me; the path of knowledge (*jñāna-yoga*) for men of discrimination (*sāṁkhyas*) and the path of works (*karma-yoga*) for men of action (*yogins*).

Not by abstention from actions does a man gain freedom, and not by mere renunciation does he attain perfection.

No one can remain, even for a moment, without performing some action. Everyone is made to act helplessly by the *guṇas* born of *prakṛti.*

He who controls his organs of action, but dwells in his mind on the objects of the senses; that man is deluded and is called a hypocrite.

But he who controls the senses by the mind, O Arjuna, and, without attachment, engages the organs of action in *karma-yoga,* he excels.

Perform thy allotted work, for action is superior to inaction; even the maintenance of thy body cannot be accomplished without action.

This world is in bondage to *karma,* unless *karma* is performed for the sake of sacrifice. For the sake of that, O Arjuna, perform thy action free from attachment. (III, 3–9)

[Kṛṣṇa goes on to explain the necessity of his own divine action and the need for human agents to surrender their action to him in order to be free from their ego-based, desire-driven lower self.]

There is nothing in the three worlds, O Arjuna, to be done by Me, nor anything unobtained that needs to be obtained; yet I continue in action.

For if I, unwearied, were not always in action, O Arjuna, men everywhere would follow my path (example).

If I did not perform action, these worlds would be destroyed, and I should be the author of confusion and would destroy these people.

As the ignorant act with attachment to their work, O Arjuna, so the wise man should act but without attachment, desiring to maintain the order of the world.

Let no wise man unsettle the minds of the ignorant who are attached to action. Acting with discipline, he should make all action attractive.

All actions are performed by the *guṇas* of *prakṛti* alone. But he who is deluded by egoism thinks, "I am the doer."

He who knows the true essence of the separation of the soul from both the guṇas and actions, O Arjuna, and that it is the guṇas which act upon the guṇas, he is not attached to action.

Those who are deluded by the guṇas of *prakṛti* are attached to the action of the guṇas. But the man who knows the whole should not unsettle the ignorant who know only a part.

Surrendering all actions to Me, with thy consciousness fixed on the supreme Self, being free from desire and selfishness, fight freed from thy sorrow. (III, 22–30)

Then by what is a man impelled to (commit) sin against his will, as if compelled by force, O Kṛṣṇa?

The Blessed Lord said:

This is desire, this is wrath, born of the *guṇa* of passion, all-devouring and very sinful. Know that this is the enemy here.

As fire is covered by smoke, as a mirror by dust, and as an embryo is enveloped by the womb, so this knowledge is covered by that passion.

Knowledge is enveloped, O Arjuna, by this constant enemy of the knower, by this insatiable flame of desire.

The senses, the mind, the understanding are said to be its basis. With these it bewilders the embodied soul, covering its knowledge.

Therefore, O Arjuna, having in the beginning controlled thy senses, slay this evil destroyer of spiritual and practical knowledge. (III, 36–41) . . .

[The question is then raised regarding the very nature of action, and the principles of *karma-yoga* are further elaborated upon.]

What is action? What is inaction? About this even the wise are confused. Therefore I will declare to thee what action is, knowing which thou shalt be freed from evil.

One must understand the nature of action, and one must understand the nature of wrong action, and one must understand the nature of inaction: hard to understand is the way of action.

He who sees inaction in action and action in inaction, he is wise among men; he does all actions harmoniously.

He whose undertakings are all free from desire and will, whose actions are burned up in the fire of knowledge, him the wise call learned.

Having abandoned attachment to the fruits of action, always content and independent, he does nothing even though he is engaged in action.

Having no desires, with his mind and self controlled, abandoning all possessions, performing action with the body alone, he commits no sin.

He who is content with what comes by chance, who has passed beyond the pairs of opposites, who is free from jealousy and is indifferent to success and failure, even when he is acting he is not bound.

The action of a man who is rid of attachment, who is liberated, whose mind is firmly established in knowledge, who performs action as a sacrifice, is completely dissolved. (IV, 16–23)

[Kṛṣṇa shifts from a straightforward presentation of *karma-yoga* to an account of the principles of *jñāna-yoga*, the way of knowledge that overcomes and obliterates all ignorance.]

Even if thou art among sinners the worst sinner of all, thou shalt cross over all evil by the boat of knowledge alone.

As the fire which is kindled makes its fuel into ashes, O Arjuna, so the fire of knowledge makes all actions into ashes.

There is no purifier in this world equal to wisdom. He who is perfected in *yoga* finds it in the self in the course of time.

He who has faith, who is intent on it (knowledge) and who has controlled his senses, obtains knowledge and having obtained it, goes quickly to the highest peace.

But the ignorant man who is without faith and of a doubting nature perishes. For the doubting self, there is not this world, nor the next, nor happiness.

Actions do not bind him who has renounced actions in *yoga*, who has cast away doubt by knowledge, who possesses himself, O Arjuna.

Therefore having cut away, with the sword of knowledge, this doubt in thy heart that is born of ignorance, resort to *yoga* and arise, O Arjuna. (IV, 36–42)

[Arjuna becomes confused, for the way of knowledge seems to involve a setting aside of all one's duties as a social being. Kṛṣṇa explains that the path of action and the path of knowledge are not really incompatible.]

Arjuna said:

Thou praisest renunciation of actions, O Kṛṣṇa, and again (*karma*) *yoga*. Tell me definitely which one of these is the better.

The Blessed Lord said:

Renunciation (of works) and the unselfish performance of works (*karma-yoga*) both lead to the highest happiness. But of these two the unselfish performance of works is better than the renunciation of works.

He who neither hates nor desires should be known as the eternal renouncer; free from the pairs of opposites, O Arjuna, he is easily released from bondage.

Children, not the wise, speak of renunciation and *yoga* as separate; for he who is well established in one obtains the fruit of both.

That place which is obtained by the *sāṁkhyas* is also gained by the *yogins*. He who sees that *sāṁkhya* and *yoga* are one, he truly sees.

Renunciation, O Arjuna, is difficult to attain without *yoga*. The sage who is disciplined in *yoga* soon goes to Brahman.

He who is disciplined in *yoga* and is pure in soul, who is ruler of his self, who has conquered his senses, whose self becomes the Self of all beings, he is not affected by acting. (V, 1–7)

The all-pervading Spirit does not take on the sin or good work of anyone. Knowledge is enveloped by ignorance; by this creatures are bewildered.

But of those in whom ignorance is destroyed by knowledge, for them knowledge illumines the highest Self like the sun.

Thinking on that (highest Self), their self fixed on that, established in that, devoted to that, they go to where there is no returning, their sins destroyed by knowledge.

Sages look equally on a Brahmin endowed with knowledge and breeding, or on a cow, an elephant, and even a dog and an outcaste.

Even here on earth, creation is conquered by those whose minds are established in equality. Brahman is spotless and is the same to all. Therefore they are established in Brahman.

One should not rejoice when obtaining the pleasant, nor be agitated when obtaining the unpleasant. Unbewildered, with firm intelligence, the knower of Brahman is established in Brahman.

The self who is unattached to external contacts finds happiness in the Self. Being joined by *yoga* to Brahman, he attains imperishable happiness.

The enjoyments which are born of contacts with objects are only sources of sorrow. These have a beginning and end, O Arjuna; the wise man does not rejoice in them.

He who is able to endure here on earth, even before he is liberated from the body, the force that springs from desire and anger, he is disciplined, he is the happy man.

He who is happy within, whose joy is within and whose light is within; that *yogin* becomes Brahman and attains to the bliss of Brahman.

The seers whose sins are destroyed, whose dualities (doubts) are dispelled, whose selves are disciplined and who rejoice in the welfare of all beings, attain to the bliss of Brahman.

To these holy men who have destroyed desire and anger, who have controlled their minds, who know the Self, the bliss of Brahman is near. (V, 15–26)

[Kṛṣṇa then gives a rather elaborate account of his own comprehensive divine nature and the need for Arjuna to grasp this in order to achieve the state of devotion that is necessary to complete the reconciliation of knowledge and unattached action.]

Hear, O Arjuna, how, by attaching thy mind to Me, and by practicing *yoga,* with reliance upon Me, thou shalt know Me entirely, without doubt.

I will declare to thee in full this wisdom together with knowledge which, when known, nothing more in this world remains to be known.

Among thousands of men perchance one strives for perfection, and of those who strive and are successful, perhaps one knows Me in essence.

This is My divided eightfold nature: earth, water, fire, wind, ether, mind, intellect and self-consciousness.

This is My lower nature. Know My other higher nature, O Arjuna, which is the life-soul by which this world is supported.

Learn that all beings arise from this higher and lower nature of Mine. I am the origin of the whole world and also its dissolution.

Nothing exists higher than Me, O Arjuna. All this (universe) is strung on Me like jewels on a string. (VII, 1–7)

The foolish think of Me, the unmanifest, as having (only) come into manifestation; not knowing My higher nature which is immutable and supreme.

I am not revealed to all, being covered by My power of illusion. This world is deluded and does not recognize Me, the unborn and imperishable.

I know beings that are past, that are present and that are yet to be, O Arjuna, but no one knows Me.

All beings are born to confusion, O Arjuna, and are deluded by the dualities that originate from desire and hatred.

But those men of virtuous deeds whose sins are ended and who are freed from the delusion of opposites, worship Me with steadfast resolve.

Those who strive for liberation from old age and death and have taken refuge in Me know Brahman entirely and the Supreme Self and all action.

Those who know Me together with My material and divine domains and the highest sacrifice; they, of balanced mind, know Me even at the time of death. (VII, 24–30)

From the world of Brahmā downwards, all worlds are reborn, O Arjuna; but having come to Me, O Arjuna, there is no rebirth.

They who know that the day of Brahmā is of a thousand ages and that the night of Brahmā is of a thousand ages, they are the persons who know what day and night are.

From the unmanifest, all manifestations come forth at the coming of day, and at the coming of night, they dissolve in that same thing, called the unmanifest.

This same multitude of beings, coming forth repeatedly, dissolves helplessly in the coming of night, O Arjuna, and comes forth in the coming of day.

But higher than that unmanifest state, there is another unmanifested eternal being who does not perish when all beings perish.

This unmanifested state is called the Indestructible. They call that the highest goal which, having obtained, they return not. That is My highest abode.

This is the supreme spirit, O Arjuna, obtainable by unswerving devotion, in whom all beings abide and by whom all this is pervaded. (VIII, 16–22)

I will declare to thee, who are uncomplaining, this deepest secret of wisdom combined with knowledge, knowing which thou shalt be delivered from evil.

This is sovereign knowledge, a sovereign secret, the highest purifier, understood immediately, righteous, very easy to practice and imperishable.

Men who have no faith in this law, O Arjuna, do not attain Me but return to the path of ceaseless birth and rebirth.

By Me, in My unmanifested form, all this world is pervaded. All beings rest in Me but I do not rest in them.

And yet beings do not rest in Me: behold My divine mystery. My Self, which is the source of beings, sustains all beings but does not rest in them.

Just as the great wind, blowing everywhere abides in the ether, so all beings abide in Me; know thou that.

All beings, O Arjuna, enter into My material nature at the end of a world cycle, and I send them forth again at the beginning of a new cycle.

Taking hold of My own material nature, I send forth again and again all this multitude of beings which are helpless, by the force of My material nature.

And these actions do not bind Me, O Arjuna; I am seated as one who is indifferent, unattached to these actions.

With Me as supervisor, *prakṛti* sends forth all moving and unmoving things; by this cause, O Arjuna, the world revolves. (IX, 1–10)

But the great-souled, O Arjuna, who abide in the divine nature, worship Me with undeviating mind, knowing Me as the imperishable source of all beings.

Always glorifying Me and striving with steadfast resolve, and honoring Me with devotion, they worship Me ever-disciplined. (IX, 13–14)

The worshipers of the gods go to the gods; the worshipers of the ancestors go to the ancestors; sacrificers of the spirits go to the spirits; and those who sacrifice to Me come to Me.

Whoever offers Me a leaf, a flower, a fruit or water with devotion, I accept that offering of devotion from the pure in heart.

Whatever thou doest, whatever thou eatest, whatever thou offerest, whatever thou givest, whatever austerities thou performest, do that, O Arjuna, as an offering to Me.

Thus thou shalt be freed from the bonds of action which produce good and evil fruits; disciplined by the *yoga* of renunciation, thou shalt be liberated and come to Me.

I am equal to all beings, there is none hateful nor dear to Me. But those who worship Me with devotion, they are in Me and I am in them.

Even if a man of very evil conduct worships Me with undivided devotion, he too must be considered righteous, for he has resolved rightly.

Quickly he becomes a righteous self and obtains eternal peace; O Arjuna, know thou that My devotee never perishes. (IX, 25–31)

[Arjuna understands intellectually the nature and extent of divinity but asks Kṛṣṇa to show him directly his divine nature—which Kṛṣṇa does in a stupendous vision, as described by an interlocutor. The vision shows vividly the destructive as well as creative sides of divine being. Kṛṣṇa then goes on to explain further the intricacies of his divine nature as it controls all human experience and calls upon Arjuna to be a "mere instrument" of his will.]

Arjuna said.

As a favor to me Thou hast spoken about the supreme mystery called the Self; and by Thy words my delusion is dispelled.

The origin and dissolution of beings have been heard by me in detail from Thee, O Lotus-eyed one, and also Thy imperishable greatness.

As Thou declarest Thyself, so it is, O Supreme Lord. I desire to see Thy godly form, O Purushottama!

If Thou thinkest that it can be seen by me, O Lord, then reveal Thy immortal Self to me, O Lord of Yoga!

The Blessed Lord said:

Behold, O Arjuna, My forms, by hundreds and by thousands, manifold and divine, of various colors and shapes. . . .

Behold today the whole world, of moving and unmoving things, united in My body, O Arjuna, and whatever else thou desirest to see.

But thou canst not see Me with thine own eye. I give thee a divine eye. Behold My divine *yoga*. . . .

Of many mouths and eyes, of many marvelous visions, of many divine ornaments, of many uplifted weapons;

Wearing divine garlands and garments with divine perfumes and ointments, full of all wonders, radiant, infinite, His face is turned everywhere.

If the light of a thousand suns were to spring forth simultaneously in the sky, it would be like the light of that great Being.

There Arjuna beheld the whole world, divided into many parts, all united in the body of the God of gods.

Then filled with amazement, his hair standing erect, Arjuna bowed down his head to the God and with hands folded in salutation said:

Arjuna said:

I see all the gods in Thy body, O God, and also the various kinds of beings: Brahmā, the Lord, seated on the lotus seat, and all the sages and divine serpents.

I see Thee, with many arms, stomachs, mouths, and eyes, everywhere infinite in form; I see no end nor middle nor beginning of Thee, O Lord of all, O universal form!

I behold Thee with diadem, club and discus as a mass of light shining everywhere with the radiance of flaming fire and the sun, difficult to regard, beyond all measure.

Thou art the imperishable, the highest to be known; Thou art the final resting place of this universe; Thou art the immortal guardian of eternal law; Thou art, I think, the primal spirit.

I behold Thee without beginning, middle or end, of infinite power, of innumerable arms, the moon and sun as Thine eyes, Thy face as a shining fire, burning this universe with Thy radiance.

This space between heaven and earth and all the quarters of the sky is pervaded by Thee alone; seeing this Thy wondrous, terrible form, the triple world trembles, O great one!

These hosts of gods enter Thee and some, affrighted, invoke Thee with folded hands, and hosts of great seers and perfected ones crying "Hail!" praise Thee with magnificent hymns. . . .

Seeing Thy great form, of many mouths and eyes, O mighty-armed one, of many arms, thighs and feet, of many bellies, of many terrible tusks, the worlds tremble, and so do I.

Seeing Thee touching the sky and blazing with many colors, with opened mouths and shining enormous eyes, my inmost self is shaken and I find no strength nor peace, O Vishnu!

Seeing Thy mouths, terrible with tusks, like time's devouring fire, I know not the directions of the sky and I find no security. Have mercy, O Lord of gods, Abode of the world!

And these sons of Dhṛtarāṣṭra, all of them, together with the hosts of kings, Bhīṣma, Droṇa, and also Karṇa together with our chief warriors.

Are rushing into Thy mouths, dreadful with terrible tusks. Some are seen with pulverized heads, stuck between Thy teeth.

As the many water currents of rivers race headlong to the ocean, so these heroes of the world of men enter into Thy flaming mouths.

As moths swiftly enter a blazing fire and perish there, so these creatures swiftly enter Thy mouths and perish.

Swallowing all the worlds from every side, Thou lickest them up with Thy flaming mouths; Thy fierce rays fill the whole world with radiance and scorch it, O Vishnu!

Tell me who Thou art with so terrible a form! Salutation to Thee, O best of gods, be merciful! I wish to know Thee, the primal one; for I do not understand Thy ways.

The Blessed Lord said:

Time am I, the world destroyer, matured, come forth to subdue the worlds here. Even without thee, all the warriors arrayed in the opposing armies shall cease to be.

Therefore stand up and win fame. Conquering thy enemies, enjoy a prosperous kingdom. By Me they have already been slain. Be thou the mere instrument, O Arjuna.

Slay thou Droṇa, Bhīṣma, Jayadratha, Karṇa, and the other warrior-heroes too, who have already been slain by Me. Be not distressed, fight! Thou shalt conquer thy enemies in battle. [XI, 1–34] . . .

[Arjuna is still somewhat confused regarding the proper object of devotion, the personal divine being as shown in the vision vouchsafed him or the impersonal unmanifest principle of all being. Kṛṣṇa allows that a pure path of knowledge is the most difficult discipline and that *karma-yoga*, grounded in a more personal style of devotion, is in fact for those "most learned in *yoga*."]

Arjuna said:

Those devotees who are always disciplined and honor Thee, and those who worship the Imperishable and the Unmanifest—which of these are more learned in *yoga?*

The Blessed Lord said:

Those who, fixing their mind on Me, worship Me with complete discipline and with supreme faith, them I consider to be the most learned in *yoga*.

But those who worship the Imperishable, the Undefinable, the Unmanifested, the Omnipresent, the Unthinkable, the Immovable, the Unchanging, the Constant,

And have restrained all their senses, and are equal-minded and rejoice in the welfare of all beings—they also obtain Me.

The difficulty of those whose minds are fixed on the Unmanifested is much greater; the goal of the Unmanifested is hard for the embodied to attain.

But those who renounce all actions in Me and are intent on Me, who worship with complete discipline and meditate on Me.

These, whose thoughts are fixed on Me, I quickly lift up from the ocean of death and rebirth, O Arjuna. (XII, 1–7)

[Kṛṣṇa then explains in greater detail his "lower nature" as manifest in nature itself and its implications for the completion of the path of action and the fulfillment of one's social nature.]

The Blessed Lord said:

This body, O Arjuna, is called the field, and he who knows this is called the knower of the field by those who know him.

Know Me as the Knower of the field in all fields, O Arjuna; the knowledge of the field and the knower of the field, this I hold to be real knowledge.

Hear from Me briefly what the field is, what its nature is, what its modifications are, whence it comes, who he (the knower of the field) is and what his powers are.

This has been sung by the seers in many ways; in various hymns distinctly and also in the well-reasoned and definite words of the aphorisms about Brahman.

The gross elements, the I-sense, the intellect and also the unmanifested, the ten senses and one (the mind) and the five objects of the senses;

Desire, hatred, pleasure, pain, the organism, intelligence and firmness; this, briefly described, is the field together with its modifications. (XIII, 1–6)

I will declare that which is to be known, by knowing which one gains immortality. It is the beginningless supreme Brahman who is called neither being nor non-being.

With his hands and feet everywhere, with eyes, heads and mouths on all sides, with his ears everywhere; he dwells in the world, enveloping all.

Appearing to have the qualities of all the senses, and yet free from all the senses; unattached and yet supporting all; free from the *guṇas* and yet enjoying the *guṇas,*

It is outside and within all beings. It is unmoving and moving. It is too subtle to be known. It is far away and it is also near.

It is undivided and yet seems to be divided in all beings. It is to be known as supporting all beings and as absorbing and creating them.

It is also, it is said, the light of lights beyond darkness; it is knowledge, the object of knowledge, and the goal of knowledge; it is seated in the hearts of all. (XIII, 12–17)

Know that both *prakṛti* and *puruṣa* are beginningless; and know also that modifications and the *guṇas* are born of *prakṛti.*

Prakṛti is said to be the cause of the generation of causes and agents, and *puruṣa* is said to be the cause of the experience of pleasure and pain.

The *puruṣa* abiding in *prakṛti* experiences the *guṇas* born of *prakṛti.* Attachment to the *guṇas* is the cause of his births in good and evil wombs.

The highest spirit in this body is said to be, the witness, the consenter, the supporter, the experiencer, the great Lord, the supreme Self.

He who knows the *puruṣa* and *prakṛti* together with its *guṇas,* though in whatever state he may exist, he is not born again.

Some by meditation see the Self in the self by the self; others by the *yoga* of discrimination, and still others by the *yoga* of action.

Yet others, not knowing this but hearing it from others, honor it, and they too cross beyond death through their devotion to the scripture which they have heard.

Whatever being is born, immovable or moving, know, O Arjuna, that it (arises) from the union of the field and the knower of the field.

He who sees the supreme Lord abiding equally in all beings, not perishing when they perish, he truly sees. (XIII, 19–27)

There are two spirits in this world: the perishable and the imperishable. The perishable is all beings and the imperishable is called Kūṭastha (the unchanging).

But there is another, the highest Spirit (*puruṣottama*) called the supreme Self, who, as the imperishable Lord, enters into the three worlds and sustains them.

Since I transcend the perishable and am higher even than the imperishable, I am renowned in the world and in the Vedas as the highest Spirit.

He who undeluded thus knows Me as the highest Spirit is the knower of all; he worships Me with his whole being, O Arjuna.

Thus the most secret doctrine has been spoken by Me, O sinless one. Being enlightened about this, one will have true enlightenment and will have done his work, O Arjuna. (XV, 16–20)

A man obtains perfection by being devoted to his own proper action. Hear then how one who is intent on his own action finds perfection.

By worshipping him, from whom all beings arise and by whom all this is pervaded, through his own proper action, a man attains perfection.

Better is one's own *dharma*, though imperfect, than the *dharma* of another, well performed. One does not incur sin when doing the action prescribed by one's own nature.

One should not abandon his natural-born action, O Arjuna, even if it be faulty, for all undertakings are clouded with faults as fire by smoke.

He whose intelligence is unattached everywhere, whose self is conquered, who is free from desire, he obtains, through renunciation, the supreme perfection of actionlessness.

Learn from me, briefly, O Arjuna, how he who has attained perfection, also attains to Brahman, the highest state of wisdom.

Disciplined with a pure intelligence, firmly controlling oneself, abandoning sound and other sense-objects and throwing aside passion and hatred;

Dwelling in solitude, eating little, controlling speech, body and mind, constantly engaged in the *yoga* of meditation and taking refuge in dispassion;

Freed from egotism, force, arrogance, desire, anger and possession; unselfish, peaceful—he is fit to become Brahman.

Having become Brahman, tranquil in the Self, he neither grieves nor desires. Regarding all beings as equal, he attains supreme devotion to Me.

By devotion he knows Me, what my measure is and what I am essentially; then, having known Me essentially, he enters forthwith into Me.

Ever performing all actions, taking refuge in Me, he obtains by My grace the eternal, imperishable abode.

Renouncing with thy thought all actions to Me, intent on Me, taking refuge in the *yoga* of intellect, fix thy mind constantly on Me.

If thy mind is on Me, thou shalt, by My grace, cross over all obstacles; but if, from egotism, thou wilt not listen, thou shalt perish.

If, centered in egotism, thou thinkest "I will not fight," vain is this thy resolution; *prakṛti* will compel thee.

That which thou wishest not to do, through delusion, O Arjuna, that thou shalt do helplessly, bound by thine own action born of thy nature.

The Lord abides in the hearts of all beings, O Arjuna, causing all beings to revolve by His power as if they were mounted on a machine.

Go to Him alone for shelter with all thy being, O Arjuna. By His grace, thou shalt obtain supreme peace and the eternal abode.

Thus the wisdom, more secret than all secrets, has been declared to thee by Me. Having considered it fully, do as thou choosest. (XVIII, 45–63)

Confucius

Confucianism, as we have seen, lays great stress on the social dimensions of person-hood. This tradition in Chinese thought was also deeply concerned with governance and realized that the social and political were intertwined and mutually involved. The ideal ruler for Confucianism was at the same time a fulfillment of the ideal for hu-mankind.

The following selections from Confucius's *Analects,* translated by Arthur Waley, make evident this intimate relationship between being the right kind of person and rightfully exercising political power. The exposition of Confucius's teaching by the contemporary American philosopher Herbert Fingarette, which follows the brief selections, shows clearly some of the differences that obtain between the communitarian thinking of Confucius and our Western commitment to individual choice and responsibility.

The Ideal Person and Ruler

The Master said, He who rules by moral force (*tê*) is like the pole-star, which re-mains in its place while all the lesser stars do homage to it. . . .

The Master said, Govern the people by regulations, keep order among them by chastisements, and they will flee from you, and lose all self-respect. Govern them by moral force, keep order among them by ritual and they will keep their self-respect and come to you of their own accord.

The Master said, At fifteen I set my heart upon learning. At thirty, I had planted my feet firm upon the ground. At forty, I no longer suffered from perplexities. At fifty, I knew what were the biddings of Heaven. At sixty, I heard them with docile ear. At seventy, I could follow the dictates of my own heart; for what I desired no longer overstepped the boundaries of right. . . .

The Master said, In the presence of a good man, think all the time how you may learn to equal him. In the presence of a bad man, turn your gaze within! . . .

Reprinted with the permission of Simon & Schuster from *Analects of Confucius,* translated by Arthur Waley (New York: Macmillan, 1938).

Of Tzu-ch'an the Master said that in him were to be found four of the virtues that belong to the Way of the true gentleman. In his private conduct he was courteous, in serving his master he was punctilious, in providing for the needs of the people he gave them even more than their due; in exacting service from the people, he was just. . . .

The Master said, Who expects to be able to go out of a house except by the door? How is it then that no one follows this Way of ours?

The Master said, When natural substance prevails over ornamentation, you get the boorishness of the rustic. When ornamentation prevails over natural substance, you get the pedantry of the scribe. Only when ornament and substance are duly blended do you get the true gentleman. . . .

The Master said, A Divine Sage I cannot hope ever to meet; the most I can hope for is to meet a true gentleman. The Master said, A faultless man I cannot hope ever to meet; the most I can hope for is to meet a man of fixed principles. Yet where all around I see Nothing pretending to be Something, Emptiness pretending to be Fullness, Penury pretending to be Affluence, even a man of fixed principles will be none too easy to find. . . .

The Master said, Is Goodness indeed so far away? If we really wanted Goodness, we should find that it was at our very side. . . .

Tzu-lu asked how one should serve ghosts and spirits. The Master said, Till you have learnt to serve men, how can you serve ghosts? Tzu-lu then ventured upon a question about the dead. The Master said, Till you know about the living, how are you to know about the dead? . . .

Jan Jung asked about Goodness. The Master said, Behave when away from home as though you were in the presence of an important guest. Deal with the common people as though you were officiating at an important sacrifice. Then there will be no feelings of opposition to you, whether it is the affairs of a State that you are handling or the affairs of a Family. . . .

Duke Ching of Ch'i asked Master K'ung about government. Master K'ung replied saying, Let the prince be a prince, the minister a minister, the father a father and the son a son. The Duke said, How true! For indeed when the prince is not a prince, the minister not a minister, the father not a father, the son not a son, one may have a dish of millet in front of one and yet not know if one will live to eat it. . . .

The Master said, The gentleman calls attention to the good points in others; he does not call attention to their defects. The small man does just the reverse of this.

Chi K'ang-tzu asked Master K'ung about the art of ruling. Master K'ung said, Ruling . . . is straightening. . . . If you lead along a straight way, who will dare go by a crooked one? . . .

Once when Fan Ch'ih was taking a walk with the Master under the trees at the Rain Dance altars, he said, May I venture to ask about "piling up moral force," "repairing shortcomings" and "deciding when in two minds"? The Master said, An excellent question. "The work first; the reward afterwards"; is not that piling up moral force? "Attack the evil that is within yourself; do not attack the evil that is in others." Is not this "repairing shortcomings"?

"Because of a morning's blind rage
To forget one's own safety
And even endanger one's kith and kin"

is that not a case of "divided mind"? . . .

The Master said, Once a man has contrived to put himself aright, he will find no difficulty at all in filling any government post. But if he cannot put himself aright, how can he hope to succeed in putting others right? . . .

The "Duke" of Shê addressed Master K'ung saying, In my country there was a man called Upright Kung. His father appropriated a sheep, and Kung bore witness against him. Master K'ung said, In my country the upright men are of quite another sort. A father will screen his son, and a son his father—which incidentally does involve a sort of uprightness.

Fan Ch'ih asked about Goodness. The Master said, In private life, courteous, in public life, diligent, in relationships, loyal. This is a maxim that no matter where you may be, even amid the barbarians of the east or north, may never be set aside.

HERBERT FINGARETTE

A Way without a Crossroads

Confucius in his teachings in the *Analects* does not elaborate on the language of choice or responsibility. He occasionally uses terms roughly akin to these. But they are not developed or elaborated in the ways so characteristic of their central import in Western philosophical and religious understanding of man. To be specific, Confucius does not elaborate the language of choice and responsibility as these are intimately intertwined with the idea of the ontologically ultimate power of the individual to select from genuine alternatives to create his own spiritual destiny, and with the related ideas of spiritual guilt, and repentance or retribution for such guilt.

Precisely because we of the West are so deeply immersed in a world conceived in just such terms, it is profitable for us to see the world in quite another way, in Confucius's way. He was, after all, profoundly concerned to understand man and man's place in society. He was dedicated to defining and illuminating what we would call moral issues. He was a great and an original teacher. How, then, could Confucius omit this whole complex of notions centering around "choice" and "responsibility"?

We must recognize at once that the absence of a developed language of choice and responsibility does not imply a failure to choose or to be responsible. Some men were more responsible than others in Confucius's day as in ours. It is also obvious that men made choices in ancient China. I am not so sure we can speak as confidently about guilt, repentance or retributive punishment in the sense we use these words, but also the realities which we use these words to designate did not exist. The notion of punishment, which did exist in ancient China, was that of deterrent punishment—not due retribution to cleanse guilt, but a stern "lesson" or literal crippling which would deter future malfeasance.

However, without arguing this latter point here, we can allow that in the case of "choice" and "responsibility," the realities they designate did indeed exist. Yet, although we in the West have an elaborated language in which to express these realities and to trace out their inner shape and dynamics in detail, Confucius (and his contemporaries) did not possess such a language. And they had no significant concern with these moral realities so central to their contemporaries, the peoples of Greece and the Near East.

Perhaps the most revealing way to begin to bring out this "omission" is to consider the primary imagery in the *Analects*. It centers around the *"Tao."* Tao is a Way, a path, a road, and by common metaphorical extensions it becomes in ancient China the right Way of life, the Way of governing, the ideal Way of human existence, the Way of the Cosmos, the generative-normative Way (Pattern, path, course) of existence as such. (In the *Analects, "Tao"* never takes its rare but possible alternative sense as "word" or "speak.")

The imagery in the *Analects* is dominated by the metaphor of traveling the road. Written characters that occur typically and frequently in the text are those meaning path, way, walk, tracks, follow, go through, from, to, enter, leave, arrive, advance, upright, crooked, level, smooth, stop, position.

The notion of a Way is, not surprisingly, congenial to the central Confucian notion of *li*, rite or ceremony. *Li,* for Confucius, is the explicit and detailed pattern of that great ceremony which is social intercourse, the humane life. The transition from the image of walking the true Path uprightly to carrying out a ceremony properly is an easy and congenial one. We may even think of *li* as the map or the specific road-system which is *Tao.*

It is easy, if one is so inclined, to develop this path-imagery to bring in the notions of choice, decision, responsibility. We should need only to introduce the derivative image of the crossroads, an obvious elaboration of *Tao* imagery to us. Yet this image, so perfectly suited, so plainly available for use as a metaphor for choice, is *never* used in the *Analects.*

Indeed the image of the crossroads is so natural and even insistently available as an element of any richly elaborated path-imagery that only the most profound commitment to the idea of the cosmos as basically unambiguous, as a single, definite order, could make it possible to ignore in the metaphor the image of the crossroads as a challenge to the traveler on the Way. This Confucian commitment to a single, definite order is also evident when we note what Confucius sees as the alternative to rightly treading the true Path: it is to walk crookedly, to get lost or to abandon the Path. That is, the only "alternative" to the one Order is disorder, chaos.

Where does one finally arrive if one follows the Way? Is there a goal that puts an end to the travel? The imagery of Confucius does not lead us to dwell upon the person arriving at a destined or ideal place, whether it be depicted as harbor, home or golden city. Instead, the spiritually noble man arrives at a condition rather than a place, the condition of following the Way without effort and properly. He arrives at that tranquil state that comes from appreciating that it is the following of the Way itself that is of ultimate and absolute value. Thus in this respect it does not take time to "reach" the goal since one does not have to arrive at any particular point on the map: to reach the goal is simply to set oneself to treading the Path now—properly, with correct appreciation of its intrinsic and ultimate significance.

One can be truly following the Way at whatever the level of one's personal development and skill in the Way, whatever the level of one's learning—for a wholehearted commitment to learning the Way is itself the Way for those who are not yet perfected in the Way. However, although the learner may be following the Way for the learner, he cannot rest; his burden is heavy for he is the apprentice, not yet the Master, the *jen* man, the man perfected in *li*, the truly noble man.

The basic conception of man in the *Analects* is that he is a being born into the world—more especially into society—with the potentiality to be shaped into a truly human form. There is, to begin with, the raw stuff, the raw material. This must be elaborated by learning and culture, shaped and controlled by *li*. Either this "cutting, filing, chiseling and polishing" (1:15) is done well or poorly. If it is well done, through painstaking and properly directed effort by the person and good training by his teachers, then to that extent he will walk straight upon the Way. If there is a failure to shape according to the ideal, then by virtue of this defect he will deviate from the Way.

Thus there is no *genuine* option: either one follows the Way or one fails. To take any other "route" than the Way is not a genuine road but a failure through weakness to follow *the* route. Neither the doctrine nor the imagery allows for choice, if we mean by choice a selection, by virtue of the agent's powers, of one out of several equally real options. Instead it puts the task in terms of either using one's powers to walk the Way or being too weak, *without* power, and of going crookedly nowhere, falling or weaving about pointlessly in quest of the mirages of profit, advantage and personal comfort.

It is true that the Master said: "If a man doesn't constantly ask himself, 'What about this, what about this?' I can do nothing about him." (15:15) Our own tendency, reading this isolated remark, may be to read this as a concern with choice. But it need not be so at all. It need not be read as "What about this—which of the alternatives, to do it or not to do it, shall I choose?" Instead, one may suppose that the notion of equally valid alternatives is not implied, that there is presumed to be only one right thing to do and that the question then means in effect, "What about this, *is* it right; is it the Way?" Put in more general terms, the task is not conceived as a choice but as the attempt to characterize some object or action as objectively right or not. The moral task is to make a proper classification, to locate an act within the scheme of *li*.

There are two passages in the *Analects* in which Confucius comments on a matter that can be rendered as a mind "deluded" or in "error" or in "doubt," but which Waley translates as a matter of "deciding when in two minds." Although Waley's translation makes choice or decision the issue, the Master's elaboration of the notion reveals, I believe, that Waley's rendering is misleading for purposes of a philosophical understanding of Confucius. In both passages (12:10, 12:21), the meaning is not that of a mind in doubt as to which course to choose but of a person being inconsistent in his desires or acts. Paraphrasing the theme of these texts: one wants someone—perhaps a relative—to live and prosper, but out of anger, one wishes that he perish or one actually endangers him out of a blind rage. In such conflict, the task is not posed as one of *choosing* or *deciding* but of distinguishing or *discriminating* *(pien)* the inconsistent inclinations. Furthermore, in each passage, we have no doubt about which inclination is the right one when we have discriminated one from the other. In short, the task is posed in terms of knowledge rather than choice. *Huo,* the key term in the passages, means here "deluded or *led astray* by an un-*li* inclination or tendency." It is not doubt as to which to choose to do.

There is one another passage in the *Analects* that is of particular interest in connection with choice. More than any other passage, this one seems to me to present a situation where the issue, as we would define it, is one of internal conflict in the moral code, a conflict to be resolved by personal choice. We are told (13:18) of a man called "Upright" Kung whose father stole a sheep. Kung testified against his father. The Duke, who reports the case to Confucius, is proud of what he considers to be Kung's uprightness. But Confucius disagrees tactfully, remarking that in his country the son who would protect his father is the one who is considered upright.

The passage could be a model one for posing the need for choice between two conflicting moral requirements. A Westerner would almost inevitably elaborate on it by emphasizing that in this case we do have knowledge (it is right to respect the law; it is right to protect one's parents; both are profound obligations), but when two profound duties conflict, *we* must choose. And it is in this necessity to make a critical choice that lies the seed of tragedy, of responsibility, of guilt and remorse. But this way of seeing the matter, so obvious a possibility to us, is not even suggested by Confucius. It is the very obviousness of this view of the matter that makes Confucius's failure to show any recognition of it the more blatant. We could have no better proof than this that the problem of genuine choice among real alternatives never occurred to Confucius, or at least never clearly occurred to him as a fundamental moral task. Confucius merely announces the way *he* sees the matter, putting it tactfully by saying it is the custom in [the state of] Li. There is nothing to suggest a decisional problem; everything suggests that there is a defect of knowledge, a simple error of moral judgment on the Duke's part.

We are supported in the view that Confucius saw nothing distinctive in this sort of situation, i.e., the sort of situation that we see as distinctively posing a choice, by the fact that in all the *Analects* there is mentioned only one such case. We know there must have been many such situations in the actual daily life of the Chinese of those times—times of exceptionally great social turmoil and transformations. Furthermore, when we take into account Confucius's stature as a moralist and his insightfulness into human nature, his failure to see or to mention the problem of internal moral conflict in such a case as this can only be accounted for by supposing that his interests, ideas, concerns, in short his entire moral and intellectual orientation, was in another direction.

Any task that is as conceivable as that of *choosing* can also be formulated, instead, in terms of the Confucian task. This is the task of objectively classifying the *prima facie* alternative paths within the order of *li,* of discovering which is the true Path and of detecting which is only an apparent path, perhaps a clearing in the brush leading nowhere except into brambles. We need only make the tacit assumption that there *is* a Way, a self-consistent, self-authenticating way of universal scope.

The notion of choice as a central feature of man's existence is only one element in a closely related complex of notions, and the absence of such a concept of choice reflects the absence of the rest of this complex. Among the chief notions closely linked to choice are moral responsibility, guilt, deserved (retributive) punishment and repentance.

Sometimes when we speak of a person as responsible for something, we refer merely to his role as a critical causal factor in bringing it about. The problem of meaning here is complex, but the general drift in this usage is to treat responsibility as a matter of production or causality rather than moral obligation.

This causal notion of responsibility is quite familiar to the ancient Chinese. There is no lack of explicit discussion of the question who or what brought about a certain state of affairs. But of course it is not discussed under a heading translatable as "responsibility." For the root sense of the latter term is the moral one, and its use with respect to mere causality is a de-moralized derivative use. The root of "responsible" is of course not "cause" or "produce" but "respond"; the root question is: Who must respond for the way things go? One who is obligated to respond for the way things go will have some actual or potential causal connection with the way things go, but not everyone who has a causal connection with the way things go is obligated to respond for how they do.

The intense concern of Confucius that a person should carry out his duties and act according to what is right reflects one aspect of our notion of responsibility. But if this were all that was characteristic of our notion of responsibility, it would be a redundancy—another way of saying that one should carry out one's duties and act rightly. What gives distinct content to the idea of responsibility is derived from the root "response." Herein lies the peculiarly personal commitment—*I* answer for this deed; it is mine—and this in turn links the notion of (moral) responsibility to those of guilt, deserved punishment and repentance. It is the one who must respond whose response may involve guilt, acceptance of punishment, repentance, restitution or merit, pride, reward.

The issues in the West can become confused because of a certain sort of utilitarian view to the effect that responsibility is ultimately a purely causal notion. On this view, "responsibility" ought to be considered merely as a matter of diagnosing past causes in order to influence future events; sanctions and reward are assignable anywhere in the human causal chain that promises future prevention. If present sanctions will deter future malfeasance, then they are justified; if sanctions will not deter, or if in a particular case they would increase tendencies to malfeasance, then countersanctions are indicated. The ground for and value of repentance lie entirely in the future deterrent consequences of repentance, not in any relation to the moral aspect of the past deed. Such value as guilt-feelings have must on this view be justified by an analogous rationale. Subtler and more complex forms of utilitarian views have been emphasized in recent philosophical discussion, but these do not eliminate the possibility of the type of confusion so evidently generated by the simpler view. The fact that Confucius uses language that pertains to sanctions for lawbreaking has led translators to render this as "punishment" and naturally misleads the unalerted reader to suppose that Confucius understood and used our concept of punishment (with its root implication of moral guilt).

The view that never appears in Confucius, the view that is peculiar to the Graeco-Hebraic-Christian tradition and for the most part profoundly contrasting with utilitarianism, is that punishment is justified not simply by its consequences but because it is *deserved* by virtue of what went before. Punishment is an appropriate moral response to prior guilty wrongdoing by a morally responsible agent. Repentance, in turn, is not simply a device which is appropriate or not depending on *its* psychological consequences; it is repentance *for* the past deed. Repentance is a moral response to a past wrongdoing for which one is morally responsible. Guilt is a moral (or spiritual) property accruing by virtue of accomplished wrong.

If punishment is given and received as a genuine moral experience, it is a kind of payment of a moral debt—a clearing of the slate. Of course a person may as a consequence also be inclined to be more averse to similar future wrongdoing, to the guilt-feeling it involves as well as to the quite nonmoral discomfort and the pain of the punishment. And if repentance is genuine, it constitutes an expression of repugnance with oneself for one's former course of conduct, an acknowledgment of moral guilt, and therefore it is expressed in a recommitment to a different course in the future. Thus normally the *consequences* of guilt, punishment and repentance upon moral character and upon morality-related behavior are likely to be salutary. There is a utilitarian value here. But the moral *ground* for each, that which gives it its moral status, is the past wrongdoing for which one was (morally) responsible. Were "punishment," "guilt" and "repentance" to be unrelated to prior moral wrong for which the person was responsible, we would have social engineering rather than morality—and this was precisely why Confucius took the use of "punishments" as a main target and saw his own positive teaching as in direct contrast.

For Confucius moral education consists in learning the codes of *li*, in studying literature, music and the civilizing arts in general. One's own effort provides the "push," but it is the intrinsic nobility of the goal that provides the "pull." It is by *being* a spiritually noble man that the teacher—or Prince—draws others into the direction of the Way. It is the Way that has power, and this power is effortless, invisible, magical. It is characteristic of the *Analects* that in every case, except for one clearly late "Legalist" insertion (13:3), the use of sanctions and punishment is explicitly contrasted as the undesirable alternative to the use of virtue (*te*), of humaneness (*jen*), of ceremonial propriety (*li*) and of such related strategies as "yielding" (*jang*). The *Analects* present the issue flatly: either one can govern by *li* and "yielding" or one can't (4:13); if one can't, then there is no use deceiving ourselves, and we might as well turn to "punishment," to sanctions and rewards. For these can influence peo-ple in a coercive way or by payment; but they are not truly human (i.e., moral) ways, nor do they establish a truly human life. Lacking any concept of moral guilt, or of moral responsibility as the ground for guilt and hence punishment as *moral* retribu-tion, Confucius could see no humane potentiality in the use of sanctions.

We should not suppose that the contrary, pro-"utilitarian" point of view on these issues was alien to the Chinese mind of the times rather than being a view whose re-jection by Confucius was distinctive of his own viewpoint. Confucius's outlook was in obvious contrast to that of a rival group which soon became very powerful, the so-called Legalists. Typically the latter taught that reliance on anything but the stick or the carrot was sentimental self-deception. They thought the moral approach a sham and ultimately a snare for the user.

> For the tiger is able to subdue the dog because of its claws and fangs. If the tiger abandons its claws and fangs and lets the dog use them, it will be subdued by the dog. Similarly, the ruler controls his ministers through punishment and kindness (i.e., the "advantages" of "congratulations and rewards").

This Legalist text contrasts flatly with the Confucian teaching: the Master said, govern the people by regulations, keep order among them by punishments, and they will evade shamelessly. Govern them by moral force (*te*), keep order among them by ritual (*li*), and there will be not only shame but correctness (2:3).

There is tacit agreement, however, that punishment, if it has any role at all, has the purely utilitarian role of practical deterrent and not of moral desert. More to the point: the notion of punishment as *moral desert* does not even arise in either the *Analects* or Legalist thought. We must, therefore, avoid reading moral meaning into the term here.

Furthermore, as has been suggested already—and it now calls for more detailed comment—there is developed in the *Analects* no notion of guilt and repentance as a moral response to one's wrongdoing. It is recognized that one may regret for prac-tical reasons one's previous actions; one may change course and follow the Way. But the "inward" stain of guilt is absent. It will, as usual, repay us to consider in a little detail some apparent exceptions to this thesis, not merely in order to support the thesis but to see better how to read the text rather than reading our own ideas into the text.

One group of passages in the *Analects* deals with "shame" (*ch'ih*), another group deals with inner flaws; a final passage seems to call for inward self-accusation. All of these, therefore, at least suggest a quasi-explicit concern with moral responsibility and guilt-related notions.

One reference to shame (*ch'ih*) has already been cited: where one relies on pun-ishment (i.e., fear), there is no shame; where one relies on *te*, there is shame. (2:3) *Te* may be rendered as the power of virtue, or as the virtue of one who is *jen* and fol-lows *li;* it is the power or virtue inherent in the Way. It is to be contrasted with phys-ical or coercive power. Thus the passage cited, as well as others, makes it clear that shame is conceived by Confucius as a moral response. And this raises the question whether the term *ch'ih* really amounts to "guilt" rather than "shame." *Ch'ih* is certainly the closest that Confucius comes to mentioning anything like guilt. The word, therefore, calls for careful examination.

The notion *ch'ih* occurs in several contexts. One group of remarks deals with the concern for or the possession of material advantages for themselves alone—e.g., good clothes, good food, wealth. [4:9, 8:13(3); 9:26(1); 14:1] These, when acquired by departing from the Way, deserve *ch'ih*. Another group of comments concerns one's public commitments and *ch'ih* from the failure to keep them. [4:22; 14:29(1)] Another group concerns *ch'ih* deserved for excess in speech, appearance, obsequiousness, pride and dissembling. [4:22; 5:14; 5:24; 14:29(1)] Finally, and more generally, *ch'ih* is a specifically moral response several times paired with disgrace (*ju*), and in these contexts it seems to be the analogue in private conduct of the public officer's acting with disgrace in his official role. (1:13; 13:20)

If we are unaware of the crucial differences in perspective, these texts on *ch'ih* lend themselves easily to an assimilation of Confucian "shame" with Western "guilt." Yet the differences are crucial with respect to the issues that concern us here. Although *ch'ih* is definitely a moral concept and designates a moral condition or response, the moral relation to which it corresponds is that of the person to his status and role as defined by *li*. *Ch'ih* thus looks "outward," not "inward." It is a matter of the spoken but empty word, of the immorally gained material possession, of the excessive in appearance and in conduct. It is not, as is guilt, a matter of the inward state, of repugnance at inner corruption, of self-denigration, of the sense that one is as a person, and independently of one's public status and repute, mean or reprehensible.

It would be a basic error, however, to assume that shame is concerned with "mere appearances" rather than moral realities. The Confucian concept of shame is a genuinely moral concept, but it is oriented to morality as centering in *li*, traditionally ceremonially defined social comportment, rather than to an inner core of one's being, "the self." The violation of the moral order is thus of the essence in Confucian shame no less than in Western guilt. A personal response, a morally infused feeling-tone is also crucial in both cases. But the direction in which one turns to interpret and to deal with this feeling is different in the two cases. True, the ground for guilt is some immoral act or betrayal of someone other than oneself, but the object of guilt is oneself. Ultimately, guilt is an attack upon oneself, whereas shame is an attack upon some specific action or outer condition. Shame is a matter of "face," of embarrassment, of social status. Shame says, "change your ways; you have lost honor or dignity." Guilt says, "change yourself; you are infected." A St. Augustine can speak of the "disease of my soul," of its "wound," of "sticking in the mire," of being plucked out of the mire and washed by God, of being soul-sick and monstrous. It takes no demonstration to remind even the casual reader of Confucius that such imagery, or analogous tone, is alien to the *Analects*. . . .

In the preceding commentary on the text, I have considered the possibility that Confucius does concern himself in substance with choice, responsibility, punishment as moral desert, guilt and repentance. The conclusions reached may be summarized as follows. Although the opportunity for explicitly and richly elaborating the notion of choice is latent in the central imagery of the Path, that opportunity is with remarkable thoroughness ignored. And, although there are isolated references to a moral illness, self-accusations, and inner examination—each potentially so fertile and apt for use by one concerned with responsibility, guilt and repentance—none of these is developed or in any way further remarked upon by Confucius. They remain isolated, *ad hoc* metaphors, very possibly with an ironic or topical meaning in their original context, a meaning now lost in the cryptic saying handed down to us. Finally, although there is more frequent and systematic reference to shame, this is associated with specific external possessions, conduct or status; it is a moral sentiment focused upon one's status and conduct in relation to the world rather than an inward charge against one's stained, corrupt self. The absence of the choice-responsibility-guilt complex of concepts, taken in the textual context, warrants the inference in connection with such an insightful philosopher of human nature and morality, that the concepts in question and their related imagery, were not rejected by Confucius but rather were simply not present in his thinking at all.

The language and imagery that *is* elaborated and that forms the main frame of Confucius's thought presents a different but intelligible and harmonious picture to us. Man is not an ultimately autonomous being who has an inner and decisive power, intrinsic to him, a power to select among real alternatives and thereby to shape a life for himself. Instead he is born as "raw material" who must be civilized by education and thus become a truly human man. To do this he must aim at the Way, and the Way must—through its nobility and the nobility of those who pursue it—attract him. This outcome is not conceived as one that enhances a personal power as over against society or the physical environment, but rather as one that sharpens and steadies a person's "aim" or orientation to the point where he can undeviatingly walk the one true Way: he is a civilized human being. Walking the Way incarnates in him the vast spiritual dignity and power that reside in the Way. One who walks the Way rather than going astray, who does so "naturally," "yielding" rather than forcing, such a man lives a life of personal dignity and fulfillment, of social harmony with others based on mutual respect allowing to each just such a life.

Therefore the central moral issue for Confucius is not the responsibility of a man for deeds he has by his own free will chosen to perform, but the factual questions of whether a man is properly taught the Way and whether he has the desire to learn diligently. The proper response to a failure to conform to the moral order (*li*) is not self-condemnation for a free and responsible, though evil, choice, but self-reeducation to overcome a mere defect, a lack of power, in short a lack in one's "formation." The Westerner's inclination to press at this point the issue of personal responsibility for lack of diligence is precisely the sort of issue that is never even raised in the *Analects*.

To summarize finally in a schematic way, moral problems resolve into one of four forms for Confucius: (1) the wrongdoer is not well enough educated to be able to recognize and properly classify what is according to the Way and what is not; (2) the wrongdoer has not yet learned the requisite skills to follow the Way in some respect; (3) the wrongdoer has not *persisted* in the required effort (this is conceived as a matter of strength, not choice); (4) the wrongdoer knows enough to go through some of the motions, but he is not totally committed to the Way, and he is then either erratic or he systematically perverts the outer forms of *li* to serve personal profit.

Confucius's vision provides no basis for seeing man as a being of tragedy, of inner crisis and guilt; but it does provide a socially oriented, action-oriented view which provides for personal dignity. Moreover, when we place the comments made here in the larger context of Confucius's view of man, a context further discussed in the other essays in this book, we see then that the images of the inner man and of his inner conflict are not essential to a concept of man as a being whose dignity is the consummation of a life of subtlety and sophistication, a life in which human conduct can be intelligible in natural terms and yet be attuned to the sacred, a life in which the practical, the intellectual and the spiritual are equally revered and are harmonized in the one act—the act of *li*.

Kant

Immanuel Kant (1724–1804) was one of the most brilliant thinkers in the history of Western philosophy; some indeed hold that he is simply the most important philosopher since Aristotle. He was born in Köningsberg, Prussia, and is said not to have wandered beyond a forty-mile radius of his birthplace during his lifetime and to have been very methodical in his habits, taking a walk at exactly the same time every day. Kant's intellect, however, certainly moved freely and insightfully across many areas and was hardly bound in any way by rigid conventions or habits of thought.

"What ought I to do?" is the central question that informs Kant's thinking in ethics. He believes that we can indeed answer this question without having to refer to any alleged objective notion of what is good for humankind that might be based on our shared beliefs or our actual native desires, preferences, and needs. Kant holds that by purely rational means we can secure the grounds for a universal morality.

He begins his *Foundations of the Metaphysics of Morals*, from which the following selections have been taken, with a discussion of a "good will," a will that is good in itself and pure in its motives, and that intends a principle for acting in accordance with duty. We need, Kant argues, to identify those rational principles that hold for all human beings irrespective of their inclinations, their particular social relations, or their historical-cultural placement. He calls the moral law that can be so rationally grounded the "categorical imperative." This takes several forms in Kant, including the more religiously grounded version, which states that one must always act in such a way as to treat another person and oneself as an end and never as a mere means; and the most contentious form, which holds that one should act only on those principles that can, without contradiction, be willed for everyone. I must, for instance, fulfill the promises I make, the debts I owe, and so on, if it can be shown that if I were to act otherwise I would undermine the very idea of what a "promise" or "debt" entails; in short, that they would lose all meaning and validity if everyone were allowed to take exception to them.

Duty and Morality

Nothing in the world—indeed nothing even beyond the world—can possibly be conceived which could be called good without qualification except a *good will*. Intelligence, wit, judgment, and the other talents of the mind, however they may be named, or courage, resoluteness, and perseverance as qualities of temperament, are doubtless in many respects good and desirable. But they can become extremely bad and harmful if the will, which is to make use of these gifts of nature and which in its special constitution is called character, is not good. It is the same with the gifts of fortune. Power, riches, honor, even health, general well-being, and the contentment with one's condition which is called happiness, make for pride and even arrogance if there is not a good will to correct their influence on the mind and on its principles of action so as to make it universally comfortable to its end. It need hardly be mentioned that the sight of a being adorned with no feature of a pure and good will, yet enjoying uninterrupted prosperity, can never give pleasure to a rational impartial observer. Thus the good will seems to constitute the indispensable condition even of worthiness to be happy.

Some qualities seem to be conducive to this good will and can facilitate its action, but, in spite of that, they have no intrinsic unconditional worth. They rather presuppose a good will, which limits the high esteem which one otherwise rightly has for them and prevents their being held to be absolutely good. Moderation in emotions and passions, self-control, and calm deliberation not only are good in many respects but even seem to constitute a part of the inner worth of the person. But however unconditionally they were esteemed by the ancients, they are far from being good without qualification. For without the principle of a good will they can become extremely bad, and the coolness of a villain makes him not only far more dangerous but also more directly abominable in our eyes than he would have seemed without it.

The good will is not good because of what it effects or accomplishes or because of its adequacy to achieve some proposed end; it is good only because of its willing, i.e., it is good of itself. And, regarded for itself, it is to be esteemed incomparably higher than anything which could be brought about by it in favor of any inclination or even of the sum total of all inclinations. . . .

We have, then, to develop the concept of a will which is to be esteemed as good of itself without regard to anything else. It dwells already in the natural sound understanding and does not need so much to be taught as only to be brought to light. In the estimation of the total worth of our actions it always takes first place and is the condition of everything else. In order to show this, we shall take the concept of duty. It contains that of a good will, though with certain subjective restrictions and hindrances; but these are far from concealing it and making it unrecognizable, for they rather bring it out by contrast and make it shine forth all the brighter.

From *Foundations of the Metaphysics of Morals* by Immanuel Kant, translated by Lewis White Beck and with critical essays edited by Robert Paul Wolff (Indianapolis: Bobbs-Merrill Educational Publ., 1969).

I here omit all actions which are recognized as opposed to duty, even though they may be useful in one respect or another, for with these the question does not arise at all as to whether they may be carried out *from* duty, since they conflict with it. I also pass over the actions which are really in accordance with duty and to which one has no direct inclination, rather executing them because impelled to do so by another inclination. For it is easily decided whether an action in accord with duty is performed from duty or for some selfish purpose. It is far more difficult to note this difference when the action is in accordance with duty and, in addition, the subject has a direct inclination to do it. For example, it is in fact in accordance with duty that a dealer should not overcharge an inexperienced customer, and wherever there is much business the prudent merchant does not do so, having a fixed price for everyone, so that a child may buy of him as cheaply as any other. Thus the customer is honestly served. But this is far from sufficient to justify the belief that the merchant has behaved in this way from duty and principles of honesty. His own advantage required this behavior; but it cannot be assumed that over and above that he had a direct inclination to the purchaser and that, out of love, as it were, he gave none an advantage in price over another. Therefore the action was done neither from duty nor from direct inclination but only for a selfish purpose.

On the other hand, it is a duty to preserve one's life, and moreover everyone has a direct inclination to do so. But for that reason the often anxious care which most men take of it has no intrinsic worth, and the maxim of doing so has no moral import. They preserve their lives according to duty, but not from duty. But if adversities and hopeless sorrow completely take away the relish for life, if an unfortunate man, strong in soul, is indignant rather than despondent or dejected over his fate and wishes for death, and yet preserves his life without loving it and from neither inclination nor fear but from duty—then his maxim has a moral import.

To be kind where one can is duty, and there are, moreover, many persons so sympathetically constituted that without any motive of vanity or selfishness they find an inner satisfaction in spreading joy, and rejoice in the contentment of others which they have made possible. But I say that, however dutiful and amiable it may be, that kind of action has no true moral worth. It is on a level with [actions arising from] other inclinations, such as the inclination to honor, which, if fortunately directed to what in fact accords with duty and is generally useful and thus honorable, deserve praise and encouragement but no esteem. For the maxim lacks the moral import of an action done not from inclination but from duty. But assume that the mind of that friend to mankind was clouded by a sorrow of his own which extinguished all sympathy with the lot of others and that he still had the power to benefit others in distress, but that their need left him untouched because he was preoccupied with his own need. And now suppose him to tear himself, unsolicited by inclination, out of this dead insensibility and to perform this action only from duty and without any inclination—then for the first time his action has genuine moral worth. Furthermore, if nature has put little sympathy in the heart of a man, and if he, though an honest man, is by temperament cold and indifferent to the sufferings of others, perhaps because he is provided with special gifts of patience and fortitude and expects or even requires that others should have the same—and such a man would certainly not be the meanest product of nature—would not he find in himself a source from which to give himself a far higher worth than he could have got by having a good-natured temperament? This is unquestionably true even though nature did not make him philanthropic, for it is just here that the worth of the character is brought out, which is morally and incomparably the highest of all: he is beneficent not from inclination but from duty.

To secure one's own happiness is at least indirectly a duty, for discontent with one's condition under pressure from many cares and amid unsatisfied wants could easily become a great temptation to transgress duties. But without any view to duty all men have the strongest and deepest inclination to happiness, because in this idea all inclinations are summed up. But the precept of happiness is often so formulated that it definitely thwarts some inclinations, and men can make no definite and certain concept of the sum of satisfaction of all inclinations which goes under the name of happiness. It is not to be wondered at, therefore, that a single inclination, definite as to what it promises and as to the time at which it can be satisfied, can outweigh a fluctuating idea, and that, for example, a man with the gout can choose to enjoy what he likes and to suffer what he may, because according to his calculations at least on this occasion he has not sacrificed the enjoyment of the present moment to a perhaps groundless expectation of a happiness supposed to lie in health. But even in this case, if the universal inclination to happiness did not determine his will, and if health were not at least for him a necessary factor in these calculations, there yet would remain, as in all other cases, a law that he ought to promote his happiness, not from inclination but from duty. Only from this law would his conduct have true moral worth.

It is in this way, undoubtedly, that we should understand those passages of Scripture which command us to love our neighbor and even our enemy, for love as an inclination cannot be commanded. But beneficence from duty, when no inclination impels it and even when it is opposed by a natural and unconquerable aversion, is practical love, not pathological love; it resides in the will and not in the propensities of feeling, in principles of action and not in tender sympathy; and it alone can be commanded.

[Thus the first proposition of morality is that to have moral worth an action must be done from duty.] The second proposition is: An action performed from duty does not have its moral worth in the purpose which is to be achieved through it but in the maxim by which it is determined. Its moral value, therefore, does not depend on the realization of the object of the action but merely on the principle of volition by which the action is done without any regard to the objects of the faculty of desire. From the preceding discussion it is clear that the purposes we may have for our actions and their effects as ends and incentives of the will cannot give the actions any unconditional and moral worth. Wherein, then, can this worth lie, if it is not in the will in relation to its hoped-for effect? It can lie nowhere else than in the principle of the will, irrespective of the ends which can be realized by such action. For the will stands, as it were, at the crossroads halfway between its a priori principle which is formal and its a posteriori incentive which is material. Since it must be determined by something, if it is done from duty it must be determined by the formal principle of volition as such since every material principle has been withdrawn from it.

The third principle, as a consequence of the two preceding, I would express as follows: Duty is the necessity of an action executed from respect for law. I can certainly have an inclination to the object as an effect of the proposed action, but I can never have respect for it precisely because it is a mere effect and not an activity of a will. Similarly, I can have no respect for any inclination whatsoever, whether my own or that of another; in the former case I can at most approve of it and in the latter I can even love it, i.e., see it as favorable to my own advantage. But that which is connected with my will merely as ground and not as consequence, that which does not serve my inclination but overpowers it or at least excludes it from being considered in making a choice—in a word, law itself—can be an object of respect and thus a command. Now as an act from duty wholly excludes the influence of inclination and therewith every object of the will, nothing remains which can determine the will objectively except the law, and nothing subjectively except pure respect for this practical law. This subjective element is the maxim that I ought to follow such a law even if it thwarts all my inclinations.

Thus the moral worth of an action does not lie in the effect which is expected from it or in any principle of action which has to borrow its motive from this expected effect. For all these effects (agreeableness of my own condition, indeed even the promotion of the happiness of others) could be brought about through other causes and would not require the will of a rational being, while the highest and unconditional good can be found only in such a will. Therefore, the preeminent good can consist only in the conception of the law in itself (which can be present only in a rational being) so far as this conception and not the hoped-for effect is the determining ground of the will. This pre-eminent good, which we call moral, is already present in the person who acts according to this conception, and we do not have to look for it first in the result.

But what kind of a law can that be, the conception of which must determine the will without reference to the expected result? Under this condition alone the will can be called absolutely good without qualification. Since I have robbed the will of all impulses which could come to it from obedience to any law, nothing remains to serve as a principle of the will except universal conformity of its action to law as such. That is, I should never act in such a way that I could not also will that my maxim should be a universal law. Mere conformity to law as such (without assuming any particular law applicable to certain actions) serves as the principle of the will, and it must serve as such a principle if duty is not to be a vain delusion and chimerical concept. The common reason of mankind in its practical judgments is in perfect agreement with this and has this principle constantly in view.

Let the question, for example, be: May I, when in distress, make a promise with the intention not to keep it? I easily distinguish the two meanings which the question can have, viz., whether it is prudent to make a false promise, or whether it conforms to my duty. Undoubtedly the former can often be the case, though I do see clearly that it is not sufficient merely to escape from the present difficulty by this expedient, but that I must consider whether inconveniences much greater than the present one may not later spring from this lie. Even with all my supposed cunning, the consequences cannot be so easily foreseen. Loss of credit might be far more disadvantageous than the misfortune I now seek to avoid, and it is hard to tell whether it might not be more prudent to act according to a universal maxim and to make it a habit not to promise anything without intending to fulfill it. But it is soon clear to me that such a maxim is based on an apprehensive concern with consequences.

To be truthful from duty, however, is an entirely different thing from being truthful out of fear of disadvantageous consequences, for in the former case the concept of the action itself contains a law for me, while in the latter I must first look about to see what results for me may be connected with it. For to deviate from the principle of duty is certainly bad, but to be unfaithful to my maxim of prudence can sometimes be very advantageous to me, though it is certainly safer to abide by it. The shortest but most infallible way to find the answer to the question as to whether a deceitful promise is consistent with duty is to ask myself: Would I be content that my maxim (of extricating myself from difficulty by a false promise) should hold as a universal law for myself as well as for others? And could I say to myself that everyone may make a false promise when he is in difficulty from which he otherwise cannot escape? I immediately see that I could will the lie but not a universal law to lie. For with such a law there would be no promises at all, inasmuch as it would be futile to make a pretense of my intention in regard to future actions to those who would not believe this pretense or—if they overhastily did so—who would pay me back in my own coin. Thus my maxim would necessarily destroy itself as soon as it was made universal law.

I do not, therefore, need any penetrating acuteness in order to discern what I have to do in order that my volition may be morally good. Inexperienced in the course of the world, incapable of being prepared for all its contingencies, I ask myself only: Can I will that my maxim becomes a universal law? If not, it must be rejected, not because of any disadvantage accruing to myself or even to others, but because it cannot enter as a principle into a possible universal legislation, and reason extorts from me an immediate respect for such legislation. I do not as yet discern on what it is grounded (a question the philosopher may investigate), but I at least understand that it is an estimation of the worth which far outweighs all the worth of whatever is recommended by the inclinations, and that the necessity of my actions from pure respect for the practical law constitutes duty. To duty every other motive must give place, because duty is the condition of a will good in itself, whose worth transcends everything. . . .

The will is thought of as a faculty of determining itself to action in accordance with the conception of certain laws. Such a faculty can be found only in rational beings. That which serves the will as the objective ground of its self-determination is an end, and, if it is given by reason alone, it must hold alike for all rational beings. On the other hand, that which contains the ground of the possibility of the action, whose result is an end, is called the means. The subjective ground of desire is the incentive, while the objective ground of volition is the motive. Thus arises the distinction between subjective ends, which rest on incentives, and objective ends, which depend on motives valid for every rational being. Practical principles are formal when they disregard all subjective ends; they are material when they have subjective ends, and thus certain incentives, as their basis. The ends which a rational being arbitrarily proposes to himself as consequences of his action are material ends and are without exception only relative, for only their relation to a particularly constituted faculty of desire in the subject gives them their worth. And this worth cannot, therefore, afford any universal principles for all rational beings or valid and necessary principles for every volition. That is, they cannot give rise to any practical laws. All these relative ends, therefore, are grounds for hypothetical imperatives only.

But suppose that there were something the existence of which in itself had absolute worth, something which, as an end in itself, could be a ground of definite laws. In it and only in it could lie the ground of a possible categorical imperative, i.e., of a practical law.

Now, I say, man and, in general, every rational being exists as an end in himself and not merely as a means to be arbitrarily used by this or that will. In all his actions, whether they are directed to himself or to other rational beings, he must always be regarded at the same time as an end. All objects of inclinations have only a conditional worth, for if the inclinations and the needs founded on them did not exist, their object would be without worth. The inclinations themselves as the sources of needs, however, are so lacking in absolute worth that the universal wish of every rational being must be indeed to free himself completely from them. Therefore, the worth of any objects to be obtained by our actions is at all times conditional. Beings whose existence does not depend on our will but on nature, if they are not rational beings, have only a relative worth as means and are therefore called "things"; on the other hand, rational beings are designated "persons" because their nature indicates that they are ends in themselves, i.e., things which may not be used merely as means. Such a being is thus an object of respect and, so far, restricts all [arbitrary] choice. Such beings are not merely subjective ends whose existence as a result of our action has a worth for us, but are objective ends, i.e., beings whose existence in itself is an end. Such an end is one for which no other end can be substituted, to which these beings should serve merely as means. For, without them, nothing of absolute worth could be found, and if all worth is conditional and thus contingent, no supreme practical principle for reason could be found anywhere.

Thus if there is to be a supreme practical principle and a categorical imperative for the human will, it must be one that forms an objective principle of the will from the conception of that which is necessarily an end for everyone because it is an end in itself. Hence this objective principle can serve as a universal practical law. The ground of this principle is: rational nature exists as an end in itself. Man necessarily thinks of his own existence in this way; thus far it is a subjective principle of human actions. Also every other rational being thinks of his existence by means of the same rational ground which holds also for myself; thus it is at the same time an objective principle from which, as a supreme practical ground, it must be possible to derive all laws of the will. The practical imperative, therefore, is the following: At so that you treat humanity, whether in your own person or in that of another, always as an end and never as a means only. Let us now see whether this can be achieved.

To return to our previous examples:

First, according to the concept of necessary duty to one's self, he who contemplates suicide will ask himself whether his action can be consistent with the idea of humanity as an end in itself. If, in order to escape from burdensome circumstances, he destroys himself, he uses a person merely as a means to maintain a tolerable condition up to the end of life. Man, however, is not a thing, and thus not something to be used merely as a means; he must always be regarded in all his actions as an end in himself. Therefore, I cannot dispose of man in my own person so as to mutilate, corrupt, or kill him. (It belongs to ethics proper to define more accurately this basic principle so as to avoid all misunderstanding, e.g., as to the amputation of limbs in order to preserve myself, or to exposing my life to danger in order to save it; I must, therefore, omit them here.)

Second, as concerns necessary or obligatory duties to others, he who intends a deceitful promise to others sees immediately that he intends to use another man merely as a means, without the latter containing the end in himself at the same time. For he whom I want to use for my own purposes by means of such a promise cannot possibly assent to my mode of acting against him and cannot contain the end of this action in himself. This conflict against the principle of other men is even clearer if we cite examples of attacks on their freedom and property. For then it is clear that he who transgresses the rights of men intends to make use of the persons of others merely as a means, without considering that, as rational beings, they must always be esteemed at the same time as ends, i.e., only as beings who must be able to contain in themselves the end of the very same action. . . .

This principle of humanity and of every rational creature as an end in itself is the supreme limiting condition on freedom of the actions of each man. It is not borrowed from experience, first, because of its universality, since it applies to all rational beings generally and experience does not suffice to determine anything about them; and, secondly, because in experience humanity is not thought of (subjectively) as the end of men, i.e., as an object which we of ourselves really make our end. Rather it is thought of as the objective end which should constitute the supreme limiting condition of all subjective ends, whatever they may be. Thus this principle must arise from pure reason. Objectively the ground of all practical legislation lies (according to the first principle) in the rule and in the form of universality, which makes it capable of being a law (at most a natural law); subjectively, it lies in the end. But the subject of all ends is every rational being as an end in itself (by the second principle); from this there follows the third practical principle of the will as the supreme condition of its harmony with universal practical reason, viz., the idea of the will of every rational being as making universal law.

By this principle all maxims are rejected which are not consistent with the universal lawgiving of will. The will is thus not only subject to the law but subject in such a way that it must be regarded also as self-legislative and only for this reason as being subject to the law (of which it can regard itself as the author). . . .

If we now look back upon all previous attempts which have ever been undertaken to discover the principle of morality, it is not to be wondered at that they all had to fail. Man was seen to be bound to laws by his duty, but it was not seen that he is subject only to his own, yet universal, legislation, and that he is only bound to act in accordance with his own will, which is, however, designed by nature to be a will giving universal laws. For if one thought of him as subject only to a law (whatever it may be), this necessarily implied some interest as a stimulus or compulsion to obedience because the law did not arise from his will. Rather, his will was constrained by something else according to a law to act in a certain way. By this strictly necessary consequence, however, all the labor of finding a supreme ground for duty was irrevocably lost, and one never arrived at duty but only at the necessity of action from a certain interest. This might be his own interest or that of another, but in either case the imperative always had to be conditional and could not at all serve as a moral command. This principle I will call the principle of *autonomy* of the will in contrast to all other principles which I accordingly count under *heteronomy.*

The concept of each rational being as a being that must regard itself as giving universal law through all the maxims of its will, so that it may judge itself and its actions from this standpoint, leads to a very fruitful concept, namely, that of a *realm of ends.*

By "realm" I understand the systematic union of different rational beings through common laws. Because laws determine ends with regard to their universal validity, if we abstract from the personal difference of rational beings and thus from all content of their private ends, we can think of a whole of all ends in systematic connection, a whole of rational beings as ends in themselves as well as of the particular ends which each may set for himself. This is a realm of ends, which is possible on the aforesaid principles. For all rational beings stand under the law that each of them should treat himself and all others never merely as means but in every case also as an end in himself. Thus there arises a systematic union of rational beings through common objective laws. This is a realm which may be called a realm of ends (certainly only an ideal), because what these laws have in view is just the relation of these beings to each other as ends and means.

Mill

*John Stuart Mill (1806–1873) was born in London and educated by his famous fa-
ther James Mill, who was also a philosopher. John Stuart was a precocious child.
He studied Greek at the age of three and Plato at the age of eight; at the age of
twenty, however, he suffered a nervous breakdown, from which happily he later
recovered. Mill is best known for his work in logic, ethics, and politics. He has
been enormously influential in popular thinking about the importance of liberty
and the need to take into account our actual human needs and desires in framing our conceptions of the good life.*

Mill's thinking on ethics follows the principles of utilitarianism laid down by his predecessor Jeremy Bentham (1748–1832). Bentham argued for the primacy of pleasure in
determining the aim of human life; in this he considered not only the pleasures of individuals but those that are conducive to the happiness of most persons. In extending
and refining this teaching, Mill argues that the idea of a calculated *quantity* of pleasure
needs to be supplemented by a concern for the *quality* of pleasure in order to insure
the greatest human happiness. Having a strong faith in the basic decency and reasonableness of most persons, Mill insists that a majority can readily agree on which pleasures, in the long if not always in the short run, offer the richest and deepest
satisfactions, and that in any event those reflective persons who have had the opportunity to experience the widest range of pleasures would be in the best position to
judge their relative value.

Utilitarianism has been, and in one form or other continues to be, the main alternative in modern Western thinking to a Kantian rational ethics of duty. It looks to the actual consequences of human actions rather than to formal principles of a rational will.
Kantian ethics has often been criticized for its abstractness and "empty formalism";
Mill's, on the other hand, has been critiqued for its apparent inability to ground principles of conduct in our shared and, we believe, justified higher moral values. The application of utilitarian principles, it is argued, oftentimes seems to be at odds with our
intuitive moral conviction that, quite apart from their presumed consequences, certain
actions are intrinsically good and others inherently evil, and the fact that some persons
may determine that certain pleasures seem to make for happiness is no guarantee of
their moral worth.

The following selections are taken from Mill's *Utilitarianism* (1861), the most popular
and still one of the strongest defenses of this ethical doctrine.

Principles of Utilitarianism

The creed which accepts as the foundation of morals *utility*, or the *greatest happiness principle*, holds that actions are right in proportion as they tend to promote happiness, wrong as they tend to produce the reverse of happiness. By "happiness" is intended pleasure, and the absence of pain; by "unhappiness," pain, and the privation of pleasure. To give a clear view of the moral standard set up by the theory, much more requires to be said; in particular, what things it includes in the ideas of pain and pleasure; and to what extent this is left an open question. But these supplementary explanations do not affect the theory of life on which this theory of morality is grounded—namely, that pleasure, and freedom from pain, are the only things desirable as ends; and that all desirable things (which are as numerous in the utilitarian as in any other scheme) are desirable either for the pleasure inherent in themselves, or as means to the promotion of pleasure and the prevention of pain.

Now such a theory of life excites in many minds, and among them in some of the most estimable in feeling and purpose, inveterate dislike. To suppose that life has (as they express it) no higher end than pleasure—no better and nobler object of desire and pursuit—they designate as utterly mean and groveling; as a doctrine worthy only of swine, to whom the followers of Epicurus were, at a very early period, contemptuously likened; and modern holders of the doctrine are occasionally made the subject of equally polite comparisons by its German, French, and English assailants.

When thus attacked, the Epicureans have always answered that it is not they but their accusers who represent human nature in a degrading light; since the accusation supposes human beings to be capable of no pleasures except those of which swine are capable. If this supposition were true, the charge could not be gainsaid, but would then be no longer an imputation; for if the sources of pleasure were precisely the same to human beings and to swine, the rule of life which is good enough for the one would be good enough for the other. The comparison of the Epicurean life to that of beasts is felt as degrading, precisely because a beast's pleasures do not satisfy a human being's conceptions of happiness. Human beings have faculties more elevated than the animal appetites, and when once made conscious of them, do not regard anything as happiness which does not include their gratification. I do not, indeed, consider the Epicureans to have been by any means faultless in drawing out their scheme of consequences from the utilitarian principle. To do this in any sufficient manner, many Stoic, as well as Christian elements require to be included. But there is no known Epicurean theory of life which does not assign to the pleasures of the intellect, of the feelings and imagination, and of the moral sentiments, a much higher value as pleasures than to those of mere sensation. . . .

If I am asked what I mean by difference of quality in pleasures, or what makes one

From *Utilitarianism* by John Stuart Mill (New York: Bobbs-Merrill, 1957; originally published in *Fraser's Magazine*, October 1861).

pleasure more valuable than another merely as a pleasure, except its being greater in amount, there is but one possible answer. Of two pleasures, if there be one to which all or almost all who have experience of both give a decided preference, irrespective of any feeling of moral obligation to prefer it, that is the more desirable pleasure. If one of the two is, by those who are competently acquainted with both, placed so far above the other that they prefer it, even though knowing it to be attended with a greater amount of discontent, and would not resign it for any quantity of the other pleasure which their nature is capable of, we are justified in ascribing to the preferred enjoyment a superiority in quality, so far outweighing quantity as to render it, in comparison, of small amount. . . .

It may be objected that many who are capable of the higher pleasures, occasionally, under the influence of temptation, postpone them to the lower. But this is quite compatible with a full appreciation of the intrinsic superiority of the higher. Men often, from infirmity of character, make their election for the nearer good, though they know it to be the less valuable; and this is no less when the choice is between two bodily pleasures, than when it is between bodily and mental. They pursue sensual indulgences to the injury of health, though perfectly aware that health is the greater good. It may be further objected that many who begin with youthful enthusiasm for everything noble, as they advance in years sink into indolence and selfishness. But I do not believe that those who undergo this very common change, voluntarily choose the lower description of pleasures in preference to the higher. I believe that before they devote themselves exclusively to the one, they have already become incapable of the other. Capacity for the nobler feelings is in most natures a very tender plant, easily killed, not only by hostile influences, but by mere want of sustenance; and in the majority of young persons it speedily dies away if the occupations to which their position in life has devoted them, and the society into which it has thrown them, are not favorable to keeping that higher capacity in exercise. Men lose their high aspirations as they lose their intellectual tastes, because they have not time or opportunity for indulging them; and they addict themselves to inferior pleasures not because they deliberately prefer them, but because they are either the only ones to which they have access or the only ones which they are any longer capable of enjoying. It may be questioned whether anyone who has remained equally susceptible to both classes of pleasures, ever knowingly and calmly preferred the lower; though many, in all ages, have broken down in an ineffectual attempt to combine both.

From this verdict of the only competent judges I apprehend there can be no appeal. On a question which is the best worth having of two pleasures, or which of two modes of existence is the most grateful to the feelings, apart from its moral attributes and from its consequences, the judgment of those who are qualified by knowledge of both, or, if they differ, that of the majority among them, must be admitted as final. And there need be the less hesitation to accept this judgment respecting the quality of pleasures, since there is no other tribunal to be referred to even on the question of quantity. What means are there of determining which is the acutest of two pains, or the intensest of two pleasurable sensations, except the general suffrage of those who are familiar with both? Neither pains nor pleasures are homogeneous, and pain is always heterogeneous with pleasure. What is there to decide whether a particular pleasure is worth purchasing at the cost of a particular pain, except the feelings and judgment of the experienced? When, therefore, those feelings and judgment declare the pleasures derived from the higher faculties to be preferable *in kind,* apart from the question of intensity, to those of which the animal nature, disjoined from the higher faculties, is suspectible, they are entitled on this subject to the same regard. . . .

According to the "greatest happiness principle," as above explained, the ultimate end, with reference to and for the sake of which all other things are desirable (whether we are considering our own good or that of other people), is an existence exempt as far as possible from pain, and as rich as possible in enjoyments, both in point of quantity and quality; the test of quality, and the rule for measuring it against quantity, being the preference felt by those who in their opportunities of experience, to which must be added their habits of self-consciousness and self-observation, are best furnished with the means of comparison. This, being, according to the utilitarian opinion, the end of human action, is necessarily also the standard of morality; which may accordingly be defined, the rules and precepts for human conduct, by the observance of which an existence such as has been described might be, to the greatest extent possible, secured to all mankind; and not to them only, but, so far as the nature of things admits, to the whole sentient creation. . . .

I must again repeat, what the assailants of utilitarianism seldom have the justice to acknowledge, that the happiness which forms the utilitarian standard of what is right in conduct, is not the agent's own happiness, but that of all concerned. As between his own happiness and that of others, utilitarianism requires him to be as strictly impartial as a disinterested and benevolent spectator. In the golden rule of Jesus of Nazareth, we read the complete spirit of the ethics of utility. To do as you would be done by, and to love your neighbor as yourself, constitute the ideal perfection of utilitarian morality. As the means of making the nearest approach to this ideal, utility would enjoin, first, that laws and social arrangements should place the happiness, or (as speaking practically it may be called) the interest, of every individual, as nearly as possible in harmony with the interest of the whole; and secondly, that education and opinion, which have so vast a power over human character, should so use that power has to establish in the mind of every individual an indissoluble association between is own happiness and the good of the whole—especially between his own happiness and the practice of such modes of conduct, negative and positive, as regard for the universal happiness prescribes; so that not only he may be unable to conceive the possibility of happiness to himself, consistently with conduct opposed to the general good, but also that a direct impulse to promote the general good may be in every individual one of the habitual motives of action, and the sentiments connected therewith may fill a large and prominent place in every human being's sentient existence. If the impugners of the utilitarian morality represented it to their own minds in this its true character, I know not what recommendation possessed by any other morality they could possibly affirm to be wanting to it; what more beautiful or more exalted developments of human nature any other ethical system can be supposed to foster, or what springs of action, not accessible to the utilitarian, such systems rely on for giving effect to their mandates.

The objectors to utilitarianism cannot always be charged with representing it in a discreditable light. On the contrary, those among them who entertain anything like a just idea of its disinterested character sometimes find fault with its standard as being too high for humanity. They say it is exacting too much to require that people shall always act from the inducement of promoting the general interests of society. But this is to mistake the very meaning of a standard of morals, and confound the rule of action with the motive of it. It is the business of ethics to tell us what are our duties, or by what test we may know them; but no system of ethics requires that the sole motive of all we do shall be a feeling of duty; on the contrary, ninety-nine hundredths of all our actions are done from other motives, and rightly so done, if the rule of duty does not condemn them. It is the more unjust to utilitarianism that this particular misapprehension should be made a ground of objection to it, inasmuch as utilitarian moralists have gone beyond almost all others in affirming that the motive has nothing to do with the morality of the action, though much with the worth of the agent. He who saves a fellow creature from drowning does what is morally right, whether his motive be duty, or the hope of being paid for his trouble; he who betrays the friend that trusts him, is guilty of a crime, even if his object be to serve another friend to whom he is under great obligations. But to speak only of actions done from the motive of duty, and in direct obedience to principle: it is a misapprehension of the utilitarian mode of thought, to conceive it as implying that people should fix their minds upon so wide a generality as the world, or society at large. The great majority of good actions are intended not for the benefit of the world, but for that of individuals, of which the good of the world is made up; and the thoughts of the most virtuous man need not on these occasions travel beyond the particular persons concerned, except so far as is necessary to assure himself that in benefiting them he is not violating the rights, that is, the legitimate and authorized expectations, of anyone else. The multiplication of happiness is, according to the utilitarian ethics, the object of virtue: the occasions on which any person (except one in a thousand) has it in his power to do this on an extended scale, in other words to be a public benefactor, are but exceptional, and on these occasions alone is he called on to consider public utility; in every other case, private utility, the interest or happiness of some few persons, is all he has to attend to. Those alone the influence of whose actions extends to society in general, need concern themselves habitually about so large an object. In the case of abstinences indeed—of things which people forbear to do from moral considerations, though the consequences in the particular case might be beneficial—it would be unworthy of an intelligent agent not to be consciously aware that the action is of a class which, if practiced generally, would be generally injurious, and that this is the ground of the obligation to abstain from it. The amount of regard for the public interest implied in this recognition is no greater than is demanded by every system of morals, for they all enjoin to abstain from whatever is manifestly pernicious to society.

Nietzsche

*Friedrich Nietzsche (1844–1900), in his examination of culture and morality, ex-
hibited great insight into the psychological drives that motivate us. Many scholars consider Nietzsche to be a precursor of Freud, and, in any event, he has had
an enormous influence upon many movements in twentieth-century philosophy, literature, and art. The son of a Lutheran pastor, Nietzsche showed great
promise in his student days as a classical philologist and became a professor of
philology in Basel, Switzerland, at the remarkable age of twenty-five. Over time
his focus shifted from philological issues to philosophical ones, and he abandoned his academic career in favor of becoming a completely independent
thinker. Nietzsche's best known works include* The Birth of Tragedy *(1872),* Thus
Spake Zarathustra *(1883–85),* Beyond Good and Evil *(1887), and* The Genealogy of
Morals *(1887).*

Although often characterized as a supreme immoralist, Nietzsche is in fact clearly ob-
sessed with ethical issues. He puts forth, on the basis of a thoroughgoing, and rather
strident, critique of modern Christian-based moral values, an ethical vision that glorifies
the possibilities of (at least some) human beings to achieve a profound insight into, and
understanding of, the full creative potentialities of their nature. Nietzsche's *Übermensch*—unhappily often translated as "superman"—is one who leaves behind or
"overcomes" the "herd" or "slave" morality of common folk who have been brain-
washed by Christianity to live dull, resentful lives of duty and submissive conformity and
sets a new ethical course for himself and others, a "master morality," that is claimed to
be "beyond good and evil."

Nietzsche's view departs quite radically, then, from the rational aim of happiness put
forward by Aristotle, the theistically grounded ethic of duty set forth by the *Gītā*, the
thoroughly social-political account given by Confucius, the formalist universalistic argument of Kant, and the pleasure-based—"vulgar," according to Nietzsche—consequen-
tialist thinking of Mill. To say that his views are controversial is to put it mildly. His
unremitting attack on herd morality and on democracy and his celebration of diversity
and creativity nevertheless have presented a strong challenge to any way of thinking
that upholds traditional Western ethical values, moral practices, and political ideologies.

On the Natural History of Morals

Philosophers one and all have, with a strait-laced seriousness that provokes laughter, demanded something much higher, more pretentious, more solemn of themselves as soon as they have concerned themselves with morality as a science: they wanted to furnish the *rational ground* of morality—and every philosopher hitherto has believed he has furnished this rational ground; morality itself, however, was taken as "given." How far from their clumsy pride was that apparently insignificant task left in dust and mildew, the task of description, although the most delicate hands and senses could hardly be delicate enough for it! It was precisely because moral philosophers knew the facts of morality only somewhat vaguely in an arbitrary extract or as a chance abridgement, as morality of their environment, their class, their church, the spirit of their times, their climate and zone of the earth, for instance—it was precisely because they were ill informed and not even very inquisitive about other peoples, ages and former times, that they did not so much as catch sight of the real problems of morality—for these come into view only if we compare *many* moralities. Strange though it may sound, in all "science of morals" hitherto the problem of morality itself has been *lacking:* the suspicion was lacking that there was anything problematic here. What philosophers called "the rational ground of morality" and sought to furnish was, viewed in the proper light, only a scholarly form of *faith* in the prevailing morality, a new way of *expressing* it, and thus itself a fact within a certain morality, indeed even in the last resort a kind of denial that this morality *ought* to be conceived of as a problem—and in any event the opposite of a testing, analysis, doubting and vivisection of this faith. . . .

Quite apart from the value of such assertions as "there exists in us a categorical imperative" one can still ask: what does such an assertion say of the man who asserts it? There are moralities which are intended to justify their authors before others; other moralities are intended to calm him and make him content with himself; with others he wants to crucify and humiliate himself; with others he wants to wreak vengeance, with others hide himself, with others transfigure himself and set himself on high; this morality serves to make its author forget, that to make him or something about him forgotten; many moralists would like to exercise power and their creative moods on mankind; others, Kant perhaps among them, give to understand with their morality: "what is worthy of respect in me is that I know how to obey—and things *ought* to be no different with you!"—in short, moralities too are only a *sign-language of the emotions.* . . .

There is something in Plato's morality which does not really belong to Plato but is only to be met with in his philosophy, one might say in spite of Plato: namely Socratism, for which he was really too noble. "No one wants to do injury to himself,

---

From *Beyond Good and Evil* by Friedrich Nietzsche, translated by R. J. Hollingdale (Penguin Classics, 1973; revised edition, 1990). Translation copyright © R. J. Hollingdale, 1973, 1990.

therefore all badness is involuntary. For the bad man does injury to himself: this he would not do if he knew that badness is bad. Thus the bad man is bad only in consequence of an error; if one cures him of his error, one necessarily makes him— good."—This way of reasoning smells of the *mob,* which sees in bad behaviour only its disagreeable consequences and actually judges "it is *stupid* to act badly"; while it takes "good" without further ado to be identical with "useful and pleasant." In the case of every utilitarian morality one may conjecture in advance a similar origin and follow one's nose: one will seldom go astray.—Plato did all he could to interpret something refined and noble into his teacher's proposition, above all himself—he, the most intrepid of interpreters, who picked up the whole of Socrates only in the manner of a popular tune from the streets, so as to subject it to infinite and impossible variations: that is, to make it into all his own masks and multiplicities. . . .

The old theological problem of "faith" and "knowledge"—or, more clearly, of instinct and reason—that is to say, the question whether in regard to the evaluation of things instinct deserves to have more authority than rationality, which wants to evaluate and act according to reasons, according to a "why?," that is to say according to utility and fitness for a purpose—this is still that old moral problem which first appeared in the person of Socrates and was already dividing the minds of men long before Christianity. Socrates himself, to be sure, had, with the taste appropriate to his talent—that of a superior dialectician—initially taken the side of reason; and what indeed did he do all his life long but laugh at the clumsy incapacity of his noble Athenians, who were men of instinct, like all noble men, and were never able to supply adequate information about the reasons for their actions? Ultimately, however, in silence and secrecy, he laughed at himself too: he found in himself, before his more refined conscience and self-interrogation, the same difficulty and incapacity. But why, he exhorted himself, should one therefore abandon the instincts! One must help both them *and* reason to receive their due—one must follow the instincts, but persuade reason to aid them with good arguments. This was the actual *falsity* of that great ironist, who had so many secrets; he induced his conscience to acquiesce in a sort of self-outwitting: fundamentally he had seen through the irrational aspect of moral judgment.—Plato, more innocent in such things and without the craftiness of the plebeian, wanted at the expenditure of all his strength—the greatest strength any philosopher has hitherto had to expend!—to prove to himself that reason and instinct move of themselves towards *one* goal, towards the good, towards "God"; and since Plato all theologians and philosophers have followed the same path—that is to say, in moral matters instinct, or as the Christians call it "faith," or as I call it "the herd," has hitherto triumphed. One might have to exclude Descartes, the father of rationalism (and consequently the grandfather of the Revolution), who recognized only the authority of reason: but reason is only an instrument, and Descartes was superficial. . . .

The diversity of men is revealed not only in the diversity of their tables of what they find good, that is to say in the fact that they regard diverse goods worth striving for and also differ as to what is more or less valuable, as to the order of rank of the goods they all recognize—it is revealed even more in what they regard as actually *having* and *possessing* what they find good. In regard to a woman, for example, the more modest man counts the simple disposal of her body and sexual gratification as a sufficient and satisfactory sign of having, of possession; another, with a more jealous and demanding thirst for possession, sees the "question-mark," the merely apparent quality of such a having and requires subtler tests, above all in order to know whether the woman not only gives herself to him but also gives up for his sake what she has or would like to have—: only *thus* does she count to him as "possessed." A third, however, is not done with jealousy and desire for having even then; he asks himself whether, when the woman gives up everything for him, she does not perhaps do so for a phantom of him: he demands that she know him to the very heart before she is able to love him at all, he dares to let himself be unravelled—. He feels that his beloved is fully in his possession only when she no longer deceives herself about him but loves him as much for his devilry and hidden insatiability as she does for his goodness, patience, and spirituality. . . .

So long as the utility which dominates moral value-judgements is solely that which is useful to the herd, so long as the object is solely the preservation of the community and the immoral is sought precisely and exclusively in that which seems to imperil the existence of the community: so long as that is the case there can be no "morality of love of one's neighbour." Supposing that even there a constant little exercise of consideration, pity, fairness, mildness, mutual aid was practised, supposing that even at that stage of society all those drives are active which are later honourably designated "virtues" and are finally practically equated with the concept "morality": in that era they do not yet by any means belong to the domain of moral valuations— they are still *extra-moral*. An act of pity, for example, was during the finest age of Rome considered neither good nor bad, neither moral nor immoral; and even if it was commended, this commendation was entirely compatible with a kind of involuntary disdain, as soon, that is, as it was set beside any action which served the welfare of the whole, of the *res publica*. Ultimately "love of one's neighbour" is always something secondary, in part conventional and arbitrarily illusory, when compared with *fear of one's neighbour*. Once the structure of society seems to have been in general fixed and made safe from external dangers, it is this fear of one's neighbour which again creates new perspectives of moral valuation. There are certain strong and dangerous drives, such as enterprisingness, foolhardiness, revengefulness, craft, rapacity, ambition, which had hitherto had not only to be honoured from the point of view of their social utility—under different names, naturally, from those chosen here—but also mightily developed and cultivated (because they were constantly needed to protect the community as a whole against the enemies of the community as a whole); these drives are now felt to be doubly dangerous—now that the diversionary outlets for them are lacking—and are gradually branded as immoral and given over to calumny. The antithetical drives and inclinations now come into moral honour; step by step the herd instinct draws its conclusions. How much or how little that is dangerous to the community, dangerous to equality, resides in an opinion, in a condition or emotion, in a will, in a talent, that is now the moral perspective: here again fear is the mother of morality. When the highest and strongest drives, breaking passionately out, carry the individual far above and beyond the average and lowlands of the herd conscience, the self-confidence of the community goes to pieces, its faith in itself, its spine as it were, is broken: consequently it is precisely these drives which are most branded and calumniated. Lofty spiritual independence, the will to stand alone, great intelligence even, are felt to be dangerous; everything that raises the individual above the herd and makes his neighbour quail is henceforth called *evil*; the fair, modest, obedient, self-effacing disposition, the *mean and average* in desires, acquires moral names and honours. Eventually, under very peaceful conditions, there is less and less occasion or need to educate one's feelings in severity and sternness; and now every kind of severity, even severity in justice, begins to trouble the conscience; a stern and lofty nobility and self-responsibility is received almost as an offence and awakens mistrust, "the lamb," even more "the sheep," is held in higher and higher respect. There comes a point of morbid mellowing and over-tenderness in the history of society at which it takes the side even of him who harms it, the *criminal,* and does so honestly and wholeheartedly. Punishment that seems to it somehow unfair—certainly the idea of "being punished" and "having to punish" is unpleasant to it, makes it afraid. "It is not enough to render him *harmless?* why punish him as well? To administer punishment is itself dreadful!"—with this question herd morality, the morality of timidity, draws its ultimate conclusion. Supposing all danger, the cause of fear, could be abolished, this morality would therewith also be abolished: it would no longer be necessary, it would no longer *regard itself* as necessary!—He who examines the conscience of the present-day European will have to extract from a thousand moral recesses and hiding-places always the same imperative, the imperative of herd timidity: "we wish that there will one day *no longer be anything to fear*!" One day—everywhere in Europe the will and way to *that* day is now called "progress."

Let us straight away say once more what we have already said a hundred times: for ears today offer such truths—*our* truths—no ready welcome. We know well enough how offensive it sounds when someone says plainly and without metaphor that man is an animal; but it will be reckoned almost a *crime* in us that precisely in regard to men of "modern ideas" we constantly employ the terms "herd," "herd instinct," and the like. But what of that! we can do no other: for it is precisely here that our new insight lies. We have found that in all principal moral judgements Europe has become unanimous, including the lands where Europe's influence predominates: one manifestly *knows* in Europe what Socrates thought he did not know, and what that celebrated old serpent once promised to teach—one "knows" today what is good and evil. Now it is bound to make a harsh sound and one not easy for ears to hear when we insist again and again: that which here believes it knows, that which here glorifies itself with its praising and blaming and calls itself good, is the instinct of the herd-animal man: the instinct which has broken through and come to predominate and prevail over the other instincts and is coming to do so more and more in proportion to the increasing physiological approximation and assimilation of which it is the symptom. *Morality is in Europe today herd-animal morality*—that is to say, as we understand the thing, only *one* kind of human morality beside which, before which, after which many other, above all *higher*, moralities are possible or ought to be possible. But against such a "possibility," against such an "ought," this morality defends itself with all its might: it says, obstinately and stubbornly, "I am morality itself, and nothing is morality besides me!"—indeed, with the aid of a religion which has gratified and flattered the sublimest herd-animal desires, it has got to the point where we discover even in political and social institutions an increasingly evident expression of this morality: the *democratic* movement inherits the Christian. But that the tempo of this movement is much too slow and somnolent for the more impatient, for the sick and suffering of the said instinct, is attested by the ever more frantic baying, the ever more undisguised fang-baring of the anarchist dogs which now rove the streets of European culture: apparently the reverse of the placidly industrious democrats and revolutionary ideologists, and even more so of the stupid philosophasters and brotherhood fanatics who call themselves socialists and want a "free society," they are in fact at one with them all in their total and instinctive hostility towards every form of society other than that of the *autonomous* herd (to the point of repudiating even the concepts "master" and "servant" . . .); at one in their tenacious opposition to every special claim, every special right and privilege (that is to say, in the last resort to *every* right: for when everyone is equal no one will need any "rights"—); at one in their mistrust of punitive justice (as if it were an assault on the weaker, an injustice against the necessary consequence of all previous society—); but equally at one in the religion of pity, in sympathy with whatever feels, lives, suffers (down as far as the animals, up as far as "God"—the extravagance of "pity for God" belongs in a democratic era—); at one, one and all, in the cry and impatience of pity, in mortal hatred for suffering in general, in their almost feminine incapacity to remain spectators of suffering, to *let* suffer; at one in their involuntary gloom and sensitivity, under whose spell Europe seems threatened with a new Buddhism; at one in their faith in the morality of *mutual* pity, as if it were morality in itself and the pinnacle, the *attained* pinnacle of man, the sole hope of the future, the consolation of the present and the great redemption from all the guilt of the past—at one, one and all, in their faith in the community as the *saviour*, that is to say in the herd, in "themselves". . . .

We, who have a different faith—we, to whom the democratic movement is not merely a form assumed by political organization in decay but also a form assumed by man in decay, that is to say in diminishment, in process of becoming mediocre and losing his value: whither must *we* direct our hopes?—Towards *new philosophers*, we have no other choice; towards spirits strong and original enough to make a start on antithetical evaluations and to revalue and reverse "eternal values"; towards heralds and forerunners, towards men of the future who in the present knot together the constraint which compels the will of millennia on to *new* paths. To teach man the future of man as his *will*, as dependent on a human will, and to prepare for great enterprises and collective experiments in discipline and breeding so as to make an end of that gruesome dominion of chance and nonsense that has hitherto been called "history"—the nonsense of the "greatest number" is only its latest form—: for that a new kind of philosopher and commander will some time be needed, in face of whom whatever has existed on earth of hidden, dreadful and benevolent spirits may well look pale and dwarfed. It is the image of such leaders which hovers before *our* eyes—may I say that aloud, you free spirits? The circumstances one would have in part to create, in part to employ, to bring them into existence; the conjectural paths and tests by virtue of which a soul could grow to such height and power it would feel *compelled* to these tasks; a revaluation of values under whose novel pressure and hammer a conscience would be steeled, a heart transformed to brass, so that it might endure the weight of such a responsibility; on the other hand, the need for such leaders, the terrible danger they might not appear or might fail or might degenerate—these are *our* proper cares and concerns, do you know that, you free spirits? These are the heavy, remote thoughts and thunder clouds that pass across *our* life's sky. There are few more grievous pains than once to have beheld, divined, sensed, how an extraordinary man missed his way and degenerated: but he who has the rare eye for the collective danger that "man" himself *may degenerate*, he who, like us, has recognized the tremendous fortuitousness which has hitherto played its game with the future of man—a game in which no hand, not even a "finger of God" took any part!—he who has divined the fatality that lies concealed in the idiotic guilelessness and blind confidence of "modern ideas," even more in the whole of Christian-European morality: he suffers from a feeling of anxiety with which no other can be compared—for he comprehends in a *single* glance all that which, given a favourable accumulation and intensification of forces and tasks, could be *cultivated out of man,* he knows with all the knowledge of his conscience how the greatest possibilities in man are still unexhausted and how often before the type man has been faced with strange decisions and new paths—he knows even better from his most painful memories against what wretched things an evolving being of the highest rank has hitherto usually been shattered and has broken off, sunk and has itself become wretched. The *collective degeneration of man* down to that which the socialist dolts and blockheads today see as their "man of the future"—as their ideal!—this degeneration and diminution of man to the perfect herd animal (or, as they say, to the man of the "free society"), this animalization of man to the pygmy animal of equal rights and equal pretensions is *possible,* there is no doubt about that! He who has once thought this possibility through to the end knows one more kind of disgust than other men do—and perhaps also a new *task*!

Plato

Plato's political views were set forth strikingly in his most important work, the *Republic*, where he focuses attention upon the concept of justice. "In what does a just society consist?" Plato asks. He answers that it is one in which each citizen performs his work and participates in the social order in a manner appropriate to his nature. Plato would agree with the *Bhagavad Gītā* that each person has his *dharma*, his duty or the "law" of his nature, albeit Plato would disagree with the Indian theistic basis on which this view was grounded.

Plato looks for those virtues that support an ideal state and appeals to the traditional Greek ones of wisdom, bravery, temperance, and justice. When exploring the nature of justice he sets forth the organization of an ideal society as composed of those who are most gifted, through their natural inclination and education, to be the bearers of wisdom and thus to be the rulers or "guardians" of the state; those who exhibit the quality of bravery appropriate to their being members of the warrior class; and those who rightfully belong to the more ordinary group of traders, merchants, and craftsmen—with all the classes to bear temperance as a harmonizing quality. Members of each class should be educated according to their abilities and the functions they need to perform in the society.

It is always interesting and instructive to ask to what extent our own contemporary liberal democracy still retains features of Plato's Republic in modern dress.

The Nature of the Ideal State

I take it that our state, having been founded and built upon the right lines, is good in the complete sense of the word.

It must be.

Obviously, then, it is wise, brave, temperate, and just.

Obviously.

Then if we find some of these qualities in it, the remainder will be the one we have not found. It is as if we were looking somewhere for one of any four things: if

From *The Republic of Plato*, translated by F. M. Cornford (1941). Reprinted by permission of Oxford University Press.

we detected that one immediately, we should be satisfied; whereas if we recognized the other three first, that would be enough to indicate the thing we wanted; it could only be the remaining one. So here we have four qualities. Had we not better follow that method in looking for the one we want?

Surely.

To begin then: the first quality to come into view in our state seems to be its wisdom; and there appears to be something odd about this quality.

What is there odd about it?

I think the state we have described really has wisdom; for it will be prudent in counsel, won't it?

Yes.

And prudence in counsel is clearly a form of knowledge; good counsel cannot be due to ignorance and stupidity.

Clearly.

But there are many and various kinds of knowledge in our commonwealth. There is the knowledge possessed by the carpenters or the smiths, and the knowledge how to raise crops. Are we to call the state wise and prudent on the strength of these forms of skill?

No; they would only make it good at furniture-making or working in copper or agriculture.

Well then, is there any form of knowledge, possessed by some among the citizens of our new-founded commonwealth, which will enable it to take thought, not for some particular interest, but for the best possible conduct of the state as a whole in its internal and external relations?

Yes, there is.

What is it, and where does it reside?

It is precisely that art of guardianship which resides in those Rulers whom we just now called Guardians in the full sense.

And what would you call the state on the strength of that knowledge?

Prudent and truly wise.

And do you think there will be more or fewer of these genuine Guardians in our state than there will be smiths?

Far fewer.

Fewer, in fact, than any of those other groups who are called after the kind of skill they possess?

Much fewer.

So if a state is constituted on natural principles, the wisdom it possesses as a whole will be due to the knowledge residing in the smallest part, the one which takes the lead and governs the rest. Such knowledge is the only kind that deserves the name of wisdom, and it appears to be ordained by nature that the class privileged to possess it should be the smallest of all.

Quite true.

Here then we have more or less made out one of our four qualities and its seat in the structure of the commonwealth.

To my satisfaction, at any rate.

.   .   .

Next there is courage. It is not hard to discern that quality or the part of the community in which it resides so as to entitle the whole to be called brave.

Why do you say so?

Because anyone who speaks of a state as either brave or cowardly can only be thinking of that part of it which takes the field and fights in its defence; the reason being, I imagine, that the character of the state is not determined by the bravery or cowardice of the other parts.

No.

Courage, then, is another quality which a community owes to a certain part of itself. And its being brave will mean that, in this part, it possesses the power of preserving, in all circumstances, a conviction about the sort of things that it is right to be afraid of—the conviction implanted by the education which the lawgiver has established. Is not that what you mean by courage?

I do not quite understand. Will you say it again?

I am saying that courage means preserving something.

Yes, but what?

The conviction, inculcated by lawfully established education, about the sort of things which may rightly be feared. When I added "in all circumstances," I meant preserving it always and never abandoning it, whether under the influence of pain or of pleasure, of desire or of fear. . . .

Two qualities, I went on, still remain to be made out in our state, temperance and the object of our whole inquiry, justice. . . .

. . . At first sight, temperance seems more like some sort of concord or harmony than the other qualities did.

How so?

Temperance surely means a kind of orderliness, a control of certain pleasures and appetites. People use the expression, "master of oneself," whatever that means, and various other phrases that point the same way.

Quite true.

Is not "master of oneself" an absurd expression? A man who was master of himself would presumably be also subject to himself, and the subject would be master; for all these terms apply to the same person.

No doubt.

I think, however, the phrase means that within the man himself, in his soul, there is a better part and a worse; and that he is his own master when the part which is better by nature has the worse under its control. It is certainly a term of praise; whereas it is considered a disgrace, when, through bad breeding or bad company, the better part is overwhelmed by the worse, like a small force outnumbered by a multitude. A man in that condition is called a slave to himself and intemperate.

Probably that is what is meant.

Then now look at our newly founded state and you will find one of these two conditions realized there. You will agree that it deserves to be called master of itself, if temperance and self-mastery exist where the better part rules the worse.

Yes, I can see that is true.

It is also true that the great mass of multifarious appetites and pleasures and pains will be found to occur chiefly in children and women and slaves, and, among free men so called, in the inferior multitude; whereas the simple and moderate desires which, with the aid of reason and right belief, are guided by reflection, you will find only in a few, and those with the best inborn dispositions and the best educated.

Yes, certainly.

Do you see that this state of things will exist in your commonwealth, where the desires of the inferior multitude will be controlled by the desires and wisdom of the superior few? Hence, if any society can be called master of itself and in control of pleasure and desires, it will be ours.

Quite so.

On all these grounds, then, we may describe it as temperate. Furthermore, in our state, if anywhere, the governors and the governed will share the same conviction on the question who ought to rule. Don't you think so?

I am quite sure of it.

Then, if that is their state of mind, in which of the two classes of citizens will temperance reside—in the governors or in the governed?

In both, I suppose.

So we were not wrong in divining a resemblance between temperance and some kind of harmony. Temperance is not like courage and wisdom, which made the state wise and brave by residing each in one particular part. Temperance works in a different way; it extends throughout the whole gamut of the state, producing a consonance of all its elements from the weakest to the strongest as measured by any standard you like to take—wisdom, bodily strength, numbers, or wealth. So we are entirely justified in identifying with temperance this unanimity or harmonious agreement between the naturally superior and inferior elements on the question which of the two should govern, whether in the state or the individual.

I fully agree.

Good, said I. We have discovered in our commonwealth three out of our four qualities, to the best of our present judgment. What is the remaining one, required to make up its full complement of goodness? For clearly this will be justice. . . .

. . . You remember how, when we first began to establish our commonwealth and several times since, we have laid down, as a universal principle, that everyone ought to perform the one function in the community for which his nature best suited him. Well I believe that that principle, or some form of it, is justice.

We certainly laid that down.

Yes, and surely we have often heard people say that justice means minding one's own business and not meddling with other men's concerns; and we have often said so ourselves.

We have.

Well, my friend, it may be that this minding of one's own business, when it takes a certain form, is actually the same thing as justice. Do you know what makes me think so?

No, tell me.

I think that this quality which makes it possible for the three we have already considered, wisdom, courage, and temperance, to take their place in the commonwealth, and so long as it remains present secures their continuance, must be the remaining one. And we said that, when three of the four were found, the one left over would be justice.

It must be so.

Well now, if we had to decide which of these qualities will contribute most to the excellence of our commonwealth, it would be hard to say whether it was the unanimity of rulers and subjects, or the soldier's fidelity to the established conviction about what is, or is not, to be feared, or the watchful intelligence of the Rulers; or whether its excellence were not above all due to the observance by everyone, child or woman, slave or freeman or artisan, ruler or ruled, of this principle that each one should do his own proper work without interfering with others.

It would be hard to decide, no doubt.

It seems, then, that this principle can at any rate claim to rival wisdom, temperance, and courage as conducing to the excellence of a state. And would you not say that the only possible competitor of these qualities must be justice?

Yes, undoubtedly.

Here is another thing which points to the same conclusion. The judging of lawsuits is a duty that you will lay upon your Rulers, isn't it?

Of course.

And the chief aim of their decisions will be that neither party shall have what belongs to another or be deprived of what is his own.

Yes.

Because that is just?

Yes.

So here again justice admittedly means that a man should possess and concern himself with what properly belongs to him.

True.

Again, do you agree with me that no great harm would be done to the community by a general interchange of most forms of work, the carpenter and the cobbler exchanging their positions and their tools and taking on each other's jobs, or even the same man undertaking both?

Yes, there would not be much harm in that.

But I think you will also agree that another kind of interchange would be disastrous. Suppose, for instance, someone whom nature designed to be an artisan or tradesman should be emboldened by some advantage, such as wealth or command of votes or bodily strength, to try to enter the order of fighting men; or some member of that order should aspire, beyond his merits, to a seat in the council-chamber of the Guardians. Such interference and exchange of social positions and tools, or the attempt to combine all these forms of work in the same person, would be fatal to the commonwealth.

Most certainly.

Where there are three orders, then, any plurality of functions or shifting from one order to another is not merely utterly harmful to the community, but one might fairly call it the extreme of wrongdoing. And you will agree that to do the greatest of wrongs to one's own community is injustice.

Surely.

This, then, is injustice. And, conversely, let us repeat that when each order—tradesman, Auxiliary, Guardian—keeps to its own proper business in the commonwealth and does its own work, that is justice and what makes a just society.

I entirely agree.

Taoism

Taoism bases its fundamental principles upon two primary texts, the *Tao Te Ching* (*The Way and Its Power*) and the *Chuang Tzu* (*Master Chuang*), which were collected and edited about 300 B.C.E. The *Tao Te Ching* is believed to be the work of Lao Tzu (sixth century B.C.E.), about whom little is known. It is a profound philosophic and poetic exposition of both a theory of statecraft and a way of spiritual life.

Traditionally, both in China and in the West, a sharp contrast has often been drawn between Taoism and Confucianism. Whereas the Confucians stressed the social character of persons, the need for political and social hierarchy, cultural refinement, and ritual, the Taoists questioned all authority and conventional wisdom and emphasized the freedom, equality, and naturalness of individual human beings. Much recent scholarship has come to see closer affinities between Confucianism and Taoism than this traditional view indicates, however, particularly with regard to the political concerns of Taoism. Although considerable differences do obtain between Confucianism and Taoism, the latter is also clearly concerned with the moral dimensions of statecraft and especially with the ethical qualities appropriate to rulership, qualities that bear interesting comparison with those argued for by Plato.

As made evident by the following brief selections from the *Tao Te Ching*, which set forth the nature of sagehood, the ideals of simplicity and spiritual passivity and adhering to the natural "way" (the *Tao* of the world) Taoist writings are often highly elusive and paradoxical in expression. This is nowhere more evident than in its teaching regarding "no action" or *wu wei*. The *Tao Te Ching* seems to suggest that the person who possesses genuine power (*te*) need never exercise coercion as such but by virtue of being an authoritative sage, quite naturally brings harmony to society.

LAO TZU

The Natural Way

Not to honour men of worth will keep the people from contention; not to value goods which are hard to come by will keep them from theft; not to display what is desirable will keep them from being unsettled of mind.

Therefore in governing the people, the sage empties their minds but fills their bellies, weakens their wills but strengthens their bones. He always keeps them innocent of knowledge and free from desire, and ensures that the clever never dare to act.

Do that which consists in taking no action, and order will prevail. . . .

The best of all rulers is but a shadowy presence to his subjects.
> Next comes the ruler they love and praise;
> Next comes one they fear;
> Next comes one with whom they take liberties.

When there is not enough faith, there is lack of good faith.
> Hesitant, he does not utter words lightly.
> When his task is accomplished and his work done
> The people all say, "It happened to us naturally". . . .

Govern the state by being straightforward; wage war by being crafty; but win the empire by not being meddlesome.
How do I know that it is like that? By means of this.
> The more taboos there are in the empire
> The poorer the people;
> The more sharpened tools the people have
> The more benighted the state;
> The more skills the people have
> The further novelties multiply;
> The better known the laws and edicts
> The more thieves and robbers there are.

Hence the sage says,
> I take no action and the people are transformed of themselves;
> I prefer stillness and the people are rectified of themselves;
> I am not meddlesome and the people prosper of themselves;
> I am free from desire and the people of themselves become simple like the uncarved block. . . .

> In ruling the people and in serving heaven it is best for a ruler to be sparing.
> It is because he is sparing
> That he may be said to follow the way from the start;

Following the way from the start he may be said to accumulate an abundance
 of virtue;
Accumulating an abundance of virtue there is nothing he cannot overcome;
When there is nothing he cannot overcome, no one knows his limit;
When no one knows his limit
He can possess a state;
When he possesses the mother of a state
He can then endure.
This is called the way of deep roots and firm stems by which one lives to see
 many days. . . .

A large state is the lower reaches of a river—
The place where all the streams of the world unite.
In the union of the world,
The female always gets the better of the male by stillness.
Being still, she takes the lower position.
Hence the large state, by taking the lower position, annexes the small state;
The small state, by taking the lower position, affiliates itself to the large state.
Thus the one, by taking the lower position, annexes;
The other, by taking the lower position, is annexed.
All that the large state wants is to take the other under its wing;
All that the small state wants is to have its services accepted by the other.
If each of the two wants to find its proper place,
It is meet that the large should take the lower position. . . .

Of old those who excelled in the pursuit of the way did not use it to enlighten the
people but to hoodwink them. The reason why the people are difficult to govern is
that they are too clever.
Hence to rule a state by cleverness
Will be to the detriment of the state;
Not to rule a state by cleverness
Will be a boon to the state.
These two are models.
Always to know the models
Is known as mysterious virtue.
Mysterious virtue is profound and far-reaching,
But when things turn back it turns back with them.
Only then is complete conformity realized. . . .

The people are hungry:
It is because those in authority eat up too much in taxes
That the people are hungry.
The people are difficult to govern:
It is because those in authority are too fond of action
That the people are difficult to govern.
The people treat death lightly:

It is because the people set too much store by life
That they treat death lightly.
It is just because one has no use for life that one is wiser than the man who values life. . . .

In the world there is nothing more submissive and weak than water. Yet for attacking that which is hard and strong nothing can surpass it. This is because there is nothing that can take its place.

That the weak overcomes the strong,
And the submissive overcomes the hard,
Everyone in the world knows yet no one can put this knowledge into practice.
Therefore the sage says,

One who takes on himself the humiliation of the state
Is called a ruler worthy of offering sacrifices to the gods of earth and millet;
One who takes on himself the calamity of the state
Is called a king worthy of dominion over the entire empire.
Straightforward words
Seem paradoxical. . . .

Reduce the size and population of the state. Ensure that even though the people have tools of war for a troop or a battalion they will not use them; and also that they will be reluctant to move to distant places because they look on death as no light matter.

Even when they have ships and carts, they will have no use for them; and even when they have armour and weapons, they will have no occasion to make a show of them.

Bring it about that the people will return to the use of the knotted rope,

Will find relish in their food
And beauty in their clothes,
Will be content in their abode
And happy in the way they live.
Though adjoining states are within sight of one another, and the sound of dogs barking and cocks crowing in one state can be heard in another, yet the people of one state will grow old and die without having had any dealings with those of another.

Kropotkin

Peter Alekseievitch Kropotkin (1842–1921) was a Russian aristocrat who became a revolutionary anarchist. Believing in the intrinsic goodness of humanity, he claimed that a person's natural inclination to aid and cooperate with others rendered all forms of government superfluous. Kropotkin based his concept of mutual aid on the theory of evolution formulated by Darwin, arguing that the abolition of all governmental power is the natural end of the evolutionary process. Kropotkin's works include Memoirs of a Revolutionist *and* Mutual Aid.

Taoism is sometimes, probably erroneously, characterized as being anarchistic; the work of Kropotkin is always, and rightfully, so described. Anarchism has taken several forms throughout history, but anarchists generally share a strong aversion to authoritarianism in all dimensions of social experience, especially governmental, and strive to find ways in which human beings can cooperate with each other free from any kind of coercion. Some anarchists have advocated violent revolutionary action to achieve the abolition of all governmental authority; others have urged some kind of nonviolent passive resistance; still others have simply gone about the business of trying to form and sustain small communities of like-minded persons. Kropotkin was involved in revolutionary activity and during czarist rule suffered exile from his native Russia as a result.

In the following selection from his writings, the argument is made against the validity of any imposed law and form of punishment. What, one may ask, does his argument purport to tell us about the nature of humankind and the kind of education that is necessary for social harmony?

An Anarchist's View of Law and Authority

In existing States a fresh law is looked upon as a remedy for evil. Instead of themselves altering what is bad, people begin by demanding a *law* to alter it. If the road between two villages is impassable, the peasant says:—"There should be a law about parish roads." If a park-keeper takes advantage of the want of spirit in those who fol-

Reprinted from *Kropotkin's Revolutionary Pamphlets*, ed. Roger N. Baldwin. Vanguard Press, New York, 1927. Originally published London, 1886.

low him with servile observance and insults one of them, the insulted man says, "There should be a law to enjoin more politeness upon park-keepers." If there is stagnation in agriculture or commerce, the husbandman, cattle-breeder, or corn speculator argues, "It is protective legislation that we require." Down to the old clothesman there is not one who does not demand a law to protect his own little trade. If the employer lowers wages or increases the hours of labor, the politician in embryo exclaims, "We must have a law to put all that to rights." In short, a law everywhere and for everything! A law about fashions, a law about mad dogs, a law about virtue, a law to put a stop to all the vices and all the evils which result from human indolence and cowardice.

We are so perverted by an education which from infancy seeks to kill in us the spirit of revolt, and to develop that of submission to authority; we are so perverted by this existence under the ferrule of a law, which regulates every event in life—our birth, our education, our development, our love, our friendship—that, if this state of things continues, we shall lose all initiative, all habit of thinking for ourselves. Our society seems no longer able to understand that it is possible to exist otherwise than under the reign of law, elaborated by a representative government and administered by a handful of rulers. And even when it has gone so far as to emancipate itself from the thralldom, its first care has been to reconstitute it immediately. "The Year I of Liberty" has never lasted more than a day, for after proclaiming it men put themselves the very next morning under the yoke of law and authority.

Indeed, for some thousands of years, those who govern us have done nothing but ring the changes upon "Respect for law, obedience to authority." This is the moral atmosphere in which parents bring up their children, and school only serves to confirm the impression. Cleverly assorted scraps of spurious science are inculcated upon the children to prove necessity of law; obedience to the law is made a religion; moral goodness and the law of the masters are fused into one and the same divinity. The historical hero of the schoolroom is the man who obeys the law, and defends it against rebels. . . .

The confused mass of rules of conduct called law, which has been bequeathed to us by slavery, serfdom, feudalism, and royalty, has taken the place of those stone monsters, before whom human victims used to be immolated, and whom slavish savages dared not even touch lest they should be slain by the thunderbolts of heaven.

This new worship has been established with especial success since the rise to supreme power of the middle class—since the great French Revolution. Under the ancient régime, men spoke little of laws; unless, indeed, it were, with Montesquieu, Rousseau and Voltaire, to oppose them to royal caprice. Obedience to the good pleasure of the king and his lackeys was compulsory on pain of hanging or imprisonment. But during and after the revolutions, when the lawyers rose to power, they did their best to strengthen the principle upon which their ascendancy depended. The middle class at once accepted it as a dyke to dam up the popular torrent. The priestly crew hastened to sanctify it, to save their bark from foundering amid the breakers. Finally the people received it as an improvement upon the arbitrary authority and violence of the past.

To understand this, we must transport ourselves in imagination into the eighteenth century. Our hearts must have ached at the story of the atrocities committed by the all-powerful nobles of that time upon the men and women of the people before we can understand what must have been the magic influence upon the peasant's mind of the words, "Equality before the law, obedience to the law without distinction of birth or fortune." He who until then had been treated more cruelly than a beast, he who had never had any rights, he who had never obtained justice against the most revolting actions on the part of a noble, unless in revenge he killed him and was hanged—he saw himself recognized by this maxim, at least in theory, at least with regard to his personal rights, as the equal of his lord. Whatever this law might be, it promised to affect lord and peasant alike; it proclaimed the equality of rich and poor before the judge. The promise was a lie, and today we know it; but at that period it was an advance, a homage to justice, as hypocrisy is a homage rendered to truth. This is the reason that when the saviors of the menaced middle class (the Robespierres and the Dantons) took their stand upon the writings of the Rousseaus and the Voltaires, and proclaimed "respect for law, the same for every man," the people accepted the compromise; for their revolutionary impetus had already spent its force in the contest with a foe whose ranks drew closer day by day; they bowed their neck beneath the yoke of law to save themselves from the arbitrary power of their lords.

The middle class has ever since continued to make the most of this maxim, which with another principle, that of representative government, sums up the whole philosophy of the bourgeois age, the nineteenth century. It has preached this doctrine in its schools, it has propagated it in its writings, it has moulded its art and science to the same purpose, it has thrust its beliefs into every hole and corner—like a pious Englishwoman, who slips tracts under the door—and it has done all this so successfully that today we behold the issue in the detestable fact that men who long for freedom begin the attempt to obtain it by entreating their masters to be kind enough to protect them by modifying the laws which these masters themselves have created!

But times and tempers are changed. Rebels are everywhere to be found who no longer wish to obey the law without knowing whence it comes, what are its uses, and whither arises the obligation to submit to it, and the reverence with which it is encompassed. The rebels of our day are criticizing the very foundations of society which have hitherto been held sacred, and first and foremost amongst them that fetish, law.

The critics analyze the sources of law, and find there either a god, product of the terrors of the savage, and stupid, paltry and malicious as the priests who vouch for its supernatural origin, or else, bloodshed, conquest by fire and sword. They study the characteristics of law, and instead of perpetual growth corresponding to that of the human race, they find its distinctive trait to be immobility, a tendency to crystallize what should be modified and developed day by day. They ask how law has been maintained, and in its service they see the atrocities of Byzantinism, the cruelties of the Inquisition, the tortures of the middle ages, living flesh torn by the lash of the executioner, chains, clubs, axes, the gloomy dungeons of prisons, agony, curses and tears. In our own days they see, as before, the axe, the cord, the rifle, the prison; on the one hand, the brutalized prisoner, reduced to the condition of a caged beast by the debasement of his whole moral being, and on the other, the judge, stripped of every feeling which does honor to human nature, living like a visionary in a world of legal fictions, revelling in the infliction of imprisonment and death, without even suspecting, in the cold malignity of his madness, the abyss of degradation into which he has himself fallen before the eyes of those whom he condemns.

They see a race of law-makers legislating without knowing what their laws are about; today voting a law on the sanitation of towns, without the faintest notion of hygiene, tomorrow making regulations for the armament of troops, without so much as understanding a gun; making laws about teaching and education without ever having given a lesson of any sort, or even an honest education to their own children; legislating at random in all directions, but never forgetting the penalties to be meted out to ragamuffins, the prison and the galleys, which are to be the portion of men a thousand times less immoral than these legislators themselves.

Finally, they see the jailer on the way to lose all human feeling, the detective trained as a blood-hound, the police spy despising himself; "informing," metamorphosed into a virtue; corruption, erected into a system; all the vices, all the evil qualities of mankind countenanced and cultivated to insure the triumph of law.

All this we see, and, therefore, instead of inanely repeating the old formula, "Respect the law," we say, "Despise law and all its attributes!" In place of the cowardly phrase, "Obey the law," our cry is "Revolt against all laws!"

Only compare the misdeeds accomplished in the name of each law with the good it has been able to effect, and weigh carefully both good and evil, and you will see if we are right.

Han Fei Tzu

Han Fei Tzu (280–233 B.C.E.), prince of the state of Han, is regarded as the culmi-nating representative of the school of Chinese thought known as Legalism, which was concerned primarily with the nature of political power, the execution of statecraft, and the application of law. Han Fei Tzu was delegated by his state to become an advisor to the king of a powerful neighboring state, Ch'in. He was initially quite successful in his appointed role, but due to machinations against him by a jealous minister, Han Fei Tzu was put to death in prison.

The direct antithesis to the kind of anarchism propounded by Kropotkin may be seen in the school of Legalism. Within the Chinese context itself, it stands in opposition mainly to Confucianism, which, as we have seen, advocates the idea that humankind is essen-tially good by virtue of persons being endowed naturally with capacities for moral sen-sitivity and the ability to achieve virtue. A well-regulated society thus is one in which the ruler in particular embodies virtue to the highest extent. Han Fei Tzu holds otherwise, believing that people are disposed toward selfishness and thus need to be closely reg-ulated in order to preserve the social order. Laws must be set forth clearly and applied equally. The rulers must be forceful and powerful and enact both punishments and re-wards to guarantee the "straightening" of the people.

Legalism

The severe household has no fierce slaves, but it is the affectionate mother who has spoiled sons. From this I know that awe-inspiring power can prohibit violence and that virtue and kindness are insufficient to end disorder. When the sage rules the state, he does not depend on people to do good for him, but utilizes their inability to do wrong. If he depends on people to do good for him, we cannot even count ten within the state, but if he utilizes the people's inability to do wrong, the whole coun-try may be regulated. A ruler makes use of the majority and neglects the minority, and so he does not devote himself to virtue but to law.

From *Han Fei Tzu* in Chan, Wing-tsit, comp. and trans., *A Source Book in Chinese Philosophy*. Copyright © 1963 renewed © Princeton University Press. Reprinted by permission of Princeton University Press.

If we had to depend on an arrow being absolutely straight by nature, there would be no arrow in a hundred generations. If we had to depend on a piece of wood being perfectly round by nature, there would not be any wheel in a thousand generations. There is not one naturally straight arrow or naturally round piece of wood in a hundred generations, and yet in every generation people ride carriages and shoot birds. Why? Because of the application of the methods of straightening and bending. Although there is a naturally straight arrow or a naturally round piece of wood [once in a hundred generations] which does not depend on any straightening or bending, the skilled workman does not value it. Why? Because it is not just one person who wishes to ride and not just one shot that the archer wishes to shoot. Similarly, the enlightened ruler does not value people who are naturally good and who do not depend on reward and punishment. Why? Because the laws of the state must not be neglected and government is not for only one man. . . .

The important thing for the ruler is either laws or statecraft. A law is that which is enacted into the statute books, kept in government offices, and proclaimed to the people. Statecraft is that which is harbored in the ruler's own mind so as to fit all situations and control all ministers. Therefore for law there is nothing better than publicity, whereas in statecraft, secrecy is desired. . . .

The means by which the enlightened ruler controls his ministers are none other than the two handles. The two handles are punishment and kindness *(te)*. What do we mean by punishment and kindness? To execute is called punishment and to offer congratulations or rewards is called kindness. Ministers are afraid of execution and punishment but look upon congratulations and rewards as advantages. Therefore, if a ruler himself applies punishment and kindness, all ministers will fear his power and turn to the advantages. As to treacherous ministers, they are different. They would get [the handle of punishment] from the ruler [through flattery and so forth] and punish those whom they hate and get [the handle of kindness] from the ruler and reward those whom they love. If the ruler does not see to it that the power of reward and punishment proceeds from himself but instead leaves it to his ministers to apply reward and punishment, then everyone in the state will fear the ministers and slight the ruler, turn to them to get away from the ruler. This is the trouble of the ruler who loses the handles of punishment and kindness.

For the tiger is able to subdue the dog because of its claws and fangs. If the tiger abandons its claws and fangs and lets the dog use them, it will be subdued by the dog. Similarly, the ruler controls his ministers through punishment and kindness. If the ruler abandons his punishment and kindness and lets his ministers use them, he will be controlled by the ministers. . . .

Whenever a ruler wants to suppress treachery, he must examine the correspondence between actuality and names. Actuality and names refer to the ministers' words and deeds. When a minister presents his words, the ruler assigns him a task in accordance with his words and demands accomplishments specifically from that work. If the results correspond to the task and the task to the words, he should be rewarded. If the accomplishments do not correspond to the task or the task not to the words, he will be punished. If the minister's words are big but his accomplishment is small, he will be punished. The punishment is not for the small accomplishment but for the fact that the accomplishment does not correspond to the words. If the minister's words are small and his accomplishments are big, he will also be punished. It is not that the ruler is not pleased with the big accomplishments but he considers the failure of the big accomplishments to correspond to the words worse than the big accomplishments themselves. Therefore he is to be punished. . . .

Moreover, people are submissive to power and few of them can be influenced by the doctrines of righteousness. Confucius was a sage known throughout the empire. He cultivated his own character and elucidated his doctrines and traveled extensively within the four seas (China). People within the four seas loved his doctrine of humanity and praised his doctrine of righteousness. And yet only seventy people became his devoted pupils. The reason is that few people value humanity and it is difficult to practice righteousness. That was why in the wide, wide world there were only seventy who became his devoted pupils and only one (Confucius) who could practice humanity and righteousness. . . .

What are mutually incompatible should not exist together. To reward those who kill their enemies in battle and at the same time to exalt acts of kindness and benevolence, to bestow honors and offices to those who capture cities and at the same time to believe in the doctrine of universal love, to sharpen weapons and strengthen troops as preparation for emergency and at the same time to praise the style of flowing robes and ornamental girdles (worn by the literati), to enrich the state through agriculture and to depend on the army to resist the enemy and at the same time highly to value men of letters, to neglect the people who respect the ruler and are afraid of the law and at the same time to support men like knights-errant and assassins—how can an orderly and strong state result from such self-contradictory acts? The state supports scholars and knights-errant in time of peace, but when emergency arises it has to use soldiers. Thus those who have been benefited by the government cannot be used by it and those used by it have not been benefited. This is the reason why those who serve take their work lightly and the number of traveling scholars increases every day. This is the reason why the world has become disorderly.

What is now called a worthy person is one who practices correctness and faithfulness. What is called wisdom consists of subtle and unfathomable doctrines. Such subtle and unfathomable doctrines are difficult even for men of highest intelligence to understand. If what men of highest intelligence find to be difficult to understand is used to become laws for the people, the people will find them impossible to understand. When you have not even coarse rice to eat, don't look for refined grains and meat. When you don't even have rags to wear, don't wait for fancy embroidery. For in governing a state, when urgent matters have not been accomplished, efforts should not be directed toward things that can wait. If in governmental measures one neglects ordinary affairs of the people and what even the simple folks can understand, but admires the doctrines of the highest wisdom, that would be contrary to the way of orderly government. Therefore subtle and unfathomable doctrines are no business of the people. . . . Therefore the way of the enlightened ruler is to unify all laws but not to seek for wise men and firmly to adhere to statecraft but not to admire faithful persons. Thus laws will never fail and no officials will ever commit treachery or deception.

In regard to the words [of traveling scholars], rulers of today like their arguments but do not find out if they correspond to facts. In regard to the application of these words to practice, they praise their fame but do not demand accomplishment. Therefore there are many in the world whose talks are devoted to argumentation and who are not thorough when it comes to practical utility. That is why even when the hall of the ruler is full of scholars who praise ancient kings and preach humanity and righteousness, the government is still not free from disorder. In their deeds scholars struggle for eminence but there is nothing in them that is suitable for real accomplishment. Therefore wise scholars withdraw to caves and decline the offering of positions. Inevitably armies become weak and the government becomes disorderly. What is the reason? The reason is that what the people praise and what the ruler respects are those techniques that bring disorder to the state. . . .

Therefore in the state of the enlightened ruler, there is no literature of books and records but the laws serve as the teaching. There are no sayings of ancient kings but the officials act as teachers. And there are no rash acts of the assassin; instead, courage will be demonstrated by those who decapitate the enemy [in battle]. Consequently, among the people within the borders of the state, whoever talks must follow the law, whoever acts must aim at accomplishment, and whoever shows courage must do so entirely in the army. Thus the state will be rich when at peace and the army will be strong when things happen. These are the materials for the true king. . . .

Locke

John Locke (1632–1704) was the father of British empiricism—which claimed that all human knowledge derives from sense experience rather than from reason as such—in addition to being an important political theorist. He advocated a constitutional form of government, rejecting the idea of the divine right of kings, which was the received view of his time. Educated at Oxford, he obtained a degree in medicine and became a physician. Locke also joined various political groups thought to be highly radical for espousing constitutionalism, and as a result he spent long periods of time on the Continent. After the Whig Revolution in 1688, Locke returned to England. His key works were his monumental An Essay on Human Understanding *and his* Two Treatises on Civil Government, *both of which were published in 1690.*

Locke is often credited with establishing many of the principles that have informed the kind of liberal democracy we are familiar with today, especially regarding the rights of individual citizens to their property and the pursuit of their own aims and goals with minimum interference from the state. In his treatises on government, Locke traces the origins of political societies with reference to a notion that became increasingly popular in political theory, that of a "state of nature" wherein, prior to the formation of societies, people were free from all constraint. People unite into commonwealths and place themselves under governmental control in order to be secure from the power struggles that would inevitably ensue in the state of nature, especially with respect to their property, which is the fruit of their own labor. In short, we consent to become members of a social order and must come to some agreement regarding the standards of behavior appropriate to citizenship and the extent of power to be granted to elected officials. These issues seem to arise continually in every democratic society, especially in times of rapidly changing economic circumstances and international conflicts and tensions.

The Origins and Nature of Political Societies

God, who hath given the world to men in common, hath also given them reason to make use of it to the best advantage of life and convenience. The earth and all that is therein is given to men for the support and comfort of their being. And though all the fruits it naturally produces, and beasts it feeds, belong to mankind in common, as they are produced by the spontaneous hand of Nature, and nobody has originally a private dominion exclusive of the rest of mankind in any of them, as they are thus in their natural state, yet being given for the use of men, there must of necessity be a means to appropriate them some way or other before they can be of any use, or at all beneficial, to any particular men. The fruit or venison which nourishes the wild Indian, who knows no enclosure, and is still a tenant in common, must be his, and so his—i.e., a part of him, that another can no longer have any right to it before it can do him any good for the support of his life.

Though the earth and all inferior creatures be common to all men, yet every man has a "property" in his own "person." This nobody has any right to but himself. The "labor" of his body and the "work" of his hands, we may say, are properly his. Whatsoever, then, he removes out of the state that Nature hath provided and left it in, he hath mixed his labor with it, and joined to it something that is his own, and thereby makes it his property. It being by him removed from the common state Nature placed it in, it hath by this labor something annexed to it that excludes the common right of other men. For this "labor" being the unquestionable property of the laborer, no man but he can have a right to what that is once joined to, at least where there is enough, and as good left in common for others.

He that is nourished by the acorns he picked up under an oak, or the apples he gathered from the trees in the wood, has certainly appropriated them to himself. Nobody can deny but the nourishment is his. I ask, then, when did they begin to be his? when he digested? or when he ate? or when he boiled? or when he brought them home? or when he picked them up? And it is plain, if the first gathering made them not his, nothing else could. That labor put a distinction between them and common. That added something to them more than Nature, the common mother of all, had done, and so they became his private right. And will anyone say he had no right to those acorns or apples he thus appropriated because he had not the consent of all mankind to make them his? Was it a robbery thus to assume to himself what belonged to all in common? If such a consent as that was necessary, man had starved, notwithstanding the plenty God had given him. We see in commons, which remain so by compact, that it is the taking any part of what is common, and removing it out of the state Nature leaves it in, which begins the property, without which the common is of no use. And the taking of this or that part does not depend on the express consent of all the commoners. Thus, the grass my horse has bit, the turfs my servant has cut, and the ore I have digged in any place, where I have a right to them

From *Second Treatise on Civil Government* by John Locke (1690).

John Locke. The New York Public
Library Picture Collection.

in common with others, become my property without the assignation or consent of
anybody. The labor that was mine, removing them out of that common state they
were in, hath fixed my property in them. . . .

. . . When any number of men have, by the consent of every individual, made a community, they have thereby made that community one body, with a power to act as
one body, which is only by the will and determination of the majority. For that which
acts any community, being only the consent of the individuals of it, and it being one
body, must move one way, it is necessary the body should move that way whither the
greater force carries it, which is the consent of the majority, or else it is impossible it
should act or continue one body, one community, which the consent of every individual that united into it agreed that it should; and so everyone is bound by that
consent to be concluded by the majority. And therefore we see that in assemblies
empowered to act by positive laws where no number is set by that positive law which
empowers them, the act of the majority passes for the act of the whole, and of course
determines as having, by the law of Nature and reason, the power of the whole.

And thus every man, by consenting with others to make one body politic under
one government, puts himself under an obligation to everyone of that society to
submit to the determination of the majority, and to be concluded by it; or else this
original compact, whereby he with others incorporates into one society, would sig-

nify nothing, and be no compact if he be left free and under no other ties than he was in before in the state of Nature. For what appearance would there be of any compact? What new engagement if he were no farther tied by any decrees of the society than he himself thought fit and did actually consent to? This would be still as great a liberty as he himself had before his compact, or anyone else in the state of Nature, who may submit himself and consent to any acts of it if he thinks fit.

Every man being, as has been showed, naturally free, and nothing being able to put him into subjection to any earthly power, but only his own consent, it is to be considered what shall be understood to be a sufficient declaration of a man's consent to make him subject to the laws of any government. There is a common distinction of an express and a tacit consent, which will concern our present case. Nobody doubts but an express consent of any man, entering into any society, makes him a perfect member of that society, a subject of that government. The difficulty is, what ought to be looked upon as a tacit consent, and how far it binds—i.e., how far anyone shall be looked on to have consented, and thereby submitted to any government, where he has made no expressions of it at all. And to this I say, that every man that hath any possession or enjoyment of any part of the dominions of any government doth hereby give his tacit consent, and is as far forth obliged to obedience to the laws of that government, during such enjoyment, as anyone under it, whether this his possession be of land to him and his heirs forever, or a lodging only for a week; or whether it be barely traveling freely on the highway; and, in effect, it reaches as far as the very being of anyone within the territories of that government.

If man in the state of Nature be so free as has been said, if he be absolute lord of his own person and possessions, equal to the greatest and subject to nobody, why will he part with his freedom, this empire, and subject himself to the dominion and control of any other power? To which it is obvious to answer, that though in the state of Nature he has such a right, yet the enjoyment of it is very uncertain and constantly exposed to the invasion of others; for all being kings as much as he, every man his equal, and the greater part no strict observers of equity and justice, the enjoyment of the property he has in this state is very unsafe, very insecure. This makes him willing to quit this condition which, however free, is full of fears and continual dangers; and it is not without reason that he seeks out and is willing to join in society with others who are already united, or have a mind to unite for the mutual preservation of their lives, liberties and estates, which I call by the general name—property.

The great and chief end, therefore, of men uniting into commonwealths, and putting themselves under government, is the preservation of their property; to which in the state of Nature there are many things wanting.

Firstly, there wants an established, settled, known law, received and allowed by common consent to be the standard of right and wrong, and the common measure to decide all controversies between them. For though the law of Nature be plain and intelligible to all rational creatures, yet men, being biased by their interest, as well as ignorant for want of study of it, are not apt to allow of it as a law binding to them in the application of it to their particular cases.

Secondly, in the state of Nature there wants a known and indifferent judge, with authority to determine all differences according to the established law. For everyone in that state being both judge and executioner of the law of Nature, men being partial to themselves, passion and revenge is [*sic*] very apt to carry them too far, and with too much heat in their own cases, as well as negligence and unconcernedness, make them too remiss in other men's.

Thirdly, in the state of Nature there often wants power to back and support the sentence when right, and to give it due execution. They who by any injustice offended will seldom fail where they are able by force to make good their injustice. Such resistance many times makes the punishment dangerous, and frequently destructive to those who attempt it.

Thus mankind, notwithstanding all the privileges of the state of Nature, being but in an ill condition while they remain in it are quickly driven into society. Hence it comes to pass, that we seldom find any number of men live any time together in this state. The inconveniences that they are therein exposed to by the irregular and uncertain exercise of the power every man has of punishing the transgressions of others, make them take sanctuary under the established laws of government, and therein seek the preservation of their property. It is this makes them so willingly give up everyone his single power of punishing to be exercised by such alone as shall be appointed to it amongst them, and by such rules as the community, or those authorized by them to that purpose, shall agree on. And in this we have the original right and rise of both the legislative and executive power as well as of the governments and societies themselves. . . .

But though men when they enter into society give up the equality, liberty, and executive power they had in the state of Nature into the hands of the society, to be so far disposed of by the legislative as the good of the society shall require, yet it being only with an intention in everyone the better to preserve himself, his liberty and property (for no rational creature can be supposed to change his condition with an intention to be worse), the power of the society or legislative constituted by them can never be supposed to extend farther than the common good, but is obliged to secure everyone's property by providing against those three defects above mentioned that made the state of Nature so unsafe and uneasy. And so, whoever has the legislative or supreme power of any commonwealth, is bound to govern by established standing laws, promulgated and known to the people, and not by extemporary decrees, by indifferent and upright judges, who are to decide controversies by those laws; and to employ the force of the community at home only in the execution of such laws, or abroad to prevent or redress foreign injuries and secure the community from inroads and invasion. And all this to be directed to no other end but the peace, safety, and public good of the people. . . .

The great end of men's entering into society being the enjoyment of their properties in peace and safety, and the great instrument and means of that being the laws established in that society, the first and fundamental positive law of all commonwealths is the establishing of the legislative power, as the first and fundamental natural law which is to govern even the legislative. Itself is the preservation of the society and (as far as will consist with the public good) of every person in it. This legislative is not only the supreme power of the commonwealth, but sacred and unalterable in the hands where the community have once placed it. Nor can any edict of anybody else, in what form soever conceived, or by what power soever backed, have the force and obligation of a law which has not its sanction from that legislative which the public has chosen and appointed; for without this the law could not have that which is absolutely necessary to its being a law, the consent of the society, over whom nobody can have a power to make laws but by their own consent and by authority received from them; and therefore all the obedience, which by the most solemn ties anyone can be obliged to pay, ultimately terminates in this supreme power, and is directed by those laws which it enacts. . . .

Though the legislative, whether placed in one or more, whether it be always in being or only by intervals, though it be the supreme power in every commonwealth, yet, first, it is not, nor can possibly be, absolutely arbitrary over the lives and fortunes of the people. For it being but the joint power of every member of the society given up to that person or assembly which is legislator, it can be no more than those persons had in a state of Nature before they entered into society, and gave it up to the community. For nobody can transfer to another more power than he has in himself, and nobody has an absolute arbitrary power over himself, or over any other, to destroy his own life, or take away the life or property of another. . . .

The reason why men enter into society is the preservation of their property; and the end while they choose and authorize a legislative is that there may be laws made, and rules set, as guards and fences to the properties of all the society, to limit the power and moderate the dominion of every part and member of the society. For since it can never be supposed to be the will of the society that the legislative should have a power to destroy that which everyone designs to secure by entering into society, and for which the people submitted themselves to legislators of their own making: whenever the legislators endeavor to take away and destroy the property of the people, or to reduce them to slavery under arbitrary power, they put themselves into a state of war with the people, who are thereupon absolved from any farther obedience, and are left to the common refuge which God hath provided for all men against force and violence. Whensoever, therefore, the legislative shall transgress this fundamental rule of society, and either by ambition, fear, folly, or corruption, endeavor to grasp themselves, or put into the hands of any other, an absolute power over the lives, liberties, and estates of the people, by this breach of trust they forfeit the power the people had put into their hands for quite contrary ends, and it devolves to the people, who have a right to resume their original liberty, and by the establishment of a new legislative (such as they shall think fit), provide for their own safety and security, which is the end for which they are in society.

Mill

In his well-known and ever-popular *On Liberty* (1859), John Stuart Mill extends his utilitarianism with a ringing endorsement of the central value of political liberty for a democratic society concerned for the welfare of the greatest number of people. According to Mill, the only justification for interfering with the liberty of others to carry out their intended action is self-protection or the prevention of harm to others. A free society is one that guarantees freedom of speech and endorses the values attendant upon an open exchange of ideas, even when these ideas appear false and contrary to received opinion. Mill extols individuality and diversity and celebrates with as little qualification as possible the good of human freedom.

The Good of Human Freedom

CHAPTER 1   INTRODUCTORY

The object of this Essay is to assert one very simple principle, as entitled to govern absolutely the dealings of society with the individual in the way of compulsion and control, whether the means used be physical force in the form of legal penalties or the moral coercion of public opinion. That principle is, that the sole end for which mankind are warranted, individually or collectively, in interfering with the liberty of action of any of their number, is self-protection. That the only purpose for which power can be rightfully exercised over any member of a civilized community, against his will, is to prevent harm to others. His own good, either physical or moral, is not a sufficient warrant. He cannot rightfully be compelled to do or forbear because it will be better for him to do so, because it will make him happier, because, in the opinions of others, to do so would be wise, or even right. There are good reasons for remonstrating with him, or reasoning with him, or persuading him, or entreating him, but not for compelling him, or visiting him with any evil, in case he do otherwise. To justify that, the conduct from which it is desired to deter him must be cal-

---

From *On Liberty* by John Stuart Mill (London, 1859).

culated to produce evil to some one else. The only part of the conduct of any one, for which he is amenable to society, is that which concerns others. In the part which merely concerns himself, his independence is, of right, absolute. Over himself, over his own body and mind, the individual is sovereign. . . .

It is proper to state that I forgo any advantage which could be derived to my argument from the idea of abstract right, as a thing independent of utility. I regard utility as the ultimate appeal on all ethical questions; but it must be utility in the largest sense, grounded on the permanent interests of man as a progressive being. Those interests, I contend, authorize the subjection of individual spontaneity to external control, only in respect to those actions of each, which concern the interest of other people. If any one does an act hurtful to others, there is a *prima facie* case for punishing him, by law, or, where legal penalties are not safely applicable, by general disapprobation. There are also many positive acts for the benefit of others, which he may rightfully be compelled to perform; such as, to give evidence in a court of justice; to bear his fair share in the common defence, or in any other joint work necessary to the interest of the society of which he enjoys the protection; and to perform certain acts of individual beneficence, such as saving a fellow creature's life, or interposing to protect the defenceless against ill-usage, things which whenever it is obviously a man's duty to do, he may rightfully be made responsible to society for not doing. A person may cause evil to others not only by his actions but by his inaction, and in either case he is justly accountable to them for the injury. The latter case, it is true, requires a much more cautious exercise of compulsion than the former. To make any one answerable for doing evil to others, is the rule; to make him answerable for not preventing evil, is comparatively speaking, the exception. Yet there are many cases clear enough and grave enough to justify that exception. In all things which regard the external relations of the individual, he is *de jure* amenable to those whose interests are concerned, and if need be, to society as their protector. There are often good reasons for not holding him to the responsibility; but these reasons must arise from the special expediencies of the case: either because it is a kind of case in which he is on the whole likely to act better, when left to his own discretion, than when controlled in any way in which society have it in their power to control him, or because the attempt to exercise control would produce other evils, greater than those which it would prevent. When such reasons as these preclude the enforcement of responsibility, the conscience of the agent himself should step into the vacant judgment-seat, and protect those interests of others which have no external protection; judging himself all the more rigidly, because the case does not admit of his being made accountable to the judgment of his fellow-creatures.

But there is a sphere of action in which society, as distinguished from the individual, has, if any, only an indirect interest; comprehending all that portion of a person's life and conduct which affects only himself, or, if it also affects others, only with their free, voluntary, and undeceived consent and participation. When I say only himself, I mean directly, and in the first instance: for whatever affects himself, may affect others *through* himself; and the objection which may be grounded on this contingency, will receive consideration in the sequel. This, is the appropriate region of human liberty. It comprises, first, the inward domain of consciousness, demanding liberty of conscience, in the most comprehensive sense; liberty of thought and feeling; absolute freedom of opinion and sentiment on all subjects, practical or speculative, scientific, moral, or theological. The liberty of expressing and publishing opinions may seem to fall under a different principle, since it belongs to that part of the conduct of an individual which concerns other people; but, being almost of as much importance as the liberty of thought itself, and resting in great part on the same reasons, is practically inseparable from it. Secondly, the principle requires liberty of tastes and pursuits; of framing the plan of our life to suit our own character; of doing as we like, subject to such consequences as may follow; without impediment from our fellow-creatures, so long as what we do does not harm them, even though they should think our conduct foolish, perverse, or wrong. Thirdly, from this liberty of each individual, follows the liberty, within the same limits, of combination among individuals; freedom to unite, for any purpose not involving harm to others: the persons combining being supposed to be of full age, and not forced or deceived.

No society in which these liberties are not, on the whole, respected, is free, whatever may be its form of government; and none is completely free in which they do not exist absolute and unqualified. The only freedom which deserves the name, is that of pursuing our own way, so long as we do not attempt to deprive others of theirs, or impede their efforts to obtain it. Each is the proper guardian of his own health, whether bodily, or mental and spiritual. Mankind are greater gainers by suffering each other to live as seems good to themselves, than by compelling each to live as seems good to the rest. . . .

CHAPTER 2   OF THE LIBERTY OF THOUGHT AND DISCUSSION

The time, it is to be hoped, is gone by when any defence would be necessary of the "liberty of the press" as one of the securities against corrupt or tyrannical government. No argument, we may suppose, can now be needed, against permitting a legislature or an executive, not identified in interest with the people, to prescribe opinions to them, and determine what doctrines or what arguments they shall be allowed to hear. This aspect of the question, besides, has been so often and so triumphantly enforced by preceding writers, that it needs not be specially insisted on in this place. Though the law of England, on the subject of the press, is as servile to this day as it was in the time of the Tudors, there is little danger of its being actually put in force against political discussion, except during some temporary panic, when fear of insurrection drives ministers and judges from their propriety; and, speaking generally, it is not, in constitutional countries, to be apprehended, that the government, whether completely responsible to the people or not, will often attempt to control the expression of opinion, except when in doing so it makes itself the organ of the general intolerance of the public. Let us suppose, therefore, that the government is entirely at one with the people, and never thinks of exerting any power of coercion unless in agreement with what it conceives to be their voice. But I deny the right of the people to exercise such coercion, either by themselves or by their government. The power itself is illegitimate. The best government has no more title to it than the worst. It is as noxious, or more noxious, when exerted in accordance with public opinion, than when in opposition to it. If all mankind minus one, were of one opinion, and only one person were of the contrary opinion, mankind would be no more justified in silencing that one person, than he, if he had the power, would be justified in silencing mankind. Were an opinion a personal possession of no value except to the owner; if to be obstructed in the enjoyment of it were simply a private injury, it would make some difference whether the injury was inflicted only on a few persons or on many. But the peculiar evil of silencing the expression of an opinion is, that it is robbing the human race; posterity as well as the existing generation; those who dissent from the opinion, still more than those who hold it. If the opinion is right, they are deprived of the opportunity of exchanging error for truth: if wrong, they lose, what is almost as great a benefit, the clearer perception and livelier impression of truth, produced by its collision with error. . . .

In order more fully to illustrate the mischief of denying a hearing to opinions because we, in our own judgment, have condemned them, it will be desirable to fix down the discussion to a concrete case; and I choose, by preference, the cases which are least favorable to me—in which the argument against freedom of opinion, both on the score of truth and on that of utility, is considered the strongest. Let the opinions impugned be the belief in a God and in a future state, or any of the commonly received doctrines of morality. To fight the battle on such ground, gives a great advantage to an unfair antagonist; since he will be sure to say (and many who have no desire to be unfair will say it internally), Are these the doctrines which you do not deem sufficiently certain to be taken under the protection of law? Is the belief in a God one of the opinions, to feel sure of which, you hold to be assuming infallibility? But I must be permitted to observe, that it is not the feeling sure of a doctrine (be it what it may) which I call an assumption of infallibility. It is the undertaking to decide that question *for others,* without allowing them to hear what can be said on the contrary side. And I denounce and reprobate this pretension not the less, if put forth on the side of my most solemn convictions. However positive any one's persuasion may be, not only of the falsity, but of the pernicious consequences—not only of the pernicious consequences, but (to adopt expressions which I altogether condemn) the immorality and impiety of an opinion; yet if, in pursuance of that private judgment, though backed by the public judgment of his country or his contemporaries, he prevents the opinion from being heard in its defence, he assumes infallibility. And so far from the assumption being less objectionable or less dangerous because the opinion is called immoral or impious, this is the case of all others in which it is most fatal. These are exactly the occasions on which the men of one generation commit those dreadful mistakes, which excite the astonishment and horror of posterity. It is among such that we find the instances memorable in history, when the arm of the law has been employed to root out the best men and the noblest doctrines; with deplorable success as to the men, though some of the doctrines have survived to be (as if in mockery) invoked, in defense of similar conduct towards those who dissent from *them,* or from their received interpretation. . . .

Let us now pass to the second division of the argument, and dismissing the supposition that any of the received opinions may be false, let us assume them to be true, and examine into the worth of the manner in which they are likely to be held, when their truth is not freely and openly canvassed. However unwillingly a person who has a strong opinion may admit the possibility that his opinion may be false, he ought to be moved by the consideration that however true it may be, if it is not fully, frequently, and fearlessly discussed, it will be held as a dead dogma, not a living truth.

There is a class of persons (happily not quite so numerous as formerly) who think it enough if a person assents undoubtingly to what they think true, though he has no knowledge whatever of the grounds of the opinion, and could not make a tenable defence of it against the most superficial objections. Such persons, if they can once get their creed taught from authority, naturally think that no good, and some harm, comes of its being allowed to be questioned. Where their influence prevails, they make it nearly impossible for the received opinion to be rejected wisely and considerately, though it may still be rejected rashly and ignorantly; for to shut out discussion entirely is seldom possible, and when it once gets in, beliefs not grounded on conviction are apt to give way before the slightest semblance of an argument. Waiving, however, this possibility—assuming that the true opinion abides in the mind, but abides as a prejudice, a belief independent of, and proof against, argument—this is not the way in which truth ought to be held by a rational being. This is not knowing the truth. Truth, thus held is but one superstition the more, accidentally clinging to the words which enunciate a truth. . . .

It still remains to speak of one of the principal causes which make diversity of opinion advantageous, and will continue to do so until mankind shall have entered a stage of intellectual advancement which at present seems at an incalculable distance. We have hitherto considered only two possibilities: that the received opinion may be false, and some other opinion, consequently, true; or that, the received opinion being true, a conflict with the opposite error is essential to a clear apprehension and deep feeling of its truth. But there is a commoner case than either of these; when the conflicting doctrines, instead of being one true and the other false, share the truth between them; and the nonconforming opinion is needed to supply the remainder of the truth, of which the received doctrine embodies only a part. Popular opinions, on subjects not palpable to sense, are often true, but seldom or never the whole truth. They are a part of the truth; sometimes a greater, sometimes a smaller part, but exaggerated, distorted, and disjoined from the truths by which they ought to be accompanied and limited. Heretical opinions, on the other hand, are generally some of these suppressed and neglected truths, bursting the bonds which kept them down, and either seeking reconciliation with the truth contained in the common opinion, or fronting it as enemies and setting themselves up, with similar exclusiveness, as the whole truth. The latter case is hitherto the most frequent, as in the human mind, one-sidedness has always been the rule, and many-sidedness of exception. Hence, even in revolutions of opinion, one part of the truth usually sets while another rises. Even progress, which ought to superadd, for the most part only substitutes one partial and incomplete truth for another; improvement consisting chiefly in this, that the new fragment of truth is more wanted, more adapted to the needs of the time, than that which it displaces. Such being the partial character of prevailing opinions, even when resting on a true foundation; every opinion which embodies somewhat of the portion of truth which the common opinion omits, ought to be considered precious, with whatever amount of error and confusion that truth may be blended. . . .

We have now recognized the necessity to the mental well-being of mankind (on which all their other well-being depends) of freedom of opinion, and freedom of the expression of opinion, on four distinct grounds; which we will now briefly recapitulate.

First, if any opinion is compelled to silence, that opinion may, for aught we can certainly know, be true. To deny this is to assume our own infallibility.

Secondly, though the silenced opinion be an error, it may, and very commonly does, contain a portion of truth; and since the general or prevailing opinion on any subject is rarely or never the whole truth, it is only by the collision of adverse opinions that the remainder of the truth has any chance of being supplied.

Thirdly, even if the received opinion be not only true, but the whole truth; unless it is suffered to be, and actually is, vigorously and earnestly contested, it will, by most of those who receive it, be held in the manner of a prejudice, with little comprehension or feeling of its rational grounds. And not only this, but fourthly, the meaning of the doctrine itself will be in danger of being lost, or enfeebled, and deprived of its vital effect on the character and conduct: the dogma becoming a mere formal profession, inefficacious for good, but cumbering the ground, and preventing the growth of any real and heartfelt conviction from reason or personal experience.

CHAPTER 3   OF INDIVIDUALITY, AS ONE OF THE ELEMENTS OF WELL-BEING

Such being the reasons which make it imperative that human beings should be free to form opinions, and to express their opinions without reserve; and such the baneful consequences to the intellectual, and through that to the moral nature of man, unless this liberty is either conceded, or asserted in spite of prohibition; let us next examine whether the same reasons do not require that men should be free to act upon their opinions—to carry these out in their lives, without hindrance, either physical or moral, from their fellow-men, so long as it is at their own risk and peril. This last proviso is of course indispensable. No one pretends that actions should be as free as opinions. On the contrary, even opinions lost their immunity, when the circumstances in which they are expressed are such as to constitute their expression a positive instigation to some mischievous act. An opinion that corn-dealers are starvers of the poor, or that private property is robbery, ought to be unmolested when simply circulated through the press, but may justly incur punishment when delivered orally to an excited mob assembled before the house of a corn-dealer, or when handed about among the same mob in the form of a placard. Acts, of whatever kind, which, without justifiable cause, do harm to others, may be, and in the more important cases absolutely require to be, controlled by the unfavorable sentiments, and, when needful, by the active interference of mankind. The liberty of the individual must be thus far limited; he must not make himself a nuisance to other people. But if he refrains from molesting others in what concerns them, and merely acts according to his own inclination and judgment in things which concern himself, the same reasons which show that opinion should be free, prove also that he should be allowed, without molestation, to carry his opinions into practice at his own cost. That mankind are not infallible; that their truths, for the most part, are only half-truths; that unity of opinion, unless resulting from the fullest and freest comparison of opposite opinions, is not desirable, and diversity not an evil, but a good, until mankind are much more capable than at present of recognizing all sides of the truth, are principles applicable to men's modes of action, not less than to their opinions. As it is useful that while mankind are imperfect there should be different opinions, so is it that there should be different experiments of living; that free scope should be given to varieties of character, short of injury to others; and that the worth of different modes of life should be proved practically, when any one thinks fit to try them. It is desirable, in short, that in things which do not primarily concern others, individuality should assert itself. Where, not the person's own character, but the traditions or customs of other people are the rule of conduct, there is wanting one of the principal ingredients of human happiness, and quite the chief ingredient of individual and social progress. . . .

CHAPTER 4   OF THE LIMITS TO THE AUTHORITY OF THE STATE OVER THE INDIVIDUAL

What, then, is the rightful limit to the sovereignty of the individual over himself? Where does the authority of society begin? How much of human life should be assigned to individuality, and how much to society?

Each will receive its proper share, if each has that which more particularly concerns it. To individuality should belong the part of life in which it is chiefly the individual that is interested; to society, the part which chiefly interests society.

Though society is not founded on a contract, and though no good purpose is answered by inventing a contract in order to deduce social obligations from it, every one who receives the protection of society owes a return for the benefit, and the fact of living in society renders it indispensable that each should be bound to observe a certain line of conduct towards the rest. This conduct consists, first, in not injuring the interests of one another; or rather certain interests, which, either by express legal provision or by tacit understanding, ought to be considered as rights; and secondly, in each person's bearing his share (to be fixed on some equitable principle) of the labors and sacrifices incurred for defending the society or its members from injury and molestation. These conditions society is justified in enforcing, at all costs to those who endeavor to withold fulfilment. Nor is this all that society may do. The acts of an individual may be hurtful to others, or wanting in due consideration for their welfare, without going the length of violating any of their constituted rights. The offender may then be justly punished by opinion, though not by law. As soon as any part of a person's conduct affects prejudicially the interests of others, society has jurisdiction over it, and the question whether the general welfare will or will not be promoted by interfering with it, becomes open to discussion. But there is no room for entertaining any such question when a person's conduct affects the interests of no persons besides himself, or needs not affect them unless they like (all the persons concerned being of full age, and the ordinary amount of understanding). In all such cases there should be perfect freedom, legal and social, to do the action and stand the consequences.

It would be a great misunderstanding of this doctrine, to suppose that it is one of selfish indifference, which pretends that human beings have no business with each other's conduct in life, and that they should not concern themselves about the well-doing or well-being of one another, unless their own interest is involved. Instead of any diminution, there is need of a great increase of disinterested exertion to promote the good of others. But disinterested benevolence can find other instruments to persuade people to their good, than whips and scourges, either of the literal or the metaphorical sort. I am the last person to undervalue the self-regarding virtues; they are only second in importance, if even second, to the social. It is equally the business of education to cultivate both. But even education works by conviction and persuasion as well as by compulsion, and it is by the former only that, when the period of education is past, the self-regarding virtues should be inculcated. Human beings owe to each other help to distinguish the better from the worse, and encouragement to choose the former and avoid the latter. They should be forever stimulating each other to increased exercise of their higher faculties, and increased direction of their feelings and aims towards wise instead of foolish, elevating instead of degrading, objects and contemplations. But neither one person, nor any number of persons, is warranted in saying to another human creature of ripe years, that he shall not do with his life for his own benefit what he chooses to do with it. He is the person most interested in his own well-being: the interest which any other person, except in cases of strong personal attachment, can have in it, is trifling, compared with that which he himself has; the interest which society has in him individually (except as to his conduct to others) is fractional, and altogether indirect: while, with respect to his own feelings and circumstances, the most ordinary man or woman has means of knowledge immeasurably surpassing those that can be possessed by anyone else. The interference of society to overrule his judgment and purposes in what only regards himself, must be grounded on general presumptions; which may be altogether wrong, and even if right, are as likely as not to be misapplied to individual cases, by persons no better acquainted with the circumstances of such cases than those are who look at them merely from without. In this department, therefore, of human affairs, Individuality has its proper field of action. In the conduct of human beings towards one another, it is necessary that general rules should for the most part be observed, in order that people may know what they have to expect; but in each person's own concerns, his individual spontaneity is entitled to free exercise. Considerations to aid his judgment, exhortations to strengthen his will, may be offered to him, even obtruded on him, by others; but he, himself, is the final judge. All errors which he is likely to commit against advice and warning, are far outweighed by the evil of allowing others to constrain him to what they deem his good. . . .

What I contend for is, that the inconveniences which are strictly inseparable from the unfavorable judgment of others, are the only ones to which a person should ever be subjected for that portion of his conduct and character which concerns his own good, but which does not affect the interests of others in their relations with him. Acts injurious to others require a totally different treatment. Encroachment on their rights; infliction on them of any loss or damage not justified by his own rights; falsehood or duplicity in dealing with them; unfair or ungenerous use of advantages over them; even selfish abstinence from defending them against injury—these are fit objects of moral reprobation, and, in grave cases, of moral retribution and punishment. And not only these acts, but the dispositions which lead to them, are properly immoral, and fit subjects of disapprobation which may rise to abhorrence. Cruelty of disposition; malice and ill-nature; that most anti-social and odious of all passions, envy; dissimulation and insincerity; irascibility on insufficient cause, and resentment disproportioned to the provocation; the love of domineering over others; the desire to engross more than one's share of advantages . . . ; the pride which derives gratification from the abasement of others; the egotism which thinks self and its concerns more important than everything else, and decides all doubtful questions in his own favor—these are moral vices, and constitute a bad and odious moral character: unlike the self-regarding faults previously mentioned, which are not properly immoralities, and to whatever pitch they may be carried, do not constitute wickedness. They may be proofs of any amount of folly, or want of personal dignity and self-respect; but they are only a subject of moral reprobation when they involve a breach of duty to others, for whose sake the individual is bound to have care for himself. What are called duties to ourselves are not socially obligatory, unless circumstances render them at the same time duties to others. The term duty to oneself, when it means anything more than prudence, means self-respect or self-development; and for none of these is any one accountable to his fellow-creatures, because for none of them is it for the good of mankind that he be held accountable to them. . . .

The distinction here pointed out between the part of a person's life which concerns only himself, and that which concerns others, many persons will refuse to admit. How (it may be asked) can any part of the conduct of a member of society be a matter of indifference to the other members? No person is an entirely isolated being; it is impossible for a person to do anything seriously or permanently hurtful to himself, without mischief reaching at least to his near connections, and often far beyond them. If he injures his property, he does harm to those who directly or indirectly derived support from it, and usually diminishes, by a greater or less amount, the general resources of the community. If he deteriorates his bodily or mental faculties, he not only brings evil upon all who depended on him for any portion of their happiness, but disqualifies himself for rendering the services which he owes to his fellow-creatures generally; perhaps becomes a burden on their affection or benevolence; and if such conduct were very frequent, hardly any offence that is committed would detract more from the general sum of good. Finally, if by his vices or follies a person does no direct harm to others, he is nevertheless (it may be said) injurious by his example; and ought to be compelled to control himself, for the sake of those whom the sight or knowledge of his conduct might corrupt or mislead.

And even (it will be added) if the consequences of misconduct could be confined to the vicious or thoughtless individual, ought society to abandon to their own guidance those who are manifestly unfit for it? If protection against themselves is confessedly due to children and persons under age, is not society equally bound to afford it to persons of mature years who are equally incapable of self-government? If gambling, or drunkenness, or incontinence, or idleness, or uncleanliness, are as injurious to happiness, and as great a hindrance to improvement, as many or most of the acts prohibited by law, why (it may be asked) should not law, so far as is consistent with practicability and social convenience, endeavor to repress these also? And as a supplement to the unavoidable imperfections of law, ought not opinion at least to organize a powerful police against these vices, and visit rigidly with social penalties those who are known to practice them? There is no question here (it may be said) about restricting individuality, or impeding the trial of new and original experiments in living. The only thing it is sought to prevent are things which have been tried and condemned from the beginning of the world until now; things which experience has shown not to be useful or suitable to any person's individuality. There must be some length of time and amount of experience, after which a moral or prudential truth may be regarded as established: and it is merely desired to prevent generation after generation from falling over the same precipice which has been fatal to their predecessors.

I fully admit that the mischief which a person does to himself, may seriously affect, both through their sympathies and their interests, those nearly connected with him, and in a minor degree, society at large. When, by conduct of this sort, a person is led to violate a distinct and assignable obligation to any other person or persons, the case is taken out of the self-regarding class, and becomes amenable to moral disapprobation in the proper sense of the term. If, for example, a man, through intemperance or extravagance, becomes unable to pay his debts, or, having undertaken the moral responsibility of a family, becomes from the same cause incapable of supporting or educating them, he is deservedly reprobated, and might be justly punished; but it is for the breach of duty to his family or creditors, not for the extravagance. If the resources which ought to have been devoted to them, had been diverted from them for the most prudent investment, the moral culpability would have been the same. George Barnwell murdered his uncle to get money for his mistress, but if he had done it to set himself up in business, he would equally have been hanged. Again, in the frequent case of a man who causes grief to his family by addiction to bad habits, he deserves reproach for his unkindness or ingratitude; but so he may for cultivating habits not in themselves vicious, if they are painful to those with whom he passes his life, or who from personal ties are dependent on him for their comfort. Whoever fails in the consideration generally due to the interests and feelings of others, not being compelled by some more imperative duty, or justified by allowable self-preference, is a subject of moral disapprobation for that failure, but not for the cause of it, nor for the errors, merely personal to himself, which may have remotely led to it. In like manner, when a person disables himself, by conduct purely self-regarding, from the performance of some definite duty incumbent on him to the public, he is guilty of a social offence. No person ought to be punished simply for being drunk; but a soldier or a policeman should be punished for being drunk on duty. Whenever, in short, there is a definite damage, or a definite risk of damage, either to an individual or to the public, the case is taken out of the province of liberty, and placed in that of morality or law.

But with regard to the merely contingent, or, as it may be called, constructive injury which a person causes to society, by conduct which neither violates any specific duty to the public, nor occasions perceptible hurt to any assignable individual except himself; the inconvenience is one which society can afford to bear, for the sake of the greater good of human freedom.

Rawls

John Rawls (born 1921) is the foremost political philosopher currently working in the United States. He received his Ph.D. from Princeton University and since 1976 has taught philosophy at Harvard University. Rawls developed a full-fledged ethical-political theory in his acclaimed work A Theory of Justice (1971), which has given rise to extended analysis, criticism, and commentary.

In his seminal article "Justice as Fairness" (1958), selections from which appear below, Rawls develops his "contractarian" view of justice as the central concept for political theory. His thinking is clearly within the liberal democratic tradition associated with Locke and Mill, although he is less concerned with historical notions of a state of nature and more with the conceptual principles that establish fairness in social-political relations. Identifying the underpinnings of equality among persons and determining how inequalities in social and economic position and in the exercise of power, can be justified become the fundamental concerns informing his argument.

Justice as Fairness

It might seem as first sight that the concepts of justice and fairness are the same, and that there is no reason to distinguish them, or to say that one is more fundamental than the other. I think that this impression is mistaken. In this paper I wish to show that the fundamental idea in the concept of justice is fairness; and I wish to offer an analysis of the concept of justice from this point of view. To bring out the force of this claim, and the analysis based upon it, I shall then argue that it is this aspect of justice for which utilitarianism, in its classical form, is unable to account, but which is expressed, even if misleadingly, by the idea of the social contract.

To start with I shall develop a particular conception of justice by stating and commenting upon two principles which specify it, and by considering the circumstances and conditions under which they may be thought to arise. The principles defining this conception, and the conception itself, are, of course, familiar. It may be possi-

From "Justice as Fairness" by John Rawls, *The Philosophical Review,* vol. LXVII (1958).

ble, however, by using the notion of fairness as a framework, to assemble and to look at them in a new way. Before stating this conception, however, the following preliminary matters should be kept in mind.

Throughout I consider justice only as a virtue of social institutions, or what I shall call practices. The principles of justice are regarded as formulating restrictions as to how practices may define positions and offices, and assign thereto powers and liabilities, rights and duties. Justice as a virtue of particular actions or of persons I do not take up at all. It is important to distinguish these various subjects of justice, since the meaning of the concept varies according to whether it is applied to practices, particular actions, or persons. These meanings are, indeed, connected, but they are not identical. I shall confine my discussion to the sense of justice as applied to practices, since this sense is the basic one. Once it is understood, the other senses should go quite easily.

Justice is to be understood in its customary sense as representing but *one* of the many virtues of social institutions, for these may be antiquated, inefficient, degrading, or any number of other things, without being unjust. Justice is not to be confused with an all inclusive vision of a good society; it is only one part of any such conception. It is important, for example, to distinguish that sense of equality which is an aspect of the concept of justice from that sense of equality which belongs to a more comprehensive social ideal. There may well be inequalities which one concedes are just, or at least not unjust, but which, nevertheless, one wishes, on other grounds, to do away with. I shall focus attention, then, on the usual sense of justice in which it is essentially the elimination of arbitrary distinctions and the establishment, within the structure of a practice, of a proper balance between competing claims. . . .

The conception of justice which I want to develop may be stated in the form of two principles as follows: first, each person participating in a practice, or affected by it, has an equal right to the most extensive liberty compatible with a like liberty for all; and second, inequalities are arbitrary unless it is reasonable to expect that they will work out for everyone's advantage, and provided the positions and offices to which they attach, or from which they may be gained, are open to all. These principles express justice as a complex of three ideas: liberty, equality, and reward for services contributing to the common good.

The term "person" is to be construed variously depending on the circumstances. On some occasions it will mean human individuals, but in others it may refer to nations, provinces, business firms, churches, teams, and so on. The principles of justice apply in all these instances, although there is a certain logical priority to the case of human individuals. As I shall use the term "person," it will be ambiguous in the manner indicated.

The first principle holds, of course, only if other things are equal: that is, while there must always be a justification for departing from the initial position of equal liberty (which is defined by the pattern of rights and duties, powers and liabilities, established by a practice), and the burden of proof is placed on him who would depart from it, nevertheless, there can be, and often there is, a justification for doing so. Now, that similar particular cases, as defined by a practice, should be treated similarly as they arise, is part of the very concept of a practice; it is involved in the notion of an activity in accordance with rules. The first principle expresses an analogous conception, but as applied to the structure of practices themselves. It holds, for example, that there is a presumption against the distinctions and classifications made by legal systems and other practices to the extent that they infringe on the original and equal liberty of the persons participating in them. The second principle defines how this presumption may be rebutted. . . .

The second principle defines what sorts of inequalities are permissible; it specifies how the presumption laid down by the first principle may be put aside. Now by inequalities it is best to understand not *any* differences between offices and positions, but differences in the benefits and burdens attached to them either directly or indirectly, such as prestige and wealth, or liability to taxation and compulsory services. Players in a game do not protest against there being different positions, such as batter, pitcher, catcher, and the like, nor to there being various privileges and powers as specified by the rules; nor do the citizens of a country object to there being the different offices of government such as president, senator, governor, judge, and so on, each with their special rights and duties. It is not differences of this kind that are normally thought of as inequalities, but differences in the resulting distribution established by a practice, or made possible by it, of the things men strive to attain or avoid. Thus they may complain about the pattern of honors and rewards set up by a practice (e.g., the privileges and salaries of government officials) or they may object to the distribution of power and wealth which results from the various ways in which men avail themselves of the opportunities allowed by it (e.g., the concentration of wealth which may develop in a free price system allowing large entrepreneurial or speculative gains).

It should be noted that the second principle holds that an inequality is allowed only if there is reason to believe that practice with the inequality, or resulting in it, will work for the advantage of *every* party engaging in it. Here it is important to stress that *every* party must gain from the inequality. Since the principle applies to practices, it implies that the representative man in every office or position defined by a practice, when he views it as a going concern, must find it reasonable to prefer his condition and prospects with the inequality to what they would be under the practice without it. The principle excludes, therefore, the justification of inequalities on the grounds that the disadvantages of those in one position are outweighed by the greater advantages of those in another position. This rather simple restriction is the main modification I wish to make in the utilitarian principle as usually understood. When coupled with the notion of a practice, it is a restriction of consequence, and one which some utilitarians, e.g., Hume and Mill, have used in their discussions of justice without realizing apparently its significance, or at least without calling attention to it. Why it is a significant modification of principle, changing one's conception of justice entirely, the whole of my argument will show.

Further, it is also necessary that the various offices to which special benefits or burdens attach are open to all. It may be, for example, to the common advantage, as just defined, to attach special benefits to certain offices. Perhaps by doing so the requisite talent can be attracted to them and encouraged to give its best efforts. But any offices having special benefits must be won in a fair competition in which contestants are judged on their merits. If some offices were not open, those excluded would normally be justified in feeling unjustly treated, even if they benefited from the greater efforts of those who were allowed to compete for them. . . .

. . . Justice is the virtue of practices where there are assumed to be competing interests and conflicting claims, and where it is supposed that persons will press their rights on each other. That persons are mutually self-interested in certain situations and for certain purposes is what gives rise to the question of justice in practices covering those circumstances. Amongst an association of saints, if such community could really exist, the disputes about justice could hardly occur; for they would all work selflessly together for one end, the glory of God as defined by their common religion, and reference to this end would settle every question of right. The justice of practices does not come up until there are several different parties (whether we think of these as individuals, associations, or nations and so on, is irrelevant) who do press their claims on one another, and who do regard themselves as representatives of interests which deserve to be considered. . . .

Again, in contrast to the various conceptions of the social contract, the several parties do not establish any particular society or practice; they do not covenant to obey a particular sovereign body or to accept a given constitution. Nor do they, as in the theory of games (in certain respects a marvelously sophisticated development of this tradition), decide on individual strategies adjusted to their circumstances in the game. What the parties do is to *jointly* acknowledge certain *principles* of appraisal relating to their common *practices* either as already established or merely proposed. They accede to standards of judgment, not to a given practice; they do not make any specific agreement, or bargain, or adopt a particular strategy. The subject of their acknowledgment is, therefore, very general indeed; it is simply the acknowledgment of certain principles of judgment, fulfilling certain general conditions, to be used in criticizing the arrangement of their common affairs. The relations of mutual self-interest between the parties who are similarly circumstanced mirror the conditions under which questions of justice arise, and the procedure by which the principles of judgment are proposed and acknowledged reflects the constraints of having a morality. Each aspect, then, of the preceding hypothetical account serves the purpose of bringing out a feature of the notion of justice. One could, if one liked, view the principles of justice as the "solution" of this highest order "game" of adopting, subject to the procedure described, principles of argument for all coming particular "games" whose peculiarities one can in no way foresee. But this comparison, while no doubt helpful, must not obscure the fact that this highest order "game" is of a special sort. Its significance is that its various pieces represent aspects of the concept of justice.

Finally, I do not, of course, conceive the several parties as necessarily coming together to establish their common practices for the first time. Some institutions may, indeed, be set up *de novo*; but I have framed the preceding account so that it will apply when the full complement of social institutions already exists and represents the result of a long period of development. Nor is the account in any way fictitious. In any society where people reflect on their institutions they will have an idea of what principles of justice would be acknowledged under the conditions described, and there will be occasions when questions of justice are actually discussed in this way. Therefore if their practices do not accord with these principles, this will affect the quality of their social relations. For in this case there will be some recognized situations wherein the parties are mutually aware that one of them is being forced to accept what the other would concede is unjust. The foregoing analysis may then be thought of as representing the actual quality of relations between persons as defined by practices accepted as just. In such practices the parties acknowledge the principles on which it is constructed, and the general recognition of this fact shows itself in the absence of resentment and in the sense of being justly treated. Thus one common objection to the theory of the social contract, its apparently historical and fictitious character, is avoided.

That the principles of justice may be regarded as arising in the manner described illustrates an important fact about them. Not only does it bring out the idea that justice is a primitive moral notion in that it arises once the concept of morality is imposed on mutually self-interested agents similarly circumstanced, but it emphasizes that, fundamental to justice, is the concept of fairness which relates to right dealing between persons who are cooperating with or competing against one another, as when one speaks of fair games, fair competition, and fair bargains. The question of fairness arises when free persons, who have no authority over one another, are engaging in a joint activity and amongst themselves settling or acknowledging the rules which define it and which determine the respective shares in its benefits and burdens. A practice will strike the parties as fair if none feels that, by participating in it, they or any of the others are taken advantage of, or forced to give in to claims which they do not regard as legitimate. This implies that each has a conception of legitimate claims which he thinks it reasonable for others as well as himself to acknowledge. If one thinks of the principles of justice as arising in the manner described, then they do define this sort of conception. A practice is just or fair, then, when it satisfies the principles which those who participate in it could propose to one another for mutual acceptance under the afore-mentioned circumstances. Persons engaged in a just, or fair, practice can face one another openly and support their respective positions, should they appear questionable, by reference to principles which it is reasonable to expect each to accept.

It is this notion of the possibility of mutual acknowledgment of principles by free persons who have no authority over one another which makes the concept of fairness fundamental to justice. Only if such acknowledgment is possible can there be true community between persons in their common practices; otherwise their relations will appear to them as founded to some extent on force. If, in ordinary speech, fairness applies more particularly to practices in which there is a choice whether to engage or not (e.g., in games, business competition), and justice to practices in which there is no choice (e.g., in slavery), the element of necessity does not render the conception of mutual acknowledgment inapplicable, although it may make it much more urgent to change unjust than unfair institutions. For one activity in which one can always engage is that of proposing and acknowledging principles to one another supposing each to be similarly circumstanced; and to judge practices by the principles so arrived at is to apply the standard of fairness to them.

Now if the participants in a practice accept its rules as fair, and so have no complaint to lodge against it, there arises a prima facie duty (and a corresponding prima facie right) of the parties to each other to act in accordance with the practice when it falls upon them to comply. When any number of persons engage in a practice, or conduct a joint undertaking according to rules, and thus restrict their liberty, those who have submitted to these restrictions when required have the right to a similar acquiescence on the part of those who have benefited by their submission. These conditions will obtain if a practice is correctly acknowledged to be fair, for in this case all who participate in it will benefit from it. . . .

The conception at which we have arrived, then, is that the principles of justice may be thought of as arising once the constraints of having a morality are imposed upon rational and mutually self-interested parties who are related and situated in a special way. A practice is just if it is in accordance with the principles which all who participate in it might reasonably be expected to propose or to acknowledge before one another when they are similarly circumstanced and required to make a firm commitment in advance without knowledge of what will be their peculiar condition, and thus when it meets standards which the parties could accept as fair should occasion arise for them to debate its merits. Regarding the participants themselves, once persons knowingly engage in a practice which they acknowledge to be fair and accept the benefits of doing so, they are bound by the duty of fair play to follow the rules when it comes their turn to do so, and this implies a limitation on their pursuit of self-interest in particular cases.

Gandhi

Mahatma Gandhi (1869–1948), the great Indian social thinker and political activist, was born in India, studied law in England from 1887 to 1891, and in 1893 moved to South Africa, where he worked to change laws that discriminated against Indians. At the advent of World War I, he returned to India and supported the British war effort, but after the war Gandhi became active in the Home Rule movement and over the next twenty years used civil disobedience as his primary weapon in his quest to end British rule in India. In 1947 India became an independent nation largely as a result of Gandhi's efforts. Unfortunately he had little time to guide the formation of the new government, since in January of 1948 Gandhi was assassinated by a Hindu fanatic.

Gandhi allowed that he was strongly influenced in his thought and practice by such diverse thinkers as Leo Tolstoy, the Russian novelist who advocated a kind of religious socialism in his late years, and Henry David Thoreau, the nineteenth-century American civil disobedient. Gandhi in turn exerted great influence on movements such as the nonviolent civil rights action in the United States of which the Reverend Martin Luther King, Jr., was a notable leader. Throughout his long activist career Gandhi urged *satyagraha,* by which he meant the power of truth and justice to prevail over evil. This was to be accomplished by means of appealing to and awakening, through one's own selfless nonviolent suffering, those same values within one's oppressive opponent. Gandhi developed his ideas on truth-power and nonviolence (*ahiṁsa*) and on the organizing of large numbers of people for social-political action in the context of British colonialism and what he perceived to be the striking inequities in traditional Hindu practice, especially with respect to the lowest classes. He was largely successful in realizing his dream of a free India, but his ideal of a society devoted to the principles of cooperation and brotherhood among all of its members has quite clearly yet to be realized anywhere.

    The selection that follows is taken from Gandhi's account of his work, *Young India* (1919–1922).

Nonviolence as a Political Method

No country has ever risen without being purified through the force of suffering. The mother suffers so that her child may live. The condition of wheat growing is that the seed grain should perish. Life comes out of Death. . . .

When a person claims to be nonviolent, he is expected not to be angry with one who has injured him. He will not wish him harm; he will wish him well; he will not swear at him; he will not cause him any physical hurt. He will put up with all the injury to which he is subjected by the wrongdoer. Thus Nonviolence is complete innocence. Complete Nonviolence is complete absence of ill will against all that lives. It therefore embraces even subhuman life, not excluding noxious insects or beasts. They have not been created to feed our destructive propensities. If we only knew the mind of the Creator, we should find their proper place in His creation. Nonviolence is therefore in its active form good will toward all life. It is pure Love. I read it in the Hindu scriptures, in the Bible, in the Koran.

Nonviolence is a perfect state. It is a goal toward which all mankind moves naturally though unconsciously. Man does not become divine when he personifies innocence in himself. Only then does he become truly man. In our present state, we are partly men and partly beasts and in our ignorance and even arrogance say that we truly fulfill the purpose of our species, when we deliver blow for blow and develop the measure of anger required for the purpose. We pretend to believe that retaliation is the law of our being, whereas in every scripture we find that retaliation is nowhere obligatory but only permissible. It is restraint that is obligatory. Retaliation is indulgence requiring elaborate regulating. Restraint is the law of our being. For highest perfection is unattainable without highest restraint. Suffering is thus the badge of the human tribe.

What then is the meaning of Noncoöperation in terms of the Law of Suffering? We must voluntarily put up with the losses and inconveniences that arise from having to withdraw our support from a Government that is ruling against our will. Possession of power and riches is a crime under an unjust government; poverty in that case is a virtue, says Thoreau. It may be that, in the transition state, we may make mistakes; there may be avoidable suffering. These things are preferable to national emasculation. We must refuse to wait for the wrong to be righted till the wrongdoer has been roused to a sense of his iniquity. We must not, for fear of ourselves or others having to suffer, remain participators in it. But we must combat the wrong by ceasing to assist the wrongdoer directly or indirectly. . . .

We have chosen a method that compels us to turn, each one of us, our face toward God. Noncoöperation presumes that our opponent with whom we noncoöperate resorts to methods which are as questionable as the purpose he seeks to fulfill by such methods. We shall therefore find favor in the sight of God only by choosing methods which are different in kind from those of our opponents. This is a big claim we have made for ourselves, and we can attain success within the short time appointed by us, only if our methods are in reality radically different from those of the Government.

Hence the foundation of our movement rests on complete Nonviolence, whereas violence is the final refuge of the Government. And as no energy can be created without resistance, our nonresistance to Government violence must bring the latter to a standstill. But our Nonviolence to be true, must be in word, thought, and deed. I am not a visionary. I claim to be a practical idealist. The religion of Nonviolence is not meant merely for the Rishis [the ancient seers and sages] and saints. It is meant for the common people as well. Nonviolence is the law of our species as violence is the law of the brute. The spirit lies dormant in the brute and he knows no law but that of physical might. The dignity of man requires obedience to a higher law—to the strength of the spirit.

I have therefore ventured to place before India the ancient law of self-sacrifice. For, Satyagraha and its offshoots, Noncoöperation and civil resistance, are nothing but new names for the law of suffering. The Rishis, who discovered the law of Nonviolence in the midst of violence, were greater geniuses than Newton. They were themselves greater warriors than Wellington. Having themselves known the use of arms, they realized their uselessness and taught a weary world that its salvation lay not through violence but through Nonviolence. . . .

I do believe that, where there is only a choice between cowardice and violence, I would advise violence. Thus when my eldest son asked me what he should have done, had he been present when I was almost fatally assaulted in 1908, whether he should have run away and seen me killed or whether he should have used his physical force which he could and wanted to use, and defended me, I told him that it was his duty to defend me even by using violence. Hence it was that I took part in the Boer War, the so-called Zulu rebellion and the late War. Hence also do I advocate training in arms for those who believe in the method of violence. I would rather have India resort to arms in order to defend her honor than that she should in a cowardly manner become or remain a helpless witness to her own dishonor. . . .

Nonviolence presupposes ability to strike. It is a conscious, deliberate restraint put upon one's desire for vengeance. But vengeance is any day superior to passive, effeminate, and helpless submission. Forgiveness is higher still. Vengeance too is weakness. The desire for vengeance comes out of fear of harm, imaginary or real. A man who fears no one on earth would consider it troublesome even to summon up anger against one who is vainly trying to injure him.

Nonviolence and cowardice go ill together. I can imagine a fully armed man to be at heart a coward. Possession of arms implies an element of fear, if not cowardice. But true Nonviolence is an impossibility without the possession of unadulterated fearlessness. If we are unmanly today, we are so, not because we do not know how to strike, but because we fear to die. He is no follower of Mahavira, the apostle of Jainism, or of Buddha or of the Vedas who, being afraid to die, takes flight before any danger, real or imaginary, all the while wishing that somebody else would remove the danger by destroying the person causing it. He is no follower of Ahimsa who does not care a straw if he kills a man by inches by deceiving him in trade, or who would protect by force of arms a few cows and make away with the butcher or who, in order to do a supposed good to his country, does not mind killing off a few officials. All these are actuated by hatred, cowardice, and fear.

I object to violence because when it appears to do good, the good is only temporary; the evil it does is permanent. I do not believe that the killing of even every Englishman can do the slightest good to India. The millions would be just as badly off as they are today, if someone made it possible to kill off every Englishman tomorrow. The responsibility is more ours than that of the English for the present state of things. The English will be powerless to do evil if we will but be good. Hence my incessant emphasis on reform from within. History teaches one that those who have, no doubt with honest motives, ousted the greedy by using brute force against them, have in their turn become a prey to the disease of the conquered. From violence done to the foreign ruler, violence to our own people whom we may consider to be obstructing the country's progress is an easy natural step. Whatever may have been the result of violent activities in other countries and without reference to the philosophy of Nonviolence, it does not require much intellectual effort to see that if we resort to violence for ridding society of the many abuses which impede our progress, we shall add to our difficulties and postpone the day of freedom. The people unprepared for reforms because unconvinced of their necessity will be maddened with rage over their coercion, and will seek the assistance of the foreigner in order to retaliate. Has not this been happening before our eyes for the past many years of which we have still painfully vivid recollections?

The beauty of Satyagraha, of which Noncoöperation is but a chapter, is that it is available to either side in a fight; that it has checks that automatically work for the vindication of truth and justice for that side, whichever it may be, that has truth and justice in preponderating measure. It is as powerful and faithful a weapon in the hand of the capitalist as in that of the laborer. It is as powerful in the hands of the government, as in that of the people, and will bring victory to the government, if people are misguided or unjust, as it will win the battle for the people if the government be in the wrong. Quick disorganization and defeat are bound to be the fate of bolstered-up cases and artificial agitations, if the battle is fought with Satyagraha weapons. Suppose the people are unfit to rule themselves, or are unwilling to sacrifice for a cause, then, no amount of noise will bring them victory in Noncoöperation.

Science teaches us that a lever cannot move a body unless it has got a resting point outside the body against which it is applied. Similarly, in order to overcome evil one must stand wholly outside it, on the firm, solid ground of unadulterated good. The methods of violence, again, have not only failed in their purpose but have produced an effect opposite to what they were intended to produce. Because, when once physical force comes on the scene, it calls forth a superior physical force which subdues it for the time being. Then it puts forth more force and the chain of violence lengthens and strengthens. This method is wrong because it overlooks the fundamental fact that evil can never be overcome with evil, it ceases only through good. . . .

The only way of curing disease is to remove the causes thereof. Let people purify themselves, let them cease to indirectly participate in the evil of the state and it will disappear by itself. Self-purification, then, and not violence, or reform is the real remedy. To purify oneself by withdrawing coöperation from the state: this is the great doctrine of Noncoöperation.

Noncoöoperation is not a movement of brag, bluster, or bluff. It is a test of our sincerity. It requires solid and silent self-sacrifice. It challenges our honesty and our capacity for national work. It is a movement that aims at translating ideas into action. And the more we do, the more we find that much more must be done than we had expected. And this thought of our imperfection must make us humble. A Noncoöperationist strives to compel attention and to set an example not by his violence, but by his unobtrusive humility. He allows his solid action to speak for his creed. His strength lies in his reliance upon the correctness of his position. And the conviction of it grows more in his opponent when he least interposes his speech between his action and his opponent. Speech, especially when it is haughty, betrays want of confidence and it makes one's opponent sceptical about the reality of the act itself. Humility therefore is the key to quick success. I hope that every Noncoöperationist will recognize the necessity of being humble and self-restrained. . . .

We have long been accustomed to think that power comes only through legislative assemblies. I have regarded this belief as a grave error brought about by inertia or hypnotism. A superficial study of British history has made us think that all power percolates to the people from parliaments. The truth is that power resides in the people and it is entrusted for the time being to those whom they may choose as their representatives. Parliaments have no power or even existence independently of the people. . . . Civil disobedience is the storehouse of power. Imagine a whole people unwilling to conform to the laws of the legislature, and prepared to suffer the consequences of noncompliance. They will bring the whole legislative and executive machinery to a standstill. The police and the military are of use to coerce minorities however powerful they may be. But no police or military coercion can bend the resolute will of a people, out for suffering to the uttermost.

The rule of the majority has a narrow application: one should yield to the majority in matters of detail. But it is slavery to be amenable to the majority, no matter what its decisions are. Democracy is not a state in which people act like sheep. Under democracy individual liberty of opinion and action is jealously guarded.

I look upon an increase in the power of the state with the greatest fear, because, although while apparently doing good by minimizing exploitation, it does the greatest harm to mankind by destroying individuality which lies at the root of all programs. The state represents violence in a concentrated and organized form. The individual has a soul, but as the state is a soulless machine, it can never be weaned from violence to which it owes its very existence.

To me political power is not an end but one of the means of enabling people to better their condition in every department of life. Political power means capacity to regulate national life through national representatives. If national life becomes so perfect as to become self-regulated, no representation becomes necessary. There is then a state of enlightened anarchy. In such a state everyone is his own ruler. He rules himself in such a manner that he is never a hindrance to his neighbor. In the ideal state, therefore, there is no political power because there is no state. But the ideal is never fully realized in life. Hence the classical statement of Thoreau that that government is best which governs the least.

PART
III

WHAT DO I KNOW?
WHAT IS TRUTH?

Philosophers have stated repeatedly that philosophy is a *rational* enterprise. But just what is this "rationality" that we value so highly and that is still taken to be that which, in virtue of our possessing it, distinguishes us from the rest of the animal world and guarantees us a unique place in the scheme of things? What are its possibilities and limitations in enabling us to secure genuine knowledge and truth? And in what precisely do this knowledge and truth that we strive to attain consist?

It has been a common assumption in Western thinking throughout much of its history that there is a single, universal rationality for all humankind, although to be sure it can be realized in varying degrees among different peoples and different individuals, and that this rationality is essential and central to the attaining of all knowledge. So-called rational men of good will, it is believed, should in principle be able to come to agreement on, if not full understanding about, any conceptual issue of importance.

Now, of course, there have always been those who are critical of this "pretension" regarding the universality and centrality of reason and who have argued instead for the superiority of our creative imagination, or feeling, or will, or intuition; and most recently psychoanalytic theory believes this pretension has been exposed at its roots. "We rationalize rather than reason," so the slogan goes, which is to say that based on nonrational considerations we are always predisposed to believe in certain things and that we then hunt around for reasons to justify those beliefs.

But none of this has involved directly the idea of there being possible valid alternative modes or styles of rationality; it has been rather a contest between an alleged universal reason and various irrational or nonrational forces or powers. It was not perhaps until the West was able to take seriously the achievements of non-Western cultures in their own terms, and that women's voices that argued for a different style of rational thought were being heard, that the real possibility of "alternative rationalities" presented itself.

With respect to non-Western traditions, in Indian philosophy (especially as exemplified in Advaita Vedānta), in parallel with its thinking about the self a distinction is drawn between two levels of knowledge and truth: first, the level of our everyday perceivings and conceivings, as these are language-based and category-informed—the "conventional" level; second, the level of our deepest insight, which discloses the real character of the world and of ourselves—the higher, spiritual level. These two levels, it is said, are incommensurable, which is to say that there are no real connections between them, for the higher level "negates" the lower, conventional one. What this means is that although conventional truth—knowledge that is justified by correct reasoning and perceiving—has its own integrity (e.g., if you want to know if it is raining, you look and see directly or infer indirectly from certain signs; you don't expect to find the answer from the exercise of a higher intuition), nevertheless this whole system of truth and knowledge is seen to be inherently partial and incomplete and is accordingly disvalued in the light of a higher, overwhelming sense of reality. Conventional truth is based on distinctions between subject and object (to think means to think *about* something), and it is grounded in temporality (it takes time to think) and in linguistic categories (we always perceive and conceive in terms of various labels, designations, and so on). These distinctions and conditions no longer obtain when the highest insight is achieved. At that level, knower and known are simply one.

At the lower, conventional level, Indian thinking, as we will see, does not depart radically from Western thinking regarding the fulfillment of various conditions for correct perception and conception, albeit it has its own distinctive and highly interesting "pragmatic" way of working this out. The major difference, which we may note for purposes of general cultural background, between the model of rationality in orthodox Indian thought and that of the West is evident on the higher, spiritual level—for in the former the authority of scripture (*śruti*) is said to obtain. This is a very complex theme in Indian thought, and one that is particularly difficult for those educated in Western styles of thought to comprehend. To be sure, in the West we have had, especially in the medieval period, extensive discussions about the relation between reason and revelation, between our own human powers of thinking and divine wisdom given to us in holy scripture. But in the Indian context we have this very special situation that scripture, the Veda, is said to be eternal and authorless. It does not arise from either a human or divine source—in fact, it does not "arise" at all; it simply has always been. The ancient seers, it is said, received scripture as part of their own spiritual experience, and this scripture has subsequently been transmitted through countless generations by an uninterrupted series of teachers. And it is scripture, the Veda, that is the supreme authority regarding matters of the higher knowledge. Reason is bound to the conventional level, and although it might be useful in preparing one to accept and to understand the highest wisdom, it is useless by itself to bring one to that wisdom. For this we must rely on the authority of the Veda. "Authority" here, however, does not mean that which requires blind obedience; rather it means that which has always been in the immediacy of one's own experience, which one is to recover. In the West, on the whole, we believe knowledge to be fundamentally a matter of *discovery;* for traditional Indian thought, it is a matter of *recovery*—of reestablishing oneself in relation to the truth of reality.

In contrast to both the Indian and the Western traditions, the Chinese tradition, in addition to having a rather unique style of rationality based on correlative thinking, takes a quite different stand. Authority, for the predominant Confucian tradi-

The Thinker by Edward Hagedorn. Photo used with permission of Stuart Denenberg, President, Denenberg Fine Arts, Inc., San Francisco.

tion, has to do not with an eternal, authorless scripture but with those who are taken to be "authoritative" individuals—those who, as we have seen, embody the virtues subscribed to in the tradition. *Who* says what and not just what is said are central to determining the truth of what is said. The same sentence could be uttered by a fool and a sage, but it would mean two quite different things and could have different truth-values. For the Chinese knowledge and truth generally are thus highly personal in character. Westerners, on the other hand, as we have seen, tend to believe in the autonomy of reason and hence in the *impersonal* character of truth and knowledge; Indians believe as well in the universality of perception and conception at the conventional level, while allowing, of course, for the expert testimony of a trustworthy person and the *nonpersonal* nature of truth at the higher spiritual level.

Closely tied to this are the differences in the relationship between reason and morality that are thought to obtain in the various traditions. In the West generally—and this is epitomized in our notions and beliefs about science—the pursuit of knowledge is an end in itself. We might indeed employ reason to justify our moral beliefs and to decide all manner of public issues concerning the usefulness of the pursuit of specified forms of knowledge (e.g., what kinds of research ought to be funded), but we insist that the moral as such cannot intrude in the actual search for knowledge. For the Chinese this claim is quite astounding, and its absence in traditional Chinese thought may be one of the reasons that theoretical science did not develop in China in the manner in which it did in the West. In general, for the Confucian tradition what is worthy of study is that which is able to contribute to the development of a person's moral consciousness or ethical sensitivity. Also unlike the Indians, for whom knowledge of a special kind alone is liberating and is said to bring about a "transvaluation of values" that discloses that which is worth knowing, the Chinese pursue knowledge of any kind only insofar as they deem it conducive to human betterment.

In the selected readings that follow, some of the specific differences between various traditions will be made evident, as will differences within the traditions themselves. Whenever we search for the nature of reason, the sources of knowledge, and the nature of truth, we are embarked on one of the most difficult and challenging areas of philosophical inquiry—one that many philosophers believe is foundational to all philosophical thinking.

Tiles

Mary Tiles is a professor of philosophy at the University of Hawaii. She specializes in the philosophy and history of mathematics, epistemology, and the philosophy of science, and has published several books and many articles in these areas.

In her "Images of Reason in Western Culture," Tiles shows clearly that in the West several differing models of rationality, rather than a single conception, were developed. She explicates these models in terms of the images or metaphors of the tree, which symbolizes branching, and the lyre, which suggests harmony, and finally the computer, which, with its calculations, has become "the dominant metaphor for reason in Western culture."

Images of Reason in Western Culture

The tree, the lyre and the computer are images which have contributed to the conception of reason in Western culture. The tree and the lyre have played this role since about the first century A.D. Even the basic idea of a computer, or a mechanical "reasoning" device, has a longer history than most people would imagine, and can be traced back at least as far as the thirteenth century Catalan philosopher Ramon Lull. I shall briefly explore these metaphors as a way of highlighting various strands which have been, and continue to be, woven together in a variety of ways to produce Western conceptions of reason.

Western culture has traditionally looked to classical Greece for its origins and its inspirations, and in particular, to the works of Plato and Aristotle. These two philosophers played a key role in moulding Western conceptions of reason. Although Plato and Aristotle agree that reason is the highest human faculty and agree in distinguishing reason from emotion, the head from the heart, their work gave rise to two significantly different conceptions of reason, and hence, also of reason-

From the proceedings of a symposium on "Alternative Rationalies" sponsored by the Society for Asian and Comparative Philosophy and held at the University of Hawaii at Manoa, 1992. Reprinted with the permission of the author.

ing and knowledge. The spirit of the opposition between Platonic and Aristotelian ideals can be summed up in two slogans, "Divide and rule" (Aristotelian) and "Unify and harmonize" (Platonic). This, naturally, represents an oversimplification because in Plato's dialogues there is use of divide and rule strategies. The characterization is based not so much on the actual works of Aristotle and Plato but on how they were read in medieval and renaissance Europe. The process of division is one of branching, hence the tree metaphor. The lyre symbolizes the particular kind of harmony which impressed Plato.

TREES

The kind of rational structure which is given prominence in Aristotle's works and which came to dominate Scholastic thought is the structure of a classificatory system—a hierarchical structure of names for kinds of things organized into genera and species. To identify an object—give it its correct name—is to locate it in a classificatory system. This location is determined by the definition of the term (a definition which gives an account of what it is to be a thing of that kind, an account of its essence). For example, the definition of a whale includes the fact that it is a sea-dwelling mammal. The definition of mammal includes the fact that it is a warm-blooded vertebrate which bears live young. The animal kingdom itself might be conceived as exhibiting the following sort of tree structure.

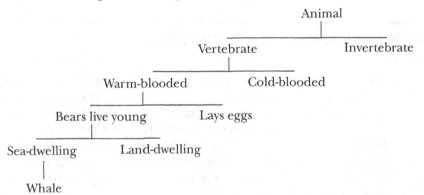

This is a hierarchical order based on qualitative similarities and differences. A key assumption underlying such an order is that a thing cannot both have and lack a given quality—the requirement of non-contradiction. Non-contradiction is therefore fundamental to this kind of rational order. Anyone working within it who asserts a contradiction will be accused of irrationality.

Knowledge of definitions (of essences) coupled with the principle of non-contradiction can serve as the foundation for further, rationally demonstrable, knowledge. One can show, for example, that it would be false to claim that some mammals are invertebrate by noting that being vertebrate is part of the definition of what it is to be a mammal. This means that no mammal can be invertebrate. Aristotle's syllogistic logic gives a complete catalogue of the simple inferences that can move one around, in, and allow one to take advantage of knowledge of such classificatory systems. For example:

Whales are mammals.	Whales are mammals.
Mammals are warm-blooded.	Mammals do not lay eggs.
Therefore, whales are warm-blooded.	Therefore, whales do not lay eggs.

Things other than plants or animals can also be seen as organized in this type of structure.

In case this should seem to be a rather antiquated and played out metaphor, it is worth pointing out that essentially the same conception, including the same logical principles used by Aristotle, form the basis of the quite recently developed logic programming language called "Prolog." Programming in this language amounts to giving the database a hierarchical, tree-like, structure. The computer is then able to use general principles for finding its way around such a structure to give answers to questions relating to things mentioned in the database. Here we already see a connection between trees and computers. We will come back to computers shortly.

LYRES

The notion of harmony introduces a rather different conception of rational order and of consistency or coherence, one which is not founded on the opposition of contrary qualities or between possession and lack of a given quality. Harmony is an intrinsically relational concept. From the Pythagoreans onwards, the notion of harmony was linked with the idea of a rational, mathematical order via the notion of a ratio. This idea started with the Pythagorean discovery that the note sounded by a vibrating string depends on its length, and that harmonic combinations of notes correspond to simple arithmetic relations between string lengths.

Interval	Ratio
octave	2:1
fifth	3:2
fourth	4:3

These same relationships were further found to hold for the notes produced by vibrating columns of air (as in wind instruments). Now, a note in itself is neither harmonious nor discordant, it is only the mutual relationship between notes which produces harmony or discord. Discord is not logically impossible, but is the product of disagreement and disorder. It was thought to mark a departure from reason, from the ideal order. Similarly a string has a length, but this length has no number except in relation to some other thing with length which is used to measure it. To measure is thus to determine the ratio of one thing to another. The importance of finding ratios is that it lets you measure one thing in terms of another. If one knows

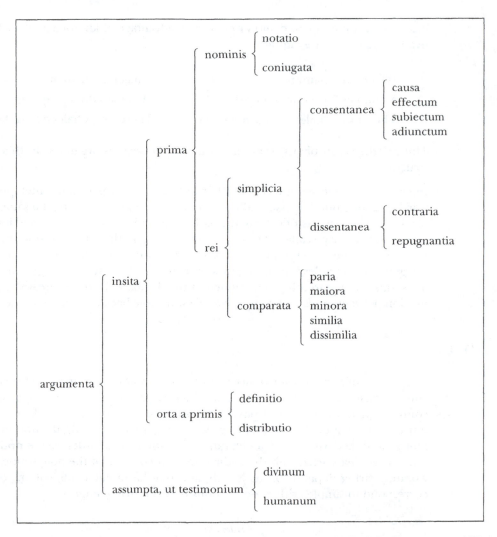

Table from *Training in Dialectic* by Peter Ramus (1547). This is the kind of classificatory tree which became very popular in the 16th and 17th centuries.

that the ratio of A to B is the same as that of B to C, that A is one inch long and B two inches long, then one can conclude that C is four inches long. If A:B = B:C and A:B = 1:2, then B:C = 1:2 = 2:*x*. If one knows that the area of a circle stands in a fixed ratio to its radius – area = πr^2, then to determine the area of a circle one need only measure its radius. Through a sequence of such reasoning, one actual measurement can fix many other quantities. In other words, ratios extend knowledge of one thing through the system of relations to many other things not directly known. This was, and is, very important in astronomy, for example, because we are not in a position to make direct measurements of the heavenly bodies or their motions. The modern

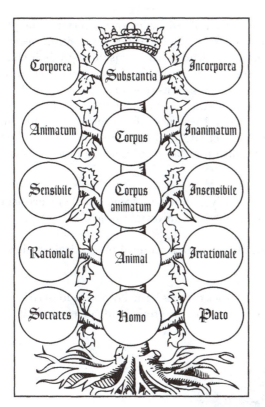

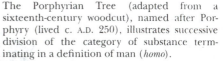

The Porphyrian Tree (adapted from a sixteenth-century woodcut), named after Porphyry (lived c. A.D. 250), illustrates successive division of the category of substance terminating in a definition of man (*homo*).

scientific conception of a law of nature as something which is expressed by means of an equation such as $e = mc^2$ embodies the same idea. Here the ratio of energy (e) to mass (m) is required to be constant [equal to the value of square of the velocity of light (c)].

Ratios exist only as relationships. To look for rational order as a system of ratios is therefore to be directed away from individual things to the whole which they compose and to the structure of their relationships. Structures of relationships can be repeatedly realized in different materials (vibrating strings and vibrating air columns, for example).

This view does not dispense with seeking knowledge of the natures of things and their attributes. Ratios can exist only between things which have some (measurable) attribute in common. What the notion of harmony introduces is the idea that there is another structure, another rational order to be discerned beneath the classificatory order of genera and species. A. N. Whitehead has written that "Classification is a halfway house between the immediate concreteness of the individual thing and the complete abstraction of mathematical notions."

The natural philosopher looks for definitions of terms, identifies things and distinguishes them one from another only in order to discern the underlying structure which they form—the harmoniously unified order of universal principles which underlies the diversity of appearances. He distinguishes parts within the whole only in order to find out how they are related, and so discerns through their changing diversity the unchanging unity—the variously realized harmonious structure of relationships, which can ultimately be expressed as relations between numbers. This is the ancient idea of *harmonia mundi* (the harmony of the world). We find it expressed frequently in the sixteenth and seventeenth centuries by figures important to the development of modern science such as Kepler and Newton. John Dee, who wrote the preface to the first English translation of Euclid's *Elements of Geometry* in 1570, for example says:

> "The entire universe is like a lyre tuned by some excellent artificer, whose strings are the separate species of the universal whole...."

We also find it expressed by Edward Witten, a modern theoretical physicist, talking about string theory:

> "... in most of the string theories there is basically one kind of string. You see, one kind of string can excite many different kinds of motion. If you think

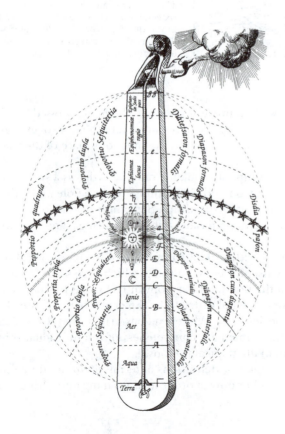

The universal lyre or monochord, adapted from *Metaphysics and Cosmic Origins* (1617) by Robert Fludd.

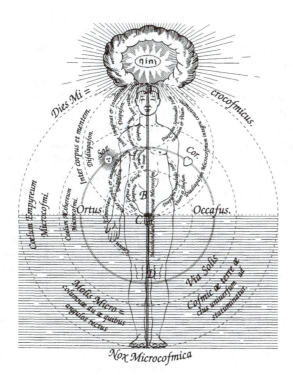

The Diapason, adapted from Fludd's *Arts and Sciences* (1618), illustrates the complex of analogies by which the microcosm (human) and the macrocosm (the cosmos) reflect each other.

about a violin, a violin string, when you play on it can vibrate at many different frequencies, called harmonics. . . . In the case of the violin string the different harmonics correspond to different sounds. In the case of a superstring, the different harmonics correspond to different elementary particles. The electron, the graviton, the photon, the neutrino and all the others are different harmonics of a fundamental string just as the different overtones of a violin string are different harmonics of one string."

In fact modern science represents a particularly fruitful weaving together of the impulse to find rational order by describing, dividing and classifying in ever more minute detail; and the impulse to seek a single, unitary order based on a few fundamental laws which determine the "harmonics" of the world.

As Whitehead expresses it, "It is this union of passionate interest in the detailed facts with equal devotion to abstract generalization which forms the novelty in our present society."

COMPUTERS

If modern scientific rationality is a tapestry woven from Aristotelian and Platonic threads, where does the computer fit in, and why has this now come to be perhaps the dominant metaphor for reason in Western culture? I remarked at the beginning that the idea of a reasoning machine was not at all new. In fact it is a very natural outgrowth of the two conceptions just outlined. Moreover, the idea that a computer embodies rationality in a superhuman form is a consequence of the way in which the philosophies of Plato and Aristotle were Christianized.

Both the conceptions outlined above presume that there is a rational order to be discerned in the world. Once the order is known and is laid out, rules can be written for moving around it, and these rules are such that their correct application does not require understanding of the particular subject matter to which they are applied. Calculations with numbers and their ratios work the same way, and must follow the same rules, whether one is dealing with pieces of chalk or planets. Aristotle's achievement was to show that there are analogous rules for "calculating" with general terms. This, for example, led Leibniz to suggest the project of devising an ideal language, one where the way the words were written would indicate how they related to other words, just as the way a numeral is written in decimal notation immediately enables us to relate it to other numbers written in the same notation.

Leibniz suggested that if such a language could be devised, then any dispute could be settled by the parties first of all agreeing on the facts of the case and then "calculating" the answer to the disputed question. In the Christian version, if the world has a rational order, it is because it was created by a supremely rational being, God. The master-plan, the rational order, is ever-present in the mind of God. It is also assumed that human reason is the same in kind as God's. The only difference is that His intellect is infinite, whereas that of any human being is finite. Modern computers may not embody infinite intellects, but they can certainly contain within them representations of more complex systems than human beings can hold in their minds. Computers can also "calculate" their way around these representations in ways which no human being could sustain. Humans get tired, bored, make mistakes, etc. Computers suffer none of these defects. They thus appear as demi-gods on our cultural scene—alternately feared and worshipped.

Do computers give us an accurate picture of human rationality or even of rationality in Western culture? I would suggest not. We would be forgetting the practical, technical rationality which was essential to bring such devices into being. It is also characteristic of Western culture to be intellectualist and elitist in its ideology. The practical wisdom of the craftsman, artisan and engineer [has] received scant attention in the writings of those concerned with cultural ideals. Yet what has really been uniquely characteristic of Western culture is that it has married scientific theory with technological practice in the manner which has produced the various industrial revolutions which have occurred since the nineteenth century. To this extent the computer does stand as an appropriate symbol of Western rationality, but it is not an embodiment of it.

Plato

In *The Republic*, Plato presents his famous "divided line," in which he sets forth in a hierarchical manner the ways in which we perceive the world and acquire knowledge, and his "allegory of the cave" (see Part IV), in which he shows how through rigorous intellectual effort the philosopher is able to attain that vision of the Good that liberates one from mere appearances and that serves to order and place all other kinds of knowing.

The section of Plato's masterpiece that follows is introduced by the translator F. M. Cornford.

F. M. CORNFORD

Introduction to the Four Stages of Cognition

[Plato] contrasted the realm of sensible appearances and shifting beliefs with the realm of eternal and unchanging Forms, dominated (as we now know) by the Good. The philosopher was he whose affections were set on knowledge of that real world. The Guardians' primary education in literature and art was mainly confined to the world of appearance and belief, though it culminated in the perception of "images" of the moral ideals, the beauty of which would excite love for the individual person in whose soul they dwelt. The higher intellectual training now to be described is to detach the mind from appearances and individuals and to carry it across the boundary between the two worlds and all the way beyond to the vision of the Good.

The allegory is here prefaced by a diagram. A line is divided into two parts, whose inequality symbolizes that the visible world has a lower degree of reality and truth than the intelligible. Each part is then subdivided in the same proportion as the whole line (this $A + B : C + D = A : B = C : D$). The four sections correspond to four states of mind or modes of cognition, each clearer and more certain than the one below.

The lower part $(A + B)$ is at first called "the Visible," . . . the wide sense . . . ; so it

From *The Republic of Plato*, translated by F. M. Cornford (1941). Reprinted by permission of Oxford University Press.

includes the "many conventional notions of the multitude" about morality. It is the physical and moral world as apprehended by those "lovers of appearance" who do not recognize the absolute ideals which Plato calls real.

(A) The lowest form of cognition is called *eikasia*. The word defies translation, being one of those current terms to which Plato gives a peculiar sense, to be inferred from the context. It is etymologically connected with *eikon* = image, likeness, and with *eikos* = likely, and it can mean either likeness (representation) or likening (comparison) or estimation of likelihood (conjecture). Perhaps "imagining" is the least unsatisfactory rendering. It seems to be the wholly unenlightened state of mind which takes sensible appearances and current moral notions at their face value. . . .

(B) The higher section stands for common-sense belief (*pistis*) in the reality of the visible and tangible things commonly called substantial. In the moral sphere it would include "correct beliefs without knowledge," such as the young Guardians were taught to hold. True beliefs are sufficient guides for action, but are insecure until based on knowledge of the reasons for them.

Higher education is to effect an escape from the prison of appearances by training the intellect, first in mathematics, and then in moral philosophy. (C) The lower section of the intelligible contains the subject-matter of the mathematical sciences. (Two characteristics of mathematical procedure are mentioned: (a) the use of visible diagrams and models as imperfect illustrations of the objects and truths of pure thought. Here is a sort of bridge carrying the mind across from the visible thing to the intelligible reality, which it must learn to distinguish. (b) Each branch of mathematics starts from unquestioned assumptions (postulates, axioms, definitions) and reasons from them deductively. The premises may be true and the conclusions may follow, but the whole structure hangs in the air until the assumptions themselves shall have been shown to depend on an unconditional principle. (This may be con-

	OBJECTS		STATES OF MIND
	The Good		
			Intelligence (*noesis*) or
INTELLIGIBLE WORLD	Forms	D	Knowledge (*episteme*)
	Mathematical objects	C	Thinking (*dianoia*)
WORLD OF APPEARANCES	Visible Things	B	Belief (*pistis*)
	Images	A	Imagining (*eikasia*)

jectured to be Unity itself, an aspect of the Good.) Meanwhile the state of mind is *dianoia,* the ordinary word for "thought" or "thinking," here implying a degree of understanding which falls short of perfect knowledge. *Dianoia* suggests discursive thinking or reasoning from premiss to conclusion, whereas *noesis* is constantly compared to the immediate act of vision and suggests rather the direct intuition or apprehension of its object.

(D) The higher method is called Dialectic. . . . In the *Republic* it simply means the technique of philosophic conversation (dialogue) carried on by question and answer and seeking to render, or to receive from a respondent, an "account" (*logos*) of some Form, usually a moral Form such as Justice in this dialogue. At this stage visible illustrations are no longer available, and the movement at first is not downward, deducing conclusions from premisses, but upward, examining the premisses themselves and seeking the ultimate principle on which they all depend. It is suggested that, if the mind could ever rise to grasp the supreme Form, it might then descend by a deduction confirming the whole structure of moral and mathematical knowledge. The state of mind is called intelligence or rational intuition (*noesis*) and knowledge (*episteme*) in the full sense.

PLATO

Four Stages of Cognition: The Line

Conceive, then, that there are these two powers I speak of, the Good reigning over the domain of all that is intelligible, the Sun over the visible world—or the heaven as I might call it; only you would think I was showing off my skill in etymology. At any rate you have these two orders of things clearly before your mind: the visible and the intelligible?

I have.

Now take a line divided into two unequal parts, one to represent the visible order, the other the intelligible; and divide each part again in the same proportion, symbolizing degrees of comparative clearness or obscurity. Then (A) one of the two sections in the visible world will stand for images. By images I mean first shadows, and then reflections in water or in close-grained, polished surfaces, and everything of that kind, if you understand.

Yes, I understand.

Let the second section (B) stand for the actual things of which the first are likenesses, the living creatures about us and all the works of nature or of human hands.

So be it.

Will you also take the proportion in which the visible world has been divided as

From *The Republic of Plato,* translated by F. M. Cornford (1941). Reprinted by permission of Oxford University Press.

corresponding to degrees of reality and truth, so that the likeness shall stand to the original in the same ratio as the sphere of appearances and belief to the sphere of knowledge?

Certainly.

Now consider how we are to divide the part which stands for the intelligible world. There are two sections. In the first (C) the mind uses as images those actual things which themselves had images in the visible world; and it is compelled to pursue its inquiry by starting from assumptions and travelling, not up to a principle, but down to a conclusion. In the second (D) the mind moves in the other direction, from an assumption up towards a principle which is not hypothetical; and it makes no use of the images employed in the other section, but only of Forms, and conducts its inquiry solely by their means.

I don't quite understand what you mean.

Then we will try again; what I have just said will help you to understand. (C) You know, of course, how students of subjects like geometry and arithmetic begin by postulating odd and even numbers, or the various figures and the three kinds of angle, and other such data in each subject. These data they take as known; and, having adopted them as assumptions, they do not feel called upon to give any account of them to themselves or to anyone else, but treat them as self-evident. Then, starting from these assumptions, they go on until they arrive, by a series of consistent steps, at all the conclusions they set out to investigate.

Yes, I know that.

You also know how they make use of visible figures and discourse about them, though what they really have in mind is the originals of which these figures are images: they are not reasoning, for instance, about this particular square and diagonal which they have drawn, but about *the* Square and *the* Diagonal; and so in all cases. The diagrams they draw and the models they make are actual things, which may have their shadows or images in water; but now they serve in their turn as images, while the student is seeking to behold those realities which only thought can apprehend.

True.

This, then, is the class of things that I spoke of as intelligible, but with two qualifications: first, that the mind, in studying them, is compelled to employ assumptions, and, because it cannot rise above these, does not travel upwards to a first principle; and second, that it uses as images those actual things which have images of their own in the section below them and which, in comparison with those shadows and reflections, are reputed to be more palpable and valued accordingly.

I understand: you mean the subject-matter of geometry and of the kindred arts.

(D) Then by the second section of the intelligible world you may understand me to mean all that unaided reasoning apprehends by the power of dialectic, when it treats its assumptions, not as first principles, but as *hypotheses* in the literal sense, things "laid down" like a flight of steps up which it may mount all the way to something that is not hypothetical, the first principle of all; and having grasped this, may turn back and, holding on to the consequences which depend upon it, descend at last to a conclusion, never making use of any sensible object, but only of Forms, moving through Forms from one to another, and ending with Forms.

I understand, he said, though not perfectly; for the procedure you describe sounds like an enormous undertaking. But I see that you mean to distinguish the field of intelligible reality studied by dialectic as having a greater certainty and truth than the subject-matter of the "arts," as they are called, which treat their assumptions as first principles. The students of these arts are, it is true, compelled to exercise thought in contemplating objects which the senses cannot perceive; but because they start from assumptions without going back to a first principle, you do not regard them as gaining true understanding about those objects, although the objects themselves, when connected with a first principle, are intelligible. And I think you would call the state of mind of the students of geometry and other such arts, not intelligence, but thinking, as being something between intelligence and mere acceptance of appearances.

You have understood me quite well enough, I replied. And now you may take, as corresponding to the four sections, these four states of mind: *intelligence* for the highest, *thinking* for the second, *belief* for the third, and for the last *imagining*. These you may arrange as the terms in a proportion, assigning to each a degree of clearness and certainty corresponding to the measure in which their objects possess truth and reality.

I understand and agree with you. I will arrange them as you say.

Descartes

In *A Discourse on Method,* René Descartes argues for the universality of reason in human beings and shares with Plato the idea—although it is understood rather differently—of a distinction to be drawn between everyday opinion and genuine knowledge. The former is based essentially on custom; the latter on the exercise of reason. While introducing here something of his own intellectual biography, Descartes proffers his rational, analytic method of demonstration, which moves from those simple beliefs that are assured by the clarity and distinctness of mind by which they are held, through a careful movement of thought comparable to that of a geometer, to the attainment of complex but certain knowledge. Descartes clearly embodies the rationalist persuasion in philosophy that, in many forms, persists to the present day.

The Universality and Method of Reason

Good sense is, of all things among men, the most equally distributed; for every one thinks himself so abundantly provided with it, that those even who are the most difficult to satisfy in everything else, do not usually desire a larger measure of this quality than they already possess. And in this it is not likely that all are mistaken: the conviction is rather to be held as testifying that the power of judging aright and of distinguishing truth from error, which is properly what is called good sense or reason, is by nature equal in all men; and that the diversity of our opinions, consequently, does not arise from some being endowed with a larger share of reason than others, but solely from this, that we conduct our thoughts along different ways, and do not fix our attention on the same objects. For to be possessed of a vigorous mind is not enough; the prime requisite is rightly to apply it. The greatest minds, as they are capable of the highest excellences, are open likewise to the greatest aberrations; and those who travel very slowly may yet make far greater progress, provided they keep always to the straight road, than those who, while they run, forsake it.

For myself, I have never fancied my mind to be in any respect more perfect than

From *A Discourse on Method* by René Descartes, translated by John Veitch, in *The Rationalists* (n.d.). Reprinted with acknowledgment to Doubleday & Company, Inc.

those of the generality; on the contrary, I have often wished that I were equal to some others in promptitude of thought, or in clearness and distinctness of imagination, or in fulness and readiness of memory. And besides these, I know of no other qualities that contribute to the perfection of the mind; for as to the reason or sense, inasmuch as it is that alone which constitutes us men, and distinguishes us from the brutes, I am disposed to believe that it is to be found complete in each individual; and on this point to adopt the common opinion of philosophers, who say that the difference of greater and less holds only among the *accidents,* and not among the *forms* or *natures of individuals* of the same *species.* . . .

From my childhood, I have been familiar with letters; and as I was given to believe that by their help a clear and certain knowledge of all that is useful in life might be acquired, I was ardently desirous of instruction. But as soon as I had finished the entire course of study, at the close of which it is customary to be admitted into the order of the learned, I completely changed my opinion. For I found myself involved in so many doubts and errors, that I was convinced I had advanced no farther in all my attempts at learning, than the discovery at every turn of my own ignorance. And yet I was studying in one of the most celebrated schools in Europe, in which I thought there must be learned men, if such were anywhere to be found. I had been taught all that others learned there; and not contented with the sciences actually taught us, I had, in addition, read all the books that had fallen into my hands, treating of such branches as are esteemed the most curious and rare. I knew the judgment which others had formed of me; and I did not find that I was considered inferior to my fellows, although there were among them some who were already marked out to fill the places of our instructors. And, in fine, our age appeared to me as flourishing, and as fertile in powerful minds as any preceding one. I was thus led to take the liberty of judging of all other men by myself, and of concluding that there was no science in existence that was of such a nature as I had previously been given to believe. . . .

. . . I took into account also the very different character which a person brought up from infancy in France or Germany exhibits, from that which, with the same mind originally, this individual would have possessed had he lived always among the Chinese or with savages, and the circumstance that in dress itself the fashion which pleased us ten years ago, and which may again, perhaps, be received into favour before ten years have gone, appears to us at this moment extravagant and ridiculous. I was thus led to infer that the ground of our opinions is far more custom and example than any certain knowledge. . . . I could, however, select from the crowd no one whose opinions seemed worthy of preference, and thus I found myself constrained, as it were, to use my own reason in the conduct of my life.

But like one walking alone and in the dark, I resolved to proceed so slowly and with such circumspection, that if I did not advance far, I would at least guard against falling. I did not even choose to dismiss summarily any of the opinions that had crept into my belief without having been introduced by reason, but first of all took sufficient time carefully to satisfy myself of the general nature of the task I was setting myself, and ascertain the true method by which to arrive at the knowledge of whatever lay within the compass of my powers.

Among the branches of philosophy, I had, at an earlier period, given some attention to logic, and among those of the mathematics to geometrical analysis and algebra,—three arts or sciences which ought, as I conceived, to contribute something to my design. But, on examination, I found that, as for logic, its syllogisms and the majority of its other precepts are of avail rather in the communication of what we already know . . . than in the investigation of the unknown; and although this science contains indeed a number of correct and very excellent precepts, there are, nevertheless, so many others, and these either injurious or superfluous, mingled with the former, that it is almost quite as difficult to effect a severance of the true from the false as it is to extract a Diana or a Minerva from a rough block of marble. Then as to the analysis of the ancients and the algebra of the moderns, besides that they embrace only matters highly abstract, and, to appearance, of no use, the former is so exclusively restricted to the consideration of figures, that it can exercise the understanding only on condition of greatly fatiguing the imagination; and, in the latter, there is so complete a subjection to certain rules and formulas, that there results an art full of confusion and obscurity calculated to embarrass, instead of a science fitted to cultivate the mind. By these considerations I was induced to seek some other method which would comprise the advantages of the three and be exempt from their defects. And as a multitude of laws often only hampers justice, so that a state is best governed when, with few laws, these are rigidly administered; in like manner, instead of the great number of precepts of which logic is composed, I believed that the four following would prove perfectly sufficient for me, provided I took the firm and unwavering resolution never in a single instance to fail in observing them.

The *first* was never to accept anything for true which I did not clearly know to be such; that is to say, carefully to avoid precipitancy and prejudice, and to comprise nothing more in my judgment than what was presented to my mind so clearly and distinctly as to exclude all ground of doubt.

The *second,* to divide each of the difficulties under examination into as many parts as possible, and as might be necessary for its adequate solution.

The *third,* to conduct my thoughts in such order that, by commencing with objects the simplest and easiest to know, I might ascend by little and little, and, as it were, step by step, to the knowledge of the more complex; assigning in thought a certain order even to those objects which in their own nature do not stand in a relation of antecedence and sequence.

And the *last,* in every case to make enumerations so complete and reviews so general, that I might be assured that nothing was omitted.

The long chains of simple and easy reasonings by means of which geometers are accustomed to reach the conclusions of their most difficult demonstrations, had led me to imagine that all things, to the knowledge of which man is competent, are mutually connected in the same way, and that there is nothing so far removed from us as to be beyond our reach, or so hidden that we cannot discover it, provided only we abstain from accepting the false for the true, and always preserve in our thoughts the order necessary for the deduction of one truth from another. And I had little difficulty in determining the objects with which it was necessary to commence, for I was already persuaded that it must be with the simplest and easiest to know, and, considering that of all those who have hitherto sought truth in the sciences, the mathematicians alone have been able to find any demonstrations, that is, any certain and evident reasons, I did not doubt but that such must have been the rule of their investigations. I resolved to commence, therefore, with the examination of the simplest objects, not anticipating, however, from this any other advantage than that to be found in accustoming my mind to the love and nourishment of truth, and to a distaste for all such reasonings as were unsound. But I had no intention on that account of attempting to master all the particular sciences commonly denominated mathematics: but observing that, however different their objects, they all agree in considering only the various relations or proportions subsisting among those objects, I thought it best for my purpose to consider these proportions in the most general form possible, without referring them to any objects in particular, except such as would most facilitate the knowledge of them, and without by any means restricting them to these, that afterwards I might thus be the better able to apply them to every other class of objects to which they are legitimately applicable. Perceiving further, that in order to understand these relations I should sometimes have to consider them one by one, and sometimes only to bear them in mind, or embrace them in the aggregate, I thought that, in order the better to consider them individually, I should view them as subsisting between staight lines, than which I could find no objects more simple, or capable of being more distinctly represented to my imagination and senses; and on the other hand, that in order to retain them in the memory, or embrace an aggregate of many, I should express them by certain characters the briefest possible. In this way I believed that I could borrow all that was best both in geometrical analysis and in algebra, and correct all the defects of the one by help of the other.

And, in point of fact, the accurate observance of these few precepts gave me, I take the liberty of saying, such ease in unravelling all the questions embraced in these two sciences, that in the two or three months I devoted to their examination, not only did I reach solutions of questions I had formerly deemed exceedingly difficult, but even as regards questions of the solution of which I continued ignorant, I was enabled, as it appeared to me, to determine the means whereby, and the extent to which, a solution was possible; results attributable to the circumstance that I commenced with the simplest and most general truths, and that thus each truth discovered was a rule available in the discovery of subsequent ones. Nor in this perhaps shall I appear too vain, if it be considered that, as the truth on any particular point is one, whoever apprehends the truth, knows all that on that point can be known. The child, for example, who has been instructed in the elements of arithmetic, and has made a particular addition, according to rule, may be assured that he has found, with respect to the sum of the numbers before him, all that in this instance is within the reach of human genius. Now, in conclusion, the method which teaches adherence to the true order, and an exact enumeration of all the conditions of the thing sought includes all that gives certitude to the rules of arithmetic.

But the chief ground of my satisfaction with this method, was the assurance I had of thereby exercising my reason in all matters, if not with absolute perfection, at least with the greatest attainable by me: besides, I was conscious that by its use my mind was becoming gradually habituated to clearer and more distinct conceptions of its objects; and I hoped also, from not having restricted this method to any particular matter, to apply it to the difficulties of the other sciences, with not less success than to those of algebra. I should not, however, on this account have ventured at once on the examination of all the difficulties of the sciences which presented themselves to me, for this would have been contrary to the order prescribed in the method, but observing that the knowledge of such is dependent on principles borrowed from philosophy, in which I found nothing certain, I thought it necessary first of all to endeavour to establish its principles. And because I observed, besides, that an inquiry of this kind was of all others of the greatest moment, and one in which precipitancy and anticipation in judgment were most to be dreaded, I thought that I ought not to approach it till I had reached a more mature age (being at the time but twenty-three), and had first of all employed much of my time in preparation for the work, as well by eradicating from my mind all the erroneous opinions I had up to that moment accepted, as by amassing variety of experience to afford materials for my reasonings, and by continually exercising myself in my chosen method with a view to increase skill in its application.

Leibniz

Gottfried Wilhelm Leibniz (1646–1716) is considered to be one of the most renowned thinkers of the seventeenth century, having made significant contributions to mathematics (he was a discoverer of the differential calculus), jurisprudence, history, and physics as well as philosophy. He corresponded and conversed with the major thinkers of his time and traveled extensively throughout Europe. Among his many important philosophical works are Discourse on Metaphysics *(1686) and* Monadology *(1714).*

Carrying forward Descartes's rationalist program, Leibniz argues for the complete autonomy of the rational mind, since "nothing can be taught us of which we have not already in our minds the idea." He strongly favors Plato over Aristotle, who, in his account of the origin of knowledge, looked to sense experience as the source of what we know. Leibniz celebrates Plato's dialogue *Meno,* wherein he showed how an ignorant slave boy could reason adequately to arrive at various truths of geometry.

The Kinds and the Source of Knowledge

WHAT CLEAR AND OBSCURE, DISTINCT AND CONFUSED, ADEQUATE AND INADEQUATE, INTUITIVE AND ASSUMED KNOWLEDGE IS, AND THE DEFINITION OF NOMINAL, REAL, CAUSAL AND ESSENTIAL

In order to understand better the nature of ideas it is necessary to touch somewhat upon the various kinds of knowledge. When I am able to recognize a thing among others, without being able to say in what its differences or characteristics consist, the knowledge is confused. Sometimes indeed we may know clearly, that is without being in the slightest doubt, that a poem or a picture is well or badly done because there is in it an "I know not what" which satisfies or shocks us. Such knowledge is not

From *Discourse on Metaphysics* by Gottfried Leibniz, translated by George Montgomery, with revisions by Albert R. Chandler, in *The Rationalists* (n.d.). Reprinted with acknowledgment to Doubleday & Company, Inc.

yet distinct. It is when I am able to explain the peculiarities which a thing has, that the knowledge is called distinct. Such is the knowledge of an assayer who discerns the true gold from the false by means of certain tests or marks which make up the definition of gold. But distinct knowledge has degrees, because ordinarily the conceptions which enter into the definitions will themselves be in need of definition, and are only known confusedly. When at length everything which enters into a definition or into distinct knowledge is known distinctly, even back to the primitive conception, I call that knowledge adequate. When my mind understands at once and distinctly all the primitive ingredients of a conception, then we have intuitive knowledge. This is extremely rare as most human knowledge is only confused or indeed assumed. . . .

IDEAS ARE ALL STORED UP WITHIN US: PLATO'S DOCTRINE OF REMINISCENCE

In order to see clearly what an idea is, we must guard ourselves against a misunderstanding. Many regard the idea as the form or the differentiation of our thinking, and according to this opinion we have the idea in our mind, in so far as we are thinking of it, and each separate time that we think of it anew we have another idea although similar to the preceding one. Some, however, take the idea as the immediate object of thought, or as a permanent form which remains even when we are no longer contemplating it. As a matter of fact our soul has the power of representing to itself any form or nature whenever the occasion comes for thinking about it, and I think that this activity of our soul is, so far as it expresses some nature, form or essence, properly the idea of the thing. This is in us, and is always in us, whether we are thinking of it or no. (Our soul expresses God and the universe and all essences as well as all existences.) This position is in accord with my principles that naturally nothing enters into our minds from outside.

It is a bad habit we have of thinking as though our minds receive certain messengers, as it were, or as if they had doors or windows. We have in our minds all those forms for all periods of time because the mind at every moment expresses all its future thoughts and already thinks confusedly of all that of which it will ever think distinctly. Nothing can be taught us of which we have not already in our minds the idea. This idea is as it were the material out of which the thought will form itself. This is what Plato has excellently brought out in his doctrine of reminiscence, a doctrine which contains a great deal of truth, provided that it is properly understood and purged of the error of pre-existence, and provided that one does not conceive of the soul as having already known and thought at some other time what it learns and thinks now. Plato has also confirmed his position by a beautiful experiment. He introduces [*Meno*] a boy, whom he leads by short steps, to extremely difficult truths of geometry bearing on incommensurables, all this without teaching the boy anything, merely drawing out replies by a well arranged series of questions. This shows that the soul virtually knows those things, and needs only to be reminded (animadverted) to recognize the truths. Consequently it possesses at least the idea upon

Gottfried Wilhelm Leibniz. New York
Public Library Picture Collection.

which those truths depend. We may say even that it already possesses those truths, if
we consider them as the relations of the ideas.

IN WHAT RESPECT OUR SOULS CAN BE COMPARED TO BLANK
TABLETS AND HOW CONCEPTIONS ARE DERIVED
FROM THE SENSES

Aristotle preferred to compare our souls to blank tablets prepared for writing, and
he maintained that nothing is in the understanding which does not come through
the senses. This position is in accord with the popular conceptions, as Aristotle's approach usually is. Plato thinks more profoundly. Such tenets or practicologies are
nevertheless allowable in ordinary use somewhat in the same way as those who accept the Copernican theory still continue to speak of the rising and setting of the
sun. . . . It is always false to say that all our conceptions come from the so-called external senses, because those conceptions which I have of myself and of my thoughts,
and consequently of being, of substance, of action, of identity, and of many others
come from an inner experience.

Locke

John Locke, as one of the founders of the British tradition of empiricism, strongly opposed the kind of rationalism advocated by Descartes and Leibniz. Looking to sense experience as the primary source of our ideas, Locke wants, as he says, "to inquire into the original, certainty, and extent of *human knowledge*, together with the grounds and degrees of *belief, opinion,* and *assent."* He allows that we must be content with that knowledge to which our understanding is suited.

Locke is concerned with our "ideas," by which he means "whatsoever is the *object* of the understanding when a man thinks," and he is intent upon showing that none of our genuine ideas are "innate" in the rationalistic sense of preceding all our experience as part of a natural mental endowment. There is, for Locke, no "hard-wiring" of the mind that necessitates our having various primitive notions, categories, or principles that are universally accepted. On the contrary, it is by means of our senses and our powers of self-reflection that we receive all the materials from which we are able to acquire simple ideas and form complex ones and attain whatever truths through observation and reasoning that we are able to possess.

In its general commitment to sense experience, if not in its precise description regarding how we actually acquire ideas, Locke's empiricism has been an enduring force in modern philosophy and has set the course for many of the debates and arguments that persist in contemporary philosophy.

The Origin of Knowledge in Sense Experience

Since it is the *understanding* that sets man above the rest of sensible beings, and gives him all the advantage and dominion which he has over them, it is certainly a subject, even for its nobleness, worth our labour to inquire into. The understanding, like the eye, whilst it makes us see and perceive all other things, takes no notice on itself; and it requires art and pains to set it at a distance and make it its own object. But whatever be the difficulties that lie in the way of this inquiry, whatever it be that keeps us so much in the dark to ourselves, sure I am that all the light we can let in upon our minds, all the acquaintance we can make with our own understandings, will not only

From *An Essay Concerning Human Understanding* by John Locke (London: E. Holt, 1689).

be very pleasant, but bring us great advantage in directing our thoughts in the search of other things.

This, therefore, being my purpose—to inquire into the original, certainty, and extent of *human knowledge,* together with the grounds and degrees of *belief, opinion, and assent*—I shall not at present meddle with the physical consideration of the mind, or trouble myself to examine wherein its essence consists, or by what motions of our spirits or alterations of our bodies we come to have any *sensation* by our organs, or any *ideas* in our understandings, and whether those ideas do in their formation, any or all of them, depend on matter or not. These are speculations which, however curious and entertaining, I shall decline, as lying out of my way in the design I am now upon. It shall suffice to my present purpose to consider the discerning faculties of a man, as they are employed about the objects which they have to do with. . . .

It is therefore worthwhile to search out the bounds between opinion and knowledge; and examine by what measures, in things whereof we have no certain knowledge, we ought to regulate our assent and moderate our persuasion. In order whereunto I shall pursue this following method:—

First I shall inquire into the original of those *ideas,* notions, or whatever else you please to call them, which a man observes, and is conscious to himself he has in his mind; and the ways whereby the understanding comes to be furnished with them.

Secondly, I shall endeavour to show what *knowledge* the understanding hath by those ideas; and the certainty, evidence, and extent of it.

Thirdly, I shall make some inquiry into the nature and grounds of *faith* or *opinion:* whereby I mean that assent which we give to any proposition as true, of whose truth yet we have not certain knowledge. And here we shall have occasion to examine the reasons and degrees of *assent.*

If by this inquiry into the nature of the understanding, I can discover the powers thereof; how far they reach; to what things they are in any degree proportionate; and where they fail us, I suppose it may be of use to prevail with the busy mind of man to be more cautious in meddling with things exceeding its comprehension; to stop when it is at the utmost extent of its tether; and to sit down in a quiet ignorance of those things which, upon examination, are found to be beyond the reach of our capacities. We should not then perhaps be so forward, out of an affectation of an universal knowledge, to raise questions, and perplex ourselves and others with disputes about things to which our understandings are not suited, and of which we cannot frame in our minds any clear or distinct perceptions, or whereof (as it has perhaps too often happened) we have not any notions at all. If we can find out how far the understanding can extend its view; how far it has faculties to attain certainty, and in what cases it can only judge and guess, we may learn to content ourselves with what is attainable by us in this state. . . .

. . . The Candle that is set up shines bright enough for all our purposes. The discoveries we can make with this ought to satisfy us; and we shall then use our understandings right, when we entertain all objects in that way and proportion that they are suited to our faculties, and upon those grounds they are capable of being proposed to us; and not peremptorily or intemperately require demonstration, and demand certainty, where probability only is to be had, and which is sufficient to govern all our concernments. If we will disbelieve everything, because we cannot certainly know all things, we shall do much what as wisely as he who would not use his legs, but sit still and perish, because he had no wings to fly.

When we know our own strength, we shall the better know what to undertake with hopes of success; and when we have well surveyed the *powers* of our own minds, and made some estimate what we may expect from them, we shall not be inclined either to sit still, and not set our thoughts on work at all, in despair of knowing anything; nor on the other side, question everything, and disclaim all knowledge, because some things are not to be understood. . . . Our business here is not to know all things, but those which concern our conduct. If we can find out those measures, whereby a rational creature, put in that state in which man is in this world, may and ought to govern his opinions, and actions depending thereon, we need not to be troubled that some other things escape our knowledge.

This was that which gave the first rise to this *Essay* concerning the understanding. For I thought that the first step towards satisfying several inquiries the mind of man was very apt to run into was to take a survey of our own understandings, examine our own powers, and see to what things they were adapted. Till that was done I suspected we began at the wrong end, and in vain sought for satisfaction in a quiet and sure possession of truths that most concerned us, whilst we let loose our thoughts into the vast ocean of Being; as if all that boundless extent were the natural and undoubted possession of our understandings wherein there was nothing exempt from its decisions, or that escaped its comprehension. Thus men, extending their inquiries beyond their capacities, and letting their thoughts wander into those depths where they can find no sure footing, it is no wonder that they raise questions and multiply disputes, which, never coming to any clear resolution, are proper only to continue and increase their doubts, and to confirm them at last in perfect scepticism. Whereas, were the capacities of our understandings well considered, the extent of our knowledge once discovered, and the horizon found which sets the bounds between the enlightened and dark parts of things, between what is and what is not comprehensible by us, men would perhaps with less scruple acquiesce in the avowed ignorance of the one, and employ their thoughts and discourse with more advantage and satisfaction in the other.

Thus much I thought necessary to say concerning the occasion of this Inquiry into human Understanding. But, before I proceed on to what I have thought on this subject, I must here in the entrance beg pardon of my reader for the frequent use of the word *idea,* which he will find in the following treatise. It being that term which, I think, serves best to stand for whatsoever is the *object* of the understanding when a man thinks, I have used it to express whatever is meant by *phantasm, notion, species,* or *whatever it is which the mind can be employed about in thinking,* and I could not avoid frequently using it.

I presume it will be easily granted me, that there are such *ideas* in men's minds: everyone is conscious of them in himself; and men's words and actions will satisfy him that they are in others.

Our first inquiry then shall be how they come into the mind.

.   .   .

It is an established opinion amongst some men, that there are in the understanding certain *innate principles;* some primary notions, characters, as it were stamped upon the mind of man, which the soul receives in its very first being, and brings into the world with it. It would be sufficient to convince unpredjudiced readers of the falseness of this supposition, if I should only show (as I hope I shall in the following parts of this Discourse) how men, barely by the use of their natural faculties, may attain to all the knowledge they have, without the help of any innate impressions; and may arrive at certainty, without any such original notions or principles. For I imagine any one will easily grant that it would be impertinent to suppose the ideas of colours innate in a creature to whom God hath given sight, and a power to receive them by the eyes from external objects: and no less unreasonable would it be to attribute several truths to the impressions of nature, and innate characters, when we may observe in ourselves faculties fit to attain as easy and certain knowledge of them as if they were originally imprinted on the mind.

But because a man is not permitted without censure to follow his own thoughts in the search of truth when they lead him ever so little out of the common road, I shall set down the reasons that made me doubt of the truth of that opinion, as an excuse for my mistake, if I be in one, which I leave to be considered by those who, with me, dispose themselves to embrace truth wherever they find it.

There is nothing more commonly taken for granted than that there are certain *principles,* both *speculative* and *practical,* (for they speak of both), universally agreed upon by all mankind: which therefore, they argue, must needs be the constant impressions which the souls of men receive in their first beings, and which they bring into the world with them, as necessarily and really as they do any of their inherent faculties.

This argument, drawn from universal consent, has this misfortune in it, that if it were true in matter of fact that there were certain truths wherein all mankind agreed, it would not prove them innate, if there can be any other way shown how men may come to that universal agreement in the things they do consent in, which I presume may be done.

But, which is worse, this argument of universal consent, which is made use of to prove innate principles, seems to me a demonstration that there are none such: because there are none to which all mankind give an universal assent. I shall begin with the speculative, and instance in those magnified principles of demonstration, 'Whatsoever is, is,' and 'It is impossible for the same thing to be and not to be', which, of all others, I think have the most allowed title to innate. These have so settled a reputation of maxims universally received that it will no doubt be thought strange if any one should seem to question it. But yet I take liberty to say, that these propositions are so far from having an universal assent, that there are a great part of mankind to whom they are not so much as known.

For, first, it is evident, that all children and idiots have not the least apprehension or thought of them. And the want of that is enough to destroy that universal assent which must needs be the necessary concomitant of all innate truths: it seeming to me near a contradiction to say, that there are truths imprinted on the soul which it perceives or understands not: imprinting, if it signify anything, being nothing else but the making certain truths to be perceived. For to imprint anything on the mind without the mind's perceiving it seems to me hardly intelligible. If therefore children and idiots have souls, have minds, with those impressions upon them, *they* must unavoidably perceive them, and necessarily know and assent to these truths; which since they do not, it is evident that there are no such impressions. For if they are not notions naturally imprinted, how can they be innate? and if they are notions imprinted, how can they be unknown? To say a notion is imprinted on the mind, and yet at the same time to say, that the kind is ignorant of it, and never yet took notice of it, is to make this impression nothing. . . . He therefore that talks of innate notions in the understanding cannot (if he intend thereby any distinct sort of truths) mean such truths to be in the understanding as it never perceived, and is yet wholly ignorant of. For if these words "to be in the understanding" have any propriety, they signify to be understood. So that to be in the understanding, and not to be understood, to be in the mind and never to be perceived, is all one as to say anything is and is not in the mind or understanding. If therefore these two propositions, "Whatsoever is, is," and "It is impossible for the same thing to be and not to be," are by nature imprinted, children cannot be ignorant of them: infants, and all that have souls, most necessarily have them in their understandings, know the truth of them, and assent to it.

To avoid this it is usually answered that all men know and assent to them *when they come to the use of reason,* and this is enough to prove them innate. I answer:

Doubtful expressions, that have scarce any significance, go for clear reasons to those who, being prepossessed, take not the pains to examine even what they themselves say. For, to apply this answer with any tolerable sense to our present purpose, it must signify one of these two things: either that as soon as men come to the use of reason these supposed native inscriptions come to be known and observed by them, or else, that the use and exercise of men's reason assists them in the discovery of these principles, and certainly makes them known to them.

If they mean that by the use of reason men may discover these principles, and that this is sufficient to prove them innate, their way of arguing will stand thus, viz. that whatever truths reason can certainly discover to us, and make us firmly assent to, those are all naturally imprinted on the mind, since that universal assent, which is made the mark of them amounts to no more but this—that by the use of reason we are capable to come to a certain knowledge of and assent to them, and, by this means, there will be no difference between the maxims of the mathematicians and theorems they deduce from them: all must be equally allowed innate; they being all discoveries made by the use of reason, and truths that a rational creature may certainly come to know, if he apply his thoughts rightly that way.

But how can these men think the use of reason necessary to discover principles that are supposed innate, when reason (if we may believe them) is nothing else but the faculty of deducing unknown truths from principles of propositions that are already known? That certainly can never be thought innate which we have need of reason to discover, unless as I have said, we will have all the certain truths that reason ever teaches us to be innate. We may as well think the use of reason necessary to make our eyes discover visible objects, as that there should be need of reason, or the exercise thereof, to make the understanding see what is originally engraven on it, and cannot be in the understanding before it be perceived by it. So that to make reason discover those truths thus imprinted is to say that the use of reason discovers to a man what he knew before: and if men have those innate impressed truths originally, and before the use of reason, and yet are always ignorant of them till they come to the use of reason, it is in effect to say that men know and know them not at the same time. . . .

Those who will take the pains to reflect with a little attention on the operations of the understanding will find that this ready assent of the mind to some truths depends not either on native inscription or the use of reason, but on a faculty of the mind quite distinct from both of them, as we shall see hereafter. Reason, therefore, having nothing to do in procuring our assent to these maxims, if by saying, that "men know and assent to them when they come to the use of reason," be meant, that the use of reason assists us in the knowledge of these maxims, it is utterly false; and were it true, would prove them not to be innate.

If by knowing and assenting to them "when we come to the use of reason," be meant, that this is the time when they come to be taken notice of by the mind, and that as soon as children come to the use of reason they come also to know and assent to these maxims, this also is false and frivolous. First, it is false because it is evident these maxims are not in the mind so early as the use of reason; and therefore the coming to the use of reason is falsely assigned as the time of their discovery. How many instances of the use of reason may we observe in children a long time before they have any knowledge of this maxim, "That it is impossible for the same thing to be and not to be"? And a great part of illiterate people and savages pass many years, even of their rational age, without ever thinking on this and the like general propositions. I grant, men come not to the knowledge of these general and more abstract truths, which are thought innate, till they come to the use of reason; and I add, nor then neither. Which is so because till after they come to the use of reason, those general abstract ideas are not framed in the mind, about which those general maxims are, which are mistaken for innate principles, but are indeed discoveries made and verities introduced and brought into mind by the same way, and discovered by the same steps, as several other propositions, which nobody was ever so extravagant as to suppose innate. . . . I allow therefore, a necessity that men should come to the use of reason before they get the knowledge of those general truths; but deny that men's coming to the use of reason is the time of their discovery. . . .

The senses at first let in *particular* ideas, and furnish the yet empty cabinet, and the mind by degrees growing familiar with some of them, they are lodged in the memory, and names got to them. Afterwards, the mind proceeding further, abstracts them, and by degrees learns the use of general names. In this manner the mind comes to be furnished with ideas and language, the *materials* about which to exercise its discursive faculty. And the use of reason becomes daily more visible, as these materials that give it employment increase. But though the having of general ideas and the use of general words and reason usually grow together, yet I see not how this any way proves them innate. The knowledge of some truths, I confess, is very early in the mind; but in a way that shows them not to be innate. For, if we will observe, who shall find it still to be about ideas, not innate, but acquired; it being about those first which are imprinted by external things, with which infants have earliest to do, which make the most frequent impressions on their senses. In ideas thus got, the mind discovers that some agree and others differ, probably as soon as it has any use of memory; as soon as it is able to retain and perceive distinct ideas. But whether it be then or no, this is certain, it does so long before it has the use of words; or comes to that which we commonly call "the use of reason." For a child knows as certainly before it can speak the difference between the ideas of sweet and bitter (i.e., that sweet is not bitter), as it knows afterwards (when it comes to speak) that wormwood and sugarplums are not the same thing. . . .

Every man being conscious to himself that he thinks, and that which his mind is applied about whilst thinking being the *ideas* that are there, it is past doubt that men have in their minds several ideas—such as are those expressed by the words *whiteness, hardness, sweetness, thinking, motion, man, elephant, army, drunkenness,* and others: it is in the first place then to be inquired, *How he comes by them?* . . .

Let us then suppose the mind to be, as we say, white paper, void of all characters, without any ideas—How comes it to be furnished? Whence comes it by that vast store which the busy and boundless fancy of man has painted on it with an almost endless variety? Whence has it all the *materials* of reason and knowledge? To this I answer, in one word, from *experience.* In that all our knowledge is founded; and from that it ultimately derives itself. Our observation employed either about external sensible objects or about the internal operations of our minds perceived and reflected on by ourselves, is that which supplies our understandings with all the *materials* of thinking. These two are the fountains of knowledge from whence all the ideas we have, or can naturally have, do spring.

First, our Senses, conversant about particular sensible objects, do convey into the mind several distinct perceptions of things, according to those various ways wherein those objects do affect them. And thus we come by those *ideas* we have of *yellow, white, heat, cold, soft, hard, bitter, sweet,* and all those which we call sensible qualities; which when I say the senses convey into the mind, I mean, they from external objects convey into the mind what produces those perceptions. This great source of most of the ideas we have, depending wholly upon our senses, and derived by them to the understanding, I call *sensation.*

Secondly, the other fountain from which experience furnisheth the understanding with ideas is the perception of the operations of our own mind within us, as it is employed about the ideas it has got which operations, when the soul comes to reflect on and consider, do furnish the understanding with another set of ideas, which could not be had from things without. And such are *perception, thinking, doubting, believing, reasoning, knowing, willing,* and all the different actings of our own minds—which we being conscious of, and observing in ourselves, do from these receive into our understandings as distinct ideas as we do from bodies affecting our senses. This source of ideas every man has wholly in himself; and though it be not sense, as having nothing to do with external objects, yet it is very like it, and might properly enough be called *internal sense.* But as I call the other Sensation, so I call this *reflection,* the ideas it affords being such only as the mind gets by reflecting on its own operations within itself. By reflection then, in the following part of this discourse, I would be understood to mean, that notice which the mind takes of its own operations, and the manner or not; and the operations of our minds will not let us be without, at least, some obscure notions of them. No man can be wholly ignorant of what he does when he thinks. These simple ideas, when offered to the mind, the understanding can no more refuse to have, nor alter when they are imprinted, nor blot them out and make new ones itself, than a mirror can refuse, alter or obliterate the images or ideas which the objects set before it do therein produce. As the bodies that surround us do diversely affect our organs, the mind is forced to receive the impressions, and cannot avoid the perception of those ideas that are annexed to them.

The better to understand the nature, manner, and extent of our knowledge, one thing is carefully to be observed concerning the ideas we have, and that is, that some of them are *simple* and some *complex*.

Though the qualities that affect our senses are, in the things themselves, so united and blended that there is no separation, no distance between them, yet it is plain that the ideas they produce in the mind enter by the senses simple and unmixed. For, though the sight and touch often take in from the same object, at the same time, different ideas—as a man sees at once motion and colour [and] the hand feels softness and warmth in the same piece of wax—yet the simple ideas thus united in the same subject are as perfectly distinct as those that come in by different senses. The coldness and hardness which a man feels in a piece of ice being as distinct ideas in the mind as the smell and whiteness of a lily, or as the taste of sugar and smell of a rose. And there is nothing can be plainer to a man than the clear and distinct perception he has of those simple ideas; which, being each in itself uncompounded, contains in it nothing but *one uniform appearance of conception in the mind,* and is not distinguishable into different ideas.

These simple ideas, the materials of all our knowledge, are suggested and furnished to the mind only by those two ways above mentioned, viz. sensation and reflection. When the understanding is once stored with these simple ideas, it has the power to repeat, compare, and unite them, even to an almost infinite variety, and so can make at pleasure new complex ideas. But it is not in the power of the most exalted wit, or enlarged understanding, by any quickness or variety of thought, to *invent* or *frame* one new simple idea in the mind, not taken in by the ways before mentioned: nor can any force of the understanding *destroy* those that are there. The dominion of man, in this little world of his own understanding being much what the same as it is in the great world of visible things, wherein his power, however managed by art and skill, reaches no farther than to compound and divide the materials that are made to his hand, but can do nothing towards the making the least particle of new matter, or destroying one atom of what is already in being. The same inability will every one find in himself, who shall go about to fashion in his understanding one simple idea, not received in by his senses from external objects, or by reflection from the operations of his own mind about them. I would have any one try to fancy any taste which had never affected his palate, or frame the idea of a scent he had never smelt: and when he can do this, I will also conclude that a blind man hath ideas of colours, and a deaf man true distinct notions of sounds.

Kant

Immanuel Kant is usually credited with working out the first and most important synthesis between rationalism and empiricism, and thereby, so he claimed, doing for philosophy what Copernicus did for science—revolutionizing the way in which as rational beings we regard our place in nature. His system was developed primarily in his three "critiques"—the *Critique of Pure Reason* (1781), the *Critique of Practical Reason* (1788), and the *Critique of Judgment* (1790). Kant argues that we possess various modes of *a priori* knowledge that precede all experience, with the senses always providing their contents. Conception without perception, he insists, is empty; perception without conception is blind. Kant is concerned with justifying the claims of science and with setting the precise boundaries of that about which we can properly reason.

For Kant, then, the world appears to us as it does because of the nature of our own minds that structure all experience in certain ways. We set up the rules by which we order our experience spatially, temporally, and causally. The principles of mathematics and the laws of science are true because we essentially make them so. But our reasoning powers, according to Kant (as will be shown in Part IV), cannot extend beyond our experience, beyond the world that we constitute through the necessary operations of our own minds.

In the following selection from the *Critique of Pure Reason*, Kant argues for the necessity of *a priori* knowledge and draws carefully a distinction, which has haunted Western philosophy ever since, between analytic and synthetic judgments—between those that are essentially definitional in nature (e.g., "All bodies are extended") and thus add nothing new to our knowledge of the concept, from those that (e.g., "All bodies are heavy"), provide new knowledge.

A Priori *Knowledge and Analytic and Synthetic Judgments*

There can be no doubt that all our knowledge begins with experience. For how should our faculty of knowledge be awakened into action did not objects affecting our senses partly of themselves produce representations, partly arouse the activity of our understanding to compare these representations, and, by combining or separating them, work up the raw material of the sensible impressions into that knowledge of objects which is entitled experience? In the order of time, therefore, we have no knowledge antecedent to experience, and with experience all our knowledge begins.

But though all our knowledge begins with experience, it does not follow that it all arises out of experience. For it may well be that even our empirical knowledge is made up of what we receive through impressions and of what our own faculty of knowledge (sensible impressions serving merely as the occasion) supplies from itself. If our faculty of knowledge makes any such addition, it may be that we are not in a position to distinguish it from the raw material, until with long practice of attention we have become skilled in separating it.

This, then, is a question which at least calls for closer examination, and does not allow of any off-hand answer:—whether there is any knowledge that is thus independent of experience and even of all impressions of the senses. Such knowledge is entitled *a priori*, and distinguished from the *empirical*, which has its sources *a posteriori*, that is, in experience.

The expression *"a priori"* does not, however, indicate with sufficient precision the full meaning of our question. For it has been customary to say, even of much knowledge that is derived from empirical sources, that we have it or are capable of having it *a priori*, meaning thereby that we do not derive it immediately from experience, but from a universal rule—a rule which is itself, however, borrowed by us from experience. Thus we would say of a man who undermined the foundations of his house, that he might have known *a priori* that it would fall, that is, that he need not have waited for the experience of its actual falling. But still he could not know this completely *a priori*. For he had first to learn through experience that bodies are heavy, and therefore fall when their supports are withdrawn.

In what follows, therefore, we shall understand by *a priori* knowledge, not knowledge independent of this or that experience, but knowledge absolutely independent of all experience. Opposed to it is empirical knowledge, which is knowledge possible only *a posteriori*, that is, through experience. *A priori* modes of knowledge are entitled pure when there is no admixture of anything empirical. Thus, for instance, the proposition, "every alteration has its cause," while an *a priori* proposition,

From *Critique of Pure Reason* by Immanuel Kant, translated by Norman Kemp Smith (1929). Reprinted by permission of Macmillan Press Ltd.

is not a pure proposition, because alteration is a concept which can be derived only from experience.

WE ARE IN POSSESSION OF CERTAIN MODES OF *A PRIORI* KNOWLEDGE, AND EVEN THE COMMON UNDERSTANDING IS NEVER WITHOUT THEM

What we here require is a criterion by which to distinguish with certainty between pure and empirical knowledge. Experience teaches us that a thing is so and so, but not that it cannot be otherwise. First, then, if we have a proposition which in being thought is thought as *necessary*, it is an *a priori* judgment; and if, besides, it is not derived from any proposition except one which also has the validity of a necessary judgment, it is an absolutely *a priori* judgment. Secondly, experience never confers on its judgments true or strict, but only assumed and comparative *universality*, through induction. We can properly only say, therefore, that, so far as we have hitherto observed, there is no exception to this or that rule. If, then, a judgment is thought with strict universality, that is, in such manner that no exception is allowed as possible, it is not derived from experience, but is valid absolutely *a priori*. Empirical universality is only an arbitrary extension of a validity holding in most cases to one which holds in all, for instance, in the proposition, "all bodies are heavy." When, on the other hand, strict universality is essential to a judgment, this indicates a special source of knowledge, namely, a faculty of *a priori* knowledge. Necessity and strict universality are thus sure criteria of *a priori* knowledge, and are inseparable from one another. But since in the employment of these criteria the contingency of judgments is sometimes more easily shown than their empirical limitation, or, as sometimes also happens, their unlimited universality can be more convincingly proved than their necessity, it is advisable to use the two criteria separately, each by itself being infallible.

Now it is easy to show that there actually are in human knowledge judgments which are necessary and in the strictest sense universal, and which are therefore pure *a priori* judgments. If an example from the sciences be desired, we have only to look to any of the propositions of mathematics; if we seek an example from the understanding in its quite ordinary employment, the proposition, "every alteration must have a cause," will serve our purpose. In the latter case, indeed, the very concept of a cause so manifestly contains the concept of a necessity of connection with an effect and of the strict universality of the rule, that the concept would be altogether lost if we attempted to derive it, as Hume has done, from a repeated association of that which happens with that which precedes, and from a custom of connecting representations, a custom originating in this repeated association, and constituting therefore a merely subjective necessity. Even without appealing to such examples, it is possible to show that pure *a priori* principles are indispensable for the possibility of experience, and so to prove their existence *a priori*. For whence could experience derive its certainty, if all the rules, according to which it proceeds, were always themselves empirical, and therefore contingent? Such rules could hardly be regarded as first principles. At present, however, we may be content to have established the fact that our faculty of knowledge does have a pure employment, and to have shown what are the criteria of such an employment.

Such *a priori* origin is manifest in certain concepts, no less than in judgments. If we remove from our empirical concept of a body, one by one, every feature in it which is [merely] empirical, the colour, the hardness or softness, the weight, even the impenetrability, there still remains the space which the body (now entirely vanished) occupied, and this cannot be removed. Again, if we remove from our empirical concept of any object, corporeal or incorporeal, all properties which experience has taught us, we yet cannot take away that property through which the object is thought as substance or as inhering in a substance (although this concept of substance is more determinate than that of an object in general). Owing, therefore, to the necessity with which this concept of substance forces itself upon us, we have no option save to admit that it has its seat in our faculty of *a priori* knowledge.

THE DISTINCTION BETWEEN ANALYTIC AND SYNTHETIC JUDGMENTS

In all judgments in which the relation of a subject to the predicate is thought (I take into consideration affirmative judgments only, the subsequent application to negative judgments being easily made), this relation is possible in two different ways. Either the predicate *B* belongs to the subject *A*, as something which is (covertly) contained in this concept *A*; or *B* lies outside the concept *A*, although it does indeed stand in connection with it. In the one case I entitle the judgment analytic, in the other synthetic. Analytic judgments (affirmative) are therefore those in which the connection of the predicate with the subject is thought through identity; those in which this connection is thought without identity should be entitled synthetic. The former, as adding nothing through the predicate to the concept of the subject, but merely breaking it up into those constituent concepts that have all along been thought in it, although confusedly, can also be entitled explicative. The latter, on the other hand, add to the concept of the subject a predicate which has not been in any wise thought in it, and which no analysis could possibly extract from it; and they may therefore be entitled ampliative. If I say, for instance, "All bodies are extended," this is an analytic judgment. For I do not require to go beyond the concept which I connect with "body" in order to find extension as bound up with it. To meet with this predicate, I have merely to analyze the concept, that is, to become conscious to myself of the manifold which I always think in that concept. The judgment is therefore analytic. But when I say, "All bodies are heavy," the predicate is something quite different from anything that I think in the mere concept of body in general; and the addition of such a predicate therefore yields a synthetic judgment.

Judgments of experience, as such, are one and all synthetic. For it would be absurd to found an analytic judgment on experience. Since, in framing the judgment, I must not go outside my concept, there is no need to appeal to the testimony of experience in its support. That a body is extended is a proposition that holds *a priori* and is not empirical. For, before appealing to experience, I have already in the concept of body all the conditions required for my judgment. I have only to extract from it, in accordance with the principle of contradiction, the required predicate, and in so doing can at the same time become conscious of the necessity of the judgment—and that is what experience could never have taught me. On the other hand, though I do not include in the concept of a body in general the predicate "weight," none the less this concept indicates an object of experience through one of its parts, and I can add to that part other parts of this same experience, as in this way belonging together with the concept. From the start I can apprehend the concept of body analytically through the characters of extension, impenetrability, figure, etc., all of which are thought in the concept. Now, however, looking back on the experience from which I have derived this concept of body, and finding weight to be invariably connected with the above characters, I attach it as a predicate to the concept; and in doing so I attach it synthetically, and am therefore extending my knowledge. The possibility of the synthesis of the predicate "weight" with the concept of "body" thus rests upon experience. While the one concept is not contained in the other, they yet belong to one another, though only contingently, as parts of a whole, namely, of an experience which is itself a synthetic combination of intuitions.

But in *a priori* synthetic judgments this help is entirely lacking: [I do not here have the advantage of looking around in the field of experience.] Upon what, then, am I to rely, when I seek to go beyond the concept, *A,* and to know that another concept *B* is connected with it? Through what is the synthesis made possible? Let us take the proposition, "Everything which happens has its cause." In the concept of "something which happens," I do indeed think an existence which is preceded by a time, etc., and from this concept analytic judgments may be obtained. But the concept of a "cause" lies entirely outside the other concept, and signifies something different from "that which happens," and is not therefore in any way contained in this latter representation. How come I then to predicate of that which happens something quite different, and to apprehend that the concept of cause, though not contained in it, yet belongs, and indeed necessarily belongs, to it? What is here the unknown = *X* which gives support to the understanding when it believes that it can discover outside the concept *A* a predicate *B* foreign to this concept, which it yet at the same time considers to be connected with it? It cannot be experience, because the suggested principle has connected the second representation with the first, not only with greater universality, but also with the character of necessity, and therefore completely *a priori* and on the basis of mere concepts. Upon such synthetic, that is, ampliative principles, all our *a priori* speculative knowledge must ultimately rest; analytic judgments are very important, and indeed necessary, but only for obtaining that clearness in the concepts which is requisite for such a sure and wide synthesis as will lead to a genuinely new addition to all previous knowledge. . . .

THE HIGHEST PRINCIPLE OF ALL ANALYTIC JUDGMENTS

The universal, though merely negative, condition of all our judgments in general, whatever be the content of our knowledge, and however it may relate to the object is that they be not self-contradictory; for if self-contradictory, these judgments are in themselves, even without reference to the object, null and void. But even if our judgment contains no contradiction, it may connect concepts in a manner not borne out by the object, or else in a manner for which no ground is given, either *a priori* or *a posteriori*, sufficient to justify such judgment, and so may still, in spite of being free from all inner contradiction, be either false or groundless.

. . . The proposition that no predicate contradictory of a thing can belong to it, is entitled the principle of contradiction, and is a universal, though merely negative, criterion of all truth. For this reason it belongs only to logic. It holds of knowledge, merely as knowledge in general, irrespective of content; and asserts that the contradiction completely cancels and invalidates it.

But it also allows of a positive employment, not merely, that is, to dispel falsehood and error (so far as they rest on contradiction), but also for the knowing of truth. For, *if the judgment is analytic,* whether negative or affirmative, its truth can always be adequately known in accordance with the principle of contradiction. The reverse of that which as concept is contained and is thought in the knowledge of the object, is always rightly denied. But since the opposite of the concept would contradict the object, the concept itself must necessarily be affirmed of it.

The principle of contradiction must therefore be recognized as being the universal and completely sufficient *principle of all analytic knowledge;* but beyond the sphere of analytic knowledge it has, as a *sufficient* criterion of truth, no authority and no field of application. The fact that no knowledge can be contrary to it without self-nullification, makes this principle a *conditio sine qua non,* but not a determining ground, of the truth of our [non-analytic] knowledge. Now in our critical enquiry it is only with the synthetic portion of our knowledge that we are concerned; and in regard to the truth of this kind of knowledge we can never look to the above principle for any positive information, though, of course, since it is inviolable, we must always be careful to conform to it.

Although this famous principle is thus without content and merely formal, it has sometimes been carelessly formulated in a manner which involves the quite unnecessary admixture of a synthetic element. The formula runs: It is impossible that something should *at one and the same time* both be and not be. Apart from the fact that the apodeictic certainty, expressed through the word "impossible," is superfluously added—since it is evident of itself from the [very nature of the] proposition—the proposition is modified by the condition of time. It then, as it were, asserts: A thing = A, which is something = B, cannot at the same time be not-B, but may very well in succession be both B and not-B. For instance, a man who is young cannot at the same time be old, but may very well at one time be young and at another time not-young, that is, old. The principle of contradiction, however, as a merely logical principle, must not in any way limit its assertions to time-relations. The above formula is therefore completely contrary to the intention of the principle. The misunderstanding results from our first of all separating a predicate of a thing from the concept of that thing, and afterwards connecting this predicate with its opposite—a procedure which never occasions a contradiction with the subject but only with the predicate which has been synthetically connected with that subject, and even then only when both predicates are affirmed at one and the same time. If I say that a man who is unlearned is not learned, the condition, *at one and the same time,* must be added; for he who is at one time unlearned can very well at another be learned. But if I say, no unlearned man is learned, the proposition is analytic, since the property, unlearnedness, now goes to make up the concept of the subject, and the truth of the negative judgment then becomes evident as an immediate consequence of the principle of contradiction, without requiring the supplementary condition, *at one and the same time.* This, then, is the reason why I have altered its formulation, namely, in order that the nature of an analytic proposition be clearly expressed through it.

Code

Lorraine Code is a professor at York University in Ontario, Canada, and director of its graduate program in philosophy. A leading feminist philosopher, Code has au-thored Epistemic Responsibility *(1987),* What Can She Know? Feminist Theory and the Construction of Knowledge *(1991), and* Rhetorical Spaces: Essays on (Gendered) Locations *(1995).*

The various discussions about what we can know and how we come to know what we take to be genuine knowledge have all explicitly or implicitly accepted some kind of ob-jectivity—a belief that what is true holds for everyone irrespective of who they are as particular persons or members of particular groups. In recent times, and for a variety of reasons, many feminist philosophers have been in the forefront of movements ques-tioning what they regard as the *presumption* of this objectivity, especially in science. The ideal of objectivity, they claim, disguises the real assumptions at work by select members of the society who have their own interests, their own needs for control, and their own "agendas," as the term is often used today.

Code argues here for the need to take subjectivity into account in our philosophical understanding of the meaning of knowledge and truth, but by "subjectivity" she does *not* mean mere private fancy or personal caprice. Commonalities, she believes, can be secured and truths can be articulated, so that we can avoid the pitfalls of both "rela-tivism" and "absolutism" as these terms are usually defined and understood.

Taking Subjectivity into Account

The project of remapping the epistemic terrain that I envisage is subversive, even anarchistic, in challenging and seeking to displace some of the most sacred princi-ples of standard Anglo-American epistemologies. It abandons the search for and de-nies the possibility of the disinterested and dislocated view from nowhere. More

From "Taking Subjectivity into Account" by Lorraine Code, in *Feminist Epistemologies,* edited by Linda Al-coff and Elizabeth Potter (1993). Reprinted by permission of Routledge. This essay also appears in *Rhetorical Spaces: Essays on (Gendered) Locations* (New York: Routledge, 1995).

subversively, it asserts the political investedness of most knowledge-producing activity and insists upon the accountability—the epistemic responsibilities—of knowing subjects to the community, not just to the evidence.

Because my engagement in the project is specifically prompted by a conviction that *gender* must be put in place as a primary analytic category, I started by assuming that it is impossible to sustain the presumption of gender-neutrality that is central to standard epistemologies: the presumption that gender has nothing to do with knowledge, that the mind has no sex, that reason is alike in all men, and man "embraces" woman. But gender is not an enclosed category, for it is always interwoven with such other sociopolitical-historical locations as class, race, and ethnicity, to mention only a few. It is experienced differently, and it plays differently into structures of power and dominance at its diverse intersections with other specificities. From these multiply describable locations, the world looks quite different from the way it might look from nowhere. Homogenizing those differences under a range of standard or typical instances always invites the question, "standard or typical for whom?" Answers to that question must necessarily take subjectivity into account. . . .

Feminist critiques of epistemology and philosophy of science/social science have demonstrated that the ideals of the autonomous reasoner—the dislocated, disinterested observer—and the epistemologies they inform are the artifacts of a small, privileged group of educated, usually prosperous, white men. Their circumstances enable them to believe that they are materially and even affectively autonomous and to imagine that they are nowhere or everywhere, even as they occupy an unmarked position of privilege. Moreover, the ideals of rationality and objectivity that have guided and inspired theorists of knowledge throughout the history of western philosophy have been constructed through processes of excluding the attributes and experiences commonly associated with femaleness and underclass social status: emotion, connection, practicality, sensitivity, and idiosyncracy. These systematic excisions of "otherness" attest to a presumed—and willed—belief in the stability of a social order that the presumers have good reasons to believe that they can ensure, because they occupy the positions that determine the norms of conduct and enquiry. Yet all that these convictions demonstrate is that ideal objectivity is a generalization from the *subjectivity* of quite a small social group, albeit a group that has the power, security, and prestige to believe that it can generalise its experiences and normative ideals across the social order, thus producing a group of like-minded practitioners ("we") and dismissing "others" as deviant, aberrant ("they"). . . .

. . . Issues about the implicit politics of "we-saying" infect even the work of such an antifoundationalist, anti-objectivist, anti-individualist as Richard Rorty, whom many feminists are tempted to see as an ally in their successor-epistemology projects. Again, the manner in which these issues arise is instructive.

In that part of his work with which feminist and other revisionary epistemologists rightly find an affinity, Rorty develops a sustained argument to the effect that the "foundational" (for which read "empiricist-positivist and rationalist") projects of western philosophy have been unable to fulfill their promise. That is to say, they have not been successful in establishing their claims that knowledge must—and can—be grounded in absolute truth and that necessary and sufficient conditions can be ascertained. Rorty turns his back on the (in his view) ill-conceived project of seeking absolute epistemic foundations to advocate a process of "continuing conversation rather than discovering truth." . . . It will move away from the search for foundations to look within communally created and communably available history, tradition, and culture for the only possible bases for truth claims. Relocating questions about knowledge and truth to positions within the conversations of humankind does seem to break the thrall of objectivist detachment and to create a forum for dialogic, cooperative debate of the epistemological issues of everyday, practical life. Yet the question is how open that forum would—or could—be; who would have a voice in Rorty's conversations? . . .

. . . The very goal of achieving "as much intersubjective agreement as possible," of extending "the reference of 'us' as far as we can," with the belief that tolerance will do the job when conflicts arise, is unlikely to convince members of groups who have never felt solidarity with the representers of the self-image of the society. The very promise of inclusion in the extension of that "we" is as likely to occasion anxiety as it is to offer hope. Naming ourselves as "we" empowers us, but it always risks disempowering others. The we-saying, then, of assumed or negotiated solidarity must always be submitted to critical analysis.

Now it is neither surprising nor outrageous that epistemologies should derive out of specific human interests. Indeed, it is much less plausible to contend that they do not; human cognitive agents, after all, have made them. Why would they not bear the marks of their makers? Nor does the implication of human interests in theories of knowledge, prima facie, invite censure. It does alert epistemologists to the need for case-by-case analysis and critique of the sources out of which claims to objectivity and neutrality are made. More pointedly, it forces the conclusion that if the ideal of objectivity cannot pretend to have been established in accordance with its own demands, then it has no right to the theoretical hegemony to which it lays claim.

Central to the program of taking subjectivity into account that feminist epistemological inquiry demands, then, is a critical analysis of that very politics of "we-saying" that objectivist epistemologies conceal from view.

. . . My contention that subjectivity has to be taken into account takes issue with the belief that epistemologists need only to understand the conditions for propositional, observationally derived knowledge, and all the rest will follow. It challenges the concomitant belief that epistemologists need only to understand how such knowledge claims are made and justified by individual, autonomous, self-reliant reasoners to understand all the rest. Such beliefs derive from conceptions of detached and faceless cognitive agency that mask the variability of the experiences and practices from which knowledge is constructed. . . .

The epistemic and moral/political ideals that govern inquiry in technologically advanced, capitalist, free-enterprise western societies are an amalgam of liberal-utilitarian moral values and the empiricist-positivist intellectual values that I have been discussing in this essay. These ideals and values shape both the intellectual enterprises that the society legitimates and the language of liberal individualism that maps out the rhetorical spaces where those enterprises are carried out. The ideal of tolerance and openness is believed to be the right attitude from which, initially, to approach truth claims. It combines with the assumptions that objectivity and value-neutrality govern the rational conduct of scientific and social-scientific research to produce the philosophical commonplaces of late twentieth-century anglo-American societies, not just in "the academy" but in the public perception—the "common sense." . . .

. . . The scope of epistemological investigation has to expand to merge with moral-political inquiry, acknowledging that "facts" are always confused with values and that both facts and values are open to ongoing critical debate. It would be necessary to demonstrate the innocence of descriptions (their derivation from pure data) and to show the perfect congruence of descriptions with "the described" in order to argue that descriptive theories have no normative force. Their assumed innocence licenses an evasion of the accountability that socially concerned communities have to demand of their producers of knowledge. Only the most starkly positivistic epistemology merged with the instrumental rationality it presupposes could presume that inquirers are accountable only to the evidence. Evidence is *selected*, not found, and selection procedures are open to scrutiny. Nor can critical analysis stop there, for the funding and institutions that enable inquirers to pursue certain projects and not others explicitly legitimize the work. So the lines of accountability are long and interwoven; only a genealogy of their multiple strands can begin to unravel the issues.

What, then, should occur within epistemic communities to ensure that scientists and other knowers cannot conceal bias and prejudice or claim *a right not to know* about their background assumptions and the significance of their locations?

The crux of my argument is that the phenomenon of the disinterested inquirer is the exception rather than the rule; there are no dislocated truths, and some facts about the locations and interests at the source of inquiry are always pertinent to questions about freedom and accountability. Hence I am arguing, with Naomi Scheman, that

> Feminist epistemologists and philosophers of science [who] *along with others who have been the objects of knowledge-as-control* [have to] understand and . . . pose alternatives to the epistemology of modernity. As it has been central to this epistemology to guard its products from contamination by connection to the particularities of its producers, it must be central to the work of its critics and to those who would create genuine alternatives to remember those connections. . . .

There can be no doubt that research is—often imperceptibly—shaped by presuppositions and interests external to the inquiry itself, which cannot be filtered out by standard, objective, disinterested epistemological techniques. . . .

Equally central, then, to a feminist epistemological program of taking subjectivity into account are case-by-case analyses of the political and other structural circumstances that generate projects and lines of inquiry. Feminist critique—with critiques that center on other marginalizing structures—needs to act as an "experimental control" in epistemic practice so that every inquiry, assumption, and discovery is analyzed for its place in and implications for the prevailing sex/gender system, in its intersections with the systems that sustain racism, homophobia, and ethnocentrism. The burden of proof falls upon inquirers who claim neutrality. In all "objective" inquiry, the positions and power relations of *gendered* and otherwise located subjectivity have to be submitted to piece-by-piece scrutiny that will vary according to the field of research. The task is intricate, because the subjectivity of the inquirer is always also implicated and has to be taken into account. Hence, the inquiry is at once critical and self-critical. But this is no monologic, self-sufficient enterprise. Conclusions are reached and immoderate subjective omissions and commissions become visible in dialogic processes among inquirers and—in social science—between inquirers and the subjects of their research.

It emerges from this analysis that although the ideal objectivity of the universal knower is neither possible nor desirable, a realistic commitment to achieving empirical adequacy that engages in situated analyses of the subjectivities of both the knower and (where appropriate) the known is both desirable and possible. . . .

Traditionally, theories of knowledge tend to be derived from the experiences of uniformly educated, articulate, epistemically "positioned" adults who introspect retrospectively to review what they must once have known most simply and clearly. Locke's *tabula rasa* is one model; Descartes's radical doubt is another. Yet this introspective process consistently bypasses the epistemic significance of early experiences with other people, with whom the relations of these philosophers must surely have been different from their relations to objects in their environment. As Seyla Benhabib wryly notes, it is a strange world from which this picture of knowledge is derived: a world in which "individuals are grown up before they have been born; in which boys are men before they have been children; a world where neither mother, nor sister, nor wife exist." Whatever the historical variations in childraising practices, evidence implicit in (similarly evolving) theories of knowledge points to a noteworthy constancy. In separated adulthood, the knowledge that enables a knower to give or withhold trust as a child—and hence to survive—is passed over as unworthy of philosophical notice. It is tempting to conclude that theorists of knowledge must either be childless or so disengaged from the rearing of children as to have minimal developmental awareness. Participators in childraising could not easily ignore the primacy of knowing and being known by other people in cognitive development, nor could they denigrate the role such knowledge plays throughout an epistemic history. In view of the fact that disengagement throughout a changing history and across a range of class and racial boundaries has been possible primarily for *men* in western societies, this aspect of the androcentricity of objectivist epistemologies is not surprising. . . .

Problems about determining criteria for justifying claims to know another person—the utter unavailability of necessary and sufficient conditions, the complete inadequacy of *S*-knows-that-*p* paradigms—must account for philosophical reluctance to count this as knowledge that bears epistemological investigation. Yet my suggestion that such knowledge is a model for a wide range of knowledge and is not merely inchoate and unmanageable recommends itself the more strongly in view of the extent to which cognitive practice is grounded upon such knowledge. I am thinking not just of everyday interactions with other people, but of the specialized knowledge—such as Rushton's—that claims institutional authority. Educational theory and practice, psychology, sociology, anthropology, law, some aspects of medicine and philosophy, politics, history, and economics all depend for their credibility upon knowing people. Hence it is all the more curious that observation-based knowledge of material objects and the methodology of the physical sciences hold such relatively unchallenged sway as the paradigm—and paragon—of intellectual achievement. The results of according continued veneration to observational paradigms are evident in the reductive approaches of behaviorist psychology. They are apparent in parochial impositions of meaning upon the practices of other cultures which is still characteristic of some areas of anthropology, and in the simple translation of present-day descriptions into past cultural contexts that characterizes some historical and archaeological practice. But feminist, hermeneutic, and postmodern critiques are slowly succeeding in requiring objectivist social scientists to reexamine their presuppositions and practices. In fact, it is methodological disputes within the social sciences—and the consequent unsettling of positivistic hegemony—that . . . have set the stage for the development of a productive, post-modern approach to epistemology for contemporary feminists.

I am not proposing that knowing other people should become *the* new epistemological paradigm but rather that it has a strong claim to exemplary status in the epistemologies that feminist and other case-by-case analyses will produce. I am proposing further that if epistemologists require a model drawn from "scientific" inquiry, then a reconstructed, interpretive social science, liberated from positivistic constraints, will be a better resource than natural science—or physics—for knowledge as such. . . .

The project I am proposing, then, requires a new *geography* of the epistemic terrain: one that is no longer primarily a physical geography, but a population geography that develops qualitative analyses of subjective positions and identities and the sociopolitical structures that produce them. Because differing social positions generate variable constructions of reality and afford different perspectives on the world, the revisionary stages of this project will consist of case-by-case analyses of the knowledge produced in specific social positions. These analyses derive from a recognition that knowers are always *somewhere*—and at once limited and enabled by the specificities of their locations. It is an interpretive project, alert to the possibility of finding generalities and commonalities within particulars and hence of the explanatory potential that opens up when such commonalities can be delineated. But it is wary of the reductivism that results when commonalities are presupposed or forced. It has no ultimate foundation, but neither does it float free, because it is grounded in experiences and practices, in the efficacy of dialogic negotiation and of action.

All of this having been said, my argument in this essay points to the conclusion that necessary and sufficient conditions for establishing empirical knowledge claims cannot be found, at least where experientially significant knowledge is at issue.

Hence it poses the question whether feminist epistemologists must, after all, "come out" as relativists. In view of what I have been arguing, the answer to that question will have to be a qualified "yes." Yet the relativism that my argument generates is sufficiently nuanced and sophisticated to escape the scorn—and the anxiety—that "relativism, after all" usually occasions. To begin with, it refuses to occupy the negative side of the traditional absolutism/relativism dichotomy. It is at once realist, rational, and significantly objective; hence it is not forced to define itself within or against the oppositions between realism and relativism, rationality and relativism, or objectivism and relativism. Moreover, it takes as its starting point a recognition that the "positive" sides of these dichotomies have been caricatured to affirm a certainty that was never rightfully theirs.

The opponents of relativism have been so hostile, so thoroughly scornful in their dismissals, that it is no wonder that feminists, well aware of the folk-historical identification of women with the forces of unreason, should resist the very thought that the logic of feminist emancipatory analyses points in that direction. Feminists know, if they know anything at all, that they have to develop the best possible explanations—the "truest" explanations—of how things are if they are to intervene effectively in social structures and institutions. The intransigence of material circumstances constantly reminds them that their world-making possibilities are neither unconstrained nor infinite; they have to be able to produce accurate, transformative analyses of things as they *are*. In fact, many feminists are vehement in their resistance to relativism precisely because they suspect—not without reason— that only the supremely powerful and privileged, the self-proclaimed sons of God, could believe that they can make the world up as they will and practice that supreme tolerance in whose terms all possible constructions of reality are equally worthy. Their fears are persuasive. Yet even at the risk of speaking within the oppositional mode, it is worth thinking seriously about the alternative. For there is no doubt that only the supremely powerful and privileged could believe, in the face of all the evidence to the contrary, that there is only one true view, and it is theirs; that they alone have the resources to establish universal, incontrovertible, and absolute Truth. . . .

The position I am advocating is one for which knowledge is always *relative to* (i.e., a perspective *on*, a standpoint *in*) specifiable circumstances. Hence it is constrained by a realist, empiricist commitment according to which getting those circumstances right is vital to effective action.

Ames

Roger T. Ames is a professor of philosophy and director of the Center for Chinese Studies at the University of Hawaii.

In his "Images of Reason in Chinese Culture," Ames makes evident the differences between the dominant conceptions of rationality in the West and in the Chinese tradition. He sets in rather sharp opposition the "logical sense of order" typical of Western thinking, with its penchant for an external and eternal structure of invariable principles or laws, and the Chinese "aesthetic" manner of ordering things and relations according to more spontaneous, self-directing processes. The very language of Chinese rationality, Ames shows, "has more to do with 'mapping' and 'unravelling' than with the grasping of some underlying formal essence presupposed in classical Western epistemology."

Images of Reason in Chinese Culture

The prominent French sinologist, Jacques Gernet, argues that when the two civilizations of China and Europe, having developed almost entirely independently of each other, first made contact in about 1600, the seeming inaptitude of the Chinese for understanding Christianity and more importantly, the philosophic edifice that undergirded it, was not simply an uneasy difference in the encounter between disparate intellectual traditions. It was a far more profound difference in mental categories and modes of thought, and particularly, a fundamental difference in the Chinese conception of human agency. Much of what Christianity and Western philosophy had to say to the Chinese was, for the Chinese, quiet literally nonsense— given their own philosophic commitments, they could not think it. And the Jesuits interpreted this difference in ways of thinking quite specifically as ineptness in reasoning, logic and dialectic.

The West fared little better in its opportunity to appreciate and to appropriate

From the proceedings of a symposium on "Alternative Rationalities" sponsored by the Society for Asian and Comparative Philosophy and held at the University of Hawaii at Manoa, 1992. Reprinted with the permission of the author.

Chinese culture. In fact, it fared so badly that the very word "Chinese" in the English language has come to denote "confusion," "incomprehensibility," "impenetrability"—a sense of order inaccessible to the Western mind. The degree of difference between our dominant sense of order and the "æsthetic" order prevalent in the Chinese world view has plagued our encounter with this antique culture from the start. . . .

To explore the Chinese philosophy in pursuit of some functional equivalent of rationality, then, we will, at the very least, have to recognize that we are dealing with a fundamentally different world view. And the more distant Chinese "rationality" is from our own conceptions, the more likely it is that our own languages will have difficulty in accommodating our discussion of it. As a device for sorting out this difference, I want to contrast a "logical" sense of order with an "æsthetic" order. This distinction is useful in bringing into relief certain features of the dominant Indo-European world view and the Chinese alternative to it, and can be extended to focus important differences between dualistic and correlative modalities of thinking, and the kinds of "reasoning" that attend them.

The signal and recurring feature of what we can call the "logical" sense of order dominating the development of our philosophical and religious orthodoxy is the presumption that there is something permanent, perfect, objective, and universal that disciplines the world of change and guarantees natural and moral order—some originative and determinative *arche*, an eternal realm of Platonic *eidos* or "ideas," the One True God of the Judeo-Christian universe, a transcendental strongbox of invariable principles or laws, an analytic method for discerning clear and distinct ideas. The model of a single-ordered world where the unchanging source of order stands independent of, sustains, and ultimately provides explanation for the sensible world is a familiar and dominant presupposition in our tradition.

Our sense of order, then, dating back to a pre-Socratic pursuit of some underlying *arche*, tends to be cosmogonic, assuming an initial beginning, and privileging the primal, unchanging principle that causes and explains that origin and everything that issues from it. Hence the weight given to analytic thinking, linear, causal explanations and the dualistic categories in which these explanations are couched. There is implicit in this world view a primacy given to some transcendent principle which presides as a top-down, disciplining order guaranteeing unity and intelligibility, whether this principle exists external to us as Deity or internal to us as the hardwiring of some essential nature. It is a "given"—a source of order independent of our own actions and experience.

In describing the largely failed encounter between the Jesuit missionaries and the Chinese intellectuals, Gernet ascribes the mutual misunderstanding to this contrast between externally imposed "logical" order assumed in our tradition, and the Chinese assumption that order is immanent in and inseparable from a spontaneously changing world.

Believing that the universe possesses within itself its own organizational principles and its own creative energy, the Chinese maintained something that was quite scandalous from the point of view of Western scholastic reason, namely that "matter" itself is intelligent—not, clearly enough, with a conscious and reflective intelligence as we usually conceive it, but with a spontaneous intelligence which makes it possible for the *yin* and the *yang* to come together and guides the infinite combinations of these two opposite sources of energy.

With the Chinese, then, we begin from a dynamic, autogenerative, and self-directing world of uniquely different particulars where order is immanent and emergent. *Yin* and *yang* is a familiar metaphor in the tradition—literally, the shady side and the sunny side of a hill—which is used to express contrast and difference. The nature of the opposition captured in this metaphor is fundamental in the culture. It is a basic correlative pairing which expresses the mutuality, interdependence, diversity, and creative efficacy of the dynamic *relationships* that are deemed immanent in, pattern, and valorize the world. The full range of difference in the world—intellectual and physical, change and continuity, quality and quantity, nobility and baseness, fact and value, substance and accident—is explicable through these correlative and complementary relationships. *Yin* and *yang* as correlatives are not universal principles characterizing some essential feature of phenomena, but are *ad hoc* explanatory categories that report on interactions among immediate concrete things of the world. . . .

The language of a classical Chinese rationality has more to do with "mapping" and "unravelling" than with the grasping of some underlying formal essence presupposed in classical Western epistemology. Where in the classical Western model, the formal essence reduces the many to one, in the Chinese model, one evokes many. Each phenomenon in suggesting other similar phenomena has the multivalence of poetic images. *Yin* and *yang* as the characterization of a particular relationship invariably entail a perception from some particular perspective that enables us to unravel patterns of relatedness and interpret our circumstances. They provide a vocabulary for sorting out the relationships among things as they come together and constitute themselves in unique compositions.

Order is not imposed from without, but is inherent in the process of existence itself, as are the rings of the tree trunk, the veins of the stone, the cadence of the ocean. "Causes" are not external to act upon an inert world, but internal to a dynamic process of change in which "that which causes" and "that which is caused" is not a legitimate distinction. If "reasoning" is the discovery of reasons or causes, how does it work in such a world? And how is it different from our own?

In both the classical Chinese corpus and the modern language, the closest term that approximates "reason" is *li*. I want to give an account of how the conventional translations of *li* as either "reason" or "principle," while foregrounding our philosophical importances, pay the unacceptable penalty of concealing precisely those meanings which are most essential to an appreciation of its differences.

Philosophically, the most familiar uses of *li* lie somewhere in the cluster "reasoning" or "rationale" (A. S. Cua), "principle" (W. T. Chan), "organism" (J. Needham), and "coherence" (W. Peterson). To focus the meaning of this term, we need to first identify what is inappropriate in each of these renderings, and then to determine how *li* in fact expresses something of each of them.

Among these several alternative translations used for *li*, "reason" or "rationale," although philosophically as protean as "principle" for our own tradition, unwarrantedly restrict *li* to a notion of human consciousness and tend to introduce distinctions such as animate and inanimate, agency and act, intelligible and sensible. In fact, *li* denotes a coherence and regularity which, although brought into greatest focus by the human mind, is characteristic of the world at large. . . . This is not to suggest that this tradition denies the biological basis of human experience, but to claim that, for it, the structure of human rationality is importantly contingent—an ongoing process specific to social, cultural, and of course, natural conditions. Rather than entailing the discovery of reasons that reveal some pattern of linear causality as a basis for understanding, *li* suggests an awareness of those constitutive relationships which condition each thing, and which, through patterns of correlation, make its world meaningful and intelligible. All things evidence a degree of coherence as their claim to uniqueness and complexity, as well as their claim to continuity with the rest of their world.

In contrast with knowing as the grasping of what is essential—the making present of the being or *logos* of beings—knowing in a Confucian world involves a tracing out without obstruction of the correlated details and the extended pattern of relationships which obtain among them. Instead of a classical rationalistic epistemology dependent upon the categories of rational faculty—substance and accident, necessity and contingency, essence and attribute, and linear causal chains—Confucian knowing has as its goal a comprehensive and unobstructed awareness of interdependent conditions and their latent, vague possibilities, where the meaning and value of each element is a function of its own particular network of relationships.

The most common translation of *li* is "principle," or Needham's biological twist on "principle"—"organism." It is what, in our tradition, human reason seeks out to make the world intelligible. This rendering is appropriate to the extent that *li* identifies an inherent structure of organization and development in the world. The inappropriate side of this rendering is that from the early days of Matteo Ricci, it has, for the Western student of Chinese culture, evoked an unfortunate association with the Platonic *eidos* or its Aristotelian variant to translate Chinese philosophy into an alternative hypostatized idealism.

Li, far from being some independent and immutable originative principle that disciplines a recalcitrant world, is the fabric of order immanent in the dynamic process of experience. For this reason, it is neither exclusively subjective or objective—"psychology" is translated into Chinese as "the *li* of the heart-and-mind," but then "physics" is "the study of the *li* of things and events." *Li* then does not entail the distinction between the intelligible and the sensible so familiar to us from the Greek and Christian traditions.

Another condition of *li* which separates it rather clearly from our common understanding of "principle" is that *li* is both a unity and a multiplicity. *Li* is the coherence of any "member of a set, all the members of a set, or the set as whole." This description reflects both the uniqueness of each particular and the continuities that obtain among them. *Li* then is the defining character or ethos of a given community, or any other such composition.

There is another point at which *li* departs from "principle." In our tradition, the discovery of originative and determinative principle enables us to give causal and rational accounts. Principle, in addition to being a basis for causal explanations, provides us with a schema for classifying things and subsuming one thing under another. The investigation of *li,* by contrast, is to seek out patterns which relate things, and to discover resonances between things that make correlations and categorization possible. The nature of classification in the Chinese case is juxtaposition through some identifiable similarity—putting different things side by side—rather than identifying essentially determined "kinds" of things. As Needham points out, "things influence one another not by acts of mechanical causation, but by a kind of 'inductance'. . . ." Things are continuous with one another, and thus are interdependent conditions for each other. In a tradition which begins from the assumption that existence is a dynamic process, the "causes" of things are resident in themselves rather than being external to them, and the project of giving reasons for things or events requires a mapping out of the conditions that sponsor them. If we report night follows day, we are pointing at a contrast and complementarity we detect in the passing of a day which provides some kind of understanding. Where we are identifying this day as a condition of this night, we are not asserting that night is "caused" by day in any strict sense. This day causes itself. Ironically, the more comprehensive we are in this project of mapping—the more *yins* and *yangs* we call into service in establishing both contrast and complement—the more complex and in some ways more ambiguous our explanation becomes.

Another feature of *li* that requires mention is the often noted fact it is both descriptive and normative—both how things are and how they ought to be. The "oughtness" here, however, does not entail some ideal order beyond that which is available through analogizing with and aspiring after cultural and historical models. The ideals reside in history. In this sense, *li* must be clearly distinguished from teleological design. In this hierarchical world view, things are most easily construed teleonomically at the basest levels. Human beings are much more predictable biologically than they are culturally.

One important consequence that follows from this alternative notion of "reasoning" is a far less severe separation between reasoning as discovery and imagining as creativity. In a world view that does not entertain as fundamental a reality/appearance distinction, imagination has a more respectable status. As the act of generating meaning by circumscribing, isolating, and composting "things," "imaging" prompts the very differentia and character of reality.

Perhaps a useful analogy for this sense of imaging is the traditional art of calligraphy. The personal style of the calligraphy as contrasted with the text is non-referential and non-representational—yet it is revealing of the artist himself. His moods, his time, his joy and pain, his place—all are resident in the Chinese character. One's calligraphy is biographical. But in much the same way as the Confucian sage, one's biography transmits the tradition rather than one's own idiosyncracies. . . .

Reasoning is irreducibly experiential. And as experience, it is culturally and historically constructed. While we tend to associate "knowing" with the mind of the individual knower, an alternative model would see knowledge, especially where it is importantly imagistic, emerging from out of the social and cultural dynamics of experience in the world. "Knowing" is *chih tao*—knowing the "way," a specific cultural tradition. Reasoning is not seen as some superordinate human faculty which, in different situations and under varied conditions, takes on its cultural particularity. Rather, a career of experience shapes one's reasoning and makes it profoundly particular. Rationality is formed dialectically amid cultural and social forces, both shaping and being shaped by them. Valid reasoning in Confucius is the discovery and articulation of appropriate and efficacious historical instances of reasonableness.

Russell

The most prevalent theory about the nature of truth in both philosophical and every-day thinking is the so-called correspondence theory of truth: a statement or belief is true if it accords with, copies, represents—"corresponds" to—some state of affairs or expresses some fact in the world. "It is now raining" is true if indeed, upon examination, it is seen or rightly inferred to be the case. Facts are thus taken to be independent of us. Truth means, as Aristotle put it, "to say of what is that it is, and of what is not that it is not" (*Metaphysics:* 1011:26), or as the contemporary American philosopher Roderick Chisholm writes: "Our question [What is truth?] is easy to answer if we allow ourselves a certain metaphysical assumption.... The assumption is that *states of affairs* may be said to exist or not to exist and that every belief and assertion . . . is a belief or assertion, with respect to some state of affairs, that that state of affairs exists" (*Theory of Knowledge:* 1966, p. 103).

Theories of truth, it should be noted, are not on the whole concerned with asking how we can know whether a particular belief is true or false but with asking what is *meant* by the very question of whether a belief is true or false. In short, theories of truth ask, "What is truth?" and not, "Which of my beliefs are true?"

In arguing that "truth consists in some form of correspondence between belief and fact," Bertrand Russell presents rather rigorous criteria for what "correspondence" itself means and offers criticisms of the rival coherence theory of truth, which will be argued for in the next selection by Brand Blanshard.

The Correspondence Theory of Truth

We know that on very many subjects different people hold different and incom-patible opinions: hence some beliefs must be erroneous. Since erroneous beliefs are often held just as strongly as true beliefs, it becomes a difficult question how they are to be distinguished from true beliefs. How are we to know, in a given case, that our belief is not erroneous? That is a question of the very greatest difficulty, to which no completely satisfactory answer is possible. There is, however, a pre-

From *The Problems of Philosophy* by Bertrand Russell (1912). Reprinted by permission of Oxford University Press.

liminary question which is rather less difficult, and that is: What do we *mean* by truth and falsehood? . . .

. . . We are not asking how we can know whether a belief is true or false: we are asking what is meant by the question whether a belief is true or false. It is to be hoped that a clear answer to this question may help us obtain an answer to the question what beliefs are true, but for the present we ask only "What is truth?" and "What is falsehood?" not "What beliefs are true?" and "What beliefs are false?" It is very important to keep these different questions entirely separate, since any confusion between them is sure to produce an answer which is not really applicable to either.

There are three points to observe in the attempt to discover the nature of truth, three requisites which any theory must fulfill.

(1) Our theory of truth must be such as to admit of its opposite, falsehood. A good many philosophers have failed adequately to satisfy this condition: they have constructed theories according to which all our thinking ought to have been true, and have then had the greatest difficulty in finding a place for falsehood. In this respect our theory of belief must differ from our theory of acquaintance, since in the case of acquaintance it was not necessary to take account of any opposite.

(2) It seems fairly evident that if there were no beliefs there could be no falsehood, and no truth either, in the sense in which truth is correlative to falsehood. If we imagine a world of mere matter, there would be no room for falsehood in such a world, and although it would contain what may be called "facts," it would not contain any truths, in the sense in which truths are things of the same kind as falsehoods. In fact, truth and falsehood are properties of beliefs and statements: hence a world of mere matter, since it would contain no beliefs or statements, would also contain no truth or falsehood.

(3) But, as against what we have just said, it is to be observed that the truth or falsehood of a belief always depends upon something which lies outside the belief itself. If I believe that Charles I died on the scaffold, I believe truly, not because of any intrinsic quality of my belief, which could be discovered by merely examining the belief, but because of an historical event which happened two and a half centuries ago. If I believe that Charles I died in his bed, I believe falsely: no degree of vividness in my belief, or of care in arriving at it, prevents it from being false, again because of what happened long ago, and not because of any intrinsic property of my belief. Hence, although truth and falsehood are properties of beliefs, they are properties dependent upon the relations of the beliefs to other things, not upon any internal quality of the beliefs.

The third of the above requisites leads us to adopt the view—which has on the whole been commonest among philosophers—that truth consists in some form of correspondence between belief and fact. It is, however, by no means an easy matter to discover a form of correspondence to which there are no irrefutable objections. By this partly—and partly by the feeling that, if truth consists in a correspondence of thought with something outside thought, thought can never know when truth has been attained—many philosophers have been led to try to find some definition of truth which shall not consist in relation to something wholly outside belief. The most important attempt at a definition of this sort is the theory that truth consists in *coherence.* It is said that the mark of falsehood is failure to cohere in the body of our beliefs, and that it is the essence of a truth to form part of the completely rounded system which is The Truth.

There is, however, a great difficulty in this view, or rather two great difficulties. The first is that there is no reason to suppose that only *one* coherent body of beliefs is possible. It may be that, with sufficient imagination, a novelist might invent a past for the world that would perfectly fit on to what we know, and yet be quite different from the real past. In more scientific matters, it is certain that there are often two or more hypotheses which account for all the known facts on some subject, and although, in such cases, men of science endeavor to find facts which will rule out all the hypotheses except one, there is no reason why they should always succeed.

In philosophy, again, it seems not uncommon for two rival hypotheses to be both able to account for all the facts. Thus, for example, it is possible that life is one long dream, and that the outer world has only that degree of reality that the objects of dreams have; but although such a view does not seem inconsistent with known facts, there is no reason to prefer it to the comon-sense view, according to which other people and things do really exist. Thus coherence as the definition of truth fails because there is no proof that there can be only one coherent system.

The other objection to this definition of truth is that it assumes the meaning of "coherence" known, whereas, in fact, "coherence" presupposes the truth of the laws of logic. Two propositions are coherent when both may be true, and are incoherent when one at least must be false. Now in order to know whether two propositions can both be true, we must know such truths as the law of contradiction. For example, the two propositions "this tree is a beech" and "this tree is not a beech," are not coherent, because of the law of contradiction. But if the law of contradiction itself were subjected to the test of coherence, we should find that, if we choose to suppose it false, nothing will any longer be incoherent with anything else. Thus the laws of logic supply the skeleton or framework within which the test of coherence applies, and they themselves cannot be established by this test.

For the above two reasons, coherence cannot be accepted as giving the *meaning* of truth, though it is often a most important *test* of truth after a certain amount of truth has become known.

Hence we are driven back to *correspondence with fact* as constituting the nature of truth. It remains to define precisely what we mean by "fact," and what is the nature of the correspondence which must subsist between belief and fact, in order that belief may be true.

In accordance with our three requisites, we have to seek a theory of truth which (1) allows truth to have an opposite, namely falsehood, (2) makes truth a property of beliefs, but (3) makes it a property wholly dependent upon the relation of the beliefs to outside things.

The necessity of allowing for falsehood makes it impossible to regard belief as a relation of the mind to a single object, which could be said to be what is believed. If belief were so regarded, we should find that, like acquaintance, it would not admit of the opposition of truth and falsehood, but would have to be always true. This may be made clear by examples. Othello believes falsely that Desdemona loves Cassio. We cannot say that this belief consists in a relation to a single object, "Desdemona's love for Cassio," for if there were such an object, the belief would be true. There is in fact no such object, and therefore Othello cannot have any relation to such an object. Hence his belief cannot possibly consist in a relation to this object.

It might be said that his belief is a relation to a different object, namely "that Desdemona loves Cassio"; but it is almost as difficult to suppose that there is such an object as this, when Desdemona does not love Cassio, as it was to suppose that there is "Desdemona's love for Cassio." Hence it will be better to seek for a theory of belief which does not make it consist in a relation of the mind to a single object.

It is common to think of relations as though they always held between *two* terms, but in fact this is not always the case. Some relations demand three terms, some four, and so on. Take, for instance, the relation "between." So long as only two terms come in, the relation "between" is impossible: three terms are the smallest number that render it possible. York is between London and Edinburgh; but if London and Edinburgh were the only places in the world, there could be nothing which was between one place and another. Similarly *jealousy* requires three people: there can be no such relation that does not involve three at least. Such a proposition as "A wishes B to promote C's marriage with D" involves a relation of four terms; that is to say, A and B and C and D all come in, and the relation involved cannot be expressed otherwise than in a form involving all four. Instances might be multiplied indefinitely, but enough has been said to show that there are relations which require more than two terms before they can occur.

The relation involved in *judging* or *believing* must, if falsehood is to be duly allowed for, be taken to be a relation between several terms, not between two. When Othello believes that Desdemona loves Cassio, he must not have before his mind a single object, "Desdemona's love for Cassio," or "that Desdemona loves Cassio," for that would require that there should be objective falsehoods, which subsist independently of any minds; and this, though not logically refutable, is a theory to be avoided if possible. Thus it is easier to account for falsehood if we take judgment to be a relation in which the mind and the various objects concerned all occur severally; that is to say, Desdemona and loving and Cassio must all be terms in the relation which subsists when Othello believes that Desdemona loves Cassio. This relation, therefore, is a relation of four terms, since Othello also is one of the terms of the relation. When we say that it is a relation of four terms, we do not mean that Othello has a certain relation to Desdemona, and has the same relation to loving and also to Cassio. This may be true of some other relation than believing; but believing, plainly, is not a relation which Othello has to *each* of the three terms concerned, but to *all* of them together: there is only one example of the relation of believing involved, but this one example knits together four terms. Thus the actual occurrence, at the moment when Othello is entertaining his belief, is that the relation called "believing" is knitting together into one complex whole the four terms Othello, Desdemona, loving, and Cassio. What is called belief or judgment is nothing but this relation of believing or judging, which relates a mind to several things other than itself. An *act* of belief or of judgment is the occurrence between certain terms at some particular time, of the relation of believing or judging.

We are now in a position to understand what it is that distinguishes a true judgment from a false one. For this purpose we will adopt certain definitions. In every act of judgment there is a mind which judges, and there are terms concerning which it judges. We will call the mind the *subject* in the judgment, and the remaining terms the *objects*. Thus, when Othello judges that Desdemona loves Cassio, Othello is the subject, while the objects are Desdemona and loving and Cassio. The subject and the objects together are called the *constituents* of the judgment. It will be observed that the relation of judging has what is called a "sense" or "direction." We may say, metaphorically, that it puts its objects in a certain *order*, which we may indicate by means of the order of the words in the sentence. . . .

We spoke of the relation called "judging" or "believing" as knitting together into one complex whole the subject and the objects. In this respect, judging is exactly like every other relation. Whenever a relation holds between two or more terms, it unites the terms into a complex whole. If Othello loves Desdemona, there is such a complex whole as "Othello's love for Desdemona." The terms united by the relation may be themselves complex, or may be simple, but the whole which results from their being united must be complex. Wherever there is a relation which relates certain terms, there is a complex object formed of the union of those terms; and conversely, wherever there is a complex object, there is a relation which relates its constituents. When an act of believing occurs, there is a complex, in which "believing" is the uniting relation, and subject and objects are arranged in a certain order by the "sense" of the relation of believing. Among the objects, as we saw in considering "Othello believes that Desdemona loves Cassio," one must be a relation—in this instance, the relation "loving." But this relation, as it occurs in the act of believing, is not the relation which creates the unity of the complex whole consisting of the subject and the objects. The relation "loving," as it occurs in the act of believing, is one of the objects—it is a brick in the structure, not the cement. The cement is the relation "believing." When the belief is *true*, there is another complex unity, in which the relation which was one of the objects of the belief relates the other objects. Thus, e.g., if Othello believes *truly* that Desdemona loves Cassio, then there is a complex unity, "Desdemona's love for Cassio," which is composed exclusively of the *objects* of the belief, in the same order as they had in the belief, with the relation which was one of the objects occurring now as the cement that binds together the other objects of the belief. On the other hand, when a belief is *false*, there is no such complex unity composed only of the objects of the belief. If Othello believes *falsely* that Desdemona loves Cassio, then there is no such complex unity as "Desdemona's love for Cassio."

Thus a belief is *true* when it *corresponds* to a certain associated complex, and *false* when it does not. Assuming, for the sake of definiteness, that the objects of the belief are two terms and a relation, the terms being put in a certain order by the "sense" of the believing, then if the two terms in that order are united by the relation into a complex, the belief is true; if not, it is false. This constitutes the definition of truth and falsehood that we were in search of. Judging or believing is a certain complex unity of which a mind is a constituent; if the remaining constituents, taken in the order which they have in the belief, form a complex unity, then the belief is true; if not, it is false.

Thus although truth and falsehood are properties of beliefs, yet they are in a sense extrinsic properties, for the condition of the truth of a belief is something not involving beliefs, or (in general) any mind at all, but only the *objects* of the belief. A mind, which believes, believes truly when there is a *corresponding* complex not involving the mind, but only its objects. This correspondence ensures truth, and its absence entails falsehood. Hence we account simultaneously for the two facts that beliefs *(a)* depend on minds for their *existence, (b)* do not depend on minds for their *truth.*

We may restate our theory as follows: If we take such a belief as "Othello believes that Desdemona loves Cassio," we will call Desdemona and Cassio the *object-terms,* and loving the *object-relation.* If there is a complex unity "Desdemona's love for Cassio," consisting of the object-terms related by the object-relation in the same order as they have in the belief, then this complex unity is called the *fact corresponding to the belief.* Thus a belief is true when there is a corresponding fact, and is false when there is no corresponding fact.

Blanshard

Brand Blanshard (1892–1987) was educated at the University of Michigan, Colum-
bia, Oxford, and Harvard, and was Sterling Professor of Philosophy at Yale. He
worked within the rational idealist tradition of philosophy, which upheld the be-
lief that there is a single rational whole or structure of the universe to which our
human reason aspires to grasp. Blanshard's major works include The Nature of
Thought *(1939) and* Reason and Analysis *(1962).*

The main criticism that has often been directed to any correspondence theory of truth, and one that Blanshard levels with considerable force, is that there is no way open to us actually to compare a statement with a state of affairs that is not itself already mediated by language and thought. We do not and cannot see bare facts. The coherence theory of truth advocated by Blanshard argues instead that truth, which is what thought aims to reach, consists ideally in a single comprehensive system of ideas, a system that we approximate in attaining our various forms of knowledge. Truth for us then consists in the degree to which our beliefs cohere with each other in a rational order. A completely satisfactory system, Blanshard argues, would be one in which "every proposition would be entailed by the others. . . . The integration would be so complete that no part could be seen for what it was without seeing its relation to the whole, and the whole itself could be understood only through the contribution of every part."

Coherence as the Nature of Truth

The view that truth *is* coherence rests on a theory of the relation of thought to reality, and since this is the central problem of the theory of knowledge, to begin one's discussion by assuming the answer to it or by trying to make one out of whole cloth would be somewhat ridiculous. . . . First we shall state in *résumé* the relation of thought to reality . . . and sketch the theory of truth implicit in it. We shall then take up one by one the objections to this theory and ask if they can pass muster.

From *The Nature of Thought* by Brand Blanshard, vol. 2 (1939). Reprinted by permission of George, Allen & Unwin, an imprint of HarperCollins Publishers Limited.

To think is to seek understanding. And to seek understanding is an activity of mind that is marked off from all other activities by a highly distinctive aim. This aim . . . is to achieve systematic vision, so to apprehend what is now unknown to us as to relate it, and relate it necessarily, to what we know already. We think to solve problems; and our method of solving problems is to build a bridge of intelligible relation from the continent of our knowledge to the island we wish to include in it. Sometimes this bridge is causal, as when we try to explain a disease; sometimes teleological, as when we try to fathom the move of an opponent over the chess board; sometimes geometrical, as in Euclid. But it is always systematic; thought in its very nature is the attempt to bring something unknown or imperfectly known into a subsystem of knowledge, and thus also into that larger system that forms the world of accepted beliefs. That is what explanation is. *Why* is it that thought desires this ordered vision? Why should such a vision give satisfaction when it comes? To these questions there is no answer, and if there were, it would be an answer only because it had succeeded in supplying the characteristic satisfaction to this unique desire.

But may it not be that what satisfies thought fails to conform to the real world? Where is the guarantee that when I have brought my ideas into the form my ideal requires, they should be *true?* . . . To think of a thing is to get that thing itself in some degree within the mind. To think of a colour or an emotion is to have that within us which if it *were developed and completed,* would identify itself with the object. In short, if we accept its own report, thought is related to reality as the partial to the perfect fulfilment of a purpose. The more adequate its grasp the more nearly does it approximate, the more fully does it realize in itself, the nature and relations of its objects.

Thought thus appears to have two ends, one immanent, one transcendent. On the one hand it seeks fulfilment in a special kind of satisfaction, the satisfaction of systematic vision. On the other hand it seeks fulfilment in its object. . . . Unless they are accepted as one, we could see no alternative to scepticism. If the pursuit of thought's own ideal were merely an elaborate self-indulgence that brought us no nearer to reality, or if the apprehension of reality did not lie in the line of thought's interest, or still more if both of these held at once, the hope of knowledge would be vain. . . . It has been the steadfast assumption of science whenever it came to an unsolved problem that there was a key to it to be found, that if things happened thus rather than otherwise they did so for a cause or reason, and that if this were not forthcoming it was never because it was lacking, but always because of a passing blindness in ourselves. Reflection has assumed that pursuit of its own immanent end is not only satisfying but revealing, that so far as the immanent end is achieved we are making progress toward the transcendent end as well. Indeed, that these ends coincide is the assumption of every act of thinking whatever. To think is to raise a question; to raise a question is to seek an explanation; to seek an explanation is to assume that one may be had; so to assume is to take for granted that nature in that region is intelligible. Certainly the story of advancing knowledge unwinds as if self-realization in thought meant also a coming nearer to reality. . . .

•   •   •

. . . Truth is the approximation of thought to reality. It is thought on its way home. Its measure is the distance thought has travelled, under guidance of its inner compass, toward that intelligible system which unites its ultimate object with its ultimate end. Hence at any given time the degree of truth in our experience as a whole is the degree of system it has achieved. The degree of truth of a particular proposition is to be judged in the first instance by its coherence with experience as a whole, ultimately by its coherence with that further whole, all-comprehensive and fully articulated, in which thought can come to rest.

But it is time we defined more explicitly what coherence means. . . . Certainly this ideal goes far beyond mere consistency. Fully coherent knowledge would be knowledge in which every judgement entailed, and was entailed by, the rest of the system. Probably we never find in fact a system where there is so much interdependence. What it means may be clearer if we take a number of familiar systems and arrange them in a series tending to such coherence as a limit. At the bottom would be a junk-heap, where we could know every item but one and still be without any clue as to what that remaining item was. Above this would come a stone-pile, for here you could at least infer that what you would find next would be a stone. A machine would be higher again, since from the remaining parts one could deduce not only the general character of a missing part, but also its special form and function. This is a high degree of coherence, but it is very far short of the highest. You could remove the engine from a motor-car while leaving the other parts intact, and replace it with any one of thousands of other engines, but the thought of such an interchange among human heads or hearts shows at once that the interdependence in a machine is far below that of the body. Do we find then in organic bodies the highest conceivable coherence? Clearly not. Though a human hand, as Aristotle said, would hardly be a hand when detached from the body, still it would be something definite enough; and we can conceive systems in which even this something would be gone. Abstract a number from the number series and it would be a mere unrecognizable x; similarly, the very thought of a straight line involves the thought of the Euclidean space in which it falls. It is perhaps in such systems as Euclidean geometry that we get the most perfect examples of coherence that have been constructed. If any proposition were lacking, it could be supplied from the rest; if any were altered, the repercussions would be felt through the length and breadth of the system. Yet even such a system as this falls short of ideal system. Its postulates are unproved; they are independent of each other, in the sense that none of them could be derived from any other or even from all the others together; its clear necessity is bought by an abstractness so extreme as to have left out nearly everything that belongs to the character of actual things. A completely satisfactory system would have none of these defects. No proposition would be arbitrary, every proposition would be entailed by the others jointly and even singly, no proposition would stand outside the system. The integration would be so complete that no part could be seen for what it was without seeing its relation to the whole, and the whole itself could be understood only through the contribution of every part. . . .

Now if we accept coherence as the test of truth, does that commit us to any conclusions about the *nature* of truth or reality? I think it does, though more clearly about reality than about truth. It is past belief that the fidelity of our thought to reality should be rightly measured by coherence if reality itself were not coherent. To say that the nature of things may be *in*coherent, but we shall approach the truth about it precisely so far as our thoughts become coherent, sounds very much like nonsense. And providing we retained coherence as the test, it would still be nonsense even if truth were conceived as correspondence. On this supposition we should have truth when, our thought having achieved coherence, the correspondence was complete between that thought and its object. But complete correspondence between a coherent thought and an incoherent object seems meaningless. It is hard to see, then, how anyone could consistently take coherence as the test of truth unless he took it also as a character of reality.

Does acceptance of coherence as a test commit us not only to a view about the nature of truth? . . .

Suppose that, accepting coherence as the test, one rejects it as the nature of truth in favour of some alternative; and let us assume, for example, that this alternative is correspondence. This, we have said, is incoherent; why? Because if one holds that truth is correspondence, one cannot intelligibly hold either that it is tested by coherence or that there is any dependable test at all. . . . In the end, the only test of truth that is not misleading is the special nature or character that is itself constitutive of truth.

Feeling that this is so, the adherents of correspondence sometimes insist that correspondence shall be its own test. But then the second difficulty arises. If truth does consist in correspondence, no test can be sufficient. For in order to know that experience corresponds to fact, we must be able to get at that fact, unadulterated with idea, and compare the two sides with each other. . . . When we try to lay hold of it, what we find in our hands is a judgement which is obviously not itself the indubitable fact we are seeking, and which must be checked by some fact beyond it. To this process there is no end. And even if we did get at the fact directly, rather than through the veil of our ideas, that would be no less fatal to correspondence. This direct seizure of fact presumably gives us truth, but since that truth no longer consists in correspondence of idea with fact, the main theory has been abandoned. In short, if we can know fact only through the medium of our own ideas, the original forever eludes us; if we can get at the facts directly, we have knowledge whose truth is not correspondence. The theory is forced to choose between scepticism and self-contradiction . . .

The theory that truth *consists* in coherence must now be developed more specifically. The theory has been widely attacked, and the average reader will not improbably come to it with numerous and dark suspicions. . . .

It is objected, first, that the view entails scepticism. What is it that our judgements must cohere with in order to be true? It is a system of knowledge complete and all-inclusive. But obviously that is beyond us—very probably forever beyond us. If to know anything as true, which means simply to know it, requires that we should see its relation to the total of possible knowledge, then we neither do nor can know anything.

The answer lies partly in an admission, partly in an explanation. The admission is that the theory does involve a degree of scepticism regarding our present knowledge and probably all future knowledge. In all likelihood there will never be a proposition of which we can say, "This that I am asserting, with precisely the meaning I now attach to it, is absolutely true." Such a conclusion may bring disappointment, but disappointment is not discredit. And in the light of the history of science, this refusal to claim absoluteness for our knowledge appears even as a merit. . . .

We may reply, secondly, with an explanation, which comes essentially to this, that the coherence theory, like other theories, needs to be applied with some common sense. While the truth of a judgement does consist in the last resort in its relations to a completed system, no sensible person would claim to know these in detail, or deny the judgement *any* truth till he did know them, any more than he would deny some beauty to a picture because it failed of beauty absolute. The system we actually work with is always less than *the* whole; at the best it is the mass of scientific knowledge bearing on the point in question; on the average it is a cloudy congeries of memories, suggestions and inferences, ill-organized in the extreme, and yet capable of subconscious mobilization and use. And for all of us, except in rare moments, the interest in truth is satisfied by exercise within these limits. . . .

This answers by implication another objection to the theory. It is said that a truth once true must be always true, whereas on the coherence theory what *was* true may now be false, and what is now true may become false with expanding knowledge. That which coheres with the knowledge of an earlier time may conflict with the knowledge of a later time. Thus propositions may put on truth or falsity, and take them off again, with changing scientific fashions; which is absurd.

But the objection is baseless. The measure of truth, which, judged by the ultimate standard, belongs to the proposition "x is y" is quite unalterable, for the coherence theory as for its critics. But as just admitted, we cannot in practice make use of that ultimate standard, and are compelled to fall back on a second best. What the ultimate standard means *in practice* is the system of present knowledge as apprehended by a particular mind. That system changes; hence what coheres with it at one time may not cohere with it at another; thus in practice we shall be justified in accepting at one time what later we must reject. This is all true, but where is the inconsistency? We have neither said nor implied that truth itself changes. What we have said is that while truth as measured by the ultimate standard is unchanging, our knowledge of that truth does change—which is a very different thing. . . .

This answer suggests a third objection. We have held that while the truth of any particular proposition must be tested by its coherence with present knowledge, the truth of this knowledge as a whole could be measured only by its approximation to an absolute system. But it has been charged that "approximation" covers a surrender to correspondence. For do we not really mean by this that our present system is true so far as it *corresponds* to the further reality, and false so far as it fails of this? . . .

. . . Thought, we have insisted, *is* its object realized imperfectly, and a system of thought is true just so far as it succeeds in embodying that end which thought in its very essence is seeking to embody. If we want analogies for the relation of our thought to the system that forms its end, we should leave aside such things as mirrors and number systems and their ways of conforming to objects, and think of the relation between seed and flower, or between the sapling and the tree. Does the sapling *correspond* to the tree that emerges from it? If you say it does, we shall agree that a system of thought may correspond to reality. If, as seems far more likely, you say it does not, and that to use "correspondence" of such a relation is confusing, then you are at one with us in considering "correspondence" a misdescription of the relation we have in mind. . . .

We come now to an objection more frequently made than any we have been considering. Granting that propositions, to be true, must be coherent with each other, may they not be coherent without being true? Are there not many systems of high unity and inclusiveness, which nevertheless are false? We have seen, for example, that there are various systems of geometry each of which seems to be as coherent internally as the others. Since they are mutually inconsistent, not more than one of them can be true, and there are many mathematicians who would say that *none* of them are true; yet if truth lies merely in coherence, are we not compelled to take all of them as true? Again, a novel, or a succession of novels such as Galsworthy's *Forsyte Saga,* may create a special world of characters and events which is at once extremely complex and internally consistent; does that make it the less fictitious? To say that it does would imply that if we could only dream constantly enough and consistently enough our dreams would literally come true.

This objection, like so many other annihilating criticisms, would have more point if anyone had ever held the theory it demolishes. But if intended to represent the coherence theory as responsibly advocated, it is a gross misunderstanding. That theory does not hold that any and every system is true, no matter how abstract and limited; it holds that one system only is true, namely the system in which everything real and possible is coherently included. How one can find in this the notion that a system would still give truth if, like some arbitrary geometry, it disregarded experience completely, it is not easy to see.

The objection gains point, however, when it goes on to inquire whether all that is actual might not be embraced in more than one system. When a murder is committed, there may be two theories of the crime which do complete and equal justice to all the known facts and yet are inconsistent with each other. Is it not conceivable similarly that there should be two perfect but conflicting systems in which all known and knowable facts should fall into place? If so, our standard would require us to say that both were true; yet since they conflict, this would be absurd. Now we might reply that such a contingency, though possible, is highly improbable. In the case of the murder, every new bit of evidence narrows the range of available hypotheses, and it does not even occur to us that if we knew *all* the relevant facts we might find ourselves at the end with conflicting theories. If such an issue is improbable where the facts are so few, is it not far more improbable where the facts are infinitely many? . . .

·   ·   ·

It may be said that such a view is a "rationalization" of conservatism. "We are to accept whatever agrees with the body of received belief, and reject whatever disagrees. But the great advances in human knowledge have been precisely those in which the mind broke loose from the received system, set up claims that ran counter to it, and in spite of opposition and derision made them good. Scientific progress, like political, has sometimes come through revolutions. But how can revolutions occur, how can there be any but the most trivial sort of progress, if it is acknowledged in advance that nothing can be true which does not accord with what is already established?". . .

But the critic is here limiting in arbitrary fashion the body of beliefs from which we start. He is assuming that the only beliefs it contains are beliefs of the first order. By "beliefs of the first order" are meant beliefs about any objects of direct experience such as tables and chairs; by "beliefs of the second order" are meant beliefs about these beliefs. Now, of course, scientific observation runs counter very frequently to established beliefs of the first order, and if these alone were decisive, the new result would have to go. Take, as a recent example, one of the observations by which the general theory of relativity was verified. It was implied in this theory that as light rays passed the sun on their journey from distant stars they would be bent by the sun's attraction, and hence that stars seen under such conditions would appear to be slightly displaced from their normal positions. Accordingly observers waited impatiently for a moment when an eclipse of the sun would render such stars visible. When it came, they found the stars displaced as Einstein had predicted. The positions actually seen conflicted with those required by Newtonian astronomy; and it may be said that if truth is to be measured by its accord with existing belief, the new observations would have had to be rejected. But at this point beliefs of the second order enter the scene. We not only hold beliefs about tables and chairs, the sun and the stars; we also hold *beliefs about the technique of acquiring beliefs.* We believe that perceptual judgements made under conditions exclusive of bias, ambiguity, and vagueness are more to be relied upon than judgements made only casually. Now let us suppose that such careful observations as the one described are rejected because of their conflict with accepted "fact." Consistency would require us to hold that *all* observations made with similar care and accuracy must be set down as giving uncertainty and perhaps falsehood, and that would conflict with the very important second-order belief just mentioned. We are thus left in a position where acceptance of the observed result would conflict with our first-order beliefs, while rejection of it would conflict with an important second-order belief; and it may be thought that the first-order beliefs would win by their sheer volume. This is a mistake. For if the second-order belief goes, an enormous mass of first-order beliefs will obviously go with it. If every judgement made under conditions as stringent as those described must be called in question, is there any perceptual judgement that can be any longer relied on? A policy that would reject such judgements consistently would involve science in general ruin. To be sure, if they are accepted, certain old first-order beliefs must be revised, but this is as nothing to the chaos that would follow from a loss of faith in the observations of science. Thus stability itself demands that the new results be given admission.

The charge of conservatism is thus a mistake. It assumes that the system we must take as base is a system of first-order beliefs. But we have seen that when beliefs of the second order are included, as they have every right to be, we have a system that provides for its own correction. . . .

Coherence means more than consistency. It means not only that the various constituents entering into the system of truth are compatible with each other, but also that they necessitate each other. The system assumed is a system ideally perfect, for nothing less than this would satisfy intelligence as stable beyond rectification. In such a system there would be no loose ends. Difference anywhere would be reflected in difference everywhere.

Now it has been held that this ideal is merely a cloud-castle, that it can never be made to embrace the facts of our actual disorderly world. There are many who would freely admit that nothing exists or occurs out of relation to *some* other things, but would regard the view that everything is related by necessity to *everything* else as demonstrably false. If the fact is that Bishop Stubbs died in his bed, this surely might be false without everything else being false that is now accepted as true.

Now it is obvious that we cannot show *in detail* that a difference anywhere in the system of truth must be reflected everywhere; we do not know enough, nor is it likely we ever shall. But we can do something else that is as near to this as can be reasonably asked. We can show that in the system of truth, *so far as reflected in our knowledge,* such interconnection holds, and that the denial of an apparently isolated judgement does in fact have implications for every other. The argument is as follows: When I say that Bishop Stubbs died in his bed, or indeed when I say anything, I always do so on evidence. This evidence may be hard or easy to bring to light, but it is there invariably; I never simply discharge judgements into the air with no ground or warrant at all. And by the rules of hypothetical argument, to admit the falsity of a judgement is to throw doubt upon its ground. Indeed it is to do more. It is to throw doubt, if I am consistent, upon *all* evidence of this kind and degree. Now the evidence on which it is believed that Bishop Stubbs died a natural death is of the kind and degree that would be accepted without hesitation by any historian or scientist. It is the sort of evidence on which science and history generally rest. Hence if I deny this proposition, and thus call in question the value of this sort of evidence, I must in consistency call in question most science and history also. And that would shatter my world of knowledge. Thus the truth about Bishop Stubbs is anything but isolated. However unimportant practically, it is so entangled with my system of beliefs that its denial would send repercussions throughout the whole.

James

William James (1842–1910), a member of the illustrious James family (his brother was the famous novelist Henry James), was a seminal force in American philosophy and psychology. He received a degree in medicine from Harvard University, where he later became a professor of philosophy and psychology. He wrote extensively on metaphysics, ethics, the philosophy of religion, and psychology. Among his principal works are Principles of Psychology *(1890),* The Varieties of Religious Experience *(1902),* Pragmatism: A New Name for Some Old Ways of Thinking *(1907), and* Essays in Radical Empiricism *(1912).*

One of the central tenets of pragmatism—that school of American thought whose leading founding members include James, Charles Sanders Peirce, and John Dewey—is that truth is something that *happens* to an idea, that truth is *made*. In opposition to both correspondence and coherence theories, pragmatism holds that truth is what "works"; true ideas are those that we can verify in experience. Impatient with notions that truth is some kind of atemporal relationship as such between statements and reality, pragmatism looks to the situations in which we actually ask various questions and resolve various doubts. " *'The true,' "* James argues, *". . . is only the expedient in the way of our thinking, just as 'the right' is only the expedient in the way of our behaving."*

The leading founders of pragmatism differed among themselves in a number of important ways, but they shared strongly the basic attitude and spirit regarding truth as set forth in James's influential essay on the subject. It is interesting to look carefully at the way in which James, although clearly opposed to correspondence and coherence notions, nevertheless incorporates various aspects of these opposing theories in his own thinking about truth.

The Pragmatic Conception of Truth

Truth, as any dictionary will tell you, is a property of certain of our ideas. It means their "agreement," as falsity means their disagreement, with "reality." Pragmatists and intellectualists both accept this definition as a matter of course. They begin to quarrel only after the question is raised as to what may precisely be meant by the term "agreement," and what by the term "reality," when reality is taken as something for our ideas to agree with.

In answering these questions the pragmatists are more analytic and painstaking, the intellectualists more off-hand and irreflective. The popular notion is that a true idea must copy its reality. Like other popular views, this one follows the analogy of the most usual experience. Our true ideas of sensible things do indeed copy them. Shut your eyes and think of yonder clock on the wall, and you get just such a true picture or copy of its dial. But your idea of its "works" (unless you are a clockmaker) is much less of a copy, yet it passes muster, for it in no way clashes with the reality. Even though it should shrink to the mere word "works," that word still serves you truly; and when you speak of the "time-keeping function" of the clock, or of its spring's "elasticity," it is hard to see exactly what your ideas can copy.

You perceive that there is a problem here. Where our ideas cannot copy definitely their object, what does agreement with that object mean? Some idealists seem to say that they are true whenever they are what God means that we ought to think about that object. Others hold the copy-view all through, and speak as if our ideas possessed truth just in proportion as they approach to being copies of the Absolute's eternal way of thinking.

These views, you see, invite pragmatistic discussion. But the great assumption of the intellectualists is that truth means essentially an inert static relation. When you've got your true idea of anything, there's an end of the matter. You're in possession; you *know;* you have fulfilled your thinking destiny. You are where you ought to be mentally; you have obeyed your categorical imperative; and nothing more need follow on that climax of your rational destiny. Epistemologically you are in stable equilibrium.

Pragmatism, on the other hand, asks its usual question. "Grant an idea or belief to be true," it says, "what concrete difference will its being true make in any one's actual life? How will the truth be realized? What experiences will be different from those which would obtain if the belief were false? What, in short, is the truth's cash-value in experiential terms?"

The moment pragmatism asks this question, it sees the answer: *True ideas are those that we can assimilate, validate, corroborate and verify. False ideas are those that we can not.* That is the practical difference it makes to us to have true ideas; that, therefore, is the meaning of truth, for it is all that truth is known-as.

This thesis is what I have to defend. The truth of an idea is not a stagnant prop-

From *Pragmatism* by William James (New York: Longmans, Green & Co., 1907).

erty inherent in it. Truth *happens* to an idea. It *becomes* true, is *made* true by events. Its verity *is* in fact an event, a process: the process namely of its verifying itself, its veri-*fication*. Its validity is the process of its valid-*ation*.

But what do the words verification and validation themselves pragmatically mean? They again signify certain practical consequences of the verified and validated idea. It is hard to find any one phrase that characterizes these consequences better than the ordinary agreement-formula—just such consequences being what we have in mind whenever we say that our ideas "agree" with reality. They lead us, namely, through the acts and other ideas which they instigate, into or up to, or towards, other parts of experience with which we feel all the while—such feeling being among our potentialities—that the original ideas remain in agreement. The connexions and transitions come to us from point to point as being progressive, harmonious, satisfactory. This function of agreeable leading is what we mean by an idea's verification. . . .

. . . the possession of true thoughts means everywhere the possession of invaluable instruments of action; and that our duty to gain truth, so far from being a blank command from out of the blue, or a "stunt" self-imposed by our intellect, can account for itself by excellent practical reasons.

The importance to human life of having true beliefs about matters of fact is a thing too notorious. We live in a world of realities that can be infinitely useful or infinitely harmful. Ideas that tell us which of them to expect count as the true ideas in all this primary sphere of verification, and the pursuit of such ideas is a primary human duty. The possession of truth, so far from being here an end in itself, is only a preliminary means towards other vital satisfactions. If I am lost in the woods and starved, and find what looks like a cow-path, it is of the utmost importance that I should think of a human habitation at the end of it, for if I do so and follow it, I save myself. The true thought is useful here because the house which is its object is useful. The practical value of true ideas is thus primarily derived from the practical importance of their objects to us. Their objects are, indeed, not important at all times. I may on another occasion have no use for the house; and then my idea of it, however verifiable, will be practically irrelevant, and had better remain latent. Yet since almost any object may some day become temporarily important, the advantage of having a general stock of *extra* truths, of ideas that shall be true of merely possible situations, is obvious. We store such extra truths away in our memories, and with the overflow we fill our books of reference. Whenever such an extra truth becomes practically relevant to one of our emergencies, it passes from cold-storage to do work in the world and our belief in it grows active. You can say of it then either that "it is useful because it is true" or that "it is true because it is useful." Both these phrases mean exactly the same thing, namely that here is an idea that gets fulfilled and can be verified. True is the name for whatever idea starts the verification-process, useful is the name for its completed function in experience. True ideas would never have been singled out as such, would never have acquired a class-name, least of all a name suggesting value, unless they had been useful from the outset in this way.

From this simple cue pragmatism gets her general notion of truth as something essentially bound up with the way in which one moment in our experience may lead us towards other moments which it will be worth while to have been led to. Primarily, and on the common-sense level, the truth of a state of mind means this function of *a leading that is worth while.* When a moment in our experience, of any kind whatever, inspires us with a thought that is true, that means that sooner or later we dip by that thought's guidance into the particulars of experience again and make advantageous connexion with them. This is a vague enough statement, but I beg you to retain it, for it is essential.

Our experience meanwhile is all shot through with regularities. One bit of it can warn us to get ready for another bit, can "intend" or be "significant of" that remoter object. The object's advent is the significance's verification. Truth, in these cases, meaning nothing but eventual verification, is manifestly incompatible with waywardness on our part. Woe to him whose beliefs play fast and loose with the order which realities follow in his experience; they will lead him nowhere or else make false connexions.

By "realities" or "objects" here, we mean either things of common sense, sensibly present, or else common-sense relations, such as dates, places, distances, kinds, activities. Following our mental image of a house along the cow-path, we actually come to see the house; we get the image's full verification. *Such simply and fully verified leadings are certainly the originals and prototypes of the truth-process.* Experience offers indeed other forms of truth-process, but they are all conceivable as being primary verifications arrested, multiplied or substituted one for another.

Take, for instance, yonder object on the wall. You and I consider it to be a "clock," altho no one of us has seen the hidden works that make it one. We let our notion pass for true without attempting to verify. If truths mean verification-process essentially, ought we then to call such unverified truths as this abortive? No, for they form the overwhelmingly large number of the truths we live by. Indirect as well as direct verifications pass muster. Where circumstantial evidence is sufficient, we can go without eye-witnessing. Just as we here assume Japan to exist without ever having been there, because it *works* to do so, everything we know conspiring with the belief, and nothing interfering, so we assume that thing to be a clock. We *use* it as a cock, regulating the length of our lecture by it. The verification of the assumption here means its leading to no frustration or contradiction. Verifi-*ability* of wheels and weights and pendulum is as good as verification. For one truth-process completed there are a million in our lives that function in this state of nascency. They turn us *towards* direct verification; lead us into the *surroundings* of the objects they envisage; and then, if everything runs on harmoniously, we are so sure that verification is possible that we omit it, and are usually justified by all that happens.

Truth lives, in fact, for the most part on a credit system. Our thoughts and beliefs "pass," so long as nothing challenges them, just as bank-notes pass so long as nobody refuses them. But this all point to direct face-to-face verifications somewhere, without which the fabric of truth collapses like a financial system with no cash-basis whatever. You accept my verification of one thing, I yours of another. We trade on each other's truth. But beliefs verified concretely by *somebody* are the posts of the whole superstructure.

Another great reason—beside economy of time—for waiving complete verification in the usual business of life is that all things exist in kinds and not singly. Our world is found once for all to have that peculiarity. So that when we have once directly verified our ideas about one specimen of a kind, we consider ourselves free to apply them to other specimens without verification. A mind that habitually discerns the kind of thing before it, and acts by the law of the kind immediately, without pausing to verify, will be a "true" mind in ninety-nine out of a hundred emergencies, proved so by its conduct fitting everything it meets, and getting no refutation.

Indirectly or only potentially verifying processes may thus be true as well as full verification-processes. They work as true processes would work, give us the same advantages, and claim our recognition for the same reasons. All this on the common-sense level of matters of fact, which we are alone considering.

But matters of fact are not our only stock in trade. *Relations among purely mental ideas* form another sphere where true and false beliefs obtain, and here the beliefs are absolute, or unconditional. When they are true they bear the name either of definitions or of principles. It is either a principle or a definition that 1 and 1 make 2, that 2 and 1 make 3, and so on; that white differs less from gray than it does from black; that when the cause begins to act the effect also commences. Such propositions hold of all possible "ones," of all conceivable "whites" and "grays" and "causes." The objects here are mental objects. Their relations are perceptually obvious at a glance, and no sense-verification is necessary. Moreover, once true, always true, of those same mental objects. Truth here has an "eternal" character. If you can find a concrete thing anywhere that is "one" or "white" or "gray" or an "effect," then your principles will everlastingly apply to it. It is but a case of ascertaining the kind, and then applying the law of its kind to the particular object. You are sure to get truth if you can but name the kind rightly, for your mental relations hold good of everything of that kind without exception. If you then, nevertheless, failed to get truth concretely, you would say that you had classed your real objects wrongly.

In this realm of mental relations, truth again is an affair of leading. We relate one abstract idea with another, framing in the end great systems of logical and mathematical truth, under the respective terms of which the sensible facts of experience eventually arrange themselves, so that our eternal truths hold good of realities also. This marriage of fact and theory is endlessly fertile. What we say is here already true in advance of special verification, *if we have subsumed our objects rightly.* Our ready-made ideal framework for all sorts of possible objects follows from the very structure of our thinking. We can no more play fast and loose with these abstract relations than we can do so with our sense-experiences. They coerce us; we must treat them consistently, whether or not we like the results. The rules of addition apply to our debts as rigorously as to our assets. The hundredth decimal of π, the ratio of the circumference to its diameter, is predetermined ideally now, tho no one may have computed it. If we should ever need the figure in our dealings with an actual circle we should need to have it given rightly, calculated by the usual rules; for it is the same kind of truth that those rules elsewhere calculate.

Between the coercions of the sensible order and those of the ideal order, our mind is thus wedged tightly. Our ideas must agree with realities, be such realities concrete or abstract, be they facts or be they principles, under penalty of endless inconsistency and frustration.

So far, intellectualists can raise no protest. They can only say that we have barely touched the skin of the matter.

Realities mean, then, either concrete facts, or abstract kinds of thing and relations perceived intuitively between them. They furthermore and thirdly mean, as things that new ideas of ours must no less take account of, the whole body of other truths already in our possession. But what does "agreement" with such threefold realities mean?—to use again the definition that is current.

Here it is that pragmatism and intellectualism begin to part company. Primarily, no doubt, to agree means to copy, but we saw that the mere word "clock" would do instead of a mental picture of its works, and that of many realities our ideas can only be symbols and not copies. "Past time," "power," "spontaneity,"—how can our mind copy such realities?

To "agree" in the widest sense with a reality *can only mean to be guided either straight up to it or into its surroundings, or to be put into such working touch with it as to handle either it or something connected with it better than if we disagreed.* Better either intellectually or practically! And often agreement will only mean the negative fact that nothing contradictory from the quarter of that reality comes to interfere with the way in which our ideas guide us elsewhere. To copy a reality is, indeed, one very important way of agreeing with it, but it is far from being essential. The essential thing is the process of being guided. Any idea that helps us to *deal*, whether practically or intellectually, with either the reality or its belongings, that doesn't entangle our progress in frustrations, that *fits*, in fact, and adapts our life to the reality's whole setting, will agree sufficiently to meet the requirement. It will hold true of that reality.

Thus, *names* are just as "true" or "false" as definite mental pictures are. They set up similar verification-processes, and lead to fully equivalent practical results.

All human thinking gets discursified; we exchange ideas; we lend and borrow verifications, get them from one another by means of social intercourse. All truth thus gets verbally built out, stored up, and made available for every one. Hence, we must *talk* consistently just as we must *think* consistently: for both in talk and thought we deal with kinds. Names are arbitrary, but once understood they must be kept to. We mustn't now call Abel "Cain" or Cain "Abel." If we do, we ungear ourselves from the whole book of Genesis, and from all its connexions with the universe of speech and fact down to the present time. We throw ourselves out of whatever truth that entire system of speech and fact may embody.

The overwhelming majority of our true ideas admit of no direct or face-to-face verification—those of past history, for example, as of Cain and Abel. The stream of time can be remounted only verbally, or verified indirectly by the present prolongations or effects of what the past harbored. Yet if they agree with these verbalities and effects, we can know that our ideas of the past are true. *As true as past time itself was*, so true was Julius Caesar, so true were antediluvian monsters, all in their proper dates and settings. That past time itself was, is guaranteed by its coherence with everything that's present. True as the present *is*, the past *was* also.

Agreement thus turns out to be essentially an affair of leading—leading that is useful because it is into quarters that contain objects that are important. True ideas lead us into useful verbal and conceptual quarters as well as directly up to useful sensible termini. They lead to consistency, stability and flowing human intercourse. They lead away from eccentricity and isolation, from foiled and barren thinking. The untrammelled flowing of the leading-process, its general freedom from clash and contradiction, passes for its indirect verification; but all roads lead to Rome, and in the end and eventually, all true processes must lead to the face of directly verifying sensible experiences *somewhere*, which somebody's ideas have copied.

Such is the large loose way in which the pragmatist interprets the word agreement. He treats it altogether practically. He lets it cover any process of conduction from a present idea to a future terminus, provided only it run prosperously. It is only thus that "scientific" ideas, flying as they do beyond common sense, can be said to agree with their realities. It is, as I have already said, *as if* reality were made of ether, atoms or electrons, but we mustn't think so literally. The term "energy" doesn't even pretend to stand for anything "objective." It is only a way of measuring the surface of phenomena so as to string their changes on a simple formula.

Yet in the choice of these man-made formulas we can not be capricious with impunity any more than we can be capricious on the common-sense practical level. We must find a theory that will *work;* and that means something extremely difficult; for our theory must mediate between all previous truths and certain new experiences. It must derange common sense and previous belief as little as possible, and it must lead to some sensible terminus or other that can be verified exactly. To "work" means both these things; and the squeeze is so tight that there is little loose play for any hypothesis. Our theories are wedged and controlled as nothing else is. Yet sometimes alternative theoretic formulas are equally compatible with all the truths we know, and then we choose between them for subjective reasons. We choose the kind of theory to which we are already partial; we follow "elegance" or "economy." Clerk-Maxwell somewhere says it would be "poor scientific taste" to choose the more complicated of two equally well-evidenced conceptions; and you will also agree with him. Truth in science is what gives us the maximum possible sum of satisfactions, taste included, but consistency both with previous truth and with novel fact is always the most imperious claimant. . . .

. . . Truth for us is simply a collective name for verification-processes, just as health, wealth, strength, etc., are names for other processes connected with life, and also pursued because it pays to pursue them. Truth is *made*, just as health, wealth and strength are made, in the course of experience.

Here rationalism is instantaneously up in arms against us. I can imagine a rationalist to talk as follows:

"Truth is not made," he will say; "it absolutely obtains, being a unique relation that does not wait upon any process, but shoots straight over the head of experience, and hits its reality every time. Our belief that yon thing on the wall is a clock is true already, altho no one in the whole history of the world should verify it. The bare quality of standing in that transcendent relation is what makes any thought true that possesses it, whether or not there be verification. You pragmatists put the cart before the horse in making truth's being reside in verification-processes. These are merely signs of its being, merely our lame ways of ascertaining after the fact, which of our ideas already has possessed the wondrous quality. The quality itself is timeless, like all essences and natures. Thoughts partake of it directly, as they partake of falsity or of irrelevancy. It can't be analyzed away into pragmatic consequences." . . .

"The true," to put it very briefly, *is only the expedient in the way of our thinking, just as* *"the right" is only the expedient in the way of our behaving.* Expedient in almost any fashion; and expedient in the long run and on the whole of course; for what meets expediently all the experience in sight won't necessarily meet all farther experiences equaly satisfactorily. Experience, as we know, has ways of *boiling over*, and making us correct our present formulas.

The "absolutely" true, meaning what no farther experience will ever alter, is that ideal vanishing-point towards which we imagine that all our temporary truths will some day converge. It runs on all fours with the perfectly wise man, and with the absolutely complete experience; and, if these ideals are ever realized, they will all be realized together. Meanwhile we have to live to-day by what truth we can get to-day, and be ready to-morrow to call it falsehood. Ptolemaic astronomy, euclidean space, aristotelian logic, scholastic metaphysics, were expedient for centuries, but human experience has boiled over those limits, and we now call these things only relatively true, or true within those borders of experience. "Absolutely" they are false; for we know that those limits were casual, and might have been transcended by past theorists just as they are by present thinkers.

Datta and Potter

D. M. Datta, a twentieth-century Indian philosopher, was formerly professor of philosophy at Patna University. He is best known for his Six Ways of Knowing *and his* Introduction to Indian Philosophy.

Karl H. Potter was educated at the University of California at Berkeley and Harvard University. He is presently a professor of philosophy at the University of Washington. He is an acknowledged authority on Indian philosophy and the editor of the multivolume Encyclopedia of Indian Philosophy.

In contrast to both classical Western and Chinese notions of rationality, knowledge, and the nature of truth (although probably closer in spirit to the Western rather than to the Chinese), Indian characterizations have their own distinctive insights. Datta sets forth various conceptions to be found in the Indian tradition, concentrating in particular on the Vedāntic school, which emphasizes that valid knowing is that which is "uncontradicted" in experience. Potter elaborates on Datta's presentation and proffers a clear account of the various kinds of knowledge accepted in Indian philosophy in general and the style of argumentation it developed, one that is akin to, but significantly different from, classical Western logic.

D. M. DATTA

Indian Conceptions of Knowledge and Knowing

Western Philosophy generally recognizes two sources of knowledge—Perception and Inference. But Indian Philosophy presents a variety of opinions on this matter. . . .

But before taking up the problems of our study proper, it is necessary to discuss in brief the Indian conceptions of knowledge (pramā) and the methods of knowing (pramāṇa), because they underlie all epistemological discussions.

From *The Six Ways of Knowing* by D. M. Datta (1960). Reprinted by permission of University of Calcutta Press.

The Sanskrit word jñāna stands for all kinds of cognition irrespective of the question of truth and falsehood. But the word pramā is used to designate only a true cognition . . . as distinct from a false one. . . . In English the word knowledge implies a cognition attended with belief. If, therefore, a cognition turns out to be false, belief in it is immediately withdrawn and as such it should cease to be called knowledge. Consequently knowledge, strictly speaking, should always stand only for a cognition that is true, uncontradicted or unfalsified. The ordinary division of knowledge into true knowledge and false knowledge should, therefore, be considered as an instance of loose thinking; the word true as applied to knowledge would then be a tautology, and the word false positively contradictory—false knowledge being only a name for falsified knowledge, which is another name for no knowledge.

If this logical meaning of the word knowledge be consistently and rigidly adhered to, knowledge will exactly correspond to the word pramā. Pramā is generally defined as a cognition having the twofold characteristics of truth and novelty. . . .

As regards the first characteristic, truth, all schools of Indian philosophy are unanimous. Every philosopher holds that truth should be the differentia of knowledge or pramā. But views as regards the meaning of truth vary, and consequently the mark of a pramā is variously expressed. Broadly speaking there are at least four different views about truth.

According to one view the truth of knowledge consists in its practical value. A true cognition is, therefore, variously defined as that which reveals an object that serves some purpose . . . or leads to the achievement of some end, or which favours a successful volition. . . . This view will at once be seen to resemble the modern pragmatic theory of the West. It is mostly held by the Buddhists, but other writers also occasionally support it.

Another view, that we find chiefly in the Nyāya [a "realist" school of Indian philosophy] works, regards truth as the faithfulness with which knowledge reveals its object. True knowledge is, therefore, defined as that which informs us of the existence of something in a place where it really exists, or which predicates of something a character really possessed by it. This view resembles the correspondence theory of Western realists.

A third view, which is incidentally referred to by many writers, regards truth as a harmony of experience. . . . A true knowledge, according to this view, would be one which is in harmony with other experiences. This view again resembles the Western theory of coherence.

The Advaita school of Vedānta, however, favours a fourth view according to which the truth of knowledge consists in its non-contradictedness. The correspondence view of truth cannot directly prove itself. The only way to prove correspondence is to fall back on the foreign method of consilience or coherence—that is to infer the existence of a real correspondence between knowledge and reality from the facts of the harmony of experience. But all that we can legitimately infer from the harmony of knowledge with the rest of our experience up to that time, is not that the knowledge is absolutely free from error, but that it is not yet contradicted. For we do not know that we shall not have in future any experience that can falsify our present knowledge. As regards the pragmatic test of causal efficiency, the Advaitins argue that even a false cognition may, and sometimes does, lead to the fufilment of a purpose. One of the examples they cite to support their view is the case of a distant bright jewel which emits lustre. We mistake the lustre for the jewel and, desiring to get the mistaken object of our knowledge, approach it and actually get the jewel. In this case, therefore, the knowledge of lustre as the jewel—which is clearly a false cognition—leads to the attainment of the jewel and thereby satisfies our purpose, though eventually we come also to know that the initial cognition which caused our action was itself false. We can multiply instances of this kind. The hypothesis that the earth is stationary and the sun is moving has been working quite satisfactorily for ages; on the basis of this cognition many of our actions are performed and purposes attained. It is only its conflict with astronomical phenomena that enables us to detect its falsity.

It is found, therefore, that the pragmatic view of truth is not tenable. The correspondence view has ultimately to fall back on the consilience or coherence theory which, when subjected to strict scrutiny, has to yield the result that truth, as ascertained by it, consists only in its noncontradictedness.

According to the Advaitins, therefore, pramā or knowledge must have as one of its characteristics truth; and the truth of pramā consists in its content being uncontradicted.

The second characteristic of pramā or knowledge is, as we have already said, novelty. It is not sufficient that knowledge should be true, it is also necessary that the content of knowledge should be new or previously unacquired. . . .

The special source of a particular pramā or knowledge is called pramāṇa. Pramāṇa is defined as the karaṇa of a pramā. A karaṇa is conceived as the *unique* or special cause through the *action* of which a particular effect is produced. In the case of perceptual knowledge, for example, a sense-organ (in the case of an external perception) or the mind (in the case of an internal perception) is said to be the karaṇa or instrumental cause. There are many causes, e.g. the mind, the sense-organ, etc., the existence of which is necessary for the production of perceptual knowledge of an external object. But of these, the mind is a cause the existence of which is common to all sorts of knowledge, perceptual and inferential; so it cannot be regarded as a special cause. The special cause here is the particular sense-organ involved in that perception, because it is not common to other kinds of knowledge; it is peculiar to external perception alone.

A cause, to be called karaṇa, must not be merely unique . . . it must also possess some active function. . . . The contact of the sense-organ with its object is undeniably a cause of perception. It is also unique; the instrumentality of sense-contact is present in perception alone. But still it is not called the karaṇa of perception, because it is itself a function or action of the sense-organ and as such does not possess a further function.

A pramāṇa is, then, such an active and unique cause (karaṇa) of a pramā or knowledge.

KARL POTTER

Good Reasons in Philosophical Discussions

I cannot here hope to catalogue every kind of argument that is used in Indian philosophical writings. I shall try to discuss some of those forms of argument which occur frequently enough so that the Indians have given them names or stock phrases to mark them out for memory's sake. . . .

This chapter, then, constitutes an introduction to Indian logic. In the West we usually use the word "logic" in philosophy to mean formal logic, the working of formal or deductive reasoning as in the syllogism. It is probable that Indian philosophy never demarcated formal from informal logic, and the terminology used to characterize the theory of argumentation shows this. The general theory of argument in India is called *nyāya*. As a part of the early discussions on the topic of argumentation, there was developed a way of expressing any inference intended for the purpose of demonstrating a thesis for general consumption. This *nyāya* "syllogism," as it is sometimes called nowadays, bears a superficial resemblance to the Aristotelian categorical syllogism, but is actually quite different in nature, as we shall shortly see. Another part of *nyāya* consists in what is known as *tarka*. *Tarka* is the use of various and assorted forms of reasons to indicate absurdity in the opponent's thesis. It is the negative side of argumentation, and as such was seldom granted the status of a means of correct knowledge (*pramāṇa*) in most Indian systems, while inference (*anumāna*), which has a positive use in establishing propositions, is regularly denominated a means of correct knowledge. Different philosophers have held distinct views about the number and nature of the various *pramāṇas*, views I do not intend to review here. Briefly, however, the other most important *pramāṇas*, besides inference and *tarka*, are perception (*pratyakṣa*) and what is called *āgama* or *śabda*, which consists in knowledge gained from hearing authoritative words, which usually means the *śruti* or sacred scriptures, such as the Vedas and Upanishads. . . .

PERCEPTION

Under this heading we may think of all those arguments which make appeal to what is directly experienced. "Perception" is perhaps too limited a word to stand duty as translation of *pratyakṣa*. All sources of immediate experience, and not only the awareness born of the functioning of the sense-organs, are included here (although there are those who would limit perception to knowledge born of sensation). . . .

Nevertheless, all schools of Indian philosophy take perception as a legitimate *pramāṇa* or valid means of knowledge, since there are some events that we directly perceive which are clearly part of the scope of any adequate philosophy system. To

---

From *Presuppositions of India's Philosophies* by Karl H. Potter (1963). Reprinted by permission of Prentice-Hall Publishers. Copyright © 1963 Prentice-Hall, Inc.

put it negatively, if someone produced a map or conceptual scheme in argument for the possibility of freedom, and if this map or scheme had no place in it for the direct experiences of human beings, then it would be proper to criticize the map or scheme on just this ground. Positively put, this means that a philosopher's demonstration that something implied by his map or scheme is in fact regularly experienced by human beings is a point in favor of his system. . . .

INFERENCE

Whereas perception gives us immediate knowledge, inference gives us only mediate knowledge. It depends upon perceptions of various kinds. Nevertheless, it is a distinct instrument of knowledge in its own right according to most schools of Indian thought, since it establishes judgments about objects and facts which are not directly confronted by the knower.

In considering the Indian account of inference, we must constantly guard against assimilating it to the Western conception of formal or deductive logic. I shall have more to say about this in a moment, but I mention it now so that the reader will not wonder at the "peculiarity" of the formulation that is about to be introduced.

The Structure of an Inference

Let us begin by examining a stock example of an inference. You and I are standing on a hillside overlooking a valley, and on the hillside across the way we see smoke billowing upwards. "There's a fire on that hill," I say to you, "because there's smoke. You know, you've seen fiery things smoking before, e.g., kitchens, and furthermore one never sees smoke where there's no fire, for example in a lake." (This illustration, like most textbook illustrations, is slightly simpleminded, since I would in such a situation hardly have to explain in such detail the reasons for my conclusion; still, in giving a simple example one cannot avoid being somewhat simplistic.)

The argument just quoted has five *terms* and three *members*. Let us state the argument formally:

Hypothesis: That mountain (is) fire-possessing.
Reason: (Because) that mountain (is) smoke-possessing.
Examples: (a) (as in) kitchen
              (b) (unlike) lake.

The three members of this inference are the hypothesis (*pratijñā*, the reason (*hetu*), and the example(s) (*dṛṣṭānta*). The five terms are (1) that mountain, (2) fire-possessing, (3) smoke-possessing, (4) kitchen, and (5) lake.

I have underlined the five terms to emphasize something about which one may be easily misled. I have called these five things "terms," and this may lead one to think that I am talking about the words or phrases "that mountain," "fire-possessing," etc. But the Indians conceive inference to be, not about words, but about the things to which the words refer, i.e., to classes of things. Thus each of the five terms underlined are to be considered as classes of things, and can well be pictured as circles—a device I shall avail myself of shortly.

(1) That mountain is a unit class, a class with exactly one member, namely that particular mountain you and I are looking at. Any class which functions in the position that mountain does in this inference, appearing in both the hypothesis and the reason as first element, is called in Sanskrit the *pakṣa*. We shall sometimes abbreviate this term to *p*.

(2) The second term is the class of all those things which possess fire—of all fiery things, as we might say. The class which functions as fire-possessing does in this inference, being the second element in the hypothesis, is called in Sanskrit the *sādhya* or thing to be proved. We shall abbreviate this term as *s*.

(3) The third term is the class of all things which smoke, or possess smoke—all smoking things. Any class which functions as smoke-possessing does in the stock inference, which appears as the second element in the second member, is called the *hetu*, and we shall abbreviate this term as *h*. (Note that the second member and the third term both go under the same name, *hetu*. Do not let this confuse you.)

(4) The fourth term, kitchen, is the class of all kitchens. It is offered as the first of the two examples, as a positive case of something which is both smoky and fiery. In Sanskrit this term is called the *sapakṣa*, which we shall abbreviate as *sp*.

(5) The fifth term, lake, is the class of all lakes. It is the second of the two examples, and is offered as negative proof, as something which is neither smoky nor fiery, helping to show that where smokiness is, fieriness is too. The Sanskrit for this negative example is *vipakṣa*, abbreviated as *vp*.

As was said, it is possible to symbolize these five terms by means of circles. Then the members can be pictured as follows:

Hypothesis: That mountain (is) fire-possessing
            p   (is)   *s*

Figure 1

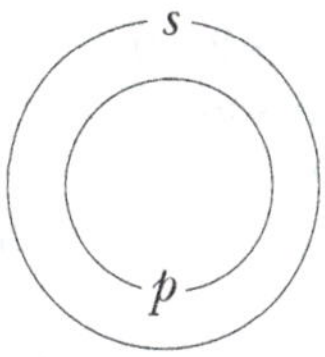

Reason: (because) that mountain (is) smoke-possessing
                       p   (is)   *h*

Figure 2

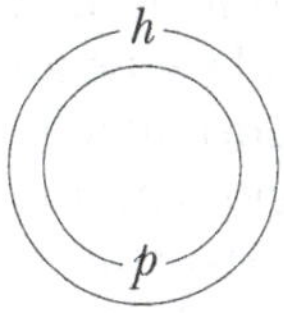

Examples: (a) (as in) <u>kitchen</u> (which overlaps <u>fire-possessing</u>
                                     and <u>smoke-possessing</u>)
             (as in)   *sp*   (which overlaps *s* and *h*)

Figure 3

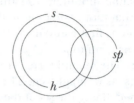

(b) (unlike) <u>lake</u> (which class falls completely outside of
                              <u>fire-possessing</u> and <u>smoke-possessing</u>)
     (unlike)   *vp*   (which excludes *s* and *h*)

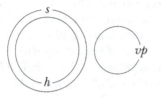

Figure 4

The combination of all these relationships,

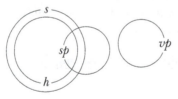

Figure 5

is what an inference asserts, i.e., what one putting forth the inference claims. Obviously, that someone asserts an inference does not mean that what he asserts is the case; there are sound inferences and unsound ones. A *sound* inference is an inference which asserts what is actually the case; an *unsound* inference is one which asserts something which is not the case.

Soundness of an inference is one thing; validity is another. To say that an argument is *valid* is to say that it passes certain tests of validity; but unless these tests exhaust the ways in which an inference may fail to represent what is the case, an argument may be valid but yet unsound, since it remains possible that it fails to picture the world accurately. Every invalid argument is unsound, but an argument may be valid and yet be unsound.

It is important to recognize that the Indian inference is not a formal or deductive type of argument. Indian rules of validity, as we shall see, do not bear merely upon the formal structure of an inference's members, but also upon the truth or falsity of the claims each member is used to make.

A Western categorical syllogism may be a valid inference even though its members be false. E.g., "everyone in this room is over ten feel tall; Jones is in this room; therefore Jones is over ten feel tall" is a valid argument even though no one in this room is over ten feet tall, or for that matter even though Jones is not in this room. Validity means something different in Western syllogistic logic from what it does here.

In examining an Indian inference, then, the first part of the task is to formulate the argument properly; the second is to test its members against certain criteria of validity.

Formulating the Argument

The first task is fairly simple in most cases, although one must be careful. The first thing to do, given an argument in ordinary language, is to identify the terms in class-terminology. Thus, for example, take the old (Western) chestnut "All men are mortal; Socrates is a man; therefore Socrates is mortal." The terms here are Socrates (a unit class), man, and mortal things. The hypothesis is that Socrates is mortal, i.e., that the unit class Socrates is included within the class mortal things. The reason is that Socrates is a man, i.e., that Socrates is included within the class man. The "major premiss," "All men are mortal," does not appear in the inference when properly formulated; if this argument were seriously offered and defended, one would normally go on to offer examples which are intended to provide evidence for the major premiss, but in the form of inference we are considering, that premiss is not enunciated.

Next, take a more complicated argument: "It must have rained upstream, for this river is rising just the way the Ganges does when there's a cloudburst in the Himalayas, and rivers don't rise when the weather in their upper parts has been dry." Here, in order to identify the terms, we do well to consider exactly what is being asserted as our hypothesis and reason. What is being asserted is that it has recently rained upstream, and the reason is that this river is rising. We want to reformulate these two assertions so that their first element is the same class—for p must appear in both the hypothesis and the reason as the first term. Furthermore, temporal distinctions seem to be in point, since the argument links what happened then with what is happening now. Therefore we may formulate the argument as follows:

> Hypothesis: this-river-now events (is included within) events closely following upstream-raining events.
>
> Reason: (because) this-river-now events (is included within) rising-river events.
>
> Examples: (a) (as in) Ganges events.
> (b) (unlike) events on rivers closely following times when it has been dry upstream.

Here, then, our terms are:

> p—this-river-now events
> s—events closely following upstream-raining events

h—rising-river events

sp—Ganges events

vp—events on rivers closely following times when it has been dry upstream.

It is not always easy to identify the correct parameters in terms of which to formulate an argument, as this last illustration shows.

No special kind of problem arises in formulating an argument which contains negative terms. For example, "there is no fire on that mountain, because there is no smoke" may be rendered as

Hypothesis: that mountain (is) non-fire-possessing

Reason: (because) that mountain (is) non-smoke-possessing.

A more complicated instance is the following: "There is no jar here, because one is not perceived, although the conditions of perception are fulfilled." The *paksa* in this case is the particular place referred to as "here." Thus this goes over into

Hypothesis: this place (is) non-jar-possessing

Reason: (because) this place (is a) place where, although the conditions of perception are fulfilled, jar is not perceived.

The *hetu* here, it will be noted, is quite complex, but despite its complexity the words clearly pick out a class, a class whose members are all those places where the (relevant) conditions of perception are fulfilled and no jar is perceived. . . .

. . . in many cases the acceptability of an inference depends on agreement upon certain facts of experience ("perception"), an agreement which can frequently be obtained; but where such agreement cannot be obtained—and these are the cases of fundamental philosophical importance—other courts of appeal must be resorted to.

When one confronts ultimate differences of opinion on such basic matters, the considerations Indians called *tarka* come into play. Some logicians include these reasons under the rubric of inference also; the decision how to classify *tarka* reasons is not one we have to reach here, however. It is sufficient for us to note merely that *tarka* reasons are brought into the picture precisely when the question shifts from how things are common-sensically supposed to be structured or how we do talk in common speech to the question of how things ought to be mapped or how we ought to talk in an "improved language." . . .

VERBAL AUTHORITY (*śabda*)

It is well accepted by everyone, I suppose, that whatever the wisdom of the practice may be, one tends to believe what he is told unless or until he has some reason to suspect the source of his information. Some Indian logicians interpret "verbal authority" in this more or less innocuous way. But that is not the natural way of interpreting the term. It is usually understood as "what is heard from a reliable person," and is sometimes replaced by terms such as *āgama* or *śruti,* meaning "what is heard from sacred authorities."

Most of the philosophers of India rely on some texts or other of hoary vintage and saintly pre-eminence. Many Buddhists rely on the Pāli canon, which contains the words of the Buddha. The Jains have their sacred scriptures. And the Hindu philosophers as a general rule account the Vedas, including those Upanishads whose style and manner testifies to their ancient origin, as authoritative. They will also admit the authoritative character of certain other texts, notably, for example, the Bhagavadgītā.

There can be no doubt about the tremendous weight that the classical philosophers of India have placed on such authoritative scriptures. But when one examines the use made of appeals to the texts, one comes to the conclusion that the argument from authority is not as dogmatic as Westerners are frequently prone to believe. In effect what happens is that philosophers regularly appeal to authorities who say what they wish to say in more elegant language than they can muster. And when it appears that a sacred text runs counter to one's thesis, it is necessary to reconstrue the passage; one is not allowed just to ignore it.

PART

IV

WHAT IS REALITY?

In the ancient collection of hymns known as the Veda, one finds this marvelous expression of wonder regarding the very origin of the world and the recognition of the inadequacy—even for the gods—of knowing what it is:

Who knows for certain? Who shall here declare it?
Whence was it born, and whence came this creation?
The gods were born after this world's creation:
Then who can know from whence it has arisen?

None knoweth whence creation has arisen;
And whether he has or has not produced it;
He who surveys it in the highest heaven,
He only knows, or haply he may know not.
(*Rig Veda*, X, 129, translated by A. A. Macdonell)

From the dawn of human reflection people in all cultures have asked: What is the origin of the world? Was the world created? And if so, how and by whom? Or did it evolve in some primordial way simply from natural principles? Or indeed is the world uncreated, having perhaps always been? Mythologies everywhere address this issue of the origin of the world, and it remains very much a part of modern philosophy and contemporary science. Related to the question of origin is that of the nature of space and time: Are they actual realities or, in some way or other, merely human ways of seeing and organizing our experience? Is nature itself material, a physical substance, or something entirely mental and insubstantial? These questions

293

in turn readily give rise to others: is the universe ordered in a rational, lawlike manner, or is it inherently irrational or nonrational? Questions of this type are usually thought to be *cosmological*, involving as they do a systematic interpretation of the nature of the universe as a whole.

Another set of questions that humankind is disposed to raise concerns the very nature of reality. Is reality *one*, a single basic unity, or *many*, a set of distinct and separate existences? What distinguishes what is real from what is only apparent? Is reality primarily in a flux, always changing, or is it fundamentally permanent, forever retaining its basic character? Are there levels and degrees of reality? Is nature uniform throughout in its constitution, or is it hierarchical, manifesting greater and less realities and values? These questions are usually thought to be *ontological* (from the Greek *on*, "being," + *logos*, "logic"), involving as they do the most basic issues having to do with reality and existence.

Cosmology and ontology are in turn usually taken to be the main branches of *metaphysics*. The term "metaphysics" derives from the Greek *meta ta physica*, which literally means "after the physics," and was the name given to an untitled group of texts written by Aristotle that his editor placed after his works on physics. Aristotle, as we will see, understood "metaphysics" to be "first philosophy," the most basic inquiry into what he called "being *qua* being." In medieval times the term came to mean the inquiry into those things that came "after" nature in the sense of being more remote from ordinary human experience but nevertheless fundamental to all experience. This sense persisted far into the modern era; for example, the nineteenth-century German philosopher Arthur Schopenhauer states that "by *metaphysics* I understand all so-called knowledge that goes beyond the possibility of experience, and so beyond nature or the given phenomenal appearance of things, in order to give information about that by which, in some sense or other, this experience or nature is conditioned, or in popular language, about that which is hidden behind nature, and renders nature possible" ("On Man's Need for Metaphysics" in The World as Will and Representation, translated by E. F. J. Payne).

Today the term "metaphysics" has both a general positive philosophical usage and a negative or derogatory one: positively it refers to that domain of philosophy that deals precisely with the kind of cosmological and ontological questions indicated; negatively it connotes mere idle, unverifiable speculation, an escape from what is actual and pressing in our experience. The term today has, unfortunately, also become associated with the occult. Most large bookstores now have a separate section on "metaphysics," which includes works on tarot cards, crystal gazing, and the rest. In any event metaphysics has certainly been frequently regarded as the very core of philosophy and has as well been challenged, especially in modern times, as being beyond the reach of the human mind.

Assuming that the enterprise of metaphysics does have positive significance and value, the question then naturally arises as to how we may judge the truth or adequacy of any particular system or view. Very few, if any, metaphysicians today would claim absolute validity for their position, for they recognize clearly enough that our experience is subject to change and that our knowledge is always advancing, and sometimes retreating, with new discoveries and revolutions in our ways of organizing conceptually our experience. We thus tend, it would seem, to evaluate a metaphysical system or viewpoint with regard to the following: (1) its *comprehensiveness*—Does it attend properly to all the significant dimensions of experience?; (2) its *coherence*—Does it bring our fundamental cosmological and ontological ideas together in a meaningful order without contradiction and skillfully draw out the implications of its basic principles?; and (3) the depth and originality of its *insight*—Does it open new ways of understanding the nature of reality and the universe?

Historically, there have been several rather distinct kinds of metaphysics, namely those associated in the West in varying degrees with Plato and Aristotle. There have also been several ways in which limits to metaphysical speculation have been put forward, namely those associated with Kant and with various linguistically oriented thinkers in both traditional Asian cultures and the contemporary West.

Platonic metaphysics introduced in a highly sophisticated way the distinction (which has never quite left us) between "appearance" and "reality," between an ever-changing world of sense-based experience and an unchanging domain of true ideas. Platonism has also been the natural home, as it were, for various forms of metaphysical idealism—doctrines that stress the centrality and priority of mind or spirit—and for all manner of dualisms between the mental and the material, the mind and the body. The Platonic tendency in metaphysics is present whenever perfection of form takes precedence over the crudities of material content and whenever reality is believed to be attainable through rational insight and discipline.

Aristotelian metaphysics, on the other hand, tends to embody the "naturalistic" spirit in philosophy, which aligns itself more with science than with poetry and holds that we can learn through experience the distinguishing features by which we identify and classify the various kinds of things of the world and the principles of their orderly development. The Aristotelian tendency in metaphysics—what William James thought to be the "tough-minded" as opposed to the "tender-minded" Platonic approach—looks for the explanation of the world within the world. It wants to lay hold of the first principles that inform all experience and the terms and qualities natural to all being. In its more extreme expression, it favors some kind of materialistic or physicalist perspective that would account for everything in terms of a material structure or process.

A third kind of metaphysics may also be identified, which, while linked historically in the West with Platonism (as articulated by his follower Plotinus), has a distinctive character of its own, and which, while often called "mystical," may more properly be called simply "nondualistic." Reality in this tradition—which has taken several different forms in Asian thought—is defined as that which is "beyond being" and is realized as such only in intense spiritual experience. Reality is said to be one, without distinction (nondual), and is, as we have seen with Vedānta, understood to be identical without our own essential human being.

Each broad tendency in metaphysics gives rise to its own special problems and concerns—for the Platonic: What precisely is the relation between eternal ideas and particular things?; for the Aristotelian: What are the immanent principles of things that cut across all the particular sciences?; for the Plotinian: Why is there, or why do we believe there is, an independent world of sense-experience at all?

As indicated, both in the West and in Asian cultures there have been various attempts to circumscribe the enterprise of metaphysics and in some instances to deny its very possibility. In the West, Kant is usually credited with exposing the pretensions of speculative metaphysics to attain certitude by means of rational demonstration alone or by some kind of "intellectual intuition." He confined metaphysics to examining the conditions for the possibility of all experience without its being able to claim any knowledge or access into the world as it is in itself.

In any event, many philosophers do believe that metaphysics in the sense of holding beliefs about the fundamental character of the world is unavoidable, for such beliefs, it is said, do ground all other notions we may have regarding ourselves, our knowledge, our values, and our conduct. Steeped as it is in the mystery of being, metaphysics is an enduring response to the wonder of existence that continually haunts human consciousness. As we review representative kinds of metaphysical thinking in the readings that follow, we might very well ponder this very issue regarding the foundational character of metaphysics and the apparent inevitability of having to deal with the basic cosmological, ontological, and, as we will see, "religious" questions that confront us.

Heidegger

Martin Heidegger (1889–1976), was one of the most brilliant and controversial philosophers of the twentieth century. His life was dedicated to "the pursuit of being," which took many twists and turns in his work. Regarded as an existential philosopher for his early and most important work, Being and Time *(1927), in which he placed great emphasis on the character of our human existence, our temporality, our finitude, and our struggle to attain authentic being, Heidegger later turned to poetry as a source for a new language appropriate to his insights into the nature of being. During the Nazi era in Germany, Heidegger was considered a Nazi sympathizer for his willingness to serve as the rector of a major German university and to voice fascist sentiments. Many efforts have been made by scholars to interpret this phase of his life and its relation to his philosophy.*

In *An Introduction to Metaphysics* (1953), Heidegger raises what he sees to be the most far-reaching, deepest, and fundamental question of metaphysics: Why is there something instead of nothing? It is not so much a question to be answered definitively with precision as it is one that expresses our wonder at the very fact of being. Its consideration requires us, according to Heidegger, to leap away from the unreflective sense of security we have in the world and to face directly the basic uncertainties of our existence. It is, in short, an "existential" question, one that takes hold of us in a way that allows an opening up, a movement toward, the very source of the question in the profound mystery of being.

The Fundamental Question of Metaphysics

Why are there essents* rather than nothing? That is the question. Clearly it is no ordinary question. "Why are there essents, why is there anything at all, rather than nothing?"—obviously this is the first of all questions, though not in a chronological

*"Essents" = "existents," "things that are."

sense. Individuals and peoples ask a good many questions in the course of their historical passage through time. They examine, explore, and test a good many things before they run into the question "Why are there essents rather than nothing?" Many men never encounter this question, if by encounter we mean not merely to hear and read about it as an interrogative formulation but to ask the question, that is, to bring it about, to raise it, to feel its inevitability.

And yet each of us is grazed at least once, perhaps more than once, by the hidden power of this question, even if he is not aware of what is happening to him. The question looms in moments of great despair, when things tend to lose all their weight and all meaning becomes obscured. Perhaps it will strike but once like a muffled bell that rings into our life and gradually dies away. It is present in moments of rejoicing, when all the things around us are transfigured and seem to be there for the first time, as if it might be easier to think they are not than to understand that they are and are as they are. The question is upon us in boredom, when we are equally removed from despair and joy, and everything about us seems so hopelessly commonplace that we no longer care whether anything is or is not—and with this the question "Why are there essents rather than nothing?" is evoked in a particular form.

But this question may be asked expressly, or, unrecognized as a question, it may merely pass through our lives like a brief gust of wind; it may press hard upon us, or, under one pretext or another, we may thrust it away from us and silence it. In any case it is never the question that we ask first in point of time.

But it is the first question in another sense—in regard to rank. This may be clarified in three ways. The question "Why are there essents rather than nothing?" is first in rank for us first because it is the most far reaching, second because it is the deepest, and finally because it is the most fundamental of all questions.

It is the widest of all questions. It confines itself to no particular essent of whatever kind. The question takes in everything, and this means not only everything that is present in the broadest sense but also everything that ever was or will be. The range of this question finds its limit only in nothing, in that which simply is not and never was. Everything that is not nothing is covered by this question, and ultimately even nothing itself; not because it is *something*, since after all we speak of it, but because it *is* nothing. Our question reaches out so far that we can never go further. We do not inquire into this and that, or into each essent in turn, but from the very outset into the essent as a whole, or, as we say for reasons to be discussed below: into the essent as such in its entirety.

This broadest of questions is also the deepest: Why are there essents . . . ? Why, that is to say, on what ground? from what source does the essent derive? on what ground does it stand? The question is not concerned with particulars, with what essents are and of what nature at any time, here and there, with how they can be changed, what they can be used for, and so on. The question aims at the ground of what is insofar as it is. To seek the ground is to try to get to the bottom; what is put in question is thus related to the ground. . . .

Finally, this broadest and deepest question is also the most fundamental. What do we mean by this? If we take the question in its full scope, namely the essent as such in its entirety, it readily follows that in asking this question we keep our distance from every particular and individual essent, from every this and that. For we mean the essent as a whole, without any special preference. Still, it is noteworthy that in this questioning *one* kind of essent persists in coming to the fore, namely the men who ask the question. But the question should not concern itself with any particular essent. In the spirit of its unrestricted scope, all essents are of equal value. An elephant in an Indian jungle "is" just as much as some chemical combustion process at work on the planet Mars, and so on.

Accordingly, if our question "Why are there essents rather than nothing?" is taken in its fullest sense, we must avoid singling out any special, particular essent, including man. For what indeed is man? Consider the earth within the endless darkness of space in the universe. By way of comparison it is a tiny grain of sand; between it and the next grain of its own size there extends a mile or more of emptiness; on the surface of this grain of sand there lives a crawling, bewildered swarm of supposedly intelligent animals, who for a moment have discovered knowledge. And what is the temporal extension of a human life amid all the millions of years? Scarcely a move of the second hand, a breath. Within the essent as a whole there is no legitimate ground for singling out this essent which is called mankind and to which we ourselves happen to belong. . . .

. . . This question and all the questions immediately rooted in it, the questions in which this one question unfolds—this question "why" is incommensurable with any other. It encounters the search for its own why. At first sight the question "Why the why?" looks like a frivolous repetition ad infinitum of the same interrogative formulation, like an empty and unwarranted brooding over words. Yes, beyond a doubt, that is how it looks. The question is only whether we wish to be taken in by this superficial look and so regard the whole matter as settled, or whether we are capable of finding a significant event in this recoil of the question "why" upon itself.

But if we decline to be taken in by surface appearances we shall see that this question "why," this question as to the essent as such in its entirety, goes beyond any mere playing with words, provided we possess sufficient intellectual energy to make the question actually recoil into its "why"—for it will not do so of its own accord. In so doing we find out that this privileged question "why" has its ground in a leap through which man thrusts away all the previous security, whether real or imagined, of his life. The question is asked only in this leap; it *is* the leap; without it there is no asking. . . . Our questioning is not yet the leap; for this it must undergo a transformation; it still stands perplexed in the face of the essent. Here it may suffice to say that the leap in this questioning opens up its own source—with this leap the question arrives at its own ground. We call such a leap, which opens up its own source, the original source or origin <Ur-sprung>, the finding of one's own ground. It is because the question "Why are there essents rather than nothing?" breaks open the ground for all authentic questions and is thus at the origin <Ursprung> of them all that we must recognize it as the most fundamental of all questions.

Plato

In his "Allegory of the Cave," which immediately follows his presentation of the "divided line" in *The Republic,* Plato shows vividly by means of a parable how the philosopher as metaphysician seeks an enlightenment that discloses both the nature of reality as the Good and the appearance-only status of the world of our ordinary experience. The latter is represented as an underground cave where persons are chained from childhood facing a wall upon which are cast shadows of moving objects from a source of light behind them that they take to be real. The parable indicates the progressive movement from this illusory state of mind to the vision of the Good and recounts the difficulty one who has been vouchsafed such a vision has in returning to the world of appearances.

The Allegory of the Cave

Next, said I, here is a parable to illustrate the degrees in which our nature may be enlightened or unenlightened. Imagine the condition of men living in a sort of cavernous chamber underground, with an entrance open to the light and a long passage all down the cave. Here they have been from childhood, chained by the leg and also by the neck, so that they cannot move and can see only what is in front of them, because the chains will not let them turn their heads. At some distance higher up is the light of a fire burning behind them; and between the prisoners and the fire is a track with a parapet built along it, like the screen at a puppet-show, which hides the performers while they show their puppets over the top.

I see, said he.

Now behind this parapet imagine persons carrying along various artificial objects, including figures of men and animals in wood or stone or other materials, which project above the parapet. Naturally, some of these persons will be talking, others silent.

It is a strange picture, he said, and a strange sort of prisoners.

Like ourselves, I replied; for in the first place prisoners so confined would have seen nothing of themselves or of one another, except the shadows thrown by the fire-light on the wall of the Cave facing them, would they?

Not if all their lives they had been prevented from moving their heads.

And they would have seen as little of the objects carried past.

Of course.

Now, if they could talk to one another, would they not suppose that their words referred only to those passing shadows which they saw?

Necessarily.

And suppose their prison had an echo from the wall facing them? When one of the people crossing behind them spoke, they could only suppose that the sound came from the shadow passing before their eyes.

No doubt.

In every way, then, such prisoners would recognize as reality nothing but the shadows of those artificial objects.

Inevitably.

Now consider what would happen if their release from the chains and the healing of their unwisdom should come about in this way. Suppose one of them set free and forced suddenly to stand up, turn his head, and walk with eyes lifted to the light; all these movements would be painful, and he would be too dazzled to make out the objects whose shadows he had been used to see. What do you think he would say, if someone told him that what he had formerly seen was meaningless illusion, but now, being somewhat nearer to reality and turned towards more real objects, he was getting a truer view? Suppose further that he were shown the various objects being carried by and were made to say, in reply to questions, what each of them was. Would he not be perplexed and believe the objects now shown him to be not so real as what he formerly saw?

Yes, not nearly so real.

And if he were forced to look at the fire-light itself, would not his eyes ache, so that he would try to escape and turn back to the things which he could see distinctly, convinced that they really were clearer than these other objects now being shown to him?

Yes.

And suppose someone were to drag him away forcibly up the steep and rugged ascent and not let him go until he had hauled him out into the sunlight, would he not suffer pain and vexation at such treatment, and, when he had come out into the light, find his eyes so full of its radiance that he could not see a single one of the things that he was now told were real?

Certainly he would not see them all at once.

He would need, then, to grow accustomed before he could see things in that upper world. At first it would be easiest to make out shadows, and then the images of men and things reflected in water, and later on the things themselves. After that, it would be easier to watch the heavenly bodies and the sky itself by night, looking at the light of the moon and stars rather than the Sun and the Sun's light in the daytime.

Yes, surely.

Last of all, he would be able to look at the Sun and contemplate its nature, not as it appears when reflected in water or any alien medium, but as it is in itself in its own domain.

No doubt.

And now he would begin to draw the conclusion that it is the Sun that produces the seasons and the course of the year and controls everything in the visible world, and moreover is in a way the cause of all that he and his companions used to see.

Clearly he would come at last to that conclusion.

Then if he called to mind his fellow prisoners and what passed for wisdom in his former dwelling-place, he would surely think himself happy in the change and be sorry for them. They may have had a practice of honouring and commending one another, with prizes for the man who had the keenest eye for the passing shadows and the best memory for the order in which they followed or accompanied one another, so that he could make a good guess as to which was going to come next. Would our released prisoner be likely to covet those prizes or to envy the men exalted to honour and power in the Cave? Would he not feel like Homer's Achilles, that he would far sooner "be on earth as a hired servant in the house of a landless man" or endure anything rather than go back to his old beliefs and live in the old way?

Yes, he would prefer any fate to such a life.

Now imagine what would happen if he went down again to take his former seat in the Cave. Coming suddenly out of the sunlight, his eyes would be filled with darkness. He might be required once more to deliver his opinion on those shadows, in competition with the prisoners who had never been released, while his eyesight was still dim and unsteady; and it might take some time to become used to the darkness. They would laugh at him and say that he had gone up only to come back with his sight ruined; it was worth no one's while even to attempt the ascent. If they could lay hands on the man who was trying to set them free and lead them up, they would kill him.

Yes, they would.

Every feature in this parable . . . is meant to fit our earlier analysis. The prison dwelling corresponds to the region revealed to us through the sense of sight, and the fire-light within it to the power of the Sun. The ascent to see the things in the upper world you may take as standing for the upward journey of the soul into the region of the intelligible; then you will be in possession of what I surmise, since that is what you wish to be told. Heaven knows whether it is true; but this, at any rate, is how it appears to me. In the world of knowledge, the last thing to be perceived and only with great difficulty is the essential Form of Goodness. Once it is perceived, the conclusion must follow that, for all things, this is the cause of whatever is right and good; in the visible world it gives birth to light and to the lord of light, while it is itself sovereign in the intelligible world and the parent of intelligence and truth. Without having had a vision of this Form no one can act with wisdom, either in his own life or in matters of state.

Chuang Tzu

Chuang Tzu (c. 399–295 B.C.E.), the famous Taoist philosopher, is usually accorded equal status and importance with Lao Tzu, the author of the Tao Te Ching. *Much of Chuang Tzu's life is shrouded in legend, but it is clear from his work that he emphasized that side of Taoism that in the West has so often been taken as essential to that tradition, namely its apolitical attitude, its concern for establishing a close relationship with nature, and its adherence to the Tao as a deep and mysterious process informing all of life.*

Chuang Tzu's writings are even more elusive and paradoxical than those of Lao Tzu, replete as they are with anecdotes that humorously show how the wise avoid all political engagement, especially the taking of high government positions, and with comments that call into question many of the settled habits of "logical" thinking that ignore the radical relativity of all genuine thought. In his well-known discussion of dream experience, Chuang Tzu, somewhat in the spirit of Plato, shows the difficulties one has in distinguishing dreams from actuality, illusion from reality.

Dreaming and Awakening

When we dream we do not know that we are dreaming. In our dreams we may even interpret our dreams. Only after we are awake do we know we have dreamed. Finally there comes a great awakening, and then we know life is a great dream. But the stupid think they are awake all the time, and believe they know it distinctly. Are we (honorable) rulers? Are we (humble) shepherds? How vulgar! Both Confucius and you were dreaming. When I say you were dreaming, I am also dreaming. This way of talking may be called perfectly strange. If after ten thousand generations we could meet one great sage who can explain this, it would be like meeting him in as short a time as in a single morning or evening.

"Suppose you and I argue. If you beat me instead of my beating you, are you really right and am I really wrong? If I beat you instead of your beating me, am I really right and are you really wrong? Or are we both partly right and partly wrong? Or are we both wholly right and wholly wrong? Since between us neither you nor I know which is right, others are naturally in the dark. Whom shall we ask to arbitrate? If we ask someone who agrees with you, since he has already agreed with you, how can he arbitrate? If we ask someone who agrees with me, since he has already agreed with me, how can he arbitrate? If we ask someone who disagrees with both you and me to arbitrate, since he has already disagreed with you and me, how can he arbitrate? If we ask someone who agrees with both you and me to arbitrate, since he has already agreed with you and me, how can he arbitrate? Thus among you, me, and others, none knows which is right. Shall we wait for still others? The great variety of sounds are relative to each other just as much as they are not relative to each other. To harmonize them in the functioning of Nature and leave them in the process of infinite evolution is the way to complete our lifetime."

"What is meant by harmonizing them with the functioning of Nature?"

"We say this is right or wrong, and is so or is not so. If the right is really right, then the fact that it is different from the wrong leaves no room for argument. If what is so is really so, then the fact that it is different from what is not so leaves no room for argument. Forget the passage of time (life and death) and forget the distinction of right and wrong. Relax in the realm of the infinite and thus abide in the realm of the infinite."

The Shade asks the Shadow, "A little while ago you moved, and now you stop. A little while ago you sat down and now you stand up. Why this instability of purpose?"

"Do I depend on something else to be this way?" answered the Shadow. "Does that something on which I depend also depend on something else? Do I depend on anything any more than a snake depends on its discarded scale or a cicada on its new wings? How can I tell why I am so or why I am not so?"

Once I, Chuang Chou [Tzu], dreamed that I was a butterfly and was happy as a butterfly. I was conscious that I was quite pleased with myself, but I did not know that I was Chou. Suddenly I awoke, and there I was, visibly Chou. I do not know whether it was Chou dreaming that he was a butterfly or the butterfly dreaming that it was Chou. Between Chou and the butterfly there must be some distinction. [But one may be the other.] This is called the transformation of things.

Aristotle

Aristotle's collection of treatises that his editor entitled the *Metaphysics* is one of his most difficult and important works. He wanted to determine the most basic, comprehensive principles that govern and inform all natural processes and to establish precisely in what things the universe consists. "Metaphysics," for Aristotle, goes beyond all other sciences, as it alone deals with what he calls "being *as* being."

Aristotle puts forward many fundamental concepts regarding the nature of being in his works *Metaphysics*, *Categories*, and *Physics*, but the central idea is that of "substance," which he defines in several ways. In its "primary" sense it is a particular, concrete thing rather than any quality that might be attributed to it (say, a particular person as such); in its "secondary" sense it refers to those things within which the objects of the primary sense would be included, such as the idea of a species ("man" in general), which includes both the concrete individual person and the genera ("animal") that includes the species "man."

A substance for Aristotle is further characterized as that which is the bearer of change and which as such underlies and supports various qualities; as that which is capable of independent existence; and, linguistically, as that which is a logical subject in a proposition to which various predicates might be attributed. In explaining how changes in substances occur, Aristotle develops an account of *causality*. He identifies four main types of causes: (1) the *material*, the basic stuff out of which something is made (say, the stone from which a statue is created); (2) the *formal*, the pattern or idea according to which an object is to be constituted (the design of the statue in the artist's mind); (3) the *efficient*, the actual means that are employed to realize the form (the sculptor employing his tools to fashion the work); and (4) the *final*, the end or purpose of the process (the fully realized statue). Aristotle's notion of cause clearly encompasses a great deal more than what we tend to mean by the term today, which in scientific explanation is restricted for the most part to what Aristotle conceives as the efficient cause. Aristotle is concerned with having a metaphysical understanding of all the basic features that are responsible for change, and he believes that everything has an end to which it aspires to realize in its full actuality.

A Metaphysical Understanding of Being

There is a science which investigates being as being and the attributes which belong to this in virtue of its own nature. Now this is not the same as any of the so-called special sciences; for none of these others treats universally of being as being. They cut off a part of being and investigate the attribute of this part; this is what the mathematical sciences for instance do. Now since we are seeking the first principles and the highest causes, clearly there must be some thing to which these belong in virtue of its own nature. If then those who sought the elements of existing things were seeking these same principles, it is necessary that the elements must be elements of being not by accident but just because it *is* being. Therefore it is of being as being that we also must grasp the first causes.

There are many senses in which a thing may be said to "be," but all that "is" is related to one central point, one definite kind of thing, and is not said to "be" by a mere ambiguity. Everything which is healthy is related to health, one thing in the sense that it preserves health, another in the sense that it produces it, another in the sense that it is a symptom of health, another because it is capable of it. And that which is medical is relative to the medical art, one thing being called medical because it possesses it, another because it is naturally adapted to it, another because it is a function of the medical art. And we shall find other words used similarly to these. So, too, there are many senses in which a thing is said to be, but all refer to one starting-point; some things are said to be because they are substances, others because they are affections of substance, others because they are a process towards substance, or destructions or privations or qualities of substance, or productive or generative of substance, or of things which are relative to substance, or negations of one of these things or of substance itself. It is for this reason that we say even of non-being that it *is* non-being. As, then, there is one science which deals with all healthy things, the same applies in the other cases also. For not only in the case of things which have one common notion does the investigation belong to one science, but also in the case of things which are related to one common nature; for even these in a sense have one common notion. It is clear then that it is the work of one science also to study the things that are, *qua* being.—But everywhere science deals chiefly with that which is primary, and on which the other things depend, and in virtue of which they get their names. If, then, this is substance, it will be of substances that the philosopher must grasp the principles and the causes. . . .

There are several senses in which a thing may be said to "be," . . . for in one sense the "being" meant is "what a thing is" or a "this," and in another sense it means a quality or quantity or one of the other things that are predicated as these are. While "being" has all these senses, obviously that which "is" primarily is the "what," which

From *Metaphysics* in *The Oxford Translation of Aristotle*, edited by W. D. Ross (1941). Reprinted with permission of Oxford University Press.

indicates the substance of the thing. For when we say of what quality a thing is, we say that it is good or bad, not that it is three cubits long or that it is a man; but when we say *what* it is, we do not say "white" or "hot" or "three cubits long," but "a man" or "a god." And all other things are said to be because they are, some of them, quantities of that which *is* in this primary sense, others qualities of it, others affections of it, and others some other determination of it. And so one might even raise the question whether the words "to walk," "to be healthy," "to sit" imply that each of these things is existent, and similarly in any other case of this sort; for none of them is either self-subsistent or capable of being separated from substance, but rather, if anything, it is that which walks or sits or is healthy that is an existent thing. Now these are seen to be more real because there is something definite which underlies them (i.e. the substance or individual), which is implied in such a predicate; for we never use the word "good" or "sitting" without implying this. Clearly then it is in virtue of this category that each of the others also *is*. Therefore that which is primarily, i.e., not in a qualified sense but without qualification must be substance.

The Category of Substance

Substance, in the truest and primary and most definite sense of the word, is that which is neither predicable of a subject nor present in a subject; for instance, the individual man or horse. But in a secondary sense those things are called substances within which, as species, the primary substances are included; also those which, as genera, include the species. For instance, the individual man is included in the species "man," and the genus to which the species belongs is "animal"; these, therefore—that is to say, the species "man" and the genus "animal"—are termed secondary substances.

It is plain from what has been said that both the name and the definition of the predicate must be predicable of the subject. For instance, "man" is predicated of the individual man. Now in this case the name of the species "man" is applied to the individual, for we use the term "man" in describing the individual; and the definition of "man" will also be predicated of the individual man, for the individual man is both man and animal. Thus, both the name and the definition of the species are predicable of the individual.

With regard, on the other hand, to those things which are present in a subject, it is generally the case that neither their name nor their definition is predicable of that in which they are present. Though, however, the definition is never predicable, there is nothing in certain cases to prevent the name being used. For instance, "white" being present in a body is predicated of that in which it is present, for a body

From *Categories* in *The Oxford Translation of Aristotle*, edited by W. D. Ross (1941). Reprinted with permission of Oxford University Press.

is called white: the definition, however, of the color "white" is never predicable of the body.

Everything except primary substances is either predicable of a primary substance or present in a primary substance. This becomes evident by reference to particular instances which occur. "Animal" is predicated of the species "man," therefore of the individual man, for if there were no individual man of whom it could be predicated, it could not be predicated of the species "man," at all. Again, colour is present in body, therefore in individual bodies, for if there were no individual body in which it was present, it could not be present in body at all. Thus everything except primary substances is either predicated of primary substances, or is present in them, and if these last did not exist, it would be impossible for anything else to exist.

Of secondary substances, the species is more truly substance than the genus, being more nearly related to primary substance. For if any one should render an account of what a primary substance is, he would render . . . a more instructive account, and one more proper to the subject, by stating the species than by stating the genus. Thus, he would give a more instructive account of an individual man by stating that he was man than by stating that he was animal, for the former description is peculiar to the individual in a greater degree, while the latter is too general. Again, the man who gives an account of the nature of an individual tree will give a more instructive account by mentioning the species "tree" than by mentioning the genus "plant."

Moreover, primary substances are most properly called substances in virtue of the fact that they are the entities which underlie everything else, and that everything else is either predicated of them or present in them. Now the same relation which subsists between primary substance and everything else subsists also between the species and the genus: for the species is to the genus as subject is to predicate, since the genus is predicated of the species, whereas the species cannot be predicated of the genus. Thus we have a second ground for asserting that the species is more truly substance than the genus.

Of species themselves, except in the case of such as are genera, no one is more truly substance than another. We should not give a more appropriate account of the individual man by stating the species to which he belonged, than we should of an individual horse by adopting the same method of definition. In the same way, of primary substances, no one is more truly substance than another; an individual man is not more truly substance than an individual ox.

It is, then, with good reason that of all that remains, when we exclude primary substances, we concede to species and genera alone the name "secondary substance," for these alone of all the predicates convey a knowledge of primary substance. For it is by stating the species or the genus that we appropriately define any individual man; and we shall make our definition more exact by stating the former than by stating the latter. All other things that we state, such as that he is white, that he runs, and so on, are irrelevant to the definition. Thus it is just that these alone, apart from primary substances, should be called substances.

Further, primary substances are most properly so called, because they underlie and are the subjects of everything else. Now the same relation that subsists between primary substance and everything else subsists also between the species and the genus to which the primary substance belongs, on the one hand, and every attribute which is not included within these, on the other. For these are the subjects of all such. If we call an individual man "skilled in grammar," the predicate is applicable also to the species and to the genus to which he belongs. This law holds good in all cases.

It is a common characteristic of all substance that it is never present in a subject. For primary substance is neither present in a subject nor predicated of a subject; while, with regard to secondary substances, it is clear from the following arguments (apart from others) that they are not present in a subject. For "man" is predicated of the individual man, but is not present in any subject: for manhood is not present in the individual man. In the same way, "animal" is also predicated of the individual man, but is not present in him. Again, when a thing is present in a subject, though the name may quite well be applied to that in which it is present, the definition cannot be applied. Yet of secondary substances, not only the name, but also the definition, applies to the subject: we should use both the definition of the species and that of the genus with reference to the individual man. Thus substance cannot be present in a subject.

Yet this is not peculiar to substance, for it is also the case that differentiae cannot be present in subjects. The characteristics "terrestrial" and "two-footed" are predicated of the species "man," but not present in it. For they are not *in* man. Moreover, the definition of the differentia may be predicated of that of which the differentia itself is predicated. For instance, if the characteristic "terrestrial" is predicated of the species "man," the definition also of that characteristic may be used to form the predicate of the species "man": for "man" is terrestrial.

The fact that the parts of substances appear to be present in the whole, as in a subject, should not make us apprehensive lest we should have to admit that such parts are not substances: for in explaining the phrase "being present in a subject," we stated that we meant "otherwise than as parts in a whole." . . .

All substance appears to signify that which is individual. In the case of primary substance this is indisputably true, for the thing is a unit. In the case of secondary substances, when we speak, for instance, of "man" or "animal," our form of speech gives the impression that we are here also indicating that which is individual, but the impression is not strictly true; for a secondary substance is not an individual, but a class with a certain qualification; for it is not one and single as a primary substance is; the words "man," "animal," are predicable of more than one subject.

Yet species and genus do not merely indicate quality, like the term "white"; "white" indicates quality and nothing further, but species and genus determine the quality with reference to a substance: they signify substance qualitatively differentiated. The determinate qualification covers a larger field in the case of the genus than in that of the species: he who uses the word "animal" is herein using a word of wider extension than he who uses the word "man."

Another mark of substance is that it has no contrary. What could be the contrary of any primary substance, such as the individual man or animal? It has none. Nor can the species or the genus have a contrary. Yet this characteristic is not peculiar to substance, but is true of many other things, such as quantity. There is nothing that forms the contrary of "two cubits long" or of "three cubits long," or of "ten," or of any such term. A man may contend that "much" is the contrary of "little," or "great" of "small," but of definite quantitative terms no contrary exists.

Substance, again, does not appear to admit of variation of degree. I do not mean by this that one substance cannot be more or less truly substance than another, for it has already been stated that this is the case; but that no single substance admits of varying degrees within itself. For instance, one particular substance, "man," cannot be more or less man either than himself at some other time or than some other man. One man cannot be more man than another, as that which is white may be more or less white than some other white object, or as that which is beautiful may be more or less beautiful than some other beautiful object. The same quality, moreover, is said to subsist in a thing in varying degrees at different times. A body, being white, is said to be whiter at one time than it was before, or, being warm, is said to be warmer or less warm than at some other time. But substance is not said to be more or less that which it is: a man is not more truly a man at one time than he was before, nor is anything, if it is substance, more or less what it is. Substance, then, does not admit of variation of degree.

The most distinctive mark of substance appears to be that, while remaining numerically one and the same, it is capable of admitting contrary qualities. From among things other than substance, we should find ourselves unable to bring forward any which possessed this mark. Thus, one and the same colour cannot be white and black. Nor can the same one action be good and bad: this law holds good with everything that is not substance. But one and the self-same substance, while retaining its identity, is yet capable of admitting contrary qualities. The same individual person is at one time white, at another black, at one time warm, at another cold, at one time good, at another bad. This capacity is found nowhere else, though it might be maintained that a statement or opinion was an exception to the rule. The same statement, it is agreed, can be both true and false. For if the statement "he is sitting" is true, yet, when the person in question has risen, the same statement will be false. The same applies to opinions. For if any one thinks truly that a person is sitting, yet, when that person has risen, this same opinion, if still held, will be false. Yet although this exception may be allowed, there is, nevertheless, a difference in the manner in which the thing takes place. It is by themselves changing that substances admit contrary qualities. It is thus that that which was hot becomes cold, for it has entered into a different state. Similarly that which was white becomes black, and that which was bad good, by a process of change; and in the same way in all other cases it is by changing that substances are capable of admitting contrary qualities. But statements and opinions themselves remain unaltered in all respects: it is by the alteration in the facts of the case that the contrary quality comes to be theirs. The statement "he is sitting" remains unaltered, but it is at one time true, at another false, according to circumstances. What has been said of statements applies also to opinions. Thus, in respect of the manner in which the thing takes place, it is the peculiar mark of substance that it should be capable of admitting contrary qualities; for it is by itself changing that it does so.

If, then, a man should make this exception and contend that statements and opinions are capable of admitting contrary qualities, his contention is unsound. For statements and opinions are said to have this capacity, not because they themselves undergo modification, but because this modification occurs in the case of something else. The truth or falsity of a statement depends on facts, and not on any power on the part of the statement itself of admitting contrary qualities. In short, there is nothing which can alter the nature of statements and opinions. As, then, no change takes place in themselves, these cannot be said to be capable of admitting contrary qualities.

But it is by reason of the modification which takes place within the substance itself that a substance is said to be capable of admitting contrary qualities; for a substance admits within itself either disease or health, whiteness or blackness. It is in this sense that it is said to be capable of admitting contrary qualities.

To sum up, it is a distinctive mark of substance, that, while remaining numerically one and the same, it is capable of admitting contrary qualities, the modification taking place through a change in the substance itself.

Let these remarks suffice on the subject of substance.

The Nature of Causality

. . . we must proceed to consider causes, their character and number. Knowledge is the object of our inquiry, and men do not think they know a thing till they have grasped the "why" of it (which is to grasp its primary cause). So clearly we too must do this as regards both coming to be and passing away and every kind of physical change, in order that, knowing their principles, we may try to refer to these principles each of our problems.

In one sense, then, (1) that out of which a thing comes to be and which persists, is called "cause," e.g. the bronze of the statue, the silver of the bowl, and the genera of which the bronze and the silver are species.

In another sense (2) the form or the archetype, i.e. the statement of the essence, and its genera, are called "causes" (e.g. of the octave the relation of 2 : 1, and generally number), and the parts in the definition.

Again (3) the primary source of the change or coming to rest; e.g. the man who gave advice is a cause, the father is cause of the child, and generally what makes of what is made and what causes change of what is changed.

Again (4) in the sense of end or "that for the sake of which" a thing is done, e.g. health is the cause of walking about. ("Why is he walking about?" we say. "To be healthy," and, having said that, we think we have assigned the cause.) The same is

From *Physics* in *The Oxford Translation of Aristotle*, edited by W. D. Ross (1941). Reprinted with permission of Oxford University Press.

true also of all the intermediate steps which are brought about through the action of something else as means towards the end, e.g. reduction of flesh, purging, drugs, or surgical instruments are means towards health. All these things are "for the sake of" the end, though they differ from one another in that some are activities, others instruments.

This then perhaps exhausts the number of ways in which the term "cause" is used.

Vaiśeṣika

The Vaiśeṣika system or school of Indian philosophy was founded by an ancient thinker Kaṇāda, who authored the *Vaiśeṣika-sūtra*. Praśastapāda, a fourth-century philosopher, in turn authored the *Padārthadharmasaṁgraha*, a commentary on Kaṇāda's work, but one that is actually an independent exposition of the teachings of this school and from which the following selections are taken.

The Vaiśeṣika philosophy elaborated a system of categories that bears a striking resemblance to the work of Aristotle. The six categories or basic notions required to account for all objects of experience that were originally put forward by the school are those of substance, quality, action, generality, individuality, and inherence. They—and their subdivisions—are set forth in very concise terms, with a certain prominence given to the category of substance. Substances are conceived of as being the only things that can be "inhered" in without "inhering" in something else, which is to say, in Aristotle's terms, that they have independent existence. The universe is composed of substances that possess various qualities and thus serve as their substrates.

Wilhelm Halbfass, a professor of South Asian Studies at the University of Pennsylvania and an authority on this school, explains rightly that for the Vaiśeṣika system, just as for Aristotle, the various categories not only classify the elements of all being but refer as well to various linguistic and cognitive structures of our own minds. They tell us as much about ourselves as about the nature of reality.

PRAŚASTAPĀDA

Categories in the Vaiśeṣika System

ENUMERATION AND CLASSIFICATION OF CATEGORIES

Question:—"Which are the categories, 'substance and the rest'?"

Answer:—Among these the substances are—earth, water, light, air, ether, time, space, self (or soul), and mind. These, mentioned in the *sūtra* [aphorism of Kaṇāda] by their general as well as specific names, are nine only; as besides these none other is mentioned by name.

The qualities are:—colour, taste, odour, touch, number, dimension, separateness, conjunction, disjunction, distance, proximity, intellect, pleasure, pain, desire, aversion, and effort; these are the seventeen that are directly mentioned in the *sūtra*. The word "*ca*" (and) (in the *sūtra*), however, indicates the other seven: viz., gravity, fluidity, viscidity, faculty [speed] [*saṁskāra*], the two-fold invisible force [*dharma* and *adharma*, virtue and vice], and sound. These make up the twenty-four qualities.

Throwing upwards, throwing downwards, contracting, expanding, and going— these are the only five actions . . . : all such actions as gyrating, evacuating, quivering, flowing upwards, transverse falling, falling downwards, rising, and the like, being only particular forms of going, and not forming distinct classes by themselves.

Of generality, or community [universality], there are two kinds, the higher and the lower; and it serves as the basis of inclusive or comprehensive cognition. The higher (or highest) generality is that of "being"; as it is this that extends over the largest number of things; and also because it is this alone that is a generality pure and simple, always serving, as it does, as the basis of comprehensive cognitions. The lower generalities are "substance" and the rest [quality, action, generality, individuality, and inherence], which extend over a limited number of things. These latter, being the basis of inclusive as well as exclusive cognitions, are sometimes regarded as individualities also.

Unique particularities reside in the ultimate substances. They are the factors that make for ultimate distinctions among these substances.

Inherence [*samavāya*: intimate union, coming together inseparably] is the relationship subsisting among things that are inseparable, standing to one another in the character of the container and the contained,—such relationship being the basis of the idea that "this is in that."

From *The Padārthadharmasaṁgraha* by Praśastapāda, in Radhakrishnan, Sarvepalli, and Moore, Charles E.; *A Source Book of Indian Philosophy.* Copyright © 1957 renewed. Reprinted by permission of Princeton University Press.

SIMILARITIES AND DISSIMILARITIES AMONG CATEGORIES

To all the six categories belong the properties of being-ness, predicability, and cognisability.

The character of being dependent (upon something else) belongs to all things except the eternal [ultimate] substances.

To the five, substance and the rest [quality, action, generality, and individuality], belong the characters of inherability and plurality.

To the five, quality and the rest [action, generality, individuality, and inherence], also belong the character of being devoid of qualities, and that of being without action [chiefly motion].

To the three, substance and the rest [quality and action], belong the relationship with being, the character of having communities [universals] and individualities. . . .

The character of being an effect and that of being non-eternal belong only to those (substances, qualities, and actions) that have causes.

The quality of being the cause belongs to all (substances, qualities, and actions) except the "atomic measure," &c.

The character of subsisting in substances (belongs to substances, qualities, and actions) with the exception of the eternal substances.

The three beginning with generality [individuality and inherence] have the character—of having their sole being within themselves, having *buddhi* or the cognitive faculty as their sole indicator, of not being an effect, of not being the cause, of having no particular generalities, of being eternal, and of not being expressible by the word "*artha*" (thing).

> "Having *buddhi* as their sole indicator": i.e., their only proof lies in the intellect . . . whereas for the existence of substance and the rest [quality, action, generality, individuality, and inherence], we would have other grounds for our belief—in the shape of the effects brought about by these, for instance.

All the nine, earth and the rest, have the character of— (1) belonging to the class "substance," (2) self-productiveness or bringing about effects in themselves, (3) having qualities, (4) not being destructible by their causes and effects, and (5) being connected with ultimate individualities.

The character of not being dependent and that of being eternal belong to all (substances) except those that are made up of certain constituent parts.

To earth, water, fire, air, soul, and mind, belongs the character of being many, and also that of having lower or less extensive generalities [sub-species].

To earth, water, fire, air, and mind, belong the character of having actions, being corporeal, having distance and proximity, and having speed.

To *ākāśa* (ether), time and space belong the characters of—being all-pervasive, having the largest dimensions, and being the common receptacle of all corporeal things.

To the five beginning with earth [water, fire—or light—, air, and ether] belong the characters of—being material, being the main material principle of the sense-organs, and being endowed with such specific qualities as are each perceptible by each of the external organs of perception.

WILHELM HALBFASS

The Vaiśeṣika Categories

The Vaiśeṣika answer to the question *What is there?* is well known and easily accessible in traditional Indian presentations or modern surveys. A few brief and general reminders will be sufficient. The basic claim is that all entities can be listed and classified under certain fundamental "titles" or "categories" (*padārtha*). The classical version of this list of categories, which is found in Praśastapāda's *Padārtha-dharmasaṃgraha* and reproduced in numerous later documents of the Vaiśeṣika or of the allied Nyāya and Vaiśeṣika systems can be summarized as follows.

There are six fundamental categories, or divisions of reality: substance (*dravya*), quality (*guṇa*), motion (*karman*), universal (*sāmānya*), particularity (*viśeṣa*), and inherence (*samavāya*). . . . These six categories are further specified and subdivided as follows.

There are nine substances or classes of substances: earth, water, fire, air, ether (*ākāśa*), space, time, souls (*ātman*), and mental organs (*manas*). The first four of these are elemental substances; they consist of indivisible, invisible, and indestructible atoms (*aṇu, paramāṇu*). The atoms form aggregates and constitute those composite and noneternal material things with which we are dealing in our practical and empirical lives. Ether, space, and time are nonatomic, unitary, all-pervasive, indestructible substances. The souls, too, are omnipresent and eternal, whereas the "mental organs" (*manas*) are equally eternal, but of atomic dimension, that is, infinitely small.

There are twenty-four qualities: color, taste, smell, and touch; number, dimension, separateness (*pṛthaktva*), conjunction, and disjunction; proximity (i.e., priority in space or time) and distance (posteriority); cognition, pleasure, pain, desire, aversion, and effort; gravity, liquidity, viscidity, disposition (*saṃskāra*); merit and demerit (i.e., good and bad karma); and sound. Some of these qualities are coextensive and coeval with their substrates, whereas others have only a momentary existence. Some can occur in all substances, whereas others are confined to specific substrates. Most qualities reside in one individual substrate, but some, such as conjunction and number, may reside in several entities jointly and simultaneously; all are nonrecurrent quality-particulars.

Motion (*karman*), which may inhere in atoms and their aggregates (i.e., composite physical bodies), but also in the mental organs, is of five different types: moving upward, moving downward, bending, stretching, and simple locomotion (*gamana*).

Universals (*sāmānya*), such as "substanceness," "qualityness," "horseness," "whiteness," and so on, are recurrent generic properties in substances, qualities, and motions. They account for the fact that numerically different individual entities can be associated with an identical concept, referred to by a common term, identified as members of the same class, and distinguished from members of other classes. The supreme, that is, most inclusive, universal is "beingness" or reality (*sattā*); it inheres in all substances, qualities, and motions. Lower, more specific universals (*sāmānya-viśeṣa*) have an exclusive as well as inclusive function.

Particularities (*viśeṣa*; more specifically, *antyaviśeṣa*) are ultimate factors of individual identity. They reside exclusively in the eternal, noncomposite substances, that is, in the individual atoms, souls, and mental organs, and in the unitary substances ether, space, and time. They account for the irreducible identity and distinctness of each of these entities.

Inherence (*samavāya*) is the relationship between entities that cannot occur separately. It is the one omnipresent principle of cooccurrence and coalescence that integrates parts and wholes, particulars and universals, substances, qualities, and motions. It accounts for the fact that we are dealing with concrete things, instead of isolated world constituents. . . .

We have used the term *padārtha* and translated it as "category." . . . We have also seen that the Vaiśeṣika itself distinguishes *padārtha* terminologically from *artha*, "object." What then is a *padārtha*, and what do we mean by *category*?

Henry Thomas Colebrooke, the European pioneer of the study of Indian philosophy and the first to summarize in English the basic teachings of the Vaiśeṣika system, rendered *padārtha* as "predicament" or "category." . . . Max Müller, in one of his earliest publications, made the association with Aristotle more explicit. In his view, Kaṇāda's list of padārthas and Aristotle's doctrine of categories have the same purpose and meaning: They try to establish "what can ultimately be predicated of the objects." . . . The precise meaning and function of Aristotle's concept of *katēgoría* continues to be controversial and elusive. In one sense, his categories are "the highest genera," *ta genikóata*, the most fundamental and most pervasive classes and types of entities. But they appear also as forms of predication and even as different meanings of being. There are, of course, many other, supposedly less ambiguous versions of the doctrine of categories in the history of Western thought. In some versions, the categories appear as forms of thought or speech or as conditions of the possibility of experience; in other versions, they are presented as divisions of reality itself. There is no need for us to adopt any specific doctrine of categories or to eliminate all ambiguity from the concept. "Categoriology," just as ontology itself, does not have an authoritative state of latest research nor a clearly recognizable direction of progress. What is important is to be aware that the concept of category suggests an approach to reality that is not direct and straightforward, but involves an awareness of, or reference to, linguistic and cognitive structures. Language, thought, and reality meet in the philosophical concept of category. Categories may be "highest genera," but they do not simply classify elements, natural species, or other groups of individual entities. They involve a different sense of distinction and analysis. . . .

For Praśastapāda, the *padārthas* are the most comprehensive units of enumeration, the ultimate divisions of reality, and the most basic correlates of thought and speech. They are not structures or projections of language and thought. Praśastapāda himself says that *astitva*, "isness" (i.e., factuality, objectivity), *jñeyatva*, "knowability," and *abhidheyatva*, "nameability," "denotability" are common denominators of all six categories. The categories are the direct correlates of *uddeśa*, "enunciation," "listing"; that is, the first step in Praśastapāda's twofold procedure. They are not the products of definition, abstraction, and analysis. The categories are not natural species; yet they are supposed to represent divisions that are equally real and objective. Praśastapāda does not discuss the relationship of the Vaiśeṣika padārthas with the grammatical categories "noun," "adjective," "verb," and so on, and he does not consider the possibility of a linguistic derivation of his categories. The actual correspondences are, nonetheless, intriguing, and they have been noticed by traditional Indian grammarians and philosophers as well as by modern scholars.

Kant

In the introduction to Kant's analysis of *a priori* knowledge and the limits of reason, it was pointed out that Kant argued that we set the rule by which our experience is ordered, and that we cannot go beyond experience so constituted. This translates metaphysically into his famous distinction between the "phenomenal" and the "noumenal." By the phenomenal, Kant means the entire domain of our sense-based, ordered experience, by the noumenal, he means the world as it is in itself. Because we ourselves order the world we experience and lack intuitive capacities for going beyond it, things as they are in themselves—the noumenal—remain inaccessible to us. The question Kant faces, and which many scholars believe he has failed to answer, is how we can draw a boundary between the knowable and the unknowable, between appearance and reality, unless in some way we are able to find ourselves, as it were, on both sides of the boundary. Kant argues that for rational understanding the only meaningful sense of the noumenal is a negative or limiting one that sets the boundary beyond which our reason and knowledge cannot go.

Phenomena and Noumena

We have seen that everything which the understanding derives from itself is, though not borrowed from experience, at the disposal of the understanding solely for use in experience. The principles of pure understanding . . . contain nothing but what may be called the pure schema of possible experience. For experience obtains its unity only from the synthetic unity which the understanding originally and of itself confers upon the synthesis of imagination in its relation to apperception. . . . But although these rules of understanding are not only true *a priori*, but are indeed the source of all truth (that is, of the agreement of our knowledge with objects), inasmuch as they contain in themselves the ground of the possibility of experience viewed as the sum of all knowledge wherein objects can be given to us, we are not satisfied with the exposition merely of that which is true, but likewise demand that

From *Critique of Pure Reason* by Immanuel Kant, translated by Norman Kemp Smith (1929). Reprinted by permission of Macmillan Press Ltd.

account be taken of that which we desire to know. If, therefore, from this critical enquiry we learn nothing more than what, in the merely empirical employment of understanding, we should in any case have practised without any such subtle enquiry, it would seem as if the advantage derived from it by no means repays the labour expended. The reply may certainly be made that in the endeavour to extend our knowledge a meddlesome curiosity is far less injurious than the habit of always insisting, before entering on any enquiries, upon antecedent proof of the utility of the enquiries—an absurd demand, since prior to completion of the enquiries we are not in a position to form the least conception of this utility, even if it were placed before our eyes. There is, however, one advantage which may be made comprehensible and of interest even to the most refractory and reluctant learner, the advantage, that while the understanding, occupied merely with its empirical employment, and not reflecting upon the sources of its own knowledge, may indeed get along quite satisfactorily, there is yet one task to which it is not equal, that, namely, of determining the limits of its employment, and of knowing what it is that may lie within and what it is that lies without its own proper sphere. This demands just those deep enquiries which we have instituted. If the understanding in its empirical employment cannot distinguish whether certain questions lie within its horizon or not, it can never be assured of its claims or of its possessions, but must be prepared for many a humiliating disillusionment, whenever, as must unavoidably and constantly happen, it oversteps the limits of its own domain, and loses itself in opinions that are baseless and misleading.

If the assertion, that the understanding can employ its various principles and its various concepts solely in an empirical and never in a transcendental manner, is a proposition which can be known with certainty, it will yield important consequences. The transcendental employment of a concept in any principle is its application to things *in general and in themselves*; the empirical employment is its application *merely to appearances*; that is, to objects of a possible experience. That the latter application of concepts is alone feasible is evident from the following considerations. We demand in every concept, first, the logical form of a concept (of thought) in general, and secondly, the possibility of giving it an object to which it may be applied. In the absence of such object, it has no meaning and is completely lacking in content, though it may still contain the logical function which is required for making a concept out of any data that may be presented. Now the object cannot be given to a concept otherwise than in intuition; for though a pure intuition can indeed precede the object *a priori*, even this intuition can acquire its object, and therefore objective validity, only through the empirical intuition of which it is the mere form. Therefore all concepts, and with them all principles, even such as are possible *a priori*, relate to empirical intuitions, that is, to the data for a possible experience. Apart from this relation they have no objective validity, and in respect of their representations are a mere play of imagination or of understanding. Take, for instance, the concepts of mathematics, considering them first of all in their pure intuitions. Space has three dimensions; between two points there can be only one straight line, etc. Although all these principles, and the representation of the object with which this science occupies itself, are generated in the mind completely *a pri-*

ori, they would mean nothing, were we not always able to present their meaning in appearances, that is, in empirical objects. We therefore demand that a bare concept be *made sensible*, that is, that an object corresponding to it be presented in intuition. Otherwise the concept would, as we say, be without *sense*, that is, without meaning. The mathematician meets this demand by the construction of a figure, which, although produced *a priori*, is an appearance present to the senses. In the same science the concept of magnitude seeks its support and sensible meaning in number, and this in turn in the fingers, in the beads of the abacus, or in strokes and points which can be placed before the eyes. The concept itself is always *a priori* in origin, and so likewise are the synthetic principles or formulas derived from such concepts; but their employment and their relation to their professed objects can in the end be sought nowhere but in experience, of whose possibility they contain the formal conditions.

That this is also the case with all categories and the principles derived from them, appears from the following consideration. We cannot define any one of them in any real fashion, that is, make the possibility of their object understandable, without at once descending to the conditions of sensibility, and so to the form of appearances—to which, as their sole objects, they must consequently be limited. For if this condition be removed, all meaning, that is, relation to the object, falls away; and we cannot through any example make comprehensible to ourselves what sort of a thing is to be meant by such a concept.

The concept of magnitude in general can never be explained except by saying that it is that determination of a thing whereby we are enabled to think how many times a unit is posited in it. But this how-many-times is based on successive repetition, and therefore on time and the synthesis of the homogeneous in time. Reality, in contradistinction to negation, can be explained only if we think time (as containing all being) as either filled with being or as empty. If I leave out permanence (which is existence in all time), nothing remains in the concept of substance save only the logical representation of a subject—a representation which I endeavour to realise by representing to myself something which can exist only as subject and never as predicate. But not only am I ignorant of any conditions under which this logical pre-eminence may belong to anything; I can neither put such a concept to any use, nor draw the least inference from it. . . .

From all this it undeniably follows that the pure concepts of understanding can *never* admit of *transcendental* but *always* only of *empirical* employment, and that the principles of pure understanding can apply only to objects of the senses under the universal conditions of a possible experience, never to things in general without regard to the mode in which we are able to intuit them.

Accordingly the Transcendental Analytic leads to this important conclusion, that the most the understanding can achieve *a priori* is to anticipate the form of a possible experience in general. And since that which is not appearance cannot be an object of experience, the understanding can never transcend those limits of sensibility within which alone objects can be given to us. Its principles are merely rules for the exposition of appearances. . . .

It may be advisable, therefore, to express the situation as follows. The pure categories, apart from formal conditions of sensibility, have only transcendental meaning; nevertheless they may not be employed transcendentally, such employment being in itself impossible, inasmuch as all conditions of any employment in judgments are lacking to them, namely, the formal conditions of the subsumption of any ostensible object under these concepts. Since, then, as pure categories merely, they are not to be employed empirically, and cannot be employed transcendentally, they cannot, when separated from all sensibility, be employed in any manner whatsoever, that is, they cannot be applied to any ostensible object. They are the pure form of the employment of understanding in respect of objects in general, that is, of thought; but since they are merely its form, through them alone no object can be thought or determined. . . .

If by "noumenon" we mean a thing so far as it is *not an object of our sensible intuition*, and so abstract from our mode of intuiting it, this is a noumenon in the *negative* sense of the term. But if we understand by it an *object* of a *non-sensible* intuition, we thereby presuppose a special mode of intuition, namely, the intellectual, which is not that which we possess, and of which we cannot comprehend even the possibility. This would be "noumenon" in the *positive* sense of the term.

. . . At the same time the understanding is well aware that in viewing things in this manner, as thus apart from our mode of intuition, it cannot make any use of the categories. For the categories have meaning only in relation to the unity of intuition in space and time; and even this unity they can determine, by means of general *a priori* connecting concepts, only because of the mere ideality of space and time. In cases where this unity of time is not to be found, and therefore in the case of the noumenon, all employment, and indeed the whole meaning of the categories, entirely vanishes; for we have then no means of determining whether things in harmony with the categories are even possible. . . . The possibility of a thing can never be proved merely from the fact that its concept is not self-contradictory, but only through its being supported by some corresponding intuition. If, therefore, we should attempt to apply the categories to objects which are not viewed as being appearances, we should have to postulate an intuition other than the sensible, and the object would thus be a noumenon in the *positive sense*. Since, however, such a type of intuition, intellectual intuition, forms no part whatsoever of our faculty of knowledge, it follows that the employment of the categories can never extend further than to the objects of experience. Doubtless, indeed, there are intelligible entities corresponding to the sensible entities; there may also be intelligible entities to which our sensible faculty of intuition has no relation whatsoever; but our concepts of understanding, being mere forms of thought for our sensible intuition, could not in the least apply to them. That, therefore, which we entitle "noumenon" must be understood as being such only in a *negative* sense.

Vedānta

As we have seen, the Vedānta tradition in Indian philosophy, is based on the teachings of the ancient Upaniṣads and in the school known as Advaita Vedānta asserts the identity of the self (ātman) and an absolute, undifferentiated reality, or Brahman. The chief proponent of Advaita Vedānta was the philosopher Śaṃkara, who was born in the southern Indian state of Kerala in 788 and is believed to have lived only to the age of thirty-two or thirty-eight. During his short life, he wrote extensively, traveled widely throughout India debating his rivals, and set the course for Vedāntic studies for many centuries. In the following selection, Eliot Deutsch sets forth the way in which this major school of Indian thought understands the very special relation that is said to obtain between Brahman and the world. This is followed by brief selections from Śaṃkara's most important philosophical work, which also discusses this issue.

ELIOT DEUTSCH

Brahman and the World

As a spider spreads and withdraws (its thread) . . . so out of the Immutable does the phenomenal universe arise.

Crave to know that from which all beings take birth, that from which being born they live, and that towards which they move and into which they merge. That is Brahman.

One of the most basic questions taken up in the Upaniṣads, which later becomes perhaps the central problem of classical, systematic Vedānta, is: What is the relation that obtains between Brahman and the world? Or in what sense is Brahman, the Absolute, the creator of the world? The Upaniṣadic answer to this question is multiform. Numerous descriptions of creation are proffered, most of which follow a

From *Advaita Vedānta: A Philosophical Reconstruction* by Eliot Deutsch (1969). First published by the East-West Center Press (1969). Reprinted by permission of University of Hawaii Press. Copyright © East-West Center Press.

Sāṃkhyan-type model of emanation. At the same time the Upaniṣads affirm repeatedly that Brahman is "one only without a second," that Brahman is a state of being wherein all distinctions between self, world, and God are transcended and are obliterated. Classical Advaita Vedānta likewise treats the question in various ways and suggests different answers to it. There is nevertheless a substantial core of doctrine and attitude that is shared by most, if not all, Advaitins. Following Śaṃkara, these Advaitins explain the relation between Brahman and the world in terms of *satkāryavāda*, the theory that the effect pre-exists in its cause, with Brahman (as Īśvara "the Lord") as the material and efficient cause of the world; and in terms of *vivartavāda*, the theory that the effect is only an apparent manifestation of its cause. These theories have their background in the concepts of *māyā* (illusion), *avidyā* (ignorance), and *adhyāsa* (superimposition).

I

In the immediate, intuitive experience of non-duality, Brahman presents itself as the fullness of being, as self-luminous consciousness, and as infinite bliss (*saccidānanda*). The complex world of our ordinary experience disappears in the pure white light of a spiritual simplicity. All distinctions, contradictions, and multiplicities are transcended and are obliterated. In Brahman-experience . . . there is the awareness that true reality belongs only to the content of that experience; that "anything beside Brahman lacks full reality."

It follows, then, that the existence of, or our perception of, an independent, substantial world of real objects, persons, and processes must be grounded in some pervasive error. We take the unreal for the real and the real for the unreal. This is *māyā*.

Whenever the "I," "me," or "mine" is present, according to Advaita, there also is *māyā*. *Māyā* is all experience that is constituted by, and follows from, the distinction between subject and object, between self and non-self.

Whenever we transform the impersonal into the personal, that is, when we make Brahman something or someone who cares, we bring about an association of the impersonal with *māyā*. *Māyā* is the ontic-noetic state wherein limitations (*upādhis*) are imposed upon Reality.

All attachments, aversions, fears, dreams, and semidreams are touched with *māyā*. All memories, cognitions, percepts, and logics are grounded in *māyā*. *Māyā* is whenever we fail to realize the oneness of the Real.

And *māyā* is beginningless for time arises only within it; it is unthinkable for all thought is subject to it; it is indescribable for all language results from it. The level of Appearance is thus *māyā*. . . .

Following the ancient Vedic usage of *māyā* as a mysterious, deceptive power of the gods, the Advaitin, metaphysically conceives of *māyā* as that power of Brahman by which the world of multiplicity comes into existence. *Māyā* is a creative power until one realizes the truth of the sole reality of Brahman. One of the analogies favored by the Advaitin to clarify this is that of the magician and his trick; and here already a transition is made into the epistemological. When a magician makes one thing appear as something else, or when he seemingly produces something from nothing, we are deluded by it; we mistake appearance for reality—but not the magician. For us the illusion is caused by the power of the magician and by our ignorance; for the magician there is no illusion at all. And just as the magician creates illusions that are not binding upon him and that last as long as the experiencer is in ignorance, so Brahman conjures up a world show of phenomena that disappears upon the attainment of knowledge (*jñāna, vidyā*). Metaphysically, *māyā* is that mysterious power of Brahman that deludes us into taking the empirical world as reality. Epistemologically, *māyā* is ignorance (*avidyā*). It has the power of concealing reality and also of misrepresenting or distorting reality. Not only do we fail to perceive Brahman, but we also substitute something else in its place, viz., the phenomenal world. *Māyā* is thus not merely a negative designation, a privation of vision; it is positive so far as it produces an illusion.

For Advaita Vedānta, then, the phenomenal world is *māyā*, and it is produced by *māyā*. But it is not on that account merely a figment of one's imagination. . . . Advaitic thinkers hold that a subjective idealism is not the proper philosophical expression or consequence of a doctrine of *māyā*. So far as a separate subject exists, so does the object that is experienced by it. Duality is transcended only in an experience that is different in kind from what takes place in the subject/; object situation. Śaṃkara writes:

> There could be no non-existence (of external entities) because external entities are actually perceived. . . .
>
> An external entity is invariably perceived in every cognition such as pillar, wall, a pot or a piece of cloth. It can never be that what is actually perceived is non-existent.

No one, in other words, perceives merely his own perception: existence must be attributed to external objects because they are cognized as such. The world, then, "appears to be real as long as the non-dual Brahman, which is the basis of all, is not known."

What is meant then by calling the world an illusion and at the same time ascribing existence to it? The answer is that for Advaita Vedānta the term "real" means that which is permanent, eternal, infinite, . . . is . . . never subrated at any time by another experience—and Brahman alone fits this meaning. The world then is not real, but it is not wholly unreal. The unreal or non-being . . . is that which never appears as an objective datum of experience because of its self-contradictoriness. In the words of the *Bhagavadgītā*: ". . . of the non-real there is no coming to be; of the real there is no ceasing to be." The world that is distinguished from true reality (*sat*) and from complete non-reality (*asat*) has then an apparent or practical reality, which is called *vyavahārika*. *Vyavahārika* is the level of *māyā* that denotes the totality or errors caused by *avidyā*. It is . . . other than the real or the unreal; or . . . indescribable in terms of being and non-being.

Both in the writings of Śaṃkara and in those of post-Śaṃkara Advaitins, the terms "*māyā*" and "*avidyā*" come to be used interchangeably, with *avidyā* actually taking precedence over *māyā* in the explanation of bondage and freedom. When asked, "What is the cause of our bondage, of our not realizing Brahman?" the answer most frequently given is *avidyā*, ignorance. And in describing the process of *avidyā*,

Śaṁkara introduces one of his most significant and interesting notions, that of *ad-hyāsa . . .*, which means "superimposition."

In the Introduction to his commentary on the *Brahma-sūtras*, Śaṁkara defines superimposition as the "apparent presentation [to consciousness] by way of remembrance of something previously perceived in something else." "It is," he goes on to say, "the unreal assumption about the attributes of one thing as being the attributes of some other thing." And again, *adhyāsa* "is the notion of *that* in something which is *not-that*: just as it is, for example, when a person superimposes on his self attributes external to his own self. . . ." Superimposition takes place, then, when the qualities of one thing not immediately present to consciousness are, through memory, given to, or projected upon, another thing that is present to consciousness and are identified with it. In the stock example of the rope and the snake, the rope (the thing immediately present to consciousness) is taken as a snake through the erroneous attribution of qualities remembered from previous perceptions (of snakes). The judgment that expresses this illusion, i.e., the judgment, "this is a snake," is the result of a positive identification between what is remembered and what is perceived.

The main or primary application of *adhyāsa* is made with respect to the self. It is the superimposition on the Self (Ātman, Brahman) of what does not properly belong to the Self (finitude, change) and the superimposition on the non-self of what does properly belong to the Self (infinitude, eternality) that constitute *avidyā*. "It is by adopting the reciprocal superimposition of the self and the non-self," writes Śaṁkara, "that all world conduct and Vedic (ritualistic) actions . . . are promoted." Vidyāraṇa in his *Pañcadaśī* asks: "What is the obstruction that prevents the recognition of the self?" And answers: "It is the superimposition of what does not really exist and is not self-evident on the Self. . . ." And: "Those who do not see clearly attribute causation to Brahman, and assign the characteristics of Brahman, such as existence, to Ishvara, the creator of the universe."

II

Brahman, or Īśvara (Brahman with attributes; Brahman become personalized as Deity), is said to be the cause of the world, then, so far as Brahman is the ground or locus of all superimpositions; so far, that is to say, as we are subject to *māyā, avidyā*. A special application of *adhyāsa* is just this superimposition of activity upon Brahman and the superimposition of effects upon causes. We assume that the cause (Brahman) actually transforms itself into an effect (the world of change and multiplicity) or that the effect, having an independent reality, is radically different in nature from the cause.

This brings us back to the central question, What is the relation that obtains between Brahman and the world? The Advaitic answer to this question, with its background in *māyā, avidyā,* and *adhyāsa*, is set forth in terms of two closely interrelated theories: the general theory of *satkāryavāda*, the theory that the effect preexists in its cause; and the special theory of *vivartavāda*, that the effect is only a manifestation or appearance of the cause.

Before these theories are taken up in our own terms, in order to understand their philosophical import it is necessary that some of the specific arguments that have been put forward in their behalf be examined first. Śaṃkara argues first of all that *satkāryavāda*—the theory that an effect is nothing more than its material cause and ontologically is not-different from it—corresponds to the actual facts of perceptual experience; that perception presents the relation between (material) cause and effect as one of non-difference.

> Such non-difference between cause and effect does happen to be directly perceived. It is this way:—In the case of a cloth which is a construction of threads, we do not of course perceive merely an effect, viz., the cloth as such, as apart from the threads themselves, but what we actually and directly see are merely the threads only in their condition as warps and woofs. . . .

This fact of our perception is further supported, according to Śaṃkara, by practical experience. If particular effects were not already latent in particular causes, then it would be possible for any given effect to issue from any cause; and this is clearly not the case.

> Our ordinary experience tells us that milk, clay and gold are taken by people in order to produce out of them curds, jars, and ornaments, respectively. No one who wants curds will expect to have it out of clay, nor will anyone expect to have jars out of milk. This means that the effect exists in the cause prior to its production. For had the effect been really non-existent before its production, there is no reason why curds [could not] be produced out of milk alone or jars out of clay. Besides, all the effects being equally non-existent, anything might come out of anything else.

In further criticism of *asatkāryavāda* (the theory that effects do not pre-exist in their causes), Śaṃkara argues that it would lead to an infinite regress . . ., for the granting of independence to two distinct realities—the cause and the effect—requires the positing of a third entity which is the relation of invariable concomitance that holds between them. And then this third entity (which must be distinct from the two terms that it relates) requires a fourth relating entity that would relate the third entity with each of the first two terms, and so on to a fifth, sixth, . . .

> Even in the assumption of a Samavāya relation (invariable concomitance) if it is understood that there is a relation as between the Samavāya, on the one hand, and the two entities between which such Samavāya exists . . ., on the other, then such another Samavāya relation of that, and then still such another Samavāya relation of that, *ad infinitum*, will have to be imagined, and hence the predicament of a *regressus ad infinitum* would result. . . .

The last major argument that Śaṃkara uses is also drawn from experience. He argues that a mere change in outward form does not constitute a fundamental change in substance. An effect, to be sure, is different from its cause in outward appearance, for otherwise no distinction would be made in the first place. But this does not mean that there are two distinct realities, the one "cause," the other "effect." A change in form is not a change in reality, for in spite of changes in form, a substance is recognized as a single reality.

> A thing as such does not become another different thing altogether, by merely appearing in a different aspect. Devadatta, whose hands and legs are (at one time) in a fixed position, and Devadatta whose hands and legs are (at some other time) in an extended position, and who is thus seen to be in such different attitudes (at different times), does not merely on that account become different persons, because he is still recognizable as the same one person.

III

But what do these arguments actually prove? They establish that within the phenomenal world one cannot make an ontological distinction between cause and effect; that an effect is nothing but a set of conditions, that it is nothing but the cause itself, albeit seen in a different form or state: the arguments do not prove anything as far as the relation between the world and Brahman is concerned; they suggest only that the world may be seen as an effect of Brahman, which is Brahman itself in a different form.

The main purport of the arguments establishing *satkāryavāda* therefore is practical. In terms of the requirements of spiritual experience, it is believed that without the extension of Brahman in the world (Brahman in this context becoming Īśvara or Lord) there could be no transition between the world and Brahman for one who is caught up in the world. The world of names and forms is ordinarily seen by us to be different from Brahman, and in order to free ourselves from it, we must affirm a spiritual ground for our experience and look upon the creative power that sustains and controls this experience as our own ideal mode of action. If one's view of the world is such that the world is taken as completely self-explanatory, self-sufficient, and real, then one would hardly to encouraged to seek a transcendence of it.

Whether seen as a theoretical necessity or as a practical requirement, Īśvara is thus taken by the Advaitin, from the standpoint of the phenomenal world, as the material and efficient cause of the world. "Those who think about creation (*sṛṣṭi*)," Śaṃkara writes, "think that creation is the expansion of Īśvara." And the nature of this "expansion" is quite unlike anything that a Western (Judaeo-Christian) theologian would affirm. "The activity of the Lord," Śaṃkara maintains, ". . . may be supposed to be mere sport (*līlā*), proceeding from his own nature, without reference to any purpose."

The concept of *līlā*, of play or sport, seeks to convey that Īśvara creates (sustains and destroys) worlds out of the sheer joy of doing so. Answering to no compelling necessity, his creative act is simply a release of energy for its own sake. Creation is not informed by any selfish motive. It is spontaneous, without any purpose. No moral consequences attach to the creator in his activity, for *līlā* is precisely different in kind from all action which yields results that are binding upon, and which determine, the actor. It is simply the Divine's nature to create just as it is man's nature to breathe in and out. *Līlā* thus removes all motive, purpose, and responsibility from

Īsvara in his creative activity. Having no need to create and having no consequences attach to his action, Īsvara cannot be held responsible for the actions that arise subsequently within the fields of his creation. *Līlā* avoids thereby any problem of evil of the sort associated with Judaeo-Christian theism, and it sets aside as meaningless any question of why Īsvara creates in the first place. There can be no "why" to creation.

IV

Still *satkāryavāda* and Īsvara's sportive activity are true only phenomenally: they are negated in Brahman-experience where no distinction at all is perceived between cause and effect. *Satkāryavāda* thus prepares the way for the affirmation of *vivartavāda*, the theory that the effect is only an apparent manifestation of its cause.

As pointed out before, Advaita is not alone in its adherence to *satkāryavāda*. The Sāmkara system likewise explains the cause-effect relation in its terms; but whereas the Sāmkara goes on to assume that the effect not only pre-exists in the cause but is an actual transformation (*parināma*) of it, Advaita argues that the effect is nothing but an apparent manifestation of the cause, that "A thing is not rendered as being a thing having parts, merely by imagining through Nescience (Avidyā) that it has different aspects. The moon, for instance, does not in fact become more than one, merely because she appears to be more than one, to an eye affected by double vision."

That which is One cannot in reality become Many, it can only appear to be Many—and this through superimposition grounded in our ignorance. If the cause (Brahman) actually transformed itself into an effect different from it (the phenomenal world *qua* phenomenal world), then the effect would still have an independent reality in that there would be a metaphysical basis for some kind of distinction between them. But Brahman, the "cause," is alone Real; hence, "an effect is merely a name made current by speech." And thus

> Brahma appears to become susceptible of (i.e., appears to be the basis of) all phenomenal behaviour by way of modifications etc., by reason of the distinctions of aspects or forms characterized by names and forms imagined through Nescience . . . while in its truest nature Brahma subsists only in its unmodified aspect and is beyond all phenomenal behaviour. . . .

V

In sum: for Advaita Vedānta, the creation or evolution of the world, as indeed the status of the world itself, is only an apparent truth. Creation may be considered a positive activity of Brahman only from the *vyavahārika* or empirical point of view; only to the extent that we are subject to *māyā, avidyā*, and are engaged in the activities of *adhyāsa*. When in this condition one attempts to understand the relation between Brahman and the world, one is compelled rationally to uphold creation in terms of *satkāryavāda*—the theory that the effect pre-exists in its cause—that Brahman is the material and efficient cause of the world. Further, when seen from this standpoint and in terms of the requirements of spiritual experience, Brahman becomes Īśvara, the creative Lord who calls forth worlds, maintains them, and re-absorbs them as *līlā*, as sport or play. Īśvara's distinctive activity is thus an outpouring of energy for its own sake. There is no purpose to creation, as Īśvara has no need that is to be fulfilled in creation. He is a free, unlimited power.

But having arrived at all of this within *māyā*, one cannot ascribe ultimacy to it. Creation is only apparent change, it is not a modification of Brahman in reality, and hence *vivartavāda*. From the standpoint of Brahman-experience, from the standpoint of Brahman itself, there is no creation: Reality is non-dual.

The whole import of *vivartavāda* then is to bring the mind away from its involvement in *māyā*, away from the need to ask the question about the relation between Brahman and the world, the asking of which implies the recognition of the world as a separate entity, to its experiencing directly the Reality that is Brahman. The world is first affirmed as an empirical reality, an affirmation which, apart from its inherent philosophical justification, avoids a subjective idealism that would overcome duality without self-transcendence; and secondly as an "effect" of Brahman which again, apart from its logical justification, has the practical value of bringing the mind that is attached to the world into an awareness of Brahman as its cause. *Vivartavāda* then affirms the appearance-only status of the effect and thus points the way to the subration of the world in Brahman through "de-superimposition," through the reducing of effects back into their causes. This leads the mind to Brahman, to Reality, where all questions of the relation between it and something else are silenced.

ŚAMKARA

Brahman as the Creative Principle of the World

We . . . declare that the omniscient, omnipotent Brahman, whose essence is eternal pure cognition and freedom, and which is additional to, i.e. different from the embodied Self, is the creative principle of the world. The faults . . . , such as doing what is not beneficial, and the like, do not attach to that Brahman; for as eternal freedom is its characteristic nature, there is nothing either beneficial to be done by it or non-beneficial to be avoided by it. Nor is there any impediment to its knowledge and power; for it is omniscient and omnipotent. The embodied Self, on the other hand, is of a different nature, and to it the mentioned faults adhere. . . . Moreover, as soon as, in consequence of the declaration of non-difference contained in such passages as "that art thou," the consciousness of non-difference arises in us, the transmigratory state of the individual soul and the creative quality of Brahman vanish at once,

From *Brahmasūtrabhāṣya* by Śaṃkara, translated by George Thibaut in *A Source Book of Advaita Vedānta*, edited by Eliot Deutsch and J. A. B. van Buitenen (1971). Reprinted by permission of University of Hawaii Press. Copyright © 1971 by University of Hawaii Press.

the whole phenomenon of plurality, which springs from wrong knowledge, being sublated by perfect knowledge, and what becomes then of the creation and the faults of not doing what is beneficial, and the like? For that this entire apparent world, in which good and evil actions are done, &c, is a mere illusion, owing to the non-discrimination of (the Self's) limiting adjuncts, viz. a body, and so on, which spring from name and form the presentations of Nescience [ignorance], and does in reality not exist at all, we have explained more than once. The illusion is analogous to the mistaken notion we entertain as to the dying, being born, being hurt, &c. of ourselves (our Selfs; while in reality the body only dies, is born, &c.). And with regard to the state in which the appearance of plurality is not yet sublated, it follows from passages declaratory of such difference (as, for instance, "That we must search for," &c.) that Brahman is superior to the individual soul; whereby the possibility of faults adhering to it is excluded.

As among minerals, which are all mere modifications of earth, nevertheless great variety is observed, some being precious gems, such as diamonds, lapis lazuli, &c., others, such as crystals and the like, being of medium value, and others again stones only fit to be flung at dogs or crows; and as from seeds which are placed in one and the same ground various plants are seen to spring, such as sandalwood and cucumbers, which show the greatest difference in their leaves, blossoms, fruits, fragrancy, juice, &c.; and as one and the same food produces various effects, such as blood and hair; so the one Brahman also may contain in itself the distinction of the individual Selfs and the highest Self, and may produce various effects. Hence the objections imagined by others (against the doctrine of Brahman being the cause of the world) cannot be maintained. Further arguments are furnished by the fact of all effects having, as Scripture declares, their origin in speech only, and by the analogous instance of the variety of dream phantoms (while the dreaming person remains one).

Your assertion that the intelligent Brahman alone, without a second, is the cause of the world cannot be maintained, on account of the observation of employment (of instruments). For in ordinary life we see that potters, weavers, and other handicraftsmen produce jars, cloth, and the like, after having put themselves in possession of the means thereto by providing themselves with various implements, such as clay, staffs, wheels, string, &c.; Brahman, on the other hand, you conceive to be without any help; how then can it act as a creator without providing itself with instruments to work with?—We therefore maintain that Brahman is not the cause of the world.

This objection is not valid, because causation is possible, in consequence of a peculiar constitution of the causal substance, as in the case of milk. Just as milk and water turn into curds and ice respectively, without any extraneous means, so it is in the case of Brahman also. And if you object to this analogy for the reason that milk, in order to turn into curds, does require an extraneous agent, viz. heat, we reply that milk by itself also undergoes a certain amount of definite change, and that its turning is merely accelerated by heat. If milk did not possess that capability of itself, heat could not compel it to turn; for we see that air or ether, for instance, is not compelled by the action of heat to turn into sour milk. By the co-operation of auxiliary means the milk's capability of turning into sour milk is merely completed. The absolutely complete power of Brahman, on the other hand, does not require to be supplemented by any extraneous help. . . .

. . . We maintain that the (alleged) break in Brahman's nature is a mere figment of Nescience. By a break of that nature a thing is not really broken up into parts, not any more than the moon is really multiplied by appearing double to a person of defective vision. By that element of plurality which is the fiction of Nescience, which is characterised by name and form, which is evolved as well as non-evolved, which is not to be defined either as the Existing or the Non-existing, Brahman becomes the basis of this entire apparent world with its changes, and so on, while in its true and real nature it at the same time remains unchanged, lifted above the phenomenal universe. And as the distinction of names and forms, the fiction of Nescience, originates entirely from speech only, it does not militate against the fact of Brahman being without parts.—Nor have the scriptural passages which speak of Brahman as undergoing change the purpose of teaching the fact of change; for such instruction would have no fruit. They rather aim at imparting instruction about Brahman's Self as raised above this apparent world; that being an instruction which we know to have a result of its own. . . .

Another objection is raised against the doctrine of an intelligent cause of the world.—The intelligent highest Self cannot be the creator of the sphere of this world, "on account of actions having a purpose."—We know from ordinary experience that man, who is an intelligent being, begins to act after due consideration only, and does not engage even in an unimportant undertaking unless it serves some purpose of his own; much less so in important business. There is also a scriptural passage confirming this result of common experience, "Verily everything is not dear that you may love everything; but that you may love the Self therefore everything is dear" (Bṛhadāraṇyaka Upaniṣad II, 4, 5). Now the undertaking of creating the sphere of this world, with all its various contents, is certainly a weighty one. If, then, on the one hand, you assume it to serve some purpose of the intelligent highest Self, you thereby sublate its self-sufficiency vouched for by Scripture; if, on the other hand, you affirm absence of motive on its part, you must affirm absence of activity also.—Let us then assume that just as sometimes an intelligent person when in a state of frenzy proceeds, owing to his mental aberration, to action without a motive, so the highest Self also created this world without any motive.—That, we reply, would contradict the omniscience of the highest Self, which is vouched for by Scripture.—Hence the doctrine of the creation proceeding from an intelligent Being is untenable.

. . . We see in every-day life that certain doings of princes or other men of high position who have no unfulfilled desires left have no reference to any extraneous purpose, but proceed from mere sportfulness, as, for instance, their recreations in places of amusement. We further see that the process of inhalation and exhalation is going on without reference to any extraneous purpose, merely following the law of its own nature. Analogously, the activity of the Lord also may be supposed to be mere sport, proceeding from his own nature, without reference to any purpose. For on the ground neither of reason nor of Scripture can we construe any other purpose of the Lord. Nor can his nature be questioned.—Although the creation of this world appears to us a weighty and difficult undertaking, it is mere play to the Lord, whose power is unlimited. And if in ordinary life we might possibly, by close scrutiny, detect some subtle motive, even for sportful action, we cannot do so with regard to the actions of the Lord, all whose wishes are fulfilled, as Scripture says.—Nor can it be said that he either does not act or acts like a senseless person; for Scripture affirms the fact of the creation on the one hand, and the Lord's omniscience on the other hand. And, finally, we must remember that the scriptural doctrine of creation does not refer to the highest reality; it refers to the apparent world only, which is characterised by name and form, the figments of Nescience, and it, moreover, aims at intimating that Brahman is the Self of everything.

In order to strengthen the tenet which we are at present defending, we follow the procedure of him who shakes a pole planted in the ground (in order to test whether it is firmly planted), and raise another objection against the doctrine of the Lord being the cause of the world.—The Lord, it is said, cannot be the cause of the world, because, on that hypothesis, the reproach of inequality of dispensation and cruelty would attach to him. Some beings, viz. the gods and others, he renders eminently happy; others, as for instance the animals, eminently unhappy; to some again, as for instance men, he allots an intermediate position. To a Lord bringing about such an unequal condition of things, passion and malice would have to be ascribed, just as to any common person acting similarly; while attributes would be contrary to the essential goodness of the Lord. . . . Moreover, as the infliction of pain and the final destruction of all creatures would form part of his dispensation, he would have to be taxed with great cruelty, a quality abhorred by low people even. For these two reasons Brahman cannot be the cause of the world.

The Lord, we reply, cannot be reproached with inequality of dispensation and cruelty, "because he is bound by regards." If the Lord on his own account, without any extraneous regards, produced this unequal creation, he would expose himself to blame; but the fact is, that in creating he is bound by certain regards, i.e. he has to look to merit and demerit. Hence the circumstance of the creation being unequal is due to the merit and demerit of the living creatures created, and is not a fault for which the Lord is to blame. The position of the Lord is to be looked on as analogous to that of Parjanya, the Giver of rain. For as Parjanya is the common cause of the production of rice, barley, and other plants, while the difference between the various species is due to the various potentialities lying hidden in the respective seeds, so the Lord is the common cause of the creation of gods, men, &c., while the differences between these classes of beings are due to the different merit belonging to the individual souls. Hence the Lord, being bound by regards, cannot be reproached with inequality of dispensation and cruelty. . . .

But—an objection is raised—the passage, "Being only this was in the beginning, one, without a second," affirms that before the creation there was no distinction and consequently no merit on account of which the creation might have become unequal. And if we assume the Lord to have been guided in his dispensations by the actions of living beings subsequent to the creation, we involve ourselves in the circular reasoning that work depends on diversity of condition of life, and diversity of condition again on work. The Lord may be considered as acting with regard to religious merit after distinction had once arisen; but as before that the cause of inequality, viz. merit, did not exist, it follows that the first creation must have been free from inequalities.

This objection we meet by the remark, that the transmigratory world is without beginning.—The objection would be valid if the world had a beginning; but as it is without beginning, merit and inequality are, like seed and sprout, caused as well as causes, and there is therefore no logical objection to their operation. . . .

The beginninglessness of the world recommends itself to reason. For if it had a beginning it would follow that, the world springing into existence without a cause, the released souls also would again enter into the circle of transmigratory existence; and further, as then there would exist no determining cause of the unequal dispensation of pleasure and pain, we should have to acquiesce in the doctrine of rewards and punishments being allotted, without reference to previous good or bad actions. That the Lord is not the cause of the inequality, has already been remarked. Nor can Nescience by itself be the cause, as it is of a uniform nature. On the other hand, Nescience may be the cause of inequality, if it be considered as having regard to merit accruing from action produced by the mental impressions of wrath, hatred, and other afflicting passions. Without merit and demerit nobody can enter into existence, and again, without a body merit and demerit cannot be formed; so that—on the doctrine of the world having a beginning—we are led into a logical see-saw. The opposite doctrine, on the other hand, explains all matters in a manner analogous to the case of the seed and sprout, so that no difficulty remains.

Spinoza

Baruch Spinoza (1632–1677) was born in Amsterdam to Jewish parents who had fled Portugal to escape religious persecution. At this time Amsterdam was one of the most tolerant places in Europe with regard to religious beliefs. Spinoza received traditional rabbinic training; however, when he was eighteen, he began to study the "new science" of Copernicus, Galileo, and Descartes, and in his later creative work sought to base his philosophy on a number of their ideas regarding the workings of nature. Although Spinoza's work has come to be regarded as deeply spiritual, he was banned from his synagogue as a result of his highly unorthodox views. He made his living as a humble lens grinder but remained very much aware of the intellectual and political currents of his time. His major philosophical work, the Ethics, *was published posthumously in 1677.*

In his *Ethics*, Spinoza is concerned with the question, In what do human freedom and perfection consist? In addressing this question, he sets forth a comprehensive vision of reality and human nature, a view that shares certain features with Vedāntic philosophy but that departs from it in a number of significant ways, chiefly in its avoidance of any doctrine of *māyā* (illusion).

Spinoza views reality as a single substance—which he defines as "that which is in itself, and is conceived through itself." He calls this God or Nature, an impersonal, rational whole or unity of all being. God or Nature, for Spinoza, is grounded in the necessity of its own nature—following the mechanistic science of his time, it might be said that it cannot be other than it is—and is made known to us only through its attributes of thought (mind) and extension (body). Nature thus represents both the creative principle of all finite things and the totality of those things themselves. God has no free will of his own and is not independent of the universe, and hence cannot be regarded as its creator. The rational order of the universe, according to Spinoza, is, nevertheless, the very essence of our own being and is that which can be realized by us in the highest exercise of our reason.

Following a kind of geometric method, Spinoza presents his remarkable vision by means of definitions, axioms, propositions, and proofs. He is a strict rationalist in his deductive method as well as being a naturalist and a man of deep spiritual convictions.

Concerning God

DEFINITIONS

I. By that which is *self-caused*, I mean that of which the essence involves existence, or that of which the nature is only conceivable as existent.

II. A thing is called *finite after its kind*, when it can be limited by another thing of the same nature; for instance, a body is called finite because we always conceive another greater body. So, also, a thought is limited by another thought, but a body is not limited by thought, nor a thought by body.

III. By *substance*, I mean that which is in itself, and is conceived through itself: in other words, that of which a conception can be formed independently of any other conception.

IV. By *attribute*, I mean that which the intellect perceives as constituting the essence of substance.

V. By *mode*, I mean the modifications of substance, or that which exists in, and is conceived through, something other than itself.

VI. By *God*, I mean a being absolutely infinite—that is, a substance consisting in infinite attributes, of which each expresses eternal and infinite essentiality.

Explanation.—I say absolutely infinite, not infinite after its kind: for, of a thing infinite only after its kind, infinite attributes may be denied; but that which is absolutely infinite, contains in its essence whatever expresses reality, and involves no negation.

VII. That thing is called free, which exists solely by the necessity of its own nature, and of which the action is determined by itself alone. On the other hand, that thing is necessary, or rather constrained, which is determined by something external to itself to a fixed and definite method of existence or action.

VIII. By *eternity*, I mean existence itself, in so far as it is conceived necessarily to follow solely from the definition of that which is eternal.

Explanation.—Existence of this kind is conceived as an eternal truth, like the essence of a thing, and, therefore, cannot be explained by means of continuance or time, though continuance may be conceived without a beginning or end.

AXIOMS

I. Everything which exists, exists either in itself or in something else.

II. That which cannot be conceived through anything else must be conceived through itself.

From *The Ethics* by Spinoza, translated by R. H. M. Elves, in *The Rationalists* (n.d.). Reprinted with acknowledgment to Doubleday & Company, Inc.

III. From a given definite cause an effect necessarily follows; and, on the other hand, if no definite cause be granted, it is impossible that an effect can follow.

IV. The knowledge of an effect depends on and involves the knowledge of a cause.

V. Things which have nothing in common cannot be understood, the one by means of the other; the conception of one does not involve the conception of the other.

VI. A true idea must correspond with its ideate or object.

VII. If a thing can be conceived as non-existing, its essence does not involve existence.

PROPOSITIONS

PROP. I. *Substance is by nature prior to its modifications.*

Proof.—This is clear from Deff. iii. and v.

PROP. II. *Two substances, whose attributes are different, have nothing in common.*

Proof.—Also evident from Def. iii. For each must exist in itself, and be conceived through itself; in other words, the conception of one does not imply the conception of the other.

PROP. III. *Things which have nothing in common cannot be one the cause of the other.*

Proof.—If they have nothing in common, it follows that one cannot be apprehended by means of the other (Ax. v.), and, therefore, one cannot be the cause of the other (Ax. iv.). *Q.E.D.*

PROP. IV. *Two or more distinct things are distinguished one from the other either by the difference of the attributes of the substances, or by the difference of their modifications.*

Proof.—Everything which exists, exists either in itself or in something else (Ax. i.),—that is (by Deff. iii. and v.), nothing is granted in addition to the understanding, except substance and its modifications. Nothing is, therefore, given besides the understanding, by which several things may be distinguished one from the other, except the substances, or, in other words (see Ax. iv.), their attributes and modifications. *Q.E.D.*

PROP. V. *There cannot exist in the universe two or more substances having the same nature or attribute.*

Proof.—If several distinct substances be granted, they must be distinguished one from the other, either by the difference of their attributes, or by the difference of their modifications (Prop. iv.). If only by the difference of their attributes, it will be granted that there cannot be more than one with an identical attribute. If by the difference of their modifications—as substance is naturally prior to its modifications (Prop. i.),—it follows that setting the modifications aside, and considering substance in itself, that is truly, (Deff. iii. and vi.), there cannot be conceived one substance different from another,—that is (by Prop. iv.), there cannot be granted several substances, but one substance only. *Q.E.D.*

PROP. VI. *One substance cannot be produced by another substance.*

Proof.—It is impossible that there should be in the universe two substances with an identical attribute, *i.e.* which have anything common to them both (Prop. ii.), and, therefore (Prop. iii.), one cannot be the cause of another, neither can one be produced by the other. *Q.E.D.*

Corollary.—Hence it follows that a substance cannot be produced by anything external to itself. For in the universe nothing is granted, save substances and their modifications (as appears from Ax. i. and Deff. iii. and v.). Now (by the last Prop.) substance cannot be produced by another substance, therefore it cannot be produced by anything external to itself. *Q.E.D.* This is shown still more readily by the absurdity of the contradictory. For, if substance be produced by an external cause, the knowledge of it would depend on the knowledge of its cause (Ax. iv.), and, (by Def. iii.) it would itself not be substance.

PROP. VII. *Existence belongs to the nature of substance.*

Proof.—Substance cannot be produced by anything external (Corollary, Prop. vi.), it must, therefore, be its own cause—that is, its essence necessarily involves existence, or existence belongs to its nature.

PROP. VIII. *Every substance is necessarily infinite.*

Proof.—There can only be one substance with an identical attribute, and existence follows from its nature (Prop. vii.); its nature, therefore, involves existence, either as finite or infinite. It does not exist as finite, for (by Def. ii.) it would then be limited by something else of the same kind, which would also necessarily exist (Prop. vii.); and there would be two substances with an identical attribute, which is absurd (Prop. v.). It therefore exists as infinite. *Q.E.D.*

Note I.—As finite existence involves a partial negation, and infinite existence is the absolute affirmation of the given nature, it follows (solely from Prop. vii.) that every substance is necessarily infinite.

Note II.—No doubt it will be difficult for those who think about things loosely, and have not been accustomed to know them by their primary causes, to comprehend the demonstration of Prop. vii.: for such persons make no distinction between the modifications of substances and the substances themselves, and are ignorant of the manner in which things are produced; hence they attribute to substances the beginning which they observe in natural objects. Those who are ignorant of true causes, make complete confusion—think that trees might talk just as well as men— that men might be formed from stones as well as from seed; and imagine that any form might be changed into any other. So, also, those who confuse the two natures, divine and human, readily attribute human passions to the deity, especially so long as they do not know how passions originate in the mind. But, if people would consider the nature of substance, they would have no doubt about the truth of Prop. vii. In fact, this proposition would be a universal axiom, and accounted a truism. For, by substance, would be understood that which is in itself, and is conceived through itself—that is, something of which the conception requires not the conception of anything else; whereas modifications exist in something external to themselves, and a conception of them is formed by means of a conception of the thing in which they exist. Therefore, we may have true ideas of non-existent modifications; for, although they may have no *actual* existence apart from the conceiving intellect, yet their essence is so involved in something external to themselves that they may through it be conceived. Whereas the only truth substances can have, external to the intellect, must consist in their existence, because they are conceived through themselves. Therefore, for a person to say that he has a clear and distinct—that is, a true—idea of a substance, but that he is not sure whether such substance exists, would be the same as if he said that he had a true idea, but was not sure whether or not it was false (a little consideration will make this plain); or if anyone affirmed that substance is created, it would be the same as saying that a false idea was true—in short, the height of absurdity. It must, then, necessarily be admitted that the existence of substance as its essence is an eternal truth. And we can hence conclude by another process of reasoning—that there is but one such substance. I think that this may profitably be done at once; and, in order to proceed regularly with the demonstration, we must premise:—

1. The true definition of a thing neither involves nor expresses anything beyond the nature of the thing defined. From this it follows that—

2. No definition implies or expresses a certain number of individuals, inasmuch as it expresses nothing beyond the nature of the thing defined. For instance, the definition of a triangle expresses nothing beyond the actual nature of a triangle: it does not imply any fixed number of triangles.

3. There is necessarily for each individual existent thing a cause why it should exist.

4. This cause of existence must either be contained in the nature and definition of the thing defined, or must be postulated apart from such definition.

It therefore follows that, if a given number of individual things exist in nature, there must be some cause for the existence of exactly that number, neither more nor less. For example, if twenty men exist in the universe (for simplicity's sake, I will suppose them existing simultaneously, and to have had no predecessors), and we want to account for the existence of these twenty men, it will not be enough to show the cause of human existence in general; we must also show why there are exactly twenty men, neither more nor less: for a cause must be assigned for the existence of each individual. Now this cause cannot be contained in the actual nature of man, for the true definition of man does not involve any consideration of the number twenty. Consequently, the cause for the existence of these twenty men, and, consequently, of each of them, must necessarily be sought externally to each individual. Hence we may lay down the absolute rule, that everything which may consist of several individuals must have an external cause. And, as it has been shown already that existence appertains to the nature of substance, existence must necessarily be included in its definition; and from its definition alone existence must be deducible. But from its definition (as we have shown, Notes 2, 3), we cannot infer the existence of several substances; therefore it follows that there is only one substance of the same nature. *Q.E.D.*

PROP. IX. *The more reality or being a thing has, the greater the number of its attributes* (Def. iv.).

PROP. X. *Each particular attribute of the one substance must be conceived through itself.*

Proof.—An attribute is that which the intellect perceives of substance, as constituting its essence (Def. iv.), and, therefore, must be conceived through itself (Def. iii.). *Q.E.D.*

Note.—It is thus evident that, though two attributes are, in fact, conceived as distinct—that is, one without the help of the other—yet we cannot, therefore, conclude that they constitute two entities, or two different substances. For it is the nature of substance that each of its attributes is conceived through itself, inasmuch as all the attributes it has have always existed simultaneously in it, and none could be produced by any other; but each expresses the reality or being of substance. It is, then, far from an absurdity to ascribe several attributes to one substance: for nothing in nature is more clear than that each and every entity must be conceived under some attribute, and that its reality or being is in proportion to the number of its attributes expressing necessity or eternity and infinity. Consequently it is abundantly clear, that an absolutely infinite being must necessarily be defined as consisting in infinite attributes, each of which expresses a certain eternal and infinite essence. . . .

APPENDIX

In the foregoing I have explained the nature and properties of God. I have shown that he necessarily exists, that he is one: that he is, and acts solely by the necessity of his own nature; that he is the free cause of all things, and how he is so; that all things are in God, and so depend on him, that without him they could neither exist nor be conceived; lastly, that all things are predetermined by God, not through his free will or absolute fiat, but from the very nature of God or infinite power. I have further, where occasion offered, taken care to remove the prejudices, which might impede the comprehension of my demonstrations. Yet there still remain misconceptions not a few, which might and may prove very grave hindrances to the understanding of the concatenation of things, as I have explained it above. I have therefore thought it worth while to bring these misconceptions before the bar of reason.

All such opinions spring from the notion commonly entertained, that all things in nature act as men themselves act, namely, with an end in view. It is accepted as certain, that God himself directs all things to a definite goal (for it is said that God made all things for man, and man that he might worship him). I will, therefore, consider this opinion, asking first, why it obtains general credence, and why all men are naturally so prone to adopt it? Secondly, I will point out its falsity; and, lastly, I will show how it has given rise to prejudices about good and bad, right and wrong, praise and blame, order and confusion, beauty and ugliness, and the like. However, this is not the place to deduce these misconceptions from the nature of the human mind: it will be sufficient here, if I assume as a starting point, what ought to be universally admitted, namely, that all men are born ignorant of the causes of things, that all have the desire to seek for what is useful to them, and that they are conscious of such desire. Herefrom it follows, first, that men think themselves free inasmuch as they are conscious of their volitions and desires, and never even dream, in their ignorance, of the causes which have disposed them so to wish and desire. Secondly, that men do all things for an end, namely, for that which is useful to them, and which they seek. Thus it comes to pass that they only look for a knowledge of the final causes of events, and when these are learned, they are content, as having no cause for further doubt. If they cannot learn such causes from external sources, they are compelled to turn to considering themselves, and reflecting what end would have induced them personally to bring about the given event, and thus they necessarily judge other natures by their own. Further, as they find in themselves and outside themselves many means which assist them not a little in their search for what is useful, for instance, eyes for seeing, teeth for chewing, herbs and animals for yielding food, the sun for giving light, the sea for breeding fish, &c., they come to look on the whole of nature as a means for obtaining such conveniences. Now as they are aware, that they found these conveniences and did not make them, they think they have cause for believing, that some other being has made them for their use. As they look upon things as means, they cannot believe them to be self-created; but, judging from the means which they are accustomed to prepare for themselves, they are bound to believe in some ruler or rulers of the universe endowed with human freedom, who have arranged and adapted everything for human use. They are bound to estimate the nature of such rulers (having no information on the subject) in accordance with their own nature, and therefore they assert that the gods ordained everything for the use of man, in order to bind man to themselves and obtain from him the highest honour. Hence also it follows, that everyone thought out for himself, according to his abilities, a different way of worshipping God, so that God might love him more than his fellows, and direct the whole course of nature for the satisfaction of his blind cupidity and insatiable avarice. Thus the prejudice developed into superstition, and took deep root in the human mind; and for his reason everyone strove most zealously to understand and explain the final causes of things; but in their endeavour to show that nature does nothing in vain, *i.e.*, nothing which is useless to man, they only seem to have demonstrated that nature, the gods, and men are all made together. Consider, I pray you, the result: among the many helps of nature they were bound to find some hindrances, such as storms, earthquakes, diseases, &c.: so they declared that such things happen, because the gods are angry at some wrong done them by men, or at some fault committed in their worship. Experience day by day protested and showed by infinite examples, that good and evil fortunes fall to the lot of pious and impious alike; still they would not abandon their inveterate prejudice, for it was more easy for them to class such contradictions among other unknown things of whose use they were ignorant, and thus to retain their actual and innate condition of ignorance, than to destroy the whole fabric of their reasoning and start afresh. They therefore laid down as an axiom, that God's judgments far transcend human understanding. Such a doctrine might well have sufficed to conceal the truth from the human race for all eternity, if mathematics had not furnished another standard of verity in considering solely the essence and properties of figures without regard to their final causes. There are other reasons (which I need not mention here) besides mathematics, which might have caused men's minds to be directed to these general prejudices, and have led them to the knowledge of the truth.

I have now sufficiently explained my first point. There is no need to show at length, that nature has no particular goal in view, and that final causes are mere human figments. . . . However, I will add a few remarks, in order to overthrow this doctrine of a final cause utterly. That which is really a cause it considers as an effect, and *vice versâ*: it makes that which is by nature first to be last, and that which is highest and most perfect to be most imperfect. Passing over the questions of cause and priority as self-evident . . . that that effect is most perfect which is produced immediately by God; the effect which requires for its production several intermediate causes is, in that respect, more imperfect. But if those things which were made immediately by God were made to enable him to attain his end, then the things which come after, for the sake of which the first were made, are necessarily the most excellent of all.

Further, this doctrine does away with the perfection of God: for, if God acts for an object, he necessarily desires something which he lacks. Certainly, theologians and metaphysicians draw a distinction between the object of want and the object of assimilation; still they confess that God made all things for the sake of himself, not for the sake of creation. They are unable to point to anything prior to creation, except God himself, as an object for which God should act, and are therefore driven to admit (as they clearly must), that God lacked those things for whose attainment he created means, and further that he desired them.

We must not omit to notice that the followers of this doctrine, anxious to display their talent in assigning final causes, have imported a new method of argument in proof of their theory—namely, a reduction, not to the impossible, but to ignorance; thus showing that they have no other method of exhibiting their doctrine. For example, if a stone falls from a roof on to someone's head, and kills him, they will demonstrate by their new method, that the stone fell in order to kill the man; for, if it had not by God's will fallen with that object, how could so many circumstances (and there are often many concurrent circumstances) have all happened together by chance? Perhaps you will answer that the event is due to the facts that the wind was blowing, and the man was walking that way. "But why," they will insist, "was the wind blowing, and why was the man at that very time walking that way?" If you again answer, that the wind had then sprung up because the sea had begun to be agitated the day before, the weather being previously calm, and that the man had been invited by a friend, they will again insist: "But why was the sea agitated, and why was the man invited at that time?" So they will pursue their questions from cause to cause, till at last you take refuge in the will of God—in other words, the sanctuary of ignorance. So, again, when they survey the frame of the human body, they are amazed; and being ignorant of the causes of so great a work of art, conclude that it has been fashioned, not mechanically, but by divine and supernatural skill, and has been so put together that one part shall not hurt another.

Hence anyone who seeks for the true causes of miracles, and strives to understand natural phenomena as an intelligent being, and not to gaze at them like a fool, is set down and denounced as an impious heretic by those, whom the masses adore as the interpreters of nature and the gods. Such persons know that, with the removal of ignorance, the wonder which forms their only available means for proving and preserving their authority would vanish also. But I now quit this subject, and pass on to my third point.

After men persuaded themselves, that everything which is created is created for their sake, they were bound to consider as the chief quality in everything that which is most useful to themselves, and to account those things the best of all which have the most beneficial effect on mankind. Further, they were bound to form abstract notions for the explanation of the nature of things, such as *goodness, badness, order, confusion, warmth, cold, beauty, deformity,* and so on; and from the belief that they are free agents arose the further notions *praise* and *blame, sin* and *merit.*

I will speak of these latter hereafter, when I treat of human nature; the former I will briefly explain here.

Everything which conduces to health and the worship of God they have called *good,* everything which hinders these objects they have styled *bad;* and inasmuch as those who do not understand the nature of things do not verify phenomena in any way, but merely imagine them after a fashion, and mistake their imagination for understanding, such persons firmly believe that there is an *order* in things, being really ignorant both of things and their own nature. When phenomena are of such a kind, that the impression they make on our senses requires little effort of imagination, and can consequently be easily remembered, we say that they are *well-ordered;* if the contrary, that they are *ill-ordered* or *confused.* Further, as things which are easily imagined are more pleasing to us, men prefer order to confusion—as though there were any order in nature, except in relation to our imagination—and say that God has created all things in order; thus, without knowing it, attributing imagination to God, unless, indeed, they would have it that God foresaw human imagination, and arranged everything, so that it should be most easily imagined. If this be their theory, they would not, perhaps, be daunted by the fact that we find an infinite number of phenomena, far surpassing our imagination, and very many others which confound its weakness. But enough has been said on this subject. The other abstract notions are nothing but modes of imagining, in which the imagination is differently affected, though they are considered by the ignorant as the chief attributes of things, inasmuch as they believe that everything was created for the sake of themselves; and, according as they are affected by it, style it good or bad, healthy or rotten and corrupt. For instance, if the motion which objects we see communicate to our nerves be conducive to health, the objects causing it are styled *beautiful;* if a contrary motion be excited, they are styled *ugly.*

Things which are perceived through our sense of smell are styled fragrant or fetid; if through our taste, sweet or bitter, full-flavoured or insipid; if through our touch, hard or soft, rough or smooth, &c.

Whatsoever affects our ears is said to give rise to noise, sound, or harmony. In this last case, there are men lunatic enough to believe, that even God himself takes pleasure in harmony; and philosophers are not lacking who have persuaded themselves, that the motion of the heavenly bodies gives rise to harmony—all of which instances sufficiently show that everyone judges of things according to the state of his brain, or rather mistakes for things the forms of his imagination. We need no longer wonder that there have arisen all the controversies we have witnessed, and finally scepticism: for, although human bodies in many respects agree, yet in very many others they differ; so that what seems good to one seems bad to another; what seems well ordered to one seems confused to another; what is pleasing to one displeases another, and so on. I need not further enumerate, because this is not the place to treat the subject at length, and also because the fact is sufficiently well known. It is commonly said: "So many men, so many minds; everyone is wise in his own way; brains differ as completely as palates." All of which proverbs show, that men judge of things according to their mental disposition, and rather imagine than understand: for, if they understood phenomena, they would, as mathematics attest, be convinced, if not attracted, by what I have urged.

We have now perceived, that all the explanations commonly given of nature are mere modes of imagining, and do not indicate the true nature of anything, but only the constitution of the imagination; and, although they have names, as though they were entities, existing externally to the imagination, I call them entities imaginary rather than real; and, therefore, all arguments against us drawn from such abstractions are easily rebutted.

Many argue in this way. If all things follow from a necessity of the absolutely perfect nature of God, why are there so many imperfections in nature? such, for instance, as things corrupt to the point of putridity, loathsome deformity, confusion, evil, sin, &c. But these reasoners are, as I have said, easily confuted, for the perfection of things is to be reckoned only from their own nature and power; things are not more or less perfect, according as they delight or offend human senses, or according as they are serviceable or repugnant to mankind. To those who ask why God did not so create all men, that they should be governed only by reason, I give no answer but this: because matter was not lacking to him for the creation of every degree of perfection from highest to lowest; or, more strictly, because the laws of his nature are so vast, as to suffice for the production of everything conceivable by an infinite intelligence. . . .

Such are the misconceptions I have undertaken to note; if there are any more of the same sort, everyone may easily dissipate them for himself with the aid of a little reflection.

Dōgen

Dōgen (1200–1253) was a Japanese monk who is credited as being the founder of the Sōtō branch of Zen Buddhism, which emphasized meditative practices as well as direct insight. While studying in China under the guidance of a master, Dōgen experienced a profound religious awakening wherein he achieved a state called satori, *or Zen enlightenment. He returned to Japan to teach what he had discovered and reform what he considered to be corrupt practices and doctrines of Buddhism in his native land. Dōgen's main work, the* Shōbōgenzō, *is often regarded as one of the most brilliant philosophical texts in the Japanese tradition.*

Saint Augustine, the influential early Christian theologian, states that "we all know what time is until we are called upon to explain it." In the West, through the influence of Christian thinking, with its concern with the destiny of humankind, and early modern science, with its predilection for mechanical explanations, we have come to accept the notion that time consists of a series of successive moments, that time is linear, "moving" from the past through the present to the future in an inexorable way. There have, however, been many conflicting theories regarding the ontological status of time so conceived, from Newton's claim—which has become deeply entrenched in most persons' understanding—that time is an absolute, objective reality, to Kant's insistence that time is only something that we employ as a means of ordering and organizing our experience. In other traditions, and going back as well to earlier thinking in the West, cyclical notions about the meaning of time tend to dominate, and metaphysical questions are raised regarding its significance and ontological status. In both Western thought, especially among the Greeks, and much Asian thinking, which is highly ritually oriented, there is also a concern to distinguish between time as a quantifiable measure (*chronos*) and time as a qualitative feature of experience, the timely—the right time to do something (*kairos*).

One of the most radical, fascinating, and elusive theories of time, which combines these two dimensions, is put forward by Dōgen, who argues that being and time are so intimately connected that it makes no sense to say that events occur in time, but rather that happenings always define the very temporality that is present. Spring *is* the blooming of flowers, not the time or the season as such when flowers bloom. Dōgen's concept of *uji*, or "being-time," also involves a kind of eternal present, so that any specific temporal occasion is at once all-time. The totality of time is implicated in every act of being.

Being Time (Uji)

So-called *time of being* means time is already being; all being is time. . . . The length and brevity of the twenty-four hours, though not as yet measured, is called twenty-four hours. Because the direction and course of their going and coming are obvious, people don't doubt them—yet though they don't doubt them, this is not to say that they know them. Because sentient beings' doubting of things which they don't know is not fixed, the future course of their doubting does not necessarily accord with their doubts of the present. It's just that doubting is for the moment *time*.

Self is arrayed as the whole world. You should perceive that each point, each thing of this *whole world* is an individual *time*. The mutual noninterference of things is like the mutual noninterference of *times*. For this reason there is *arousal of minds at the same time*, there is *arousal of times in the same mind*. Cultivating practice and achieving enlightenment are also like this. Arraying self, self sees this—such is the principle of *self* being *time*.

Because it is the principle of *being such*, there are *myriad forms, a hundred grasses* on *the whole earth*. You should learn that each *single blade of grass*, each *single form*, is on *the whole earth*. Such *going and coming* is the starting point of cultivation of practice. . . . Because it is only *right at such a time*, therefore *being time* is all *the whole time*. *Being grass* and *being form* are both time. In the time of *time's time* there is *the whole of being, the whole world*. For a while try to visualize whether or not there is *the whole being, the whole world* apart from the present time.

In spite of this, when people are ordinary folk who have not studied the Buddha's teaching, the views they have are such that when they hear the expression *a time of being* . . . they think, "Even though those mountains and rivers may exist still, I have passed them and am now in the vermillion tower of the jewel palace—the mountains and rivers and I are as far apart as sky and earth." However, the truth is not just this one line of reasoning alone. In the time one climbed the mountains and crossed the rivers, there was oneself. There must be *time* in oneself. Since oneself exists, *time* cannot leave. If time is not the appearances of going and coming, the time of climbing a mountain is the *immediate present of being time*. If time preserves the appearances of going and coming, there is in oneself the *immediate present* of *being time*—this is *being time*. Does not that *time* of *climbing mountain and crossing rivers* swallow up this *time* of the *vermillion tower of the jewel palace*? Does it not spew it forth?

. . . The principle of *yesterday and today* is just the time of directly entering the mountains and gazing out over the thousand peaks, the myriad peaks—it is not a matter of having passed. . . . Though it seems to be elsewhere, it is *right now*. So pines are *time* too; bamboo is *time* too.

One should not understand time only as flying away; one should not only get the idea that flying away is the function of time. If time only were to fly, then there

From *Shōbōgenzō: Zen Essays by Dōgen*, translated by Thomas Clearly (1986). Reprinted by permission of University of Hawaii Press.

would be gaps. Not having heard of the path of *being time* is because of learning only that it has passed. To tell the gist of it, all existences in the whole world, while being lined up, are individual times. Because it is *being time*, it is *my being time*.

In *being time* there is the quality of passage. That is, it passes from today to tomorrow, it passes from today to yesterday, it passes from yesterday to today, it passes from today to today, it passes from tomorrow to tomorrow.

Because passage is a quality of time, past and present time doesn't pile up, doesn't accumulate in a row. . . . Since self and others are *time*, cultivation and realization are times. *Going into the mud, going into the water* is similarly *time*. . . .

Even forms which seem to slip by are *being*. Furthermore, if you leave it at that, being the period of manifestation of *slipping by*, it is the *abiding in position of being time*. Don't stir it as nonexistence, don't insist on it as existence. Only conceiving of time as passing one way, one doesn't understand it as not yet having arrived. Though understanding is *time*, it has no relation drawn by another. . . . Even recognizing *remaining in position*, who can express the preservation of *already being such*? Even if they have long expressed it as *such*, still everyone gropes for the appearance of its countenance. If we leave ordinary people's being *being time* at that, then even enlightenment and nirvana are only *being time* which is merely the appearance of going and coming. . . .

Passage is, for example, like spring: in spring there are numerous appearances—this is called *passage*. You should learn that it *passes through* without any external thing. For example, the *passage* of spring necessarily *passes through* spring. Though *passage* is not spring, because it is the *passage* of spring, *passage* has *accomplished the Way* in the *time* of spring. You should examine thoroughly in whatever you are doing. In speaking of *passage*, if you think that the objective realm is outside and the phenomenon which *passes through* passes a million worlds to the east through a billion eons, in thinking thus you are not concentrating wholly on the study of the Buddha Way.

Cārvāka

In both Western and Asian cultures metaphysical theories called "materialism" have frequently been put forward and represent quite clearly a strong intellectual need to encompass all the things of the universe and the objects of our experience, including ourselves, into a single scheme or mode of explanation. Materialism, in all of its many forms, holds that everything is essentially material in nature: what we call our mind is really only our brain, a sunset is actually only a play of physical elements and forces, and so on. Physical substance, in short, is the only reality; everything throughout the universe is, in principle, reducible to it.

While there have been crude forms of materialism as well as highly sophisticated ones (as often exemplified today in studies that model mental behavior on computer-like functions of information inputs and outputs), nevertheless quite typically materialistic perspectives have taken a very dim view indeed of religious claims regarding the nature of the soul, human immortality, and the like. Even in ancient India, the home of spiritual values par excellence, a materialistic system of thought was put forward and, although most of the texts of this school have been lost, was sufficiently influential that its opponents felt compelled to deal with it. This Indian school was known as Cārvāka, but it is sometimes called Lokāyata, which refers to "those who are attached to the world."

The cārvākins based their materialism on a kind of radical epistemological empiricism that held that all knowledge is restricted to our sense perceptions and that inferential reasoning—the kind of logic developed, as we have seen, in the Nyāya school—cannot be justified. Deduction provides no new knowledge; induction may never yield anything that is certain.

Critics of materialism in both the West and India have always insisted that the doctrine itself cannot be put forward except by assuming the reality of the mind and the validity of reasoning and by accepting that our experience, in all of its richness and diversity, can never be reduced to a physical base as such: experiences of feeling love, of planning a future, of valuing one thing over another, and so on, have qualitative features of their own. Nevertheless, as it is said in the following selection from a sixteenth-century compendium of the different schools of Indian philosophy by the scholar Mādhava, the majority of human beings do hold to the dictum that one should, as we might express it, "eat, drink, and be merry, for tomorrow you may die."

MĀDHAVA

The Cārvāka System

The efforts of Cārvāka are indeed hard to be eradicated, for the majority of living beings hold by the current refrain—

> While life is yours, live joyously;
> None can escape Death's searching eye:
> When once this frame of ours they burn,
> How shall it e'er again return?

The mass of men, in accordance with the Śāstras [Sciences] of policy and enjoyment, considering wealth and desire the only ends of man, and denying the existence of any object belonging to a future world, are found to follow only the doctrine of Cārvāka. Hence another name for that school is Lokāyata,—a name well accordant with the thing signified. . . .

In this school the four elements, earth, etc., are the original principles; from these alone, when transformed into the body, intelligence is produced. . . .

The soul is only the body distinguished by the attribute of intelligence, since there is no evidence for any soul distinct from the body, as such cannot be proved, since this school holds that perception is the only source of knowledge and does not allow inference, etc.

The only end of man is enjoyment produced by sensual pleasures. Nor may you say that such cannot be called the end of man as they are always mixed with some kind of pain, because it is our wisdom to enjoy the pure pleasure as far as we can, and to avoid the pain which inevitably accompanies it; just as the man who desires fish takes the fish with their scales and bones, and having taken as many as he wants, desists; or just as the man who desires rice, takes the rice, straw and all, and having taken as much as he wants, desists. It is not therefore for us, through a fear of pain, to reject the pleasure which our nature instinctively recognises as congenial. Men do not refrain from sowing rice, because forsooth there are wild animals to devour it; nor do they refuse to set the cooking-pots on the fire, because forsooth there are beggars to pester us for a share of the contents. If any one were so timid as to forsake a visible pleasure, he would indeed be foolish like a beast, as has been said by the poet—

> The pleasure which arises to men from contact with sensible objects,
> Is to be relinquished as accompanied by pain,—such is the reasoning of fools;
> The berries of paddy, rich with the finest white grains,

From *The Sarva-Darśana Saṃgraha* by Mādhava, translated by E. B. Cowell and A. E. Gough (London: Kegan Paul, 1904).

What man, seeking his true interest, would fling away because covered with husk and dust?

If you object that, if there be no such thing as happiness in a future world, then how should men of experienced wisdom engage in the agnihotra [fire sacrifice] and other sacrifices, which can only be performed with great expenditure of money and bodily fatigue, your objection cannot be accepted as any proof to the contrary, since the agnihotra, etc., are only useful as means of livelihood, for the Veda is tainted by the three faults of untruth, self-contradiction, and tautology. . . .

> The Agnihotra, the three Vedas, the ascetic's three staves, and smearing one-self with ashes,—
> Brihaspati says, these are but means of livelihood for those who have no manliness nor sense.

Hence it follows that there is no other hell than mundane pain produced by purely mundane causes, as thorns, etc.; the only Supreme is the earthly monarch whose existence is proved by all the world's eyesight; and the only Liberation is the dissolution of the body. By holding the doctrine that the soul is identical with the body, such phrases as "I am thin," "I am black," etc., are at once intelligible, as the attributes of thinness, etc., and self-consciousness will reside in the same subject [the body]; like and the use of the phrase "my body" is metaphorical. . . .

All this has been thus summed up—

> In this school there are four elements, earth, water, fire, and air;
> And from these four elements alone is intelligence produced,—
> Just like the intoxicating power from kinwa [a grain], etc., mixed together;
> Since in "I am fat," "I am lean," these attributes abide in the same subject,
> And since fatness, etc., reside only in the body, it alone is the soul and no other,
> And such phrases as "my body" are only significant metaphorically.

"Be it so," says the opponent; "your wish would be gained if inference, etc., had no force of proof; but then they have this force; else, if they had not, then how, on perceiving smoke, should the thoughts of the intelligent immediately proceed to fire; or why, on hearing another say, 'There are fruits on the bank of the river,' do those who desire fruit proceed at once to the shore?"

All this, however, is only the inflation of the world of fancy.

Those who maintain the authority of inference accept the *sign* or middle term as the causer of knowledge, which middle term must be found in the minor and be itself invariably connected with the major. Now this invariable connection must be a relation destitute of any condition accepted or disputed; and this connection does not possess its power of causing inference by virtue of its *existence*, as the eye, etc., are the cause of perception, but by virtue of its being *known*. What then is the means of this connection's being known?

We will first show that it is not *perception*. Now perception is held to be of two kinds, external and internal. The former is not the required means; for although it is possible that the actual contact of the senses and the object will produce the knowledge of the particular object thus brought in contact, yet as there can never be such contact in the case of the past or the future, the universal proposition which was to embrace the invariable connection of the middle and major terms in every case becomes impossible to be known. Nor may you maintain that this knowledge of the universal proposition has the general class as its object, because if so, there might arise a doubt as to the existence of the invariable connection in this particular case.

Nor is internal perception the means, since you cannot establish that the mind has any power to act independently towards an external object, since all allow that it is dependent on the external senses, as has been said by one of the logicians, "The eye, etc., have their objects as described; but mind externally is dependent on the others."

Nor can *inference* be the means of the knowledge of the universal proposition, since in the case of this inference we should also require another inference to establish it, and so on, and hence would arise the fallacy of an *ad infinitum* retrogression.

Again, this same absence of a condition, which has been given as the definition of an invariable connection, can itself never be known; since it is impossible to establish that all conditions must be objects of perception; and therefore, although the absence of perceptible things may be itself perceptible, the absence of non-perceptible things must be itself non-perceptible; and thus, since we must here too have recourse to inference, etc., we cannot leap over the obstacle which has already been planted to bar them. Again, we must accept as the definition of the condition, "it is that which is reciprocal or equipollent in extension with the major term though not constantly accompanying the middle." These three distinguishing clauses, "not constantly accompanying the middle term," "constantly accompanying the major term," and "being constantly accompanied by it" are needed. . . .

But since the knowledge of the condition must here precede the knowledge of the condition's absence, it is only when there is the knowledge of the condition, that the knowledge of the universality of the proposition is possible, *i.e.*, a knowledge in the form of such a connection between the middle term and major term as is distinguished by the absence of any such condition; and on the other hand, the knowledge of the condition depends upon the knowledge of the invariable connection. Thus we fasten on our opponents as with adamantine glue the thunder-bolt-like fallacy of reasoning in a circle. Hence by the impossibility of knowing the universality of a proposition it becomes impossible to establish inference, etc.

The step which the mind takes from the knowledge of smoke, etc., to the knowledge of fire, etc., can be accounted for by its being based on a former perception or by its being an error; and that in some cases this step is justified by the result, is accidental just like the coincidence of effects observed in the employment of gems, charms, drugs, etc.

From this it follows that fate, etc., do not exist, since these can only be proved by inference. But an opponent will say, if you thus do not allow adrishta [an unseen force], the various phenomena of the world become destitute of any cause. But we cannot accept this objection as valid, since these phenomena can all be produced spontaneously from the inherent nature of things. Thus it has been said—

> The fire is hot, the water cold, refreshing cool the breeze of morn;
> By whom came this variety? from their own nature was it born.

And all this has been also said by Brihaspati—

> There is no heaven, no final liberation, nor any soul in another world. . . .

Hence in kindness to the mass of living beings must we fly for refuge to the doctrine of Cārvāka. Such is the pleasant consummation.

Yogācāra Buddhism

At the opposite end, as it were, on the metaphysical spectrum from materialism is the philosophical system known as "subjective idealism." Its main proponent in the West was George Berkeley, who lived in the eighteenth century (and to whom we will turn next), and in India the fifth-century Buddhist philosopher Vasubandhu. Both Berkeley and Vasubandhu, in their quite different ways, argued that everything is mental rather than material; that the very idea of "matter" is precisely an "idea" and is never itself an object of direct experience.

Subjective idealism seems at first to be in direct contradiction to common sense. We all believe, and act accordingly, that there is an objective world that is independent of ourselves and is made up of real objects that interact in lawlike ways. Can all this be merely the stuff of our own ideas? As we will see, Berkeley develops many strong, and to some, convincing, arguments in support of his position, while offering, however, a way out of what appears to be insuperable difficulties by appealing to the reality of God. Vasubandhu, a proponent of the subjective idealism that was developed in the so-called later Mahāyāna tradition of Buddhism in the school named *Yogācāra* or *Vijñānavāda* (mind only), is unrelenting in his thoroughgoing claim that what we take to be objectively given is only a projection of our own consciousness—that quite literally there is only mind. Consciousness is a stream of ideas that is sufficient, as it were, unto itself. The existence of a perceived object cannot, it is argued, be different from our perception of it, which is to say, from the perceiving mind itself. In explaining how this can make sense, how an ordered world with its regularities can appear at all, Vasubandhu argues that within the stream of consciousness we find impressions, the *saṃskāras* of our past experience, that come forward appropriately under the right circumstances as "objects" of consciousness. These impressions have their seat or home, as it were, in a kind of collective consciousness, or "storehouse consciousness" (*ālaya-vijñāna*), that in its various movement contains the seeds of all experience. This "absolute" consciousness can, it is believed, be realized as such, and the mental states that arise from it can accordingly be controlled and freedom of consciousness attained.

It is important to understand that for Yogācāra Buddhism the "mind-only" theory as such is believed to have practical efficacy in promoting the attainment of *nirvāṇa*, for if there is only the mind, why should one be attached to a world that in fact does not exist.

VASUBANDHU

There Is Only Mind

THE TREATISE IN TWENTY STANZAS ON REPRESENTATION-ONLY

[The *Viṁśatikā* of Vasubandhu (4th century C.E., translated by Clarence H. Hamilton.]

In the *Mahāyāna* it is established that the three worlds are representation-only. According to the scriptures it is said that the three worlds are only mind. Mind, thought, consciousness, discernment are different names. What is here spoken of as mind includes mental activities also in its meaning. "Only" excludes external objects; it does not do away with mental associates. When inner representations arise, seemingly external objects appear, as persons having bad eyes see hairs and flies. . . .

To this doctrine there are supposed objections. . . .

If representations are without real objects,
Then their spatial and temporal determination,
The indetermination of the perceiving stream of consciousness
And their action must be unfounded.

Place and time are determined as in a dream; . . .
As in dreams there is function in the loss of [semen].

That is, as in a dream although there are no real objects, yet it is in a certain place that such things as a village, a garden, a man, or a woman are seen, not in all places, and in this place it is at a certain time that this village, garden, etc., are seen, not at all times. . . .

Again as in dream, although the objects are unreal, they yet have function such as the loss of semen, etc. . . .

If you grant that from the force of deeds
Special elements are born
Which produce such transformations,
Why not admit [the process to be] consciousness? . . .

[Question] What advantage is there in this teaching of an inner meaning?

By reason of this teaching one enters into
[The doctrine of] the egolessness of the individual:

From *Viṁśatikā* and *Triṁśikā* by Vasubandhu, in Radhakrishnan, Sarvepalli, and Moore, Charles E., *A Source Book of Indian Philosophy*. Copyright © 1957 renewed Princeton University Press. Reprinted by permission of Princeton University Press.

The asserted non-substantiality of elements
One enters again by reason of the remainder of the teaching, . . .

[Question] Again, how do we know that Buddha intended such an inner meaning when he said there are bases of sense cognition? Are there not separate, really existing outer elements, having color-and-form, etc., which become severally the objects of visual, etc. consciousness?

That realm is neither one [thing],
Nor is it many atoms;
Again, it is not an agglomeration, etc.,
Because the atom is not proved.

. . . the external object cannot logically be one, because we cannot grasp the substance of the whole apart from the parts. Also it logically is not many, because we cannot apprehend the atoms separately. . . .

[Question] The existence or non-existence of anything is determined by means of proof. Among all means of proof immediate perception is the most excellent. If there are no external objects how is there this awareness of objects such as are now immediately evident to me? . . .

Immediate awareness is the same as in dreams, etc.
At the time when immediate awareness has arisen,
Seeing and its object are already non-existent;
How can it be admitted that perception exists?

[According to] those who hold the doctrine of momentariness, at the time when this awareness arises the immediate objects, visible [tangible, audible] etc. are already destroyed. How can you admit that at this time there is immediate perception?. . .

If you wish thus to prove the existence of external objects from "first experiencing, later remembering," this theory also fails. . . .

[first part] As has been said, the apparent object is a representation.
It is from this that memory arises.

[Question] If, in waking time as well as in a dream, representations may arise although there are no true objects, then, just as the world naturally knows that dream objects are non-existent, why is it not naturally known of the objects in waking time? . . .

[second part] Before we have awakened we cannot know
That what is seen in the dream does not exist.

After this, the purified knowledge of the world which is obtained takes precedence; according to the truth it is clearly understood that those objects are unreal. The principle is the same. . . .

[Conclusion]
The doctrines and implications of representation-only are of kinds infinitely diverse for decision and selection; difficult is it to fathom their profundities. Without being a Buddha, who is able to comprehend their total extent?

I, according to my ability,
Have briefly demonstrated the principles of representation-only;
Among these all [other] kinds,
Difficult to think, are reached by Buddhas [alone].

THE THIRTY VERSES ON THE MIND-ONLY DOCTRINE

[The *Triṁśikā* of Vasubandhu, translated from the Chinese version of Hsüan Tsang (596–664 c.e.) by Wing-tsit Chan.]

Because our ideation gives rise to the false ideas of the ego and *dharmas* (elements of existence),
There are various revulsions of appearances.
This ideation, depending on the mind, goes through certain transformations.
These transformations are of three kinds.

They are the consciousness of "ripening in a different life,"
The consciousness of intellection, and the consciousness of the discrimination of the objective world.
First of all, the *ālaya* (ideation-store) consciousness,
Which brings into fruition all seeds [or effects of good and evil deeds].

[In its state of pure consciousness], it is not conscious of its clingings and impressions.
In both its objective and subjective functions, it is always associated with touch,
Volition, feeling, thought, and cognition.
But it is always indifferent to its associations.

It is not affected by the darkness of ignorance or by the memory [of the distinction of good and evil].
The same is true in the case of touch, etc.
It is always flowing like a torrent,
And is abandoned in the state of the *arhat*.

The second transformation
Is called the mind-consciousness,
Which, while it depends on the ideation-store consciousness, in turn conditions it.
Its nature and characteristic consists of intellection.

It is always accompanied by the four evil desires,
Namely, ignorance of the self, view of the self [as being real and permanent],

Self-pride, and self-love,
And by touch, etc. [volition, feeling, thought, and cognition].

It is free from the memory [of the distinction of good and evil] but not from
the darkness of ignorance.
It follows its objects in their emergence and dependence.
It is abandoned by the *arhat* when he arrives at the state of complete extinc-
tion of sensation and thought,
And transcends this mundane world.

Next comes the third transformation,
Which consists of the last six categories of discrimination [the consciousness
of touch, sight, hearing, smell, taste, and the sense-center consciousness].
Its nature and characteristic consists of the discrimination of objects.
It is neither good nor evil.

Mental functions consist of general mental functions,
Particular mental functions, good functions, evil functions,
Minor evil functions, and indeterminate mental functions.
They all impress the mind in three ways [of joy, of suffering, and of indiffer-
ence].

General mental functions are touch, etc. [volition, feeling, thought, cogni-
tion].
Particular mental functions are desire,
Resolve, remembrance, concentration, and wisdom,
Each depending on different conditions.

Good mental functions are belief, sense of shame, bashfulness,
The three roots of the absence of covetousness, etc. [the absence of hatred
and the absence of attachment],
Energy, repose of mind, vigilance,
Equanimity, and non-injury.

Evil mental functions are covetousness, hatred,
Attachment, arrogance, doubt, and false view.
Minor evil mental functions are anger,
Enmity, concealment, affliction, envy, parsimony,

Deception, fraudulence, injury, pride,
Absence of the sense of shame, absence of bashfulness,
High-mindedness, low-mindedness,
Unbelief, indolence,

Idleness, forgetfulness,
Distraction, and non-discernment.
Indeterminate mental functions are repentance, drowsiness,
Reflection, and investigation, the former two composing a different class from
the latter.

Based on the mind-consciousness
The five consciousness [of the senses] manifest themselves in concomitance
  with the objective world.
Sometimes the senses manifest themselves together, and sometimes not,
Just as waves are dependent on the water.

The sense-center consciousness always arises and manifests itself,
Except when born in the realm of the absence of thought,
In the state of unconsciousness, in the two forms of concentration,
In sleep, and in that state where the spirit is depressed or absent.

Thus the various consciousness are but transformations.
That which discriminates and that which is discriminated
Are, because of this, both unreal.
For this reason, everything is mind only.

As the result of various ideations which serve as seeds,
Different transformations take place.
The revulsion-energy of these ideations
Gives rise to all sorts of discrimination.

Due to the habit-energy of various *karmas*
The habit-energy of both the six organs and their objects is influenced.
As the previous "ripening in a different life" is completed,
Succeeding "ripenings in a different life" are produced.

Because of false discriminations,
Various things are falsely discriminated.
What is grasped by such false discrimination
Has no self-nature whatsoever.

The self-nature which results from dependence on others
Is produced by the condition of discrimination.
The difference between the Absolute (perfect wisdom) and the dependent
Is that the former is eternally free from what is grasped by false discrimination.

Thus the Absolute and the dependent
Are neither the same nor different;
As in the case of impermanence and permanence,
The one can be seen only in the other.

From the three aspects of entity,
The three aspects of non-entity are established.
Therefore the Enlightened One abstrusely preached
That all *dharmas* have no entity.

The first is the non-entity of phenomenon.
The second is the non-entity of self-existence.
The last is the non-entity of the ultimate existence
Of the falsely discriminative ego and *dharmas* now to be eliminated.

The supreme truth of all *dharmas*
Is nothing other than the True Norm [suchness].
It is forever true to its nature,
Which is the true nature of mind-only.

Inasmuch as consciousness in its unawakened state
Is not in the abode of the reality of mind-only,
The six sense-organs, their objects, and the seeds of evil desires
Cannot be controlled and extirpated.

To hold something before oneself,
And to say that it is the reality of mind-only,
Is not the state of mind-only,
Because it is the result of grasping.

But when [the objective world which is] the basis of conditioning as well as the
    wisdom [which does the conditioning]
Are both eliminated,
The state of mind-only is realized,
Since the six sense-organs and their objects are no longer present.

Without any grasping and beyond thought
Is the supra-mundane wisdom [of *bodhisattva*hood].
Because of the abandonment of the habit-energy of various *karmas* and the six
    sense-organs as well as their objects,
The revulsion from relative knowledge to perfect wisdom is attained.

This is the realm of passionlessness or purity,
Which is beyond description, is good, and is eternal,
Where one is in the state of emancipation, peace, and joy.
This is the law of the Great Buddha.

Berkeley

George Berkeley (1685–1753) was born in Ireland and wrote his most significant works while he was still in his twenties. A devout Anglican, he later became bishop of Cloyne, and a strong religious commitment is evident in his work. A Treatise Concerning the Principles of Human Knowledge *(1710), from which the following selection is taken, is considered to be his most important contribution to metaphysics.*

Berkeley may be said to have developed the metaphysical implications of the view of his predecessor John Locke regarding the nature and source of human knowledge. If Locke's empiricism—the belief that all knowledge originates in sense-experience—is correct, then it follows that the senses do not give us independent material objects but rather only the stuff of our own ideas. What we call "things" are collections of sensations or ideas, and ideas can exist only in minds that perceive them. Berkeley's "subjective idealism" or immaterialism is summarized in his well-known phrase *esse est percipi*—"to be is to be perceived." When we say that something "exists" we mean, he argues, that we can see or feel it, and so on. We do not mean that we have access to a materiality that stands apart from our sensations and that is the basis of what we do directly experience. The only thing whose existence he denies, Berkeley asserts, "is that which *philosophers* call matter or corporeal substance." The things of the world, according to Berkeley, remain for us as indeed the things of the world—and we can rely upon the very perdurance of our ordered world because of the existence of that one being, God, whose existence does not depend upon our sensations.

Berkeley expounds his idealist position with great clarity and force. What initially appears to many of us as nonsensical soon takes on a plausibility that challenges deeply our natural disposition toward some form of metaphysical realism.

To Be Is to Be Perceived

It is evident to anyone who takes a survey of the objects of human knowledge, that they are either ideas (1) actually imprinted on the senses, or else such as are (2) perceived by attending to the passions and operations of the mind, or lastly (3) ideas formed by help of memory and imagination, either compounding, dividing, or barely representing those originally perceived in the aforesaid ways. By sight I have the ideas of lights and colors, with their several degrees and variations. By touch I perceive hard and soft, heat and cold, motion and resistance, and of all these more and less either as to quantity or degree. Smelling furnishes me with odors, the palate with tastes, and hearing conveys sounds to the mind in all their variety of tone and composition. And as several of these are observed to accompany each other, they come to be marked by one name, and so to be reputed as one thing. Thus, for example, a certain color, taste, smell, figure, and consistence, having been observed to go together, are accounted one distinct thing, signified by the name "apple." Other collections of ideas constitute a stone, a tree, a book, and the like sensible things; which, as they are pleasing or disagreeable, excite the passions of love, hatred, joy, grief, and so forth.

But besides all that endless variety of ideas or objects of knowledge, there is likewise something which knows or perceives them, and exercises divers operations, as willing, imagining, remembering, about them. This perceiving, active being is what I call *mind, spirit, soul,* or *myself.* By which words I do not denote any one of my ideas, but a thing entirely distinct from them wherein they exist, or, which is the same thing, whereby they are perceived; for the existence of an idea consists in being perceived.

That neither our thoughts, nor passions, nor ideas formed by the imagination, exist without the mind, is what everybody will allow. And it seems no less evident that the various sensations or ideas imprinted on the sense, however blended or combined together (that is, whatever objects they compose), cannot exist otherwise than in a mind perceiving them. I think an intuitive knowledge may be obtained of this by anyone that shall attend to what is meant by the term "exist" when applied to sensible things. The table I write on I say exists—that is, I see and feel it; and if I were out of my study I should say it existed—meaning thereby that if I was in my study I might perceive it, or that some other spirit actually does perceive it. There was an odor, that is, it was smelt; there was a sound, that is, it was heard; a color or figure, and it was perceived by sight or touch. This is all that I can understand by these and the like expressions. For as to what is said of the absolute existence of unthinking things without any relation to their being perceived, that seems perfectly unintelligible. Their *esse* is *percipi,* nor is it possible they should have any existence out of the minds or thinking things which perceive them.

From *A Treatise Concerning the Principles of Human Knowledge* by George Berkeley, in *The Empiricists* (n.d.). Reprinted with acknowledgement of Doubleday & Company, Inc.

It is indeed an opinion strangely prevailing amongst men, that houses, mountains, rivers, and in a word all sensible objects, have an existence, natural or real, distinct from their being perceived by the understanding. But with how great an assurance and acquiescence soever this principle may be entertained in the world, yet whoever shall find in his heart to call it in question may, if I mistake not, perceive it to involve a manifest contradiction. For what are the forementioned objects but the things we perceive by sense? and what do we perceive *besides our own ideas or sensations*? and is it not plainly repugnant that any one of these, or any combination of them, should exist unperceived?

If we thoroughly examine this tenet it will perhaps be found at bottom to depend on the doctrine of *abstract ideas*. For can there be a nicer strain of abstraction than to distinguish the existence of sensible objects from their being perceived, so as to conceive them existing unperceived? Light and colors, heat and cold, extension and figures—in a word the things we see and feel—what are they but so many sensations, notions, ideas, or impressions on the sense? And is it possible to separate, even in thought, any of these from perception? For my part, I might as easily divide a thing from itself. I may, indeed, divide in my thoughts, or conceive apart from each other, those things which perhaps I never perceived by sense so divided. Thus I imagine the trunk of a human body without the limbs, or conceive the smell of a rose without thinking on the rose itself. So far, I will not deny, I can abstract, if that may properly be called abstraction which extends only to the conceiving separately such objects as it is possible may really exist or be actually perceived asunder. But my conceiving or imagining power does not extend beyond the possibility of real existence or perception. Hence, as it is impossible for me to see or feel anything without an actual sensation of that thing, so it is impossible for me to conceive in my thoughts any sensible thing or object distinct from the sensation or perception of it.

Some truths there are so near and obvious to the mind that a man need only open his eyes to see them. Such I take this important one to be, to wit, that all the choir of heaven and furniture of the earth, in a word all those bodies which compose the mighty frame of the world, have not any subsistence without a mind, that their *being* is to be perceived or known; that consequently so long as they are not actually perceived by me, or do not exist in my mind or that of any other created spirit, they must either have no existence at all, or else subsist in the mind of some Eternal Spirit; it being perfectly unintelligible, and involving all the absurdity of abstraction, to attribute to any single part of them an existence independent of a spirit. To be convinced of which, the reader need only reflect and try to separate in his own thoughts the *being* of a sensible thing from its *being perceived*.

From what has been said it follows there is not any other substance than *spirit*, or that which perceives. But for the fuller proof of this point, let it be considered the sensible qualities are color, figure, motion, smell, taste, etc.—that is, the ideas perceived by sense. Now, for an idea to exist in an unperceiving thing is a manifest contradiction, for to have an idea is all one as to perceive; that therefore wherein color, figure, and the like qualities exist must perceive them; hence it is clear there can be no unthinking substance or *substratum* of those ideas.

But, say you, though the ideas themselves do not exist without the mind, yet there may be things *like* them, whereof they are copies or resemblances, which things exist without the mind in an unthinking substance. I answer, an idea can be like nothing but an idea; a color or figure can be like nothing but another color or figure. If we look but never so little into our thoughts, we shall find it impossible for us to conceive a likeness except only between our ideas. Again, I ask whether those supposed originals or external things, of which our ideas are the pictures or representations, be themselves perceivable or no? If they are, then they are ideas and we have gained our point; but if you say they are not, I appeal to anyone whether it be sense to assert a color is like something which is invisible; hard or soft, like something which is intangible; and so of the rest.

Some there are who make a distinction betwixt *primary* and *secondary* qualities. By the former they mean extension, figure, motion, rest, solidity or impenetrability, and number; by the latter they denote all other sensible qualities, as colors, sounds, tastes, and so forth. The ideas we have of these they acknowledge not to be the resemblances of anything existing without the mind, or unperceived, but they will have our ideas of the primary qualities to be patterns or images of things which exist without the mind, in an unthinking substance which they call *matter*. By *matter*, therefore, we are to understand an inert, senseless substance, in which extension, figure, and motion do actually subsist. But it is evident from what we have already shown, that extension, figure, and motion are only ideas existing in the mind, and that an idea can be like nothing but another idea, and that consequently neither they nor their archetypes can exist in an unperceiving substance. Hence, it is plain that the very notion of what is called *matter*, or *corporeal substance*, involves a contradiction in it.

They who assert that figure, motion, and the rest of the primary or original qualities do exist without the mind in unthinking substances, do at the same time acknowledge that color, sounds, heat, cold, and suchlike secondary qualities, do not; which they tell us are sensations existing in the mind alone, that depend on and are occasioned by the different size, texture, and motion of the minute particles of matter. This they take for an undoubted truth, which they can demonstrate beyond all exception. Now, if it be certain that those original qualities are inseparably united with the other sensible qualities, and not, even in thought, capable of being abstracted from them, it plainly follows that they exist only in the mind. But I desire anyone to reflect and try whether he can, by any abstraction of thought, conceive the extension and motion of a body without all other sensible qualities. For my own part, I see evidently that it is not in my power to frame an idea of a body extended and moving, but I must withal give it some color or other sensible quality which is acknowledged to exist only in the mind. In short, extension, figure, and motion, abstracted from all other qualities, are inconceivable. Where therefore the other sensible qualities are, there must these be also, to wit, in the mind and nowhere else.

Again, *great* and *small, swift* and *slow,* are allowed to exit nowhere without the mind, being entirely relative, and changing as the frame or position of the organs of sense varies. The extension therefore which exists without the mind is neither great nor small, the motion neither swift nor slow, that is, they are nothing at all. But, say you, they are extension in general, and motion in general: thus we see how much the tenet of extended movable substances existing without the mind depends on the strange doctrine of *abstract ideas*. And here I cannot but remark how nearly the vague and indeterminate description of matter or corporeal substance, which the modern philosophers are run into by their own principles, resembles that antiquated and so much ridiculed notion of *materia prime*, to be met with in Aristotle and his followers. Without extension solidity cannot be conceived; since therefore it has been shewn that extension exists not in an unthinking substance, the same must also be true of solidity.

That *number* is entirely the creature of the mind, even though the other qualities be allowed to exist without, will be evident to whoever considers that the same thing bears a different denomination of number as the mind views it with different respects. Thus, the same extension is one, or three, or thirty-six, according as the mind considers it with reference to a yard, a foot, or an inch. Number is so visibly relative, and dependent on men's understanding, that it is strange to think how anyone should give it an absolute existence without the mind. We say one book, one page, one line; all these are equally units, though some contain several of the others. And in each instance, it is plain, the unit relates to some particular combination of ideas arbitrarily put together by the mind. . . .

I shall farther add that, after the same manner as modern philosophers prove certain sensible qualities to have no existence in matter, or without the mind, the same thing may be likewise proved of all other sensible qualities whatsoever. Thus, for instance, it is said that heat and cold are affections only of the mind, and not at all patterns of real beings, existing in the corporeal substances which excite them, for that the same body which appears cold to one hand seems warm to another. Now, why may we not as well argue that figure and extension are not patterns or resemblances of qualities existing in matter, because to the same eye at different stations, or eyes of a different texture at the same station, they appear various, and cannot therefore be the images of anything settled and determinate without the mind? Again, it is proved that sweetness is not really in the sapid thing, because the thing remaining unaltered the sweetness is changed into bitter, as in case of a fever or otherwise vitiated palate. Is it not as reasonable to say that motion is not without the mind, since if the succession of ideas in the mind become swifter, the motion, it is acknowledged, shall appear slower without any alteration in any external object?
. . .

If we inquire into what the most accurate philosophers declare themselves to mean by *material substance*, we shall find them acknowledge they have no other meaning annexed to those sounds but the idea of *Being in general*, together with the relative notion of its supporting accidents. The general idea of Being appeareth to me the most abstract and incomprehensible of all other; and as for its supporting accidents, this, as we have just now observed, cannot be understood in the common sense of those words; it must therefore be taken in some other sense, but what that is they do not explain. So that when I consider the two parts or branches which make the signification of the words *material substance*, I am convinced there is no distinct meaning annexed to them. But why should we trouble ourselves any farther, in discussing this material *substratum* or support of figure and motion, and other sensible qualities? Does it not suppose they have an existence without the mind? And is not this a direct repugnancy, and altogether inconceivable?

But though it were possible that solid, figured, movable substances may exist without the mind, corresponding to the ideas we have of bodies, yet how is it possible for us to know this? Either we must know it by sense or by reason. As for our senses, by them we have the knowledge only of our sensations, ideas, or those things that are immediately perceived by sense, call them what you will; but they do not inform us that things exist without the mind, or unperceived, like to those which are perceived. This the materialists themselves acknowledge. It remains therefore that if we have any knowledge at all of external things, it must be by reason, inferring their existence from what is immediately perceived by sense. But what reason can induce us to believe the existence of bodies without the mind, from what we perceive, since the very patrons of matter themselves do not pretend there is any necessary connection betwixt them and our ideas? I say it is granted on all hands (and what happens in dreams, frenzies, and the like, puts it beyond dispute) that *it is possible we might be affected with all the ideas we have now, though there were no bodies existing without, resembling them.* Hence, it is evident the supposition of external bodies is not necessary for the producing our ideas; since it is granted they are produced sometimes, and might possibly be produced always in the same order we see them in at present, without their concurrence. . . .

I am afraid I have given cause to think I am needlessly prolix in handling this subject. For, to what purpose is it to dilate on that which may be demonstrated with the utmost evidence in a line or two, to anyone that is capable of the least reflection? It is but looking into your own thoughts, and so trying whether you can conceive it possible for a sound, or figure, or motion, or color to exist without the mind or unperceived. This easy trial may perhaps make you see that what you contend for is a downright contradiction. Insomuch that I am content to put the whole upon this issue: if you can but conceive it possible for one extended movable substance, or, in general, for any one idea, or anything like an idea, to exist otherwise than in a mind perceiving it, I shall readily give up the cause; and, as for all that compages of external bodies you contend for, I shall grant you its existence, though you cannot either give me any reason why you believe it exists, or assign any use to it when it is supposed to exist. I say, the bare possibility of your opinion's being true shall pass for an argument that it is so.

But, say you, surely there is nothing easier than for me to imagine trees, for instance, in a park, or books existing in a closet, and nobody by to perceive them. I answer, you may so, there is no difficulty in it; but what is all this, I beseech you, more than framing in your mind certain ideas which you call books and trees, and the same time omitting to frame the idea of anyone that may perceive them? But do not you yourself perceive or think of them all the while? This therefore is nothing to the purpose; it only shews you have the power of imagining or forming ideas in your mind: but it doth not shew that you can conceive it possible the objects of your thought may exist without the mind. To make out this, it is necessary that you conceive them existing unconceived or unthought of, which is a manifest repugnancy. When we do our utmost to conceive the existence of external bodies, we are all the while only contemplating our own ideas. But the mind taking no notice of itself, is deluded to think it can and doth conceive bodies existing unthought of or without the mind, though at the same time they are apprehended by or exist in itself. A little attention will discover to anyone the truth and evidence of what is here said, and make it unnecessary to insist on any other proofs against the existence of *material substance.* . . .

I find I can excite ideas in my mind at pleasure, and vary and shift the scene as oft as I think fit. It is no more than willing, and straightway this or that idea arises in my fancy; and by the same power it is obliterated and makes way for another. This making and unmaking of ideas doth very properly denominate the mind active. Thus much is certain and grounded on experience; but when we think of unthinking agents or of exciting ideas exclusive of volition, we only amuse ourselves with words.

But, whatever power I may have over my own thoughts, I find the ideas actually perceived by sense have not a like dependence on my will. When in broad daylight I open my eyes, it is not in my power to choose whether I shall see or no, or to determine what particular objects shall present themselves to my view; and so likewise as to the hearing and other senses, the ideas imprinted on them are not creatures of my will. There is therefore some other will or spirit that produces them.

The ideas of sense are more strong, lively, and distinct than those of the imagination; they have likewise a steadiness, order, and coherence, and are not excited at random, as those which are the effects of human wills often are, but in a regular train or series, the admirable connection whereof sufficiently testifies the wisdom and benevolence of its Author. Now the set rules or established methods wherein the mind we depend on excites in us the ideas of sense, are called the *laws of nature;* and these we learn by experience, which teaches us that such and such ideas are attended with such and such other ideas, in the ordinary course of things.

This gives us a sort of foresight which enables us to regulate our actions for the benefit of life. And without this we should be eternally at a loss: we could not know how to act anything that might procure us the least pleasure, or remove the least pain of sense. That food nourishes, sleep refreshes, and fire warms us; that to sow in the seed-time is the way to reap in the harvest; and, in general, that to obtain such or such ends, such or such means are conducive—all this we know, not by discovering any necessary connection between our ideas, but only by the observation of the settled laws of nature, without which we should be all in uncertainty and confusion, and a grown man no more know how to manage himself in the affairs of life than an infant just born. . . .

The ideas imprinted on the senses by the Author of nature are called *real things;* and those excited in the imagination, being less regular, vivid, and constant, are more properly termed *ideas,* or *images* of *things,* which they copy and represent. But then our sensations, be they never so vivid and distinct, are nevertheless ideas, that is, they exist in the mind, or are perceived by it, as truly as the ideas of its own framing. The ideas of sense are allowed to have more reality in them, that is, to be more strong, orderly, and coherent than the creatures of the mind; but this is no argument that they exist without the mind. They are also less dependent on the spirit, or thinking substance which perceives them, in that they are excited by the will of another and more powerful spirit; yet still they are *ideas*, and certainly no idea, whether faint or strong, can exist otherwise than in a mind perceiving it.

Before we proceed any farther it is necessary we spend some time in answering objections which may probably be made against the principles we have hitherto laid down. In doing of which, if I seem too prolix to those of quick apprehensions, I hope it may be pardoned, since all men do not equally apprehend things of this nature, and I am willing to be understood by everyone.

First, then, it will be objected that by the foregoing principles all that is real and substantial in nature is banished out of the world, and instead thereof a chimerical scheme of *ideas* takes place. All things that exist, exist only in the mind, that is, they are purely notional. What therefore becomes of the sun, moon, and stars? What must we think of houses, rivers, mountains, trees, stones; nay, even of our own bodies? Are all these but so many chimeras and illusions on the fancy? To all which, and whatever else of the same sort may be objected, I answer that by the principles premised we are not deprived of any one thing in nature. Whatever we see, feel, hear, or anywise conceive or understand remains as secure as ever, and is as real as ever. . . .

I do not argue against the existence of any one thing that we can apprehend either by sense or reflection. That the things I see with my eyes and touch with my hands do exist, really exist, I make not the least question. The only thing whose existence we deny is that which *philosophers* call matter or corporeal substance. And in doing of this there is no damage done to the rest of mankind, who, I dare say, will never miss it. The atheist indeed will want the color of an empty name to support his impiety; and the philosophers may possibly find they have lost a great handle for trifling and disputation.

If any man thinks this detracts from the existence or reality of things, he is very far from understanding what hath been premised in the plainest terms I could think of. Take here an abstract of what has been said. There are spiritual substances, minds, or human souls, which will or excite ideas in themselves at pleasure; but these are faint, weak, and unsteady in respect of others they perceive by sense— which, being impressed upon them according to certain rules or laws of nature, speak themselves the effects of a mind more powerful and wise than human spirits. These latter are said to have more *reality* in them than the former; by which is meant that they are more affecting, orderly, and distinct, and that they are not fictions of the mind perceiving them. And in this sense the sun that I see by day is the real sun, and that which I imagine by night is the idea of the former. In the sense here given of "reality" it is evident that every vegetable, star, mineral, and in general each part of the mundane system, is as much as a real being by our principles as by any other. Whether others mean anything by the term "reality" different from what I do, I entreat them to look into their own thoughts and see. . . .

But after all, say you, it sounds very harsh to say we eat and drink ideas, and are clothed with ideas. I acknowledge it does so; the word "idea" not being used in common discourse to signify the several combinations of sensible qualities which are called "things"; and it is certain that any expression which varies from the familiar use of language will seem harsh and ridiculous. But this doth not concern the truth of the proposition, which in other words is no more than to say, we are fed and clothed with those things which we perceive immediately by our senses. The hardness or softness, the color, taste, warmth, figure, or suchlike qualities, which combined together constitute the several sorts of victuals and apparel, have been shewn to exist only in the mind that perceives them; and this is all that is meant by calling them "ideas"; which word if it was as ordinarily used as "things," would sound no harsher nor more ridiculous than it. I am not for disputing about the propriety, but the truth of the expression. If therefore you agree with me that we eat and drink and are clad with the immediate objects of sense, which cannot exist unperceived or without the mind, I shall readily grant it is more proper or conformable to custom that they should be called things rather than ideas.

If it be demanded why I make use of the word "idea," and do not rather in compliance with custom call them "thing"; I answer, I do it for two reasons:—first, because the term "thing" in contradistinction to "idea," is generally supposed to denote somewhat existing without the mind; secondly, because "thing" hath a more comprehensive signification than "idea," including spirit or thinking things as well as ideas. Since therefore the objects of sense exist only in the mind, and are withal thoughtless and inactive, I chose to mark them by the word "idea," which implies those properties. . . .

. . . It may perhaps be objected that—though it be clear from what has been said that there can be no such thing as an inert, senseless, extended, solid, figured, movable substance existing without the mind, such as philosophers describe matter— yet, if any man shall leave out of his idea of matter the positive ideas of extension, figure, solidity and motion, and say that he means only by that word an inert, senseless substance, that exists without the mind or unperceived, which is the *occasion of our ideas,* or at the presence whereof God is pleased to excite ideas in us: it doth not appear but that matter taken in this sense may possibly exist. In answer to which I say, first, that it seems no less absurd to suppose a substance without accidents, than it is to suppose accidents without a substance. But secondly, though we should grant this unknown substance may possibly exist, yet where can it be supposed to be? That it exists not in the mind is agreed; and that it exists not in place is no less certain— since all place or extension exists only in the mind, as hath been already proved. It remains therefore that it exists nowhere at all. . . .

You will perhaps say that matter, though it be not perceived by us, is nevertheless perceived by God, to whom it is the occasion of exciting ideas in our minds. For, say you, since we observe our sensations to be imprinted in an orderly and constant manner, it is but reasonable to suppose there are certain constant and regular occasions of their being produced. That is to say, that there are certain permanent and distinct parcels of matter, corresponding to our ideas, which, though they do not excite them in our minds, or anywise immediately affect us, as being altogether passive and unperceivable to us, they are nevertheless to God, by whom they are perceived, as it were so many occasions to remind Him when and what ideas to imprint on our minds; that so things may go on in a constant uniform manner.

In answer to this, I observe that, as the notion of matter is here stated, the question is no longer concerning the existence of a thing distinct from *spirit* and *idea*, from perceiving and being perceived; but whether there are not certain ideas of I know not what sort, in the mind of God which are so many marks or notes that direct Him how to produce sensations in our minds in a constant and regular method—much after the same manner as a musician is directed by the notes of music to produce that harmonious train and composition of sound which is called a tune, though they who hear the music do not perceive the notes, and may be entirely ignorant of them. But, this notion of matter seems too extravagant to deserve a confutation. Besides, it is in effect no objection against what we have advanced, to wit, that there is no senseless unperceived substance. . . .

It were a mistake to think that what is here said derogates in the least from the reality of things. It is acknowledged, on the received principles, that extension, motion, and in a word all sensible qualities have need of a support, as not being able to subsist by themselves. But the objects perceived by sense are allowed to be nothing but combinations of those qualities, and consequently cannot subsist by themselves. Thus far it is agreed on all hands. So that in denying the things perceived by sense an existence independent of a substance of support wherein they may exist, we detract nothing from the received opinion of their *reality*, and are guilty of no innovation in that respect. All the difference is that, according to us, the unthinking beings perceived by sense have no existence distinct from being perceived, and cannot therefore exist in any other substance than those unextended indivisible substances or *spirits* which act and think and perceive them; whereas philosophers vulgarly hold that the sensible qualities do exist in an inert, extended, unperceiving substance which they call *matter*, to which they attribute a natural subsistence, exterior to all thinking beings, or distinct from being perceived by any mind whatsoever, even the eternal mind of the Creator, wherein they suppose only ideas of the corporeal substances created by Him; if indeed they allow them to be at all created.

Russell

Around the beginning of the twentieth century there was a strong reaction among many philosophers, especially in the Anglo-American world, to metaphysical idealism in all its various forms. These new realists, as they were called, were motivated to a considerable extent, it seems, by what they regarded to be the inability of metaphysical idealism to make sense out of science, with its implicit faith in the existence of an independent, real world. They wanted to show how perception does give us genuine knowledge of objects. They agreed with their colleague, the British philosopher G. E. Moore, who in his "Refutation of Idealism" argued that "if sensations are not cases of awareness of objects, no awareness is ever awareness of anything, and we cannot be aware of other persons or even of ourselves and our own sensations."

Moore and Bertrand Russell were among the strongest realist voices of the time. Russell developed his realism from a so-called phenomenalistic theory of perception and the application of what he took to be "the logical-analytic method," Moore from a common sense notion of perception and a rather close linguistic analysis of the meaning of various key concepts.

The main problem that philosophical realism faces is how to account for errors in perception and how to avoid the possibility that all of perception is systematically misleading regarding the actual state of the world insofar as, due to the perspectival nature of sense-experience—the fact that anything is always seen from one standpoint or other—all our knowledge is necessarily partial and incomplete.

In the selection from *Our Knowledge of the External World* (1914) that follows, Russell formulates his arguments in a very lucid manner and clearly embodies the values of precision in thinking that he extols.

The Reality of the External World

Philosophy may be approached by many roads, but one of the oldest and most travelled is the road which leads through doubt as to the reality of the world of sense. In Indian mysticism, in Greek and modern monistic philosophy from Parmenides onward, in Berkeley, in modern physics, we find sensible appearance criticised and condemned for a bewildering variety of motives. The mystic condemns it on the ground of immediate knowledge of a more real and significant world behind the veil; Parmenides and Plato condemn it because its continual flux is thought inconsistent with the unchanging nature of the abstract entities revealed by logical analysis; Berkeley brings several weapons, but his chief is the subjectivity of sense-data, their dependence upon the organisation and point of view of the spectator; while modern physics, on the basis of sensible evidence itself, maintains a mad dance of electrons which has, superficially at least, very little resemblance to the immediate object of sight or touch.

Every one of these lines of attack raises vital and interesting problems.

The mystic, so long as he merely reports a positive revelation, cannot be refuted; but when he *denies* reality to objects of sense, he may be questioned as to what he means by "reality," and may be asked how their unreality follows from the supposed reality of his supersensible world. In answering these questions, he is led to a logic which merges into that of Parmenides and Plato and the idealist tradition. . . .

Berkeley's attack, as reinforced by the physiology of the sense-organs and nerves and brain, is very powerful. I think it must be admitted as probable that the immediate objects of sense depend for their existence upon physiological conditions in ourselves, and that, for example, the coloured surfaces which we see cease to exist when we shut our eyes. But it would be a mistake to infer that they are dependent upon mind, not real while we see them, or not the sole basis for our knowledge of the external world. This line of argument will be developed in the present lecture. . . .

In this lecture, I wish to apply the logical-analytic method to one of the oldest problems of philosophy, namely, the problem of our knowledge of the external world. What I have to say on this problem does not amount to an answer of a definite and dogmatic kind; it amounts only to an analysis and statement of the questions involved, with an indication of the directions in which evidence may be sought. But although not yet a definite solution, what can be said at present seems to me to throw a completely new light on the problem, and to be indispensable, not only in seeking the answer, but also in the preliminary question as to what parts of our problem may possibly have an ascertainable answer.

From *Our Knowledge of the External World*, Bertrand Russell, a Mentor Book edition (New American Library, New York, 1960). Reprinted by permission of George Allen and Unwin, Ltd., London, and with acknowledgment to the Bertrand Russell Peace Foundation and to Routledge, Chapman & Hall, Ltd., London.

In every philosophical problem, our investigation starts from what may be called "data," by which I mean matters of common knowledge, vague, complex, inexact, as common knowledge always is, but yet somehow commanding our assent as on the whole and in some interpretation pretty certainly true. In the case of our present problem, the common knowledge involved is of various kinds. There is first our acquaintance with particular objects of daily life—furniture, houses, towns, other people, and so on. Then there is the extension of such particular knowledge to particular things outside our personal experience, through history and geography, newspapers, etc. And lastly, there is the systematisation of all this knowledge of particulars by means of physical science, which derives immense persuasive force from its astonishing power of foretelling the future. We are quite wiling to admit that there may be errors of detail in this knowledge, but we believe them to be discoverable and corrigible by the methods which have given rise to our beliefs, and we do not, as practical men, entertain for a moment the hypothesis that the whole edifice may be built on insecure foundations. In the main, therefore, and without absolute dogmatism as to this or that special portion, we may accept this mass of common knowledge as affording data for our philosophical analysis. . . .

The first thing that appears when we begin to analyse our common knowledge is that some of it is derivative, while some is primitive; that is to say, there is some that we only believe because of something else from which it has been inferred in some sense, though not necessarily in a strict logical sense, while other parts are believed on their own account, without the support of any outside evidence. It is obvious that the senses give knowledge of the latter kind: the immediate facts perceived by sight or touch or hearing do not need to be proved by argument, but are completely self-evident. Psychologists, however, have made us aware that what is actually given in sense is much less than most people would naturally suppose, and that much of what at first sight seems to be given is really inferred. This applies especially in regard to our space-perceptions. For instance, we instinctively infer the "real" size and shape of a visible object from its apparent size and shape, according to its distance and our point of view. When we hear a person speaking, our actual sensations usually miss a great deal of what he says, and we supply its place by unconscious inference; in a foreign language, where this process is more difficult, we find ourselves apparently grown deaf, requiring, for example, to be much nearer the stage at a theatre than would be necessary in our own country. Thus the first step in the analysis of data, namely, the discovery of what is really given in sense, is full of difficulty. We will, however, not linger on this point; so long as existence is realised, the exact outcome does not make any very great difference in our main problem.

The next step in our analysis must be the consideration of how the derivative parts of our common knowledge arise. Here we become involved in a somewhat puzzling entanglement of logic and psychology. Psychologically, a belief may be called derivative whenever it is caused by one or more other beliefs, or by some fact of sense which is not simply what the belief asserts. Derivative beliefs in this sense constantly arise without any process of logical inference, merely by association of ideas or some equally extra-logical process. From the expression of a man's face we judge as to what he is feeling: we say we *see* that he is angry, when in fact we only see a frown. We do not judge as to his state of mind by any logical process: the judgment grows up, often without our being able to say what physical mark of emotion we actually saw. In such a case, the knowledge is derivative psychologically; but logically it is in a sense primitive, since it is not the result of any logical deduction. There may or may not be a possible deduction leading to the same result, but whether there is or not, we certainly do not employ it. If we call a belief "logically primitive" when it is not actually arrived at by a logical inference, then innumerable beliefs are logically primitive which psychologically are derivative. The separation of these two kinds of primitivenesses is vitally important to our present discussion.

When we reflect upon the beliefs which are logically but not psychologically primitive, we find that, unless they can on reflection be deduced by a logical process from beliefs which are also psychologically primitive, our confidence in their truth tends to diminish the more we think about them. We naturally believe, for example, that tables and chairs, trees and mountains, are still there when we turn our backs upon them. I do not wish for a moment to maintain that this is certainly not the case, but I do maintain that the question whether it is the case is not to be settled off-hand on any supposed ground of obviousness. The belief that they persist is, in all men except a few philosophers, logically primitive, but it is not psychologically primitive; psychologically, it arises only through our having seen those tables and chairs, trees and mountains. As soon as the question is seriously raised whether, because we have seen them, we have a right to suppose that they are there still, we feel that some kind of argument must be produced, and that if none is forthcoming, our belief can be no more than a pious opinion. We do not feel this as regards the immediate objects of sense: there they are, and, as far as their momentary existence is concerned, no further argument is required. There is accordingly more need of justifying our psychologically derivative beliefs than of justifying those that are primitive.

We are thus led to a somewhat vague distinction between what we may call "hard" data and "soft" data. This distinction is a matter of degree, and must not be pressed; but if not taken too seriously it may help to make the situation clear. I mean by "hard" data those which resist the solvent influence of critical reflection, and by "soft" data those which, under the operation of this process, become to our minds more or less doubtful. The hardest of hard data are of two sorts: the particular facts of sense, and the general truths of logic. The more we reflect upon these, the more we realise exactly what they are, and exactly what a doubt concerning them really means, the more luminously certain do they become. *Verbal* doubt concerning even these is possible, but verbal doubt may occur when what is nominally being doubted is not really in our thoughts, and only words are actually present to our minds. Real doubt, in these two cases, would, I think, be pathological. At any rate, to me they seem quite certain, and I shall assume that you agree with me in this. Without this assumption, we are in danger of falling into that universal scepticism which, as we saw, is as barren as it is irrefutable. If we are to continue philosophising, we must make our bow to the sceptical hypothesis, and, while admitting the elegant terseness of its philosophy, proceed to the consideration of other hypotheses which, though perhaps not certain, have at least as good a right to our respect as the hypothesis of the sceptic.

Applying our distinction of "hard" and "soft" data to psychologically derivative but logically primitive beliefs, we shall find that most, if not all, are to be classed as soft data. They may be found, on reflection, to be capable of logical proof, and they then again become believed, but no longer as data. As data, though entitled to a certain limited respect, they cannot be placed on a level with the facts of sense or the laws of logic. The kind of respect which they deserve seems to me such as to warrant us in hoping, though not too confidently, that the hard data may prove them to be at least probable. Also, if the hard data are found to throw no light whatever upon their truth or falsehood, we are justified, I think, in giving rather more weight to the hypothesis of their truth than to the hypothesis of their falsehood. For the present, however, let us confine ourselves to the hard data, with a view to discovering what sort of world can be constructed by their means alone.

Our data now are primarily the facts of sense (i.e. of *our own* sense-data) and the laws of logic. But even the severest scrutiny will allow some additions to this slender stock. Some facts of memory—especially of recent memory—seem to have the highest degree of certainty. Some introspective facts are as certain as any facts of sense. And facts of sense themselves must, for our present purposes, be interpreted with a certain latitude. Spatial and temporal relations must sometimes be included, for example in the case of a swift motion falling wholly within the specious present. And some facts of comparison, such as the likeness or unlikeness of two shades of colour, are certainly to be included among hard data. Also we must remember that the distinction of hard and soft data is psychological and subjective, so that, if there are other minds than our own—which at our present stage must be held doubtful—the catalogue of hard data may be different for them from what it is for us.

Certain common beliefs are undoubtedly excluded from hard data. Such is the belief which led us to introduce the distinction, namely, that sensible objects in general persist when we are not perceiving them. Such also is the belief in other people's minds: this belief is obviously derivative from our perception of their bodies, and is felt to demand logical justification as soon as we become aware of its derivativeness. Belief in what is reported by the testimony of others, including all that we learn from books, is of course involved in the doubt as to whether other people have minds at all. Thus the world from which our reconstruction is to begin is very fragmentary. The best we can say for it is that it is slightly more extensive than the world at which Descartes arrived by a similar process, since that world contained nothing except himself and his thoughts.

We are now in a position to understand and state the problem of our knowledge of the external world, and to remove various misunderstandings which have obscured the meaning of the problem. The problem really is: Can the existence of anything other than our own hard data be inferred from the existence of those data? But before considering this problem, let us briefly consider what the problem is *not*.

When we speak of the "external" world in this discussion, we must not mean "spatially external," unless "space" is interpreted in a peculiar and recondite manner.

The immediate objects of sight, the coloured surfaces which make up the visible world, are spatially external in the natural meaning of this phrase. We feel them to be "there" as opposed to "here"; without making any assumption of an existence other than hard data, we can more or less estimate the distance of a coloured surface. It seems probable that distances, provided they are not too great, are actually given more or less roughly in sight; but whether this is the case or not, ordinary distances can certainly be estimated approximately by means of the data of sense alone. The immediately given world is spatial, and is further not wholly contained within the sense-data which constitute what we perceive of our own bodies. Thus our knowledge of what is external in this sense is not open to doubt.

Another form in which the question is often put is: "Can we know of the existence of any reality which is independent of ourselves?" This form of the question suffers from the ambiguity of the two words "independent" and "self." To take the Self first: the question as to what is to be reckoned part of the Self and what is not, is a very difficult one. Among many other things which we may mean by the Self, two may be selected as specially important, namely, (1) the bare subject which thinks and is aware of objects, (2) the whole assemblage of things that would necessarily cease to exist if our lives came to an end. The bare subject, if it exists at all, is an inference, and is not part of the data; therefore this meaning of Self may be ignored in our present inquiry. The second meaning is difficult to make precise, since we hardly know what things depend upon our lives for their existence. And in this form, the definition of Self introduces the word "depend," which raises the same questions as are raised by the word "independent." Let us therefore take up the word "independent," and return to the Self later.

When we say that one thing is "independent" of another, we may mean either that it is logically possible for the one to exist without the other, or that there is no causal relation between the two such that the one only occurs as the effect of the other. The only way, so far as I know, in which one thing can be *logically* dependent upon another is when the other is *part* of the one. The existence of a book, for example, is logically dependent upon that of its pages: without the pages there would be no book. Thus in this sense the question, "Can we know of the existence of any reality which is independent of ourselves?" reduces to the question, "Can we know of the existence of any reality of which our Self is not part?" In this form, the question brings us back to the problem of defining the Self; but I think, however the Self may be defined, even when it is taken as the bare subject, it cannot be supposed to be part of the immediate object of sense; thus in this form of the question we must admit that we can know of the existence of realities independent of ourselves.

The question of causal dependence is much more difficult. To know that one kind of thing is causally independent of another, we must know that it actually occurs without the other. Now it is fairly obvious that, whatever legitimate meaning we give to the Self, our thoughts and feelings are causally dependent upon ourselves, *i.e.* do not occur when there is no Self for them to belong to. But in the case of objects of sense this is not obvious; indeed, as we saw, the common-sense view is that such objects persist in the absence of any percipient. If this is the case, then they are causally independent of ourselves; if not, not. Thus in this form the question reduces to the question whether we can know that objects of sense, or any other objects not our own thoughts and feelings, exist at times when we are not perceiving them. This form, in which the difficult word "independent" no longer occurs, is the form in which we stated the problem a minute ago.

Our question in the above form raises two distinct problems, which it is important to keep separate. First, can we know that objects of sense, or very similar objects, exist at times when we are not perceiving them? Secondly, if this cannot be known, can we know that other objects, inferable from objects of sense but not necessarily resembling them, exist either when we are perceiving the objects of sense or at any other time? This latter problem arises in philosophy as the problem of the "thing in itself," and in science as the problem of matter as assumed in physics. We will consider this latter problem first.

Owing to the fact that we feel passive in sensation, we naturally suppose that our sensations have outside causes. When I speak of the sensation or sensible object, it must be understood that I do not mean such a thing as a table, which is both visible and tangible, can be seen by many people at once, and is more or less permanent. What I mean is just that patch of colour which is momentarily seen when we look at the table, or just that particular hardness which is felt when we press it, or just that particular sound which is heard when we rap it. Each of these I call a sensible object or a sensation. Now our sense of passivity, if it really afforded any argument, would only tend to show that sensible objects must have outside causes, and both the thing-in-itself of philosophy and the matter of physics present themselves as outside causes of the sensible object. What are the grounds for this common opinion?

In each case, I think, the opinion has resulted from the combination of a belief that *something* which can persist independently of our consciousness makes itself known in sensation, with the fact that our sensations often change in ways which seem to depend upon us rather than upon anything which would be supposed to persist independently of us. At first, we believe unreflectingly that everything is as it seems to be, and that, if we shut our eyes, the objects we had been seeing remain as they were though we no longer see them. But there are arguments against this view, which have generally been thought conclusive. It is extraordinarily difficult to see just what the arguments prove; but if we are to make any progress with the problem of the external world, we must try to make up our minds as to these arguments.

A table viewed from one place presents a different appearance from that which it presents from another place. This is the language of common sense, but this language already assumes that there is a real table of which we see the appearances. Let us try to state what is known in terms of sensible objects alone, without any element of hypothesis. We find that as we walk round the table, we perceive a series of gradually changing visible objects. But in speaking of "walking round the table," we have still retained the hypothesis that there is a single table connected with all the appearances. What we ought to say is that, while we have those muscular and other sensations which make us say we are walking, our visual sensations change in a continuous way, so that, for example, a striking patch of colour is not suddenly replaced by something wholly different, but is replaced by an insensible gradation of slightly different colours with slightly different shapes. This is what we really know by experience, when we have freed our minds from the assumption of permanent "things" with changing appearances. What is really known is a correlation of muscular and other bodily sensations with changes in visual sensations.

But walking round the table is not the only way of altering its appearance. We can shut one eye, or put on blue spectacles, or look through a microscope. All these operations, in various ways, alter the visual appearance which we call that of the table. More distant objects will also alter their appearance if (as we say) the state of the atmosphere changes—if there is fog or rain or sunshine. Physiological changes also alter the appearance of things. If we assume the world of common sense, all these changes, including those attributed to physiological causes, are changes in the intervening medium. It is not quite so easy as in the former case to reduce this set of facts to a form in which nothing is assumed beyond sensible objects. Anything intervening between ourselves and what we see must be invisible: our view in every direction is bounded by the nearest visible object. It might be objected that a dirty pane of glass, for example, is visible although we can see things through it. But in this case we really see a spotted patchwork: the dirtier specks in the glass are visible, while the cleaner parts are invisible and allow us to see what is beyond. Thus the discovery that the intervening medium affects the appearances of things cannot be made by means of the sense of sight alone. . . .

The first thing to realise is that there are no such things as "illusions of sense." Objects of sense, even when they occur in dreams, are the most indubitably real objects known to us. What, then, makes us call them unreal in dreams? Merely the unusual nature of their connection with other objects of sense. I dream that I am in America, but I wake up and find myself in England without those intervening days on the Atlantic which, alas! are inseparably connected with a "real" visit to America. Objects of sense are called "real" when they have the kind of connection with other objects of sense which experience has led us to regard as normal; when they fail in this, they are called "illusions." But what is illusory is only the inferences to which they give rise; in themselves, they are every bit as real as the objects of waking life. And conversely, the sensible objects of waking life must not be expected to have any more intrinsic reality than those of dreams. Dreams and waking life, in our first efforts at construction, must be treated with equal respect; it is only by some reality not *merely* sensible that dreams can be condemned. . . .

It must be conceded to begin with that the argument in favour of the existence of other people's minds cannot be conclusive. A phantasm of our dreams will appear to have a mind—a mind to be annoying, as a rule. It will give unexpected answers, refuse to conform to our desires, and show all those other signs of intelligence to which we are accustomed in the acquaintances of our waking hours. And yet, when we are awake, we do not believe that the phantasm was, like the appearances of people in waking life, representative of a private world to which we have no direct access. If we are to believe this of the people we meet when we are awake, it must be on some ground short of demonstration, since it is obviously possible that what we call waking life may be only an unusually persistent and recurrent nightmare. It may be that our imagination brings forth all that other people seem to say to us, all that we read in books, all the daily, weekly, monthly, and quarterly journals that distract our thoughts, all the advertisements of soap and all the speeches of politicians. This *may* be true, since it cannot be shown to be false, yet no one can really believe it. Is there any *logical* ground for regarding this possibility as improbable? Or is there nothing beyond habit and prejudice?

The minds of other people are among our data, in the very wide sense in which we used the word at first. That is to say, when we first begin to reflect, we find ourselves already believing in them, not because of any argument, but because the belief is natural to us. It is, however, a psychologically derivative belief, since it results from observation of people's bodies; and along with other such beliefs, it does not belong to the hardest of hard data, but becomes, under the influence of philosophic reflection, just sufficiently questionable to make us desire some argument connecting it with the facts of sense.

The obvious argument is, of course, derived from analogy. Other people's bodies behave as ours do when we have certain thoughts and feelings; hence, by analogy, it is natural to suppose that such behaviour is connected with thoughts and feelings like our own. Someone says, "Look out!" and we find we are on the point of being killed by a motor-car; we therefore attribute the words we heard to the person in question having seen the motor-car first, in which case there are existing things of which we are not directly conscious. But this whole scene, with our inference, may occur in a dream, in which case the inference is generally considered to be mistaken. Is there anything to make the argument from analogy more cogent when we are (as we think) awake?

The analogy in waking life is only to be preferred to that in dreams on the ground of its greater extent and consistency. If a man were to dream every night about a set of people whom he never met by day, who had consistent characters and grew older with the lapse of years, he might, like the man in Calderon's play, find it difficult to decide which was the dream-world and which was the so-called "real" world. It is only the failure of our dreams to form a consistent whole either with each other or with waking life that makes us condemn them. Certain uniformities are observed in waking life, while dreams seem quite erratic. The natural hypothesis would be that demons and the spirits of the dead visit us while we sleep; but the modern mind, as a rule, refuses to entertain this view, though it is hard to see what could be said against it. On the other hand, the mystic, in moments of illumination, seems to awaken from a sleep which has filled all his mundane life: the whole world of sense becomes phantasmal, and he sees, with the clarity and convincingness that belong to our morning realisation after dreams, a world utterly different from that of our daily cares and troubles. Who shall condemn him? Who shall justify him? Or who shall justify the seeming solidity of the common objects among which we suppose ourselves to live?

The hypothesis that other people have minds must, I think, be allowed to be not susceptible of any very strong support form the analogical argument. At the same time, it is a hypothesis which systematises a vast body of facts and never leads to any consequences which there is reason to think false. There is therefore nothing to be said against its truth, and good reason to use it as a working hypothesis. When once it is admitted, it enables us to extend our knowledge of the sensible world by testimony, and thus leads to the system of private worlds which we assumed in our hypothetical construction. In actual fact, whatever we may try to think as philosophers, we cannot help believing in the minds of other people, so that the question whether our belief is justified has a merely speculative interest. And if it is justified, then there is no further difficulty of principle in that vast extension of our knowledge, beyond our own private data, which we find in science and common sense.

This somewhat meagre conclusion must not be regarded as the whole outcome of our long discussion. The problem of the connection of sense with objective reality has commonly been dealt with from a standpoint which did not carry initial doubt so far as we have carried it; most writers, consciously or unconsciously, have assumed that the testimony of others is to be admitted, and therefore (at least by implication) that others have minds. Their difficulties have arisen after this admission, from the differences in the appearance which one physical object presents to two people at the same time, or to one person at two times between which it cannot be supposed to have changed. Such difficulties have made people doubtful how far objective reality could be known by sense at all, and have made them suppose that there were positive arguments against the view that it can be so known. Our hypothetical construction meets these arguments, and shows that the account of the world given by common sense and physical science can be interpreted in a way which is logically unobjectionable, and finds a place for all the data, both hard and soft. It is this hypothetical construction, with its reconciliation of psychology and physics, which is the chief outcome of our discussion. Probably the construction is only in part necessary as an initial assumption, and can be obtained from more slender materials by the logical methods of which we shall have an example in the definitions of points, instants, and particles; but I do not yet know to what lengths this diminution in our initial assumptions can be carried.

Husserl

Edmund Husserl (1859–1938), a German philosopher and the teacher of Martin Heidegger, is considered to be the major figure in the European movement of twentieth-century philosophy known as phenomenology. A phenomenological investigation is one in which an observer is concerned with examining the objects of consciousness exactly as they appear, without bringing to the description any underlying ontological assumptions. Husserl's slogan was "Back to the things themselves." Husserl taught at several German universities but, being Jewish, lost his academic standing during the Nazi regime. His most significant works include Logical Investigations *(1900–1901)—interestingly published around the same time as Sigmund Freud's* Interpretation of Dreams—*and his* Ideas *(1913).*

Husserl believes that his phenomenological method provides a way to overcome the traditional opposition between metaphysical realism and idealism. Consciousness, he argues, is "intentional"—by which he means that it is always *of* something, whether of an actually existing object or not. Husserl's phenomenology is essentially a method that leads one from a natural, realist standpoint—the belief in a world that is made up of independent, real objects ordered in spatial and temporal relationships—through a "suspension" of this belief and then to a progressive realization of the essential character of objects as they are constituted in consciousness.

The following brief selection, which is taken from Husserl's *Ideas: General Introduction to Pure Phenomenology*, focuses on how we adopt the "natural standpoint" in our relation to the world and should give one a sense of a style of continental thinking that has been immensely influential in many areas of philosophy, from logic to aesthetics.

The Thesis of the Natural Standpoint and Its Suspension

THE WORLD OF THE NATURAL STANDPOINT: I AND MY WORLD ABOUT ME

Our first outlook upon life is that of natural human beings, imagining, judging, feeling, willing, "*from the natural standpoint.*" Let us make clear to ourselves what this means in the form of simple meditations which we can best carry on in the first person.

I am aware of a world, spread out in space endlessly, and in time becoming and become, without end. I am aware of it, that means, first of all, I discover it immediately, intuitively, I experience it. Through sight, touch, hearing, etc., in the different ways of sensory perception, corporeal things somehow spatially distributed *are for me simply there*, in verbal or figurative sense "present," whether or not I pay them special attention by busying myself with them, considering, thinking, feeling, willing. Animal beings also, perhaps men, are immediately there for me; I look up, I see them, I hear them coming towards me, I grasp them by the hand; speaking with them, I understand immediately what they are sensing and thinking, the feelings that stir them, what they wish or will. They too are present as realities in my field of intuition, even when I pay them no attention. But it is not necessary that they and other objects likewise should be present precisely in my *field of perception*. For me real objects are there, definite, more or less familiar, agreeing with what is actually perceived without being themselves perceived or even intuitively present. I can let my attention wander from the writing-table I have just seen and observed, through the unseen portions of the room behind my back to the verandah, into the garden, to the children in the summer-house, and so forth, to all the objects concerning which I precisely "know" that they are there and yonder in my immediate co-perceived surroundings—a knowledge which has nothing of conceptual thinking in it, and first changes into clear intuiting with the bestowing of attention, and even then only partially and for the most part very imperfectly.

But not even with the added reach of this intuitively clear or dark, distinct or indistinct *co-present* margin, which forms a continuous ring around the actual field of perception, does that world exhaust itself which in every waking moment is in some conscious measure "present" before me. It reaches rather in a fixed order of being into the limitless beyond. What is actually perceived, and what is more or less clearly co-present and determinate (to some extent at least), is partly pervaded, partly girt about with a *dimly apprehended depth or fringe of indeterminate reality*. I can pierce it with rays from the illuminating focus of attention with varying success. Determining rep-

From *Ideas: General Introduction to Pure Phenomenology* by Edmund Husserl, translated by W. R. Boyce Gibson (London: George Allen E. Unwin, Ltd.; New York: the Macmillan Co., 1931).

resentations, dim at first, then livelier, fetch me something out, a chain of such recollections takes shape, the circle of determinacy extends ever farther, and eventually so far that the connexion with the actual field of perception as the *immediate* environment is established. But in general the issue is a different one: an empty mist of dim indeterminacy gets studded over with intuitive possibilities or presumptions, and only the "form" of the world as "world" is foretokened. Moreover, the zone of indeterminacy is infinite. The misty horizon that can never be completely outlined remains necessarily there.

As it is with the world in its ordered being as a spatial present—the aspect I have so far been considering—so likewise is it with the world in respect to its *ordered being in the succession of time.* This world now present to me, and in every waking "now" obviously so, has its temporal horizon, infinite in both directions, its known and unknown, its intimately alive and its unalive past and future. Moving freely within the moment of experience which brings what is present into my intuitional grasp, I can follow up these connexions of the reality which immediately surrounds me. I can shift my standpoint in space and time, look this way and that, turn temporally forwards and backwards; I can provide for myself constantly new and more or less clear and meaningful perceptions and representations, and images also more or less clear, in which I make intuitable to myself whatever can possibly exist really or supposedly in the steadfast order of space and time.

Glance of a Landscape, 1926, by Paul Klee (The Philadelphia Museum of Art: Louise and Walter Arensberg Collection). Is the landscape glanced at real? Is it an "idea" in the mind of the spectator or the artist? Does it exist only in the artwork as such? Is Klee perhaps showing us that the landscape is glancing at *us*?

In this way, when consciously awake, I find myself at all times, and without my ever being able to change this, set in relation to a world which, through its constant changes, remains one and ever the same. It is continually "present" for me, and I myself am a member of it. Therefore this world is not there for me as a mere *world of facts and affairs*, but, with the same immediacy, as a *world of values, a world of goods, a practical world.* Without further effort on my part I find the things before me furnished not only with the qualities that befit their positive nature, but with value-characters such as beautiful or ugly, agreeable or disagreeable, pleasant or unpleasant, and so forth. Things in their immediacy stand there as objects to be used, the "table" with its "books," the "glass to drink from," the "vase," the "piano," and so forth. These values and practicalities, they too belong to *the constitution of the "actually present" objects as such*, irrespective of my turning or not turning to consider them or indeed any other objects. The same considerations apply of course just as well to the men and beasts in my surroundings as to "mere things." They are my "friends" or my "foes," my "servants" or "superiors," "strangers" or "relatives," and so forth.

THE "COGITO." MY NATURAL WORLD-ABOUT-ME AND THE IDEAL WORLDS-ABOUT-ME

It is then to this world, *the world in which I find myself and which is also my world-about-me*, that the complex forms of my manifold and shifting *spontaneities* of consciousness stand related: observing in the interests of research the bringing of meaning into conceptual form through description; comparing and distinguishing, collecting and counting, presupposing and inferring, the theorizing activity of consciousness, in short, in its different forms and stages. Related to it likewise are the diverse acts and states of sentiment and will: approval and disapproval, joy and sorrow, desire and aversion, hope and fear, decision and action. All these, together with the sheer acts of the Ego, in which I become acquainted with the world as *immediately* given me, through spontaneous tendencies to turn towards it and to grasp it, are included under the one Cartesian expression: *Cogito*. In the natural urge of life I live continually in *this fundamental form of all "wakeful" living*, whether in addition I do or do not assert the *cogito*, and whether I am or am not "reflectively" concerned with the Ego and the *cogitare*. If I am so concerned, a new *cogito* has become livingly active, which for its part is not reflected upon, and so not objective for me.

I am present to myself continually as someone who perceives, represents, thinks, feels, desires, and so forth; and *for the most part* herein I find myself related in present experience to the fact-world which is constantly about me. But I am not always so related, not every *cogito* in which I live has for its *cogitatum* things, men, objects or contents of one kind or another. Perhaps I am busied with pure numbers and the laws they symbolize: nothing of this sort is present in the world about me, this world of "real fact." And yet the world of numbers also is there for me, as the field of objects with which I am arithmetically busied; while I am thus occupied some numbers or constructions of a numerical kind will be at the focus of vision, girt by an arithmetical horizon partly defined, partly not; but obviously this being-there-for-me, like the being there at all, is something very different from this. *The arithmetical world is there for me only when and so long as I occupy the arithmetical standpoint.* But the *natural* world, the world in the ordinary sense of the word, is *constantly there for me*, so long as I live naturally and look in its direction. I am then at the *"natural standpoint,"* which is just another way of stating the same thing. And there is no need to modify these conclusions when I proceed to appropriate to myself the arithmetical world, and other similar "worlds," by adopting the corresponding standpoint. The natural world *still remains "present,"* I am at the natural standpoint after as well as before, and in this respect *undisturbed by the adoption of new standpoints.* If my *cogito* is active *only* in the worlds proper to the new standpoints, the natural world remains unconsidered; it is now the background for my consciousness as act, but it is *not the encircling sphere within which an arithmetical world finds its true and proper place.* The two worlds are present together but *disconnected*, apart, that is, from their relation to the Ego, in virtue of which I can freely direct my glance or my acts to the one or to the other.

THE "OTHER" EGO-SUBJECT AND THE INTERSUBJECTIVE NATURAL WORLD-ABOUT-ME

Whatever holds good for me personally, also holds good, as I know, for all other men whom I find present in my world-about-me. Experiencing them as men, I understand and take them as Ego-subjects, units like myself, and related to their natural surroundings. But this in such wise that I apprehend the world-about-them and the world-about-me objectively as one and the same world, which differs in each case only through affecting consciousness differently. Each has his place whence he sees the things that are present, and each enjoys accordingly different appearances of the things. For each, again, the fields of perception and memory actually present are different, quite apart from the fact that even that which is here intersubjectively known in common is known in different ways, is differently apprehended, shows different grades of clearness, and so forth. Despite all this, we come to understandings with our neighbours, and set up in common an objective spatio-temporal fact-world as *the world about us that is there for us all, and to which we ourselves none the less belong.*

THE GENERAL THESIS OF THE NATURAL STANDPOINT

That which we have submitted towards the characterization of what is given to us from the natural standpoint, and thereby of the natural standpoint itself, was a piece of pure description *prior to all "theory."* In these studies we stand bodily aloof from all theories, and by "theories" we here mean anticipatory ideas of every kind. Only as facts of our environment, not as agencies for uniting facts validly together, do theories concern us at all. But we do not set ourselves the task of continuing the pure description and raising it to a systematically inclusive and exhaustive characterization of the data, in their full length and breadth, discoverable from the natural standpoint (or from any standpoint, we might add, that can be knit up with the same in a common consent). A task such as this can and must—as scientific—be undertaken, and it is one of extraordinary importance, although so far scarcely noticed. Here it is not ours to attempt. For us who are striving towards the entrance-gate of phenomenology all the necessary work in this direction has already been carried out; the few features pertaining to the natural standpoint which we need are of a quite general character, and have already figured in our descriptions, and been sufficiently *and fully clarified*. We even made a special point of securing this full measure of clearness.

We emphasize a most important point once again in the sentences that follow: I find continually present and standing over against me the one spatio-temporal fact-world to which I myself belong, as do all other men found in it and related in the same way to it. This "fact-world," as the word already tells us, I find to *be out there*, and also *take it just as it gives itself to me as something that exists out there*. All doubting and rejecting of the data of the natural world leaves standing the *general thesis of the natural standpoint*. "The" world is as fact-world always there; at the most it is at odd points "other" than I supposed, this or that under such names as "illusion," "hallucination," and the like, must be struck *out of it*, so to speak; but the "it" remains ever, in the sense of the general thesis, a world that has its being out there. To know it more comprehensively, more trustworthily, more perfectly than the naïve lore of experience is able to do, and to solve all the problems of scientific knowledge which offer themselves upon its ground, that is the goal of the *sciences* of *the natural standpoint*.

PART V

WHAT IS RELIGIOUS EXPERIENCE? DOES GOD EXIST? WHY IS THERE EVIL?

The metaphysical questions concerning the origin of the world, the nature of reality, and so on have been traditionally—and in various ways still are—addressed in a religious or spiritual context. For many people throughout history, the world does not seem to be self-explanatory or sufficient in itself. Some persons have indeed devoted their lives to seeking religious fulfillment in a relationship to a personal divine being or to attaining an impersonal spiritual enlightenment; almost everyone at one time or another in their lives has asked, "Is this life of joy and suffering, pleasure and pain, accomplishment and frustration, all that is available to us?" All civilizations have developed elaborate ways of worship and meditation to establish relations to what is taken to be sacred, with these ways not infrequently dictating much of the manner in which social life is organized. In short, "religions" have developed, flourished, and floundered throughout history.

Philosophy of religion is that branch of philosophy that seeks to understand the nature of religious experience both within and apart from the religious traditions of humankind; to appraise the claims about the nature of the universe, of God, and of human beings put forward by religious thinkers; and to examine critically the fundamentally presuppositions and beliefs that inform various religious world views. Philosophy of religion thus differs from theology and from the history of religion as such in its basic concern with, and approach to, the phenomena of humankind's religious life. Unlike the theologian, the philosopher is under no obligation to defend or interpret so as to make intelligible and convincing any one tradition of religion, and unlike the historian of religion, the philosopher's interest is not centered on examining in detail the intricacies and subtleties in the development of particular religious doctrines, practices, and institutions. The philosopher instead is concerned with understanding religion as it is for many persons a central dimension of their experience and as it is a possible avenue to, or claimant of, philosophical truth.

Among the most fundamental problems in the philosophy of religion is, as one might expect, the problem of defining religion. Definition-making here is an arduous task for at least two reasons. First, it appears that it is difficult if not impossible to define religion without at the same time evaluating it. Most definitions of religion tell one more about the religious orientation of the person giving the definition than they do about the nature of what is purportedly defined. For example:

"Religion is (subjectively regarded) the recogniton of all duties as divine commands."—Kant

"Religion, being identical with the characteristic of man, is thus identical with self-consciousness—with the consciousness that man has of his [own] nature."—Ludwig Feuerbach

"The marks of genuine religion are freedom from fear and love. Freedom and love are the two features, theoretical and practical, of religion."—S. Radhakrishnan

"Religion is the vision of something which stands beyond, behind and within, the passing flux of immediate things; something which is real, and yet waiting to be realized; . . . something that gives meaning to all that passes, and yet eludes apprehension."—A. N. Whitehead

Second, there are such vast and varied phenomena that come under the label of religion—from performing burial rites to having profound experiences of love and insight—that it seems well-nigh impossible to encompass them all in a single definition. No other area of human experience, it seems, calls forth such a wide diversity and oftentimes conflicting range of experience as religion. Every manner of stupidity, fanaticism, superstition, and barbarism, as well as some of the most wonderful acts of kindness, love, and generosity, has been carried out in its name. It has been the source of many of the greatest intellectual and artistic achievements of humankind; it has also, especially in its secular institutional forms, been among the greatest barriers to a life of reason and freedom.

Huston Smith, in *The Religions of Man,* describes the situation of attempting to define or account for this enormous diversity in this way:

> A great historian of religion devoted forty years of his life to determining what the world's religions have in common and came up with two things: "Belief in God—if there be a God," and "life is worth living—sometimes."

Nevertheless, when historians look at the history of various civilizations and cultures, they usually find at least three identifiable kinds or levels of religious experience and concern. These orientations, although they frequently overlap and intertwine, differ from one another considerably and have often been at odds with each other. The three kinds, each of which is actually present in varying degrees in all organized world religions, are usually identified—in very general terms—as:

1. *Archaic or primal religion,* which tends to identify various forces of nature as unseen divine powers and seeks to control or propitiate these powers, is organized hi-

erarchically in a way that provides stability to a society, is highly ritualistic, and expresses itself in a rich texture of myths and legends.

2. *Ethical and metaphysical theism,* which involves the search for an ultimate meaning in life to be attained through relations to an infinite, transcendent creator God believed to be all powerful and good; affirmations of the dignity of each person as a creature of God's creative power; the dominance of faith in and obedience to the will of God; and the promise and hope of an eternal salvation.

3. *Mysticism,* which, in its various forms (nature, love, intellectual), is an experiential quest for a direct experience or realization of the unity or identity of the self and the divine; a contemplation of an impersonal or transpersonal state of being rather than the worship of a personal divine being; or the claim to achieve a state of insight or awareness superior to and qualitatively different from all ordinary perceptual and rational knowledge.

What do these forms of religious orientation have in common? At the least, they involve a search for and an affirmation of a fundamental spiritual reality, and assert that this reality is of supreme value and, accordingly, has an enduring claim upon one's life.

Many issues in the philosophy of religion deal with the expression of these diverse forms of religious experience in myth and in various other symbol systems, with the meaning of human freedom and immortality, and so on. For purposes of introducing this branch of philosophy we have chosen for discussion and analysis what many philosophers today regard as the two central and most interesting problems: that of the nature of religious experience, primarily in its theistic and mystical forms, and that of the role of reason in religion, especially as it involves various attempts to demonstrate the existence and reality of God and to reconcile God's goodness and power with the existence of evil.

Tillich

Paul Tillich (1886–1965) was a leading Protestant theologian who developed an immensely influential interpretation of religion that centered on the nature of faith. He is often linked with existential thinking because of his concern for the non-rational, passionate dimensions of religious experience and for the need of persons to make a deep commitment to the religious life. The language of religion, for Tillich, is "symbolic," pointing to and participating in that which it symbolizes. In an obscure but tantalizing formulation, Tillich argues that the very term "God" is a symbol for God—understood as the ground of our being and that with which we are "ultimately concerned." Tillich's major works include his monumental three-volume Systematic Theology *(1957–1963), and* Dynamics of Faith *(1957).*

Many contemporary historians and philosophers of religion as well as theologians make a rather clear distinction between "belief" and "faith" within the framework of theism. A belief expresses a statement or proposition to which one offers one's assent and is most often part of a network of belief or doctrinal creed. The most prevalent religious question people ask of one another is, "Do you believe in God?" A "yes" or a "no" or an "I don't know" suffices for an answer. Faith, on the other hand, is regarded as the living core of a religious commitment; it is the reflection of the manner in which one conducts one's life in relation to what one takes to be sacred. Someone might say "yes" to the "Do you believe?" question and quite clearly not live a life reflective of having religious faith.

Tillich argues that everyone has a general faith of one sort or another that exhibits the person's most basic values and aspirations—be it the pursuit of wealth, artistic achievement, nationalism, or whatever. This faith is made up of that with which the individual is "ultimately concerned" and is expressive of his or her personality as a whole, which in turn is informed by culture and tradition. What distinguishes religious faith is that it is "ultimately concerned" with "the ultimate." This faith calls for risk and courage, for it always takes hold of one in the context of uncertainty. Doubt, he says, "is a necessary element in it." Within the life of a community, religious faith is a passion for the infinite and becomes the awareness of holiness.

What Faith Is

FAITH AS ULTIMATE CONCERN

Faith is the state of being ultimately concerned: the dynamics of faith are the dynamics of man's ultimate concern. Man, like every living being, is concerned about many things, above all about those which condition his very existence, such as food and shelter. But man, in contrast to other living beings, has spiritual concerns—cognitive, aesthetic, social, political. Some of them are urgent, often extremely urgent, and each of them as well as the vital concerns can claim ultimacy for a human life or the life of a social group. If it claims ultimacy it demands the total surrender of him who accepts this claim, and it promises total fulfillment even if all other claims have to be subjected to it or rejected in its name. If a national group makes the life and growth of the nation its ultimate concern, it demands that all other concerns, economic well-being, health and life, family, aesthetic and cognitive truth, justice and humanity, be sacrificed. The extreme nationalisms of our century are laboratories for the study of what ultimate concern means in all aspects of human existence, including the smallest concern of one's daily life. Everything is centered in the only god, the nation—a god who certainly proves to be a demon, but who shows clearly the unconditional character of an ultimate concern.

But it is not only the unconditional demand made by that which is one's ultimate concern, it is also the promise of ultimate fulfillment which is accepted in the act of faith. The content of this promise is not necessarily defined. It can be expressed in indefinite symbols or in concrete symbols which cannot be taken literally, like the "greatness" of one's nation in which one participates even if one has died for it, or the conquest of mankind by the "saving race," etc. In each of these cases it is "ultimate fulfillment" that is promised, and it is exclusion from such fulfillment which is threatened if the unconditional demand is not obeyed.

An example—and more than an example—is the faith manifest in the religion of the Old Testament. It also has the character of ultimate concern in demand, threat and promise. The content of this concern is not the nation—although Jewish nationalism has sometimes tried to distort it into that—but the content is the God of justice, who, because he represents justice for everybody and every nation, is called the universal God, the God of the universe. He is the ultimate concern of every pious Jew, and therefore in his name the great commandment is given: "You shall love the Lord your God with all your heart, and with all your soul, and with all your might" (Deut 6:5). This is what ultimate concern means and from these words the term "ultimate concern" is derived. They state unambiguously the character of genuine faith, the demand of total surrender to the subject of ultimate concern. The

Old Testament is full of commands which make the nature of this surrender concrete, and it is full of promises and threats in relation to it. Here also are the promises of symbolic indefiniteness, although they center around fulfillment of the national and individual life, and the threat is the exclusion from such fulfillment through national extinction and individual catastrophe. Faith, for the men of the Old Testament, is the state of being ultimately and unconditionally concerned about Jahweh and about what he represents in demand, threat, and promise.

Another example—almost a counter-example, yet nevertheless equally revealing—is the ultimate concern with "success" and with social standing and economic power. It is the god of many people in the highly competitive Western culture and it does what every ultimate concern must do: it demands unconditional surrender to its laws even if the price is the sacrifice of genuine human relations, personal conviction and creative *eros*. Its threat is social and economic defeat, and its promise—indefinite as all such promises—the fulfillment of one's being. It is the breakdown of this kind of faith which characterizes and makes religiously important most contemporary literature. Not false calculations but a misplaced faith is revealed in novels like *Point of No Return*. When fulfilled, the promise of this faith proves to be empty.

Faith is the state of being ultimately concerned. The content matters infinitely for the life of the believer, but it does not matter for the formal definition of faith. And this is the first step we have to make in order to understand the dynamics of faith.

FAITH AS A CENTERED ACT

Faith as ultimate concern is an act of the total personality. It happens in the center of the personal life and includes all its elements. Faith is the most centered act of the human mind. It is not a movement of a special section or a special function of man's total being. They all are united in the act of faith. But faith is not the sum total of their impacts. It transcends every special impact as well as the totality of them and it has itself a decisive impact on each of them.

Since faith is an act of the personality as a whole, it participates in the dynamics of personal life. These dynamics have been described in many ways, especially in the recent developments of analytic psychology. Thinking in polarities, their tensions and their possible conflicts, is a common characteristic of most of them. This makes the psychology of personality highly dynamic and requires a dynamic theory of faith as the most personal of all personal acts. The first and decisive polarity in analytic psychology is that between the so-called unconscious and the conscious. Faith as an act of the total personality is not imaginable without the participation of the unconscious elements in the personality structure. They are always present and decide largely about the content of faith. But, on the other hand, faith is a conscious act and the unconscious elements participate in the creation of faith only if they are taken into the personal center which transcends each of them. If this does not happen, if unconscious forces determine the mental status without a centered act, faith does not occur, and compulsions take its place. For faith is a matter of freedom. Freedom is nothing more than the possibility of centered personal acts. The frequent discussion in which faith and freedom are contrasted could be helped by the insight that faith is a free, namely, centered act of the personality. In this respect freedom and faith are identical.

Also important for the understanding of faith is the polarity between what Freud and his school call ego and superego. The concept of the superego is quite ambiguous. On the one hand, it is the basis of all cultural life because it restricts the uninhibited actualization of the always-driving libido; on the other hand, it cuts off man's vital forces, and produces disgust about the whole system of cultural restrictions, and brings about a neurotic state of mind. From this point of view, the symbols of faith are considered to be expressions of the superego or, more concretely, to be an expression of the father image which gives content to the superego. Responsible for this inadequate theory of the superego is Freud's naturalistic negation of norms and principles. If the superego is not established through valid principles, it becomes a suppressive tyrant. But real faith, even if it uses the father image for its expression, transforms this image into a principle of truth and justice to be defended even against the "father." Faith and culture can be affirmed only if the superego represents the norms and principles of reality.

This leads to the question of how faith as a personal, centered act is related to the rational structure of man's personality which is manifest in his meaningful language, in his ability to know the true and to do the good, in his sense of beauty and justice. All this, and not only his possibility to analyze, to calculate and to argue, makes him a rational being. But in spite of this larger concept of reason we must deny that man's essential nature is identical with the rational character of his mind. Man is able to decide for or against reason, he is able to create beyond reason or to destroy below reason. This power is the power of his self, the center of self-relatedness in which all elements of his being are united. Faith is not an act of any of his rational functions, as it is not an act of the unconscious, but it is an act in which both the rational and the nonrational elements of his being are transcended.

Faith as the embracing and centered act of the personality is "ecstatic." It transcends both the drives of the nonrational unconscious and the structures of the rational conscious. It transcends them, but it does not destroy them. The ecstatic character of faith does not exclude its rational character although it is not identical with it, and it includes nonrational strivings without being identical with them. In the ecstasy of faith there is an awareness of truth and of ethical value; there are also past loves and hates, conflicts and reunions, individual and collective influences. "Ecstasy" means "standing outside of oneself"—without ceasing to be oneself—with all the elements which are united in the personal center.

A further polarity in these elements, relevant for the understanding of faith, is the tension between the cognitive function of man's personal life, on the one hand, and emotion and will, on the other hand. In a later discussion I will try to show that many distortions of the meaning of faith are rooted in the attempt to subsume faith to the one or the other of these functions. At this point it must be stated as sharply and insistently as possible that in every act of faith there is cognitive affirmation, not as the result of an independent process of inquiry but as an inseparable element in a total act of acceptance and surrender. This also excludes the idea that faith is the result of an independent act of "will to believe." There is certainly affirmation by the will of what concerns one ultimately, but faith is not a creation of the will. In the ecstasy of faith the will to accept and to surrender is an element, but not the cause. And this is true also of feeling. Faith is not an emotional outburst: this is not the meaning of ecstasy. Certainly, emotion is in it, as in every act of man's spiritual life. But emotion does not produce faith. Faith has a cognitive content and is an act of the will. It is the unity of every element in the centered self. Of course, the unity of all elements in the act of faith does not prevent one or the other element from dominating in a special form of faith. It dominates the character of faith but it does not create the act of faith.

This also answers the question of a possible psychology of faith. Everything that happens in man's personal being can become an object of psychology. And it is rather important for both the philosopher of religion and the practical minister to know how the act of faith is embedded in the totality of psychological processes. But in contrast to this justified and desirable form of a psychology of faith there is another one which tries to derive faith from something that is not faith but is most frequently fear. The presupposition of this method is that fear or something else from which faith is derived is more original and basic than faith. But this presupposition cannot be proved. On the contrary, one can prove that in the scientific method which leads to such consequences faith is already effective. Faith precedes all attempts to derive it from something else, because these attempts are themselves based on faith.

THE SOURCE OF FAITH

We have described the act of faith and its relation to the dynamics of personality. Faith is a total and centered act of the personal self, the act of unconditional, infinite and ultimate concern. The question now arises: what is the source of this all-embracing and all-transcending concern? The word "concern" points to two sides of a relationship, the relation between the one who is concerned and his concern. In both respects we have to imagine man's situation in itself and in his world. The reality of man's ultimate concern reveals something about his being, namely, that he is able to transcend the flux of relative and transitory experiences of his ordinary life. Man's experiences, feelings, thoughts are conditioned and finite. They not only come and go, but their content is of finite and conditional concern—unless they are elevated to unconditional validity. But this presupposes the general possibility of doing so; it presupposes the element of infinity in man. Man is able to understand in an immediate personal and central act the meaning of the ultimate, the unconditional, the absolute, the infinite. This alone makes faith a human potentiality.

Human potentialities are powers that drive toward actualization. Man is driven toward faith by his awareness of the infinite to which he belongs, but which he does not own like a possession. This is in abstract terms what concretely appears as the "restlessness of the heart" within the flux of life.

The unconditional concern which is faith is the concern about the unconditional. The infinite passion, as faith has been described, is the passion for the infinite. Or, to use our first term, the ultimate concern is concern about what is experienced as ultimate. In this way we have turned from the subjective meaning of faith as a centered act of the personality to its objective meaning, to what is meant in the act of faith. It would not help at this point of our analysis to call that which is meant in the act of faith "God" or a "a god." For at this step we ask: What in the idea of God constitutes divinity? The answer is: It is the element of the unconditional and of ultimacy. This carries the quality of divinity. If this is seen, one can understand why almost every thing "in heaven and on earth" has received ultimacy in the history of human religion. But we also can understand that a critical principle was and is at work in man's religious consciousness, namely, that which is really ultimate over against what claims to be ultimate but is only preliminary, transitory, finite. . . .

In terms like ultimate, unconditional, infinite, absolute, the difference between subjectivity and objectivity is overcome. The ultimate of the act of faith and the ultimate that is meant in the act of faith are one and the same. This is symbolically expressed by the mystics when they say that their knowledge of God is the knowledge God has of himself; and it is expressed by Paul when he says (I Cor. 13) that he will know as he is known, namely, by God. God never can be object without being at the same time subject. Even a successful prayer is, according to Paul (Rom. 8), not possible without God as Spirit praying within us. The same experience expressed in abstract language is the disappearance of the ordinary subject-object scheme in the experience of the ultimate, the unconditional. In the act of faith that which is the source of this act is present beyond the cleavage of subject and object. It is present as both and beyond both.

This character of faith gives an additional criterion for distinguishing true and false ultimacy. The finite which claims infinity without having it (as, e.g., a nation or success) is not able to transcend the subject-object scheme. It remains an object which the believer looks at as a subject. He can approach it with ordinary knowledge and subject it to ordinary handling. There are, of course, many degrees in the endless realm of false ultimacies. The nation is nearer to true ultimacy than is success. Nationalistic ecstasy can produce a state in which the subject is almost swallowed by the object. But after a period the subject emerges again, disappointed radically and totally, and by looking at the nation in a skeptical and calculating way does injustice even to its justified claims. The more idolatrous a faith the less it is able to overcome the cleavage between subject and object. For that is the difference between true and idolatrous faith. In true faith the ultimate concern is a concern about the truly ultimate; while in idolatrous faith preliminary, finite realties are elevated to the rank of ultimacy. The inescapable consequence of idolatrous faith is "existential disappointment," a disappointment which penetrates into the very existence of man! This is the dynamics of idolatrous faith: that it is faith, and as such, the centered act of a personality; that the centering point is something which is more or less on the periphery; and that, therefore, the act of faith leads to a loss of the center and to a disruption of the personality. The ecstatic character of even an idolatrous faith can hide this consequence only for a certain time. But finally it breaks into the open.

FAITH AND THE DYNAMICS OF THE HOLY

He who enters the sphere of faith enters the sanctuary of life. Where there is faith there is an awareness of holiness. This seems to contradict what has just been said about idolatrous faith. But it does not contradict our analysis of idolatry. It only contradicts the popular way in which the word "holy" is used. What concerns one ultimately becomes holy. The awareness of the holy is awareness of the presence of the divine, namely of the content of our ultimate concern. This awareness is expressed in a grand way in the Old Testament from the visions of the patriarchs and Moses to the shaking experiences of the great prophets and psalmists. It is a presence which remains mysterious in spite of its appearance, and it exercises both an attractive and a repulsive function on those who encounter it. . . .

FAITH AND DOUBT

We now return to a fuller description of faith as an act of the human personality, as its centered and total act. An act of faith is an act of a finite being who is grasped by and turned to the infinite. It is a finite act with all the limitations of a finite act, and it is an act in which the infinite participates beyond the limitations of a finite act. Faith is certain in so far as it is an experience of the holy. But faith is uncertain in so far as the infinite to which it is related is received by a finite being. This element of uncertainty in faith cannot be removed, it must be accepted. And the element in faith which accepts this is courage. Faith includes an element of immediate awareness which gives certainty and an element of uncertainty. To accept this is courage. In the courageous standing of uncertainty, faith shows most visibly its dynamic character.

If we try to describe the relation of faith and courage, we must use a larger concept of courage than that which is ordinarily used. Courage as an element of faith is the daring self-affirmation of one's own being in spite of the powers of "nonbeing" which are the heritage of everything finite. Where there is daring and courage there is the possibility of failure. And in every act of faith this possibility is present. The risk must be taken. Whoever makes his nation his ultimate concern needs courage in order to maintain this concern. Only certain is the ultimacy as ultimacy, the infinite passion as infinite passion. This is a reality given to the self with his own nature. It is as immediate and as much beyond doubt as the self is to the self. It *is* the self in its self-transcending quality. But there is not certainty of this kind about the content of our ultimate concern, be it nation, success, a god, or the God of the Bible: They all are contents without immediate awareness. Their acceptance as matters of ultimate concern is a risk and therefore an act of courage. There is a risk if what was considered as a matter of ultimate concern proves to be a matter of preliminary and transitory concern—as, for example, the nation. The risk to faith in one's ultimate concern is indeed the greatest risk man can run. For if it proves to be a failure, the meaning of one's life breaks down; one surrenders oneself, including truth and justice, to something which is not worth it. One has given away one's personal center without having a chance to regain it. The reaction of despair in people who have experienced the breakdown of their national claims is an irrefutable proof of the idolatrous character of their national concern. In the long run this is the inescapable result of an ultimate concern, the subject matter of which is not ultimate. And this is the risk faith must take; this is the risk which is unavoidable if a finite being affirms itself. Ultimate concern is ultimate risk and ultimate courage. It is not risk and needs no courage with respect to ultimacy itself. But it is risk and demands courage if it affirms a concrete concern. And every faith has a concrete element in itself. It is concerned about something or somebody. But this something or this somebody may prove to be not ultimate at all. Then faith is a failure in its concrete expression, although it is not a failure in the experience of the unconditional itself. A god disappears; divinity remains. Faith risks the vanishing of the concrete god in whom it believes. It may well be that with the vanishing of the god the believer breaks down without being able to re-establish his centered self by a new content of his ultimate concern. This risk cannot be taken away from any act of faith. There is only one point which is a matter not of risk but of immediate certainty and herein lies the greatness and the pain of being human; namely, one's standing between one's finitude and one's potential infinity.

All this is sharply expressed in the relation of faith and doubt. If faith is understood as belief that something is true, doubt is incompatible with the act of faith. If faith is understood as being ultimately concerned, doubt is a necessary element in it. It is a consequence of the risk of faith.

The doubt which is implicit in faith is not a doubt about facts or conclusions. It is not the same doubt which is the lifeblood of scientific research. Even the most orthodox theologian does not deny the right of methodological doubt in matters of empirical inquiry or logical deduction. A scientist who would say that a scientific theory is beyond doubt would at that moment cease to be scientific. He may believe that the theory can be trusted for all practical purposes. Without such belief no technical application of a theory would be possible. One could attribute to this kind of belief pragmatic certainty sufficient for action. Doubt in this case points to the preliminary character of the underlying theory.

There is another kind of doubt, which we could call skeptical in contrast to the scientific doubt which we could call methodological. The skeptical doubt is an attitude toward all the beliefs of man, from sense experiences to religious creeds. It is more an attitude than an assertion. For as an assertion it would conflict with itself. Even the assertion that there is no possible truth for man would be judged by the skeptical principle and could not stand as an assertion. Genuine skeptical doubt does not use the form of an assertion. It is an attitude of actually rejecting any certainty. Therefore, it can not be refuted logically. It does not transform its attitude into a proposition. Such an attitude necessarily leads either to despair or cynicism, or to both alternately. And often, if this alternative becomes intolerable, it leads to indifference and the attempt to develop an attitude of complete unconcern. But since man is that being who is essentially concerned about his being, such an escape finally breaks down. This is the dynamics of skeptical doubt. It has an awakening and liberating function, but it also can prevent the development of a centered personality. For personality is not possible without faith. The despair about truth by the skeptic shows that truth is still his infinite passion. The cynical superiority over every concrete truth shows that truth is still taken seriously and that the impact of the question of an ultimate concern is strongly felt. The skeptic, so long as he is a serious skeptic, is not without faith, even though it has no concrete content.

The doubt which is implicit in every act of faith is neither the methodological nor the skeptical doubt. It is the doubt which accompanies every risk. It is not the permanent doubt of the scientist, and it is not the transitory doubt of the skeptic, but it is the doubt of him who is ultimately concerned about a concrete content. One could call it the existential doubt, in contrast to the methodological and the skeptical doubt. It does not question whether a special proposition is true or false. It does not reject every concrete truth, but it is aware of the element of insecurity in every existential truth. At the same time, the doubt which is implied in faith accepts this insecurity and takes it into itself in an act of courage. Faith includes courage. Therefore, it can include the doubt about itself. Certainly faith and courage are not identical. Faith has other elements besides courage and courage has other functions beyond affirming faith. Nevertheless, an act in which courage accepts risk belongs to the dynamics of faith.

This dynamic concept of faith seems to give no place to that restful affirmative confidence which we find in the documents of all great religions, including Christianity. But this is not the case. The dynamic concept of faith is the result of a conceptual analysis, both of the subjective and of the objective side of faith. It is by no means the description of an always actualized state of the mind. An analysis of structure is not the description of a state of things. The confusion of these two is a source of many misunderstandings and errors in all realms of life. An example, taken from the current discussion of anxiety, is typical of this confusion. The description of anxiety as the awareness of one's finitude is sometimes criticized as untrue from the point of view of the ordinary state of the mind. Anxiety, one says, appears under special conditions but is not an ever-present implication of man's finitude. Certainly anxiety as an acute experience appears under definite conditions. But the underlying structure of finite life is the universal condition which makes the appearance of anxiety under special conditions possible. In the same way doubt is not a permanent experience within the act of faith. But it is always present as an element in the structure of faith. This is the difference between faith and immediate evidence either of perceptual or of logical character. There is no faith without an intrinsic "in spite of" and the courageous affirmation of oneself in the state of ultimate concern. This intrinsic element of doubt breaks into the open under special individual and social conditions. If doubt appears, it should not be considered as the negation of faith, but as an element which was always and will always be present in the act of faith. Existential doubt and faith are poles of the same reality, the state of ultimate concern.

The insight into this structure of faith and doubt is of tremendous practical importance. Many Christians, as well as members of other religious groups, feel anxiety, guilt and despair about what they call "loss of faith." But serious doubt is confirmation of faith. It indicates the seriousness of the concern, its unconditional character. This also refers to those who as future or present ministers of a church experience not only scientific doubt about doctrinal statements—this is as necessary and perpetual as theology is a perpetual need—but also existential doubt about the message of their church, e.g., that Jesus can be called the Christ. The criterion according to which they should judge themselves is the seriousness and ultimacy of their concern about the content of both their faith and their doubt.

FAITH AND COMMUNITY

The last remarks about faith and doubt in relation to religious creeds have led us to those problems which are ordinarily dominant in the popular mind in the discussion of faith. Faith is seen in its doctrinal formulations or in its legally dogmatic expressions. It is seen in its sociological setting more than in its character as a personal act. The historical causes of this attitude are obvious. The periods of suppression of the autonomous mind, culturally and religiously, in the name of the doctrinal formulations of a special faith, are remembered by the following generations. The life-and-death struggle of rebellious autonomy with the powers of religious suppression has left a deep scar in the "collective unconscious." This is true even in the present period, when the kind of suppression that existed at the end of the Middle Ages and in the period of the religious wars is a thing of the past. Therefore, it is not futile to defend the dynamic concept of faith against the accusation that it would lead back to new forms of orthodoxy and religious suppression. Certainly, if doubt is considered an intrinsic element of faith, the autonomous creativity of the human mind is in no way restricted. But, one will ask, is not this concept of faith incompatible with the "community of faith" which is a decisive reality in all religions? Is not the dynamic idea of faith an expression of Protestant individualism and humanistic autonomy? Can a community of faith—e.g., a church—accept a faith which includes doubt as an intrinsic element and calls the seriousness of doubt an expression of faith? And even if it could allow such an attitude in its ordinary members, how could it permit the same in its leaders?

The answers to these often rather passionately asked questions are many-sided and involved. At the present point the obvious and yet significant assertion must be made that the act of faith, like every act in man's spiritual life, is dependent on language and therefore on community. For only in the community of spiritual beings is language alive. Without language there is no act of faith, no religious experience! This refers to language generally and to the special language in every function of man's spiritual life. The religious language, the language of symbol and myth, is created in the community of the believers and cannot be fully understood outside this community. But within it, the religious language enables the act of faith to have a concrete content. Faith needs its language, as does every act of the personality; without language it would be blind, not directed toward a content, not conscious of itself. This is the reason for the predominant significance of the community of faith. Only as a member of such a community (even if in isolation or expulsion) can man have a content for his ultimate concern. Only in a community of language can man actualize his faith.

But now one will repeat the question and ask: If there is no faith without community of faith, is it not necessary that the community formulate the content of its faith in a definite way as a creedal statement and demand that every member of the community accept it? Certainly this is the way in which the creeds came into existence. This is the reason for their dogmatic and legal fixation! But this does not explain the tremendous power of these expressions of the communal faith over groups and individuals from generation to generation. Nor does it explain the fanaticism with which doubts and deviations were suppressed, not only by external power but even more by the mechanisms of inner suppression. These mechanisms had been planted into the individual mind and were most effective even without pressure from outside. In order to understand these facts we must remember that faith as the state of ultimate concern includes total surrender to the content of this concern in a centered act of the personality. This means that the existence of the personality in the ultimate sense is at stake. Idolatrous concern and devotion may destroy the center of the personality. If, as in the Christian Church, in centuries of strife the content of the communal faith has been defended against idolatrous intrusions and has been formulated as a defense against such intrusions, it is understandable that every deviation from these formulations is considered destructive for the "soul" of the Christian. He is thought to have fallen under demonic influences. Ecclesiastical punishments are attempts to save him from demonic self-destruction. In these measures the concern which is the content of faith is taken absolutely seriously. It is a matter of eternal life and death. . . .

All this drives to the question: How is a community of faith possible without suppression of the autonomy of man's spiritual life? The first answer is based on the relation of the civil authorities to the community of faith. Even if a society is practically identical with a community of faith and the actual life of the group is determined by the spiritual substance of a church, the civil authorities should as such remain neutral and risk the rise of dissident forms of faith. If they try to enforce spiritual conformity, and are successful, they have removed the risk and courage which belong to the act of faith. They have transformed faith into a behavior pattern which does not admit alternatives, and which loses its character of ultimacy even if the fulfillment of the religious duties is done with ultimate concern. However, such a situation has become rare in our period. In most societies the civil authorities have to deal with different communities of faith, unable to enforce the one or the other in all members of the society. In this case the spiritual substance of the social group is determined by the common denominator of the different groups and their common tradition. This denominator may be more secular or more religious. In any case it is an outgrowth of faith, and its expression—as in the American Constitution—is affirmed in an attitude which sometimes has the unconditional character of an ultimate concern, but more often the conditional character of a preliminary concern of highest degree. Just for this reason the civil authorities should not try to prohibit the expression of doubt about such a basic law, although they must enforce the legal consequences of it.

The second step in the solution of the problem deals with faith and doubt within the community of faith itself. The question is whether the dynamic concept of faith is incompatible with a community which needs creedal expressions of the concrete elements in its ultimate concern. The answer which follows from the preceding analyses is that no answer is possible if the character of the creed excludes the presence of doubt. The concept of the "infallibility" of a decision by a council or a bishop or a book excludes doubt as an element of faith in those who subject themselves to these authorities. They may have to struggle within themselves about their subjection; but after they have made the decision, no doubt can be admitted by them about the infallible statements of the authorities. This faith has become static, a nonquestioning surrender not only to the ultimate, which is affirmed in the act of faith, but also to its concrete elements as formulated by the religious authorities. In this way something preliminary and conditional—the human interpretation of the content of faith from the Biblical writers of the present—receives ultimacy and is elevated above the risk of doubt. The fight against the idolatrous implication of this kind of static faith was waged first by Protestantism and then, when Protestantism itself became static, by Enlightenment. This protest, however insufficient its expression, aimed originally at a dynamic faith and not at the negation of faith, not even at the negation of creedal formulations. So we stand again before the question: How can a faith which has doubt as an element within itself be united with creedal statements of the community of faith? The answer can only be that creedal expressions of the ultimate concern of the community must include their own criticism. It must become obvious in all of them—be they liturgical, doctrinal or ethical expressions of the faith of the community—that they are not ultimate. Rather, their function is to point to the ultimate which is beyond all of them. This is what I call the "Protestant principle," the critical element in the expression of the community of faith and consequently the element of doubt in the act of faith. Neither the doubt nor the critical element is always actual, but both must always be possible within the circle of faith. From the Christian point of view, one would say that the Church with all its doctrines and institutions and authorities stands under the prophetic judgment and not above it. Criticism and doubt show that the community of faith stands "under the Cross," if the Cross is understood as the divine judgment over man's religious life, and even over Christianity, though it has accepted the sign of the Cross. In this way the dynamic faith which we first have described in personal terms in applied to the community of faith. Certainly, the life of a community of faith is a continuous risk, if faith itself is understood as a risk. But this is the character of dynamic faith, and the consequence of the Protestant principle.

Otto

Rudolf Otto (1869–1937) was the most important twentieth-century Christian thinker working from a phenomenological perspective. He was concerned with describing the essential of theistic religious experience as far as possible as it occurs apart from doctrines and beliefs of a strictly rational character. Although the conceptual framework of interpretation, our rational notions of the divine nature, and so on, are of immense importance for a religious tradition, they do not by any means, according to Otto, exhaust the richness and vitality of our experience of the holy. Otto's major work, The Idea of the Holy *(1923), has become a modern classic in the philosophy of religion.*

In working out his phenomenology of theistic religious experience (with passing references to mystical experience), Otto introduces the term "numinous" as a symbol for that ineffable spiritual reality that is taken to be divine and for that religious state of mind associated with it that cannot be reduced to any other. The numinous, he maintains, cannot be adequately understood but only evoked and awakened within us. Otto examines carefully what he discerns to be the key elements—and tensions—in the numinous, such as "creature-feeling," which is experienced as a "mysterium tremendum," the profound feeling of the presence of a transcendent mystery; the elements of "awefulness," "overpoweringness," and "urgency"; and the awareness of that which is "wholly other" and the "fascination" we have toward it.

The Theistic Religious Experience

THE RATIONAL AND THE NON-RATIONAL

It is essential to every theistic conception of God, and most of all to the Christian, that it designates and precisely characterizes deity by the attributes spirit, reason, purpose, good will, supreme power, unity, selfhood. The nature of God is thus thought of by analogy with our human nature of reason and personality; only,

From *The Idea of the Holy* by Rudolf Otto, translated by John W. Harvey (1950). Reprinted by permission of Oxford University Press.

whereas in ourselves we are aware of this as qualified by restriction and limitation, as applied to God the attributes we use are "completed," i.e. thought as absolute and unqualified. Now all these attributes constitute clear and definite *concepts:* they can be grasped by the intellect; they can be analysed by thought; they even admit of definition. An object that can thus be thought conceptually may be termed *rational.* The nature of deity described in the attributes above mentioned is, then, a rational nature; and a religion which recognizes and maintains such a view of God is in so far a "rational" religion. Only on such terms is *belief* possible in contrast to mere *feeling.* And of Christianity at least it is false that "feeling is all, the name but sound and smoke";—where "name" stands for conception or thought. Rather we count this the very mark and criterion of a religion's high rank and superior value—that it should have no lack of *conceptions* about God; that it should admit knowledge—the knowledge that comes by faith—of the transcendent in terms of conceptual thought, whether those already mentioned or others which continue and develop them. . . .

But, when this is granted, we have to be on our guard against an error which would lead to a wrong and one-sided interpretation of religion. This is the view that the essence of deity can be given completely and exhaustively in such "rational" attributions as have been referred to above and in others like them. It is not an unnatural misconception. We are prompted to it by the traditional language of edification, with its characteristic phraseology and ideas; by the learned treatment of religious themes in sermon and theological instruction; and further even by our Holy Scriptures themselves. In all these cases the "rational" element occupies the foreground, and often nothing else seems to be present at all. But this is after all to be expected. All language, in so far as it consists of words, purports to convey ideas or concepts;—that is what language means;—and the more clearly and unequivocally it does so, the better the language. And hence expositions of religious truth in language inevitably tend to stress the "rational" attributes of God.

But though the above mistake is thus a natural one enough, it is none the less seriously misleading. For so far are these "rational" attributes from exhausting the idea of deity, that they in fact imply a non-rational or supra-rational Subject of which they are predicates. They are "essential" (and not merely "accidental") attributes to that subject, but they are also, it is important to notice, *synthetic* essential attributes. That is to say, we have to predicate them of a subject which they qualify, but which in its deeper essence is not, nor indeed can be, comprehended in them; which rather requires comprehension of a quite different kind. Yet, though it eludes the conceptual way of understanding, it must be in some way or other within our grasp, else absolutely nothing could be asserted of it. And even mysticism, in speaking of it as the ineffable, does not really mean to imply that absolutely nothing can be asserted of the object of the religious consciousness; otherwise, mysticism could exist only in unbroken silence, whereas what has generally been a characteristic of the mystics is their copious eloquence. . . .

And so it is salutary that we should be incited to notice that religion is not exclusively contained and exhaustively comprised in any series of "rational" assertions; and it is well worth while to attempt to bring the relation of the different "moments" of religion to one another clearly before the mind, so that its nature may become more manifest.

This attempt we are now to make with respect to the quite distinctive category of the holy or sacred.

"NUMEN" AND THE "NUMINOUS"

"Holiness"—"the holy"—is a category of interpretation and valuation peculiar to the sphere of religion. It is, indeed, applied by transference to another sphere—that of ethics—but it is not itself derived from this. While it is complex, it contains a quite specific element or "moment," which sets it apart from "the rational" in the meaning we gave to that word above, and which remains inexpressible—in the sense that it completely eludes apprehension in terms of concepts. The same thing is true (to take a quite different region of experience) of the category of the beautiful.

Now these statements would be untrue from the outset if "the holy" were merely what is meant by the word, not only in common parlance, but in philosophical, and generally even in theological usage. The fact is we have come to use the words "holy," "sacred" in an entirely derivative sense, quite different from that which they originally bore. We generally take "holy" as meaning "completely good"; it is the absolute moral attribute, denoting the consummation of moral goodness. . . .

But this common usage of the term is inaccurate. It is true that all this moral significance is contained in the word "holy," but it includes in addition—as even we cannot but feel—a clear overplus of meaning, and this it is now our task to isolate. Nor is this merely a later or acquired meaning; rather, "holy," or at least the equivalent words in Latin and Greek, in Semitic and other ancient languages, denoted first and foremost *only* this overplus: if the ethical element was present at all, at any rate it was not original and never constituted the whole meaning of the word. Any one who uses it to-day does undoubtedly always feel "the morally good" to be implied in "holy"; and accordingly in our inquiry into that element which is separate and peculiar to the idea of the holy it will be useful, at least for the temporary purpose of the investigation, to invent a special term to stand for "the holy" *minus* its moral factor or "moment," and, as we can now add, minus its "rational" aspect altogether.

It will be our endeavour to suggest this unnamed Something to the reader as far as we may, so that he may himself feel it. There is no religion in which it does not live as the real innermost core, and without it no religion would be worthy of the name. It is pre-eminently a living force in the Semitic religions, and of these again in none has it such vigour as in that of the Bible. . . . It is not, of course, disputed that these terms in all three languages connote, as part of their meaning, *good, absolute goodness*, when, that is, the notion has ripened and reached the highest state in its development. And we then use the word "holy" to translate them. But this "holy" then represents the gradual shaping and filling in with ethical meaning, or what we shall call the "schematization," of what was a unique original feeling-response, which can be in itself ethically neutral and claims consideration in its own right. And when this moment or element first emerges and begins its long development, all those expressions mean beyond all question something quite other than "the good." . . .

Accordingly, it is worth while, as we have said, to find a word to stand for this element in isolation, this "extra" in the meaning of "holy" above and beyond the meaning of goodness. By means of a special term we shall the better be able, first, to keep the meaning clearly apart and distinct, and second, to apprehend and classify connectedly whatever subordinate forms or stages of development it may show. For this purpose I adopt a word coined from the Latin *numen*. *Omen* has given us "ominous," and there is no reason why from *numen* we should not similarly form a word "numinous." I shall speak, then, of a unique "numinous" category of value and of a definitely "numinous" state of mind, which is always found wherever the category is applied. This mental state is perfectly *sui generis* and irreducible to any other; and therefore, like every absolutely primary and elementary datum, while it admits of being discussed, it cannot be strictly defined. There is only one way to help another to an understanding of it. He must be guided and led on by consideration and discussion of the matter through the ways of his own mind, until he reach the point at which "the numinous" in him perforce begins to stir, to start into life and into consciousness. We can co-operate in this process by bringing before his notice all that can be found in other regions of the mind, already known and familiar, to resemble, or again to afford some special contrast to, the particular experience we wish to elucidate. Then we must add: "This *X* of ours is not precisely *this* experience, but akin to this one and the opposite of that other. Cannot you now realize for yourself what it is?" In other words our *X* cannot, strictly speaking, be taught, it can only be evoked, awakened in the mind; as everything that comes "of the spirit" must be awakened.

THE ELEMENTS IN THE "NUMINOUS"

Creature-Feeling

The reader is invited to direct his mind to a moment of deeply-felt religious experience, as little as possible qualified by other forms of consciousness. Whoever cannot do this, whoever knows no such moments in his experience, is requested to read no farther; for it is not easy to discuss questions of religious psychology with one who can recollect the emotions of his adolescence, the discomforts of indigestion, or, say, social feelings, but cannot recall any intrinsically religious feelings. We do not blame such an one, when he tries for himself to advance as far as he can with the help of such principles of explanation as he knows, interpreting "aesthetics" in terms of sensuous pleasure, and "religion" as a function of the gregarious instinct and social standards, or as something more primitive still. But the artist, who for his part has an intimate personal knowledge of the distinctive element in the aesthetic experience, will decline his theories with thanks, and the religious man will reject them even more uncompromisingly.

Next, in the probing and analysis of such states of the soul as that of solemn worship, it will be well if regard be paid to what is unique in them rather than to what they have in common with other similar states. To be *rapt* in worship is one thing; to be morally *uplifted* by the contemplation of a good deed is another; and it is not to their common features, but to those elements of emotional content peculiar to the first that we would have attention directed as precisely as possible. . . .

Schleiermacher [a famous nineteenth-century German religious thinker] has the credit of isolating a very important element in such an experience. This is the "feeling of dependence." But this important discovery of Schleiermacher is open to criticism in more than one respect.

In the first place, the feeling or emotion which he really has in mind in this phrase is in its specific quality not a "feeling of dependence" in the "natural" sense of the word. As such, other domains of life and other regions of experience than the religious occasion the feeling, as a sense of personal insufficiency and impotence, a consciousness of being determined by circumstances and environment. The feeling of which Schleiermacher wrote has an undeniable analogy with these states of mind: they serve as an indication to it, and its nature may be elucidated by them, so that, by following the direction in which they point, the feeling itself may be spontaneously felt. But the feeling is at the same time also qualitatively different from such analogous states of mind. Schleiermacher himself, in a way, recognizes this by distinguishing the feeling of pious or religious dependence from all other feelings of dependence. His mistake is in making the distinction merely that between "absolute" and "relative" dependence, and therefore a difference of degree and not of intrinsic quality. What he overlooks is that, in giving the feeling the name "feeling of dependence" at all, we are really employing what is no more than a very close analogy. Anyone who compares and contrasts the two states of mind introspectively will find out, I think, what I mean. It cannot be expressed by means of anything else, just because it is so primary and elementary a datum in our psychical life, and therefore only definable through itself. It may perhaps help him if I cite a well-known example, in which the precise "moment" or element of religious feeling of which we are speaking is most actively present. When Abraham ventures to plead with God for the men of Sodom, he says (Gen. xviii. 27): "Behold now, I have taken upon me to speak unto the Lord, which am but dust and ashes." There you have a self-confessed "feeling of dependence," which is yet at the same time far more than, and something other than, *merely* a feeling of dependence. Desiring to give it a name of its own, I propose to call it "creature-consciousness" or creature-feeling. It is the emotion of creature, submerged and overwhelmed by its own nothingness in contrast to that which is supreme above all creatures.

It is easily seen that, once again, this phrase, whatever it is, is not a *conceptual* explanation of the matter. All that this new term, "creature-feeling," can express, is the note of submergence into nothingness before an overpowering, absolute might of some kind; whereas everything turns upon the *character* of this overpowering might, a character which cannot be expressed verbally, and can only be suggested indirectly through the tone and content of a man's feeling-response to it. And this response must be directly experienced in oneself to be understood.

We have now to note a second defect in the formulation of Schleiermacher's principle. The religious category discovered by him, by whose means he professes to determine the real content of the religious emotion, is merely a category of *self-valuation*, in the sense of self-depreciation. According to him the religious emotion would be directly and primarily a sort of *self*-consciousness, a feeling concerning oneself in a special, determined relation, viz. one's dependence. Thus, according to Schleiermacher, I can only come upon the very fact of God as the result of an inference, that is, by reasoning to a cause beyond myself to account for my "feeling of dependence." But this is entirely opposed to the psychological facts of the case. Rather, the "creature-feeling" is itself a first subjective concomitant and effect of another feeling-element, which casts it like a shadow, but which in itself indubitably has immediate and primary reference to an object outside the self.

Now this object is just what we have already spoken of as "the numinous." For the "creature-feeling" and the sense of dependence to arise in the mind the "numen" must be experienced as present as is in the case of Abraham. There must be felt a something "numinous," something bearing the character of a "numen," to which the mind turns spontaneously; or (which is the same thing in other words) these feelings can only arise in the mind as accompanying emotions when the category of "the numinous" is called into play.

The numinous is thus felt as objective and outside the self. We have now to inquire more closely into its nature and the modes of its manifestation.

"MYSTERIUM TREMENDUM"

The Analysis of "Tremendum"

We said above that the nature of the numinous can only be suggested by means of the special way in which it is reflected in the mind in terms of feeling. "Its nature is such that it grips or stirs the human mind with this and that determinate affective state." We have now to attempt to give a further indication of these determinate states. We must once again endeavour, by adducing feelings akin to them for the purpose of analogy or contrast, and by the use of metaphor and symbolic expressions, to make the states of mind we are investigating ring out, as if were, of themselves.

Let us consider the deepest and most fundamental element in all strong and sincerely felt religious emotion. Faith unto salvation, trust, love—all these are there. But over and above these is an element which may also on occasion, quite apart from them, profoundly affect us and occupy the mind with a wellnigh bewildering strength. Let us follow it up with every effort of sympathy and imaginative intuition wherever it is to be found, in the lives of those around us, in sudden, strong ebullitions of personal piety and the frames of mind such ebullitions evince, in the fixed and ordered solemnities of rites and liturgies, and again in the atmosphere that clings to old religious monuments and buildings, to temples and to churches. If we do so we shall find we are dealing with something for which there is only one appropriate expression, "*mysterium tremendum.*" The feeling of it may at times come sweeping like a gentle tide, pervading the mind with a tranquil mood of deepest worship. It may pass over into a more set and lasting attitude of the soul, continuing, as it were, thrillingly vibrant and resonant, until at last it dies away and the soul resumes its "profane," non-religious mood of everyday experience. It may burst in sudden eruption up from the depths of the soul with spasms and convulsions, or lead to the strangest excitement, to intoxicated frenzy, to transport, and to ecstasy. It has its wild and demonic forms and can sink to an almost grisly horror and shuddering. It has its crude, barbaric antecedents and early manifestations, and again it may be developed into something beautiful and pure and glorious. It may become the hushed, trembling, and speechless humility of the creature in the presence of— whom or what? In the presence of that which is a *mystery* inexpressible and above all creatures.

It is again evident at once that here too our attempted formulation by means of a concept is once more a merely negative one. Conceptually *mysterium* denotes merely that which is hidden and esoteric, that which is beyond conception or understanding, extraordinary and unfamiliar. The term does not define the object more positively in its qualitative character. But though what is enunciated in the word is negative, what is meant is something absolutely and intensely positive. This pure positive we can experience in feelings, feelings which our discussion can help to make clear to us, in so far as it arouses them actually in our hearts.

The Element of Awefulness.   To get light upon the positive *"quale"* of the object of these feelings, we must analyse more closely our phrase *mysterium tremendum,* and we will begin first with the adjective.

Tremor is in itself merely the perfectly familiar and "natural" emotion of *fear.* But here the term is taken, aptly enough but still only by analogy, to denote a quite specific kind of emotional response, wholly distinct from that of being afraid, though it so far resembles it that the analogy of fear may be used to throw light upon its nature. . . .

Before going on to consider the elements which unfold as the "tremendum" develops, let us give a little further consideration to the first crude, primitive forms in which this "numinous dread" or *awe* shows itself. It is the mark which really characterizes the so-called "religion of primitive man," and there it appears as "daemonic dread." This crudely naïve and primordial emotional disturbance, and the fantastic images to which it gives rise, are later overborne and ousted by more highly developed forms of the numinous emotion, with all its mysteriously impelling power. But even when this has long attained its higher and purer mode of expression it is possible for the primitive types of excitation that were formerly a part of it to break out in the soul in all their original naïveté and so to be experienced afresh. That this is so is shown by the potent attraction again and again exercised by the element of horror and "shudder" in ghost stories, even among persons of high all-around education. It is a remarkable fact that the physical reaction to which this unique "dread" of the uncanny gives rise is also unique, and is not found in the case of any "natural" fear or terror. We say: "My blood ran icy cold," and "my flesh crept." The "cold blood" feeling may be a symptom of ordinary, natural fear, but there is something non-natural or supernatural about the symptom of "creeping flesh." And any one who is capable of more precise introspection must recognize that the distinction between such a "dread" and natural fear is not simply one of degree and intensity. The awe or "dread" *may* indeed be so overwhelmingly great that it seems to penetrate to the very marrow, making the man's hair bristle and his limbs quake. But it may also steal upon him almost unobserved as the gentlest of agitations, a mere fleeting shadow passing across his mood. It has therefore nothing to do with intensity, and no natural fear passes over into it merely by being intensified. I may be beyond all measure afraid and terrified without there being even a trace of the feeling of uncanniness in my emotion. . . .

Though the numinous emotion in its completest development shows a world of difference from the mere "daemonic dread," yet not even at the highest level does it belie its pedigree or kindred. Even when the worship of "daemons" has long since reached the higher level of worship of "gods," these gods still retain as *numina* something of the "ghost" in the impress they make on the feelings of the worshipper, viz. the peculiar quality of the "uncanny" and "awful," which survives with the quality of exaltedness and sublimity or is symbolized by means of it. And this element, softened though it is, does not disappear even on the highest level of all, where the worship of God is at its purest. Its disappearance would be indeed an essential loss. The "shudder" reappears in a form ennobled beyond measure where the soul, held speechless, trembles inwardly to the farthest fiber of its being. It invades the mind mightily in Christian worship with the words: "Holy, holy, holy"; it breaks forth from the hymn of Tersteegen:

> God Himself is present:
> Heart, be stilled before Him:
> Prostrate inwardly adore Him.

The "shudder" has here lost its crazy and bewildering note, but not the ineffable something that holds the mind. It has become a mystical awe, and sets free as its accompaniment, reflected in self-consciousness, that "creature-feeling" that has already been described as the feeling of personal nothingness and submergence before the awe-inspiring object directly experienced.

The Element of "Overpoweringness" ("majestas").   We have been attempting to unfold the implications of that aspect of the *mysterium tremendum* indicated by the adjective, and the result so far may be summarized in two words, constituting, as before, what may be called an "ideogram," rather than a concept proper, viz. "absolute unapproachability."

It will be felt at once that there is yet a further element which must be added, that, namely, of "might," "power," "absolute overpoweringness." We will take to represent this the term *majestas,* majesty—the more readily because anyone with a feeling for language must detect a last faint trace of the numinous still clinging to the world. The *tremendum* may then be rendered more adequately *tremenda majestas,* or "aweful majesty." This second element of majesty may continue to be vividly preserved, where the first, that of unapproachability, recedes and dies away, as may be seen, for example, in mysticism. It is especially in relation to this element of majesty or absolute overpoweringness that the creature-consciousness, of which we have already spoken, comes upon the scene, as a sort of shadow or subjective reflection of it. Thus, in contrast to "the overpowering" of which we are conscious as an object over against the self, there is the feeling of one's own submergence, of being but "dust and ashes" and nothingness. And this forms the numinous raw material for the feeling of religious humility. . . .

This leads again to the mention of mysticism. No mere inquiry into the genesis of a thing can throw any light upon its essential nature, and it is hence immaterial to us how mysticism historically arose. But essentially mysticism is the stressing to a very high degree, indeed the overstressing, of the non-rational or supra-rational elements in religion; and it is only intelligible when so understood. The various phases and factors of the non-rational may receive varying emphasis, and the type of mysticism will differ according as some or others fall into the background. What we have been analysing, however, is a feature that recurs in all forms of mysticism everywhere, and it is nothing but the "creature-consciousness" stressed to the utmost and to excess, the expression meaning, if we may repeat the contrast already made, not "feeling of our createdness" but "feeling of our creaturehood," that is, the consciousness of the littleness of every creature in face of that which is above all creatures.

A characteristic common to all types of mysticism is the *Identification,* in different degrees of completeness, of the personal self with the transcendent Reality. This identification has a source of its own, with which we are not here concerned, and springs from "moments" of religious experience which would require separate treatment. "Identification" alone, however, is not enough for mysticism; it must be Identification with the Something that is at once absolutely supreme in power and reality and wholly non-rational. And it is among the mystics that we most encounter this element of religious consciousness. . . .

The Element of "Energy" or Urgency.   There is, finally, a third element comprised in those of *tremendum* and *majestas,* awefulness and majesty, and this I venture to call the "urgency" or "energy" of the numinous object. It is particularly vividly perceptible in "wrath'; and it everywhere clothes itself in symbolical expressions—vitality, passion, emotional temper, will, force, movement, excitement, activity, impetus. These features are typical and recur again and again from the daemonic level up to the idea of the "living" God. We have here the factor that has everywhere more than any other prompted the fiercest opposition to the "philosophic" God of mere rational speculation, who can be put into a definition. And for their part the philosophers have condemned these expressions of the energy of the numen, whenever they are brought on to the scene, as sheer anthropomorphism. In so far as their opponents have for the most part themselves failed to recognize that the terms they have borrowed from the sphere of human conative and affective life have merely value as analogies, the philosophers are right to condemn them. But they are wrong, in so far as, this error notwithstanding, these terms stood for a genuine aspect of the divine nature—its non-rational aspect—a due consciousness of which served to protect religion itself from being "rationalized" away. . . .

The Analysis of "Mysterium"

> *Eïn begriffener Gott ist kein Gott.*
> "A God comprehended is no God." (TERSTEEGEN.)

We gave to the object to which the numinous consciousness is directed the name *mysterium tremendum,* and we then set ourselves first to determine the meaning of the adjective *tremendum*—which we found to be itself only justified by analogy—because it is more easily analysed than the substantive idea *mysterium.* We have now to turn to this, and try, as best we may, by hint and suggestion, to get to a clearer apprehension of what it implies.

    The "Wholly Other." It might be thought that the adjective itself gives an explanation of the substantive; but this is not so. It is not merely analytical; it is a synthetic attribute to it; i.e. *tremendum* adds something not necessarily inherent in *mysterium.* It is true that the reactions in consciousness that correspond to the one readily and spontaneously overflow into those that correspond to the other; in fact, anyone sensitive to the use of words would commonly feel that the idea of "mystery" (*mysterium*) is so closely bound up with its synthetic qualifying attribute "aweful" (*tremendum*) that one can hardly say the former without catching an echo of the latter, "mystery" almost of itself becoming "aweful mystery" to us. But the passage from the one idea to the other need not by any means be always so easy. The elements of meaning implied in "awefulness" and "mysteriousness" are in themselves definitely different. The latter may so far preponderate in the religious consciousness, may stand out so vividly, that in comparison with it the former almost sinks out of sight; a case which again could be clearly exemplified from some forms of mysticism. Occasionally, on the other hand, the reverse happens, and the *tremendum* may in turn occupy the mind without the *mysterium.*

    This latter, then, needs special consideration on its own account. We need an expression for the mental reaction peculiar to it; and here, too, only one word seems appropriate, though, as it is strictly applicable only to a "natural" state of mind, it has here meaning only by analogy: it is the word "stupor." *Stupor* is plainly a different thing from *tremor;* it signifies blank wonder, an astonishment that strikes us dumb, amazement absolute. Taken, indeed, in its purely natural sense, *mysterium* would first mean merely a secret or a mystery in the sense of that which is alien to us, uncomprehended and unexplained; and so far *mysterium* is itself merely an ideogram, an analogical notion taken from the natural sphere, illustrating, but incapable of exhaustively rendering, our real meaning. Taken in the religious sense, that which is "mysterious" is—to give it perhaps the most striking expression—the "wholly other," that which is quite beyond the sphere of the usual, the intelligible, and the familiar, which therefore falls quite outside the limits of the "canny," and is contrasted with it, filling the mind with blank wonder and astonishment.

This is already to be observed on the lowest and earliest level of the religion of primitive man, where the numinous consciousness is but an inchoate stirring of the feelings. What is a really characteristic of this stage is *not*—as the theory of Animism would have us believe—that men are here concerned with curious entities, called "souls" or "spirits," which happen to be invisible. Representations of spirits and similar conceptions are rather one and all early modes of "rationalizing" a precedent experience, to which they are subsidiary. They are attempts in some way or other, it little matters how, to guess the riddle it propounds, and their effect is at the same time always to weaken and deaden the experience itself. They are the source from which springs, not religion, but the rationalization of religion, which often ends by constructing such a massive structure of theory and such a plausible fabric of interpretation, that the "mystery" is frankly excluded. Both imaginative "myth," when developed into a system, and intellectualist Scholasticism, when worked out to its completion, are methods by which the fundamental fact of religious experience is, as it were, simply rolled out so thin and flat as to be finally eliminated altogether.

Even on the lowest level of religious development the essential characteristic is therefore to be sought elsewhere than in the appearance of "spirit" representations. It lies rather, we repeat, in a peculiar "moment" of consciousness, to wit, the *stupor* before something "wholly other," whether such an other be named "spirit" or "daemon" or "deva," or be left without any name. Nor does it make any difference in this respect whether, to interpret and preserve their apprehension of this "other," men coin original imagery of their own or adapt imaginations drawn from the world of legend, the fabrications of fancy apart from and prior to any stirrings of daemonic dread. . . .

The Element of Fascination.   The qualitative *content* of the numinous experience, to which "the mysterious" stands as *form*, is in one of its aspects the element of daunting "awefulness" and "majesty," which has already been dealt with in detail; but it is clear that it has at the same time another aspect, in which it shows itself as something uniquely attractive and *fascinating*.

These two qualities, the daunting and the fascinating, now combine in a strange harmony of contrasts, and the resultant dual character of the numinous consciousness, to which the entire religious development bears witness, at any rate from the level of the "daemonic dread" onwards, is at once the strangest and most noteworthy phenomenon in the whole history of religion. The daemonic-divine object may appear to the mind an object of horror and dread, but at the same time it is no less something that allures with a potent charm, and the creature, who trembles before it, utterly cowed and cast down, has always at the same time the impulse to turn to it, nay even to make it somehow his own. The "mystery" is for him not merely something to be wondered at but something that entrances him; and beside that in it which bewilders and confounds, he feels a something that captivates and transports him with a strange ravishment, rising often enough to the pitch of dizzy intoxication. . . .

The ideas and concepts which are the parallels or "schemata" on the rational side of this non-rational element of "fascination" are love, mercy, pity, comfort; these are all "natural" elements of the common psychical life, only they are here thought as absolute and in completeness. But important as these are for the experience of religious bliss or felicity, they do not by any means exhaust it. It is just the same as with the opposite experience of religious infelicity—the experience of the "wrath" of God:—both alike contain fundamentally non-rational elements. Bliss or beatitude is more, far more, than the mere natural feeling of being comforted, of reliance, of the joy of love, however these may be heightened and enhanced. Just as "wrath," taken in a purely rational or a purely ethical sense, does not exhaust that profound element of *awefulness* which is locked in the mystery of deity, so neither does "graciousness" exhaust the profound element of *wonderfulness* and rapture which lies in the mysterious beatific experience of deity. The term "grace" may indeed be taken as its aptest designation, but then only in the sense in which it is really applied in the language of the mystics, and in which not only the "gracious intent" but "something more" is meant by the word. This "something more" has its antecedent phases very far back in the history of religions. . . .

What we Christians know as the experiences of grace and the second birth have their parallels also in the religions of high spiritual rank beyond the borders of Christianity. Such are the breaking out of the saving "Bodhi," the opening of the "heavenly eye," which is victorious over the darkness of nescience and shines out in an experience with which no other can be measured. And in all these the entirely non-rational and specific element in the beatific experience is immediately noticeable. The qualitative character of it varies widely in all these cases, and is again in them all very different from its parallels in Christianity; still in all it is very similar in intensity, and in all it is a "salvation" and an absolute "fascination," which in contrast to all that admits of "natural" expression or comparison is deeply imbued with the "over-abounding" ("exuberant") nature of the numen.

And this is also entirely true of the rapture of Nirvana, which is only in appearance a cold and negative state. It is only conceptually that "Nirvana" is a negation; it is felt in consciousness as in the strongest degree positive; it exercises a "fascination" by which its votaries are as much carried away as are the Hindu or the Christian by the corresponding objects of their worship. I recall vividly a conversation I had with a Buddhist monk. He had been putting before me methodically and pertinaciously the arguments for the Buddhist "theology of negation," the doctrine of Anātman and "entire emptiness." When he had made an end, I asked him, what then Nirvana itself is; and after a long pause came at last the single answer, low and restrained: "Bliss—unspeakable." And the hushed restraint of that answer, the solemnity of his voice, demeanour, and gesture, made more clear what was meant than the words themselves.

And so we maintain, on the one hand, . . . that the divine is indeed the highest, strongest, best, loveliest, and dearest that man can think of; but we assert on the other, . . . that God is not *merely* the ground and superlative of all that can be thought; He is in Himself a subject on His own account and in Himself.

Buber

Martin Buber (1878–1965) was a distinguished scholar of the Jewish mystical tra-dition called Hasidism and a deeply religious thinker in his own right. He was born in Vienna and studied philosophy in Vienna, Zurich, and Berlin. He taught philos-ophy at the Hebrew University of Jerusalem from 1938 to 1951.

In his widely acclaimed work *I and Thou* (1923), Buber set forth and evoked the relational character of religious experience in a clear, moving, and poetic style. He shows the ten-sion that obtains between our I-Thou relationships and our I-It forms of experience—or, to put it in terms of Kant's ethics, between our taking the objects of experience as ends in themselves and as mere means for what we want to achieve or acquire. As the ulti-mate end, God stands forth for Buber as the eternal Thou and the context, as it were, for all meaningful human relations.

The I-Thou Experience

To man the world is twofold, in accordance with his twofold attitude.

The attitude of man is twofold, in accordance with the twofold nature of the pri-mary words which he speaks.

The primary words are not isolated words, but combined words.

The one primary word is the combination *I-Thou.*

The other primary word is the combination *I-It;* wherein, without a change in the primary word, one of the words *He* and *She* can replace *It.*

Hence the *I* of man is also twofold.

For the *I* of the primary word *I-Thou* is a different *I* from that of the primary word *I-It.*

Primary words do not signify things, but they intimate relations.

Primary words do not describe something that might exist independently of them, but being spoken they bring about existence.

From *I and Thou* by Martin Buber, translated by Ronald Gregor Smith (1937). Reprinted by permission of T & T Clark Ltd.

414

Primary words are spoken from the being.

If *Thou* is said, the *I* of the combination *I-Thou* is said along with it.

If *It* is said, the *I* of the combination *I-It* is said along with it.

The primary word *I-Thou* can only be spoken with the whole being.

The primary word *I-It* can never be spoken with the whole being.

There is no *I* taken in itself, but only the *I* of the primary word *I-Thou* and the *I* of the primary word *I-It*.

When a man says *I* he refers to one or other of these. The *I* to which he refers is present when he says *I*. Further, when he says *Thou* or *It*, the *I* of one of the two primary words is present.

The existence of *I* and the speaking of *I* are one and the same thing.

When a primary word is spoken the speaker enters the word and takes his stand in it.

The life of human beings is not passed in the sphere of transitive verbs alone. It does not exist in virtue of activities alone which have some *thing* for their object.

I perceive something. I am sensible of something. I imagine something. I will something. I feel something. I think something. The life of human beings does not consist of all this and the like alone.

This and the like together establish the realm of *It*.

But the realm of *Thou* has a different basis.

When *Thou* is spoken, the speaker has no thing for his object. For where there is a thing there is another thing. Every *It* is bounded by others; *It* exists only through being bounded by others. But when *Thou* is spoken, there is no thing. *Thou* has no bounds.

When *Thou* is spoken, the speaker has no *thing*; he has indeed nothing. But he takes his stand in relation.

It is said that man experiences his world. What does that mean?

Man travels over the surface of things and experiences them. He extracts knowledge about their constitution from them: he wins an experience from them. He experiences what belongs to the things.

But the world is not presented to man by experiences alone. These present him only with a world composed of *It* and *He* and *She* and *It* again.

I experience something—If we add "inner" to "outer" experiences, nothing in the situation is changed. We are merely following the uneternal division that springs from the lust of the human race to whittle away the secret of death. Inner things or outer things, what are they but things and things!

I experience something—If we add "secret" to "open" experiences, nothing in the situation is changed. How self-confident is that wisdom which perceives a closed compartment in things, reserved for the initiate and manipulated only with the key. O secrecy without a secret! O accumulation of information! It, always It!

The man who experiences has no part in the world. For it is "in him" and not between him and the world that the experience arises.

The world has no part in the experience. It permits itself to be experienced, but has no concern in the matter. For it does nothing to the experience, and the experience does nothing to it.

As experience, the world belongs to the primary word *I-It*.
The primary word *I-Thou* establishes the world of relation.

The spheres in which the world of relation arises are three.

First, our life with nature. There the relation sways in gloom, beneath the level of speech. Creatures live and move over against us, but cannot come to us, and when we address them as *Thou*, our words cling to the threshold of speech.

Second, our life with men. There the relation is open and in the form of speech. We can give and accept the *Thou*.

Third, our life with intelligible forms. There the relation is clouded, yet it discloses itself; it does not use speech, yet begets it. We perceive no *Thou*, but none the less we feel we are addressed and we answer—forming, thinking, acting. We speak the primary word with our being, though we cannot utter *Thou* with our lips.

But with what right do we draw what lies outside speech into relation with the world of the primary word?

In every sphere in its own way, through each process of becoming that is present to us we look out toward the fringe of the eternal *Thou;* in each we are aware of a breath from the eternal *Thou;* in each *Thou* we address the eternal *Thou*.

I consider a tree.

I can look on it as a picture: stiff column in a shock of light, or splash of green shot with the delicate blue and silver of the background.

I can perceive it as movement: flowing veins on clinging, pressing pith, suck of the roots, breathing of the leaves, ceaseless commerce with earth and air—and the obscure growth itself.

I can classify it in a species and study it as a type in its structure and mode of life.

I can subdue its actual presence and form so sternly that I recognise it only as an expression of law—of the laws in accordance with which a constant opposition of forces is continually adjusted, or of those in accordance with which the component substances mingle and separate.

I can dissipate it and perpetuate it in number, in pure numerical relation.

In all this the tree remains my object, occupies space and time, and has its nature and constitution.

It can, however, also come about, if I have both will and grace, that in considering the tree I become bound up in relation to it. The tree is now no longer *It*. I have been seized by the power of exclusiveness.

To effect this it is not necessary for me to give up any of the ways in which I consider the tree. There is nothing from which I would have to turn my eyes away in order to see, and no knowledge that I would have to forget. Rather is everything, picture and movement, species and type, law and number, indivisibly united in this event.

Everything belonging to the tree is in this: its form and structure, its colours and chemical composition, its intercourse with the elements and with the stars, are all present in a single whole.

The tree is no impression, no play of my imagination, no value depending on my mood; but it is bodied over against me and has to do with me, as I with it—only in a different way.

Let no attempt be made to sap the strength from the meaning of the relation: relation is mutual.

The tree will have a consciousness, then, similar to our own? Of that I have no experience. But do you wish, through seeming to succeed in it with yourself, once again to disintegrate that which cannot be disintegrated? I encounter no soul or dryad of the tree, but the tree itself.

If I face a human being as my *Thou,* and say the primary word *I-Thou* to him, he is not a thing among things, and does not consist of things.

This human being is not *He* or *She,* bounded from every other *He* and *She,* a specific point in space and time within the net of the world; nor is he a nature able to be experienced and described, a loose bundle of named qualities. But with no neighbour, and whole in himself, he is *Thou* and fills the heavens. This does not mean that nothing exists except himself. But all else lives in *his* light.

Just as the melody is not made up of notes nor the verse of words nor the statue of lines, but they must be tugged and dragged till their unity has been scattered into these many pieces, so with the man to whom I say *Thou.* I can take out from him the colour of his hair, or of his speech, or of his goodness. I must continually do this. But each time I do it he ceases to be *Thou.*

And just as prayer is not in time but time in prayer, sacrifice not in space but space in sacrifice, and to reverse the relation is to abolish the reality, so with the man to whom I say *Thou.* I do not meet with him at some time and place or other. I can set him in a particular time and place; I must continually do it: but I set only a *He* or *She,* that is an *It,* no longer my *Thou.*

So long as the heaven of *Thou* is spread out over me the winds of causality cower at my heels, and the whirlpool of fate stays its course.

I do not experience the man to whom I say *Thou.* But I take my stand in relation to him, in the sanctity of the primary word. Only when I step out of it do I experience him once more. In the act of experience *Thou* is far away.

Even if the man to whom I say *Thou* is not aware of it in the midst of his experience, yet relation may exist. For *Thou* is more than *It* realizes. No deception penetrates here; here is the cradle of the Real Life.

This is the eternal source of art: a man is faced by a form which desires to be made through him into a work. This form is no offspring of his soul, but is an appearance which steps up to it and demands of it the effective power. The man is concerned with an act of his being. If he carries it through, if he speaks the primary word out of his being to the form which appears, then the effective power streams out, and the work arises.

The act includes a sacrifice and a risk. This is the sacrifice: the endless possibility that is offered up on the altar of the form. For everything which just this moment in play ran through the perspective must be obliterated; nothing of that may penetrate the work. The exclusiveness of what is facing it demands that it be so. This is the risk: the primary word can only be spoken with the whole being. He who gives himself to it may withhold nothing of himself. The work does not suffer me, as do the tree and the man, to turn aside and relax in the world of *It;* but it commands. If I do not serve it aright it is broken, or it breaks me.

I can neither experience nor describe the form which meets me, but only body it forth. And yet I behold it, splendid in the radiance of what confronts me, clearer than all the clearness of the world which is experienced. I do not behold it as a thing among the "inner" things nor as an image of my "fancy," but as that which exists in the present. If test is made of its objectivity the form is certainly not "there." Yet what is actually so much present as it is? And the relation in which I stand to it is real, for it affects me, as I affect it.

To produce is to draw forth, to invent is to find, to shape is to discover. In bodying forth I disclose. I lead the form across—into the world of *It.* The work produced is a thing among things, able to be experienced and described as a sum of qualities. But from time to time it can face the receptive beholder in its whole embodied form.

—What, then, do we experience of *Thou?*
—Just nothing. For we do not experience it.
—What, then, do we know of *Thou?*
—Just everything. For we know nothing isolated about it any more.

The *Thou* meets me through grace—it is not found by seeking. But my speaking of the primary word to it is an act of my being, is indeed *the* act of my being.

The *Thou* meets me. But I step into direct relation with it. Hence the relation means being chosen and choosing, suffering and action in one; just as any action of the whole being, which means the suspension of all partial actions and consequently of all sensations of actions grounded only in their particular limitation, is bound to resemble suffering.

The primary word *I-Thou* can be spoken only with the whole being. Concentration and fusion into the whole being can never take place through my agency, nor can it ever take place without me. I become through my relation to the *Thou;* as I become *I,* I say *Thou.*

All real living is meeting.

The relation to the *Thou* is direct. No system of ideas, no foreknowledge, and no fancy intervene between *I* and *Thou.* The memory itself is transformed, as it plunges out of its isolation into the unity of the whole. No aim, no lust, and no anticipation intervene between *I* and *Thou.* Desire itself is transformed as it plunges out of its dream into the appearance. Every means is an obstacle. Only when every means has collapsed does the meeting come about.

In face of the directness of the relation everything indirect becomes irrelevant. It is also irrelevant if my *Thou* is already the *It* or other *I's* ("an object of general experience"), or can become so through the very accomplishment of this act of my being. For the real, though certainly swaying and swinging, boundary runs neither between experience and non-experience, nor between what is given and what is not given, nor yet between the world of being and the world of value; but cutting indifferently across all these provinces it lies between *Thou* and *It*, between the present and the object.

The present, and by that is meant not the point which indicates from time to time in our thought merely the conclusion of "finished" time, the mere appearance of a termination which is fixed and held, but the real, filled present, exists only in so far as actual presentness, meeting, and relation exist. The present arises only in virtue of the fact that the *Thou* becomes present.

The *I* of the primary word *I-It*, that is, the *I* faced by no *Thou*, but surrounded by a multitude of "contents," has no present, only the past. Put in another way, in so far as man rests satisfied with the things that he experiences and uses, he lives in the past, and his moment has no present content. He has nothing but objects. But objects subsist in time that has been.

The present is not fugitive and transient, but continually present and enduring. The object is not duration, but cessation, suspension, a breaking off and cutting clear and hardening, absence of relation and of present being.

True beings are lived in the present, the life of objects is in the past.

Appeal to a "world of ideas" as a third factor above this opposition will not do away with its essential twofold nature. For I speak of nothing else but the real man, of you and of me, of our life and of our world—not of an *I*, or a state of being, in itself alone. The real boundary for the actual man cuts right across the world of ideas as well.

To be sure, many a man who is satisfied with the experience and use of the world of things has raised over or about himself a structure of ideas, in which he finds refuge and repose from the oncome of nothingness. On the threshold he lays aside his inauspicious everyday dress, wraps himself in pure linen, and regales himself with the spectacle of primal being, or of necessary being; but his life has no part in it. To proclaim his ways may even fill him with well-being.

But the mankind of mere *It* that is imagined, postulated, and propagated by such a man has nothing in common with a living mankind where *Thou* may truly be spoken. The noblest fiction is a fetish, the loftiest fictitious sentiment is depraved. Ideas are no more enthroned above our heads than resident in them; they wander amongst us and accost us. The man who leaves the primary word unspoken is to be pitied; but the man who addresses instead these ideas with an abstraction or a password, as if it were their name, is contemptible.

In one of the three examples it is obvious that the direct relation includes an effect on what confronts me. In art the act of the being determines the situation in which the form becomes the work. Through the meeting that which confronts me is fulfilled, and enters the world of things, there to be endlessly active, endlessly to become *It*, but also endlessly to become *Thou* again, inspiring and blessing. It is "embodied"; its body emerges from the flow of the spaceless, timeless present on the shore of existence.

The significance of the effect is not so obvious in the relation with the *Thou* spoken to men. The act of the being which provides directness in this case is usually understood wrongly as being one of feeling. Feelings accompany the metaphysical and metapyschical fact of love, but they do not constitute it. The accompanying feelings can be of greatly differing kinds. The feeling of Jesus for the demoniac differs from his feeling for the beloved disciple; but the love is the one love. Feelings are "entertained": love comes to pass. Feelings swell in man; but man dwells in his love. That is no metaphor, but the actual truth. Love does not cling to the *I* in such a way as to have the *Thou* only for its "content," its object; but love is *between I* and *Thou*. The man who does not know this, with his very being know this, does not know love; even though he ascribes to it the feelings he lives through, experiences, enjoys, and expresses. Love ranges in its effect through the whole world. In the eyes of him who takes his stand in love, and gazes out of it, men are cut free from their entanglement in bustling activity. Good people and evil, wise and foolish, beautiful and ugly, become successively real to him; that is, set free they step forth in their singleness, and confront him as *Thou*. In a wonderful way, from time to time, exclusiveness arises—and so he can be effective, helping, healing, educating, raising up, saving. Love is responsibility of an *I* for a *Thou*. In this lies the likeness—impossible in any feeling whatsoever—of all who love, from the smallest to the greatest and from the blessedly protected man, whose life is rounded in that of a loved being, to him who is all his life nailed to the cross of the world, and who ventures to bring himself to the dreadful point—to love *all men*.

Let the significance of the effect in the third example, that of the creature and our contemplation of it, remain sunk in mystery. Believe in the simple magic of life, in service in the universe, and the meaning of that waiting, that alertness, that "craning of the neck" in creatures will dawn upon you. Every word would falsify; but look! round about you beings live their life, and to whatever point you turn you come upon being.

Relation is mutual. My *Thou* affects me, as I affect it. We are moulded by our pupils and built up by our works. The "bad" man, lightly touched by the holy primary word, becomes one who reveals. How we are educated by children and by animals! We live our lives inscrutably included within the streaming mutual life of the universe.

—You speak of love as though it were the only relation between men. But properly speaking, can you take it even only as an example, since there is such a thing as hate?

—So long as love is "blind," that is, so long as it does not see a *whole* being, it is not truly under the sway of the primary word of relation. Hate is by nature blind. Only a part of a being can be hated. He who sees a whole being and is compelled to reject it is no longer in the kingdom of hate, but is in that of human restriction of the power to say *Thou*. He finds himself unable to say the primary word to the other human being confronting him. This word consistently involves an affirmation of the being addressed. He is therefore compelled to reject either the other or himself. At this barrier the entering on a relation recognises its relativity, and only simultaneously with this will the barrier be raised.

Yet the man who straighforwardly hates is nearer to relation than the man without hate and love.

But this is the exalted melancholy of our fate, that every *Thou* in our world must become an *It*. It does not matter how exclusively present the *Thou* was in the direct relation. As soon as the relation has been worked out or has been permeated with a means, the *Thou* becomes an object among objects—perhaps the chief, but still one of them, fixed in its size and its limits. In the work of art realisation in one sense means loss of reality in another. Genuine contemplation is over in a short time; now the life in nature, that first unlocked itself to me in the mystery of mutual action, can again be described, taken to pieces, and classified—the meeting-point of manifold systems of laws. And love itself cannot persist in direct relation. It endures, but in interchange of actual and potential being. The human being who was even now single and unconditioned, not something lying to hand, only present, not able to be experienced, only able to be fulfilled, has now become again a *He* or a *She*, a sum of qualities, a given quantity with a certain shape. Now I may take out from him again the colour of his hair or of his speech or of his goodness. But so long as I can do this he is no more my *Thou* and cannot yet be my *Thou* again.

Every *Thou* in the world is by its nature fated to become a thing, or continually to re-enter into the condition of things. In objective speech it would be said that every thing in the world, either before or after becoming a thing, is able to appear to an *I* as its *Thou*. But objective speech snatches only at a fringe of real life.

The *It* is the eternal chrysalis, the *Thou* the eternal butterfly—except that situations do not always follow one another in clear succession, but often there is a happening profoundly twofold, confusedly entangled.

Freud

In *Thus Spake Zarathustra* (1883–1885), Friedrich Nietzsche—through the voice of "The Madman"—declares that "God is dead":

> "Whither is God?" he [The Madman] cried. "I shall tell you. We—have killed him— you and I. . . . God is dead. God remains dead!" (translated by Walter Kaufmann)

In *Civilization and Its Discontents* (1930), Sigmund Freud—in his own voice—states that "what the ordinary man understands by his religion," that Providence is "a greatly exalted father," is "so patently infantile, so incongruous with reality, that to one whose attitude to humanity is friendly it is painful to think that the great majority of mortals will never be able to rise above this view of life" (translated by Joan Riviere).

Religion, for Freud, is an illusion, a projection of human needs upon reality. Psychologically grounded, philosophically empty, religious experience is essentially only an experience of oneself. "God is dead"—indeed for Freud, he was never anything more than a figment of human imagination.

In denigrating religion on the basis of its origin in deeply felt and rather repressed and unconscious desires and aspirations, Freud has often been criticized for committing what is called the "genetic fallacy"—the fallacy that one can measure the truth and value of various ideas by tracing them to their (often unseemly) psychological origin. It is as though one were to evaluate Einstein's $E = mc^2$ equation solely on the hypothetical grounds, say, that due to various early childhood deprivations at his mother's breast, Einstein had a compulsion to regard matter everywhere in terms of energy. The absurdity of this approach is evident. We determine the truth or value of various beliefs, claims, theories, and the like by appropriate means quite other than the examination of the psychological conditions of the holder of those beliefs and so on. Similarly, so the criticism goes, is the situation with religion. As William James, to whom we will turn again shortly, argued, it is "by their fruits ye shall know them, not by their roots." Freud, in *The Future of an Illusion* (1927), from which the selections that follow are taken, does allow that "illusions need not necessarily be false," but he goes on to assert that some religious doctrines "are so improbable, so incompatible with everything we have laboriously discovered about the reality of the world, that we may compare them . . . to delusions."

The Psychical Origin of Religious Ideas

These [religious ideas] which are given out as teachings, are not precipitates of experience or end-results of thinking: they are illusions, fulfillments of the oldest, strongest and most urgent wishes of mankind. The secret of their strength lies in the strength of those wishes. As we already know, the terrifying impression of helplessness in childhood aroused the need for protection—for protection through love—which was provided by the father; and the recognition that this helplessness lasts throughout life made it necessary to cling to the existence of a father, but this time a more powerful one. Thus the benevolent rule of a divine Providence allays our fear of the dangers of life; the establishment of a moral world-order ensures the fulfillment of the demands of justice, which have so often remained unfulfilled in human civilization; and the prolongation of earthly existence in a future life provides the local and temporal framework in which these wish-fulfillments shall take place. Answers to the riddles that tempt the curiosity of man, such as how the universe began or what the relation is between body and mind, are developed in conformity with the underlying assumptions of this system. It is an enormous relief to the individual psyche if the conflicts of its childhood arising from the father-complex—conflicts which it has never wholly overcome—are removed from it and brought to a solution which is universally accepted.

When I say that these things are all illusions, I must define the meaning of the word. An illusion is not the same thing as an error; nor is it necessarily an error. Aristotle's belief that vermin are developed out of dung (a belief to which ignorant people still cling) was an error; so was the belief of a former generation of doctors that *tabes dorsalis* is the result of sexual excess. It would be incorrect to call these errors illusions. On the other hand, it was an illusion of Columbus's that he had discovered a new sea-route to the Indies. The part played by his wish in this error is very clear. One may describe as an illusion the assertion made by certain nationalists that the Indo-Germanic race is the only one capable of civilization; or the belief, which was only destroyed by psycho-analysis, that children are creatures without sexuality. What is characteristic of illusions is that they are derived from human wishes. In this respect they come near to psychiatric delusions. But they differ from them, too, apart from the more complicated structure of delusions. In the case of delusions, we emphasize as essential their being in contradiction with reality. Illusions need not necessarily be false—that is to say, unrealizable or in contradiction to reality. For instance, a middle-class girl may have the illusion that a prince will come and marry her. This is possible; and a few such cases have occurred. That the Messiah will come and found a golden age is much less likely. Whether one classifies this belief as an illusion or as something analogous to a delusion will depend on one's personal attitude. Examples of illusions which have proved true are not easy to find, but the illusion of the alchemists that all metals can be turned into gold might be one of them. The wish to have a great deal of gold, as much gold as possible, has, it is true, been a good deal damped by our present-day knowledge of the determinants of wealth, but chemistry no longer regards the transmutation of metals into gold as impossible. Thus we call a belief an illusion when a wish-fulfillment is a prominent factor in its motivation, and in doing so we disregard its relations to reality, just as the illusion itself sets no store by verification.

Having thus taken our bearings, let us return once more to the question of religious doctrines. We can now repeat that all of them are illusions and insusceptible of proof. No one can be compelled to think them true, to believe in them. Some of them are so improbable, so incompatible with everything we have laboriously discovered about the reality of the world, that we may compare them—if we pay proper regard to the psychological differences—to delusions. Of the reality value of most of them we cannot judge; just as they cannot be proved, so they cannot be refuted. We still know too little to make a critical approach to them. The riddles of the universe reveal themselves only slowly to our investigation; there are many questions to which science to-day can give no answer. But scientific work is the only road which can lead us to a knowledge of reality outside ourselves. It is once again merely an illusion to expect anything from intuition and introspection; they can give us nothing but particulars about our own mental life, which are hard to interpret, never any information about the questions which religious doctrine finds it so easy to answer. It would be insolent to let one's own arbitrary will step into the breach and, according to one's personal estimate, declare this or that part of the religious system to be less or more acceptable. Such questions are too momentous for that; they might be called too sacred.

At this point one must expect to meet with an objection. "Well then, if even obdurate sceptics admit that the assertions of religion cannot be refuted by reason, why should I not believe in them, since they have so much on their side—tradition, the agreement of mankind, and all the consolations they offer?" Why not, indeed? Just as no one can be forced to believe, so no one can be forced to disbelieve. But do not let us be satisfied with deceiving ourselves that arguments like these take us along the road of correct thinking. If ever there was a case of a lame excuse we have it here. Ignorance is ignorance; no right to believe anything can be derived from it. In other matters no sensible person will behave so irresponsibly or rest content with such feeble grounds for his opinions and for the line he takes. It is only in the highest and most sacred things that he allows himself to do so. In reality these are only attempts at pretending to oneself or to other people that one is still firmly attached to religion, when one has long since cut oneself loose from it. Where questions of religion are concerned, people are guilty of every possible sort of dishonesty and intellectual misdemeanour. Philosophers stretch the meaning of words until they retain scarcely anything of their original sense. They give the name of "God" to some vague abstraction which they have created for themselves; having done so they can pose before all the world as deists, as believers in God, and they can even boast that they have recognized a higher, purer concept of God, notwithstanding that their

God is now nothing more than an insubstantial shadow and no longer the mighty personality of religious doctrines. Critics persist in describing as "deeply religious" anyone who admits to a sense of man's insignificance or impotence in face of the universe, although what constitutes the essence of the religious attitude is not this feeling but only the next step after it, the reaction to it which seeks a remedy for it. The man who goes no further, but humbly acquiesces in the small part which human beings play in the great world—such a man is, on the contrary, irreligious in the truest sense of the word.

To assess the truth-value of religious doctrines does not lie within the scope of the present enquiry. It is enough for us that we have recognized them as being, in their psychological nature, illusions. But we do not have to conceal the fact that this discovery also strongly influences our attitude to the question which must appear to many to be the most important of all. We know approximately at what periods and by what kind of men religious doctrines were created. If in addition we discover the motives which led to this, our attitude to the problem of religion will undergo a marked displacement. We shall tell ourselves that it would be very nice if there were a God who created the world and was a benevolent Providence, and if there were a moral order in the universe and an after-life; but it is a very striking fact that all this is exactly as we are bound to wish it to be. And it would be more remarkable still if our wretched, ignorant and downtrodden ancestors had succeeded in solving all these difficult riddles of the universe.

James

William James was keenly sensitive to the nature and possible values of a wide range of religious experience. Regarding the holding of theistic beliefs of the sort Freud compared to delusions, he argues in *The Will to Believe* (1897) that a scientific agnostic attitude that says "it is better to risk the loss of truth than suffer the chance of error" is not rational, and indeed that "a rule of thinking which would absolutely prevent me from acknowledging certain kinds of truth if those kinds of truth were really there, would be an irrational rule."

James maintained an openness to all forms of experience and was especially interested in making sense of various kinds of mysticism. In his ground-breaking *The Varieties of Religious Experience* (1902), a selection from which follows, he sets forth features or marks of mystical experience and analyzes what he takes to be examples of them.

Mysticism

First of all, then, I ask, What does the expression "mystical states of consciousness" mean? How do we part off mystical states from other states?

The words "mysticism" and "mystical" are often used as terms of mere reproach, to throw at any opinion which we regard as vague and vast and sentimental, and without a base in either facts or logic. For some writers a "mystic" is any person who believes in thought-transference, or spirit-return. Employed in this way the word has little value: there are too many less ambiguous synonyms. So, to keep it useful by restricting it, I will do what I did in the case of the word "religion," and simply propose to you four marks which, when an experience has them, may justify us in calling it mystical for the purpose of the present lectures. In this way we shall save verbal disputation, and the recriminations that generally go therewith.

1. *Ineffability.*—The handiest of the marks by which I classify a state of mind as mystical is negative. The subject of it immediately says that it defies expression, that

From *The Varieties of Religious Experience* (1902) by William James (New York: Random House, Modern Library, n.d.).

no adequate report of its contents can be given in words. It follows from this that its quality must be directly experienced; it cannot be imparted or transferred to others. In this peculiarity mystical states are more like states of feeling than like states of intellect. No one can make clear to another who has never had a certain feeling, in what the quality or worth of it consists. One must have musical ears to know the value of a symphony; one must have been in love one's self to understand a lover's state of mind. Lacking the heart or ear, we cannot interpret the musician or the lover justly, and are even likely to consider him weak-minded or absurd. The mystic finds that most of us accord to his experiences an equally incompetent treatment.

2. *Noetic quality.*—Although so similar to states of feeling, mystical states seem to those who experience them to be also states of knowledge. They are states of insight into depths of truth unplumbed by the discursive intellect. They are illuminations, revelations, full of significance and importance, all inarticulate though they remain; and as a rule they carry with them a curious sense of authority for after-time.

These two characters will entitle any state to be called mystical, in the sense in which I use the word. Two other qualities are less sharply marked, but are usually found. These are:—

3. *Transiency.*—Mystical states cannot be sustained for long. Except in rare instances, half an hour, or at most an hour or two, seems to be the limit beyond which they fade into the light of common day. Often, when faded, their quality can but imperfectly be reproduced in memory; but when they recur it is recognized; and from one recurrence to another it is susceptible of continuous development in what is felt as inner richness and importance.

4. *Passivity.*—Although the oncoming of mystical states may be facilitated by preliminary voluntary operations, as by fixing the attention, or going through certain bodily performances, or in other ways which manuals of mysticism prescribe; yet when the characteristic sort of consciousness once has set in, the mystic feels as if his own will were in abeyance, and indeed sometimes as if he were grasped and held by a superior power. This latter peculiarity connects mystical states with certain definite phenomena of secondary or alternative personality, such as prophetic speech, automatic writing, or the mediumistic trance. When these latter conditions are well pronounced, however, there may be no recollection whatever of the phenomenon, and it may have no significance for the subject's usual inner life, to which, as it were, it makes a mere interruption. Mystical states, strictly so-called, are never merely interruptive. Some memory of their content always remains, and a profound sense of their importance. They modify the inner life of the subject between the times of their recurrence. Sharp divisions in this region are, however, difficult to make, and we find all sorts of gradations and mixtures.

These four characteristics are sufficient to mark out a group of states of consciousness peculiar enough to deserve a special name and to call for careful study. Let it then be called the mystical group.

Our next step should be to gain acquaintance with some typical examples. Professional mystics at the height of their development have often elaborately organized experiences and a philosophy based thereupon. . . .

The simplest rudiment of mystical experience would seem to be that deepened sense of the significance of a maxim or formula which occasionally sweeps over one. "I've heard that said all my life," we exclaim, "but I never realized its full meaning until now." "When a fellow-monk," said Luther, "one day repeated the words of the Creed: 'I believe in the forgiveness of sins,' I saw the Scripture in an entirely new light; and straightway I felt as if I were born anew. It was as if I had found the door of paradise thrown wide open." This sense of deeper significance is not confined to rational propositions. Single words, and conjunctions of words, effects of light on land and sea, odors and musical sounds, all bring it when the mind is tuned aright. Most of us can remember the strangely moving power of passages in certain poems read when we were young, irrational doorways as they were through which the mystery of fact, the wildness and the pang of life, stole into our hearts and thrilled them. The words have now perhaps become mere polished surfaces for us; but lyric poetry and music are alive and significant only in proportion as they fetch these vague vistas of a life continuous with our own, beckoning and inviting, yet ever eluding our pursuit. We are alive or dead to the eternal inner message of the arts according as we have kept or lost this mystical susceptibility.

A more pronounced step forward on the mystical ladder is found in an extremely frequent phenomenon, that sudden feeling, namely, which sometimes sweeps over us, of having "been here before," as if at some indefinite past time, in just this place, with just these people, we were already saying just these things. As Tennyson writes:

> "Moreover, something is or seems
> That touches me with mystic gleams,
> Like glimpses of forgotten dreams—
>
> "Of something felt, like something here;
> Of something done, I know not where;
> Such as no language may declare." . . .

Somewhat deeper plunges into mystical consciousness are met with in yet other dreamy states. Such feelings as these which Charles Kingsley describes are surely far from being uncommon, especially in youth:—

> "When I walk the fields, I am oppressed now and then with an innate feeling that everything I see has a meaning, if I could but understand it. And this feeling of being surrounded with truths which I cannot grasp amounts to indescribable awe sometimes. . . . Have you not felt that your real soul was imperceptible to your mental vision, except in a few hallowed moments?"

A much more extreme state of mystical consciousness is described by J. A. Symonds; and probably more persons than we suspect could give parallels to it from their own experience.

> "Suddenly," writes Symonds, "at church, or in company, or when I was reading, and always, I think, when my muscles were at rest, I felt the approach of the

mood. Irresistibly it took possession of my mind and will, lasted what seemed an eternity, and disappeared in a series of rapid sensations which resembled the awakening from anæsthetic influence. One reason why I disliked this kind of trance was that I could not describe it to myself. I cannot even now find words to render it intelligible. It consisted in a gradual but swiftly progressive obliteration of space, time, sensation, and the multitudinous factors of experience which seem to qualify what we are pleased to call our Self. In proportion as these conditions of ordinary consciousness were subtracted, the sense of an underlying or essential consciousness acquired intensity. At last nothing remained but a pure, absolute, abstract Self. The universe became without form and void of content. But Self persisted, formidable in its vivid keenness, feeling the most poignant doubt about reality, ready, as it seemed, to find existence break as breaks a bubble round about it. And what then? The apprehension of a coming dissolution, the grim conviction that this state was the last state of the conscious Self, the sense that I had followed the last thread of being to the verge of the abyss, and had arrived at demonstration of eternal Maya or illusion, stirred or seemed to stir me up again. The return to ordinary conditions of sentient existence began by my first recovering the power of touch, and then by the gradual though rapid influx of familiar impressions and diurnal interests. At last I felt myself once more a human being; and though the riddle of what is meant by life remained unsolved, I was thankful for this return from the abyss—this deliverance from so awful an initiation into the mysteries of skepticism.

"This trance recurred with diminishing frequency until I reached the age of twenty-eight. It served to impress upon my growing nature the phantasmal unreality of all the circumstances which contribute to a merely phenomenal consciousness. Often have I asked myself with anguish, on waking from that formless state of denuded, keenly sentient being, Which is the unreality—the trance of fiery, vacant, apprehensive, skeptical Self from which I issue, or these surrounding phenomena and habits which veil that inner Self and build a self of flesh-and-blood conventionality? Again, are men the factors of some dream, the dream-like unsubstantiality of which they comprehend at such eventful moments? What would happen if the final stage of the trance were reached?"

. . . The next step into mystical states carries us into a realm that public opinion and ethical philosophy have long since branded as pathological, though private practice and certain lyric strains of poetry seem still to bear witness to its ideality. I refer to the consciousness produced by intoxicants and anæsthetics, especially by alcohol. The sway of alcohol over mankind is unquestionably due to its power to stimulate the mystical faculties of human nature, usually crushed to earth by the cold facts and dry criticisms of the sober hour. Sobriety diminishes, discriminates, and says no; drunkenness expands, unites, and says yes. It is in fact the great exciter of the *Yes* function in man. It brings its votary from the chill periphery of things to the radiant core. It makes him for the moment one with truth. Not through mere perversity do men run after it. To the poor and the unlettered it stands in the place of symphony concerts and of literature; and it is part of the deeper mystery and tragedy of life that whiffs and gleams of something that we immediately recognize as excellent should be vouchsafed to so many of us only in the fleeting earlier phases of when in its totality is so degrading a poisoning. The drunken consciousness is one bit of the mystic consciousness, and our total opinion of it must find its place in our opinion of that larger whole.

Nitrous oxide and ether, especially nitrous oxide, when sufficiently diluted with air, stimulate the mystical consciousness in an extraordinary degree. Depth beyond depth of truth seems revealed to the inhaler. This truth fades out, however, or escapes, at the moment of coming to; and if any words remain over in which it seemed to clothe itself, they prove to be the veriest nonsense. Nevertheless, the sense of a profound meaning having been there persists; and I know more than one person who is persuaded that in the nitrous oxide trance we have a genuine metaphysical revelation.

Some years ago I myself made some observations on this aspect of nitrous oxide intoxication, and reported them in print. One conclusion was forced upon my mind at that time, and my impression of its truth has ever since remained unshaken. It is that our normal waking consciousness, rational consciousness as we call it, is but one special type of consciousness, whilst all about it, parted from it by the filmiest of screens, there lie potential forms of consciousness entirely different. We may go through life without suspecting their existence; but apply the requisite stimulus, and at a touch they are there in all their completeness, definite types of mentality which probably somewhere have their field of application and adaptation. No account of the universe in its totality can be final which leaves these other forms of consciousness quite disregarded. How to regard them is the question—for they are so discontinuous with ordinary consciousness. Yet they may determine attitudes though they cannot furnish formulas, and open a region though they fail to give a map. At any rate, they forbid a premature closing of our accounts with reality. Looking back on my own experiences, they all converge towards a kind of insight to which I cannot help ascribing some metaphysical significance. The keynote of it is invariably a reconciliation. It is as if the opposites of the world, whose contradictoriness and conflict make all our difficulties and troubles, were melted into unity. Not only do they, as contrasted species, belong to one and the same genus, but *one of the species, nobler and better one, is itself the genus, and so soaks up and absorbs its opposite into itself.* This is a dark saying, I know, when thus expressed in terms of common logic, but I cannot wholly escape from its authority. . . . Those who have ears to hear, let them hear; to me the living sense of its reality only comes in the artificial mystic state of mind.

Smith

Huston Smith was for many years a professor of philosophy at the Massachusetts Institute of Technology and remains an extremely popular historian of world religions. He has appeared often on radio and television as a spokesperson for the religious values and philosophical insights to be found throughout various religious traditions.

In the highly provocative article "Do Drugs Have Religious Import?", Smith takes up the issue raised by William James regarding those dimensions of drug-induced experience that, according to James's own testimony, seem to share important features with more traditional and orthodox forms of religious experience. While trying to avoid the genetic fallacy, Smith takes a somewhat controversial position regarding the question of whether drug-induced experiences are in fact indistinguishable from genuine religious or spiritual experiences.

Do Drugs Have Religious Import?

Until six months ago, if I picked up my phone in the Cambridge area and dialed KISS-BIG, a voice would answer, "If-if." These were coincidences: KISS-BIG happened to be the letter equivalents of an arbitrarily assigned telephone number, and I.F.I.F. represented the initials of an organization with the improbable name of the International Federation for Internal Freedom. But the coincidences were apposite to the point of being poetic. "Kiss big" caught the euphoric, manic, life-embracing attitude that characterized this most publicized of the organizations formed to explore the newly synthesized consciousness-changing substances; the organization itself was surely one of the "iffy-est" phenomena to appear on our social and intellectual scene in some time. It produced the first firings in Harvard's history, an ultimatum to get out of Mexico in five days, and "the miracle of Marsh Chapel," in which, during a two-and-one-half-hour Good Friday service, ten theological stu-

From "Do Drugs Have Religious Import?" by Huston Smith, *The Journal of Philosophy,* vol. LXI, no. 18 (October 1, 1964).

dents and professors ingested psilocybin and were visited by what they generally reported to be the deepest religious experiences of their lives.

Despite the last of these phenomena and its numerous if less dramatic parallels, students of religion appear by and large to be dismissing the psychedelic drugs that have sprung to our attention in the '60s as having little religious relevance. The position taken in one of the most forward-looking volumes of theological essays to have appeared in recent years—*Soundings,* edited by A. R. Vidler—accepts R. C. Zaehner's *Mysticism Sacred and Profane* as having "fully examined and refuted" the religious claims for mescalin which Aldous Huxley sketched in *The Doors of Perception.* This closing of the case strikes me as premature, for it looks as if the drugs have light to throw on the history of religion, the phenomenology of religion, the philosophy of religion, and the practice of the religious life itself.

1. DRUGS AND RELIGION VIEWED HISTORICALLY

In his trial-and-error life explorations man almost everywhere has stumbled upon connections between vegetables (eaten or brewed) and actions (yogi breathing exercises, whirling-dervish dances, flagellations) that alter states of consciousness. From the psychopharmacological standpoint we now understand these states to be the products of changes in brain chemistry. From the sociological perspective we see that they tend to be connected in some way with religion. If we discount the wine used in Christian communion services, the instances closest to us in time and space are the peyote of The Native American [Indian] Church and Mexico's 2000-year-old "sacred mushrooms," the latter rendered in Aztec as "God's Flesh"—striking parallel to "the body of our Lord" in the Christian eucharist. . . .

2. DRUGS AND RELIGION VIEWED PHENOMENOLOGICALLY

Phenomenology attempts a careful description of human experience. The question the drugs pose for the phenomenology of religion, therefore, is whether the experiences they induce differ from religious experiences reached naturally, and if so how.

Even the Bible notes that chemically induced psychic states bear *some* resemblance to religious ones. Peter had to appeal to a circumstantial criterion—the early hour of the day—to defend those who were caught up in the Pentecostal experience against the charge that they were merely drunk: "These men are not drunk, as you suppose, since it is only the third hour of the day" (Acts 2:15); and Paul initiates the comparison when he admonishes the Ephesians not to "get drunk with wine . . . but [to] be filled with the spirit" (Ephesians 5:18). Are such comparisons, paralleled in the accounts of virtually every religion, superficial? How far can they be pushed?

Not all the way, students of religion have thus far insisted. With respect to the new drugs, Prof. R. C. Zaehner has drawn the line emphatically. "The importance of Huxley's *Doors of Perception,*" he writes, "is that in it the author clearly makes the claim that what he experienced under the influence of mescalin is closely comparable to a genuine mystical experience. If he is right, . . . the conclusions . . . are alarming." Zaehner thinks that Huxley is not right, but I fear that it is Zaehner who is mistaken.

There are, of course, innumerable drug experiences that have no religious feature; they can be sensual as readily as spiritual, trivial as readily as transforming, capricious as readily as sacramental. If there is one point about which every student of the drugs agrees, it is that there is no such thing as the drug experience *per se*— no experience that the drugs, as it were, merely secrete. Every experience is a mix of three ingredients: drug, set (the psychological make-up of the individual), and setting (the social and physical environment in which it is taken). But given the right set and setting, the drugs can induce religious experiences indistinguishable from experiences that occur spontaneously. Nor need set and setting be exceptional. The way the statistics are currently running, it looks as if from one-fourth to one-third of the general population will have religious experiences if they take the drugs under naturalistic conditions, meaning by this conditions in which the researcher supports the subject but does not try to influence the direction his experience will take. Among subjects who have strong religious inclinations to begin with, the proportion of those having religious experiences jumps to three-fourths. If they take the drugs in settings that are religious too, the ratio soars to nine in ten.

How do we know that the experiences these people have really are religious? We can begin with the fact that they say they are. The "one-fourth to one-third of the general population" figure is drawn from two sources. Ten months after they had had their experiences, 24 per cent of the 194 subjects in a study by the California psychiatrist Oscar Janiger characterized their experiences as having been religious. Thirty-two per cent of the 74 subjects in Ditman and Hayman's study reported, looking back on their LSD experience, that it looked as if it had been "very much" or "quite a bit" a religious experience; 42 per cent checked as true the statement that they "were left with a greater awareness of God, or a higher power, or ultimate reality." The statement that three-fourths of subjects having religious "sets" will have religious experiences comes from the reports of sixty-nine religious professionals who took the drugs while the Harvard project was in progress.

In the absence of (a) a single definition of religious experience acceptable to psychologists of religion generally and (b) fool-proof ways of ascertaining whether actual experiences exemplify any definition, I am not sure there is any better way of telling whether the experiences of the 333 men and women involved in the above studies were religious than by noting whether they seemed so to them. . . .

With the thought that the reader might like to test his own powers of discernment on the question being considered, I insert here a simple test I gave to a group of Princeton students following a recent discussion sponsored by the Woodrow Wilson Society:

> Below are accounts of two religious experiences. One occurred under the influence of drugs, one without their influence. Check the one you think *was* drug-induced.

I

Suddenly I burst into a vast, new, indescribably wonderful universe. Although I am writing this over a year later, the thrill of the surprise and amazement, the awesomeness of the revelation, the engulfment in an overwhelming feeling-wave of gratitude and blessed wonderment, are as fresh, and the memory of the experience is as vivid, as if it had happened five minutes ago. And yet to concoct anything by way of description that would even hint at the magnitude, the sense of ultimate reality . . . this seems such an impossible task. The knowledge which has infused and affected every aspect of my life came instantaneously and with such complete force of certainty that it was impossible, then or since, to doubt its validity.

II

All at once, without warning of any kind, I found myself wrapped in a flame-colored cloud. For an instant I thought of fire . . . the next, I knew that the fire was within myself. Directly afterward there came upon me a sense of exultation, of immense joyousness accompanied or immediately followed by an intellectual illumination impossible to describe. Among other things, I did not merely come to believe, but I saw that the universe is not composed of dead matter, but is, on the contrary, a living Presence; I became conscious in myself of eternal life. . . . I saw that all men are immortal: that the cosmic order is such that without any preadventure all things work together for the good of each and all; that the foundation principle of the world . . . is what we call love, and that the happiness of each and all is in the long run absolutely certain.

On the occasion referred to, twice as many students (46) answered incorrectly as answered correctly (23). I bury the correct answer in a footnote to preserve the reader's opportunity to test himself.*

Why, in the face of this considerable evidence, does Zaehner hold that drug experiences cannot be authentically religious? There appear to be three reasons:

1. His own experience was "utterly trivial." This of course proves that not all drug experiences are religious; it does not prove that no drug experiences are religious.

2. He thinks the experiences of others that appear religious to them are not truly so. Zaehner distinguishes three kinds of mysticism: nature mysticism, in which the soul is united with the natural world; monistic mysticism, in which the soul merges with an impersonal absolute; and theism, in which the soul confronts the living, personal God. He concedes that drugs can induce the first two species of mysticism, but not its supreme instance, the theistic. As proof, he analyzes Huxley's experience as recounted in *The Doors of Perception* to show that it produced at best a blend of nature and monistic mysticism. Even if we were to accept Zaehner's evaluation of the three forms of mysticism, Huxley's case, and indeed Zaehner's entire book, would prove only that not every mystical experience induced by the drugs is theistic. Insofar as

---

* The former experience occurred under the influence of drugs; the latter did not.

Zaehner goes beyond this to imply that drugs do not and cannot induce theistic mysticism, he not only goes beyond the evidence but proceeds in the face of it. James Slotkin reports that the peyote Indians "see visions, which may be of Christ Himself. Sometimes they hear the voice of the Great Spirit. Sometimes they become aware of the presence of God and of those personal shortcomings which must be corrected if they are to do His will." . . .

3. There is a third reason why Zaehner might doubt that drugs can induce genuinely mystical experiences. Zaehner is a Roman Catholic, and Roman Catholic doctrine teaches that mystical rapture is a gift of grace and as such can never be reduced to man's control. This may be true; certainly the empirical evidence cited does not preclude the possibility of a genuine ontological or theological difference between natural and drug-induced religious experiences. At this point, however, we are considering phenomenology rather than ontology, description rather than interpretation, and on this level there is no difference. Descriptively, drug experiences cannot be distinguished from their natural religious counterpart. When the current philosophical authority on mysticism, W. T. Stace, was asked whether the drug experience is similar to the mystical experience, he answered, "It's not a matter of its being *similar* to mystical experience; it *is* mystical experience." . . .

3. DRUGS AND RELIGION VIEWED PHILOSOPHICALLY

Why do people reject evidence? Because they find it threatening, we may suppose. Theologians are not the only professionals to utilize this mode of defense. In his *Personal Knowledge*, Michael Polanyi recounts the way the medical profession ignored such palpable facts as the painless amputation of human limbs, performed before their own eyes in hundreds of successive cases, concluding that the subjects were imposters who were either deluding their physicians or colluding with them. One physician, Esdaile, carried out about 300 major operations painlessly under mesmeric trance in India, but neither in India nor in Great Britain could he get medical journals to print accounts of his work. Polanyi attributes this closed-mindedness to "lack of a conceptual framework in which their discoveries could be separated from specious and untenable admixtures."

The "untenable admixture" in the fact that psychotomimetic drugs can induce religious experience is its apparent implicate: that religious disclosures are no more veridical than psychotic ones. For religious skeptics, this conclusion is obviously not untenable at all; it fits in beautifully with their thesis that *all* religion is at heart an escape from reality. Psychotics avoid reality by retiring into dream worlds of make-believe; what better evidence that religious visionaries do the same than the fact that identical changes in brain chemistry produce both states of mind? Had not Marx already warned us that religion is the "opiate" of the people?—apparently he was more literally accurate than he supposed. Freud was likewise too mild. He "never doubted that religious phenomena are to be understood only on the model of the neurotic symptoms of the individual." He should have said "psychotic symptoms."

So the religious skeptic is likely to reason. What about the religious believer?

Convinced that religious experiences are not fundamentally delusory, can he admit that psychotomimetic drugs can occasion them? To do so he needs (to return to Polanyi's words) "a conceptual framework in which [the discoveries can] be separated from specious and untenable admixtures," the "untenable admixture" being is this case the conclusion that religious experiences are in general delusory.

One way to effect the separation would be to argue that, despite phenomenological similarities between natural and drug-induced religious experiences, they are separated by a crucial *ontological* difference. Such an argument would follow the pattern of theologians who argue for the "real presence" of Christ's body and blood in the bread and wine of the Eucharist despite their admission that chemical analysis, confined as it is to the level of "accidents" rather than "essences," would not disclose this presence. But this distinction will not appeal to many today, for it turns on an essence-accident metaphysics which is not widely accepted. Instead of fighting a rear-guard action by insisting that if drug and non-drug religious experiences cannot be distinguished empirically there must be some transempirical factor that distinguishes them and renders the drug experience profane, I wish to explore the possibility of accepting drug-induced experiences as religious without relinquishing confidence in the truth-claims of religious experience generally.

To begin with the weakest of all arguments, the argument from authority: William James did not discount *his* insights that occurred while his brain chemistry was altered. The paragraph in which he retrospectively evaluates his nitrous oxide experiences has become classic, but it is so pertinent to the present discussion that it merits quoting once again.

> One conclusion was forced upon my mind at that time, and my impression of its truth has ever since remained unshaken. It is that our normal waking consciousness, rational consciousness as we call it, is but one special type of consciousness, whilst all about it, parted from it by the filmiest of screens, there lie potential forms of consciousness entirely different. We may go through life without suspecting their existence; but apply the requisite stimulus, and at a touch they are there in all their completeness, definite types of mentality which probably somewhere have their field of application and adaptation. No account of the universe in its totality can be final which leaves these other forms of consciousness quite disregarded. How to regard them is the question—for they are so discontinuous with ordinary consciousness. Yet they may determine attitudes though they cannot furnish formulas, and open a region though they fail to give a map. At any rate, they forbid a premature closing of our accounts with reality. Looking back on my own experiences, they all converge toward a kind of insight to which I cannot help ascribing some metaphysical significance.

To this argument from authority, I add two arguments that try to provide something by ways of reason. Drug experiences that assume a religious cast tend to have fearful and/or beatific features, and each of my hypotheses relates to one of these aspects of the experience.

Beginning with the ominous, "fear of the Lord," awe-ful features, Gordon Wasson, the New York banker-turned-mycologist, describes these as he encountered them in his psilocybin experience as follows: "Ecstasy! In common parlance . . . ecstasy is fun. . . . But ecstasy is not fun. Your very soul is seized and shaken until it tingles. After all, who will choose to feel undiluted awe? . . . The unknowing vulgar abuse the word; we must recapture its full and terrifying sense." Emotionally the drug experience can be like having forty-foot waves crash over you for several hours while you cling desperately to a life-raft which may be swept from under you at any minute. It seems quite possible that such an ordeal, like any experience of a close call, could awaken rather fundamental sentiments respecting life and death and destiny and trigger the "no atheists in foxholes" effect. Similarly, as the subject emerges from the trauma and realizes that he is not going to be insane as he had feared, there may come over him an intensified appreciation like that frequently reported by patients recovering from critical illness. "It happened on the day when my bed was pushed out of doors to the open gallery of the hospital," reads one such report:

> I cannot now recall whether the revelation came suddenly or gradually; I only remember finding myself in the very midst of those wonderful moments, beholding life for the first time in all its young intoxication of loveliness, in its unspeakable joy, beauty, and importance. I cannot say exactly what the mysterious change was. I saw no new thing, but I saw all the usual things in a miraculous new light—in what I believe is their true light. I saw for the time how wildly beautiful and joyous, beyond any words of mine to describe, is the whole of life. Every human being moving across that porch, every sparrow that flew, every branch tossing in the wind, was caught in and was a part of the whole mad ecstasy of loveliness, of joy, of importance, of intoxication of life.

If we do not discount religious intuitions because they are prompted by battlefields and *physical* crises; if we regard the latter as "calling us to our senses" more often than they seduce us into delusions, need comparable intuitions be discounted simply because the crises that trigger them are of an inner, *psychic* variety?

Turning from the hellish to the heavenly aspects of the drug experience, *some* of the latter may be explainable by the hypothesis just stated; that is, they may be occasioned by the relief that attends the sense of escape from high danger. But this hypothesis cannot possibly account for *all* the beatific episodes, for the simple reason that the positive episodes often come first, or to persons who experience no negative episodes whatever. Dr. Sanford Unger of the National Institute of Mental Health reports that among his subjects "50 to 60% will not manifest any real disturbance worthy of discussion," yet "around 75% will have at least one episode in which exaltation, rapture, and joy are the key descriptions." How are we to account for the drug's capacity to induce peak experiences, such as the following, which are *not* preceded by fear?

A feeling of great peace and contentment seemed to flow through my entire body. All sound ceased and I seemed to be floating in a great, very very still void or hemisphere. It is impossible to describe the overpowering feeling of peace, contentment, and being a part of goodness itself that I felt. I could feel my body dissolving and actually becoming a part of the goodness and peace that was all around me. Words can't describe this. I feel an awe and wonder that such a feeling could have occurred to me.

. . .

4. THE DRUGS AND RELIGION VIEWED "RELIGIOUSLY"

Suppose that drugs can induce experiences indistinguishable from religious experiences and that we can respect their reports. Do they shed any light, not (we now ask) on life, but on the nature of the religious life?

One thing they may do is throw religious experience itself into perspective by clarifying its relation to the religious life as a whole. Drugs appear able to induce religious experiences; it is less evident that they can produce religious lives. It follows that religion is more than religious experiences. This is hardly news, but it may be a useful reminder, especially to those who incline toward "the religion of religious experience"; which is to say toward lives bent on the acquisition of desired states of experience irrespective of their relation to life's other demands and components.

Despite the dangers of faculty psychology, it remains useful to regard man as having a mind, a will, and feelings. One of the lessons of religious history is that, to be adequate, a faith must rouse and involve all three components of man's nature. Religions of reason grow arid; religions of duty, leaden. Religions of experience have their comparable pitfalls, as evidenced by Taoism's struggle (not always successful) to keep from degenerating into quietism, and the vehemence with which Zen Buddhism has insisted that once students have attained *satori*, they must be driven out of it, back into the world. The case of Zen is especially pertinent here, for it pivots on an enlightenment experience—*satori*, or *kensho*—which some (but not all) Zennists say resembles LSD. Alike or different, the point is that Zen recognizes that unless the experience is joined to discipline, it will come to naught:

> Even the Buddha . . . had to sit. . . . Without *joriki*, the particular power developed through *zazen* [seated meditation], the vision of oneness attained in enlightenment . . . in time becomes clouded and eventually fades into a pleasant memory instead of remaining an omnipresent reality shaping our daily life. . . . To be able to live in accordance with what the Mind's eye has revealed through *satori* requires, like the purification of character and the development of personality, a ripening period of *zazen*.

If the religion of religious experience is a snare and a delusion, it follows that no religion that fixes its faith primarily in substances that induce religious experiences can be expected to come to a good end. What promised to be a short cut will prove to be a short circuit; what began as a religion will end as a religion surrogate. Whether chemical substances can be helpful *adjuncts* to faith is another question. The peyote-using Native American Church seems to indicate that they can be; anthropologists give this church a good report, noting among other things that members resist alcohol and alcoholism better than do nonmembers. The conclusion to which evidence currently points would seem to be that chemicals *can* aid the religious life, but only where set within a context of faith (meaning by this the conviction that what they disclose is true) and discipline (meaning diligent exercise of the will in the attempt to work out the implications of the disclosures for the living of life in the everyday, common-sense world).

Nowhere today in Western civilization are these two conditions jointly fulfilled. Churches lack faith in the sense just mentioned; hipsters lack discipline. This might lead us to forget about the drugs, were it not for one fact: the distinctive religious emotion and the emotion that drugs unquestionably can occasion—Otto's *mysterium tremendum, majestas, mysterium fascinans;* in a phrase, the phenomenon of religious awe—seems to be declining sharply. As Paul Tillich said in an address to the Hillel Society at Harvard several years ago:

> The question our century puts before us [is]: Is it possible to regain the lost dimension, the encounter with the Holy, the dimension which cuts through the world of subjectivity and objectivity and goes down to that which is not world but is the mystery of the Ground of Being?

Tillich may be right; this may be the religious question of our century. For if (as we have insisted) religion cannot be equated with religious experiences, neither can it long survive their absence.

Suzuki

D. T. Suzuki (1870–1966) is considered to be the leading interpreter of Zen Buddhism for Western readers. He was professor of Buddhist philosophy at Otani University, Kyoto, and also taught at Harvard and Columbia universities. During his long life he wrote over one hundred books on Buddhism.

Perhaps more than any other religious-philosophical tradition, Zen Buddhism emphasizes the direct and immediate insight into reality that it calls *satori*. Suzuki describes this phenomena within the framework of the Rinzai school of Zen, which calls attention to the nonrational (some would say irrational) features of this experience and insists that the experience overcomes radically all manner of analytic, intellectual comprehension. Appealing, as does the Rinzai school itself, to anecdotes and stories about Zen masters and their pupils, Suzuki shows through several vivid examples how *satori* is thought to be achieved and the boundless joy that accompanies the enlightenment that it represents.

Satori, *or Acquiring a New Viewpoint*

The object of Zen discipline consists in acquiring a new viewpoint for looking into the essence of things. If you have been in the habit of thinking logically according to the rules of dualism, rid yourself of it and you may come around somewhat to the viewpoint of Zen. You and I are supposedly living in the same world, but who can tell that the thing we popularly call a stone that is lying before my window is the same to both of us? You and I sip a cup of tea. That act is apparently alike to us both, but who can tell what a wide gap there is subjectively between your drinking and my drinking? In your drinking there may be no Zen, while mine is brim-full of it. The reason for it is: you move in a logical circle and I am out of it. Though there is in fact nothing new in the so-called new viewpoint of Zen, the term "new" is convenient to express the Zen way of viewing the world, but its use here is a condescension on the part of Zen.

This acquiring of a new viewpoint in Zen is called *satori* and its verb form is *satoru*. Without it there is no Zen, for the life of Zen begins with the "opening of *satori*." *Satori* may be defined as intuitive looking-into, in contradistinction to intellectual and logical understanding. Whatever the definition, *satori* means the unfolding of a new world hitherto unperceived in the confusion of a dualistic mind. . . .

. . . Tokusan was a great scholar of the *Diamond Sutra*. Learning that there was such a thing as Zen, ignoring all the written scriptures and directly laying hands on one's soul, he went to Ryutan to be instructed in the teaching. One day Tokusan was sitting outside trying to look into the mystery of Zen. Ryutan said, "Why don't you come in?" Replied Tokusan, "It is pitch dark." A candle was lighted and held out to Tokusan. When he was at the point of taking it Ryutan suddenly blew out the light, whereupon the mind of Tokusan was opened.

Hyakujo (Pai-chang) went out one day attending his master Baso (Ma-tsu), when they saw a flock of wild geese flying. Baso asked:

"What are they?"

"They are wild geese, sir."

"Whither are they flying?"

"They have flown away."

Baso, abruptly taking hold of Hyakujo's nose, give it a twist. Overcome with pain, Hyakujo cried out: "Oh! Oh!"

Said Baso, "You say they have flown away, but all the same they have been here from the very first."

This made Hyakujo's back wet with perspiration; he had *satori*. . . .

Kyogen (Hsiang-yen) was a disciple of Hyakujo (Pai-chang). After his master's death Kyogen went to Yisan (Kuei-shan), who had been a senior disciple of Hyakujo. Yisan asked him: "I am told that you have been studying under my late master, and also that you have remarkable intelligence. The understanding of Zen through this medium necessarily ends in intellectual analytical comprehension, which is not of much use; but nevertheless you may have had an insight into the truth of Zen. Let me have your view as to the reason of birth and death; that is, as to your own being before your parents had given birth to you."

Thus asked, Kyogen did not know how to reply. He retired into his own room and assiduously made research into the notes which he had taken of the sermons given by their late master. He failed to come across a suitable passage which he might present as his own view. He returned to Yisan and implored him to teach him in the faith of Zen, but Yisan replied: "I really have nothing to impart to you, and if I tried to do so you might have occasion to make me an object of ridicule. Besides, whatever I can tell you is my own and can never be yours." Kyogen was disappointed and considered him unkind. Finally he came to the decision to burn up all his notes and memoranda, which seemed to be of no help to his spiritual welfare, and, retiring altogether from the world, to spend the rest of his life in solitude and the simple life in accordance with Buddhist rules. He reasoned: "What is the use of studying Buddhism, which is so difficult to comprehend and which is too subtle to receive as instruction from another? I will be a plain homeless monk, troubled with no desire to master things too deep for thought." He left Yisan and built a hut near the tomb of Chu, the National Master at Nan-yang. One day he was weeding and sweeping the ground when a pebble which he had swept away struck a bamboo; the unexpected sound produced by the percussion elevated his mind to a state of *satori*. His joy was boundless. The question proposed by Yisan became transparent; he felt as if meeting his lost parents. Besides, he came to realize the kindness of Yisan in refusing him instruction, for now he realized that this experience could not have happened to him if Yisan had been unkind enough to explain things to him.

Cannot Zen be so explained that a master can lead all his pupils to enlightenment through explanation? Is *satori* something that is not at all capable of intellectual analysis? Yes, it is an experience which no amount of explanation or argument can make communicable to others unless the latter themselves had it previously. If *satori* is amenable to analysis in the sense that by so doing it becomes perfectly clear to another who has never had it, that *satori* will be no *satori*. For a *satori* turned into a concept ceases to be itself; and there will no more be a Zen experience. Therefore, all that we can do in Zen in the way of instruction is to indicate, or to suggest, or to show the way so that one's attention may be directed towards the goal. As to attaining the goal and taking hold of the thing itself, this must be done by one's own hands, for nobody else can do it for one. As regards the indication, it lies everywhere. When a man's mind is matured for *satori* it tumbles over one everywhere. An inarticulate sound, an unintelligent remark, a blooming flower, or a trivial incident such as stumbling, is the condition or occasion that will open his mind or *satori*. Apparently, an insignificant event produces an effect which in importance is altogether out of proportion. The light touch of an igniting wire, and an explosion follows which will shake the very foundation of the earth. All the causes, all the conditions of *satori* are in the mind; they are merely waiting for the maturing. When the mind is ready for some reasons or others, a bird flies, or a bell rings, and you at once return to your original home; that is, you discover your now real self. From the very beginning nothing has been kept from you, all that you wished to see has been there all the time before you, it was only yourself that closed the eye to the fact. Therefore, there is in Zen nothing to explain, nothing to teach, that will add to your knowledge. Unless it grows out of yourself no knowledge is really yours, it is only a borrowed plumage. . . .

After these remarks the following points about the opening of the mind that is called *satori* may be observed and summarized.

1. People often imagine that the discipline of Zen is to produce a state of self-suggestion through meditation. This entirely misses the mark. . . . *Satori* does not consist in producing a certain premeditated condition by intensely thinking of it. It is acquiring a new point of view for looking at things. Ever since the unfoldment of consciousness we have been led to respond to the inner and outer conditions in a certain conceptual and analytical manner. The discipline of Zen consists in upsetting this groundwork once for all and reconstructing the old frame on an entirely new basis. It is evident, therefore, that meditating on metaphysical and

symbolical statements, which are products of a relative consciousness, play no part in Zen.

2. Without the attainment of *satori* no one can enter into the truth of Zen. *Satori* is the sudden flashing into consciousness of a new truth hitherto undreamed of. It is a sort of mental catastrophe taking place all at once, after much piling up of matters intellectual and demonstrative. The piling has reached a limit of stability and the whole edifice has come tumbling to the ground, when, behold, a new heaven is open to full survey. When the freezing point is reached, water suddenly turns into ice; the liquid has suddenly turned into a solid body and no more flows freely. *Satori* comes upon a man unawares, when he feels that he has exhausted his whole being. Religiously, it is a new birth; intellectually, it is the acquiring of a new viewpoint. The world now appears as if dressed in a new garment, which seems to cover up all the unsightliness of dualism, which is called delusion in Buddhist phraseology.

3. *Satori* is the *raison d'être* of Zen without which Zen is no Zen. Therefore every contrivance, disciplinary or doctrinal, is directed toward *satori*. Zen masters could not remain patient for *satori* to come by itself; that is, to come sporadically or at its own pleasure. In their earnestness to aid their disciples in the search after the truth of Zen their manifestly enigmatical presentations were designed to create in their disciples a state of mind which would more systematically open the way to enlightenment. All the intellectual demonstrations and exhortatory persuasions so far carried out by most religious and philosophical leaders had failed to produce the desired effect, and their disciples thereby had been farther and farther led astray. Especially was this the case when Buddhism was first introduced into China, with all its Indian heritage of highly metaphysical abstractions and most complicated systems of Yoga discipline, which left the more practical Chinese at a loss as to how to grasp the center point of the doctrine of Sakyamuni. Bodhidharma, the Sixth Patriarch, Baso, and other Chinese masters noticed this fact, and the proclamation and development of Zen was the natural outcome. By them *satori* was placed above sutra-learning and scholarly discussions of the sastras and was identified with Zen itself. Zen, therefore, without *satori* is like pepper without its pungency: But there is also such a thing as too much *satori,* which is to be detested.

4. This emphasizing of *satori* in Zen makes the fact quite significant that Zen is not a system of Dhyana as practised in India and by other Buddhist schools in China. By Dhyana is generally understood a kind of meditation or contemplation directed towards some fixed thought; in Hinayana Buddhism it was the thought of transiency, while in the Mahayana it was more often the doctrine of emptiness. When the mind has been so trained as to be able to realize a state of perfect void in which there is not a trace of consciousness left, even the sense of being unconscious having departed; in other words, when all forms of mental activity are swept away clean from the field of consciousness, leaving the mind like the sky devoid of every speck of cloud, a mere broad expanse of blue, Dhyana is said to have reached its perfection. This may be called ecstasy or trance, but it is not Zen. In Zen there must be *satori;* there must be a general mental upheaval which destroys the old accumulations of intellection and lays down the foundation for a new life; there must be the

awakening of a new sense which will review the old things from a hitherto un-dreamed-of angle of observation. In Dhyana there are none of these things, for it is merely a quieting exercise of mind. As such Dhyana doubtless has its own merit, but Zen must not be identified with it.

5. *Satori* is not seeing God as he is, as might be contended by some Christian mystics. Zen has from the beginning made clear and insisted upon the main thesis, which is to see into the work of creation; the creator may be found busy moulding his universe, or he may be absent from his workshop, but Zen goes on with its own work. It is not dependent upon the support of a creator; when it grasps the reason for living a life, it is satisfied. Hoyen (Fa-yen, died 1104) of Go-so-san used to produce his own hand and ask his disciples why it was called a hand. When we know the reason, there is *satori* and we have Zen. Whereas with the God of mysticism there is the grasping of a definite object; when you have God, what is no-God is excluded. This is self-limiting. Zen wants absolute freedom, even from God. "No abiding place" means that very thing; "Cleanse your mouth when you utter the word Buddha" amounts to the same thing. It is not that Zen wants to be morbidly unholy and godless, but that it recognizes the incompleteness of a mere name. Therefore, when Yakusan (Yueh-shan, 751–834) was asked to give a lecture, he did not say a word, but instead came down from the pulpit and went off to his own room. Hyakujo merely walked forward a few steps, stood still, and then opened out his arms, which was his exposition of the great principle.

6. *Satori* is not a morbid state of mind, a fit subject for the study of abnormal psychology. If anything, it is a perfectly normal state of mind. When I speak of a mental upheaval, some may be led to consider Zen as something to be shunned by ordinary people. This is a most mistaken view of Zen, but one unfortunately often held by prejudiced critics. As Joshu declared, "Zen is your everyday thought"; it all depends on the adjustment of the hinge whether the door opens in or opens out. Even in the twinkling of an eye the whole affair is changed and you have Zen, and you are as perfect and as normal as ever. More than that, you have acquired in the meantime something altogether new. All your mental activities will now be working to a different key, which will be more satisfying, more peaceful, and fuller of joy than anything you ever experienced before. The tone of life will be altered. There is something rejuvenating in the possession of Zen. The spring flowers look prettier, and the mountain stream runs cooler and more transparent. The subjective revolution that brings about this state of things cannot be called abnormal. When life becomes more enjoyable and its expanse broadens to include the universe itself, there must be something in *satori* that is quite precious and well worth one's striving after.

Ruether

Rosemary Radford Ruether is the Georgia Harkness Professor of Applied Theology at the Garrett-Evangelical Theological Seminary in Evanston, Illinois. She has lectured widely and written extensively on feminist issues in theology. Her many works include Religion and Sexism, New Woman/New Earth, *and* Sexism and God-Talk: Toward a Feminist Theology.

Feminist religious thinkers in recent times have made evident the male-oriented character of Western theistic religions, especially with regard to their hierarchical organization and to the language and imagery in which the teachings have traditionally been presented. Apart from a rejection of this "patriarchal" model, feminist thinkers, however, have quite naturally differed among themselves as to the appropriate response to this situation. Some have favored reforming the traditions to accommodate women's experience, allowing, for example, women to have an equal place as priests, ministers, and rabbis; others have urged that these traditions, being hopelessly "androcentric" (centered on male experience), be set aside and that new practices and institutions be created for women; and still others have looked for ways to transform radically the existing structures and practices of Western theism by reexamining their histories and discovering ways to alter them at their very core.

In *Sexism and God-Talk: Toward a Feminist Theology,* Ruether seeks to set a framework for a new egalitarian Christianity that will transform those dualisms (such as spirit/nature, mind/body) of traditional theism, which have originated from a male-dominated "father" perspective, to an integrative understanding and language that are inclusive of women's religious experience.

Sexism and God-Language: Male and Female Images of the Divine

Few topics are as likely to arouse such passionate feelings in contemporary Christianity as the question of the exclusively male image of God. Liberals who have advanced to the point of accepting inclusive language for humans often exhibit a phobic reaction to the very possibility of speaking of God as "She." This emotional hostility has deep roots in the Judeo-Christian formation of the normative image of transcendent ego in the male God image. The underside of this transcendent male ego is the conquest of nature, imaged as the conquest and transcendence of the Mother. To probe the roots of this formation of the male God image, it is useful to reach back behind patriarchal monotheism to religions in which a Goddess was either the dominant divine image or was paired with the male image in a way that made both equivalent modes of apprehending the divine.

THE GODDESS IN THE ANCIENT NEAR EAST

From archaeological evidence one can conclude that the most ancient human image of the divine was female. From Paleolithic to Neolithic times and into the beginnings of ancient civilization, we find the widely diffused image of the Goddess without an accompanying male cult figure. E. O. James, in his classic book *The Cult of the Mother Goddess,* cites M. E. L. Mallowan's assertion that the "mother-goddess cult must indeed be one of the oldest and longest surviving religions of the ancient world." A second ancient cult, found in numerous Ice Age cave paintings, focuses on the Shaman, probably male, of the hunting cult, although no representation of the divine is depicted. Thus the widely diffused images of the Goddess found throughout the ancient Mediterranean world and into India and western Europe are the only archaeological clue as to how these early peoples imaged the source and powers of life on which they depended.

Their figures typically emphasize the breasts, buttocks, and enlarged abdomen of the female; face, hands, and legs are given little attention. This suggests that the Goddess is not a focus of personhood, but rather an impersonalized image of the mysterious powers of fecundity. The pregnant human female is the central metaphor for the powers of life for peoples who domesticated neither animals nor plants but were totally dependent on the spontaneous forces of the earth for gathering food. Later, when animals were domesticated, plants were sown and harvested, and humanity began to intervene in, rather than simply to depend on, the spontaneous powers of fertility, the metaphor of the Goddess continued to shape the cultural imagination. Humanity did not visualize itself as controlling these life processes so much as cooperating with them. To shape and bury in the earth images

---

of the pregnant human female continued to be humanity's primary way of experiencing mimetic cooperation with the awesome powers of life and renewal of life.

We can speak of the root human image of the divine as the Primal Matrix, the great womb within which all things, Gods and humans, sky and earth, human and nonhuman beings, are generated. Here the divine is not abstracted into some other world beyond this earth but is the encompassing source of new life that surrounds the present world and assures its continuance. This is expressed in the ancient myth of the World Egg out of which all things arise.

The ancient apprehension of Goddess as Primal Matrix has never entirely disappeared from the human religious imagination, despite the superimposition of male monotheism. It survives in the metaphor of the divine as Ground of Being. Here the divine is not "up there" as abstracted ego, but beneath and around us as encompassing source of life and renewal of life; spirit and matter are not split hierarchically. That which is most basic, matter (mother, matrix), is also most powerfully imbued with the powers of life and spirit. . . .

In the contemporary feminist reaction to patriarchal religion, the revival of the Goddess of antiquity as an alternative manifestation of the divine is much discussed. But both those who appropriate this idea and those who oppose it often incorrectly project modern dualisms on the ancient Goddess. The dualisms of nature/civilization, sexuality/spirituality, nurturance/dominance, immanence/transcendence, femininity/masculinity are taken for granted, and the Goddess is espoused or repudiated as representative of nature, sexuality, nurturance, immanence, and the feminine. The result is the creation of a Goddess religion that is the reverse of patriarchal religion.

When we look at the images of the Goddess in her various forms in the ancient texts (2800–1200 B.C.), we discover a world whose dialectics do not fall into such dualisms. Specifically, the concept of gender complementary is absent from the ancient myths. The Goddess and God are equivalent, not complementary, images of the divine. Psalms addressed to Ishtar do not address her as the embodiment of maternal, nurturing, and feminine characteristics, but as the expression of divine sovereignty and power in female form. Sexual potency and social power are found in both the Goddess and the God. There are tensions that define ancient religion—especially between chaos and cosmos, death and life—but divine forces, male and female, are ranged on both side of the dichotomies. Gender division is not yet the primary metaphor for imaging the dialectics of human existence. It is precisely this aspect of the religious world of the ancient Near East that provides the most striking alternative to the symbolic world generated by male monotheism.

MALE MONOTHEISM AND THE DUALIZING OF GENDER METAPHORS

Male monotheism has been so taken for granted in Judeo-Christian culture that the peculiarity of imaging God solely through one gender has not been recognized. But such an image indicates a sharp departure from all previous human consciousness. It is possible that the social origins of male monotheism lie in nomadic herding societies. These cultures lacked the female gardening role and tended to image God as the Sky-Father. Nomadic religions were characterized by exclusivism and an aggressive, hostile relationship to the agricultural people of the land and their religions.

Male monotheism reinforces the social hierarchy of patriarchal rule through its religious system in a way that was not the case with the paired images of God and Goddess. God is modeled after the patriarchal ruling class and is seen as addressing this class of males directly, adopting them as his "sons." They are his representatives, the responsible partners of the covenant with him. Women as wives now become symbolically repressed as the dependent servant class. Wives, along with children and servants, represent those ruled over and owned by the patriarchal class. They relate to men as he relates to God. A symbolic hierarchy is set up: God-male-female. Women no longer stand in direct relation to God; they are connected to God secondarily, through the male. This hierarchical order is evident in the structure of patriarchal law in the Old Testament, in which only the male heads of families are addressed directly. Women, children, and servants are referred to indirectly through their duties and property relations to the patriarch. In the New Testament this hierarchical "order" appears as a cosmic principle:

> But I want to understand that the head of every man is Christ, the head of a woman is her husband, and the head of Christ is God. . . . For a man ought not to cover his head, since he is the image and glory of God, but the woman is the glory of man. (1 Cor. 11:3, 7)

Male monotheism becomes the vehicle of a psychocultural revolution of the male ruling class in its relationship to surrounding reality. Whereas ancient myth had seen the Gods and Goddesses as within the matrix of one physical-spiritual reality, male monotheism begins to split reality into a dualism of transcendent Spirit (mind, ego) and inferior and dependent physical nature. Bodiless ego or spirit is seen as primary, existing before the cosmos. The physical world is "made" as an artifact by transcendent, disembodied mind or generated through some process of devolution from spirit to matter.

Both the Hebrew Genesis story and the Platonic creation story of *Timaeus* retain reminiscences of the idea of primal matter as something already existing that is ordered or shaped by the Creator God. But this now becomes the lower pole in the hierarchy of being. Thus the hierarchy of God-male-female does not merely make woman secondary in relation to God, it also gives her a negative identity in relation to the divine. Whereas the male is seen essentially as the image of the male transcendent ego or God, woman is seen as the image of the lower, material nature. Although both are seen as "mixed natures," the male identity points "above" and the female "below." Gender becomes a primary symbol for the dualism of transcendence and immanence, spirit and matter. . . .

Do traditions of the androgyny of God and the female aspect of the Trinity resolve the problem of the exclusively male image of God? Some Christian feminists feel they do. God has both mothering or feminine as well as masculine characteristics. The feminine aspect of God is to be identified particularly with the Holy Spirit. It is doubtful, however, that we should settle for a concept of the Trinity that consists of two male and one female "persons." Such a concept of God falls easily into an androcentric or male-dominant perspective. The female side of God then becomes a subordinate principle underneath the dominant image of male divine sovereignty.

We should guard against concepts of divine androgyny that simply ratify on the divine level the patriarchal split of the masculine and the feminine. In such a concept, the feminine side of God, as a secondary or mediating principle, would act in the same subordinate and limited roles in which females are allowed to act in the patriarchal social order. The feminine can be mediator or recipient of divine power in relation to creaturely reality. She can be God's daughter, the bride of the (male) soul. But she can never represent divine transcendence in all fullness. For feminists to appropriate the "feminine" side of God within this patriarchal gender hierarchy is simply to reinforce the problem of gender stereotyping on the level of God-language. We need to go beyond the idea of a "feminine side" of God . . . and question the assumption that the highest symbol of divine sovereignty still remains exclusively male.

GOD-LANGUAGE BEYOND PATRIARCHY IN THE BIBLICAL TRADITION

The Prophetic God

Although the predominantly male images and roles of God make Yahwism an agent in the sacralization of patriarchy, there are critical elements in Biblical theology that contradict this view of God. By patriarchy we mean not only the subordination of females to males, but the whole structure of Father-ruled society: aristocracy over serfs, masters over slaves, king over subjects, racial overlords over colonized people. Religions that reinforce hierarchical stratification use the Divine as the apex of this system of privilege and control. The religions of the ancient Near East link the Gods and Goddesses with the kings and queens, the priests and priestesses, the warrior and temple aristocracy of a stratified society. The Gods and Goddesses mirror this ruling class and form its heavenly counterpart. The divinities also show mercy and favor to the distressed, but in the manner of noblesse oblige.

Yahweh, as tribal God of Israel, shows many characteristics similar to those of the Near Eastern deities, as mighty king, warrior, and one who shows mercy and vindicates justice. But these characteristics are put in a new and distinct context: Yahweh is unique as the God of a tribal confederation that identifies itself as liberated slaves. The basic identity of Yahweh as God of this confederation lies in "his" historical action as the divine power that liberated these slaves from bondage and led them to a new land. This confederation is not an ethnic people, but a bonding of groups of distinct backgrounds. A core group experienced the escape from bondage in Egypt that formed the primary identity of Israel. They were joined by nomadic groups from the desert and hill peoples in Canaan in revolt against the feudal power of the city-states of the plains. Norman Gottwald reconstructs the premonarchical formation of this tribal confederation (1250–1050 B.C.). The identification of Yahweh with liberation from bondage allowed this diverse group to unite in a new egalitarian society and to revolt against the stratified feudal society of the city-states that oppressed the peasant peoples of the hills with taxes and forced labor. . . .

The New Testament contains a renewal and radicalization of prophetic consciousness, now applied to marginalized groups in a universal, nontribal context. Consequently, it is possible to recognize as liberated by God social groups overlooked in Old Testament prophecy. Class, ethnicity, and gender are now specifically singled out as the divisions overcome by redemption in Christ. In the New Testament stories, gender is recognized as an additional oppression within oppressed classes and ethnic groups. Women, the doubly oppressed within marginalized groups, manifest God's iconoclastic, liberating action in making "the last first and the first last." All women are not doubly oppressed; there are also queens and wealthy women. But women's experience of oppression has begun to become visible and to be addressed by prophetic consciousness (very likely because of the participation of women in the early Christian movement).

The Liberating Sovereign

A second antipatriarchal use of God-language occurs in the Old and New Testaments when divine sovereignty and fatherhood are used to break the ties of bondage under human kings and fathers. Abraham is called into an adoptive or covenanted relation with God only by breaking his ties with his family, leaving behind the graves of his ancestors. The God of Exodus establishes a relationship with the people that breaks their ties with the ruling overlords. As the people flee from the land of bondage, Pharaoh and his horsemen are drowned. God's kingship liberates Israel from human kings. The antimonarchical tradition inveighs against Israel's capitulation of the customs of the surrounding people by adopting kingship.

These Old Testament traditions are developed in Jesus' teaching. It has been often pointed out that Jesus uses a unique word for God. By adopting the word *Abba* for God, he affirms a primary relationship to God based on love and trust; *Abba* was the intimate word used by children in the family for their fathers. It is not fully conveyed by English terms such as *Daddy*, for it was also a term an adult could use of an older man to signify a combination of respect and affection. But is it enough to conclude from this use of *Abba* that Jesus transforms the patriarchal concept of divine fatherhood into what might be called a maternal or nurturing concept of God as loving, trustworthy parent? . . .

The Proscription of Idolatry

A third Biblical tradition that is important to a feminist theology is the proscription of idolatry. Israel is to make no picture or graven image of God; no pictorial or verbal representation of God can be taken literally. By contrast, Christian sculpture and painting represents God as a powerful old man with a white beard, even crowned and robed in the insignia of human kings or the triple tiara of the Pope. The message created by such images is that God is both similar to and represented by the patriarchal leadership, the monarchs and the Pope. Such imaging of God should be judged for what it is—as idolatry, as the setting up of certain human figures as the privileged images and representations of God. To the extent that such political and ecclesiastical patriarchy incarnates unjust and oppressive relationships, such images of God become sanctions of evil.

The proscription of idolatry must also be extended to verbal pictures. When the word *Father* is taken literally to mean that God is male and not female, represented by males and not females, then this word becomes idolatrous. The Israelite tradition is circumspect about the verbal image, printing it without vowel signs. The revelation to Moses in the burning bush gives as the name of God only the enigmatic "I am what I shall be." God is person without being imaged by existing social roles. God's being is open-ended, pointing both to what is and to what can be.

Classical Christian theology teaches that all names for God are analogies. The tradition of negative or *apophatic* theology emphasizes the unlikeness between God and human works for God. That tradition corrects the tendency to take verbal images literally; God is like but also unlike any verbal analogy. Does this not mean that male words for God are not in any way superior to or more appropriate than female analogies? God is both male and female and neither male nor female. One needs inclusive language for God that draws on the images and experiences of both genders. This inclusiveness should not become more abstract. Abstractions often conceal androcentric assumptions and prevent the shattering of the male monopoly on God-language, as in "God is not male. He is Spirit." Inclusiveness can happen only by naming God/ess in female as well as male metaphors.

Equivalent Images for God as Male and Female

Are there any Biblical examples of such naming of God/ess in female as well as male metaphors that are truly equivalent images, that is, not "feminine" aspects of a male God? The synoptic Gospels offer some examples of this in the parallel parables, which seem to have been shaped in the early Christian catechetical community. They reflect the innovation of the early Christian movement of including women equally in those called to study the Torah of Jesus. Jesus justifies this practice in the Mary-Martha story, where he defends Mary's right to study in the circle of disciples around Rabbi Jesus in the words "Mary has chosen the better part which shall not be taken from her" (Luke 10:38–42).

In the parables of the mustard seed and the leaven the explosive power of the Kingdom, which God, through Jesus, is sowing in history through small signs and deeds, is compared to a farmer sowing the tiny mustard seed that produces a great tree or a woman folding the tiny bit of leaven in three measures of flour which then causes the whole to rise (Luke 13:18–21; Matt. 13:31–33). The parables of the lost sheep and the lost coin portray God seeking the sinners despised by the "righteous" of Israel. God is compared to a shepherd who leaves his ninety-nine sheep to seek the one that is lost or to a woman with ten coins who loses one and sweeps her house diligently until she finds it. Having found it, she rejoices and throws a party for her friends. This rejoicing is compared to God's rejoicing with the angels in heaven over the repentance of one sinner (Luke 15:1–10).

These metaphors for divine activity are so humble that their significance has been easily overlooked in exegesis, but we should note several important points. First, the images of male and female in these parables are equivalent. They both stand for the same things, as paired images. One is in no way inferior to the other. Second, the images are not drawn from the social roles of the mighty, but from the activities of Galilean peasants. It might be objected that the roles of the women are stereotypical and enforce the concept of woman as housekeeper. But it is interesting that the women are never described as related to or dependent on men. The small treasure of the old woman is her own. Presumably she is an independent house-holder. Finally, and most significantly, the parallel male and female images do not picture divine action in parental terms. The old woman seeking the lost coin and the woman leavening the flour image God not as mother or father (Creator), but as seeker of the lost and transformer of history (Redeemer).

TOWARD A FEMINIST UNDERSTANDING OF GOD/ESS

The four preceding Biblical traditions may not be adequate for a feminist recon-struction of God/ess, but they are suggestive. If all language for God/ess is analogy, if taking a particular human image literally is idolatry, then male language for the divine must lose its privileged place. If God/ess is not the creator and validator of the existing hierarchical social order, but rather the one who liberates us from it, who opens up a new community of equals, then language about God/ess drawn from kingship and hierarchical power must lose its privileged place. Images of God/ess must include female roles and experience. Images of God/ess must be drawn from the activities of peasants and working people, people at the bottom of society. Most of all, images of God/ess must be transformative, pointing us back to our authentic potential and forward to new redeemed possibilities. God/ess-language cannot validate roles of men or women in stereotypic ways that justify male dominance and female subordination. Adding an image of God/ess as loving, nur-turing mother, mediating the power of the strong, sovereign father, is insufficient.

Feminists must question the overreliance of Christianity, especially modern bour-geois Christianity, on the model of God/ess as parent. Obviously any symbol of God/ess as parent should include mother as well as father. Mary Baker Eddy's in-clusive term, *Mother-Father God*, already did this one hundred years ago. Mother-Father God has the virtue of concreteness, evoking both parental images rather than moving to an abstraction (Parent), which loses effective resonance. Mother and father image God/ess as creator, as the source of our being. They point back from our own historical existence to those upon whom our existence depends. Par-ents are a symbol of roots, the sense of being grounded in the universe in those who have gone before, who underlie our own existence.

But the parent model for the divine has negative resonance as well. It suggests a kind of permanent parent-child relationship to God. God becomes a neurotic parent who does not want us to grow up. To become autonomous and responsible for our own lives is the gravest sin against God. Patriarchal theology uses the parent image for God to prolong spiritual infantilism as virtue and to make autonomy and assertion of free will a sin. Parenting in patriarchal society also becomes the way of enculturating us to the stereotypic male and female roles. The family becomes the nucleus and model of patriarchal relations in society. To that extent parenting language for God reinforces patriarchal power rather than liberating us from it. We need to start with language for the Divine as redeemer, as liberator, as one who fosters full personhood and, in that context, speak of God/ess as creator, as source of being.

Patriarchal theologies of "hope" or liberation affirm the God of Exodus, the God who uproots us from present historical systems and puts us on the road to new possibilities. But they typically do this in negation of God/ess as Matrix, as source and ground of our being. They make the fundamental mistake of identifying the ground of creation with the foundations of existing social systems. Being, matter, and nature become the ontocratic base for the evil system of what is. Liberation is liberation out of or against nature into spirit. The identification of matter, nature, and being with mother makes such patriarchal theology hostile to women as symbols of all that "drags us down" from freedom. The hostility of males to any symbol of God/ess as female is rooted in this identification of mother with the negation of liberated spirit. God/ess as Matrix is thought of as "static" immanence. A static, devouring, death-dealing matter is imaged, with horror, as extinguishing the free flight of transcendent consciousness. The dualism of nature and transcendence, matter and spirit as female against male is basic to male theology.

Feminist theology must fundamentally reject this dualism of nature and spirit. It must reject both sides of the dualism: both the image of mother-matter-matrix as "static immanence" and as the ontological foundation of existing, oppressive social systems and also the concept of spirit and transcendence as rootless, antinatural, originating in an "other world" beyond the cosmos, ever repudiating and fleeing from nature, body, and the visible world. Feminist theology needs to affirm the God of Exodus, of liberation and new being, but as rooted in the foundations of being rather than as its antithesis. The God/ess who is the foundation (at one and the same time) of our being and our new being embraces both the roots of the material substratum of our existence (matter) and also the endlessly new creative potential (spirit). The God/ess who is the foundation of our being-new being does not lead us back to a stifled, dependent self or uproot us in a spirit-trip outside the earth. Rather it leads us to the converted center, the harmonization of self and body, self and other, self and world. It is the *Shalom* of our being.

God/ess as once and future *Shalom* of being, however, is *not* the creator, founder, or sanctioner or patriarchal-hierarchical society. This world arises in revolt against God/ess and in alienation from nature. It erects a false system of alienated dualisms modeled on its distorted and oppressive social relationships. God/ess liberates us from this false and alienated world, not by an endless continuation of the same trajectory of alienation but as a constant breakthrough that points us to new possibilities that are, at the same time, the regrounding of ourselves in the primordial matrix, the original harmony. The liberating encounter with God/ess is always an encounter with our authentic selves resurrected from underneath the alienated self. It is not experienced against, but in and through relationships, healing our broken relations with our bodies, with other people, with nature. We have no adequate name for the true God/ess, the "I am who I shall become." Intimations of Her/His name will appear as we emerge from false naming of God/ess modeled on patriarchal alienation.

Pascal

Blaise Pascal (1623–1662) was a famous mathematician and religious thinker who accorded superiority to the heart over reason in religion. His best-known work is nevertheless entitled Pensées (Thoughts, *1670)*

A good deal of contemporary religious concern centers, as we have seen, on the non-rational dimensions of religious experience. Many religious thinkers are pleased to subordinate rational demonstrations for the existence of God and the like to analyses of the nature of faith as a form of passionate commitment that centers one's whole being and gives meaning and direction to one's life. Søren Kierkegaard, a nineteenth-century forerunner of modern existentialists, ridiculed any attempt to prove the existence of God when he stated that "if God does not exist it would of course be impossible to prove it; and if he does exist it would be folly to attempt it." Nevertheless, there has been an enduring interest shown in "natural theology"—the attempt to demonstrate rationally the existence of God (as conceived of in theism)—and in spite of the rather trenchant criticisms made against the various "proofs" that have been put forward, one can be assured that as long as theistic traditions persist, continuing efforts will be made to prove the existence of God.

Although not offering a "proof" as such, Pascal, in a rather playful spirit, argues that because we are severely limited intellectually when we confront an infinite universe and a God who is different in kind from us, we cannot know *what* God is or even *if* he exists, but if one has the calculating prudence of a good gambler, one will indeed wager *that* God is. In brief: if we believe in God and it turns out there is no God, we have lost nothing; if, on the other hand, God does exist and we disbelieve in him, we stand to lose much, whereas if we believe, we will win a great deal.

The Wager

If there is a God, He is infinitely incomprehensible, since, having neither parts nor limits, He has no affinity to us. We are then incapable of knowing either what He is or if He is. This being so, who will dare to undertake the decision of the question? Not we, who have no affinity to Him.

Who then will blame Christians for not being able to give a reason for their belief, since they profess a religion for which they cannot give a reason? They declare, in expounding it to the world, that it is a foolishness, *stultitiam:* and then you complain that they do not prove it! If they proved it, they would not keep their word; it is in lacking proofs that they are not lacking in sense. "Yes, but although this excuses those who offer it as such, and takes away from them the blame of putting it forward without reason, it does not excuse those who receive." Let us then examine this point, and say, "God is, or He is not." But to which side shall we incline? Reason can decide nothing here. There is an infinite chaos which separates us. A game is being played at the extremity of this infinite distance where heads or tails will turn up. What will you wager? According to reason, you can do neither the one thing nor the other; according to reason, you can defend neither of the propositions.

Do not then reprove for error those who have made a choice; for you know nothing about it. "No, but I blame them for having made, not this choice, but a choice, for again both he who chooses heads and he who chooses tails are equally at fault, they are both in the wrong. The true course is not to wager at all."

Yes; but you must wager. It is not optional. You are embarked. Which will you choose then? Let us see. Since you must choose, let us see which interests you least. You have two things to lose, the true and the good; and two things to stake, your reason and your will, your knowledge and your happiness; and your nature has two things to shun, error and misery. Your reason is no more shocked in choosing one rather than the other, since you must of necessity choose. This is one point settled. But your happiness? Let us weigh the gain and the loss in wagering that God is. Let us estimate these two chances. If you gain, you gain all; if you lose, you lose nothing. Wager, then, without hesitation that He is.—"That is very fine. Yes, I must wager; but I may perhaps wager too much."—Let us see. Since there is an equal risk of gain and of loss, if you had only to gain two lives, instead of one, you might still wager. But if there were three lives to gain, you would have to play (since you are under the necessity of playing), and you would be imprudent, when you are forced to play, not to chance your life to gain three at a game where there is an equal risk of loss and gain. But there is an eternity of life and happiness. And this being so, if there were an infinity of chances, of which one only would be for you, you would still be right in wagering one to win two, and you would act stupidly, being obliged to play, by refusing to stake one life against three at a game in which out of an infinity of chances there is one for you, if there were an infinity of an infinitely happy life to gain. But there

---

From *Pensées* by Blaise Pascal, translated by W. Trotter (London: Dent & Co., 1908).

is here an infinity of an infinitely happy life to gain, a chance of gain against a finite number of chances of loss, and what you stake is finite. It is all divided; wherever the infinite is and there is not an infinity of chances of loss against that of gain, there is no time to hesitate, you must give all. And thus, when one is forced to play, he must renounce reason to preserve his life, rather than risk it for infinite gain, as likely to happen as the loss of nothingness.

For it is no use to say it is uncertain if we will gain, and it is certain that we risk, and that the infinite distance between the *certainty* of what is staked and the *uncertainty* of what will be gained, equals the finite good which is certainly staked against the uncertain infinite. It is not so, as every player stakes a certainty to gain an uncertainty, and yet he stakes a finite certainty to gain a finite uncertainty, without transgressing against reason. There is not an infinite distance between the certainty staked and the uncertainty of the gain; that is untrue. In truth, there is an infinity between the certainty of gain and the certainty of loss. But the uncertainty of the gain is proportioned to the certainty of the stake according to the proportion of the chances of gain and loss. Hence it comes that, if there are as many risks on one side as on the other, the course is to play even; and then the certainty of the stake is equal to the uncertainty of the gain, so far is it from fact that there is an infinite distance between them. And so our proposition is of infinite force, when there is the finite to stake in a game where there are equal risks of gain and of loss, and the infinite to gain. This is demonstrable; and if men are capable of any truths, this is one.

"I confess it, I admit it. But, still, is there no means of seeing the faces of the cards?"—Yes, Scripture and the rest, etc. "Yes, but I have my hands tied and my mouth closed; I am forced to wager, and am not free. I am not released, and am so made that I cannot believe. What, then would you have me do?"

True. But at least learn your inability to believe, since reason brings you to this, and yet you cannot believe. Endeavor then to convince yourself, not by increase of proofs of God, but by the abatement of your passions. You would like to attain faith, and do not know the way; you would like to cure yourself of unbelief, and ask the remedy for it. Learn of those who have been bound like you, and who now stake all their possessions. These are people who know the way which you would follow, and who are cured of an ill of which you would be cured. Follow the way by which they began; by acting as if they believed, taking the holy water, having masses said, etc. Even this will naturally make you believe, and deaden your acuteness.—"But this is what I am afraid of."—And why? What have you to lose?

. . . Now, what harm will befall you in taking this side? You will be faithful, honest, humble, grateful, generous, a sincere friend, truthful. Certainly you will not have those poisonous pleasures, glory and luxury; but will you have not others? I will tell you that you will thereby gain in his life, and that, at each step you take on this road, you will see so great certainty of gain, so much nothingness in what you risk, that you will at last recognize that you have wagered for something certain and infinite, for which you have given nothing.

Saint Anselm

Saint Anselm (c. 1033–1109) was an archbishop of Canterbury and a strong rational defender of the faith. His main religious ideas were set forth in his works Monologion *and* Proslogion.

Two kinds of proofs for the existence of God are usually distinguished: those of an *a priori* character, which try to show how God's existence is entailed in the very idea of God, and *a posteriori* arguments, which reason from various aspects of the world as we experience it to an extranatural principle, understood to be God, that is necessary to make the world intelligible. The main *a priori* argument is known as the "ontological argument." It was initially put forward by Saint Anselm and then given a slightly different form, as we will see, in Descartes. Disagreeing with Pascal, Saint Anselm presupposes that we do have an adequate idea of God as a perfect being, "that something than which nothing greater can be conceived," and that his surpassing greatness and perfection necessitate his very existence.

This kind of ontological argument was also put forward much earlier within the Indian philosophical tradition, where in the yoga system of one Patañjali (second-century B.C.E.) it is stated that "God's (*Īśvara's*) pre-eminence is understood to be without anything equal to or excelling it. God cannot be excelled by any other pre-eminence, because the very idea of God is that which is the uttermost limit of a real and existing perfection."

In the following selection from his *Proslogion*, Saint Anselm sets forth his ontological argument and replies to one of its common criticisms made by a French monk named Gaunilo, about whom nothing is otherwise known. Anselm's argument seems to rest on the assumption that we all have a clear idea of the nature of God but that our belief in him nevertheless precedes our understanding of him: *credo ut intelligum*—"I believe in order to understand." This suggests that the force of the argument is directed toward a believer and not to someone who stands outside of the faith.

The Ontological Argument for the Existence of God

THE PROSLOGION

That God Truly Is

O Lord, you who give understanding to faith, so far as you know it to be beneficial, give me to understand that you are as we believe, and that you are what we believe.

We believe that you are something than which nothing greater can be conceived.

But is there any such nature, since "the fool has said in his heart: God is not"?

However, when this same fool hears what I say, when he hears of this something than which nothing greater can be conceived, he at least understands what he hears.

What he understands stands in relation to his understanding, even if he does not understand that it exists. For it is one thing for a thing to stand in relation to our understanding; it is another thing for us to understand that it really exists. For instance, when a painter imagines what he is about to paint, he has it in relation to his understanding. However, he does not yet understand that it exists, because he has not yet made it. After he paints it, then he both has it in relation to his understanding and understands that it exists. Therefore even the fool is convinced that something than which nothing greater can be conceived at least stands in relation to his understanding, because when he hears of it he understands it, and whatever he understands stands in relation to his understanding.

However, that than which a greater cannot be conceived can certainly not stand only in relation to the understanding. For if it at least stood only in relation to the understanding, it could be conceived to be also in reality, and this would be something greater. Therefore, if that than which a greater cannot be conceived only stood in relation to the understanding, then that than which a greater cannot be conceived would be something than which a greater can be conceived. Obviously this is impossible.

Therefore, something than which a greater cannot be conceived undoubtedly both stands in relation to the understanding and exists in reality.

That It Is Impossible to Conceive That God Is Not

This so truly is that it is impossible to think of it as not existing.

It can be conceived to be something such that we cannot conceive of it as not existing.

This is greater than something which we can conceive of as not existing.

Therefore, if that than which a greater cannot be conceived could be conceived

From Anselm, *The Proslogion;* Gaunilo, *On Behalf of the Fool;* Anselm, *Reply;* translated by Arthur C. McGill from Arthur C. McGill and John Hick, eds., *The Many-Faced Argument* (New York: The Macmillan Co., 1967). Used by permission of the publisher.

not to be, we would have an impossible contradiction: that than which a greater cannot be conceived would not be that than which a greater cannot be conceived.

Therefore something than which a greater cannot be conceived so truly is that it is impossible even to conceive of it as not existing.

This is you, O Lord our God. You so truly are that you cannot be thought not to be. And rightly so.

For if some mind could conceive of something better than you, the creature would become superior to its Creator and would judge its Creator.

This is obviously absurd. Indeed, whatever else there is, except for you alone, can be conceived not to be.

Therefore you alone, of all things, exist in the truest and greatest way . . . , for nothing else so truly exists and therefore everything else has less being.

Why, then, did the fool say in his heart: "God is not," since it is so obvious to the rational mind that you exist supremely above all things? Why, because he is a dim-witted fool.

How the Fool Said in His Heart What Cannot Be Conceived

How was the fool able to "say in his heart" what he was unable to conceive? Or how was it that he could not conceive what he said in his heart? For to "say in one's heart" and to "conceive" are the same thing.

However, if—or rather because—he really did conceive of it (since he said it in his heart) and yet did not really say it in his heart (since he was unable to conceive of it), then there must be more than one way for something to be said in one's heart, or to be conceived.

Indeed, a thing is conceived of in one way when the word signifying it is thought; in another way when the very thing itself is understood. Accordingly God can be conceived not to be in the first way, but not at all in the second. . . .

GAUNILO AND ANSELM—CRITICISM AND REPLY

Gaunilo

Consider this example. Certain people say that somewhere in the ocean there is an island which they call the "Lost Island," because of the difficulty or, rather, the impossibility of finding what does not exist. They say that it is more abundantly filled with inestimable riches and delights than the Isles of the Blessed, and that although it has no owner or inhabitant, it excels all the lands that men inhabit taken together in the unceasing abundance of its fertility.

When someone tells me that there is such an island, I easily understand what is being said, for there is nothing difficult here. Suppose, however, as as consequence of this, he then goes on to say: you cannot doubt that this island, more excellent than all lands, actually exists somewhere in reality, because it undoubtedly stands in relation to your understanding. Since it is more excellent, not simply to stand in relation to the understanding, but to be in reality as well, therefore this island must necessarily be in reality. Otherwise any other land that exists in reality would be more excellent than this island, and this island, which you understood to be the most excellent of all lands, would then not be the most excellent.

If, I repeat, someone should wish by this argument to demonstrate to me that this island truly exists and is no longer to be doubted, I would think he were joking; or, if I accepted the argument, I do not know whom I would regard as the greater fool, me for accepting it or him for supposing that he had proved the existence of this island with any kind of certainty. He should first show that this excellent island exists as a genuine and undeniably real thing, and not leave it standing in relation to my understanding as a false or uncertain something.

Anselm

My reasoning, you claim, is as if someone should say that there is an island in the ocean, which surpasses the whole earth in its fertility, but which is called a "Lost Island" because of the difficulty, or even impossibility, of finding something that does not exist, and as if he should then argue that no one can doubt that it actually does exist because the words describing it are easily understood.

I can confidently say that if anyone discovers for me something existing either in fact or in thought alone, other than "that than which a greater cannot be thought," and is able to apply the logic of my argument to it, I shall find that lost island for him and shall give it to him as something which he will never lose again.

Descartes

Descartes's version of the ontological argument stresses the idea of perfection rather than "that than which nothing greater can be conceived." He argues that just as the idea of a triangle entails its having three angles equal to two right angles, so the attribution of "existence" to God is essential to the very conception of a most perfect being.

The Ontological Argument Restated

But now, if just because I can draw the idea of something from my thought, it follows that all which I know clearly and distinctly as pertaining to this object does really belong to it, may I not derive from this an argument demonstrating the existence of God? It is certain that I no less find the idea of God, that is to say, the idea of a supremely perfect Being, in me, than that of any figure or number whatever it is; and I do not know any less clearly and distinctly that an [actual and] eternal existence pertains to this nature than I know that all that which I am able to demonstrate of some figure or number truly pertains to the nature of this figure or number, and therefore, although all that I concluded in the preceding Meditations were found to be false, the existence of God would pass with me as at least as certain as I have ever held the truths of mathematics (which concern only numbers and figures) to be.

This indeed is not at first manifest, since it would seem to present some appearance of being a sophism. For being accustomed in all other things to make a distinction between existence and essence, I easily persuade myself that the existence can be separated from the essence of God, and that we can thus conceive God as not actually existing. But, nevertheless, when I think of it with more attention, I clearly see that existence can no more be separated from the essence of God than can its having its three angles equal to two right angles be separated from the essence of a [rectilinear] triangle, or the idea of a mountain from the idea of a valley; and so

From "Of God, That He Exists," *Meditations*, V, in *The Philosophical Works of Descartes*, vol. 1, translated by Elizabeth S. Haldane and G. R. T. Ross (1911). Reprinted with the permission of Cambridge University Press.

there is not any less repugnance to our conceiving a God (that is, a Being supremely perfect) to whom existence is lacking (that is to say, to whom a certain perfection is lacking), than to conceive of a mountain which has no valley.

But although I cannot really conceive of a God without existence any more than a mountain without a valley, still from the fact that I conceive of a mountain with a valley, it does not follow that there is such a mountain in the world; similarly although I conceive of God as possessing existence, it would seem that it does not follow that there is a God which exists; for my thought does not impose any necessity upon things, and just as I may imagine a winged horse, although no horse with wings exists, so I could perhaps attribute existence to God, although no God existed.

But a sophism is concealed in this objection; for from the fact that I cannot conceive a mountain without a valley, it does not follow that there is any mountain or any valley in existence, but only that the mountain and the valley, whether they exist or do not exist, cannot in any way be separated one from the other. While from the fact that I cannot conceive God without existence, it follows that existence is inseparable from Him, and hence that He really exists; not that my thought can bring this to pass, or impose any necessity on things, but, on the contrary, because the necessity which lies in the thing itself, i.e., the necessity of the existence of God, determines me to think in this way. For it is not within my power to think of God without existence (that is, of a supremely perfect Being devoid of a supreme perfection) though it is in my power to imagine a horse either with wings or without wings.

And we must not here object that it is in truth necessary for me to assert that God exists after having presupposed that He possesses every sort of perfection, since existence is one of these, but that as a matter of fact my original supposition was not necessary, just as it is not necessary to consider that all quadrilateral figure can be inscribed in the circle; for supposing I thought this, I should be constrained to admit that the rhombus might be inscribed in the circle since it is a quadrilateral figure, which, however, is manifestly false. [We must not, I say, make any such allegations because] although it is not necessary that I should at any time entertain the notion of God, nevertheless whenever it happens that I think of a first and a sovereign Being, and, so to speak, derive the idea of Him from the storehouse of my mind, it is necessary that I should attribute to Him every sort of perfection, although I do not get so far as to enumerate them all, or to apply my mind to each one in particular. And this necessity suffices to make me conclude (after having recognized that existence is a perfection) that this first and sovereign Being really exists; just as though it is not necessary for me ever to imagine any triangle, yet, whenever I wish to consider a rectilinear figure composed only of three angles, it is absolutely essential that I should attribute to it all those properties which serve to bring about the conclusion that its three angles are not greater than two right angles, even although I may not then be considering this point in particular. But when I consider which figures are capable of being inscribed in the circle, it is in no wise necessary that I should think that all quadrilateral figures are of this number; on the contrary, I cannot even pretend that this is the case, so long as I do not desire to accept anything which I cannot conceive clearly and distinctly. And in consequence there is a great difference between the false suppositions such as this, and the true ideas born within me, the first and principal of which is that of God. For really I discern in many ways that this idea is not something factitious, and depending solely on my thought, but that it is the image of a true and immutable nature; first of all, because I cannot conceive anything but God Himself to whose essence existence [necessarily] pertains; in the second place because it is not possible for me to conceive two or more Gods in this same position; and, granted that there is one such God who now exists, I see clearly that it is necessary that He should have existed from all eternity, and that He must exist eternally; and finally, because I know an infinitude of other properties in God, none of which I can either diminish or change.

Kant

The most telling criticism against the ontological argument is put forward by Kant, who argues that it is impossible to reason properly from the idea of the nature of something to its existence, for "existence" itself is not a real predicate. We don't say "this table in front of me is six-foot long, is brown, *and exists*." "Exists" does not add to the concept of a table, and it does not tell us something about the table; rather it is positing the table with its appropriate predicates. It is quite legitimate, according to Kant, to say that *if* God exists, then he has various characteristics; but his "existence" as such cannot be demonstrated only through the meaning of "God" in terms of his characteristics such as "perfection." The structure of ideas and the domain of what exists apart from ideas are quite different things.

The Impossibility of Ontological Proof

In all ages men have spoken of an *absolutely necessary* being, and in so doing have endeavoured, not so much to understand whether and how a thing of this kind allows even of being thought, but rather to prove its existence. There is, of course, no difficulty in giving a verbal definition of the concept, namely, that it is something the non-existence of which is impossible. But this yields no insight into the conditions which make it necessary to regard the non-existence of a thing as absolutely unthinkable. It is precisely these conditions that we desire to know, in order that we may determine whether or not, in resorting to this concept, we are thinking anything at all. The expedient of removing all those conditions which the understanding indispensably requires in order to regard something as necessary, simply through the introduction of the word *unconditioned,* is very far from sufficing to show whether I am still thinking anything in the concept of the unconditionally necessary, or perhaps rather nothing at all.

Nay more, this concept, at first ventured upon blindly, and now become so completely familiar, has been supposed to have its meaning exhibited in a number of ex-

From *Critique of Pure Reason* by Immanuel Kant, translated by Norman Kemp Smith (1929). Reprinted by permission of Macmillan Press Ltd.

amples; and on this account all further enquiry into its intelligibility has seemed to be quite needless. Thus the fact that every geometrical proposition, as, for instance, that a triangle has three angles, is absolutely necessary, has been taken as justifying us in speaking of an object which lies entirely outside the sphere of our understanding as if we understood perfectly what it is that we intend to convey by the concept of that object.

All the alleged examples are, without exception, taken from *judgments,* not from *things* and their existence. But the unconditioned necessity of judgments is not the same as an absolute necessity of things. The absolute necessity of the judgment is only a conditioned necessity of the thing, or of the predicate in the judgment. The above proposition does not declare that three angles are absolutely necessary, but that, under the condition that there is a triangle (that is, that a triangle is given), three angles will necessarily be found in it. So great, indeed, is the deluding influence exercised by this logical necessity that, by the simple device of forming an *a priori* concept of a thing in such a manner as to include existence within the scope of its meaning, we have supposed ourselves to have justified the conclusion that because existence necessarily belongs to the object of this concept—always under the condition that we posit the thing as given (as existing)—we are also of necessity, in accordance with the law of identity, required to posit the existence of its object, and that this being is therefore itself absolutely necessary—and this, to repeat, for the reason that the existence of this being has already been thought in a concept which is assumed arbitrarily and on condition that we posit its object.

If, in an identical proposition, I reject the predicate while retaining the subject, contradiction results; and I therefore say that the former belongs necessarily to the latter. But if we reject subject and predicate alike, there is no contradiction; for nothing is then left that can be contradicted. To posit a triangle, and yet to reject its three angles, is self-contradictory; but there is no contradiction in rejecting the triangle together with its three angles. The same holds true of the concept of an absolutely necessary being. If its existence is rejected, we reject the thing itself with all its predicates; and no question of contradiction can then arise. There is nothing outside it that would then be contradicted, since the necessity of the thing is not supposed to be derived from anything external; nor is there anything internal that would be contradicted, since in rejecting the thing itself we have at the same time rejected all its internal properties. "God is omnipotent" is a necessary judgment. The omnipotence cannot be rejected if we posit a Deity, that is, an infinite being; for the two concepts are identical. But if we say, "There is no God," neither the omnipotence nor any other of its predicates is given; they are one and all rejected together with the subject, and there is therefore not the least contradiction in such a judgment.

We have thus seen that if the predicate of a judgment is rejected together with the subject, no internal contradiction can result, and that this holds no matter what the predicate may be. The only way of evading this conclusion is to argue that there are subjects which cannot be removed, and must always remain. That, however, would only be another way of saying that there are absolutely necessary subjects; and that is the very assumption which I have called in question, and the possibility of which the above argument professes to establish. For I cannot form the least concept of a thing which, should it be rejected with all its predicates, leaves behind a contradiction; and in the absence of contradiction I have, through pure *a priori* concepts alone, no criterion of impossibility.

Notwithstanding all these general considerations, in which every one must concur, we may be challenged with a case which is brought forward as proof that in actual fact the contrary holds, namely, that there is one concept, and indeed only one, in reference to which the not-being or rejection of its object is in itself contradictory, namely, the concept of the *ens realissimum*. It is declared that it possesses all reality, and that we are justified in assuming that such a being is possible (the fact that a concept does not contradict itself by no means proves the possibility of its object: but the contrary assertion I am for the moment willing to allow). Now [the argument proceeds] "all reality" includes existence; existence is therefore contained in the concept of a thing that is possible. If, then, this thing is rejected, the internal possibility of the thing is rejected—which is self-contradictory.

My answer is as follows. There is already a contradiction in introducing the concept of existence—no matter under what title it may be disguised—into the concept of a thing which we profess to be thinking solely in reference to its possibility. If that be allowed as legitimate, a seeming victory has been won; but in actual fact nothing at all is said: the assertion is a mere tautology. We must ask: Is the proposition that *this or that thing* (which, whatever it may be, is allowed as possible) *exists,* an analytic or a synthetic proposition? If it is analytic, the assertion of the existence of the thing adds nothing to the thought of the thing; but in that case either the thought, which is in us, is the thing itself, or we have presupposed an existence as belonging to the realm of the possible, and have then, on that pretext, inferred its existence from its internal possibility—which is nothing but a miserable tautology. The word "reality," which in the concept of the thing sounds other than the word "existence" in the concept of the predicate, is of no avail in meeting this objection. For if all positing (no matter what it may be that is posited) is entitled reality, the thing with all its predicates is already posited in the concept of the subject, and is assumed as actual; and in the predicate this is merely repeated. But if, on the other hand, we admit, as every reasonable person must, that all existential propositions are synthetic, how can we profess to maintain that the predicate of existence cannot be rejected without contradiction? This is a feature which is found only in analytic propositions, and is indeed precisely what constitutes their analytic character.

I should have hoped to put an end to these idle and fruitless disputations in a direct manner, by an accurate determination of the concept of existence, had I not found that the illusion which is caused by the confusion of a logical with a real predicate (that is, with a predicate which determines a thing) is almost beyond correction. Anything we please can be made to serve as a logical predicate; the subject can even be predicated of itself; for logic abstracts from all content. But a *determining* predicate is a predicate which is added to the concept of the subject and enlarges it. Consequently, it must not be already contained in the concept.

"*Being*" is obviously not a real predicate; that is, it is not a concept of something which could be added to the concept of a thing. It is merely the positing of a thing, or of certain determinations, as existing in themselves. Logically, it is merely the copula of a judgment. The proposition, "God is omnipotent," contains two concepts, each of which has its object—God and omnipotence. The small word "is" adds no new predicate, but only serves to posit the predicate *in its relation* to the subject. If, now, we take the subject (God), with all its predicates (among which is omnipotence), and say "God is," or "There is a God," we attach no new predicate to the concept of God, but only posit the subject in itself with all its predicates, and indeed posit it as being an *object* that stands in relation to my *concept*. The content of both must be one and the same; nothing can have been added to the concept, which expresses merely what is possible, by my thinking its object (through the expression "it is") as given absolutely. Otherwise stated, the real contains no more than the merely possible. A hundred real thalers do not contain the least coin more than a hundred possible thalers. . . .

The attempt to establish the existence of a supreme being by means of the famous ontological argument of Descartes is therefore merely so much labour and effort lost; we can no more extend our stock of [theoretical] insight by mere ideas, than a merchant can better his position by adding a few noughts to his cash account.

Aquinas

Saint Thomas Aquinas (1225–1274) constructed the most elaborate and comprehensive structure of Christian thought in the medieval period, which became the primary theological foundation for the Roman Catholic Church. His major work, the Summa Theologica, *contains a short, but exceedingly important, section devoted to proofs for the existence of God.*

Aquinas sets forth five ways to demonstrate the existence of God within the framework of *a posteriori* argumentation and develops what are called cosmological and teleological arguments. Cosmological arguments are those that reason from the causal or contingent character of the world to the existence of God, while teleological arguments are those that reason from purported design or purpose in nature to the existence of an intelligent creator. The arguments, especially the cosmological ones, are based upon many features of Aristotle's philosophy and presuppose a notion of rational intelligibility that disallows an "infinite regress" in our explanations of the world.

Following the presentation of Aquinas's arguments below, F. C. Copleston, a noted contemporary historian of philosophy and Jesuit religious thinker, offers a somewhat updated version of and commentary on the proofs for a modern reader.

Five Ways to Prove the Existence of God

The existence of God can be proved in five ways.

The first and more manifest way is the argument from motion. It is certain, and evident to our senses, that in the world some things are in motion. Now whatever is moved is moved by another, for nothing can be moved except it is in potentiality to that towards which it is moved; whereas a thing moves inasmuch as it is in act. For motion is nothing else than the reduction of something from potentiality to actuality. But nothing can be reduced from potentiality to actuality, except by something in a state of actuality. Thus that which is actually hot, as fire, makes wood, which is

From *Summa Theologica*, in *Basic Writings of Saint Thomas Aquinas*, edited by Anton C. Pegis (New York: Random House, 1945). Reprinted by permission of the Anton C. Pegis Estate.

potentially hot, to be actually hot, and thereby moves and changes it. Now it is not possible that the same thing should be at once in actuality and potentiality in the same respect but only in different respects. For what is actually hot cannot simultaneously be potentially hot; but it is simultaneously potentially cold. It is therefore impossible that in the same respect and in the same way a thing should be both mover and moved, *i.e.*, that it should move itself. Therefore, whatever is moved must be moved by another. If that by which it is moved be itself moved, then this also must needs be moved by another, and that by another again. But this cannot go on to infinity, because then there would be no first mover, and, consequently, no other mover, seeing that subsequent movers move only inasmuch as they are moved by the first mover; as the staff moves only because it is moved by the hand. Therefore it is necessary to arrive at a first mover, moved by no other; and this everyone understands to be God.

The second way is from the nature of efficient cause. In the world of sensible things we find there is an order of efficient causes. There is no case known (neither is it, indeed, possible) in which a thing is found to be the efficient cause of itself; for so it would be prior to itself, which is impossible. Now in efficient causes it is not possible to go on to infinity, because in all efficient causes following in order, the first is the cause of the intermediate cause, and the intermediate is the cause of the ultimate cause, whether the intermediate cause be several, or one only. Now to take away the cause is to take away the effect. Therefore, if there be no first cause among efficient causes, there will be no ultimate, nor any intermediate, cause. But if in efficient causes it is possible to go on to infinity, there will be no first efficient cause, neither will there be an ultimate effect, nor any intermediate efficient causes; all of which is plainly false. Therefore it is necessary to admit a first efficient cause, to which everyone gives the name of God.

The third way is taken from possibility and necessity, and runs thus. We find in nature things that are possible to be and not to be, since they are found to be generated, and to be corrupted, and consequently, it is possible from them to be and not to be. But it is impossible for these always to exist, for that which can not-be at some time is not. Therefore, if everything can not-be, then at one time there was nothing in existence. Now if this were true, even now there would be nothing in existence, because that which does not exist begins to exist only through something already existing. Therefore, if at one time nothing was in existence, it would have been impossible for anything to have begun to exist; and thus even now nothing would be in existence—which is absurd. Therefore, not all beings are merely possible, but there must exist something the existence of which is necessary. But every necessary thing either has its necessity caused by another, or not. Now it is impossible to go on to infinity in necessary things which have their necessity caused by another, as has been already proved in regard to efficient causes. Therefore we cannot but admit the existence of some being having of itself its own necessity, and not receiving it from another, but rather causing in others their necessity. This all men speak of as God.

The fourth way is taken from the gradation to be found in things. Among beings there are some more and some less good, true, noble, and the like. But *more* and *less* are predicated of different things according as they resemble in their different ways something which is the maximum, as a thing is said to be hotter according as it more nearly resembles that which is hottest; so that there is something which is truest, something best, something noblest, and, consequently, something which is most being, for those things that are greatest in truth are greatest in being, as it is written in *Metaphysics* II. Now the maximum is any genus is the cause of all in that genus, as fire, which is the maximum of heat, is the cause of all hot things, as is said in the same book. Therefore there must also be something which is to all beings the cause of their being, goodness, and every other perfection; and this we call God.

The fifth way is taken from the governance of the world. We see that things which lack knowledge, such as natural bodies, act for an end, and this is evident from their acting always, or nearly always, in the same way, so as to obtain the best result. Hence it is plain that they achieve their end, not fortuitously, but designedly. Now whatever lacks knowledge cannot move towards an end, unless it be directed by some being endowed with knowledge and intelligence; as the arrow is directed by the archer. Therefore some intelligent being exists by whom all natural things are directed to their end; and this being we call God.

F. C. COPLESTON

Commentary on the Five Ways

GOD AND CREATION

I [now] turn to Aquinas' five proofs of the existence of God. In the first proof he argues that "motion" or change means the reduction of a thing from a state of potentiality to one of act, and that a thing cannot be reduced from potentiality to act except under the influence of an agent already in act. In this sense "everything which is moved must be moved by another." He argues finally that in order to avoid an infinite regress in the chain of movers, the existence of a first unmoved mover must be admitted. "And all understand that this is God."

A statement like "all understand that this is God" or "all call this (being) God" occurs at the end of each proof, and I postpone consideration of it for the moment. As for the ruling out of an infinite regress, I shall explain what Aquinas means to reject after outlining the second proof, which is similar in structure to the first.

Whereas in the first proof Aquinas considers things as being acted upon, as being changed or "moved," in the second he considers them as active agents, as efficient causes. He argues that there is a hierarchy of efficient causes, a subordinate cause being dependent on the cause above it in the hierarchy. He then proceeds, after excluding the hypothesis of an infinite regress, to draw the conclusion that there must be a first efficient cause, "which all call God."

Now, it is obviously impossible to discuss these arguments profitably unless they are first understood. And misunderstanding of them is only too easy, since the terms and phrases used are either unfamiliar or liable to be taken in a sense other than the sense intended. In the first place it is essential to understand that in the first argument Aquinas supposes that movement or change is dependent on a "mover" acting here and now, and that in the second argument he supposes that there are efficient causes in the world which even in their causal activity are here and now dependent on the causal activity of other causes. That is why I have spoken of a "hierarchy" rather than of a "series." What he is thinking of can be illustrated in this way. A son is dependent on his father, in the sense that he would not have existed except for the causal activity of his father. But when the son acts for himself, he is not dependent here and now on his father. But he is dependent here and now on other factors. Without the activity of the air, for instance, he could not himself act, and the life-preserving activity of the air is itself dependent here and now on other factors, and they in turn on other factors. I do not say that this illustration is in all respects adequate for the purpose; but it at least illustrates the fact that when Aquinas talks about an "order" of efficient causes he is not thinking of a series stretching back into the past, but of a hierarchy of causes, in which a subordinate member is here and now dependent on the causal activity of a higher member. If I wind up my watch at night, it then proceeds to work without further interference on my part. But the activity of the pen tracing these words on the page is here and now dependent on the activity of my hand, which in turn is here and now dependent on other factors.

The meaning of the rejection of an infinite regress should now be clear. Aquinas is not rejecting the possibility of an infinite series as such. . . . he did not think that anyone had ever succeeded in showing the impossibility of an infinite series of events stretching back into the past. Therefore he does not mean to rule out the possibility of an infinite series of causes and effects, in which a given member depended on the preceding member, say X on Y, but does not, once it exists, depend here and now on the present causal activity of the preceding member. We have to imagine, not a lineal or horizontal series, so to speak, but a vertical hierarchy, in which a lower member depends here and now on the present causal activity of the member above it. It is the latter type of series, if prolonged to infinity, which Aquinas rejects. And he rejects it on the ground that unless there is a "first" member, a mover which is not itself moved or a cause which does not itself depend on the causal activity of a higher cause, it is not possible to explain the "motion" or the causal activity of the lowest member. His point of view is this. Suppress the first unmoved mover and there is no motion or change here and now. Suppress the first efficient cause and there is no causal activity here and now. If therefore we find that some things in the world are changed, there must be a first unmoved mover. And if there are efficient causes in the world, there must be a first efficient, and completely non-dependent cause. The word "first" does not mean first in the temporal order, but supreme or first in the ontological order. . . .

In the third proof Aquinas starts from the fact that some things come into being and perish, and he concludes from this that it is possible for them to exist or not to exist: they do not exist "necessarily." He then argues that it is impossible for things which are of this kind to exist always; for "that which is capable of not existing, at some time does not exist." If all things were of this kind, at some time there would be nothing. Aquinas is clearly supposing for the sake of argument the hypothesis of infinite time, and his proof is designed to cover this hypothesis. He does not say that infinite time is impossible: what he says is that if time is infinite and if all things are capable of not existing, this potentiality would inevitably be fulfilled in infinite time. There would then be nothing. And if there had ever been nothing, nothing would now exist. For no thing can bring itself into existence. But it is clear as a matter of fact that there are things. Therefore it can never have been true to say that there was literally no thing. Therefore it is impossible that all things should be capable of existing or not existing. There must, then, be some necessary being. But perhaps it is necessary in the sense that it must exist if something else exists; that is to say, its necessity may be hypothetical. We cannot, however, proceed to infinity in the series or hierarchy of necessary beings. If we do so, we do not explain the presence here and now of beings capable of existing or not existing. Therefore we must affirm the existence of a being which is absolutely necessary (*per se necessarium*) and completely independent. "And all call this being *God.*"

This argument may appear to be quite unnecessarily complicated and obscure. But it has to be seen in its historical context. As already mentioned, Aquinas designed his argument in such a way as to be independent of the question whether or not the world existed from eternity. He wanted to show that on either hypothesis there must be a necessary being. As for the introduction of hypothetical necessary beings, he wanted to show that even if there are such beings, perhaps within the universe, which are not corruptible in the sense in which a flower is corruptible, there must still be an absolutely independent being. Finally, in regard to terminology, Aquinas uses the common medieval expression "necessary being." He does not actually use the term "contingent being" in the argument and talks instead about "possible" beings; but it comes to the same thing. And though the words "contingent" and "necessary" are now applied to propositions rather than to beings, I have retained Aquinas' mode of speaking. Whether one accepts the argument or not, I do not think that there is any insuperable difficulty in understanding the line of thought.

The fourth argument is admittedly difficult to grasp. Aquinas argues that there are degrees of perfections in things. Different kinds of finite things possess different perfections in diverse limited degrees. He then argues not only that if there are different degrees of a perfection like goodness there is a supreme good to which other good things approximate but also that all limited degrees of goodness are caused by the supreme good. And since goodness is a convertible term with being, a thing being good in so far as it has being, the supreme good is the supreme being and the cause of being in all other things. "Therefore there is something which is the cause of the being and goodness and of every perfection in all other things; and this we call *God.*"

Aquinas refers to some remarks of Aristotle in the *Metaphysics;* but this argument puts one in mind at once of Plato's *Symposium* and *Republic.* And the Platonic doctrine of participation seems to be involved. Aquinas was not immediately acquainted with either work, but the Platonic line of thought was familiar to him from other writers. And it has not disappeared from philosophy. Indeed, some of those theists who reject or doubt the validity of the "cosmological" arguments seem to feel a marked attraction for some variety of the fourth way, arguing that in the recognition of objective values we implicitly recognize God as the supreme value. But if the line of thought represented by the fourth way is to mean anything to the average modern reader, it has to be presented in a rather different manner from that in which it is expressed by Aquinas who was able to assume in his readers ideas and points of view which can no longer be presupposed.

Finally, the fifth proof, if we take its statement in the *Summa theologica* together with that in the *Summa contra Gentiles,* can be expressed more or less as follows. The activity and behaviour of each thing is determined by its form. But we observe material things of very different types co-operating in such a way as to produce and maintain a relatively stable world-order or system. They achieve an "end," the production and maintenance of a cosmic order. But nonintelligent material things certainly do not co-operate consciously in view of a purpose. If it is said that they co-operate in the realization of an end or purpose, this does not mean that they intend the realization of this order in a manner analogous to that in which a man can act consciously with a view to the achievement of a purpose. Nor, when Aquinas talks about operating "for an end" in this connection, is he thinking of the utility of certain things to the human race. He is not saying, for example, that grass grows to feed the sheep and that sheep exist in order that human beings should have food and clothing. It is of the unconscious co-operation of different kinds of material things in the production and maintenance of a relatively stable cosmic system that he is thinking, not of the benefits accruing to us from our use of certain objects. And his argument is that this co-operation on the part of heterogeneous material things clearly points to the existence of an extrinsic intelligent author of this co-operation, who operates with an end in view. If Aquinas had lived in the days of the evolutionary hypothesis, he would doubtless have argued that this hypothesis supports rather than invalidates the conclusion of the argument.

No one of these arguments was entirely new, as Aquinas himself was very well aware. But he developed them and arranged them to form a coherent whole. I do not mean that he regarded the validity of one particular argument as necessarily depending on the validity of the other four. He doubtless thought that each argument was valid in its own right. But, as I have already remarked, they conform to a certain pattern, and they are mutually complementary in the sense that in each argument things are considered from a different point of view or under a different aspect. They are so many different approaches to God.

Hume

The most popular and perhaps the most devastating criticisms of the *a posteriori* arguments, especially in their teleological form, are articulated by David Hume in his posthumously published *Dialogues Concerning Natural Religion* (1777). He points out what he sees as the absurdities in an anthropomorphic conception of God and the manner in which these are embedded in the arguments for the existence of God. He maintains that this is by no means a perfect world and so does not stand in need of a supreme designer. Further, it makes no sense, according to Hume, to argue from objects of sense experience to explanatory principles that occupy a region outside of that experience.

In the *Dialogues,* it is thought that the character Philo, more than any other, represents Hume's own views.

Against the Design Argument

Now, Cleanthes, said Philo, . . . *First,* by this method of reasoning you renounce all claim to infinity in any of the attributes of the Deity. For, as the cause ought only to be proportioned to the effect, and the effect, so far as it falls under our cognizance, is not infinite, what pretensions have we, upon your suppositions, to ascribe that attribute to the Divine Being? You will still insist that, by removing Him so much from all similarity to human creatures, we give in to the most arbitrary hypothesis, and at the same time weaken all proofs of His existence.

Secondly, you have no reason, on your theory, for ascribing perfection to the Deity, even in His finite capacity, or for supposing Him free from every error, mistake, or incoherence, in His undertakings. There are many inexplicable difficulties in the works of nature which, if we allow a perfect Author to be proved a priori, are easily solved, and become only seeming difficulties from the narrow capacity of man, who cannot trace infinite relations. But according to your method of reasoning, these difficulties become all real, and, perhaps, will be insisted on as new instances of likeness to human art and contrivance. At least, you must acknowledge that it is im-

From *Dialogues Concerning Natural Religion* by David Hume in *The Empiricists* (n.d.). Reprinted with acknowledgment to Doubleday & Company, Inc.

possible for us to tell, from our limited views, whether this system contains any great faults or deserves any considerable praise if compared to other possible and even real systems. . . .

But were this world ever so perfect a production, it must still remain uncertain whether all the excellences of the work can justly be ascribed to the workman. If we survey a ship, what an exalted idea must we form of the ingenuity of the carpenter who framed so complicated, useful, and beautiful a machine? And what surprise must we feel when we find him a stupid mechanic who imitated others, and copied an art which, through a long succession of ages, after multiplied trials, mistakes, corrections, deliberations, and controversies, had been gradually improving? Many worlds might have been botched and bungled, throughout an eternity, ere this system was struck out; much labour lost, many fruitless trials made, and a slow but continued improvement carried on during infinite ages in the art of world-making. In such subjects, who can determine where the truth, nay, who can conjecture where the probability, lies, amidst a great number of hypotheses which may be proposed, and a still greater which may be imagined?

And what shadow of an argument, continued Philo, can you produce from your hypothesis to prove the unity of the Deity? A great number of men join in building a house or ship, in rearing a city, in framing a commonwealth; why may not several deities combine in contriving and framing a world? This is only so much greater similarity to human affairs. By sharing the work among several, we may so much further limit the attributes of each, and get rid of that extensive power and knowledge which must be supposed in one deity, and which, according to you, can only serve to weaken the proof of his existence. And if such foolish, such vicious creatures as man can yet often unite in framing and executing one plan, how much more those deities or demons, whom we may suppose several degrees more perfect!

To multiply causes without necessity is indeed contrary to true philosophy, but this principle applies not to the present case. Were one deity antecedently proved by your theory who were possessed of every attribute requisite to the production of the universe, it would be needless, I own (though not absurd), to suppose any other deity exist. But while it is still a question whether all these attributes are united in one subject or dispersed among several independent beings, by what phenomena in nature can we pretend to decide the controversy? Where we see a body raised in a scale, we are sure that there is in the opposite scale, however concealed from sight, some counterpoising weight equal to it; but it is still allowed to doubt whether that weight be an aggregate of several distinct bodies or one uniform united mass. And if the weight requisite very much exceeds anything which we have ever seen conjoined in any single body, the former supposition becomes still more probable and natural. An intelligent being of such vast powers and capacity as is necessary to produce the universe, or, to speak in the language of ancient philosophy, so prodigious an animal exceeds all analogy and even comprehension.

But further, Cleanthes: men are mortal, and renew their species by generation; and this is common to all living creatures. The two great sexes of male and female, says Milton, animate the world. Why must this circumstance, so universal, so essential, be excluded from those numerous and limited deities? Behold, then, the theogeny of ancient times brought back upon us.

And why not become a perfect anthropomorphite? Why not assert the deity or deities to be corporeal, and to have eyes, a nose, mouth, ears, etc.? Epicurus maintained that no man had ever seen reason but in a human figure; therefore, the gods must have a human figure. And this argument, which is deservedly so much ridiculed by Cicero, becomes, according to you, solid and philosophical.

In a word, Cleanthes, a man who follows your hypothesis is able, perhaps, to assert or conjecture that the universe sometime arose from something like design; but beyond that position he cannot ascertain one single circumstance, and is left afterwards to fix every point of his theology by the utmost license of fancy and hypothesis. This world, for aught he knows, is very faulty and imperfect, compared to a superior standard, and was only the first rude essay of some infant deity who afterwards abandoned it, ashamed of his lame performance; it is the work only of some dependent, inferior deity, and is the object of derision to his superiors; it is the production of old age and dotage in some superannuated deity, and ever since his death has run on at adventures, from the first impulse and active force which it received from him. You justly give signs of horror, Demea, at these strange suppositions; but these, and a thousand more of the same kind, are Cleanthes' suppositions, not mine. From the moment the attributes of the Deity are supposed finite, all these have place. And I cannot, for my part, think that so wild and unsettled a system of theology is, in any respect, preferable to none at all.

Flew

Antony Flew (born 1923), an emeritus English professor of philosophy, is the author and editor of many works on the philosophy of religion.

Contemporary analytic philosophy has offered some interesting challenges to traditional theology in its effort to make sense of the claim that there exists a personal, loving God. Philosophers like Antony Flew, by way of an analysis of the cognitive status of religious assertions, have argued that the very statement "God exists" has no real explanatory value, as it is formulated and adhered to in such a way by the believer that no conceivable evidence is allowed to count against it. If one says that "God is love" and holds fast to the belief by way of qualifying at every turn what is apparently meant by it when challenged with contrary evidence, the result is that the belief is not really asserting anything at all.

Theology and Falsification

Let us begin with a parable. It is a parable developed from a tale told by John Wisdom in his haunting and revelatory article "Gods." Once upon a time two explorers came upon a clearing in the jungle. In the clearing were growing many flowers and many weeds. One explorer says, "Some gardener must tend this plot." The other disagrees, "There is no gardener." So they pitch their tents and set a watch. No gardener is ever seen. "But perhaps he is an invisible gardener." So they set up a barbed-wire fence. They electrify it. They patrol with bloodhounds. . . . But no shrieks ever suggest that some intruder has received a shock. No movements of the wire ever betray an invisible climber. The bloodhounds never give cry. Yet still the Believer is not convinced. "But there is a gardener, invisible, intangible, insensible to electric shocks, a gardener who has no scent and makes no sound, a gardener who comes secretly to look after the garden which he loves." At last the Sceptic despairs, "But what remains of your original assertion? Just how does what you call an invisible, intangible, eternally elusive gardener differ from an imaginary gardener or even from no gardener at all?"

In this parable we can see how what starts as an assertion, that something exists or that there is some analogy between certain complexes of phenomena, may be reduced step by step to an altogether different status, to an expression perhaps of a "picture preference." The Sceptic says there is no gardener. The Believer says there is a gardener (but invisible, etc.). . . . The process of qualification may be checked at any point before the original assertion is completely withdrawn and something of that first assertion will remain. . . . But though the process of qualification may be, and of course usually is, checked in time, it is not always judiciously so halted. Someone may dissipate his assertion completely without noticing that he has done so. A fine brash hypothesis may thus be killed by inches, the death by a thousand qualifications.

And in this, it seems to me, lies the peculiar danger, the endemic evil, of theological utterance. Take such utterances as "God has a plan," "God created the world," "God loves us as a father loves his children." They look at first sight very much like assertions, vast cosmological assertions. Of course, this is no sure sign that they either are, or are intended to be, assertions. But let us confine ourselves to the cases where those who utter such sentences intend them to express assertion. (Merely remarking parenthetically that those who intend or interpret such utterances as crypto-commands, expressions of wishes, disguised ejaculations, concealed ethics, or as anything else but assertions, are unlikely to succeed in making them either properly orthodox or practically effective.)

Now to assert that such and such is the case is necessarily equivalent to denying that such and such is not the case. Suppose then that we are in doubt as to what someone who gives vent to an utterance is asserting, or suppose that, more radically, we are sceptical as to whether he is really asserting anything at all, one way of trying to understand (or perhaps it will be to expose) his utterance is to attempt to find what he would regard as counting against, or as being incompatible with, its truth. For if the utterance is indeed an assertion, it will necessarily be equivalent to a denial of the negation of that assertion. And anything which would count against the assertion, or which would induce the speaker to withdraw it and to admit that it had been mistaken, must be part of (or the whole of) the meaning of the negation of that assertion. And to know the meaning of the negation of an assertion, is as near as makes no matter, to know the meaning of that assertion. And if there is nothing which a putative assertion denies then there is nothing which it asserts either; and so it is not really an assertion. When the Sceptic in the parable asked the Believer, "Just how does what you call an invisible, intangible, eternally elusive gardener differ from an imaginary gardener or even from no gardener at all?" he was suggesting that the Believer's earlier statement had been so eroded by qualification that it was no longer an assertion at all.

Now it often seems to people who are not religious as if there was no conceivable event or series of events the occurrence of which would be admitted by sophisticated religious people to be a sufficient reason for conceding "There wasn't a God after all" or "God does not really love us then." Someone tells us that God loves us as a father loves his children. We are reassured. But then we see a child dying of inoperable cancer of the throat. His earthly father is driven frantic in his efforts to help, but his Heavenly Father reveals no obvious sign of concern. Some qualification is made—God's love is "not a merely human love" or it is "an inscrutable love," perhaps—and we realize that such sufferings are quite compatible with the truth of the assertion that "God loves us as a father (but, of course, . . .)." We are reassured again. But then perhaps we ask: what is his assurance of God's (appropriately qualified) love worth, what is this apparent guarantee really a guarantee against? Just what would have to happen not merely (morally and wrongly) to tempt but also (logically and rightly) to entitle us to say "God does not love us" or even "God does not exist"? . . . "What would have to occur or to have occurred to constitute for you a disproof of the love of, or of the existence of, God?"

Mackie and Hick

J. L. Mackie (1917–1981) was a professor of philosophy at Oxford University and the author of many works, including The Miracle of Theism.

John Hick (born 1922) received his education at Edinburgh University, Oxford, and Cambridge University, and was for many years the Danforth Professor of Religion at Claremont Graduate School. Among his notable works are Death and Eternal Life, An Interpretation of Religion, *and* Religious Pluralism.

It has often been observed that no aspect of human experience has called into question the nature and reality of God more than the existence of evil. If God exists, how is it possible that young children are abused and sometimes even tortured; that the Holocaust occurred; that earthquakes, floods, and tornadoes indiscriminately destroy persons and property? The *problem* of evil for theistic religion is perfectly straightforward, although for most philosophers no theological solution has been convincingly put forward. The classical formulation of the problem is: "If God is willing to prevent evil but is not able to, then he is impotent. If he is able but not willing, then he is malevolent." The problem as so formulated arises on the theistic assumption that God, the creator, is omnipotent and entirely good. Why, then, is there evil?

The term used to justify God's ways to humankind, or as John Hick puts it, "a defence of the goodness of God in face of the evil in His world," is "theodicy." Two forms of evil are usually identified in every theodicy: natural and moral, with the greater stress in our time given to the latter. Natural evil is defined simply as those happenings in nature that apparently occur without human agency or intention—the earthquakes, floods, and tornadoes; moral evil is defined precisely as those actions of human beings that are violative of human dignity and that are repugnant to what we take to be our moral sense.

Now conceptions of evil are not, of course, restricted to theism; indeed, historians of religions frequently note that different kinds of religious experience and orientations have understood the meaning of evil in rather different ways. For archaic or primal religiosity evil is generally seen as a kind of defilement, a "blackening" of the soul that requires purification, and for the mystical generally it is taken as a mark of ignorance, or incompleteness that is overcome by insight or knowledge. For both the archaic and the mystical, the fact of evil is not so much a problem to be resolved rationally by way of a theodicy as it is an actuality to be faced, understood, and overcome through different forms of social action and spiritual experience. Evil, in short, once again, is a theological-philosophical problem for theism when it arises from the need to make its basic assumptions about the nature of God coherent and commensurate with the existence of evil.

J. L Mackie, in the selection that follows, claims that no arguments have been (and by implication can ever be) put forward that will withstand criticism, for the basic reason that there is an inherent contradiction between the propositions that God is omnipotent and wholly good and that evil exists. Without identifying who historically has argued for what resolutions (e.g., Saint Augustine, who formulated the "free will" and "evil as a privation" arguments), Mackie sets forth clearly what he sees as the insuperable difficulties that any theodicy faces.

Hick, on the other hand, wants to show how "the mystery of evil, largely incomprehensible though it remains, does not render irrational a faith that has arisen, not from the inferences of natural theology, but from participation in a stream of religious experience which is continuous with that recorded in the Bible." He develops his contemporary theodicy on the assumption, going back to the Irenaean tradition in Christianity, that human beings, rather than being created by God in a "finished state," are still "in process of creation" and that goodness, the beatitude, that may come in a far-distant fulfillment justifies "the long travail of the soul-making process." Mackie, one might suppose, would respond to Hick with the charge that this is still a rather odd way for God to go about his business.

J. L. MACKIE

Evil and Omnipotence

The traditional arguments for the existence of God have been fairly thoroughly criticized by philosophers. But the theologian can, if he wishes, accept this criticism. He can admit that no rational proof of God's existence is possible. And he can still retain all that is essential to his position, by holding that God's existence is known in some other, nonrational way. I think, however, that a more telling criticism can be made by way of the traditional problem of evil. Here it can be shown, not that religious beliefs lack rational support, but that they are positively irrational, that the several parts of the essential theological doctrine are inconsistent with one another, so that the theologian can maintain his position as a whole only by a much more extreme rejection of reason than in the former case. He must now be prepared to believe, not merely what cannot be proved, but what can be *disproved* from other beliefs that he also holds.

The problem of evil, in the sense in which I shall be using the phrase, is a problem only for someone who believes that there is a God who is both omnipotent and wholly good. And it is a logical problem, the problem of clarifying and reconciling a number of beliefs: it is not a scientific problem that might be solved by further ob-

From "Evil and Omnipotence" by J. L Mackie, *Mind,* vol. LXIV, no. 254 (April 1955). Reprinted by permission of Oxford University Press.

servations, or a practical problem that might be solved by a decision or an action. These points are obvious; I mention them only because they are sometimes ignored by theologians, who sometimes parry a statement of the problem with such remarks as "Well, can you solve the problem yourself?" or "This is a mystery which may be revealed to us later" or "Evil is something to be faced and overcome, not to be merely discussed."

In its simplest form the problem is this: God is omnipotent; God is wholly good; and yet evil exists. There seems to be some contradiction between these three propositions, so that if any two of them were true the third would be false. But at the same time all three are essential parts of most theological positions: the theologian, it seems, at once *must* adhere and *cannot consistently* adhere to all three. (The problem does not arise only for theists, but I shall discuss it in the form in which it presents itself for ordinary theism.)

However, the contradiction does not arise immediately; to show it we need some additional premises, or perhaps some quasilogical rules connecting the terms "good," "evil," and "omnipotent." These additional principles are that good is opposed to evil, in such a way that a good thing always eliminates evil as far as it can, and that there are no limits to what an omnipotent thing can do. From these it follows that a good omnipotent thing eliminates evil completely, and then the propositions that a good omnipotent thing exists, and that evil exists, are incompatible.

Now once the problem is fully stated it is clear that it can be solved, in the sense that the problem will not arise if one gives up at least one of the propositions that constitute it. If you are prepared to say that God is not wholly good, or not quite omnipotent, or that evil does not exist, or that good is not opposed to the kind of evil that exists, or that there are limits to what an omnipotent thing can do, then the problem of evil will not arise for you.

There are, then, quite a number of adequate solutions of the problem of evil, and some of these have been adopted, or almost adopted, by various thinkers. For example, a few have been prepared to deny God's omnipotence, and rather more have been prepared to keep the term "omnipotence" but severely to restrict its meaning, recording quite a number of things that an omnipotent being cannot do. Some have said that evil is an illusion, perhaps because they held that the whole world of temporal, changing things is an illusion, and that what we call evil belongs only to this world, or perhaps because they held that although temporal things *are* much as we see them, those that we call evil are not really evil. Some have said that what we call evil is merely the privation of good, that evil in a positive sense, evil that would really be opposed to good, does not exist. Many have agreed with Pope that disorder is harmony not understood, and that partial evil is universal good. Whether any of these views is *true* is, of course, another question. But each of them gives an adequate solution of the problems of evil in the sense that if you accept it this problem does not arise for you, though you may, of course, have *other* problems to face. . . .

There are, in fact, many so-called solutions which purport to remove the contradiction without abandoning any of its constituent propositions. These must be fallacious, as we can see from the very statement of the problem, but it is not so easy to see in each case precisely where the fallacy lies. I suggest that in all cases the fallacy has the general form suggested above: in order to solve the problem one (or perhaps more) of its constituent propositions is given up, but in such a way that it appears to have been retained, and can therefore be asserted without qualification in other contexts. Sometimes there is a further complication: the supposed solution moves to and fro between, say, two of the constituent propositions, at one point asserting the first of these but covertly abandoning the second, at another point asserting the second but covertly abandoning the first. These fallacious solutions often turn upon some equivocation with the words "good" and "evil," or upon some vagueness about the way in which good and evil are opposed to one another, or about how much is meant by "omnipotence." I proposed to examine some of these so-called solutions, and to exhibit their fallacies in detail. Incidentally, I shall also be considering whether an adequate solution could be reached by a minor modification of one or more of the constituent propositions, which would, however, still satisfy all the essential requirements of ordinary theism.

1. "GOOD CANNOT EXIST WITHOUT EVIL" OR "EVIL IS NECESSARY AS A COUNTERPART TO GOOD"

It is sometimes suggested that evil is necessary as a counterpart to good, that if there were no evil there could be no good either, and that this solves the problem of evil. It is true that it points to an answer to the question "Why should there be evil?" But it does so only by qualifying some of the propositions that constitute the problem.

First, it sets a limit to what God can do, saying that God *cannot* create good without simultaneously creating evil, and this means either that God is not omnipotent or that there are *some* limits to what an omnipotent thing can do. It may be replied that these limits are always presupposed, that omnipotence has never meant the power to do what is logically impossible, and on the present view the existence of good without evil would be a logical impossibility. This interpretation of omnipotence may, indeed, be accepted as a modification of our original account which does not reject anything that is essential to theism, and I shall in general assume it in the subsequent discussion. It is, perhaps, the most common theistic view, but I think that some theists at least have maintained that God can do what is logically impossible. Many theists, at any rate, have held that logic itself is created or laid down by God, that logic is the way in which God arbitrarily chooses to think. (This is, of course, parallel to the ethical view that morally right actions are those which God arbitrarily chooses to command, and the two views encounter similar difficulties.) And *this* account of logic is clearly inconsistent with the view that God is bound by logical necessities—unless it is possible for an omnipotent being to bind himself, an issue which we shall consider later, when we come to the Paradox of Omnipotence. This solution of the problem of evil cannot, therefore, be consistently adopted along with the view that logic is itself created by God.

But, secondly, this solution denies that evil is opposed to good in our original sense. If good and evil are counterparts, a good thing will not "eliminate evil as far as it can." Indeed, this view suggests that good and evil are not strictly qualities of things at all. Perhaps the suggestion is that good and evil are related in much the same way as great and small. Certainly, when the term "great" is used relatively as a condensation of "greater than so-and-so," and "small" is used correspondingly, greatness and smallness are counterparts and cannot exist without each other. But in this sense greatness is not a quality, not an intrinsic feature of anything; and it would be absurd to think of a movement in favor of greatness and against smallness in this sense. Such a movement would be self-defeating, since relative greatness can be promoted only by a simultaneous promotion of relative smallness. I feel sure that no theists would be content to regard God's goodness as analogous to this—as if what he supports were not the *good* but the *better,* and as if he had the paradoxical aim that all things should be better than other things. . . .

2. "EVIL IS NECESSARY AS A MEANS TO GOOD"

It is sometimes suggested that evil is necessary for good not as a counterpart but as a means. In its simple form this has little plausibility as a solution of the problem of evil, since it obviously implies a severe restriction of God's power. It would be a *causal* law that you cannot have a certain end without a certain means, so that if God has to introduce evil as a means to good, he must be subject to at least some causal laws. This certainly conflicts with what a theist normally means by omnipotence. This view of God as limited by causal laws also conflicts with the view that causal laws are themselves made by God, which is more widely held than the corresponding view about the laws of logic. This conflict would, indeed, be resolved if it were possible for an omnipotent being to bind himself, and this possibility has still to be considered. Unless a favorable answer can be given to this question, the suggestion that evil is necessary as a means to good solves the problem of evil only by denying one of its constituent propositions, either that God is omnipotent or that "omnipotent" means what it says.

3. "THE UNIVERSE IS BETTER WITH SOME EVIL IN IT THAN IT COULD BE IF THERE WERE NO EVIL"

Much more important is a solution which at first seems to be a mere variant of the previous one, that evil may contribute to the goodness of a whole in which it is found, so that the universe as a whole is better as it is, with some evil in it, than it would be if there were no evil. This solution may be developed in either of two ways. It may be supported by an aesthetic analogy, by the fact that contrasts heighten beauty, that in a musical work, for example, there may occur discords which somehow add to the beauty of the work as a whole. Alternatively, it may be worked out in connection with the notion of progress, that the best possible organization of the universe will not be static, but progressive, that the gradual overcoming of evil by good is really a finer thing than would be the eternal unchallenged supremacy of good.

In either case, this solution usually starts from the assumption that the evil whose existence gives rise to the problem of evil is primarily what is called physical evil, that is to say, pain. In Hume's rather half-hearted presentation of the problem of evil, the evils that he stresses are pain and disease, and those who reply to him argue that the existence of pain and disease makes possible the existence of sympathy, benevolence, heroism, and the gradually successful struggle of doctors and reformers to overcome these evils. In fact, theists often seize the opportunity to accuse those who stress the problem of evil of taking a low, materialistic view of good and evil, equating these with pleasure and pain, and of ignoring the more spiritual goods which can arise in the struggle against evils. . . .

4. "EVIL IS DUE TO HUMAN FREE WILL"

Perhaps the most important proposed solution of the problem of evil is that evil is not to be ascribed to God at all, but to the independent actions of human beings, supposed to have been endowed by God with freedom of the will. . . .

. . . To explain why a wholly good God gave men free will although it would lead to some important evils, it must be argued that it is better on the whole that men should act freely, and sometimes err, than that they should be innocent automata, acting rightly in a wholly determined way. . . .

I think that this solution is unsatisfactory primarily because of the incoherence of the notion of freedom of the will: but I cannot discuss this topic adequately here, although some of my criticisms will touch upon it. . . .

. . . I should ask this: if God has made men such that in their free choices they sometimes prefer what is good and sometimes what is evil, why could he not have made men such that they always freely choose the good? If there is no logical impossibility in a man's freely choosing the good on one, or on several, occasions, there cannot be a logical impossibility in his freely choosing the good on every occasion. God was not, then, faced with a choice between making innocent automata and making beings who, in acting freely, would sometimes go wrong: there was open to him the obviously better possibility of making beings who would act freely but always go right. Clearly, his failure to avail himself of this possibility is inconsistent with his being both omnipotent and wholly good.

If it is replied that this objection is absurd, that the making of some wrong choices is logically necessary for freedom, it would seem that "freedom" must here mean complete randomness or indeterminacy, including randomness with regard to the alternatives good and evil, in other words that men's choices and consequent actions can be "free" only if they are not determined by their characters. Only on this assumption can God escape the responsibility for men's actions; for if he made them as they are, but did not determine their wrong choices, this can only be because the wrong choices are not determined by men as they are. But then if freedom is randomness, how can it be a characteristic of *will*? And, still more, how can it be the most important good? What value or merit would there be in free choices if these were random actions which were not determined by the nature of the agent? . . .

This criticism is sufficient to dispose of this solution. But besides this there is a fundamental difficulty in the notion of an omnipotent God creating men with free will, for if men's wills are really free this must mean that even God cannot control them, that is, that God is no longer omnipotent. It may be objected that God's gift of freedom to men does not mean that he *cannot* control their wills, but that he always *refrains* from controlling their wills. But why, we may ask, should God refrain from controlling evil wills? Why should he not leave men free to will rightly, but intervene when he sees them beginning to will wrongly? If God could do this, but does not, and if he is wholly good, the only explanation could be that even a wrong free act of will is not really evil, that its freedom is a value which outweighs its wrongness, so that there would be a loss of value if God took away the wrongness and the freedom together. But this is utterly opposed to what theists say about sin in other contexts. The present solution of the problem of evil, then, can be maintained only in the form that God has made men so free that he *cannot* control their wills.

This leads us to what I call the "Paradox of Omnipotence": can an omnipotent being make things which he cannot subsequently control? Or, what is practically equivalent to this, can an omnipotent being make rules which then bind himself? (These are practically equivalent because any such rules could be regarded as setting certain things beyond his control, and vice versa.) The second of these formulations is relevant to the suggestions that we have already met, that an omnipotent God creates the rules of logic or causal laws, and is then bound by them.

It is clear that this is a paradox: the questions cannot be answered satisfactorily either in the affirmative or in the negative. If we answer "Yes," it follows that if God actually makes things which he cannot control, or makes rules which bind himself, he is not omnipotent once he had made them: there are *then* things which he cannot do. But if we answer "No," we are immediately asserting that there are things which he cannot do, that is to say that he is already not omnipotent.

It cannot be replied that the question which sets this paradox is not a proper question. It would make perfectly good sense to say that a human mechanic has made a machine which he cannot control: if there is any difficulty about the question it lies in the notion of omnipotence itself.

This, incidentally, shows that although we have approached this paradox from the free-will theory, it is equally a problem for a theological determinist. No one thinks that machines have free will, yet they may well be beyond the control of their makers. The determinist might reply that anyone who makes anything determines its ways of acting, and so determines its subsequent behavior: even the human mechanic does this by his *choice* of materials and structure for his machine, though he does not know all about either of these: the mechanic thus determines, though he may not foresee, his machine's actions. And since God is omniscient, and since his creation of things is total, he both determines and foresees the ways in which his creatures will act. We may grant this, but it is beside the point. The question is not whether God *originally* determined the future actions of his creatures, but whether he can *subsequently* control their actions, or whether he was able in his original creation to put things beyond his subsequent control. Even on determinist principles the answers "Yes" and "No" are equally irreconcilable with God's omnipotence.

Before suggesting a solution of this paradox, I would point out that there is a parallel Paradox of Sovereignty. Can a legal sovereign make a law restricting its own future legislative power? For example, could the British parliament make a law forbidding any future parliament to socialize banking, and also forbidding the future repeal of this law itself? Or could the British parliament, which was legally sovereign in Australia in, say, 1899, pass a valid law, or series of laws, which made it no longer sovereign in 1933? Again, neither the affirmative nor the negative answer is really satisfactory. If we were to answer. "Yes," we should be admitting the validity of a law which, if it were actually made, would mean that parliament was no longer sovereign. If we were to answer "No," we should be admitting that there is a law, not logically absurd, which parliament cannot validly make, that is, that parliament is not now a legal sovereign. This paradox can be solved in the following way. We should distinguish between first order laws, that is laws governing the actions of individuals and bodies other than the legislature, and second order laws, that is laws about laws, laws governing the actions of the legislature itself. Correspondingly, we should distinguish two orders of sovereignty, first order sovereignty (sovereignty [1]) which is unlimited authority to make first order laws, and second order sovereignty (sovereignty [2]) which is unlimited authority to make second order laws. If we say that parliament is sovereign we might mean that any parliament at any time has sovereignty (1), or we might mean that parliament has both sovereignty (1) and sovereignty (2) at present, but we cannot without contradiction mean both that the present parliament has sovereignty (2) and that every parliament at every time has sovereignty (1), for if the present parliament has sovereignty (2) it may use it to take away the sovereignty (1) of later parliaments. What the paradox shows is that we cannot ascribe to any continuing institution legal sovereignty in an inclusive sense.

The analogy between omnipotence and sovereignty shows that the paradox of omnipotence can be solved in a similar way. We must distinguish between first order omnipotence (omnipotence [1]), that is unlimited power to act, and second order omnipotence (omnipotence [2]), that is unlimited power to determine what powers to act things shall have. Then we could consistently say that God all the time has omnipotence (1), but if so no beings at any time have powers to act independently of God. Or we could say that God at one time had omnipotence (2), and used it to assign independent powers to act to certain things, so that God thereafter did not have omnipotence (1). But what the paradox shows is that we cannot consistently ascribe to any continuing being omnipotence in an inclusive sense.

An alternative solution of this paradox would be simply to deny that God is a continuing being, that any times can be assigned to his actions at all. But on this assumption (which also has difficulties of its own) no meaning can be given to the assertion that God made men with wills so free that he could not control them. The paradox of omnipotence can be avoided by putting God outside time, but the free-will solution of the problem of evil cannot be saved in this way, and equally it remains impossible to hold that an omnipotent God *binds himself* by causal or logical laws.

CONCLUSION

Of the proposed solutions of the problem of evil which we have examined, none has stood up to criticism. There may be other solutions which require examination, but this study strongly suggests that there is no valid solution of the problem which does not modify at least one of the constituent propositions in a way which would seriously affect the essential core of the theistic position.

Quite apart from the problem of evil, the paradox of omnipotence has shown that God's omnipotence must in any case be restricted in one way or another, that unqualified omnipotence cannot be ascribed to any being that continues through time. And if God and his actions are not in time, can omnipotence, or power of any sort, be meaningfully ascribed to him?

JOHN HICK

The Irenaean Theodicy

1. THE NEGATIVE TASK OF THEODICY

At the outset of an attempt to present a Christian theodicy—a defence of the goodness of God in face of the evil in His world—we should recognize that, whether or not we can succeed in formulating its basis, an implicit theodicy is at work in the Bible, at least in the sense of an effective reconciliation of profound faith in God with a deep involvement in the realities of sin and suffering. The Scriptures reflect the characteristic mixture of good and evil in human experience. They record every kind of sorrow and suffering from the terrors of childhood to the "stony griefs of age": cruelty, torture, violence, and agony; poverty, hunger, calamitous accident; disease, insanity, folly; every mode of man's inhumanity to man and of his painfully insecure existence in the world. In these writings there is no attempt to evade the clear verdict of human experience that evil is dark, menacingly ugly, heart-rending, crushing. And the climax of this biblical history of evil was the execution of Jesus of Nazareth. Here were pain and violent destruction, gross injustice, the apparent defeat of the righteous, and the premature death of a still-young man. But further, for

From *Classical and Contemporary Readings in the Philosophy of Religion*, edited by John Hick, 2nd ed. (Englewood Cliffs, NJ: Prentice-Hall, Inc., 1970).

Christian faith, this death was the slaying of God's Messiah, the one in whom mankind was to see the mind and heart of God made flesh. Here, then, the problem of evil rises to its ultimate maximum; for in its quality this was an evil than which no greater can be conceived. And yet throughout the biblical history of evil, including even this darkest point, God's purpose of good was moving visibly or invisibly towards its far-distant fulfillment. In this faith the prophets saw both personal and national tragedy as God's austere but gracious disciplining of His people. And even the greatest evil of all, the murder of the son of God, has been found by subsequent Christian faith to be also, in an astounding paradox, the greatest good of all. . . . For this reason there is no room within the Christian thought-world for the idea of tragedy in any sense that includes the idea of finally *wasted* suffering and goodness.

In all this a Christian theodicy is latent; and our aim must be to try to draw it out explicitly. The task, like that of theology in general, is one of "faith seeking understanding," seeking in this case an understanding of the grounds of its own practical victory in the face of the harsh facts of evil. Accordingly, from the point of view of apologetics, theodicy has a negative rather than a positive function. It cannot profess to create faith, but only to preserve an already existing faith from being overcome by this dark mystery. For we cannot share the hope of the older schools of natural theology of inferring the existence of God from the evidences of nature; and one main reason for this, as David Hume made clear in his *Dialogues*, is precisely the fact of evil in its many forms. For us today the live question is whether this renders impossible a rational belief in God: meaning by this, not a belief in God that has been arrived at by rational argument (for it is doubtful whether a religious faith is ever attained in this way), but one that has arisen in a rational individual in response to some compelling element in his experience, and decisively illuminates and is illuminated by his experience as a whole. The aim of a Christian theodicy must thus be the relatively modest and defensive one of showing that the mystery of evil, largely incomprehensible though it remains, does not render irrational a faith that has arisen, not from the inferences of natural theology, but from participation in a stream of religious experience which is continuous with that recorded in the Bible.

2. THE TRADITIONAL THEODICY BASED UPON CHRISTIAN MYTH

We can distinguish, though we cannot always separate, three relevant facets of the Christian religion: Christian experience, Christian mythology, and Christian theology.

Religious experience is "the whole experience of religious persons," constituting an awareness of God acting towards them in and through the events of their lives and of world history, the interpretative element within which awareness is the cognitive aspect of faith. And distinctively *Christian experience,* as a form of this, is the Christian's seeing of Christ as his "Lord and Saviour," together with the pervasive recreative effects of this throughout his life, transforming the quality of his experience and determining his responses to other people. Christian faith is thus a distinctive consciousness of the world and of one's existence within it, radiating from and illuminated by a consciousness of God in Christ. It is because there are often a successful facing and overcoming of the challenge of evil at this level that there can, in principle at least, be an honest and serious—even though tentative and incomplete—Christian theodicy.

By *Christian mythology* I mean the great persisting imaginative pictures by means of which the corporate mind of the Church has expressed to itself the significance of the historical events upon which its faith is based, above all the life, death, and resurrection of Jesus who was the Christ. The function of these myths is to convey in universally understandable ways the special importance and meaning of certain items of mundane experience.

By *Christian theology* I mean the attempts by Christian thinkers to speak systematically about God on the basis of the data provided by Christian experience. Thus it is a fact of the Christian faith-experience that "God was in Christ"; and the various Christological theories are attempts to understand this by seeing it in the context of other factors both of faith and of nature. Again, it is another facet of this basic fact of faith that in Christ God was "reconciling the world unto Himself"; and the various atonement theories are accordingly attempts to understand this further aspect of the experience. The other departments of Christian doctrine stand in a similar relationship to the primary data of Christian experience.

In the past, theology and myth have been closely twined together. For the less men knew about the character of the physical universe the harder it was for them to identify myth as myth, as distinct from history or science. This fact has profoundly affected the development of the dominant tradition of Christian theodicy. Until comparatively recent times the ancient myth of the origin of evil of the fall of man was quite reasonably assumed to be history. The theologian accordingly accepted it as providing "hard" data, and proceeded to build his theodicy upon it. This mythological theodicy was first comprehensively developed by Augustine, and has continued substantially unchanged within the Roman Catholic Church to the present day. It was likewise adopted by the Reformers of the sixteenth century and has been virtually unquestioned as Protestant doctrine until within approximately the last hundred years. Only during this latest period has it been possible to identify as such its mythological basis, to apply a theological criticism to it, and then to go back to the data of Christian experience and build afresh, seeking a theodicy that can hope to make sense to Christians in our own and succeeding centuries. . . .

Because we can no longer share the assumption, upon which traditional Christian theodicy has been built, that the creation-fall myth is basically authentic history, we inevitably look at that theodicy critically and see in it inadequacies to which in the past piety has tended to blind the eyes of faith.

For, in general, religious myths are not adapted to the solving of problems. Their function is to illumine by means of unforgettable imagery the religious significance of some present or remembered fact of experience. But the experience which myth thus emphasizes and illumines is itself the locus of mystery. Hence it is not surprising that Christian mythology mirrors Christian experience in presenting but not resolving the profound mystery of evil. Nor is it surprising that when this pictorial presentation of the problem has mistakenly been treated as a solution to it, the "solution" has suffered from profound incoherences and contradictions.

This traditional solution (representing the theological, in distinction from the philosophical, side of Augustine's thought on the theodicy problem) finds the origin of evil . . . in the fall, which was the beginning both of sin and, as its punishment, of man's sorrows and sufferings. But this theory, so simple and mythologically satisfying, is open to insuperable scientific, moral, and logical objections. To begin with less fundamental aspects of the traditional solution, we know today that the conditions that were to cause human disease and mortality and the necessity for man to undertake the perils of hunting and the labours of agriculture and building, were already part of the natural order prior to the emergence of man and prior therefore to any first human sin, as were also the conditions causing such further "evils" as earthquake, storm, flood, drought, and pest. And, second, the policy of punishing the whole succeeding human race for the sin of the first pair is, by the best human moral standards, unjust and does not provide anything that can be recognized by these standards as a theodicy. Third, there is a basic and fatal incoherence at the heart of the mythically based "solution." The Creator is preserved from any responsibility for the existence of evil by the claim that He made men (or angels) as free and finitely perfect creatures, happy in the knowledge of Himself, and subject to no strains or temptations, but that they themselves inexplicably and inexcusably rebelled against Him. But this suggestion amounts to a sheer self-contradiction. It is impossible to conceive of wholly good beings in a wholly good world becoming sinful. To say that they do is to postulate the self-creation of evil *ex nihilo!* There must have been some moral flaw in the creature or in his situation to set up the tension of temptation; for creaturely freedom in itself and in the absence of any temptation cannot lead to sin. Thus the very fact that the creature sins refutes the suggestion that until that moment he was a finitely perfect being living in an ideal creaturely relationship to God. . . .

3. THE VALUE OF SOUL-MAKING THEODICY

. . . As well as the "majority report" of the Augustinian tradition, which has dominated Western Christendom, both Catholic and Protestant, since the time of Augustine himself, there is the "minority report" of the Irenaean tradition. This latter is both older and newer than the other, for it goes back to St. Irenaeus and others of the early Hellenistic Fathers of the Church in the two centuries prior to St. Augustine, and it has flourished again in more developed forms during the last hundred years.

Instead of regarding man as having been created by God in a finished state, as a finitely perfect being fulfilling the divine intention for our human level of existence, and then falling disastrously away from this, the minority report sees man as still in process of creation. Irenaeus himself expressed the point in terms of the (exegetically dubious) distinction between the "image" and the "likeness" of God referred to in Genesis i. 26: "Then God said, let us make man in our image, after our likeness." His view was that man as a personal and moral being already exists in the image, but has not yet been formed into the finite likeness of God. By this "likeness" Irenaeus means something more than personal existence as such; he means a certain valuable quality of personal life which reflects finitely the divine life. This represents the perfecting of man, the fulfilment of God's purpose for humanity, the "bringing of many sons to glory," the creating of "children of God" who are "fellow heirs with Christ" of his glory.

And so man, created as a personal being in the image of God, is only the raw material for a further and more difficult stage of God's creative work. This is the leading of men as relatively free and autonomous persons, through their own dealings with life in the world in which He has placed them, towards that quality of personal existence that is the finite likeness of God. . . .

In the light of modern anthropological knowledge some form of two-stage conception of the creation of man has become an almost unavoidable Christian tenet. At the very least we must acknowledge as two distinguishable stages the fashioning of *homo sapiens* as a product of the long evolutionary process, and his sudden or gradual spiritualization as a child of God. But we may well extend the first stage to include the development of man as a rational and responsible person capable of personal relationship with the personal Infinite who has created him. This first stage of the creative process was, to our anthropomorphic imaginations, easy for divine omnipotence. By an exercise of creative power God caused the physical universe to exist, and in the course of countless ages to bring forth within it organic life, and finally to produce out of organic life personal life; and when man had thus emerged out of the evolution of the forms of organic life, a creature had been made who has the possibility of existing in conscious fellowship with God. But the second stage of the creative process is of a different kind altogether. It cannot be performed by omnipotent power as such. For personal life is essentially free and self-directing. It cannot be perfected by divine fiat, but only through the uncompelled responses and willing co-operation of human individuals in their actions and reactions in the world in which God has placed them. Men may eventually become the perfected persons whom the New Testament calls "children of God," but they cannot be created ready-made as this.

The value-judgement that is implicitly being invoked here is that one who has attained to goodness by meeting and eventually mastering temptations, and thus by rightly making responsible choices in concrete situations, is good in a richer and more valuable sense than would be one created *ab initio* in a state either of innocence or of virtue. In the former case, which is that of the actual moral achievements of mankind, the individual's goodness has within it the strength of temptations overcome, a stability based upon an accumulation of right choices, and a positive and responsible character that comes from the investment of costly personal effort. I suggest, then, that it is an ethically reasonable judgement, even though in the nature of the case not one that is capable of demonstrative proof, that human goodness slowly built up through personal histories of moral effort has a value in the eyes of the Creator which justifies even the long travail of the soul-making process.

The picture with which we are working is thus developmental and teleological. Man is in process of becoming the perfected being whom God is seeking to create. However, this is not taking place—it is important to add—by a natural and inevitable evolution, but through a hazardous adventure in individual freedom. Because this is a pilgrimage within the life of each individual, rather than a racial evolution, the progressive fulfilment of God's purpose does not entail any corresponding progressive improvement in the moral state of the world. There is no doubt a development in man's ethical situation from generation to generation through the building of individual choices into public institutions, but this involves an accumulation of evil as well as of good. It is thus probable that human life was lived on much the same moral plane two thousand years ago or four thousand years ago as it is today. But nevertheless during this period uncounted millions of souls have been through the experience of earthly life, and God's purpose has gradually moved towards its fulfilment within each one of them, rather than within a human aggregate composed of different units in different generations.

If, then, God's aim in making the world is "the bringing of many sons to glory," that aim will naturally determine the kind of world that He has created. Antitheistic writers almost invariably assume a conception of the divine purpose which is contrary to the Christian conception. They assume that the purpose of a loving God must be to create a hedonistic paradise; and therefore to the extent that the world is other than this, it proves to them that God is either not loving enough or not powerful enough to create such a world. They think of God's relation to the earth on the model of a human being building a cage for a pet animal to dwell in. If he is humane he will naturally make his pet's quarters as pleasant and healthful as he can. Any respect in which the cage falls short of the veterinarian's ideal, and contains possibilities of accident or disease, is evidence of either limited benevolence or limited means, or both. Those who use the problem of evil as an argument against belief in God almost invariably think of the world in this kind of way. David Hume, for example, speaks of an architect who is trying to plan a house that is to be as comfortable and convenient as possible. If we find that "the windows, doors, fires, passages, strains, and the whole economy of the building were the source of noise, confusion, fatigue, darkness, and the extremes of heat and cold" we should have no hesitation in blaming the architect. It would be in vain for him to prove that if this or that defect were corrected greater ills would result: "still you would assert in general, that, if the architect had had skill and good intentions, he might have formed such a plan of the whole, and might have adjusted the parts in such a manner, as would have remedied all or most of these inconveniences."

But if we are right in supposing that God's purpose for man is to lead him from human *Bios,* or the biological life of man, to that quality of *Zoe,* or the personal life of eternal worth, which we see in Christ, then the question that we have to ask is not, Is this the kind of world that an all-powerful and infinitely loving being would create as an environment for his human pets? or, Is the architecture of the world the most pleasant and convenient possible? The question that we have to ask is rather, Is this the kind of world that God might make as an environment in which moral beings may be fashioned, through their own free insights and responses, into "children of God"?

Such critics as Hume are confusing what heaven ought to be, as an environment for perfected finite beings, with what this world ought to be, as an environment for beings who are in process of becoming perfected. For if our general conception of God's purpose is correct the world is not intended to be a paradise, but rather the scene of a history in which human personality may be formed towards the pattern of Christ. Men are not to be thought of on the analogy of animal pets, whose life is to be made as agreeable as possible, but rather on the analogy of human children, who are to grow to adulthood in an environment whose primary and overriding purpose is not immediate pleasure but the realizing of the most valuable potentialities of human personality.

Needless to say, this characterization of God as the heavenly Father is not a merely random illustration but an analogy that lies at the heart of the Christian faith. Jesus treated the likeness between the attitude of God to man, and the attitude of human parents at their best towards their children, as providing the most adequate way for us to think about God. And so it is altogether relevant to a Christian understanding of this world to ask, How does the best parental love express itself in its influence upon the environment in which children are to grow up? I think it is clear that a parent who loves his children, and wants them to become the best human beings that they are capable of becoming, does not treat pleasure as the sole and supreme value. Certainly we seek pleasure for our children, and take great delight in obtaining it for them; but we do not desire for them unalloyed pleasure at the expense of their growth in such even greater values as moral integrity, unselfishness, compassion, courage, humour, reverence for the truth, and perhaps above all the capacity for love. We do not act on the premise that pleasure is the supreme end of life; and if the development of these other values sometimes clashes with the provision of pleasure, then we are willing to have our children miss a certain amount of this, rather than fail to come to possess and to be possessed by the finer and more precious qualities that are possible to the human personality. A child brought up on the principle that the only or the supreme value is pleasure would not be likely to become an ethically mature adult or an attractive or happy personality. And to most parents it seems more important to try to foster quality and strength of character in their children than to fill their lives at all times with the utmost possible degree of pleasure. If, then, there is any true analogy between God's purpose for his human creatures, and the purpose of loving and wise parents for their children, we have to recognize that the presence of pleasure and the absence of pain cannot be the supreme and overriding end for which the world exists. Rather, this world must be a place of soul-making. And its value is to be judged, not primarily by the quantity of pleasure and pain occurring in it at any particular moment, but by its fitness for its primary purpose, the purpose of soul-making.

In all this we have been speaking about the nature of the world considered simply as the God-given environment of man's life. For it is mainly in this connection that the world has been regarded in Irenaean and in Protestant thought. But such a way of thinking involves a danger of anthropocentrism from which the Augustinian and Catholic tradition has generally been protected by its sense of the relative insignificance of man within the totality of the created universe. Man was dwarfed within the medieval world-view by the innumerable hosts of angels and archangels above him—unfallen rational natures which rejoice in the immediate presence of God, reflecting His glory in the untarnished mirror of their worship. However, this higher creation has in our modern world lost its hold upon the imagination. Its place has been taken, as the minimizer of men, by the immensities of outer space and by the material universe's unlimited complexity transcending our present knowledge. As the spiritual environment envisaged by Western man has shrunk, his physical horizons have correspondingly expanded. Where the human creature was formerly seen as an insignificant appendage to the angelic world, he is now seen as an equally insignificant organic excrescence, enjoying a fleeting moment of consciousness on the surface of one of the planets of a minor star. Thus the truth that was symbolized for former ages by the existence of the angelic hosts is today impressed upon us by the vastness of the physical universe, countering the egoism of our species by making us feel that this immense prodigality of existence can hardly all exist for the sake of man—though, on the other hand, the very realization that it is not all for the sake of man may itself be salutary and beneficial to man!

However, instead of opposing man and nature as rival objects of God's interest, we should perhaps rather stress man's solidarity as an embodied being with the whole natural order in which he is embedded. For man is organic to the world; all his acts and thoughts and imaginations are conditioned by space and time; and in abstraction from nature he would cease to be human. We may, then, say that the beauties and sublimities and powers, the microscopic intricacies and macroscopic vastnesses, the wonders and the terrors of the natural world and of the life that pulses through it, are willed and valued by their Maker in a creative act that embraces man together with nature. By means of matter and living flesh God both builds a path and weaves a veil between Himself and the creature made in His image. Nature thus has permanent significance; for God has set man in a creaturely environment, and the final fulfilment of our nature in relation to God will accordingly take the form of an embodied life within "a new heaven and a new earth." And as in the present age man moves slowly towards that fulfilment through the pilgrimage of his earthly life, so also "the world creation" is "groaning in travail," waiting for the time when it will be "set free from its bondage to decay."

And yet however fully we thus acknowledge the permanent significance and value of the natural order, we must still insist upon man's special character as a personal creature made in the image of God; and our theodicy must still centre upon the soul-making process that we believe to be taking place within human life.

This, then, is the starting-point from which we propose to try to relate the realities of sin and suffering to the perfect love of an omnipotent Creator. And as will become increasingly apparent, a theodicy that starts in this way must be eschatological in its ultimate bearings. That is to say, instead of looking to the past for its clue to the mystery of evil, it looks to the future, and indeed to that ultimate future to which only faith can look. Given the conception of a divine intention working in and through human time towards a fulfilment that lies in its completeness beyond human time, our theodicy must find the meaning of evil in the part that it is made to play in the eventual outworking of that purpose; and must find the justification of the whole process in the magnitude of the good to which it leads. The good that outshines all ill is not a paradise long since lost but a kingdom which is yet to come in its full glory and permanence.

Glossary

Advaita Vedānta.   The school of Indian philosophy expounded by Śaṃkara (c. seventh-eighth century), which emphasizes the identity between the self (*ātman*) and reality (*Brahman*) and the empirical status only of the individual self (*jīva*).

ahiṁsa.   "Nonviolence": for Gandhi, the means to achieve political and social ends through organized passive resistance to one's oppressors.

analytic.   Judgment or statement whose truth derives solely from the meaning of the terms used and hence adds nothing new to the knowledge of the concept; statements in which the predicate is included in the concept of the subject (e.g., "all husbands are male").

anarchism.   The political view that denies the legitimacy of governmental authority of any kind in favor of free cooperative arrangements between autonomous persons.

anātman.   "No-self": the Buddhist doctrine that denies the existence of an underlying self (*ātman*) in favor of seeing oneself as a collection of empirical constituents (e.g., mental, physical, volitional) that form a pattern of individuality.

appearance.   The world as it appears to us, usually taken as an ever-changing order of experience in contrast to an unchanging, permanent reality.

a priori.   "What comes before": propositions that are known to be true independent of experience; arguments whose conclusions are deduced from *a priori* premises.

archaic (or primal) religion.   Beliefs and practices appearing at the earliest stages of religion that emphasize the existence of a multiplicity of spiritual powers in nature and develop elaborate rituals to control or propitiate those powers.

ātman.   For Advaita Vedānta, one's true self, which is timeless and undifferentiated, a state of pure consciousness identical to the supreme reality (*Brahman*), which is without distinction of any kind.

avidyā.   "Ignorance": lack of genuine self-knowledge; false identification of oneself as being an independent, particular person that is the cause of bondage, of our not realizing reality.

buddhi.   In Indian thought, mind in its reasoning, discriminatory function that makes intellectual judgment and understanding possible.

categorical imperative.   For Kant, one's willing that one's own maxim—rule or intention—be universalizable, i.e., that everyone could follow it without contradiction; acting in such a way as to treat another person always as an end and never merely as a means.

categories.   The most basic concepts employed for understanding experience, e.g., causality.

causation.   The relations of cause and effect; for Hume, a basis for the belief that the mind is a system of different perceptions that are linked together.

clear and distinct ideas.   For Descartes, those ideas that we hold that appear to be self-evident and irrefutable.

chün-tzu.   The "superior man" or "authoritative person" in Confucianism; one who has realized the possibilities of being human (*jen*) and displays appropriate behavior (*li*) in all things.

cogito ergo sum.   "I think; therefore I am": Descartes' assertion regarding the indubitability of the consciousness of one's own existence as a thinking being.

coherence (theory of truth).   Doctrine associated historically with objective idealism that a statement or belief is true to the degree to which it fits into, "coheres" with, a system of necessary truths or with a body of established beliefs.

correspondence (theory of truth).   Doctrine that truth is a matter of establishing an accord or "correspondence" between a statement and a state of affairs or "facts" independent of it.

cosmological argument.   Argument for the existence of God that reasons from certain characteristics of the world, e.g., motion and causality, to a divine principle that alone can render those characteristics intelligible.

cosmology.   Study of the origin and nature of the universe as a whole.

darśana.   Sanskrit term for "philosophy" understood as a vision of, or perspective upon, reality and life.

dharma.   Law or duty; in Hindu thought, the responsibility one has to contribute to society according to one's capacities as determined by one's past experience and one's corresponding place in the social order.

duḥkha.   "Suffering": in Buddhism, the doctrine that all life is subject to impermanence and the frustration of human desires.

duty.   That which one ought morally to do; for Kant, the adherence to a moral law for its own sake without regard to one's own inclinations.

ego.   For Freud, the individual, waking self that seeks self-preservation and is compelled to adjust to the external conditions of experience (the "reality principle"); generally regarded as the locus for all the characteristics that make one's character or personality unique.

empiricism.   The view that all knowledge derives from sense experience; denial of the position that the human mind contains a variety of ideas or concepts independent of all experience.

esse est percipi.   "To be is to be perceived": the subjective idealist belief that to exist means to be seen or otherwise sensed as an object, and that there is no underlying matter that stands apart from our sensations of an object.

existentialism.   The view that one's self is made up of one's actions carried out against a background of total freedom; the need for each person to determine, through the choices they make, their own nature and character.

facticity. For Sartre, the totality of the conditions (the "facts")—biological, social, etc.—that hold for a particular person.

faith. The dynamic core of a religious commitment; way in which one exhibits one's relationship to the sacred; system of religious belief.

focus-field self. The view ascribed to Confucius that a person is a "field of selves" comprising social, political, personal relationships, with the family as a central focus.

four noble truths. The fundamental teaching of Buddhism that (1) all life is suffering (2) that has a cause based on selfishness and ignorance (3) that can be overcome (4) through an eightfold ethical and mental path to *nirvāṇa*.

genetic fallacy. The reduction of the truth or value of an idea to its psychological origins.

good (the idea of the). For Plato, the highest idea, grasped by pure reason, which unifies all knowledge and morality.

good will. For Kant, that will that is pure in its motives and dedicated to act in accordance with the principle of duty.

happiness. The living of a good life as individually determined; for Aristotle, the living in accordance with rational principles of virtue.

impression. For Hume and empiricism in general, the source in sense-experience, a sensation or feeling, for whatever idea we subsequently hold in the mind.

Īśvara. In Indian thought, reality as expressed or manifest as an infinite being with innumerable attributes who is taken as the cause of the world.

jen. Basic humanness or genuine humanity, the primary virtue in Confucianism.

jiva. For Vedānta, the individual self in waking, dream, and deep-sleep consciousness, as constituted by material, intellectual, emotional and volitional factors.

justice. In general, the fair sharing of the material and social benefits of being a member of a society; the impartial application of lawfully constituted rules and procedures.

karma. The principle of one's becoming the results of one's own actions through the acquiring of dispositions to act in certain ways, usually conceived of as occurring over many lives.

legalism. The political doctrine that lays stress on the right of government to set forth clear and impartial laws to constrain human behavior for the benefit of social order.

li. "Propriety," as based on feelings of respect and reverence; in Confucianism, the awareness of what is the right or appropriate way to behave in particular circumstances.

liberal democracy. The political philosophy that supports the rights of individuals to pursue their own interests as free as possible from government interference; society organized by principles of equality and the rule of law.

liberty. The political freedom to act without external constraint, usually qualified politically by regard for the rights of others.

līlā. "Sportive play": in Indian thought, the way of acting of the divine creative principle; actions carried out for their own sake, without motive or purpose.

manas.   In Indian philosophy, mind as a sense organ; the seat of perceptual consciousness.

materialism.   A metaphysical position that claims that everything in essence is material and that all mental processes can be explained and accounted for in physical terms.

māyā.   "Illusion": for Advaita Vedānta, the world as it appears to us in our ignorance of its true nature; all experience that is based on subject-object distinctions; the power that deludes us into assuming that the empirical world is reality.

mean (the).   For Aristotle, appropriate behavior that avoids excess and deficiency (e.g., courage is the mean between acting fearlessly in a mindless fashion and being a coward through fearfulness).

metaphysics.   The study of the most basic and fundamental principles that inform all experience; the inquiry into the nature of ultimate reality.

moral virtue.   For Aristotle, those excellences of character acquired through habit that enable one to act according to rational principles of the mean.

mysticism.   The religious-philosophical view that affirms the intrinsic unity or identity of persons with a spiritual reality and seeks in practice a direct realization of that unity or identity.

narrative concept of self.   MacIntyre's view that a person's identity arises from the unity of one's life story as grounded in various social and historical contexts.

natural theology.   The attempt to demonstrate rationally the existence of God.

nirvāṇa.   In Buddhism, the attainment of enlightenment through extinguishing all desires and selfish craving.

noumenal.   For Kant, the world as it is in itself and as unknowable by us.

numinous.   The religious state of mind said to be irreducible as it confronts the mystery of spiritual being; the nature of the divine as a transcendent being.

ontological argument.   A proof for the existence of God that argues from the idea of God as a perfect being, "that than which nothing greater can be conceived," to his existence.

ontology.   The study of existence or being as such; inquiry into the fundamental kinds of things that exist in the universe.

original nature.   In Confucianism (e.g., Mencius), the set of natural propensities to act benevolently, with spontaneous concern for the welfare of others.

personal identity.   Being the same person over a period of time; generally, how one identifies oneself as the particular person that one is.

phenomenology.   The descriptive method that seeks to grasp the essential character of the objects of experience; theory of consciousness that holds that all consciousness is *of* something or other.

pragmatic (theory of truth).   Doctrine according to which a belief is held to be true if it "works" in enabling us to predict and control experience, to function well, to lead richer lives; truth "happens"; it is *made,* not found.

pramāṇa.   "Means of valid knowledge" in Indian philosophy; perception and inference being the primary kinds.

rationalism. The philosophy that extols the power of reason to determine through its own methods the basic rational structure of the universe; the belief that reason can in principle explain everything within a single system of knowledge.

reality principle. For Freud, all the demands that physical nature and society make or impose upon one and to which the ego must adjust.

realism. The view that there exists a world of objects and relations external to the mind; that our perceptions are of independent objects that are ordered spatially, temporally, and causally, and about which we may have genuine knowledge.

relativism. The recognition of a variety of moralities, ways of knowing, etc., which are fundamentally different from one another and are cultural or historically specific; doctrine that there is not, and cannot be, a single correct account of reality.

resemblance. For Hume, a relation of likeness or similarity among perceptions that is produced by memory of different perceptions and that serves as one of the bases for our erroneous belief in having a personal substantial identity.

satori. In Zen Buddhism, the immediate, nonrational insight into reality.

satyagraha. For Gandhi, the power of truth and justice to overcome evil and oppression.

self-transcendence. Going beyond or overcoming the limitations of one's empirical individuality.

sex and gender. The distinction, emphasized in feminist thinking, between one's given biological makeup (sex) and the identifications that emerge (gender) from various social practices, such as upbringing and vocational opportunities.

social contract. The agreement among members of a society to adhere to certain laws and procedures to attain a system of relationships that can insure human flourishing.

soul. Greek: *psychē;* the animating or living principle, with reason as its highest form and the ground for one's immortality.

subjective idealism. The school of thought associated in the West with Berkeley and in Asia with *yogācāra* Buddhism that explains the world by reference to the mind and holds that the "mental" alone exists.

substance. Generally, the essential nature of a thing that underlies and supports its various properties; that which exists by itself and can be conceived only by itself.

substantial self. An underlying self that is conceived either as supporting various empirical qualities or as being different in kind from all ordinary experience.

superego. For Freud, all the moral rules taught to one in childhood, primarily from one's parents, which subsequently become "internalized" or accepted by one and which dictate one's sense of responsibility.

synthetic. A judgment or statement whose truth is not determined by the meaning of its terms and that therefore provides new knowledge (e.g., "a red light indicates 'stop' ").

tao. The right way of life; in Taoism, the natural-spiritual principle that is the primal source of all being and is manifest in all natural processes.

te. Moral force; in Taoism, the power inherent in virtue.

teleology.   The view that everything in the universe has a goal or purpose to which it seeks to realize or fulfill; a way of explaining some process by reference to its end or purpose.

theism.   Religious orientation, which celebrates the existence of a personal, creator God who is all-powerful and good.

theodicy.   The attempt to demonstrate the compatibility between the fact of evil in the world and the goodness and omnipotence of God.

Übermensch.   For Nietzsche, that rare person who, through the power of creative will, goes "beyond good and evil" and sets the moral standard for humankind.

uji.   "Being-time": in Zen Buddhism (Dōgen) the temporality that is intrinsic to an event and represents an eternal presence.

unconscious.   Or id: for Freud, that domain of our psychic life that remains hidden or inaccessible to ordinary waking consciousness and is the seat of instinctual desires and sexual drives.

unity of self.   The state of being a single self rather than a plurality or collection of (disparate) selves.

utilitarianism.   The moral doctrine in which the goal of action is to promote the greatest happiness (or maximum pleasure) of the greatest number of persons, and an action is therefore judged by its consequences.

Vaiśeṣika.   System of Indian philosophy that investigates the basic categories of existence; the classifications, both ontological and linguistic, that structure experience.

Vedānta.   The major tradition of Indian philosophy that bases its teachings primarily on the ancient Vedic texts known as Upaniṣads.

wu wei.   "Actionless action": in Taoism, the style of governance that emphasizes the character of the Taoist ruler and that brings about harmony without coercion.

Index